MASTERING THE NATIONAL COUNSELOR EXAMINATION AND THE COUNSELOR PREPARATION COMPREHENSIVE EXAMINATION

Bradley T. Erford

Loyola University Maryland

Danica G. Hays

Old Dominion University

Stephanie Crockett

Old Dominion University

Emily M. Miller

Loyola University Maryland

PEARSON

Boston   Columbus   Indianapolis   New York   San Francisco   Upper Saddle River
Amsterdam   Cape Town   Dubai   London   Madrid   Milan   Munich   Paris   Montreal   Toronto
Delhi   Mexico City   Sao Paulo   Sydney   Hong Kong   Seoul   Singapore   Taipei   Tokyo

Vice President and Editor-in-Chief: Jeffery W. Johnston
Senior Acquisitions Editor: Meredith D. Fossel
Editorial Assistant: Nancy Holstein
Vice President, Director of Sales and Marketing: Quinn Perkson
Senior Marketing Manager: Christopher Barry
Senior Managing Editor: Pamela D. Bennett
Senior Project Manager: Mary M. Irvin
Senior Operations Supervisor: Matt Ottenweller
Cover Designer: Candace Rowley
Cover Art: SuperStock
Full-Service Project Management: Mohinder Singh/Aptara®, Inc.
Composition: Aptara®, Inc.
Printer/Binder: Edwards Brothers Malloy
Cover Printer: Edwards Brothers Malloy
Text Font: Palatino

Every effort has been made to provide accurate and current Internet information in this book. However, the Internet and information posted on it are constantly changing, so it is inevitable that some of the Internet addresses listed in this textbook will change.

Library of Congress Cataloging-in-Publication Data
Mastering the National Counselor Examination (NCE) and the counselor preparation comprehensive examination (CPCE) / Bradley T. Erford . . . [et al].
    p. cm.
  Includes bibliographical references and index.
  ISBN-13: 978-0-13-701750-8 (alk. paper)
  ISBN-10: 0-13-701750-2 (alk. paper)
  1. Counseling psychology—Examinations, questions, etc. 2. Counseling psychology—Examinations—Study guides. I. Erford, Bradley T.
  BF636.6.M37 2011
  158'.3076—dc22

                            2010012028

Note: NCE® is a registered trademark of the National Board for Certified Counselors®, Inc. (NBCC®). National Counselor Exam™ is a trademark of the NBCC. Counselor Preparation Comprehensive Examination™ and CPCE™ are trademarks of the Center for Credentialing & Education™ (CCE®).

NBCC and CCE do not endorse or sponsor the services or products of any individuals, businesses, or other organizations. NBCC and CCE are not, in any way, responsible for such services or products, or the representations made concerning such services, products, or affiliations with other organizations or businesses.

10 9 8 7 6 5

www.pearsonhighered.com

ISBN 13: 978-0-13-701750-8
ISBN 10:   0-13-701750-2

This effort is dedicated to The One: the Giver of energy, passion, and understanding, who makes life worth living and endeavors worth pursuing and accomplishing, the Teacher of love and forgiveness. —BTE

For Owen and children of all ages—may they always dream big. —DGH

I dedicate this work to my husband, John, for his unwavering support and understanding during the writing process, and to my family, who always encouraged me to pursue my vocational aspirations. I also thank my mentors and fellow authors, Dr. Danica Hays and Dr. Bradley Erford, for recognizing my potential as a writer and providing me with the opportunity to be part of this project. —SC

To Sean and my family, for their endless support and encouragement. —EMM

ACKNOWLEDGMENTS

Meredith Fossel and Nancy Holstein of Pearson deserve special mention for their stewardship during the production of this book. Additional thanks go to Heath Lynn Silberfeld, our outstanding copy editor at Enough Said; and to Mary Irvin our project manager at Pearson, and Mohinder Singh, our project manager at Aptara, for their outstanding service. We are also grateful to the reviewers for their helpful and supportive comments: George R. Beals, Delta State University; Karla D. Carmichael, University of Alabama; Tony W. Cawthon, Clemson University; Joseph C. Ciechalski, East Carolina University; Harvey Ginsburg, Texas State University; Bette S. Katsekas, University of Southern Maine; Timothy B. Smith, Brigham Young University; and Regine Mylene Talleyrand, George Mason University.

ABOUT THE AUTHORS

Dr. Bradley T. Erford, PhD, LCPC, LPC, NCC, LP, LSP, is professor of educational specialties in the school counseling program at Loyola University Maryland. He is the editor or author of more than 15 books. His research specialization falls primarily in development and technical analysis of psychoeducational tests and has resulted in the publication of numerous refereed journal articles, book chapters, and published tests. He has held numerous leadership positions and has been honored with awards many times by the American Counseling Association (ACA) and ACA–Southern Region, the Association for Assessment in Counseling and Education (AACE), and the Maryland Association for Counseling and Development (MACD). Dr. Erford is a Licensed Clinical Professional Counselor, Licensed Professional Counselor, Nationally Certified Counselor, Licensed Psychologist, and Licensed School Psychologist. He is a graduate of the University of Virginia (Ph.D. in counselor education), Bucknell University (M.A. in school psychology), and Grove City College (B.S. in biology and psychology) and teaches courses in testing and measurement, lifespan development, school counseling, research and evaluation in counseling, and stress management.

Danica G. Hays, PhD, LPC, NCC, is an associate professor and graduate program director in the Department of Counseling and Human Services at Old Dominion University. Her research interests include qualitative methodology, assessment and diagnosis, trauma and gender issues, and multicultural and social justice concerns in counselor preparation and community mental health. She has published numerous refereed journal articles and book chapters. She is co-editor of the text *Developing Multicultural Counseling: A Systems Approach* (Pearson), associate and content editor of the *American Counseling Association Encyclopedia of Counseling* (ACA), and an author of an upcoming text, *Qualitative Inquiry in Clinical and Educational Settings* (Guilford Publications). Dr. Hays has been a faculty member at Old Dominion University since 2006 with prior teaching experience at the University of New Orleans, Argosy University–Atlanta, and Georgia State University. Her primary teaching responsibilities are master's- and doctoral-level research methods courses, assessment, and doctoral supervision. Dr. Hays has received several national awards, including the ACA Research Award, ACA Counselor Educator Advocacy Award, the Association for Assessment in Counseling and Education (AACE) AACE/MECD Award, Association for Counselor Education and Supervision (ACES) Outstanding Graduate Student Leadership Award, and Chi Sigma Iota International Fellow.

Stephanie Crockett, MS Ed, NCC, is a doctoral student in the Department of Counseling and Human Services at Old Dominion University. Prior to pursuing her doctorate, Stephanie provided vocational assistance and counseling to college students. Her research interests and specializations include career counseling, research and assessment in counseling, and counseling supervision.

Emily M. Miller, M.Ed., is professional school counselor and a graduate of the school counseling program at Loyola University Maryland. She has authored several articles and book chapters on a variety of counseling topics. She is continuing her education to become a Licensed Clinical Professional Counselor (LCPC) and Registered Play Therapist.

BRIEF CONTENTS

CONTENTS

INTRODUCTION

ABOUT *MASTERING THE NATIONAL COUNSELOR EXAM AND COUNSELOR PREPARATION COMPREHENSIVE EXAM*

Mastering the National Counselor Exam and Counselor Preparation Comprehensive Exam is a powerful resource and tool to help you prepare for two of the most important examinations in counselor preparation and credentialing: the National Counselor Examination for Licensure and Certification (NCE) and the Counselor Preparation Comprehensive Examination (CPCE). This study guide is organized into eight chapters coinciding with the Council for Accreditation of Counseling and Related Educational Programs (CACREP) core content areas:

Section 1: Professional Orientation and Ethical Practice
Section 2: Social and Cultural Foundations
Section 3: Human Growth and Development
Section 4: Career Development
Section 5: Helping Relationships
Section 6: Group Work
Section 7: Assessment
Section 8: Research and Program Evaluation

Each chapter is made up of sections addressing major topics within its CACREP core content area. Each section has five self-administered, multiple-choice questions to test your knowledge of the presented material and allow you to maximize your learning while making the reviewing of course material more manageable. This study guide also contains a glossary of key terms and several full-length practice tests to help you retain this information. Before delving into each of the CACREP core content areas, it is important to present some introductory information about the NCE and CPCE and some test-preparation and test-taking strategies for mastering the NCE and CPCE.

ABOUT THE NATIONAL COUNSELOR EXAMINATION (NCE)

To obtain certification from the National Board for Certified Counselors (NBCC), professional counselors must first pass the National Counselor Examination for Licensure and Certification (NCE), which NBCC creates and administers. Counselors who pass the exam and meet NBCC's standards of education and training are entitled to receive NBCC's general practitioner credential, the National Certified Counselor (NCC) credential. Although taking and passing the NCE is voluntary, many states require the NCE for their own licensure and credentialing purposes. One of the primary benefits of taking the NCE and working toward the NCC is that the credential is nationally recognized and strengthens the credential holder's professional reputation (NBCC, 2009b).

The NCE is a paper-and-pencil multiple-choice test. It contains 200 multiple-choice questions, which test-takers are allowed up to 4 hours to complete. The NCE aims to assess test-takers' knowledge and understanding of areas thought to be essential for effective and successful counseling practice. The NCE's test questions stem from CACREP's (2009) eight core content areas and five work behaviors. The eight content areas and the topics they cover include the following:

1. *Professional Orientation and Ethical Practice.* Professional counselors' roles and functions; history and philosophy of the counseling profession; professional credentialing; professional organizations; legal and ethical standards.
2. *Social and Cultural Foundations.* Multicultural and pluralistic trends; theories of multicultural counseling; identity development and social justice; strategies for working with and advocating for diverse populations; counselors' roles in developing cultural self-awareness.
3. *Human Growth and Development.* Theories of individual and family development across the lifespan; learning theories; personality, cognitive, and moral development; normal and abnormal behavior.
4. *Career and Lifestyle Development.* Career development theories and decision-making models; vocational assessment instruments and techniques relevant to career planning and decision making; the relationship between work, leisure, and family; career counseling for specific populations.
5. *Helping Relationships.* Wellness and prevention; essential interviewing and counseling skills; counseling theories; family theories and related interventions; counselor characteristics and behaviors that influence helping processes.
6. *Group Work.* Principles of group dynamics; theories of group counseling; group leadership styles; methods for evaluation of effectiveness.
7. *Appraisal.* Basic concepts of standardized and nonstandardized testing; statistical concepts associated with appraisal; principles of validity and reliability; interpretation of testing results; ethical and legal consideration in appraisal.
8. *Research and Program Development.* Qualitative and quantitative research designs; descriptive and inferential statistics; program evaluation and needs assessment; research's role in the use of evidence-based practices; ethical and cultural considerations in research.

The NBCC seeks to reflect the actual work that professional counselors do by incorporating work behavior categories into the NCE. The five work behaviors provide the context for the eight CACREP content areas. The work behaviors were last updated by the NBCC in 2001. The following are the five categories:

1. *Fundamentals of Counseling* refers to the use of counseling theories and fundamental counseling processes to

provide counseling to individuals, families, children, or adolescents and those who have experienced sexual or physical abuse.

2. *Assessment and Career Counseling* is concerned with the provision of career counseling and testing-related services. Assessment refers to administering achievement tests, interest inventories, aptitude tests, and intelligence tests and assisting the client with understanding test results. Career counseling refers to using print-based and computerized career resources, assisting a client in developing decision-making skills, and evaluating a client's occupational skills.

3. *Group Counseling* involves all aspects of providing group counseling. These aspects include setting group goals and procedures, observing group member behaviors, evaluating group progress, managing termination, and using group- and leader-centered group counseling leadership techniques.

4. *Programmatic and Clinical Intervention* is concerned with providing client informed consent, assessing client needs, determining client diagnosis, establishing and evaluating client goals and treatment plans, and evaluating referrals.

5. *Professional Practice Issues* refers to continuing education, reading professional counseling literature, providing supervision to counselor trainees and staff, participating in community outreach and public relations, engaging in experimental and outcome-based counseling research, writing for publication, and providing training/educational programming.

The NCE is administered throughout the United States two times each year (April and October), and each administration of the NCE involves a varying set of questions from the NCE test item bank (NBCC, 2009a). Of the 200 multiple-choice questions administered, only 160 count toward the test-takers' final score. Thus, the highest score an examinee can receive on the NCE is 160. The NBCC includes the 40 remaining questions for field-testing purposes to determine whether these 40 questions may be suitable for inclusion in future examinations. Examinees are not informed of which questions are scored. Each multiple-choice question has four answer choices, with only one correct answer per question. Test-takers are not penalized for guessing, so examinees should be sure to select an answer for each question. According to the NBCC, the questions on the test do not equally represent the eight content areas. Over the past decade, the NCE has included approximately 29 professional orientation and ethical practice items, 11 social and cultural diversity items, 12 human growth and development items, 20 career development items, 36 helping relationship items, 16 group work items, 20 assessment items, and 16 research and program evaluation items.

The minimum passing score for the NCE changes for each examination and is decided based on a modified Angoff procedure, which calculates the likelihood that a nominally skilled individual would answer each question correctly and then, based on that information, determines a cutoff score for the entire set of items. Thus, the NCE is a criterion-referenced test, and the total score is interpreted as pass or fail based on a determined cutoff score. About 8 weeks after taking the test, candidates receive their score report in the mail. The score report includes candidates' scores in each of the 13 domains (delineated above), their total score for the entire test, and the minimum passing score for the version of the NCE the examinee completed.

ABOUT THE COUNSELOR PREPARATION COMPREHENSIVE EXAMINATION (CPCE)

The Counselor Preparation Comprehensive Examination (CPCE) was created by the Research and Assessment Corporation for Counseling (RACC) and the Center for Credentialing and Education (CCE), both affiliates of NBCC, for use in colleges and universities with master's programs in counseling. Currently, over 220 colleges and universities use the CPCE for program evaluation and, frequently, as an exit exam (Center for Credentialing and Education, 2009). Results of the test give an educational institution a sense of their students' and their program's strengths and weaknesses in relation to national data. In addition, many colleges and universities use this examination to encourage their students to engage in frequent, cumulative studying and reviewing of the information learned in their courses and field experiences.

The format of the CPCE resembles the NCE. The CPCE comprises 160 questions, with 20 questions for each of the eight CACREP areas. Only 17 questions from each area count toward the test-takers' score, which means that the highest score a person can achieve on the examination is 136. Because the CPCE is based on the same eight CACREP areas as the NCE, students have the ability to simultaneously prepare for both examinations. However, the CPCE does not offer a cutoff score to indicate a passing or failing score; instead, university program faculty are left with that responsibility if they intend to use the CPCE scores for high-stakes evaluation decisions.

PREPARATION STRATEGIES FOR SUCCESS

Taking the NCE or CPCE is undoubtedly an important event in your counseling career. Although the breadth of knowledge that you are expected to learn can be overwhelming—even intimidating—mastering the domain of knowledge of essential counseling information is definitely possible. Remember, you have already learned a large portion of this information in your classes. So, to prepare for these tests, much of your time will be dedicated to reviewing previously mastered information and concepts and ensuring that you understand how to apply them. Before you start working through this study guide, consider the following strategies for success as you work toward your test date.

1. *Manage your time and plan ahead.* Neither the NCE nor CPCE lend themselves to cramming; therefore, it is much more advantageous to begin studying ahead of time. One of the easiest ways to make the tasks of learning and reviewing so much information easier is to break

up the task into manageable sections. Write out a study schedule for yourself, and plan on reviewing only small segments of information at each study session so that you do not become overwhelmed or frustrated. It may be helpful for your schedule to include when you will study (e.g., the date and time), what you will study (e.g., the material and any pages numbers), and how you will study (e.g., read, highlight key terms, answer multiple-choice questions). It is also important to schedule time off from studying. Allowing yourself to mentally recharge will help you approach the material with greater clarity and focus. Do not put yourself at a disadvantage by procrastinating.

2. *Practice.*   Practice is a key factor in preparing for both the NCE and CPCE. Specifically, it is important to be familiar with the test format and types of questions that will be asked on each exam. This study guide is packed with sample questions similar to those that you will encounter on the NCE and CPCE. The more familiar you are with applying this information to sample questions, the better prepared you will be for the actual tests.

3. *Apply rather than memorize.*   Although you may feel pressure to memorize everything word for word, doing so is not an effective study strategy. Both the NCE and CPCE will require you to apply the knowledge you have gained. Nor is it useful to memorize the test questions you review during your preparation for the exams. Each administration of the NCE and CPCE includes new questions, so you will not find any questions in this study guide that will occur exactly as written on future NCEs or CPCEs. Of course, some of the questions in this guide will resemble some of the actual questions. After all, the questions all measure the same domain of knowledge. But it is a much better use of your time to master the domain of knowledge presented in this guide than to master an item set.

4. *Employ a study strategy.*   The use of a study strategy can help you to both learn and apply the material you study. One of the most well-known strategies for retaining the material you read is Survey, Question, Read, Recite, and Review (SQ3R). Specifically, this strategy recommends first surveying the material's words in bold-face type, tables, headings, and introductory sentences. Next, you are advised to turn headings and boldface words into questions, then to read the text to answer the previously developed questions. Finally, you should restate the material in your own words and engage in an ongoing process of review. Other study strategies that can be employed to assist you in reading and reviewing the test material include taking notes, highlighting key words and phrases, reviewing key words presented in the glossary, reviewing flash cards, and forming a peer study group. Given that there are numerous study strategies and that everyone learns differently, it is important for you to find and use the strategies that will work best for you.

5. *Give yourself positive reinforcements.*   Studying for the NCE and CPCE is hard work. Be sure to reward yourself with enjoyable activities or treats as you work through the study material. Build in time between study sessions to relax, too.

6. *Apply the Premack principle to your study schedule.* The Premack principle demands that high-frequency behaviors (i.e., what people like to do) should follow low-frequency behaviors (i.e., what people don't like to do); thus, you should do what you don't want to do before you do what you do want to do! As pertains to studying for the NCE or CPCE, complete a period of study and follow it with an activity that you find more enjoyable and rewarding.

7. *Seek accommodations.*   If you have a disability and will need accommodations while taking the NCE, it is your responsibility to contact the NBCC prior to your test date. E-mails can be sent to examinations@nbcc.com, or you can contact a representative at (336) 547-0607. If you decide to send an e-mail regarding accommodations, include your name, address, phone number, and state or residence, along with your question or request. When taking the CPCE, notify your program faculty ahead of time regarding your need for accommodations.

8. *Take good care of yourself before the exam.*   Keep in mind that cramming the night before the exam will most likely make you more anxious, so try instead to engage in a relaxing activity that will calm your nerves and enable you to get a good night's sleep. So that you will be mentally alert and focused when you arrive at the test center, make sure that you are fully rested and have had a nutritious breakfast before taking the exam.

9. *Arrive prepared for the examination.*   Remember to bring several sharp #2 pencils, your admission ticket, and two forms of identification (one with a photo). If you are not familiar with the area where you will take the test, print out directions beforehand. Finally, be sure to arrive at least 30 minutes early so that you are not rushing before the exam.

TEST-TAKING STRATEGIES

With successful preparation, counselors and counselor trainees will have the necessary competence *and* confidence when taking the NCE and CPCE. In addition, mastering these exams involves several strategies to use while taking the exam itself. During the exam, remember the following:

1. *Answer all questions.*   As mentioned, you will not be penalized for guessing. If you do not know the correct answer to a question, it is better to use your common sense and guess than to leave the answer blank.

2. *Make educated guesses.*   You are better off making an educated guess about a question than leaving it blank. With no penalty for guessing, you have a 25% chance of guessing correctly, whereas if you leave the question blank you will automatically receive zero points for that question. When guessing, start by eliminating obviously incorrect answers and then use cues and common sense to infer which remaining answer makes the most sense.

3. *Pace yourself.* On the NCE, you will have 4 hours to answer 200 questions, which gives you 60 minutes for every 50 questions. Do not spend more than 1 minute on each question on your initial pass through the items. If you are unsure of the answer to a question, skip it and return to it later so that you give yourself adequate time to respond to the questions that you are sure about first.

4. *Stay calm.* No doubt you have learned some useful relaxation techniques over the years to help you through school. Likely, you have also learned counseling techniques to help your clients cope with stress. Use these skills to help you through your exam. For example, if you find yourself stressed during the test, try some deep breathing exercises, progressive muscle relaxation, positive self-talk, or visual imagery to help alleviate some of your anxiety.

5. *Think and read carefully.* Some questions on the NCE and CPCE will include qualifiers that ask you to choose the answer that is "not true" or the "best" choice. The former asks you to choose the answer that does not accurately answer the question. Regarding "best" choice questions, a question may have four answer options, several of which may seem right, and your task will be to select the choice that is *better* than all the others. Therefore, make sure you read each question and *all of the possible answer options* thoroughly before marking your response. For example, the first answer choice you read may seem correct, but perhaps the second, third, or fourth option is even better, so do not be tempted to rush through a question just because one of the first choices you read seems to fit.

6. *Skip difficult or confusing questions.* All questions are worth the same number of points, so if you are hung up on a question, skip it and come back to it later, or make a guess. Spending too much time on questions you are unsure about takes away precious time from questions to which you do know the answers.

7. *Check your answer sheet frequently.* Pay close attention to your answer sheet to be sure that you are marking answers to the correct questions, especially if you are temporarily skipping some questions. Place a question mark, hyphen, or some other symbol next to the questions you are skipping so that you do not accidentally mark that question with the answer to a different item.

8. *Keep your answer sheet neat.* If you need to write down anything to assist you in working through a question, use your response booklet. Your answer sheet will be optically scanned, so it is important that you completely color in all of your answer choices and avoid leaving stray marks on the answer sheet. If you put a question mark or hyphen next to an item you want to come back to, make sure you erase it after you have returned and filled in the answer.

9. *Stay focused.* Ignore any distractions that arise. Instead, keep your concentration centered on the test questions. Four hours is adequate time to complete the test if you maintain your focus.

10. *Keep the test in perspective.* You are not expected to receive a perfect score on these tests, and you can get many questions wrong and still pass, so do not stress out if you do not know the answer to every question. Study, practice, prepare, and try your best—that is all you can do!

CHAPTER 1

Professional Orientation
and Ethical Practice

1.1 INTRODUCTION TO PROFESSIONAL ORIENTATION AND ETHICAL PRACTICE

Professional orientation and ethical practice encompass much of the counseling curriculum. Professional counselors must become very familiar with ethical and legal practice considerations and with historical perspectives and advocacy models. Counselors also must understand the roles of professional organizations and counseling specialties in counseling practice, as well as the diverse nature of credentialing.

Administrations of the NCE include (in addition to some trial items that do not count) 29 scored items (of the 160 total, or about 18%) designed to measure professional issues and ethical practice (rank = 2 of 8; the 2nd most items of any of the eight domains). The average item difficulty index was .77 (rank = 2 of 8; 2nd easiest domain of item content), meaning that the average item in this domain was correctly answered by 77% of test-takers.

Over the past several years, administrations of the CPCE have included 17 scored items designed to measure professional issues and ethical practice, plus several trial items that do not count in your score. The average item difficulty index was .72, meaning that the average item in this domain was correctly answered by 72% of test-takers, which made this set of items among the easiest on the examination.

Council for Accreditation of Counseling and Related Educational Programs (CACREP, 2009) defined standards for Professional Orientation and Ethical Practice as follows:

studies that provide an understanding of all of the following aspects of professional functioning:

a. history and philosophy of the counseling profession;

b. professional roles, functions, and relationships with other human service providers, including strategies for interagency/interorganization collaboration and communications;

c. counselors' roles and responsibilities as members of an interdisciplinary emergency management response team during a local, regional, or national crisis, disaster, or other trauma-causing event;

d. self-care strategies appropriate to the counselor role;

e. counseling supervision models, practices, and processes;

f. professional organizations, including membership benefits, activities, services to members, and current issues;

g. professional credentialing, including certification, licensure, and accreditation practices and standards, and the effects of public policy on these issues;

h. the role and process of the professional counselor advocating on behalf of the profession;

i. advocacy processes needed to address institutional and social barriers that impede access, equity, and success for clients; and

j. ethical standards of professional organizations and credentialing bodies, and applications of ethical and legal considerations in professional counseling. (p. 9)

Each of these standards is addressed throughout Chapter 1. In the remainder of this first section of Chapter 1, we discuss key historical events in counseling; key legal issues, including important laws, abuse, and minor consent; accreditation and CACREP; advocacy counseling; health maintenance organizations (HMOs); liability insurance; licensure; and the National Board for Certified Counselors (NBCC).

1.1.1   Key Historical Events in Counseling

The counseling profession today comprises counselors who work in myriad settings, from educational institutions and hospitals to community health centers. As evidenced by the numerous counseling specializations and associations, counseling is an all-inclusive profession dedicated to meeting the needs of diverse individuals and families at every stage of the life cycle. However, the counseling profession had its genesis in the late 1800s, when it began in a much more circumscribed manner: vocational guidance. During the following decades, individuals began introducing additional approaches to counseling and types of counseling services to the public to promote the wellness of clients and students in need, and the profession slowly began expanding and changing from its vocational guidance roots. The timeline in Table 1.1 highlights some of the key historical events that transformed the counseling profession into the diverse field that it is today.

1.1.2   Key Legal Issues in Counseling

It is the responsibility of professional counselors to abide by the American Counseling Association (ACA) *Code of Ethics* (2005), which provides counselors with mandatory ethics rules they *must* follow and aspirational ethics rules they *should* follow if they want to meet the highest standards of professional practice and conduct (Herlihy & Corey, 2006). Likewise, it is also the duty of professional counselors to be knowledgeable of and adhere to applicable laws. The principal difference between ethics and laws is that ethics are developed by associations to help members practice in a reputable manner, whereas laws are included in the penal code and often carry more serious consequences when individuals fail to comply with laws (Linde, 2007). Violation of ethical standards may carry sanctions, but those penalties vary greatly and are determined by ethics committees rather than courts. Although the law trumps ethics in all circumstances, professional counselors rarely have to violate ethical standards to follow the law. When studying for the NCE or CPCE, counselors should become thoroughly familiar with the NBCC *Code of Ethics* (see http://www.nbcc.org/AssetManagerFiles/ethics/nbcc-codeofethics.pdf) and the ACA *Code of Ethics* (see http://www.counseling.org/Resources/CodeOfEthics/TP/Home/CT2.aspx; and see section 1.4) and be able to apply these ethical concepts to practice situations. This section presents an overview of some of the key legal issues that are crucial for you to be aware of, including the Family Educational Rights and Privacy Act (FERPA), Individuals with Disabilities Education Improvement Act (IDEA), U.S. Rehabilitation Act of 1973 (Section 504), Health Insurance Portability and Accountability Act (HIPAA), child abuse and neglect, and counseling minors.

1.1.2.1 FAMILY EDUCATIONAL RIGHTS AND PRIVACY ACT (FERPA)   Enacted in 1974, the **Family Educational Rights and Privacy Act (FERPA)**, also known as the Buckley Amendment, is a federal law that affects any counselor who works in an educational setting that receives funding from the U.S. Department of Education (U.S. Department of Education [USDE], 2007). Private schools, colleges, or universities that do not receive *any* funds from the USDE for *any* of their programs do not have to follow this act, but those institutions represent the minority.

Key Points of FERPA

- FERPA was created to specify the rights of parents (if the child is a minor) and nonminor students to access and examine the educational record, petition to have incorrect information found in the record amended, and ensure that certain information is not released to outside agencies without permission.
- An **educational record** refers to any document or information kept by the school relating to a student, such as attendance, achievement, behavior, activities, and assessment.
- Parents have the right to access their children's educational information until the child is 18 years old or begins college, whichever comes first, at which point the rights shift to the student.
- Educational institutions are required to obtain written permission before releasing any information in a student's educational record.
- An exception to the preceding rule is that schools have the ability to give out **directory information** about students without consent. Directory information includes the student's name, address, telephone number, date of birth, place of birth, honors or awards, and dates of attendance at the school. However, schools must send an annual notice to students and/or parents informing them that they have they right to have their information, or their child's information, barred from release.
- Educational institutions that fail to comply with FERPA may face punitive action, such as loss of federal funding.
- Professional counselors' personal notes on students, considered an expansion of the counselor's memory that are kept separate from the educational record in a secure location, are considered confidential (Linde, 2007). Students and parents do not have the right to access counselors' personal notes. That being said, *general* counseling case notes may be considered part of a student's educational record, depending on the state.

1.1.2.2 INDIVIDUALS WITH DISABILITIES EDUCATION IMPROVEMENT ACT (IDEA)   Also pertaining to counselors who work in educational settings, Individuals with Disabilities Education Improvement Act (IDEA) is a civil rights law that was passed to guarantee that students with disabilities receive the services they need to gain the benefits of education. Like FERPA, this act applies to any school that receives federal funding and prohibits educational institutions from putting any

TABLE 1.1 **Timeline of Historical Events.**

- **Late 1800s**—Vocational guidance counseling emerges as a result of the Industrial Revolution and social reform movements.
- **Early 1900s**—Frank Parsons, heralded as the father of vocational guidance, opens the Bureau of Vocational Guidance in Boston, which helps match individuals with suitable careers based on their skills and personal traits.
- **1908**—Frank Parsons dies, but his influential book *Choosing a Vocation* is published posthumously.
- **1913**—The National Vocational Guidance Association (NVGA) is founded.
- **1913**—Clifford Beers, the leader of the mental health movement, which advocated for the construction of mental health clinics and more humane treatment of institutionalized patients with psychological disorders, founds the Clifford Beers Clinic in New Haven, Connecticut, considered the first outpatient mental health clinic in America.
- **1930s**—E. G. Williamson creates the Minnesota Point of View, a trait and factor theory considered to be one of the first counseling theories.
- **1932**—The *Wagner O'Day Act* is passed, which creates U.S. Employment Services to aid the unemployed in finding work through vocational guidance.
- **1940s and 1950s**
  - Carl Rogers' humanistic approach to psychology gains widespread support in the counseling profession.
  - Soldiers return home after World War II and increase the need for counseling, readjustment, and rehabilitation services.
  - Increased numbers of counselors begin working full-time at postsecondary educational institutions, community agencies, and vocational rehabilitation centers.
  - More associations sprout up to help new counseling specializations form a unified and professional identity.
- **1952**—To gain a larger voice in the counseling field, the American Personnel and Guidance Association (APGA; since renamed the American Counseling Association [ACA]) is formed as a union among the National Vocational Guidance Association (NVGA; since renamed the National Career Development Association [NCDA]), the National Association of Guidance and Counselor Trainers (NAGCT; since renamed the Association for Counselor Education and Supervision [ACES]), the Student Personnel Association for Teacher Education (SPATE; since renamed the Counseling Association for Humanistic Education and Development [C-AHEAD]), and the American College Personnel Association (ACPA).
- **1952**—The American School Counselor Association (ASCA) is formed and becomes a division of APGA the next year.
- **1958**—Congress passes the National Defense Education Act (NDEA) in response to the launch of the *Sputnik* satellite in 1957, which signaled that the Russians were leading in the Space Race. The NDEA provides schools with increased funds to improve their curriculum and hire school counselors to pick out students showing promise in math and science.
- **1958**—The American Rehabilitation Counseling Association (ARCA), a division of APGA, is chartered.
- **1961**—APGA publishes its first code of ethics.
- **1963**—President Lyndon Johnson signs into law the *Community Mental Health Act,* which allots money for the creation of mental health centers.
- **1965**—The Association for Measurement and Evaluation in Guidance (AMEG), currently known as the Association for Assessment in Counseling and Education (AACE), is chartered as a division of APGA.
- **1966**—The National Employment Counseling Association (NECA), a division of APGA, is chartered.
- **1970s**
  - Legislation for individuals with disabilities emerges, leading to a heightened demand for rehabilitation counselors and school counselors.
  - Individuals in the counseling field publish books and articles that increase the counseling profession's interest in multicultural issues, such as cultural identity development, multicultural awareness, racism, and counseling minorities.
- **1972**—The Association for Multicultural Counseling and Development (AMCD), a division of APGA, is founded.
- **1973**—The Association for Specialists in Group Work (ASGW), a division of APGA, is created.
- **1974**—The Association for Spiritual, Ethical, and Religious Values in Counseling (ASERVIC) and the International Association of Addictions and Offender Counselors (IAAOC), both divisions of APGA, are chartered.
- **1975**—The U.S. Supreme Court's decision in *Donaldson v. O'Connor* results in the deinstitutionalization of patients in state mental hospitals. This precedent-setting decision has been one of the most significant in mental health law. It barred mental institutions from committing individuals involuntarily if they were not an immediate threat to themselves or other people.
- **1976**—Virginia is the first state to offer counselors the option to seek licensure.
- **1978**—The American Mental Health Counselors Association (AMHCA), a division of APGA, is chartered.
- **1981**—The Council for Accreditation of Counseling and Related Educational Programs (CACREP) is established to provide accreditation for master's and doctoral programs in counseling that adhere to its standards of preparation.

(Continued)

TABLE 1.1   Timeline of Historical Events. (*Continued*)

- **1982**—The National Board for Certified Counselors (NBCC), which develops and implements the first national examination to certify counselors, the National Counselor Exam (NCE), is formed by APGA.
- **1983**—APGA changes its name to the American Association of Counseling and Development (AACD).
- **1984**—The Association for Counselors and Educators in Government (ACEG), a division of AACD, is chartered.
- **1985**—Chi Sigma Iota, the international honor society for the counseling profession, is founded.
- **1986**—The Association for Adult Development and Aging (AADA), a division of AACD, is chartered.
- **1989**—The International Association of Marriage and Family Counselors (IAMFC), a division of AACD, is chartered.
- **1991**—The American College Counseling Association (ACCA), a division of AACD, is chartered.
- **1993**—AACD, formerly known as APGA, changes its name to the American Counseling Association (ACA).
- **1995**—ACA makes a major revision to its code of ethics, allowing members and divisions to submit suggestions and ideas and revising the format of the document to make it more cohesive and organized.
- **1997**—The Association for Gay, Lesbian, and Bisexual Issues in Counseling (AGLBIC) is chartered by ACA.
- **2002**—Counselors for Social Justice (CSJ), a division of ACA, is chartered.
- **2004**—The Association for Creativity in Counseling (ACC), a division of ACA, is established.
- **2005**—The most recent revision of the ACA code of ethics includes new sections on technology, end-of-life care, making diagnoses, ending practice, and choosing therapeutic interventions.
- **2007**—The AGLBIC name is changed to the Association for Lesbian, Gay, Bisexual, and Transgender Issues in Counseling (ALGBTIC).

student at a disadvantage based on a disability. It is important for professional counselors to be knowledgeable of this act if they work in an educational institution because part of their role is to advocate for the academic needs of their clients.

Key Points of IDEA

- Children are eligible to receive services under IDEA from birth until the age of 21 years.
- Counselors and educators serve as advocates for children with special education needs. School counselors are frequently part of the child study team, which evaluates a child's educational, psychological, sociological, and medical needs to determine eligibility for services.
- To qualify for eligibility under IDEA, a student must have a documented disability in at least one of the following areas: mental retardation, hearing impairment (including deafness), speech or language impairment, visual impairment (including blindness), serious emotional disturbance, orthopedic impairment, autism, traumatic brain injury, other health impairment, or specific learning disability. In addition, the student must *need* special education services as a result of a disability.
- All students with disabilities must be given **free appropriate public education (FAPE)** that addresses their individual needs and helps ready them for higher levels of education or employment.
- Every student who is eligible to receive special education services under IDEA must have an **individualized educational plan (IEP)** on file (USDE, 2000). School systems convene meetings of multidisciplinary teams to create the IEP. A student's IEP delineates what services the student will receive; when and how often; and goals for the student's learning, which are updated and reviewed yearly.

- It is required that each student's IEP ensure that the child receive the benefits of education in the **least restrictive environment (LRE)**, which was mandated to allow as many students as possible to remain in regular classrooms if their needs could be met there with only limited accommodation.
- Students covered under IDEA often are also covered under the more expansive Section 504 of the *U.S. Rehabilitation Act* of 1973.

1.1.2.3 U.S. REHABILITATION ACT OF 1973 (SECTION 504) The **U.S. Rehabilitation Act** of 1973 (**Section 504**), a civil rights act, protects individuals with disabilities from being discriminated against or denied equal access to services and opportunities because of their disability, IDEA being one of those protections. Often, in a school setting, students who do not qualify for special education services under IDEA may be eligible for accommodations under Section 504, which has a more inclusive definition of *disability*. Unlike IDEA, Section 504 applies not only to educational institutions receiving federal funds but also to any organization or employer in the United States receiving federal funds.

Key Points of Section 504

- Eligible individuals must have a physical or psychological impairment that substantially limits at least one **major life activity**. These major life activities include walking, seeing, hearing, speaking, breathing, working, performing manual tasks, learning, and caring for oneself (U.S. Department of Health and Human Services [HHS], 2000).
- To receive consideration, individuals must also be viewed as having the disability or have documentation of the disability, and it must interfere with their ability to meet their needs.

- In a school setting, when a student indicates a need, a multidisciplinary team meets to assess the students' eligibility under Section 504. If eligible, a **504 plan** is constructed, which dictates the accommodations or other special considerations the student is entitled to receive. The team looks at multiple sources of information when determining students' eligibility, including any test scores, grades, educational records, and medical documentation.
- Although there exists a whole host of possible accommodations a student may be given, a few examples of accommodations that school personnel make for eligible individuals include building ramps and installing elevators for students who are wheelchair bound or injured, giving students more time to complete tests or other classroom tasks, and allowing students to use laptop computers to take notes.

1.1.2.4 HEALTH INSURANCE PORTABILITY AND ACCOUNTABILITY ACT (HIPAA)

HIPAA is a federal law, passed in 1996, to protect the privacy of individuals' medical and mental health records. Under HIPAA, patients are given rights to control who can view their health records as well as the ability to inspect their own medical record and request that changes be incorporated (USDHHS, 2006). HIPAA applies to doctors, nurses, hospitals, clinics, insurance companies, health maintenance organizations (HMOs), Medicare, Medicaid, mental health professionals, and a variety of other health care providers. In fact, it would be difficult to find a health care provider who is *not* subject to the stipulations outlined in HIPAA, so understanding this law is essential to avoid violating the confidentiality of private client information.

Key Points of HIPAA

- All patients must be given a copy of the HIPAA **privacy policy**, which outlines their rights, with whom their **protected health information (PHI)**—that is, individually identifiable health information—might be shared, and the procedures to request that their information not be released to certain parties.
- Patients, for their part, are required to sign a document affirming that they have received information on HIPAA.
- Health organizations must secure all PHI from unauthorized individuals and organizations.
- A counselor following HIPAA must allow clients to view their records and petition for changes to the counselor's notes if they believe any information is false or inaccurate. (USDHHS, 2006)

1.1.2.5 CHILD ABUSE AND NEGLECT

The federal **Child Abuse Prevention and Treatment Act (CAPTA)** defines child abuse and neglect as "Any recent act or failure to act on the part of a parent or caretaker which results in death, serious physical or emotional harm, sexual abuse or exploitation; or, an act or failure to act which presents an imminent risk of serious harm" (Child Welfare Information Gateway, 2007).

Key Points of CAPTA

- Any counselor who suspects child abuse or neglect is required by law to report the suspicion to the local **child protective services (CPS)** agency within 72 hours from the time of first awareness of the potentially abusive or neglectful event (Linde, 2007). Counselors also must submit a written report to CPS after submitting the initial account.
- Anyone who reports suspected abuse or neglect will not be held liable, even if CPS fails to find any evidence supporting the claim during the investigation (Linde, 2007), unless a false report was filed with malicious intent.
- The ACA *Code of Ethics* (2005, B.2.a.) upholds this legal duty, allowing counselors to ethically break confidentiality to protect a client from a potentially dangerous situation.

1.1.2.6 COUNSELING MINORS

When counseling minors, particularly in a nonschool setting, it is crucial for counselors to obtain **informed consent** from the parents or legal guardian and assent, or agreement, of minors before any counseling begins. The necessity of informed consent in school systems ordinarily is dictated by local school or state policies (American School Counselor Association [ASCA], 2004).

Key Points of Informed Consent

- During the informed consent and assent process, minors and their parents must receive details on what they can expect from counseling, limitations to confidentiality, and their right to withdraw from treatment at any time (ACA, 2005, A.2.a., A.2.b., & A.2.d.).
- Informed consent should be given in writing to parents and explained by the counselor to minors in age-appropriate language so that they are able make an educated decision about whether they want to enter into the counseling relationship. Some minor children, because of substantial disability (e.g., mental retardation) or age, are unable to give assent for counseling, thus requiring special precautions in care and parental consent.
- All counselors should note that although, ethically, the child (if under the age of 18 years) should be able to expect confidentiality, parents still retain the legal right to know what their child discusses in counseling sessions should they choose to exercise that right (Linde, 2007). Therefore, counselors must carefully balance the needs of both parties to most effectively implement services and must work diligently to uphold the minor's ethical rights whenever feasible.
- Some states allow minors of a certain age to consent to various community health services, including mental health treatment, without parental consent. However, these **minor consent laws** vary among states, so it is essential to become very familiar with the laws governing the state where you are practicing or plan to practice.
- In a school setting, most professional school counselors are *not* required to obtain parental consent before delivering

counseling services to students, although professional school counselors should familiarize themselves with the policies of their state and local school boards.

1.1.3 Accreditation and the Council for Accreditation of Counseling and Related Educational Programs (CACREP)

Accreditation is a process that eligible educational institutions and organizations can elect to undergo (i.e., it is voluntary) to demonstrate that the institution meets set standards. Although accreditation applies to many careers and professions, for the purposes of this study guide, we are concerned with **educational accreditation**.

- An educational institution seeking accreditation must apply to the appropriate association. For example, for colleges and universities to have their counseling programs accredited, they apply to the **Council for Accreditation of Counseling and Related Educational Programs (CACREP)**, the association in charge of the accreditation for the majority of counseling and counseling-related programs, and undergo its accreditation process.
- The purpose of accreditation for educational institutions is to signify to the public that the accredited program's educators and curriculum adhere to specific standards of quality; only those institutions that meet the specified criteria become accredited (CACREP, 2009).
- Institutions may seek accreditation for a variety reasons:
  - It increases the institution's status and prestige.
  - It requires institutions to hold themselves accountable for the quality of their program and educators.
  - It encourages colleges and universities to continually evaluate and assess the effectiveness of their programs and make changes and improvements as necessary to ensure adherence to the standards of accreditation. Educational institutions accredited by CACREP must undergo and pass the accreditation process every 8 years to retain their certification, so the process of meeting CACREP's standards is ongoing (CACREP, 2009).
  - Students who graduate from an accredited institution may be more marketable than those students graduating from an unaccredited institution because they have succeeded in meeting specified programmatic standards.

CACREP was established in 1981 to promote excellence in counseling and counseling-related educational programs. CACREP has developed and revised educational standards over the years that institutions must meet to gain the organization's accreditation approval. These standards were created to respond to society's comprehensive needs, ensuring that institutions seeking accreditation are providing students with the necessary tools to address those needs at graduation and on entrance into the counseling profession (CACREP, 2009).

CACREP accredits master's-level programs in addiction counseling; clinical mental health counseling; marriage, couple, and family counseling; school counseling; student affairs and college counseling; and doctoral-level programs in counselor

education and supervision (CACREP, 2009). Currently, more than 220 universities in the United States have received CACREP accreditation.

1.1.3.1 CACREP APPLICATION PROCESS The following are the components of the CACREP application process (CACREP, 2009):

1. The CACREP application process requires educational institutions with a counseling or counseling-related program seeking accreditation to complete the *application* and submit a *self-study report,* which outlines how the institution meets CACREP's standards.
2. Once the application and self-study report have been received, a CACREP review board convenes a team of trained counseling professionals and educators to conduct an *on-site visit* of the institution for several days to tour the facilities and conduct extensive interviews with students, faculty, administrators, and graduates to further determine if the program adequately meets CACREP standards.
3. At the completion of the visit, the team writes a *report* delineating whether the standards were met and areas of particular strength or weakness within the program. The educational institution receives a copy of this report and is given the opportunity to respond to any comments made by the site-visit team.
4. Accreditation decisions are made by the CACREP board after reviewing an institution's application, self-study report, and site-visit report. If the program meets all the necessary criteria, the board gives the program the status of being CACREP accredited for a duration of 8 years. If the program meets most, but not all, of the standards, the board can grant accreditation for 2 years, giving the educational institution an opportunity to improve its program during the 2-year probation period, after which it may or may not receive accreditation. Finally, if the board determines that a program does not sufficiently meet its requirements, it is denied CACREP accreditation.

1.1.4 Advocacy Counseling

Advocacy counseling is concerned with supporting and promoting the needs of clients (e.g., individuals, groups, communities) and the counseling profession at all levels (local, state, regional, national). Examples of advocacy counseling include teaching clients to self-advocate, being involved in changes in public policy, writing to or meeting with policymakers about bills that affect counselors and clients, or backing licensure laws. Advocacy counseling also can take many other forms, such as educating people about the counseling profession, providing leadership and advocacy training, networking with the media to have important issues covered, and working with community organizations to meet the needs of clients.

- Advocacy follows a process that is similar to problem-solving models. Counselors must identify the problem, gather resources, create an action plan, train professionals to execute the advocacy activities and, finally, put the plan into action. Of course, throughout this process, counselors should engage in **formative evaluations** (i.e., ongoing assessment of programs and interventions) to ensure that their advocacy efforts are effectively meeting objectives.

- Counselors are expected to be advocates not only for their profession but also for their clients and to help clients overcome any barrier that is preventing them from making progress. The ACA *Code of Ethics* (2005, A.6.a.) demands that counselors empower clients to advocate for themselves when needed or that counselors advocate on their clients' behalf (with client consent) when clients are unable to do so for themselves. ACA has published "Advocacy Competencies" that counselors should be familiar with (see http://www.counseling.org/Resources).

1.1.5   Health Maintenance Organizations (HMO)

A **health maintenance organization (HMO)**, also known as a managed care organization, is a health care organization that allows members to access health and mental health services at a lower cost than many standard health insurance plans. Although members often pay only a small fee per month, a frequent criticism is that they can visit only hospitals and providers that are part of their HMO's network, and often they must receive a referral from their primary care physician before visiting any specialists, including counselors.

- A benefit for mental health providers who are part of an HMO is that they are given a stable influx of clients and are ensured payment if they follow the organization's regulations. However, a criticism of HMOs is that mental health providers must give the organization a diagnosis and detailed history of each client before the HMO will approve and pay for the treatment, perhaps infringing on the client's confidentiality (Mentor Research Institute, 2009). Mental health professionals also are often limited in how much time they have to treat clients, and they are usually required to follow specific guidelines or treatment modalities in working with their clients.

1.1.6   Liability Insurance

In the field of counseling, **liability insurance** has become something of a necessity for all counselors, counseling students, and counselor educators. In the event that professional counselors find themselves in a legal dispute or the subject of a complaint, having liability insurance can be instrumental in the protection of their assets and also greatly reduces the financial burden they may face if found guilty of **malpractice** or **negligence**. Many professional organizations, such as ACA and NBCC, offer reasonably priced liability insurance to members.

- Although counselors are urged to abide by applicable ethics codes and doing so will help decrease the likelihood of negligence or malpractice, there is always inherent risk in treating clients, and even the best-intentioned professionals can make mistakes. Even counselors who are wrongly accused of negligence or unethical behavior

will still have to respond to the claim, which is costly and can jeopardize their assets (Wheeler & Bertram, 2008).

1.1.7   Licensure

Licensure in the counseling field emerged in the 1970s in an effort to validate the counseling profession by passing state laws controlling who could legally practice counseling (Wheeler & Bertram, 2008). The underlying purpose of state licensure is to protect the public by ensuring that only qualified professionals, granted a license from the state, can legally render certain counseling services. Just as people must obtain a driver's license to legally operate a vehicle, so too must professional counselors procure a license to practice in most states. Once an individual has been licensed, he or she usually is granted the title of Licensed Professional Counselor (LPC), or a similar title as determined by a specific state's law; some examples include Licensed Clinical Professional Counselor (LCPC), Licensed Mental Health Counselor (LMHC), and Licensed Clinical Mental Health Counselor (LCMHC).

- Although the requirements for obtaining licensure vary from state to state, most states require individuals to achieve at least a master's degree from an approved institution (thereby fulfilling specific coursework requirements), accrue a certain number of years or hours of supervised clinical experience, and pass an examination, such as the NCE.
- Virginia was the first state to license professional counselors (in 1976). Now, 49 states have licensure laws.
- Although professional counselors can secure national certification, to enhance their professional credibility, through the NBCC, currently there is no nationally recognized licensure. However, a push for licensure portability is beginning to take hold within the profession (Wheeler & Bertram, 2008). Portability would establish **reciprocity** for licensed counselors. This would allow a counselor who is licensed in one state to work in another state without having to reapply for licensure or fulfill additional requirements.

1.1.8   The National Board for Certified Counselors

The **National Board for Certified Counselors (NBCC)** is the chief credentialing organization in the United States for professional counselors seeking certification. Founded in 1982 as the result of an ACA committee recommendation, NBCC is a nonprofit organization that certifies counselors who have met its criteria for education and training and have passed the **National Counselor Examination (NCE)**, which it developed and administers. The mission of NBCC is to promote and recognize counselors who meet established standards of quality in delivering counseling services.

- Certification with NBCC is voluntary, but counselors who obtain certification strengthen their professional reputation. In some cases, the certification has made counselors eligible for salary increases (NBCC, 2007a).

- NBCC offers counselors general and specialty credentialing options (NBCC, 2007a). NBCC's premier credential is the **National Certified Counselor (NCC)**. Specialties within this credential are the National Certified School Counselor (NCSC), the Certified Clinical Mental Health Counselor (CCMHC), and the Master Addictions Counselor (MAC). Candidates must first attain the NCC before they can earn a specialty credential; in some cases, though, they may apply concurrently for both the general and a specialty credential. Acquiring a specialty credential provides counselors with greater notoriety within the counseling community and can increase financial remuneration or professional opportunities.

- The NCC is NBCC's general practice credential (NBCC, 2007a). Approximately 42,000 counselors have gained this national certification. To be eligible for the NCC, the candidate must meet one of the following educational requirements: (1) be a current student in a counseling program that participates in the Graduate Student Application process, (2) have earned at least a master's degree from a CACREP-accredited program, (3) have earned at least a master's degree in a counseling field and have taken courses in the following areas: human growth and development, social/cultural foundations, helping relationships, group work, career and lifestyle development, assessment, research and program evaluation, and professional orientation and ethical practice, and have been employed in the counseling profession under supervision for 2 or more years, or (4) hold a counseling license conferred by the candidate's state board and possess at least a master's degree in a mental health field.

1.1.9 Practice Multiple-Choice Items: Introduction to Professional Orientation and Ethical Practice

1. The American Counseling Association was originally named
   a. American Association of Counseling and Development.
   b. American Personnel and Guidance Association.
   c. National Vocational Guidance Association.
   d. American Counseling Association.

2. When working with an 8-year-old child in a nonschool setting, it is ethically necessary to obtain
   a. assent from the child and informed consent from the parent.
   b. informed consent from only the child.
   c. informed consent from only the parent.
   d. informed consent from both the child and the parent.

3. When counseling minors, the legal right to confidentiality belongs to
   a. the child.
   b. the counselor.
   c. the parents or legal guardians.
   d. both the child and the parents.

4. The Buckley Amendment is also known as the
   a. Health Insurance Portability and Accountability Act.
   b. Section 504 of the U.S. Rehabilitation Act.
   c. Individuals with Disabilities Education Improvement Act.
   d. Family Educational Rights and Privacy Act.

5. All of the following statements are correct EXCEPT
   a. licensure was created to protect the public.
   b. counselors who hold a license from one state have reciprocity in every other state.
   c. Virginia was the first state to license counselors.
   d. the requirements for acquiring licensure vary from state to state.

Answer Key: 1. b; 2. a; 3. c; 4. d; 5. b.

1.2   COUNSELING SPECIALIZATIONS

The counseling profession contains a number of specializations, each of which is dedicated to addressing the needs of a particular group of people. Each specialization requires counselors to meet its specific training requirements, and all are driven by the same overarching mission to promote the growth and potential of all individuals.

A **professional counselor** works in diverse settings with diverse clientele, including colleges, hospitals, clinics, private practices, and schools. Many of the counselors from special counseling disciplines are described in the sections that follow. Other types of professional counselors not described here include career and substance abuse counselors. These specialty areas are described in other chapters of this study guide within a more specific context. Regardless of the specialization within counseling, all professional counselors are concerned with working not only to treat but also to prevent, psychological problems and to promote healthy human development throughout all stages of life. Professional counselors often work with clients to overcome developmental and unexpected life changes, come to terms with their environment, adjust to foreign situations, and find ways to improve the quality of clients' lives.

If properly trained in administration of psychological tests, professional counselors are eligible in most states to administer such tests as part of their practice. As previously mentioned, to become a professional counselor individuals must earn at least a master's degree in the field of counseling. This second section of Chapter 1 outlines the predominant counseling and related specializations currently in existence, specifically clinical mental health counseling, college admissions counseling, college counseling, rehabilitation counseling, school counseling, and other types of mental health counseling.

1.2.1   Clinical Mental Health Counseling

Mental health counselors first surfaced in the 1940s and 1950s but did not benefit from formal training or employment in significant numbers until the passing of the *Community Mental Health Act* of 1963, which provided funding for the establishment of mental health centers across the United States to provide greater access to mental health care services.

- Clinical mental health counselors work with individuals, groups, and families in many different settings, including community organizations, hospitals, drug and alcohol treatment centers, and private practices.
- Mental health counselors are trained in assessment; diagnosis; treatment planning; psychotherapy; substance abuse treatment, prevention, and intervention; crisis counseling; and brief therapy (American Mental Health Counselors Association [AMHCA], 2004).
- To become licensed as a mental health counselor, individuals must earn a master's degree in a counseling field, pass their state's required examination, and have at least 2 years of work experience under supervision (AMHCA, 2004).
- Many mental health counselors work toward the NCC credential and the CCMHC specialty credential, both granted by NBCC, to forward their careers, become eligible providers for certain insurance companies, or strengthen their professional reputation.
- The American Mental Health Counselors Association (AMHCA) is the division under ACA that serves as the professional association for mental health counselors.

1.2.2 College Admissions Counseling

College admissions counseling focuses on helping students maneuver through the college admissions process to select and, ideally, to secure entry into suitable postsecondary educational institutions.

- College admissions counselors work in a variety of settings, most commonly in colleges, universities, and high schools. Often, *professional school counselors* who work in high schools are highly involved in this process, although some high schools employ a separate counselor whose sole responsibility is to work with students interested in attending college; these individuals are usually called *college counselors,* but the role is relegated to college admissions counseling—not to the wellness and mental health roles of the college counselors discussed in the next section. *Educational consultants* are people who work outside the school district and provide college counseling services to students for a fee (National Association for College Admission Counseling, 2008). Finally, some areas have *commercial college counseling centers* that offer students a variety of services ranging from test preparation classes to assistance with college applications.
- The bulk of college admissions counseling occurs at the secondary level, particularly in students' junior and senior years, although some schools believe it is useful to integrate college counseling programs into the middle school curricula as well.
- Counselors at the high school and college levels assist students in the college admissions process through

academic advising, during which they help students choose high school courses beneficial to their postsecondary aspirations and often administer **interest assessments**, which facilitate students' personal exploration of career options in concert with their interests. College admissions counselors also work with students individually to discuss specific college options, and they work with groups to guide students in preparing to complete college applications, take the Scholastic Achievement Test (SAT) or American College Testing (ACT) examinations, and obtain financial aid, if necessary.

- The **National Association for College Admission Counseling (NACAC)** is the professional association for individuals who work in this specialization. NACAC is not affiliated with ACA.

1.2.3 College Counseling

The previous section provided an overview of college admission counseling primarily at the secondary level. *College counseling* at the postsecondary level has a much different charter, and counselors who work in this specialty have a distinct job description. Although college admissions counselors are concerned with helping students apply and gain admittance to postsecondary schools, college counselors in higher education work in *counseling centers* on college campuses to support students who have *mental health and educational concerns* that are negatively affecting their personal, social, and academic endeavors.

- Individuals working in college counseling centers are often professional counselors and psychologists who hold doctoral degrees; they may also be counseling interns. College counselors engage in individual and group counseling and serve as liaisons to community services and resources. Most college counseling services are free to students.
- College counselors help students deal with diverse issues, including homesickness, social problems, relationship issues, academic problems, stress, eating disorders, and mental illnesses. Because of the variety of issues presented to college counselors, most are trained in crisis counseling, diagnosis, and treatment planning.
- The American College Counseling Association, a division of ACA, is the professional association for counselors working in higher education.

1.2.4 Rehabilitation Counseling

A **certified rehabilitation counselor (CRC)** seeks to help individuals with disabilities work through personal and vocational issues they may encounter as a result of their impairment. A CRC's clients have wide-ranging disabilities. Some are a result of illness, although others are due to accidents, birth defects, or many other causes (U.S. Department of Labor, 2007).

- CRCs are employed in a wide range of settings, such as public vocational rehabilitation agencies, hospitals, community centers, schools, and employee assistance programs.

- After conducting a thorough assessment of the client and gathering information on the client's condition and job skills from a variety of sources, CRCs begin to work with the client to improve the quality of the client's life and help him or her cope with disabilities, find jobs that match skill levels and interests, and learn to live more independently (U.S. Department of Labor, 2007). Part of a CRC's work may also involve connecting clients with community resources, such as health care and occupational training. The ultimate goal of a CRC's work is to assist individuals with disabilities in either returning to their place of employment or finding a different vocation.
- To become a CRC, individuals must be granted certification from the Commission on Rehabilitation Counselor Certification (CRCC). Certification with CRCC is voluntary; however, some employers require rehabilitation counselors to become certified.

1.2.4.1 THE COMMISSION ON REHABILITATION COUNSELOR CERTIFICATION The **Commission on Rehabilitation Counselor Certification (CRCC)** is a nonprofit organization that was formed in 1974 to certify rehabilitation counselors who meet particular professional standards and have achieved adequate education and work experience related to rehabilitation. CRCC is the equivalent of the National Board for Certified Counselors (NBCC) for rehabilitation counselors seeking certification.

- CRCC operates with the belief that effective rehabilitation counselors work in a holistic fashion, take into consideration each client's environment and background, believe in the innate dignity of all individuals, and commit to adhering to its code of professional ethics (Commission on Rehabilitation Counselor Certification, 2003). Accordingly, requirements for certification are based around these principles.
- Eligible applicants must submit an application to CRCC and pass its examination to become certified by the organization. Once counselors have become certified, CRCC requires them to renew their certification every 5 years, which entails either retaking their exam or accumulating at least 100 hours of continuing education (Commission on Rehabilitation Counselor Certification, 2010).

1.2.5 School Counseling

Professional school counselors work in elementary, middle, and high schools to serve the *personal–social, career,* and *academic* needs of the school's students. School counseling began as a profession dedicated primarily to vocational guidance, and then school counselors began also addressing the personal–social issues of students in need through individual counseling. Since then, the role of the school counselor has undergone a substantial transformation. Today, the role of the school counselor, as outlined by the American School Counselor Association (ASCA), the division of ACA that serves as the professional association for school counselors, is

that of an educator with special training in counseling who is committed to increasing student achievement and success (ASCA, 2004).

- ASCA's main ideal is that school counselors should meet the needs of every student (ASCA, 2004), not just the ones who seek help or are referred to the counselor by teachers or parents. Implementation of a comprehensive, developmental school counseling program is accomplished through individual counseling, individual student planning, group counseling, delivering classroom guidance lessons, and consultation. In addition, ASCA urges school counselors to infuse their work with accountability, collaboration, advocacy, and leadership to ensure that all students have equal access to a high-quality education.
- To help school counseling programs meet the needs of all students, ASCA (2005) published the *ASCA National Model: A Framework for School Counseling Programs*, which provides school counselors with guidelines on how to reshape their programs to fully meet ASCA's standards and ensure that they are comprehensive, accountable, and developmental.

1.2.6 Other Types of Mental Health Counseling

A **mental health practitioner** is a person trained to treat individuals with mental health issues and mental illnesses. Many types of the professional counselors reviewed in preceding subsections are mental health practitioners, but this extensive occupational category incorporates a wide range of professionals, a handful of which are described in this section, including psychologists, psychiatrists, psychoanalysts, social workers, psychiatric nurses, and marriage and family therapists. All these professionals help individuals with similar concerns and problems, but they differ in the types of treatment that they have been educated and trained to administer in working with clients.

1.2.6.1 PSYCHOLOGISTS A **psychologist** diagnoses and treats psychological, learning, and behavioral disorders in a variety of settings, including clinics, schools, hospitals, counseling centers and private and group practice. Psychologists use interviewing and psychological testing when assessing and diagnosing client issues. Specializations within the field include clinical, counseling, and school psychology. To obtain licensure in most states, individuals must earn a doctoral degree in psychology.

1.2.6.2 PSYCHIATRISTS A **psychiatrist** is a medical doctor who works with clients with severe psychological disorders. Psychiatrists provide psychotherapy, prescribe medications, perform physical examinations, and order laboratory testing for clients. To become a psychiatrist, individuals must earn a medical degree, participate in a residency program, and pass licensure examinations.

1.2.6.3 PSYCHOANALYSTS A **psychoanalyst** helps clients resolve psychological issues through psychoanalysis—an

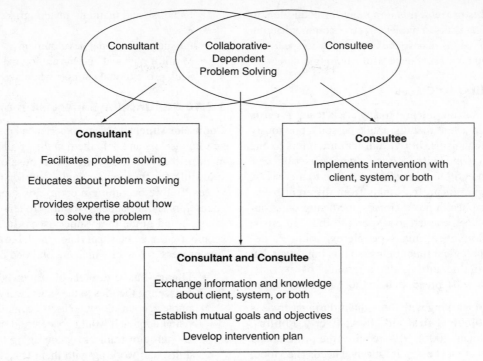

FIGURE 1.1 Consultation as a collaborative-dependent relationship.
Source: From B. T. Erford, (2011). *Transforming the school counseling profession,* 3rd ed. (p. 227). Upper Saddle River, NJ: Merrill Prentice Hall. Reprinted with permission.

intervention developed by Sigmund Freud—a long-term process that attempts to help clients remedy and alleviate their symptoms through exploring their unconscious conflicts. To become a psychoanalyst, individuals are usually required to earn a terminal degree in the mental health field, train at a psychoanalysis institute, and engage in personal psychoanalysis by a trained psychoanalyst. Psychoanalysts generally work in private practice.

1.2.6.4 SOCIAL WORKERS A **social worker** is characterized by his or her commitment to pursuing social reform, social justice, and affecting public policy. The social worker's role is one of counselor, case manager, and change agent, which is accomplished through delivering therapeutic treatments to clients, connecting clients with valuable community resources, advocating to fix societal conflicts, working with communities to develop programs to meet the needs of citizens, conducting research, and teaching. Educational requirements for social workers include a minimum of a bachelor's degree in social work.

1.2.6.5 PSYCHIATRIC NURSES **Psychiatric nursing** is a specialization within the nursing profession. Psychiatric nurses are trained to deliver counseling services to patients with severe psychological disorders, develop nursing care programs, and, in many states, prescribe medication. Individuals can pursue psychiatric nursing at the bachelor's, master's, and doctoral levels.

1.2.6.6 MARRIAGE AND FAMILY THERAPISTS A **marriage and family therapist** approaches working with individuals,

couples, and families from a systems theory perspective, helping clients to develop more effective patterns of interaction with significant others and family members. To become a marriage and family therapist, individuals must earn at least a master's degree in marriage and family therapy.

1.2.7 Interagency Collaboration

At times counselors must seek consultation and collaboration with other professionals, and even other agencies and organizations, to best meet client needs. In fact, the ACA *Code of Ethics* (2005, D.1.c.) encourages this type of interdisciplinary cooperation because it helps enrich and enhance the effectiveness of counseling interventions. However, to work successfully with others, it is important to follow a sound model. The **collaborative-interdependent consultation model** (see figure 1.1) (Erford, 2011) provides clinicians with a way to work in concert with community organizations to solve complicated problems that affect many clients on a variety of levels.

- In the collaborative-interdependent model, diverse professionals join together as *equals* to solve presenting issues of individuals. Although some consultation models require one member to serve as an expert, this model stresses the importance of all members contributing equitably. Because this model is used to solve complex problems, no one person can act as the expert, and all members are responsible for sharing their own personal knowledge and expertise, listening to the input and ideas of others, and working *interdependently* to develop a way forward.

- Throughout this process, it is important for counselors to use their helping skills to model effective communication, ensure that all members have the opportunity to speak and contribute, and preserve a respectful environment.

1.2.8 Responding to Crises

Professional counselors are integral to any crisis team. A **crisis** can be defined as any event that disrupts a person's previously effective coping mechanisms. **Individual trauma** refers to one person's ability to cope with a crisis, whereas **collective trauma** refers to an entire community's reaction to a crisis. A **crisis team** is a group of professionals from different backgrounds (e.g., mental health professionals, medical professionals, etc.) who have been trained to respond to those in crisis. Following a traumatic event, many people experience a decrease in their psychological functioning, so it is important that counselors are available during the aftermath of a crisis, whether it is local or widespread, to help those in need recover.

- One method of working with individuals during a crisis is called **psychological first aid (PFA;** Everly, Phillips, Kane, & Feldman, 2006). PFA requires the professional counselor to first meet essential survival needs (i.e., food, water, shelter, safety), then client psychological needs by using the core counseling skills (e.g., active listening, reflecting, showing empathy, etc.). Finally, the counselor should work with clients to help them establish contact with friends and family to help mitigate feelings of loneliness or isolation.
- After natural disasters, the **crisis counseling program (CCP;** Castellano & Plionis, 2006) can be used to help restore a sense of safety. Using this model, professional counselors should work with a team to identify the problem, inventory the available resources, help reduce the disorder and confusion, assist victims in adjusting to their new life situations, provide victims with support and empathy, and educate individuals about common and atypical reactions to crisis and what to do should they need extra help.
- Although two specific models have been discussed, there exist a variety of approaches that counselors can implement effectively with crisis victims, including client-centered counseling, existential counseling, cognitive-behavioral therapy, and play therapy for children. The most important aspect to keep in mind is that early intervention is the best intervention, regardless of the approach.

1.2.9 Self-Care Strategies

To function effectively with clients, it is vital that counselors take the appropriate steps to ensure that they are tending to their own personal needs and well-being. Counselors who suffer from burnout lack the ability to sufficiently meet the needs of their clients, so self-care should be a top priority. Although burnout will vary from person to person, the following activities and skills are thought to help prevent or mitigate the effects of burnout:

- Learn and implement time management skills.
- Engage regularly in enjoyable activities and hobbies.

- Establish and maintain meaningful connections with others.
- Pursue professional development.
- Monitor physical and psychological health.
- Seek professional support when needed.

1.2.10 Counselor Supervision Models

Counselor supervisors are experienced professionals who train new counselors and help them in the development and improvement of their clinical skills. All counselor supervisors are responsible for their own clients, and for those of their supervisees. Before becoming a counselor supervisor, professional counselors should undergo training to learn the necessary skills to assist and guide their supervisees. In addition, counselors should use a specific supervision model to facilitate the supervision process, a few of which are outlined briefly in this section.

- **Theory-based models of supervision** extend the basic counseling theories to the supervisory relationship. For example, a counselor who uses a cognitive-behavioral supervision approach would concentrate on teaching new skills to counselor-trainees, encouraging them to practice their skills, and working with them to help improve particular areas of weakness. A counselor using a client-centered approach would establish a warm, trusting environment where counselor-trainees feel comfortable and confident enough to practice and refine their counseling skills.
- **Developmental supervision approaches** emphasize counselor-trainees' progress through a series of stages as they become more experienced, competent, and independent. To meet the needs of the trainee at each stage, supervisors must adjust and adapt their supervisory style.
- Beyond theory-based and developmental supervision approaches, some models have been developed *specifically* for supervision. For example, the **discrimination model** requires the supervisor to be aware of the supervisee's intervention, conceptualization, and personalization skills and address supervisee needs by adopting the role of either teacher, counselor, or consultant as needed.

Supervision can occur in a variety of formats. Supervisors might meet privately with supervisees to discuss particular cases, meet with supervisees in a group format, watch videotapes of supervisee counseling sessions, and/or actually sit in during a supervisee session with a client (called a **live observation**). It is of utmost importance for counselor supervisors to establish positive, honest, and trusting working relationships with their supervisees to foster their professional growth and reduce their anxiety.

1.2.11 Practice Multiple-Choice Items: Counseling Specializations

1. CRCC certifies the following type of counselor:
   a. Clinical mental health counselors
   b. School counselors
   c. College counselors
   d. Rehabilitation counselors

2. The mental health practitioners who most commonly administer psychological testing are
   a. psychiatrists.
   b. psychologists.
   c. professional counselors.
   d. psychiatric nurses.

3. A _____ works in counseling centers at postsecondary institutions to meet the mental health and wellness needs of students.
   a. school counselor
   b. college admissions counselor
   c. college counselor
   d. clinical mental health counselor

4. By license, all _____ can prescribe medication to their clients.
   a. psychiatrists
   b. psychologists
   c. professional counselors
   d. All of the above

5. The professionals most involved in working to affect public policy are
   a. marriage and family therapists.
   b. social workers.
   c. rehabilitation counselors.
   d. school counselors.

Answer Key: 1. d; 2. b; 3. c; 4. a; 5. b.

1.3 PROFESSIONAL ORGANIZATIONS

In this third section of Chapter 1, you will find brief summaries in alphabetical order of over 20 **professional associations** and organizations important to the counseling profession, which demonstrate the scope and diversity of this profession, many of which are affiliated with ACA and represented in Figure 1.2. Professional associations serve a multitude of purposes within the counseling field. They unite members through a shared identity, advocate on behalf of the profession, provide members with professional development opportunities and access to valuable resources, and often publish journals containing current research and news about their counseling specializations.

1.3.1 American Association of State Counseling Boards

Founded in 1986 through an ACA committee recommendation, the **American Association of State Counseling Boards (AASCB)** was created to connect together states that have licensure boards in order to promote communication to the public and collaboration among states regarding licensure laws and legal matters (AASCB, 2009). The mission of AASCB is to ensure that all proficient counselors have the ability to become licensed by their state boards as well as to spark discussion and cooperation among state boards with the purpose of making the licensure process simpler and more standardized across states.

1.3.2 American College Counseling Association

The **American College Counseling Association (ACCA)**, a division of ACA, was chartered in 1991 to unify counseling professionals working at postsecondary institutions in support of the mental health and growth of students (ACCA, 2006). ACCA's mission is to bring together college counselors from all professional backgrounds to improve the profession, share ideas, encourage ethical practice, and advocate for college counseling. ACCA publishes the *Journal of College Counseling*.

1.3.3 American Counseling Association (ACA)

The **American Counseling Association (ACA)**, headquartered in Alexandria, Virginia, was first established in 1952 as the American Personnel and Guidance Association (APGA) when four autonomous associations (National Vocational Guidance Association, National Association of Guidance and Counselor Trainers, Student Personnel Association for Teacher Education, and American College Personnel Association) united to gain more of a presence in the counseling field and in governmental and legislative initiatives at the federal level. The organization changed its name in 1983 to the American Association of Counseling and Development (AACD) and again in 1993 to ACA, the name it still uses today (2009). The final name change was endorsed to demonstrate the shared affiliation of all members. Today, ACA has over 40,000 members and serves as a nationally recognized organization with 19 divisions, which represent nearly all the diverse disciplines within the counseling field. The 19 divisions are listed in Figure 1.2.

ACA's mission statement is "To enhance the quality of life in society by promoting the development of professional counselors, advancing the counseling profession and practice of counseling to promote respect for human dignity and diversity" (ACA, 2009). Working under that charter, ACA is a nonprofit organization that advocates and provides services not only for professional counselors in the United States but also for counselors in 50 other countries. With the goal of helping professional counselors, and the profession itself, ACA offers benefit and support to those in need, has created a *Code of Ethics* to which members must adhere, offers continuing educational opportunities to help members stay current in their individual area, publishes literature on topics of interest to counselors, and promotes the profession's mission in Congress and in the media.

1.3.4 American Mental Health Counselors Association

The **American Mental Health Counselors Association (AMHCA)** was formed in 1976 and became a division of ACA in 1978 to help mental health counselors establish a clear and unified identity, separate from other counseling professionals. One of AMHCA's primary goals when it formed was to begin the process of establishing licensure laws in states without licensure laws as well as to create accreditation standards for relevant counseling programs. The present vision of AMHCA is to advocate for the profession, provide members with professional

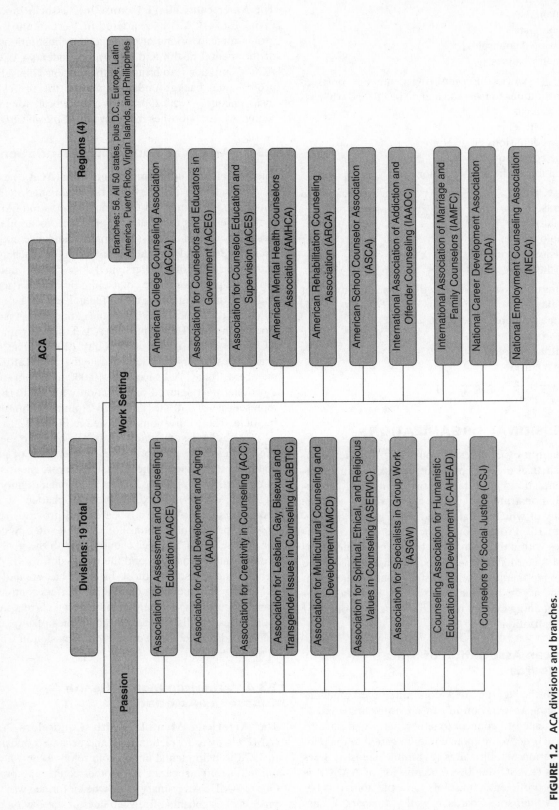

FIGURE 1.2 ACA divisions and branches.

Source: From Erford, B. T. (2010). *Orientation to the counseling profession.* Upper Saddle River, NJ: Pearson.

development opportunities, and continue promoting licensure for mental health counselors (AMHCA, 2004). AMHCA publishes the *Journal of Mental Health Counseling.*

1.3.5 American Rehabilitation Counseling Association

Founded in 1958, the **American Rehabilitation Counseling Association (ARCA)**, a division of ACA, is the professional association for rehabilitation counselors, educators, and students. The missions of ARCA are to foster quality practice, education, and research within the profession; improve the lives of people who have disabilities; advocate the removal of barriers for people with disabilities; and raise public awareness regarding rehabilitation counseling (American Rehabilitation Counseling Association, 2005). ARCA is a separate association from the National Rehabilitation Counseling Association (NRCA), although efforts have been made in the past to merge the two associations. ARCA publishes the *Rehabilitation Counseling Bulletin.*

1.3.6 American School Counselor Association

Established in 1953, the **American School Counselor Association (ASCA)**, a division of ACA, was created to serve the needs of all professional school counselors by hosting professional development classes and seminars, publishing cutting-edge research on effective programs, providing helpful and practical resources to members, and promoting ethical behavior (ASCA, 2009). The vision of ASCA is to function as the voice for school counselors, advocating on their behalf, and to provide professional school counselors with the tools they need to successfully support students. ASCA publishes *Professional School Counseling,* which keeps readers informed about research and new ideas within the school counseling field.

1.3.7 Association for Adult Development and Aging

The **Association for Adult Development and Aging (AADA)**, chartered by ACA in 1986, was created to improve the counseling services available to adults at all stages of life through advancing counselor education and preparation related to human development and aging (AADA, 2005). AADA is also committed to campaigning for higher standards of care for older adults and partners with organizations that share its mission. AADA publishes *Adultspan,* a journal that prints current research on aging and adult development.

1.3.8 Association for Assessment in Counseling and Education

The **Association for Assessment in Counseling and Education (AACE)**, a division of ACA since 1965, was founded to guide the proper development, training, and use of assessment in the realm of counseling and education (AACE, 2008). In addition, AACE backs legislation that is in alignment with its mission and encourages professional development for individuals who use diagnostic or assessment tools in their practice. AACE leaders and members have been involved in numerous committees formed to develop guidelines for the ethical use of tests and other evaluation tools, such as the "Responsibilities of Users of Standardized Tests" and ACA's "Position Statement on High Stakes Testing." AACE publishes two journals: *Measurement and Evaluation in Counseling and Development* (MECD) and *Counseling Outcome Research and Evaluation* (CORE).

1.3.9 Association for Counselor Education and Supervision

The primary goal of the **Association for Counselor Education and Supervision (ACES)** is to enhance counseling services in all specializations through the promotion of quality education, supervision, and credentialing of counselors (ACES, 2005). The vision of ACES is to support educational programs and supervisory practices that are culturally competent and shown both to be successful and to possess value to the community. ACES was one of the founding associations of ACA. ACES publishes the journal *Counselor Education and Supervision.*

1.3.10 Association for Counselors and Educators in Government

Founded in 1978, the **Association for Counselors and Educators in Government (ACEG)** became a division of ACA in 1984. Formed to connect counselors and educators working in government and military settings, ACEG's mission is to provide adequate support to its members so that counselors and educators in government can work effectively with their clients and to create a network of professionals to share ideas and give assistance to other members (ACEG, 2009).

1.3.11 Association for Creativity in Counseling

The **Association for Creativity in Counseling (ACC)** is a fairly new association; it was established in 2004 and has since become a division of ACA. ACC champions imaginative and creative approaches to counseling and comprises counseling professionals from diverse specializations, including dance, art, music, and play therapy (ACC, 2004). ACC's mission is to increase the recognition and appreciation of creative approaches to counseling within the profession, promote the use of such techniques, and determine which factors serve to increase creativity in counselors and in clients. ACC publishes the *Journal of Creativity in Mental Health.*

1.3.12 Association for Lesbian, Gay, Bisexual, and Transgender Issues in Counseling

The **Association for Lesbian, Gay, Bisexual, and Transgender Issues in Counseling (ALGBTIC)** was established in 1975 (known then as the Caucus of Gay and Lesbian Counselors) in the midst of the gay activism of the 1970s to fight in the crusade for recognition of sexual minority issues within the counseling profession (ALGBTIC, 2009).

- Originally was titled the Association for Gay, Lesbian, and Bisexual Issues in Counseling (AGLBIC), in 1997

ALGBTIC received divisional status from ACA after more than 20 years of endeavoring to gain the association's official endorsement. The same year, ALGBTIC created *Competencies for Counseling LGBT Clients,* which provides counselors with an overview of the skills counselors should possess to work effectively with these clients.

- The overriding mission of ALGBTIC is to improve the delivery of counseling services to sexual minorities and to promote professional understanding of the effect of society on lesbian, gay, bisexual, and transgender (LGBT) issues and challenges (ALGBTIC, 2009). Also at the core of ALGBTIC's mission is the attempt to remove barriers that interfere with the development of LGBT clients and to ensure that LGBT counselors and counseling students have the same access to quality education and equal professional standing as other counselors and students.
- ALGBTIC publishes *The Journal of LGBT Issues in Counseling.*

1.3.13 Association for Multicultural Counseling and Development

Created in 1972 to raise awareness about multicultural issues in counseling, the **Association for Multicultural Counseling and Development (AMCD)**, like ALGBTIC, encountered difficulty in its attempts to become a division of ACA and receive the association's official recognition and support (AMCD, 2009). However, it eventually secured divisional status.

The mission of AMCD is to foster the growth and mental health of all individuals by working to identify and eliminate obstacles preventing the development of clients, appreciate human diversity and multiculturalism, and ensure that counselors and counseling students from all backgrounds receive equal status, treatment, and access to higher education (AMCD, 2009). The *AMCD Multicultural Counseling Competencies* were published in 1992 to guide counselors in delivering effective counseling services to clients from dissimilar backgrounds. AMCD produces the *Journal of Multicultural Counseling and Development.*

1.3.14 Association for Specialists in Group Work

The **Association for Specialists in Group Work (ASGW)**, a division of ACA since 1973, was founded to serve as the international association for group workers. ASGW's undertakings are to create standards of ethical group practice, promote group work, encourage research on counseling groups, and inspire members to become leaders in the field through modeling successful techniques in group practice (ASGW, 2009). ASGW publishes the *Journal for Specialists in Group Work* as well as best practice guidelines, training standards, and multicultural group work principles.

1.3.15 Association for Spiritual, Ethical, and Religious Values in Counseling

The **Association for Spiritual, Ethical, and Religious Values in Counseling (ASERVIC)** was originally developed as a joining together of the Catholic members of APGA and Catholic guidance councils across the United States, the first of which was formed in 1951 in the Archdiocese in New York to provide guidance for students at diocesan parochial schools (ASERVIC, 2010). These two groups joined forces in 1961 to create the National Catholic Guidance Conference (NCGC), and in 1974 the NCGC was granted divisional status in APGA. The name of the organization was changed in 1993 to the name it uses today. No particular religious group controls the association, so the name change was enacted to reflect the increased diversity of members and member faiths.

The mission of ASERVIC is to promote the incorporation of spiritual, religious, and ethical values into counselors' educational programs and professional practice (ASERVIC, 2010). To help achieve this goal, ASERVIC has generated *Competencies for Integrating Spirituality into Counseling,* which is aimed at helping counselors work with clients from various religious and spiritual backgrounds in an ethical and sensitive manner. ASERVIC publishes the journal *Counseling and Values.*

1.3.16 Chi Sigma Iota

Chi Sigma Iota (CSI) is the international honor society for professional counselors, counselor educators, and counseling students. CSI was created in 1985 to foster achievement and scholarship within the profession and to acknowledge exceptional leaders in the field (Chi Sigma Iota, 2008).

- To become a member of CSI, professional counselors and counselor educators must have achieved a GPA of 3.5 or above, based on a 4.0 scale, in their counseling program and be endorsed by their chapter. In addition, they must be credentialed as counselors at either the state or national level.
- Counseling students who have completed at least one semester of full-time coursework at the graduate level in a counseling program, have attained a GPA of 3.5 or above, and have been recommended by their chapter are also eligible to join.
- Members are able to apply for CSI's award, research grant, fellowship, and internship programs.

1.3.17 Counseling Association for Humanistic Education and Development

The **Counseling Association for Humanistic Education and Development (C-AHEAD)** was formed in 1931 and became one of the founding organizations of ACA in 1952. C-AHEAD has evolved over the years to become "the heart and conscience of the counseling profession" (C-AHEAD, 2009).

- According to C-AHEAD (2009), some of the core convictions of humanistic counselors include the belief in the worth and dignity of all human beings, self-determination, the capacity for clients to make progress and enhance their own lives, and the need for clients to help others and the community to grow and improve their mental health.
- C-AHEAD attempts to look after the mental health and wellness of clients and counselors. The association

hosts a Wellness Center for counselors at each ACA convention. It also gathers donations from ACA members to support its Empty Plate Project, which gives money to a local food bank during each convention (C-AHEAD, 2009).

- C-AHEAD publishes the *Journal of Humanistic Counseling, Education, and Development.*

1.3.18   Counselors for Social Justice

Counselors for Social Justice (CSJ), a division of ACA since 2002, was established with the mission of "confronting oppressive systems of power and privilege" relevant to counselors and their clients (CSJ, 2007). CSJ aspires not only to advocate on behalf of clients but also to empower clients to fight injustices affecting them. Counselors working with a social justice philosophy recognize the necessity of considering their clients' cultural backgrounds and the social contexts in which they live when developing treatment plans and counseling goals. CSJ, in conjunction with Psychologists for Social Responsibility, publishes the *Journal for Social Action in Counseling and Psychology.*

1.3.19   International Association of Addiction and Offender Counselors

The **International Association of Addiction and Offender Counselors (IAAOC)**, a division of ACA, was chartered in 1974. The association comprises substance abuse and corrections counselors, students, and counselor educators who are dedicated to helping individuals with addictions and those who have engaged in adult or juvenile criminal behaviors (IAAOC, 2009). The mission of IAAOC is to promote suitable services for and treatment of clients addressing these issues and also to forward this counseling specialization by endorsing ongoing research, training, advocacy, prevention, and intervention related to these groups.

IAAOC was a strong proponent for the development of the Master Addictions Counselor (MAC) credential, one of NBCC's specialty credentials, which is available to counselors who have achieved advanced training and experience in addictions counseling and who have also passed the Examination for Master Addictions Counselors. IAAOC publishes the *Journal of Addictions and Offender Counseling.*

1.3.20   International Association of Marriage and Family Counselors

The **International Association of Marriage and Family Counselors (IAMFC)** was founded in 1986 at Ohio University and chartered by ACA in 1989. IAMFC's mission is to encourage leadership and distinction in marriage and family counseling. Some of IAMFC's goals include advocating on behalf of clients and the profession; disseminating helpful information to the public about couples and family counseling, thereby increasing the public knowledge of IAMFC; promoting excellence in counselor preparation that includes training in systems theory; encouraging research related to marriage and family counseling; and offering professional development opportunities to counselors (IAMFC, 2002). IAMFC publishes *The Family Journal: Counseling and Therapy for Couples and Families.*

1.3.21   National Career Development Association

The **National Career Development Association (NCDA)**, one of the founding associations of ACA in 1952, was established in 1913 to champion the career development issues faced by people of all ages and to serve as the leading association for individuals who provide career services (NCDA, 2010). NCDA is involved in creating standards of practice for career counselors, establishing ethical guidelines for counselors working in career services settings, and appraising career materials and resources. The association also advocates on behalf of its members in Congress.

- In November of each year, NCDA sponsors National Career Development Month, which aims to inspire career development professionals to celebrate and host career-related activities. During this career development month, NCDA holds a poetry and poster contest centered around a career theme that is open to children and to adults (NCDA, 2010).
- NCDA publishes *Career Development Quarterly.*

1.3.22   National Employment Counseling Association

The **National Employment Counseling Association (NECA)** was chartered by ACA in 1966. The mission of NECA is to make strides in the field of employment counseling by providing members with helpful resources, promoting research and knowledge related to effective career counseling techniques and tools to best serve job seekers and society, staying abreast of legislation affecting employment counselors, and creating a community in which professionals can network and share ideas (NECA, 2008). The *Journal of Employment Counseling* is the official journal of NECA.

1.3.23   National Rehabilitation Counseling Association

Founded in 1958, the **National Rehabilitation Counseling Association (NRCA)** was created to help individuals with disabilities become as independent and self-reliant as possible through counseling interventions and advocacy (NRCA, 2009). NRCA also works to uphold the professional standards of preparation for rehabilitation counselors set forth by CRCC and the Council of Rehabilitation Education, ensure that clients from all backgrounds receive equal services and treatment, encourage professional rehabilitation counselors to practice in an ethical manner, and advocate for licensure and certification for rehabilitation counselors. NRCA collaborated with CRCC and ARCA to develop the *Rehabilitation Counseling Code of Ethics and Scope of Practice Statement,* which guides ethical practice for the profession. NRCA publishes the *Journal of Applied Rehabilitation Counseling.*

1.3.24 Practice Multiple-Choice Items: Professional Organizations

1. The _____ is *not* a founding member of ACA.
   a. Counseling Association for Humanistic Education and Development (C-AHEAD)
   b. American School Counselor Association (ASCA)
   c. National Career Development Association (NCDA)
   d. Association for Counselor Education and Supervision (ACES)

2. The most recently established division of ACA is
   a. Association for Creativity in Counseling (ACC).
   b. Counselors for Social Justice (CSJ).
   c. Association for Lesbian, Gay, Bisexual, and Transgender Issues in Counseling (ALGBTIC).
   d. Association for Multicultural Counseling and Development (AMCD).

3. NECA and NCDA are both professional associations devoted to the specialization of
   a. career counseling.
   b. rehabilitation counseling.
   c. college counseling.
   d. marriage and family counseling.

4. The Association for Spiritual, Ethical, and Religious Values in Counseling (ASERVIC) began as an association for counselors who were
   a. Jewish.
   b. Protestant.
   c. Catholic.
   d. Baptist.

5. Members of IAAOC are committed to helping clients who
   a. are dealing with addictions.
   b. have engaged in criminal acts as adults.
   c. are juvenile delinquents.
   d. are all of the above.

Answer Key: 1. b; 2. a; 3. a; 4. c; 5. d.

1.4 ETHICAL AND LEGAL ISSUES

1.4.1 Ethics

Ethics are moral principles that guide an individual's behavior. For professional counselors, ethics and, more specifically, codes of ethics are what guide professional practice to ensure that the welfare and safety of clients and counselors are secure. According to Herlihy and Corey (2006), codes of ethics serve a variety of purposes. The most fundamental objective of codes of ethics is to give information to professionals about how to practice in an ethical manner. To behave ethically, counselors are required to familiarize themselves deeply with applicable ethical codes. Although many ethical standards are straightforward, others are more complex and ambiguous, necessitating that counselors take adequate time to ensure they understand both the content of the code and how to resolve any ethical quandaries they may encounter.

Codes of ethics are also established as accountability measures and as means to enhance professional practice (Herlihy & Corey, 2006). For example, when professions have ethical codes, they are able to hold their members liable for any breaches of ethical conduct. Also, by including in their codes not only **mandatory ethics**, which are the lowest standards to which all members must comply to behave ethically, but also **aspirational ethics**, which describe best practices, professions can inspire members to work on continually improving their own knowledge base and skills to advance their practice and the reputation of the profession itself.

1.4.1.1 PRINCIPLES OF ETHICAL CODES

Many codes of ethics embrace certain principles considered necessary for ethical conduct in that field. In the counseling profession, these principles are autonomy, nonmaleficence, beneficence, justice, and fidelity (Herlihy & Corey, 2006). When confronted with questions about ethics on the NCE or CPCE, it can be immensely helpful to think through these five principles; they will assist in determining whether an ethical violation is evident in a scenario and what a sound course of action might be in a given situation.

- **Autonomy** refers to the ability of clients to exercise free will and act independently. For counselors, this means respect for clients' rights to make their own decisions, even if the counselor does not agree with them or believe it is in their best interest.
- **Nonmaleficence** is the foundational principle on which counselors operate. It means to do no harm to clients. In any situation, counselors' first priority should be to ensure that the client is not injured—physically, mentally, or psychologically—or could potentially become injured as a result of the counselor's actions.
- **Beneficence**, in contrast to nonmaleficence, means doing only good. For counselors, this means being proactive in advancing the health and well-being of their clients.
- **Justice** is characterized by fairness. Counselors adhering to the principle of justice will not discriminate against clients and will ensure that all clients receive equal treatment.
- **Fidelity** means to be faithful and loyal. For counselors, this means facilitating trust, keeping one's word, and fulfilling any obligations they make to clients.

In some situations, these principles will contend with each other (Herlihy & Corey, 2006). In these cases, the counselor must judge which principle takes precedence.

1.4.1.2 ETHICAL DECISION MAKING

When faced with ethical dilemmas, it is also helpful to use some form of decision-making model. Herlihy and Corey (2006) describe one possible model in the *ACA Ethical Standards Casebook*, which serves as a helpful guide for counselors:

1. Identify the problem or concern.
2. Study pertinent codes of ethics and research.
3. Reflect on the principles of autonomy, nonmaleficence, beneficence, justice, and fidelity.

4. Consult with other professionals.
5. Maintain an awareness of your emotions to ensure that emotions do not cloud your judgment.
6. Include the client in the decision-making process whenever feasible.
7. Decide how you would like to see the situation resolved and brainstorm courses of action.
8. Examine the possible consequences for all courses of action and then select the one you would like to take.
9. Assess your chosen course of action.
10. Take action.

1.4.2 ACA *Code of Ethics*

As the professional association for all counselors, ACA publishes its *Code of Ethics* to serve as a basis for ethical behavior, providing counselors with a foundation and model for behavior, a useful resource when ethical questions arise, and a procedure for filing and responding to ethical complaints (ACA, 2005). Since 1961 when the first *Code of Ethics* was created, ACA's *Code of Ethics* has undergone five revisions to update both its content and format, aiming to ensure the code's continued relevance and comprehensiveness (Herlihy & Corey, 2006). As the profession evolves, so too does the ethical code, and it is the responsibility of professional counselors to stay abreast of any changes that are implemented. For example, in the most recent revision of the code in 2005, new sections were added on such topics as technology and end-of-life care. As important issues surface within the profession, ACA revises its code to ensure that professional counselors understand how best to respond.

Becoming intimately familiar with the content of the ACA and NBCC codes of ethics will prove invaluable when answering ethics questions on the NCE or CPCE. To help facilitate that process, this section of Chapter 1 summarizes the key points of the eight sections that comprise the ACA *Code of Ethics:*

A. The Counseling Relationship
B. Confidentiality, Privileged Communication, and Privacy
C. Professional Responsibility
D. Relationships with Other Professionals
E. Evaluation, Assessment, and Interpretation
F. Supervision, Training, and Teaching
G. Research and Publication
H. Resolving Ethical Issues

You should review the most current version of the ACA *Code of Ethics* prior to taking the NCE or CPCE. It can be downloaded in its entirety by visiting the following link: http://www.counseling.org/Resources/CodeOfEthics/TP/Home/CT2.aspx.

1.4.2.1 SECTION A: THE COUNSELING RELATIONSHIP

Section Highlights Counselors must:

- Keep accurate records and document their activities as required by their employer and by the law.
- Develop realistic counseling plans in conjunction with clients.
- Obtain informed consent (verbally and in writing) from clients.
- Obtain assent from those unable to give informed consent (e.g., minors).
- Seek permission to make contact and work collaboratively with any additional counselors or mental health professionals who their client is seeing.
- Avoid any romantic or sexual relationships with clients, their significant others, or their family members. In addition, counselors must not engage in any romantic or sexual relationships with previous clients, their significant others, or their family members for 5 years after the date the client was last seen professionally.
- Avoid any interactions with clients outside of the professional context unless the interaction could be potentially beneficial (e.g., attending a wedding, graduation, or funeral). If counselors decide to engage in a potentially beneficial interaction, they must gain consent from the client and document their reasoning in writing.
- Gain consent from the client before changing roles in the counseling relationship (e.g., switching from acting as an individual counselor to a family counselor).
- Advocate on behalf of clients, with their consent, to help them overcome barriers to improvement, and encourage clients to advocate on their own behalf when possible.
- Screen potential group members prior to starting a group, and only select clients whose goals align with the group's purpose.
- Assist terminally ill clients in receiving excellent end-of-life care and being involved in educated decision making regarding their care.
- Establish appropriate fees.
- Refrain from engaging in bartering unless it is fair, suggested by the client, and an admissible convention in the community.
- Exercise prudence when offered a gift from a client. Consider the potential effect on the counseling relationship before deciding to accept or decline the gift.
- Make arrangements for clients to continue to receive care in the case of extended absence, illness, or death.
- Terminate the counseling relationship when it is evident that the client no longer needs or is benefiting from treatment.
- Abide by applicable laws when engaging in technology-assisted distance counseling.
- Ensure that clients are capable of using the appropriate technology before engaging in technology-assisted distance counseling.
- Include information about technology in the informed consent process, when applicable, such as limits to confidentiality.

1.4.2.2 SECTION B: CONFIDENTIALITY, PRIVILEGED COMMUNICATION, AND PRIVACY

Section Highlights Counselors must:

- Address the issue of confidentiality in a culturally sensitive manner, inform clients of the limits to confidentiality, and refrain from divulging confidential information about clients to outside parties without client consent or a legal or ethical rationale.

- Limits to confidentiality arise when:
  - "disclosure is required to protect clients or identified others from serious and foreseeable harm" (ACA, 2005, B.2.a.). For example, if a client is threatening to hurt himself or herself or someone else, or if someone is threatening to hurt the client, counselors are ethically obligated to break confidentiality.
  - Clients disclose that they have a life-threatening and communicable disease that they may be infecting an identified other with and refuse to inform that person of their disease. However, counselors are only "justified" (ACA, 2005, B.2.b.) in breaking confidentiality under these circumstances, not required.
  - Ordered by the court.
- Communicate their plans to break confidentiality to the client, if possible and appropriate.
- Only disclose the minimum amount of information required when breaking confidentiality is necessary.
- Obtain client consent before sharing confidential information with treatment teams or third-party payers.
- Ensure that any confidential discussions with clients occur in private settings.
- Discuss confidentiality and its limits when conducting group work, marriage counseling, or family counseling.
- Recognize the rights of parents/legal guardians to access confidential information of minor clients and work in concert with parents/legal guardians to meet the needs of the minor.
- Keep records in a safe location, protected from those who do not have the authority to access them.
- Allow clients to have "reasonable access" (ACA, 2005, B.6.d.) to their records and answer any questions clients have about the information found therein.
- Obtain consent before recording a session with a client, observing a session with a client, or showing a recorded session to an outside party.
- Discuss the limits of confidentiality with research participants, and refrain from publishing information about any participants that could reveal their identities, unless consent has been obtained.
- Protect the identity of clients when consulting with other professionals, unless the client has given his or her prior consent.

1.4.2.3 SECTION C: PROFESSIONAL RESPONSIBILITY

Section Highlights **Counselors must:**

- Practice within the parameters of their education, training, and experience.
- Only accept jobs that align with their qualifications; only hire employees that are capable and qualified.
- Evaluate the effectiveness of their skills and techniques and work to improve any weaknesses identified.

- Participate in continuing education and professional development to stay informed about current techniques and procedures and to improve their effectiveness.
- Remain cognizant of their own level of functioning and abstain from performing professional duties when they are experiencing an impairment (e.g., emotional, psychological, physical) that is likely to interfere with their ability to help their clients.
- Select a "records custodian" (ACA, 2005, C.2.h.), a colleague who they will inform of their plan regarding what should happen to their records and clients in the event of their death, impairment, or discontinuation of practice.
- Truthfully represent their services in advertisements.
- Refrain from pressuring individuals with whom they are in a professional relationship to buy their products (i.e., books).
- Honestly represent their qualifications and credentials (e.g., counselors should not put the prefix "Dr." before their name if their doctoral degree is in a field unrelated to counseling).
- Denounce and avoid participation in any discriminatory behavior or sexual harassment, whether physical, verbal, or nonverbal.
- Use techniques that are "grounded in theory and/or have an empirical or scientific foundation" (ACA, 2005, C.6.e.) or else label their techniques as "developing"/"unproven" and make sure to discuss any possible risks with the client.

1.4.2.4 SECTION D: RELATIONSHIP WITH OTHER PROFESSIONALS

Section Highlights **Counselors must:**

- Show respect for professionals and organizations that use counseling procedures or techniques that are different from the ones they use.
- Strive to create positive relationships with other professionals (inside and outside of their field) to enrich their own practice and effectiveness with clients.
- Only give staff members job responsibilities for which they are trained and qualified to perform.
- Protect client confidentiality and promote the welfare of the client when working in interdisciplinary teams.
- Recognize that by accepting employment at an organization, they are indicating their accordance with that organization's practices and procedures.
- Notify their employer about any improper or unethical organizational practices that negatively affect clients, or counselors' ability to provide services, and work to change those policies.
- Refrain from firing or persecuting an employee who has revealed, in an ethical manner, improper or unethical practices within his or her organization.
- Only function in a consultative capacity in areas for which they are trained and qualified.
- Obtain informed consent before providing consultation.

- Ensure that the problem to be addressed and the goals to be worked toward during the consultation process are constructed in collaboration with the consultee.

1.4.2.5 SECTION E: EVALUATION, ASSESSMENT, AND INTERPRETATION

Section Highlights **Counselors must:**

- Safeguard client welfare by making accurate interpretations of assessment results, explaining to clients the results and their interpretations in terms they can understand, and working to ensure that other professionals do the same.
- Only use assessment tools that they are trained and qualified to use.
- Monitor the use of assessment techniques by any individuals under their supervision to ensure that they are being used appropriately.
- Obtain informed consent prior to engaging in an assessment of a client.
- Make culturally sensitive diagnoses of mental disorders.
- Consider abstaining from making a diagnosis if they think it would damage the client in any way.
- Only use assessment tools with sound psychometric properties.
- When choosing assessment tools for culturally diverse populations, exercise discretion to ensure their suitability. If counselors use assessments that were not normed on the client's population, they make sure to report the results in the appropriate context. For example, if a counselor uses an assessment for depression that was not normed on any Native American individuals, the counselor would take that into account when making an interpretation of a Native American client's results.
- Administer assessment tools "under the same conditions that were established in the standardization" (ACA, 2005, E.7.a.), document any "irregularities" or disruptions that occur during administration, and consider any irregularities or disruptions in the interpretation of results.
- Avoid making copies or replications of assessments without gaining permission from the publisher.
- Refrain from using any assessments or results from assessments that are dated or no longer used in the evaluation of a certain construct.
- Follow the appropriate, contemporary procedures when creating assessments.
- Refuse to perform forensic evaluations on current or former clients, as well as refuse to accept clients who are currently or have previously been evaluated for forensic purposes.

1.4.2.6 SECTION F: SUPERVISION, TRAINING, AND TEACHING

Section Highlights **Counselors must:**

- Observe the performance of counselors-in-training and ensure that clients' needs are being met. To that end,

counseling supervisors discuss cases with supervisees, observe live counseling sessions, and watch recorded sessions.
- Ensure that supervisees discuss the limits of confidentiality with clients in regard to the supervisory relationship.
- Complete training in supervision before supervising counselors-in-training.
- Avoid romantic or sexual relationships with supervisees.
- Refrain from entering into a supervisory relationship with family members, friends, or significant others.
- Avoid any interactions with supervisees outside of the professional context unless the interaction could be potentially beneficial (e.g., attending a wedding, graduation, or funeral). If counseling supervisors decide to engage in a potentially beneficial interaction, they must gain consent from the supervisee and document their reasoning in writing.
- Recognize that they, along with their supervisees, may end the supervisory relationship at any time provided that sufficient notice and rationale are given.
- Provide supervisees with regular formal and informal evaluation and feedback. If counseling supervisors notice that a supervisee is struggling in a certain area, they help him or her in gaining assistance to improve his or her performance.
- Propose supervisee dismissal from his or her training program if the supervisee exhibits an unreasonable lack of skill in his or her performance.
- Endorse supervisees who they believe are competent and ready for employment or to move forward in their training program.

Counselor educators must:

- Integrate information about multiculturalism into all classes to foster counselors who are culturally competent.
- Teach students about the ethical issues related to the counseling profession and their ethical obligations as students.
- Involve students in both academic coursework and supervised practical training.
- Develop procedures for assigning students to field placements, ensuring that all site supervisors are qualified to carry out their duties. In addition, counselor educators must ensure that both students and supervisors understand their responsibilities and ethical obligations.
- Give prospective students sufficient information and orientation about the counseling program's goals, requirements, and expectations.
- Use discretion when integrating activities or assignments in class that involves self-disclosure, making it clear to students that their level of self-disclosure will not affect their grade in the class.
- Provide students with regular formal and informal evaluation and feedback. If counselor educators notice that students are struggling in a certain area, they help them in gaining assistance to improve their performance.
- Refrain from engaging in romantic or sexual relationships with current students.

- Avoid any interactions with students outside of the professional context unless the interaction could be potentially beneficial (e.g., attending a wedding, graduation, or funeral). If counselor educators decide to engage in a potentially beneficial interaction, they must gain consent from the student and document their reasoning in writing.
- Promote the recruitment of diverse faculty members and students.

Counseling students must:

- Abide by the ACA *Code of Ethics* and any applicable laws.
- Recognize that their obligations to clients are the same as those of professional counselors.
- Remain aware of their own well-being and abstain from performing professional duties when they are experiencing an impairment (e.g., emotional, psychological, physical) that is likely to interfere with their ability to help their clients.

1.4.2.7 SECTION G: RESEARCH AND PUBLICATION

Section Highlights **Counselors who conduct research must:**

- Abide by relevant ethics and laws pertaining to research practices, including approval of human subjects research through an institutional review board (IRB).
- Hold themselves accountable for the safety of research participants.
- Understand that the principal researcher holds the greatest responsibility for ensuring ethical conduct, although others involved in a research project are, of course, also obligated to adhere to ethical standards.
- Take appropriate preventative measures to avoid creating disturbances in the lives of research participants.
- Obtain informed consent from research participants, ensuring that participants know that they may choose to drop out of the study at any time.
- Avoid using deception as part of a research study unless it is necessary, justifiable, and will not cause harm to the participants. After the study is complete, researchers inform the participants about the deception and the rationale for using it.
- Keep confidential any information gleaned about research participants during the study.
- Explain the exact purpose of the study to research participants once it has been completed.
- Report the results of the study to pertinent organizations, sponsors, and publications.
- Dispose, in a timely manner, of any materials related to a completed study that contains confidential information about participants.
- Recognize that romantic or sexual relationships with research participants are not permitted.
- Avoid any interactions with participants outside of the professional context unless the interaction could be potentially beneficial. If researchers decide to engage in a potentially beneficial interaction, they must gain consent from the participant and document their reasoning in writing.

- Faithfully report the results of their studies, even if the results are negative or discouraging, and include an explanation about the limitations of the study.
- Disguise the identities of participants in any information disseminated about the study, unless participants have given their consent.
- Publish enough information and detail about their study so that interested researchers can replicate it.
- Give credit in publications through such means as "joint authorship, acknowledgement, footnote statements" (ACA, 2005, G.5.d.) to individuals who have made substantial contributions to the research.
- Refrain from submitting articles for consideration to more than one publication at a time.
- Maintain author confidentiality when serving as a professional reviewer for a publication. In addition, counselors should only evaluate submissions that they are qualified to review.

1.4.2.8 SECTION H: RESOLVING ETHICAL ISSUES

Section Highlights **Counselors must:**

- Familiarize themselves with the ACA *Code of Ethics,* along with any other relevant codes of ethics (i.e., codes of ethics from other professional associations).
- Realize that not understanding the *Code of Ethics* is not a valid excuse for acting in an unethical manner while carrying out their professional duties.
- Try to resolve any conflicts that arise between the *Code of Ethics* and the law. When unable to do so, counselors may follow the law.
- Confront counselors who they believe are violating, or may be violating, the ethical code, and try to resolve the issue informally.
- Report any ethical violations that cannot be resolved informally to ACA's Ethics Committee or other applicable committees.
- Consult with colleagues, supervisors, organizations, or other professionals when in doubt about the ethical, appropriate course of action to take in a situation.
- Only file ethical complaints when they have sufficient information to back up the claim.
- Refrain from discriminating against individuals based *only* on the knowledge that they have filed ethics complaints or have had ethics complaints filed against them.
- Cooperate with any investigations made by ethics committees.

1.4.3 National Board for Certified Counselors *Code of Ethics*

The NBCC *Code of Ethics* (2005) applies directly to professional counselors who have been certified by its board. Any counselors who pass the NCE and subsequently become certified must abide by NBCC's ethical code and so, too, must any counselors aiming to become certified by NBCC. Unlike ACA's code, which provides counselors with mandatory and aspirational ethics, the NBCC code consists solely of mandatory ethics. Many of the sections of the NBCC code strongly resemble those found in the ACA code; however, some variation exists and is delineated in this section. The following seven sections comprise the NBCC ethical code:

1. Section A: General
2. Section B: Counseling Relationship
3. Section C: Counselor Supervision
4. Section D: Measurement and Evaluation
5. Section E: Research and Publication
6. Section F: Consulting
7. Section G: Private Practice.

Due to the substantial overlap between the ACA and NBCC codes, and to prevent unnecessary repetition, only elements that are unique to the NBCC code are discussed here. This section of Chapter 1 also includes any NBCC ethical standards that vary in some important way from those in the ACA code (e.g., time period for sexual and romantic relationships with clients).

1.4.3.1 SECTION A: GENERAL

Section Highlights **Certified counselors must:**

- Refrain from using the counseling relationship to meet their needs (i.e., personal or professional) to the detriment of the client.
- Avoid any romantic or sexual relationships with clients. In addition, counselors may not engage in any romantic or sexual relationships with previous clients for 2 years (remember that the ACA code requires counselors to wait at least 5 years) after the date the client was last seen professionally.
- Recognize that all professional behavior is a reflection on the counseling profession, and strive to promote and maintain the public's trust in the efficacy of counseling through ethical and legal behavior.
- Stop providing counseling services if they breach the ethical code.

1.4.3.2 SECTION B: COUNSELING RELATIONSHIP

Section Highlights **Certified counselors must:**

- Refrain from recommending their services to individuals who are "receiving similar services" (NBCC, 2005, B.2.) from another professional. If a person who is already receiving counseling services from a professional seeks additional counseling, counselors must use their judgment and discretion to decide whether to enter into a counseling relationship.
- "Take reasonable action" (NBCC, 2005, B.4.) to warn any third parties and/or contact relevant authorities when clients make serious threats to harm themselves or others.
- Understand that although the counseling records are their property, the *content* of the counseling records belongs to the *client,* which means that they must ask the client's permission before sharing any information with others.

- Permit clients to access their records, if requested.
- Retain counseling records for at least 5 years after the counseling relationship has ended, even if the client has died.
- Make certain that any client data that are stored electronically are protected and are deleted when no longer necessary.
- Remain aware of referral resources in their community should a personal impairment require them to terminate counseling services with clients. Certified counselors must always provide clients with acceptable referral options if they have to prematurely terminate the counseling relationship.
- Ensure that clients have access to other professionals who charge standard prices during and after involvement in brief counseling.
- Provide clients whom they are counseling long-distance (i.e., via the Internet) with community mental health resources in their area.
- Abide by the NBCC *Standards for Ethical Practice of Internet Counseling* when engaging in distance counseling using the Internet.
- Provide a manual for any "self-help/stand-alone computer software for use by the general public," and ensure that the software is suitable for all intended users (NBCC, 2005, B.15).

1.4.3.3 SECTION C: COUNSELOR SUPERVISION The significant elements of Section C of NBCC's ethical code are included in Section F of the ACA *Code of Ethics,* which can be reviewed in section 1.4.2.6.

1.4.3.4 SECTION D: MEASUREMENT AND EVALUATION

Section Highlights **Certified counselors must:**

- Truthfully represent the psychometric properties of any assessment instruments they discuss in communications to the public.
- Use discretion when interpreting any data from assessment instruments with inadequate technical information, and inform clients about the rationale for using such tools to evaluate them.
- Refrain from providing clients with copies of a test or training prior to their evaluation to avoid contaminating the outcomes of the test.
- Routinely check that all computer-based assessment instruments are working correctly.
- Avoid publicly disseminating any computer-based assessment instrument they have designed until its efficacy has been demonstrated.

1.4.3.5 SECTION E: RESEARCH AND PUBLICATION

Section Highlights **Certified counselors must:**

- Uphold any commitments they make to contribute to the projects or publications of another researcher (e.g., submit materials by the agreed-on deadline).

1.4.3.6   SECTION F: CONSULTING

Section Highlights **Certified counselors must:**

- Determine that they possess the requisite skills to provide effective services to consultees prior to entering into a consultative relationship.
- Avoid developing a relationship in which the consultee comes to depend on the counselor to make decisions. Certified counselors should help consultees become self-sufficient.

1.4.3.7   SECTION G: PRIVATE PRACTICE

Section Highlights **Certified counselors must:**

- Honestly represent themselves and their credentials when advertising their services.
- Refrain from including their name in "professional notices" (NBCC, 2005, G.2.) when they are not currently providing counseling services (e.g., when they are serving solely as an executive of a private practice organization).
- Make their degrees, credentials, and qualifications accessible to interested individuals.
- State their specialization and those of their co-workers when working in partnership with other professionals.

1.4.4   National Board for Certified Counselors Standards for the Ethical Practice of Internet Counseling

In addition to its standard ethical code, NBCC has developed ethical expectations for certified counselors who participate in **technology-assisted distance counseling**, which is defined as any counseling that occurs over the phone or online via e-mail, video, or chat programs (NBCC, 2007b). As technology has emerged and more clients have become interested in obtaining counseling services online, it has become important for counselors engaging in Internet counseling to understand their ethical obligations to their clients. This section provides an overview of NBCC's standards regarding Internet counseling, which differ somewhat from the standards found in the general ethical code. The three sections that comprise the NBCC *Standards for the Ethical Practice of Internet Counseling* are Internet Counseling Relationship; Confidentiality in Internet Counseling; and Legal Considerations, Licensure, and Certification. Counselors are urged to review these expectations regularly because they are subject to change periodically in response to new issues or technology (NBCC, 2007b). To access the standards in their entirety, please visit: http://www.nbcc.org/AssetManagerFiles/ethics/internetCounseling.pdf.

1.4.4.1   INTERNET COUNSELING RELATIONSHIP

Section Highlights **Internet counselors must:**

- Take appropriate steps to confirm the identity of the client (e.g., use a code word to ensure they are talking to the actual client and not someone who may be posing as the client).

- Gain consent (and confirm the identity) of a parent/legal guardian when counseling minors.
- Provide clients with ways of contacting them when they are not online or should the necessary technology fail to function properly during a session.
- Discuss with clients the limitations of technology-assisted distance counseling, such as the possibility that statements may be misinterpreted "when visual cues do not exist" (NBCC, 2007b) and how to handle those types of situations if they occur.
- Work with clients to find suitable, local mental health professionals and hotline numbers should the client need to contact someone in an emergency situation.
- Inform clients of locations in their community that provide free access to the Internet, if appropriate.
- Attempt to make their Web sites as accessible as possible to clients with disabilities.

1.4.4.2   CONFIDENTIALITY IN INTERNET COUNSELING

Section Highlights **Internet counselors must:**

- Use encryption software to secure their online communications and discuss these security measures with clients. If counselors are unable to use encryption methods, they must describe any possible limitations to confidentiality to their clients.
- Explain to clients the length of time that data (e.g., e-mails, video recordings, notes, transcripts) from their sessions will be saved.

1.4.4.3   LEGAL CONSIDERATIONS, LICENSURE, AND CERTIFICATION

Section Highlights **Internet counselors must:**

- Familiarize themselves with applicable laws related to Internet counseling, counseling minors, and reporting child abuse in their state and the state in which their clients reside. In addition, counselors should ensure that they are covered for Internet counseling under their liability insurance policies.
- Supply links on their Web sites to their licensure and certification boards.

1.4.5   Legal Issues in Counseling

Along with adhering to ethical codes, counselors must also be knowledgeable of and follow relevant legal guidelines. Some of the most consequential laws related to counselors were highlighted in section 1.1 of this chapter. In this section of Chapter 1, legal concepts and definitions are discussed. Having a clear knowledge of this information will benefit you when taking the NCE or CPCE and in your professional counseling career.

- **Liability** is the legal responsibility of the counselor to act with due care in professional practice. Counselors who neglect to practice with due care become vulnerable to legal action being taken against them.

- If clients believe that they have been injured or wronged in some way by the behavior of a counselor and want legal retribution, the client can file a tort. According to Wheeler and Bertram (2008), a **tort** is "a private injury against the person, property, or reputation of another individual that legal action is designed to set right" (p. 33). The two types of torts that are essential for counselors to be aware of are negligence and malpractice.
- Negligence and malpractice are both usually considered an **unintentional tort**, meaning that the counselor did not plan or aim to cause harm to the client (Wheeler & Bertram, 2008). However, either tort could be considered an **intentional tort** if it seems obvious that the counselor's action would result in harm to the client, even if the counselor did not intend to injure the client.
- **Negligence** occurs when counselors fail to use reasonable care in carrying out their professional duties, resulting in injury to the client. For the plaintiff to win in a negligence case, they must prove the following four components (Wheeler & Bertram, 2008):
  1. The defendant owed the plaintiff some kind of legal duty as stipulated by their counselor–client relationship.
  2. The defendant breached that legal duty.
  3. The plaintiff has an authentic injury (e.g., physical, financial, psychological).
  4. The defendant's breach of duty caused the plaintiff's injury.
- **Malpractice** occurs when professional counselors fail to provide the standard of care expected of them based on their credentials, skills, and experience (Granello & Witmer, 1998). Standard of care is often established by comparing the defendant's behavior to that expected of other professional counselors with comparable credentials in similar situations. Like a negligence case, the plaintiff is required to prove the same four components outlined above for negligence: legal duty, breach of legal duty, real injury, and causal connection between duty and injury (Wheeler & Bertram, 2008). Unlike a negligence case, however, for a malpractice lawsuit to be brought against a counselor, it is ordinarily necessary for the counselor to be licensed or certified by his or her state.
- Another type of tort is **defamation**, which occurs when a counselor mars someone's reputation through the intentional spreading of falsehoods. There are two types of defamation: libel and slander. **Libel** is defamation through writing, whereas **slander** is defamation through a spoken statement(s). It is possible for a counselor to be held liable for defamation if counseling notes, records, or communications with others about a client are erroneous, injurious to that person's reputation, and shared maliciously (Wheeler & Bertram, 2008).

1.4.6 Duty to Warn/Protect

There are limits to counselor–client confidentiality. Counselors are ethically and legally obligated to break client confidentiality under certain circumstances. Although counselors' obligations vary by state, counselors have a duty in general to protect clients from harming themselves or someone else and to protect clients from individuals who are threatening to harm them. This section provides a review of counselors' duty to warn, with specific attention given to cases of child abuse and neglect, elder abuse, domestic violence, suicide, and a discussion of the precedent-setting legal case *Tarasoff v. Regents of the University of California,* which addressed counselors' responsibilities when clients threaten to harm others.

- *Child and elder abuse/neglect.* The protocol for handling cases of potential child or elder abuse are fairly straightforward. According to Wheeler and Bertram (2008), all states legally require counselors to report any cases of suspected or known child abuse or neglect to the appropriate authorities. Likewise, almost all states also require counselors to report any suspicion of elder abuse as well as abuse of a person who is disabled or vulnerable due to a severe mental illness. Essentially, it has been decided by the courts that protecting these vulnerable groups from possible harm overrides the need for confidentiality. Counselors who fail to report these cases are likely to lose if they find themselves in a legal battle.
- *Domestic violence.* The majority of states do not have a legal requirement mandating that counselors report suspected or known domestic violence to law enforcement agencies, although some states require physicians to report suspected cases or provide patients with helpful resources or referral information. Counselors should research the domestic violence laws in their state to address these cases.
- *Suicide/Self-Harm.* As outlined in the ACA *Code of Ethics,* counselors can ethically break confidentiality when clients make serious threats to harm themselves (ACA, 2005, B.2.a.). The two moral principles that conflict in these circumstances are autonomy and beneficence (Wheeler & Bertram, 2008). However, in certain cases, such as **suicide**—the taking, whether intentionally or unintentional, of one's own life—beneficence is more important than preserving client autonomy. This means that the counselor is ethically justified in breaching confidentiality, or violating autonomy, in order to promote the ultimate welfare of the client. For clients who make overtures that could lead to suicide, it is appropriate for the counselor to breach confidentiality to protect the client by contacting the family of the client, and possibly hospitalizing the client (if the risk appears imminent). In cases of client self-harm, such as cutting (self-mutilation), counselors walk a finer line during which time autonomy may triumph (i.e., when the client's cutting is superficial and does not lead to infection).

  In both cases (suicide and self-harm), it is important for counselors to make a thorough assessment of the client's behavior, prior history, and future plans before making any decisions. As always, counselors should document any actions they take along with the rationale behind their decisions and consult with others when unsure about how to proceed. In addition, counselors should be familiar with any specific laws related to suicide in their state, particularly in relation to minors.

- *Clients who are a threat to others.* In 1974, the Supreme Court of California ruled in *Tarasoff v. Regents of the University of California* that counselors could be held legally responsible for failing to take adequate steps to warn third parties about clients who present a "serious danger of violence" to them (Wheeler & Bertram, 2008, p. 80). In 1976, the law was extended to require counselors not only to warn but also to protect third parties from serious and foreseeable harm. That is, if a client makes a serious threat to harm someone the counselor can identify, the counselor must *warn* the third party about the threat that has been made and take steps to *protect* the identified individual, such as notifying the police. Although most states have now adopted this precedent, it is important for all counselors to determine to what extent it applies in their state. For example, although the majority of states fully follow the *Tarasoff* ruling, Texas is one state that does not.
  - *Background.* The *Tarasoff* case arose after a graduate student at the University of California, Prosenjit Poddar, disclosed to his psychologist (employed by the university) his plans to kill a woman, Tatiana Tarasoff, who would not enter into a romantic relationship with him (Wheeler & Bertram, 2008). The psychologist notified campus police; however, he did not warn Tatiana Tarasoff or city police, and Poddar was released after campus officials decided that he did not seem to pose a threat. On release, Poddar proceeded to kill Tarasoff, after which her family filed a case against the psychologist, the campus police, and others at the university.

When uncertain about what course of action to take in any of these circumstances, it can be helpful to:

- Familiarize oneself with applicable laws and related court decisions.
- Review codes of ethics.
- Consult with a lawyer, colleague, or supervisor.
- Document the decisions made in relation to these cases, including an explanation of why certain decisions were made.

1.4.7 Privileged Communication/ Confidentiality

Confidentiality refers primarily to counselors' ethical duty to keep client disclosures private, whereas, **privileged communication** is a legal term that protects certain counselor–client communication in the court systems (Wheeler & Bertram, 2008). For example, in most states counselors, like doctors, are protected under privileged communication from having to reveal information about a client in a legal proceeding, even if they receive a subpoena (see explanation below). Both confidentiality and privileged communication belong to the client, meaning that a client can choose to waive his or her right to either, allowing the counselor to ethically and legally disclose private information about the client.

- Privilege varies among states, so be sure to research the laws in your area. Some states have limitations to the privileged communication statute. For example, some states do not recognize privilege in criminal court cases and child custody cases, so it is essential that one be aware of how the law is applied in one's state.
- A **subpoena** is a legal document that orders a person to appear in court to serve as a witness or to provide the court with certain documents (Wheeler & Bertram, 2008). It is not uncommon for counselors to receive subpoenas, especially in child abuse and custody cases. The most important aspect for counselors to remember is to *always* consult with an attorney before providing any information to the court in order to best protect the client's confidentiality and determine if privileged communication applies.
- In addition to seeking legal advice, the counselor should also contact the client or the client's attorney to ascertain how the client would like the counselor to proceed (Wheeler & Bertram, 2008). If the client is agreeable to the counselor providing the requested information, the counselor should ask the client to sign a written authorization. If the client does *not* want the counselor to divulge information, the counselor should ask the client's attorney to file a motion to quash the subpoena. At this point, the court will normally decide whether the counselor's information is necessary and, if so, will provide the counselor with a court order demanding the release of information. If a counselor receives both a subpoena and a court order, he or she *must* comply or be held in contempt of court. However, as outlined in the ACA *Code of Ethics,* if counselors have to share private information, they should only disclose information germane to the case and nothing more (ACA, 2005, B.2.d.).

1.4.8 Practice Multiple-Choice Items: Ethical and Legal Issues

1. A counselor who receives both a subpoena and a court order must
   a. assert privilege.
   b. request that the client's attorney immediately file a motion to quash.
   c. provide the court with the appropriate information or be held in contempt of court.
   d. only comply with the court order.

2. Libel is all of the following, EXCEPT
   a. the intentional spreading of falsehoods through spoken word.
   b. the intentional spreading of falsehood through writing.
   c. a type of defamation.
   d. addressed by tort law.

3. An ethical principle that encourages counselors to actively promote the welfare of their clients is known as
   a. justice.
   b. beneficence.
   c. autonomy.
   d. fidelity.

4. The ACA *Code of Ethics* prohibits sexual or romantic relationships between counselors and clients
   a. for 2 years after they last saw each other professionally.
   b. for 5 years after they last saw each other professionally.
   c. only until the counseling relationship has been terminated.
   d. None of the above.
5. When Internet counselors are unable to use encryption software, they are ethically required to
   a. refrain from providing their services over the Internet.
   b. be extra careful with any information they store on their computer.
   c. use code words to identify their clients.
   d. tell their clients about the potential risks involved in their online communications.

Answer Key: 1. c; 2. a; 3. b; 4. b; 5. d.

KEY POINTS FROM CHAPTER 1: PROFESSIONAL ORIENTATION AND ETHICAL PRACTICE

- The counseling profession emerged in the late 1800s in the form of vocational guidance.
- IDEA and FERPA prohibit discrimination against individuals with disabilities.
- Counselors who suspect child abuse are legally and ethically required to file a report with Child Protective Services.
- CACREP is an accreditation body that approves educational institutions with counseling programs that meet predetermined standards of quality.
- Counselors obtain liability insurance to protect their assets in the event that a negligence or malpractice case is brought against them.
- Licensure laws regulate who is allowed to practice counseling.
- NBCC offers voluntary certification to counselors who meet its criteria for education, training, and experience, and who have passed the NCE.
- The counseling profession is composed of numerous specializations and associations.
- ACA serves as the professional voice for all counselors, regardless of specialization.
- Ethical codes provide counselors with a guide for professional behavior.
- When faced with an ethical dilemma, counselors should consult codes of ethics, other professionals, applicable laws, and ethics committees, as appropriate.
- Counselors are justified in breaching confidentiality if clients make a serious and impending threat to hurt themselves or an identified third party, or if someone makes a serious and impending threat to hurt the client.
- Laws always overrule ethics.
- In malpractice and negligence cases, these four aspects are examined to determine whether the defendant is liable: legal duty between plaintiff and defendant, breach of legal duty by the defendant, injury caused to the plaintiff, and causal connection between the defendant's breach of duty and the plaintiff's injury.
- *Privileged communication* is a legal term, whereas *confidentiality* is an ethical principle.
- Malpractice is considered professional negligence. Anyone can be sued for negligence; only certain professionals can be sued for malpractice.

CHAPTER 2

Social and Cultural Diversity

2.1 INTRODUCTION TO SOCIAL AND CULTURAL DIVERSITY

Social and cultural diversity is a core subject area that addresses how culture and social justice efforts affect the counseling relationship and the worlds of clients and counselors in general. Hays and McLeod (2010) stated,

> We as a profession are attending more to the complexities of both counselors and clients in their cultural makeup, the systems by which they are surrounded, and the impact these two components have on what earlier counselors and psychotherapists viewed as "universal" expressions of mental health. In addition, we are challenging each other to address biases and assumptions we have that prevent us from forming an affirming, therapeutic alliance with clients we counsel. (p. 2)

This Council for Accreditation of Counseling and Related Educational Programs (CACREP) core area is becoming increasingly more important in counselor preparation, given that the U.S. population is steadily becoming more culturally diverse. Several racial and ethnic groups make up the population of the United States today. The predominant racial group in 2000 was White (81.0%; 69.4% non-Hispanic), followed by Black/African American (12.7%), Asian American (3.8%), and all other races (e.g., Native American, Alaska Native, Native Hawaiian making up 2.5% of the total U.S. population; U.S. Census Bureau, 2004). However, the percentage of those identifying as White is projected to decrease over the next 50 years. The overall foreign-born population in 2003 made up approximately 11% of the U.S. population. Individuals from Latin America (e.g., the Caribbean, Central America, South America) represent the largest number (53.3%) of foreign-born individuals presently in the United States.

Over the past several years, administrations of the National Counselor Examination (NCE) have included only 11 (of the 160 total, or about 7%) of the scored items (plus some trial items that do not count) designed to measure social and cultural diversity (rank = 8 of 8, the fewest items of any of the eight domains). The average item difficulty index was .69 (rank = 6 of 8, the third most challenging domain of item content), meaning that the average item in this domain was correctly answered by 69% of test-takers.

Over the past several years, administrations of the Counselor Preparation Comprehensive Exam (CPCE) have included 17 scored items designed to measure social and cultural diversity, plus several trial items that do not count in one's score. The average item difficulty index was .61, meaning that the average item in this domain was correctly answered by 61% of test-takers, making this set of items among the most difficult on the examination.

CACREP (2009, pp. 9–10) defined standards for Social and Cultural Diversity as studies that provide an understanding of the cultural context of relationships, issues, and trends in a multicultural society, including all of the following:

  a. multicultural and pluralistic trends, including characteristics and concerns within and among diverse groups nationally and internationally;
  b. attitudes, beliefs, understandings, and acculturative experiences, including specific experiential learning activities designed to foster students' understanding of self and culturally diverse clients;
  c. theories of multicultural counseling, identity development, and social justice;
  d. individual, couple, family, group, and community strategies for working with and advocating for diverse populations, including multicultural competencies;

e. counselors' roles in developing cultural self-awareness, promoting cultural social justice, advocacy and conflict resolution, and other culturally supported behaviors that promote optimal wellness and growth of the human spirit, mind, or body; and

f. counselors' roles in eliminating biases, prejudices, and processes of intentional and unintentional oppression and discrimination.

Eight major sections comprise Chapter 2, including: Introduction to Social and Cultural Diversity, Key Cultural Group Categories, Social Justice Concepts, Cultural Identity Development, Counseling Racial and Ethnic Groups, Counseling Other Cultural Groups, Crisis, Trauma, and Specialized interventions, and Additional Considerations in Multicultural Counseling Practice. But first, let's review some key historical events and ethical issues in social and cultural diversity and foundational terms.

2.1.1 Culture and Multicultural Counseling

Before moving forward, it is important to define culture and multicultural counseling. **Culture** refers to the human experience mediated by biological, psychological, historical, and political events. It includes behaviors, attitudes, feelings, and cognitions related to our identities living within the world. Culture exists on three levels: universal, group, and individual— that is, culture organizes how groups as a whole, individuals within a particular group, and individuals as a human race behave, think, and feel. Because of this, we each have a unique cultural makeup that affects our experiences in counseling and in the world.

- The extent to which a group membership is labeled as "cultural" depends on how broadly individuals define culture. For example, a broad definition might include variables such as race, ethnicity, gender, sexual orientation, educational status, language, and geographical origin. A more narrow definition might label culture as race and gender only.

- Because we have varying ways of defining culture, we may consider certain cultural group memberships as more significant to ourselves and more valued when examining mental health issues. As professional counselors, we may use a biased lens (our own cultural values) to examine client issues. Oftentimes, the dominant cultural view is regarded in counseling as more important, leading the counselor to evaluate and treat clients from this perspective and disregard individual culture. This is known as **cultural encapsulation**.

- **Multicultural counseling** may be defined as the integration of cultural identities within the counseling process. **Cultural identity** refers to the degree to which individuals identify belonging to subgroups of various cultural groups or categories—that is, how the combinations of the various cultural group memberships for the client and counselor interact to affect the counseling relationship and the process and outcome of counseling. Most counseling scholars note that all counseling is multicultural counseling in some manner.

2.1.2 Key Historical Events in Social and Cultural Diversity

Culture's role in mental health was first discussed in the 1960s and 1970s when scholars stated that the cultural identities of clients should be acknowledged because they affect clients' experiences in counseling. In addition, several wrote about the negative ways in which counselors inhibit clients' well-being when not addressing client cultural experiences in counseling sessions. Table 2.1 presents some key historical events in social and cultural diversity. This list is not intended to be exhaustive.

TABLE 2.1   Key Historical Events in Social and Cultural Diversity.

- **1962**—Gilbert Wrenn authors *The Culturally Encapsulated Counselor*.
- **1970s**—William Cross, Jr., develops one of the first racial identity development models, the Cross Nigrescence Model.
- **1990s**—Janet Helms edits *Black and White Racial Identity: Theory, Research and Practice*. This book and subsequent research make significant strides in cultural identity development research.
- **1991**—The ACA (known then as the American Association of Counseling and Development) approves the multicultural counseling competency standards (see section 2.1.3 for more information).
- **1991**—Paul Pedersen labels multiculturalism as the "fourth force" in counseling, moving to center stage the importance of culture in counseling. This force follows the three forces of psychodynamic, behaviorism, and humanism–existentialism.
- **1992**—The Multicultural Counseling Competency standards are published concurrently in the *Journal of Counseling and Development* and the *Journal of Multicultural Counseling and Development*.
- **1996**—Patricia Arredondo and colleagues operationalize the 31 multicultural counseling competency standards in a seminal article (see Arredondo et al., 1996).
- **2001**—The U.S. Department of Health and Human Services (USDHHS, 2001) publishes the Surgeon General's Report (*Mental Health: Culture, Race and Ethnicity—A Supplement to Mental Health: A Report of the Surgeon General*) that highlights significant research related to how race and ethnicity (and associated oppression and resiliency experiences) influence mental health outcomes.
- **2004**—Manivong Ratts and colleagues (Ratts, D'Andrea, & Arredondo, 2004) label social advocacy as the "fifth force" of counseling.
- **2005**—The ACA *Code of Ethics* is revised to include a greater emphasis on culture.

2.1.3 Key Ethical Issues in Social and Cultural Diversity

Attending to social and cultural diversity (and avoiding cultural encapsulation) is an ethical imperative. Avoiding cultural bias is integral to all major counseling documents, including the ACA *Code of Ethics* (ACA, 2005; see Appendix A), CACREP standards (CACREP, 2009), NBCC *Code of Ethics* (NBCC, 2005; see Appendix B), and all ACA division guidelines, to name a few. Ramsey (2009) identified several pertinent ethical challenges:

- Counselors have an ethical obligation to build their knowledge, awareness, and skills to work with culturally diverse clientele—that is, multicultural counseling competence (described in more detail in the next subsection) is a continual developmental process.
- Counselors must be aware of both the strengths and challenges of traditional counseling theories and must familiarize themselves with indigenous healing practices.
- Although counselors are charged with practicing only within the bounds of their competence, it is unlikely that counselors will be knowledgeable about every culture. However, it is important for counselors to "stretch the boundaries" (Ramsey, 2009, p. 497) of their competence to increase their cultural awareness, knowledge, and skills.
- Counselors make client referrals when the setting in which they work fails to provide for the client, and that setting cannot or will not alter its policies and procedures to cater to that client.
- Counselor educators are to be properly trained in social and cultural diversity issues and are to implement a culturally sensitive and advocacy-based curriculum.
- Counselors must consider client cultural idioms of distress and cultural bias among practitioners when evaluating client symptomology and providing clinical diagnoses.
- Counseling researchers must consider culture throughout the research process, including involving a representative sample, avoiding harm in data collection, and interpreting data in a culturally sensitive manner.

2.1.4 Multicultural Counseling Competence

Sue and colleagues (Sue et al., 1982; Sue, Arredondo, & McDavis, 1992) constructed 31 multicultural counseling competencies (MCC) (see Appendix C) to introduce counselors to more effective ways to serve clients of color, given the increasing diversity and ethical challenges that counselors face. The standards have been increasingly applied to other cultural identities, including gender, spirituality, sexual orientation, and socioeconomic status, to name a few.

- The **tripartite model of multicultural counseling** (Ponterotto, 1997) involves three components: awareness (e.g., self-awareness of values and biases), knowledge (e.g., understands client's worldview), and skills (e.g., intervenes in a culturally appropriate manner). Thus, these MCC standards guide counselors to be self-aware, examine their beliefs and attitudes regarding other cultures, understand how various forms of oppression influence counseling, appreciate other cultural norms and value systems, and skillfully employ culturally appropriate assessments and interventions (Arredondo, 1999; Sue et al., 1992). Table 2.2 provides more detail about the tripartite model.
- In developing MCC, counselors are to be familiar with two perspectives that can be considered a continuum: etic vs. emic perspectives. An **etic** perspective refers to viewing clients from a universal perspective. This likely means that an individual client's culture is minimized to focus more on basic counseling processes and strategies that apply across individuals. As there is more attention to social and cultural diversity, counselors are increasingly taking an emic perspective in their work with clients. An **emic** perspective refers to using counseling approaches that are specific to a client's culture. Thus, a counselor using an emic perspective would more likely use indigenous healing practices and look for alternative explanations of symptoms based on specific cultural expressions.

2.1.5 Communication Patterns

Communication between a counselor and client, an important aspect of multicultural counseling, affects the extent to which trust and empathy in the counseling relationship are established. Both verbal communication and nonverbal communication are important to attend to in counseling dyads.

- Most major counseling theories rely on spoken words as a primary tool for promoting growth and change. Individuals who are not fluent in the dominant language (i.e., English) may be marginalized and prevented from accessing resources and opportunities that are available to individuals who are fluent in standard English.
- Many clients who speak English as a second language may prefer to express themselves in their native language during the counseling process, and counselors should encourage clients to use the language with which they feel most comfortable expressing themselves. At a minimum, counselors must be aware of community resources for clients who do not speak the dominant language.
- Approximately 85% of communication is nonverbal (Ivey & Ivey, 2007). Even though the notion of nonverbal communication is universal across cultures, the same nonverbal expressions can have drastically different meanings in different cultures. For example, acceptable interpersonal distance and eye contact vary from culture to culture.
- Nonverbal communication includes many types:
  - **High-context communication** involves individuals relaying messages by relying heavily on surroundings; it is assumed that "many things can be left unsaid," and thus nonverbal cues create social harmony. **Low-context communication** refers to individuals communicating primarily verbally to express thoughts and feelings.
  - **Paralanguage** refers to verbal cues other than words. These may be volume, tempo, prolongation of sound, disfluencies (e.g., utterances such as *uh* and *um*), and pitch (highness or lowness of one's voice).

TABLE 2.2   Tripartite Model of Multicultural Counseling Competence.

I. Counselor awareness of own cultural values and biases

Attitudes and Beliefs: Counselors are aware of themselves and their clients as cultural beings and appreciate these cultural differences. They also understand how their cultural backgrounds affect the counseling process.

Knowledge: Culturally sensitive counselors understand how their cultural backgrounds and values impact their definitions of optimal mental health, understand how oppression affects them personally and professionally, and understand the impact these two knowledge competencies have on their clients.

Skills: Counselors recognize limitations to their MCC and seek out continuing education and personal growth experiences to increase their competencies, which include developing a nonoppressive identity.

II. Counselor awareness of client's worldview

Attitudes and Beliefs: Counselors are aware of how stereotypes and other negative reactions they hold about minority clients affect the counseling relationship, process, and outcome.

Knowledge: Counselors have knowledge of the cultural backgrounds, sociopolitical influences (e.g., acculturative stress, poverty, racism), help-seeking behaviors, within-group variation, identity development, and culturally relevant approaches specific to a particular cultural group with which they are working.

Skills: Counselors engage in personal and professional immersion experiences and research in which they can gain an understanding of unique mental health concerns and daily experiences for minority groups.

III. Culturally appropriate intervention strategies

Attitudes and Beliefs: Counselors identify and respect community-specific values (e.g., spiritual beliefs, indigenous healing practices, language preferences) and actively integrate them into counseling interventions.

Knowledge: Counselors have knowledge of the culture and current practice of counseling, its limitations for work with minorities (including existing bias in assessment and diagnostic procedures), limited accessibility for some communities, and restricted use of culturally specific and community resources.

Skills: Counselors engage in both verbal and nonverbal helping responses that are congruent with the helping style of their clients. During helping, counselors understand and articulate expectations and limitations of counseling assessments and interventions. In addition, counselors seek support and consultation from those in clients' communities in cases where healers and practitioners (e.g., language match, spiritual leadership) are appropriate and engage in social justice efforts to improve their clients' lives.

Source: From D. G. Hays & B. T. Erford (Eds.). (2010). *Developing multicultural counseling competence: A systems approach* (pp. 22–23). Columbus, OH: Pearson Merrill.

- **Kinesics** involve postures, body movements, and positions. These might include facial expressions, eye contact and gazes, and touch.
- **Chronemics** is how individuals conceptualize and act toward time. **Monochromic time** refers to an orientation toward time in a linear fashion (use of schedules, advanced planning of activities), and **polychromic time** refers to the value of time as secondary to relationships among people.
- **Proxemics** is the use of personal physical distance. The four interpersonal distance "zones" include intimate distance (0 to 18 inches), personal distance (18 inches to 4 feet), social distance (4 to 12 feet), and public distance (12 feet or more).

2.1.6 Acculturation

Acculturation is the process in which an individual (usually an immigrant) makes sense of a host culture's value system in relation to his or her own. An individual may completely embrace or reject a new culture, reject both cultures, or integrate the new culture to some degree into a current value system.

- Acculturation level is largely determined by the number of years a client has been involved in the acculturation process, the client's country of origin, and the age at which the client began the acculturation process.
- Paniagua (2005) identified four main models of acculturation with which counselors should be familiar. These include the (a) **assimilation model**, in which highly acculturated individuals identify solely with the new culture and adopt values and customs of the other, more dominant group; (b) **separation model**, in which individuals refuse to adapt to cultural values outside of their own cultural values; (c) **integration model**, or **biculturalism**, in which individuals identify with both their own culture and that of the host culture; and (d) **marginalization model**, in which individuals reject the cultural values and customs of both cultures.
- The more immigrants identify with and belong to a particular ethnic group, particularly if their ethnic values contrast with general U.S. cultural values, the more difficult the process of acculturation becomes.

2.1.7 Worldview

Worldview is defined as individuals' conceptualization of their relationship with the world. We will present two worldview models typically referenced in counseling programs.

- Sue (1978) described that individuals guide their behaviors based on two intersecting dimensions: locus of responsibility and locus of control. **Locus of responsibility** refers to what system is accountable for things that happen to individuals. An internal locus of responsibility (IR) refers to the idea that success (or failure) is viewed as an individual's own doing and is thus the result of individual systems. An external locus of responsibility (ER) refers to the notion that the social environment or external system is responsible for what happens to individuals. The second dimension, **locus of control**, is the degree of control individuals perceive they have over their environment. An internal locus of control (IC) is the belief that consequences are dependent on an individual's actions. An external locus of control (EC) refers to the notion that consequences result by chance, outside of an individual's control. These dimensions result in four worldview combinations: IR-IC, IR-EC, ER-IC, and ER-EC.
- The second worldview model was developed by Kluckhohn and Strodtbeck (1961) and contains five components that integrate in various cultures to create unique cultural worldviews:
  - *Human nature* involves the continuum that humans are basically good, bad, or both good and bad.
  - *Relationship to nature* refers to how individuals view the power of nature: harmony with nature, power over nature, or power of nature.
  - *Sense of time* relates to what aspect of time individuals focus upon: past, present, or future.
  - *Activity* is how self-expression occurs for individuals. These may include being (i.e., present oriented with an internal focus on self), being-in-becoming (i.e., present- and future-oriented goal development to create an integrated self), and doing (i.e., actively engaging in activities that are deemed important by external standards).
  - *Social relationships* involve three categories that relate to the degree of hierarchy and group focus within a culture: *lineal–hierarchal* (i.e., traditional cultures with hierarchal positions, typically patriarchal structures), *collateral–mutual* (i.e., collectivistic focus), and *individualistic* (i.e., the needs of groups are secondary to those of individuals).

2.1.8 Practice Multiple-Choice Items: Introduction to Social and Cultural Diversity

1. Labeling clients as resistant because they do not make eye contact during a counseling session might be an example of
   a. cultural encapsulation.
   b. an emic perspective.
   c. chronemics.
   d. integration.
2. _____ is NOT a component of the tripartite model of multicultural counseling competence.
   a. Knowledge
   b. Awareness
   c. Skills
   d. Relationship
3. An individual fidgeting during a counseling session is an example of what form of nonverbal communication?
   a. Chronemics
   b. Kinesics
   c. Context communication
   d. Proxemics
4. After spending 5 years in the United States, Maya believes she no longer belongs in her home culture and does not fit in the host culture. Which acculturation model best describes her acculturation level?
   a. Assimilation
   b. Biculturalism
   c. Separation
   d. Marginalization
5. The worldview that the environment accounts for actions that occur is best captured by which of Sue's (1978) dimensions?
   a. Locus of responsibility
   b. Locus of control
   c. Activity
   d. Relationship to nature

Answer Key: 1. a; 2. d; 3. b; 4. d; 5. a.

2.2 KEY CULTURAL GROUP CATEGORIES

This second section of Chapter 2 outlines several cultural group memberships. These include race, ethnicity, socioeconomic status, gender, sexual orientation, spirituality, and disability. Review Case 2.1. What cultural group categories do you notice? Circle them.

2.2.1 Race

Race describes how groups of people are thought to be identified by physical characteristics, such as a person's skin color, facial features, hair texture, or eye shape. The concept of race is a social and political classification system historically based on a genetic and biological background.

- Research, on the other hand, has shown that fewer biological differences exist between various groups and that racial categories are inappropriate and not scientifically based. Therefore, the classification of individuals based on race is now seen as more of a vehicle to allow racial discrimination to occur in a variety of forms, such as exploitation, adverse treatment, and segregation.
- The U.S. Bureau of the Census (2008) defines race as the group with which a person most closely self-identifies. Racial classifications include White, Black, Asian, Alaskan Native, and Pacific Islander. The U.S. Census also recognizes 165 racial combinations and has added a new designation entitled "Two or More Races Population." It is important to note that Hispanic/Latino is not considered to be a race but an ethnicity.

CASE 2.1
Case of Susan

Susan is a 77-year-old African American woman. She works two jobs most days of the week and is barely able to pay the bills. Susan wishes she could save money to move into a nicer house, like the one her boss has. She would have liked to have been an athlete of some sort or perhaps a coach for a female basketball team. However, she was not allowed to play sports due to a heart condition. Due to this heart malady, Susan has a parking pass for the closer spots in parking lots, but she sometimes finds people think she is undeserving of the parking spot because she looks relatively young and healthy. In fact, sometimes people are quite rude to her. Susan also tries to be very active in her church, although things have been a bit tense lately since one of Susan's children disclosed he was gay.

- One way that individuals consider someone's "race" in social interactions involves **color blindness**, or treating individuals equally by ignoring their racial group, or color of their skin, as a component of their identity. This concept was historically used in relation to the ill treatment that African Americans received and the intention that they not be judged by the tone of their skin. However, acting "color blind" presents challenges. A professional counselor who operates under this assumption is likely to perpetuate a continuing distrust of White counselors for clients of color, diminish the importance that the client's cultural background has on his or her worldview, and fail to create therapeutic goals that are met with culturally appropriate treatments.

- Color consciousness and colorism are two other important terms to know regarding race. **Color consciousness** describes the process of how Whites, in response to guilt for their role in perpetuating racial discrimination for racial minorities, focus predominantly on racial (or perceived) differences. Color consciousness can be a form of unintentional racism due to the magnification of one's position as a minority instead of attention to a presenting concern that may not have much to do with race. A positive aspect of color consciousness, however, is that this new recognition of cultural differences offers the counselor a platform from which to address the topic in the counseling relationship and to be mindful of the individual.

- **Colorism** refers to the judgment of worth based on how closely an individual's skin color approximates that of Whites. The practice of valuing more highly one who has more European American features originates from a time when African American slavery was a prominent practice and the offspring of a slave and her owner were given treatment preferential to that received by offspring who had no European features.

- **Biracial individuals** refer to those who are biological children of parents from two different racial backgrounds. For example, a **mulatto** is designated as one with both White and African lineages, and the term **mestizo** characterizes one who is born of Native American and Caucasian parents. Discrimination of biracial individuals occurred originally as a result of the **eugenics movement**, or a method to monitor a person's inborn characteristics and an attempt to keep the Caucasian race "pure" by directing who could marry and reproduce. As part of this movement, European Americans and African Americans—as well as the uneducated, those with mental illnesses, and those in poverty—could not intermarry.

- Unlike the term *biracial*, which connotes only two racial backgrounds, one who is **multiracial** is from multiple racial lineages. A multiracial family includes those with birth parents of different racial backgrounds as well as those who were brought into a family by adoption.

2.2.2 Ethnicity

Although race refers to characteristics that are biological in origin, **ethnicity** refers to a person's identification with a group of people who have a similar social or cultural background. A person's ethnicity is rather flexible, depending on changes in his or her own **ethnic identity** and experiences. Individuals from the same ethnic group may have very different ties to that group, resulting in differences in ethnic identity.

- Ethnic groups often share patterns within their culture that may take the form of a shared language, religious preference, close proximity geographically, traditions, gender, or ancestry. Subsets of a cultural group are common as well.

- Examples of ethnic groups include Arab Americans, Hispanic/Latino/as, African Americans, Italian Americans, Jewish Americans, Japanese Americans, and Irish Americans.

- **Ethnocentrism** is a concept defining a cultural group's belief that it is superior in comparison to all other cultures. Although all ethnicities may use their own as a reference against which to measure other groups, ethnocentrism carries with it the notion that a group's ethnicity is the "gold standard" by which to judge others. In the counseling profession, ethnocentrism may appear in the form of the counselor not taking a client's ethnicity into consideration when planning treatment or being prejudicial toward the client.

2.2.3 Socioeconomic Status

Socioeconomic class or status (SES) is another cultural group categorization for a counselor to consider. Individuals in each SES can have a different worldview, conceptions of problems, perceptions of themselves, and needs to be met. In particular, working-class and underclass individuals may exhibit hopelessness or addiction or may have difficulties reaching services to address their physical or mental health needs. SES includes factors such as income, financial status, educational background, resource availability (e.g., housing, clothing), and job held. SES traditionally is used to guide social roles among groups, and racial and ethnic minorities tend to be disproportionately represented in statuses with fewer resources. Even though the United States has no formal class system, as some other countries do, four classes can be identified in the United States, and each represents a distinct culture:

- *Upper-class status.* The wealthy, who have made or inherited large sums of money.
- *Middle-class status.* Able to meet immediate needs plus those that arise in the future. Are employed in technical or professional occupations.
- *Working-class status.* Live paycheck to paycheck, working to get immediate needs and bills met. Often work in service or labor industries and are placed under extreme pressure to make ends meet.
- *Underclass status.* Generally have an underpaying job or are not employed. Struggle greatly to maintain basic needs, such as food, housing, health care, and even access to transportation. Can be considered to be at the **poverty** level and also to suffer from great anxiety over how to meet their needs.
- Poverty has two other delineations: **generational poverty**, occurs when poverty has been a factor in numerous generations, and **situational poverty** occurs when the lack of resources is due to an extenuating circumstance, such as a divorce, unexpected unemployment, or a death.
- A term related to SES is **classism**, which is a form of discrimination founded on a person's social status. Classism is generally thought to have its origins in the higher classes who would try to discriminate and oppress the lower classes, but **modern classism** proposes that those of lower statuses may exhibit classism as well (Liu, Soleck, Hopps, Dunston, & Pickett, 2004). **Structural classism** promotes a current status quo or arrangement of classes. For example, it can be said to be similar to being "grandfathered" into an organization, meaning that one who is the ancestor of a predecessor at a job or at a university is automatically accepted into the fold. **Internalized classism** is the result of a person feeling shame for the class to which they belong and their "place" in society due to SES.

2.2.4 Sex and Gender

Sex and gender are two concepts that are often incorrectly used interchangeably, as are race and ethnicity. **Sex** refers to whether a person is biologically a male or a female as determined by hormones, genetics, and physical makeup. **Gender** refers to the social categories of masculinity or femininity, with placement heavily guided by culture. Individuals often base how they behave socially, and how they justify their behaviors, on gender.

- **Sex roles**—similar to the biological basis on which the definition of sex is derived—tend to focus on a person's

physiological functioning. (For example, a woman's sex role would include her ability to conceive and birth a child.) **Gender roles**, on the other hand, take into account many factors, which include expectations placed on a person by society about how someone should behave, think, and be treated, and also about what beliefs a person should hold. Gender role is a fluid concept that is different from culture to culture or one period of time to another.
- The binary system of male and female has been challenged within the past few decades, with increased attention to transgender individuals. **Transgender** refers to identity and roles that, to varying degrees, do not conform to cultural norms and expectations associated with one's biological sex. (Transgender is discussed in more detail in section 2.6.2).
- Three terms that are important to know concerning gender are *femininity, masculinity, and androgyny.* These concepts represent how society would generally characterize someone as being stereotypically female or male. **Femininity** refers to attributions that are commonly associated with a woman, such as relational, nurturing, and emotional. **Masculinity** includes the features typically affiliated with a male, such as aggression, rationality, competitiveness, and independence. **Androgyny** alludes to the meshing of both masculine and feminine properties. Sandra Bem (1974) determined that androgyny was the most ideal psychologically, a finding disputed by Broverman, Broverman, Clarkson, Rosenkrantz, and Vogel (1970), who concluded that the masculine traits were more desirable and deemed healthier.
- Bem's **gender schema theory** interprets the "why" behind an individual's placement of genders into certain categories. Bem proposed that children learn gender roles and behaviors that conform to a society's standards and color their view on what proper gender behavior is expected to be. Those with a preexisting view, or gender schema, will exhibit the stereotypical traits of the gender role in which they fall, and as such, society should remove these notions of a gender template to allow more personal freedom of choice and individuality.

2.2.5 Sexual Orientation

Sexual orientation is a multifaceted and complicated concept. Definitions of sexual orientation range from a person's biology, attitudes, and beliefs to the traditions of culture. On a more basic level, **sexual orientation** can be thought of as the way people prefer to meet their sexual needs and the object of their sexual attraction.

- Chaney and Marszalek (2010) identified four components of **sexual identity**, a term they believe more comprehensively defines sexual orientation. These four components include physical identity (biological makeup of an individual), gender identity (belief about one's gender), social sex role identity (sex roles individuals adopt due to culture), and sexual orientation identity (sexual and emotional attraction to individuals of the same and/or opposite sex). Thus, sexual orientation involves gender, although it should also be considered independently.

- Sexual orientation is generally categorized as the following orientations:
  - **Homosexual:** A person of the same sex is usually the object of sexual attraction and fantasizing. Persons with this orientation can be referred to as being "gay" or "lesbian," and they do not prefer to be called "homosexual."
  - **Heterosexual:** A person of the opposite sex is usually the object of sexual attraction and fantasizing. Also known as being "straight," this orientation is the most socially accepted.
  - **Bisexual:** A person is attracted to and fantasizes about both the opposite and the same sex. A bisexual may encounter discrimination similar to that experienced by the gay community but also may encounter resistance from the gay community.
  - **Questioning:** This is a relatively new term that refers to an individual who is questioning his or her sexual orientation and/or gender identity. The letter *Q* is used to represent this concept, although for many young people *Q* represents queer (i.e., any gender and/or sexual orientation outside the mainstream).
- **Affectional orientation** is a recent term suggested by researchers to describe sexual minorities because it broadens discussion beyond simple sexual attraction. Relationships also involve attraction based on intelligence, emotional stability, communication style, and other interpersonal factors and feelings.
- A healthy sexual identity is possessed by those who are aware of their needs and desires, able to express themselves, and content with their sexual orientation.
- **Heterosexism** is the discriminatory practice toward those who do not fall within the "mainstream" category of heterosexual. It involves imposing heterosexually based social norms and positively regarding those who abide by such norms. Some of those norms include recognizing marriage among heterosexuals, providing insurance coverage to heterosexual couples, allowing legal and financial rights to property, and valuing custody and adoption rights of heterosexuals.
- **Homophobia** refers to fear and hatred of sexual minorities, often resulting in hate crimes. **Internalized homophobia** is the process by which sexual minorities accept heterosexist messages; this can hinder their sexual identity development.
- **Homoprejudice** is a term that has recently emerged in research as scholars suggest that prejudice is more the cause of discrimination than an actual phobia per se.

2.2.6 Spirituality

Spirituality can best be understood as meaningful experiences that possibly include a relationship with a divine entity, the universe, or nature. Usually spirituality encompasses a sense of well-being and fulfillment, and it can also be said to be closely tied to a person's **soul**, or the quintessential nature of a person.

Spirituality is not to be confused with **religion**. Religion involves the actual ritualized practices that may involve a church or other organization, authority figures, and religious mores.

- Spirituality may be polytheistic (believing in many gods), monotheistic (believing in one God), or nontheistic (nonbelief in God or gods).
- There are several major types of religions:
  - *Buddhism.* Goal is increasing of awareness and understanding of life so as to reduce the anxieties of life. This state is called *nirvana* and is reached by means of meditation. Peacefulness, forbearance, and a belief in *karma* and reincarnation are further hallmarks of this faith.
  - *Christianity.* Belief in one God who sent his son Jesus Christ to die for the forgiveness of sins for all. Focuses on God's transformative love and the gift of grace to have a personal relationship with God. Forgiveness, mercy, and personal growth are further precepts of this faith.
  - *Confucianism.* Focuses on the completion of a person through lifelong educational growth concerning various aspects, including moral and cognitive. Persons are expected to conduct themselves harmoniously and humbly. Relationships, family, and tranquility in social transactions are key to Confucianism. The proper mannerisms, traditions, ethics, and regulations, called *li*, dictate these social interactions (Mio, Trimble, Arredondo, Cheatham, & Sue, 1999).
  - *Hinduism.* A "pantheistic" faith that believes in Brahman being the creator of the Earth and that all things in nature are manifestations of Brahman. Meditation is a key element in this faith, as is *karma*, or the belief that a person's actions in this life determine his or her destiny in the next life. *Karma* is the core precept of Hinduism, rather than a core focus on Brahman. Hindus believe in reincarnation and the transcendence of the self.
  - *Islam.* A faith based on the belief in Allah, who is Islam's only god, and whose doctrine was proclaimed by the messenger Muhammed in the holy book of Islam, the Koran. Abraham and the first five books of the Old Testament are also incorporated into this faith. Focus is on prayer, sharing wealth, forgiveness, benevolence, religious fasting, and making a spiritual pilgrimage to the holy city of Mecca.
  - *Judaism.* With a focus on interacting with others humbly and performing good deeds, religious Jewish clients focus on the Torah, which comprises the first five books of the Bible. Some ascribe to the more mystical Kabbalah, or the "Force of the Creator," which allows that wisdom provides growth and an opportunity to focus on the life that follows this earthly one. The focus for most Jews is solidly on actions in this life.
  - *Taoism.* Concentrates on harmony with nature, a peaceful existence with the world, and power from Dao. Taoism has three foci that include the ways of ultimate

reality, human life, and the universe. Intense study, it is believed, leads to enlightenment. Taoism also follows the precept that all humans have a moral center.

- **Agnosticism** is the belief that any ultimate being is unknown or unknowable.
- **Atheism** is the disbelief in the existence of God.
- Spirituality is an important and pervasive aspect of a person's life and has an impact on the counseling relationship. In fact, research has shown that spirituality is correlated with an increase in health, inner strength, mental well-being, and happiness. A critical aspect of many faiths is the existence of hope, which is a key element in counseling. Hope allows a client to move toward goals and believe that a positive change can be achieved.
- Complications can occur in many spheres of one's life, including the psychological, physical, emotional, cognitive, relational, or behavioral levels. **Spiritual bypass** is a term that refers to the avoidance of these problematic issues by a person "misusing their spiritual beliefs, practices, or experiences rather than address the struggle at the level at which it occurs" (Cashwell, 2010, p. 517). Although this may seem helpful in avoiding the pain in the here and now, in the long run spiritual bypass is a maladaptive practice. An example of spiritual bypass is a person driven by an inner need to cover up deep insecurities becoming overly involved in services and outreach to others instead of striving for spiritual fulfillment.

2.2.7 Disability

A mental or physical challenge that greatly limits a person's ability to function in activities of daily living is a **disability**. Examples of these impairments include diminished ability to be independent, take care of oneself, move about freely, breathe, talk, see, hear, or be educated.

- **Ableism** is the form of discrimination that afflicts this population, where people believe that one who is disabled is limited in the extent of what they can truly do and underevaluates their abilities. Although some disabilities may be readily apparent, other disabilities are not as easy to see and cause a person to have to justify themselves and their status. The U.S. government has put into place three laws—the 1973 Rehabilitation Act, the Americans with Disabilities Act in 1990, and the 2004 Individuals with Disabilities Education Improvement Act, to protect citizens with disabilities.
  - **Rehabilitation Act of 1973 (PL 93-122).** Prohibits discrimination against persons with disabilities in federally sponsored or federal programs.
  - **American with Disabilities Act (ADA) of 1990.** Prohibits discrimination of persons with disabilities in employment, public services, telecommunications, and accommodations.
  - **Individuals with Disabilities Education Improvement Act (IDEA) of 2004.** Provision of nondiscriminatory education process for children with disabilities in the least restrictive environment.

- *People-first language* is a recent move to undo the harm caused by labeling a person. For example, it's not the "disabled person" but the "person with a disability." It is important to note that the term *handicap* is no longer acceptable to use.

2.2.8 Practice Multiple-Choice Items: Key Cultural Group Categories

1. The faith that focuses on *karma* and the deity Brahman is
   a. Buddhism.
   b. Taoism.
   c. Islam.
   d. Hinduism.

2. Situational poverty is due to
   a. being poor for generations.
   b. lacking resources due to an extenuating circumstance.
   c. being poor due to geographic location.
   d. lacking money because of poor investments.

3. What socioeconomic class recognized in the United States encompasses people who are able to meet current expenses, plus plan for the future, but are not necessarily wealthy?
   a. Upper class
   b. Middle class
   c. Working class
   d. Underclass

4. The view that one's own culture is superior to another culture is called
   a. classism.
   b. ethnocentrism.
   c. racism.
   d. colorism.

5. Which law most protects children with disabilities concerning public education?
   a. ADA of 1990
   b. IDEA of 2004
   c. Rehabilitation Act of 1973
   d. Buckley Amendment

Answer Key: 1. d; 2. b; 3. b; 4. b; 5. b.

2.3 SOCIAL JUSTICE CONCEPTS

This third section of Chapter 2 discusses the premise behind social justice and related terms. **Social justice** is the belief in an equitable world for all individuals and the corresponding goal of promoting fairness by addressing privilege and oppression.

2.3.1 Social Justice

Social justice promotes working with individual clients to empower them and engage in advocacy to promote equity in society and the client's systems. Crethar (2009) outlined four main foci of social justice:

- *Equity.* Balanced allocation of services, rights, and duties within a society. Counselors promote diminishing inequity while bringing awareness and empowerment to the client.

- *Access.* Fair access to services, resources, and education that allow the individual to reach a good quality of life with the ability to make one's own decisions. Access forms the main piece of the *Bill of Rights,* which calls for equality for all citizens. It is assumed marginalized individuals (e.g., within the minority, those not experiencing White privilege) will have less access to resources than those who are not pushed aside in society.
- *Participation.* It is the right of all individuals to have their opinion taken into consideration on decisions that will influence their lives. Participation increases hope, control, motivation, and community. Counselors work to empower individuals and find appropriate resource referrals.
- *Harmony.* Working for the greater good of all of the community instead of being merely self-serving, harmony desires that each group's wants and needs be supplied fairly and evenly. Counselors should be able to work within various systems and understand the subtleties of a cultural group.
- The American Counseling Association (ACA) has created the Counselors for Social Justice Division and the ACA Advocacy Competencies, which give counselors knowledge about how to advocate against oppression.

2.3.2 Privilege and Oppression

Privilege and oppression refer to a bidirectional system in which individuals, depending largely on their cultural group combinations, experience differential levels of power, access, advantage, and social status (Hays, Chang, & Dean, 2004). Typically, cultural groups that experience oppression are various ethnic, religious, or sexual minorities; women; and those with disabilities. Those with privilege predominantly include Whites, males, able-bodied individuals, middle- to upper-class individuals, and heterosexuals.

- **Privilege** is the ability of a group to receive benefits and prestige that are not as readily available to other groups. McIntosh (1988), in a seminal article on White and male privilege, outlined everyday privileges individuals experience. These privileges tend to be unearned and involve creating oppression experiences (intentionally and unintentionally) for other cultural groups. A belief that one's group is superior is also part of privilege. Systems in which a group may experience privilege are in the workplace, judicial system, media, schools, and housing.
- **Oppression** may occur by force or deprivation. *Oppression by force* refers to imposing a role, experience, or condition on someone, whereas *oppression by deprivation* refers to not providing someone with a necessary experience or resource (Hanna, Talley, & Guindon, 2000).
- The several types of oppression include racism, sexism, heterosexism, ableism, and classism. Every cultural group category has associated "-isms" whereby individuals with

higher status within a particular group oppress those with lower status and power.
- Hanna et al. (2000) described three different levels of oppression:
  - *Primary oppression.* Obvious acts by both force and deprivation.
  - *Secondary oppression.* Oppressive acts in which individuals do not get directly involved but from which they may benefit.
  - *Tertiary oppression.* When minority group members adopt the majority opinion so they fit in. This is also known as *internalized oppression,* which is prevalent in ethnic minority literature and basically means internalizing, or taking in, the dominant message about the minority's low self-worth and importance. Tertiary oppression can lead to posttraumatic stress disorder (PTSD), mood disorders, eating disorders, drug and alcohol abuse, identity problems, and health issues.
- Double or triple jeopardy refers to individuals who are marginalized because of multiple minority statuses, such as being a racial minority and a female (**double jeopardy**) or being a racial minority, female, and having a disability (**triple jeopardy**).

2.3.3 Prejudice

Prejudice is closely related to oppression. **Prejudice** involves making assumptions about an individual and can either have positive or negative feelings attached with it, but negative prejudice is the most common connotation.

- Prejudice may affect individuals of various genders, races, financial situations, religions, and so forth. Oftentimes, the concept of phobias is intricately tied to prejudice, with fear causing prejudicial attitudes. For example, homophobia is the fear and hatred of same-sex couples that results in prejudice and oppression.
- The five stages of prejudice include different levels of severity (Allport, 1979):
  - *Antilocution.* The sharing of harmful views with those who have the same belief system, whether they are known to the person or not. Antilocution involves pure discussion, no actions.
  - *Avoidance.* Purposefully trying to not be around disliked persons.
  - *Discrimination.* Purposefully making sure individuals do not have access to resources for a better quality of life.
  - *Physical attack.* Acting either overtly violent or with violent undertones when in a high-pressure situation against a targeted group.
  - *Extermination.* Focused effort to demolish certain groups of people (e.g., genocide).
- Prejudice harms both the perpetrator (by anger and malice) and the victim (by shaming and creating feelings of isolation, suicidal or homicidal thoughts, and health problems). The creation, sustainment, and actualization of prejudice stem from three causes: individual personality, social traditions, and political system.

2.3.4 Racism

Racism is a predominant form of prejudice and oppression. **Racism** involves the belief that a group of people are inferior to one's own group due to recognized or perceived differences in physical characteristics. Racism also involves the ability to act on such beliefs overtly or covertly, intentionally or unintentionally (Ridley, 2005). *Covert racism* is not directly obvious but is done insidiously, either through conscious or unconscious motivations. For example, diagnosing a client incorrectly due to not taking client behaviors in cultural context or repeatedly not seeing clients who are in a target population are examples of unintentional and intentional covert acts of racism, respectively. *Overt racism* is a more obvious and focused prejudice, and it is never unintentional or unconscious.

- Racism occurs at three levels: individual, institutional, and cultural. *Individual racism* is the individual perspective that another race is less intelligent, inferior, and so on. These beliefs maintain racial status quo and are both unconscious and conscious. *Institutional racism* is racism perpetrated by institutions such as businesses and government. Examples of this include racial profiling by law enforcement or loan officers, or difficulty obtaining employment due to race. In addition to oppressing minority races, institutional racism benefits Whites. *Cultural racism* refers to devaluing cultural artifacts (e.g., art, media, religion) that do not approximate White cultural values.
- Consequences of racism on the victim include the inability to access resources such as medical services resulting in poorer health, lower salary and education levels, stress, and lower quality of life due to living conditions. Anger, depression, and guilt may also manifest. Victims may experience **internalized racism**, which is the taking in of majority beliefs about minority groups that will cause the minority group to believe stereotypes concerning itself, resulting in low self-esteem, feelings of worthlessness, and lowered motivation levels. Whites may experience shame, guilt, fear, and ignorance of other races and have incorrect notions about other groups.

2.3.5 Resilience

Resilience is an important social justice concept that is helpful for working with clients who experience oppression. **Resilience** is defined as "a person's ability to maintain equilibrium, adjust to distressful or disturbing circumstances, or to 'bounce back' toward a level of positive functioning in spite of (or often in response to) adverse situations" (Cheek, 2009, p. 458).

- Three characteristics are observed in persons with higher resilience: espousing hopeful attitudes and worldviews; having a supportive network of family, friends, and so forth; and having a connected and safe community with sufficient services available. It is important that professional counselors help clients build resilience within these characteristics.

2.3.6 Practice Multiple-Choice Items: Social Justice Concepts

1. Tertiary oppression is
   a. internalized oppression.
   b. not helping another who is being oppressed.
   c. committing covert acts of oppression.
   d. benefiting from oppression.

2. A resilience characteristic is
   a. not espousing upbeat attitudes and worldviews.
   b. having a supportive social network.
   c. living in an unsafe community.
   d. not being able to bounce back.

3. White privilege includes all of the following EXCEPT
   a. seeing one's race represented often in the media.
   b. being able to obtain work easily.
   c. being free from much oppression based on race.
   d. being discriminated against due to being in the majority.

4. _____ is NOT likely associated with privilege.
   a. Power
   b. Control
   c. Advantage
   d. Minority status

5. Working for the collective good of society refers to which tenet of social justice?
   a. Equity
   b. Harmony
   c. Access
   d. Participation

Answer Key: 1. a; 2. b; 3. d; 4. d; 5. b.

2.4   CULTURAL IDENTITY DEVELOPMENT

This fourth section of Chapter 2 addresses the process by which individuals identify with various cultural groups, or cultural identity development. It addresses the identity development processes for the cultural group categories of race, gender, sexual orientation, and spirituality.

- Cultural identity development is contextual. How we identify ourselves and others culturally is based on social interactions with members of different cultural groups. These interactions are guided by privilege and oppression experiences (e.g., a White individual "advances" to higher status by addressing his or her privileged racial status).
- Cultural identity development is always changing. Typically, the more frequent and culturally diverse our social interactions, the more cognitively complex our identity. And individuals can cycle through statuses or possess characteristics of multiple statuses within a particular identity model.
- The purpose of cultural identity development models is to explain individuals' process of defining themselves and how this is associated with their relationships with other cultural groups.

- A positive cultural identity has been linked to greater mental health and more effective cross-cultural relationships (Poll & Smith, 2003).
- Hays and Gray (2010) identified some common themes of the cultural identity development process that can apply to many specific identity development processes, such as racial identity or sexual identity development. These themes are (a) unawareness or denial of cultural group membership; (b) conflict or anxiety when encountering those who differ in cultural identity; (c) retreat into one's own cultural group and then cautious interaction with others; (d) integration of one's own cultural identity with other self-identities and other factors; and (e) advocation for those who belong to cultural group memberships that may experience oppression. Table 2.3 provides a list of these themes and corresponding statuses of the cultural identity development models.
- We present the identity development models independently, although individuals go through several identity development processes at a time given their multiple cultural identities.

2.4.1 Racial Identity Development

Racial identity refers to an orientation to one or more racial groups. We present five racial identity models here: two people of color racial identity development models; two White racial identity development models; and a biracial identity development model. You will note that developing one's racial identity deals partly with addressing racism issues and partly with integrating racial identity with other identities (Hays & Gray, 2010).

2.4.1.1 PEOPLE OF COLOR RACIAL IDENTITY DEVELOPMENT

The two models presented here are Cross's Nigrescence Model (Cross 1971, 1995) and Helms' People of Color Racial Identity Model (Helms, 1995). Cross was interested in the process of Blacks "becoming Black," or **Nigrescence**, and developed a racial identity model in the 1970s. This model serves as a description of stages that Blacks experience as they come to understand and embrace their Black identity. Cross's Nigrescence model is considered a guide for other racial identity development models. The statuses are as follows:

- *Preencounter.* Preexperiencing of a racial event; race or anti-Black attitudes are not viewed as important by the Black individual.
- *Encounter.* A specific experience, or encounter, that prompts the Black individual to begin to notice and question his or her racial identity.
- *Immersion-Emersion.* A response to conflict and anxiety from the Encounter status, which prompts the individual to retreat and embrace symbols and artifacts of Black identity, and then develop a more sophisticated Black identity.
- *Internalization.* The Black individual is more accepting of his racial identity and integrates it with other cultural identities (e.g., gender, sexual orientation).
- *Internalization-Commitment.* Represented by the individual being an advocate for Black issues.

TABLE 2.3   Themes of Cultural Identity Development Models.

Themes	Identity Stages/Statuses
Unawareness/ denial	Naiveté, contact (WRID)
	Pre-Encounter (POCRID)
	Personal identity (BID)
	Passive acceptance, unexamined female identity (FID)
	Unexplored commitment, diffusion (SID)
	Pre-awareness (SPID)
Conflict/anxiety	Resistance, disintegration, reintegration, pseudo-independence (WRID)
	Encounter (POCRID)
	Choice of group categorization, enmeshment/denial (BID)
	Revelation, crisis (FID)
	Identity confusion, identity tolerance, awareness (SID)
	Awakening (SPID)
Retreat into own group/interact cautiously	Redefinition, immersion/emersion (WRID)
	Immersion/emersion (POCRID)
	Embeddedness-emanation (FID)
	Identity acceptance, identity pride, identity assumption, exploration, deepening commitment, finding and applying the label of bisexuality, active exploration (SID)
Integrate cultural identity with other identities and other factors	Internalization (WRID)
	Internalization (POCRID)
	Appreciation, integration (BID)
	Synthesis, achieved female identity (FID)
	Identity synthesis, identity integration, settling into the identity, commitment, deepening and commitment, synthesis (SID)
	Recognition, integration (SPID)
Advocacy	Autonomy (WRID)
	Integrative-awareness (POCRID)
	Active commitment, moratorium/equilibrium (FID)

Note: WRID = White Racial Identity Development (Hardiman, 1994; Helms, 1995); POCRID = People of Color Racial Identity Development (Cross, 1971, 1995; Helms, 1995); BID = Biracial Identity Development (Poston, 1990); FID = Feminist Identity Development (Downing & Roush, 1985; Hoffman, 2006); SID = Sexual Identity Development (Cass, 1979; McCarn & Fassinger, 1996; Troiden, 1989; Weinberg, Williams, & Pryor, 1994; Worthington, Bielstein-Savoy, Dillion, & Vernaglia, 2002); SPID = Spiritual Identity Development (Griffith & Griggs, 2001; Poll & Smith, 2003).

Source: Hays & Gray (2010).

Helms' (1995) People of Color Racial Identity Development Model (POCRID) adopted Cross's principles and applied them to all people of color. The five statuses include the following:

- *Conformity.* Individuals of color may embrace racial stereotypes, blaming people of color for their problems. Individuals at this status may not socialize with other people of color. There is no awareness of racism.
- *Dissonance.* Individuals in this status experience a crisis that increases their awareness that racism exists. Conflict may lead individuals of color to appreciate aspects of their respective racial groups and distrust the dominant racial group (i.e., Whites).
- *Immersion/Emersion.* Similar to Cross's model, individuals in this status actively reject White culture and have increased racial pride, retreating in their own racial group practices.
- *Internalization.* Individuals increasingly identify with individuals of other oppressed identities and develop an individualized racial self-concept. Individuals interact with Whites with more flexibility and objectivity.
- *Integrative Awareness.* Individuals develop a more complex view of all racial groups and work to eliminate all forms of oppression (e.g., racism, sexism, classism). This status differs from Cross's last status, which focuses on advocacy for Black issues only.

2.4.1.2 WHITE RACIAL IDENTITY DEVELOPMENT Helms' (1995) and Hardiman's (1994) White racial identity development models are presented in this section. Helms (1995) developed a White racial identity development (WRID) model to illustrate that the general developmental issue for Whites is abandonment of entitlement—that is, Whites develop a more complex racial identity as they learn to relinquish some of the White privileges they receive. Helms' model is the most well-known and researched White racial identity development model. The statuses of the WRID model are as follows:

- *Contact.* Whites in this status are unaware that racism exists and deny race plays a role in their interactions with others.
- *Disintegration.* This status refers to when Whites become uncomfortable with the notion of racial superiority. Similar to the second status of minority racial identity development models, there is a racialized event that increases Whites' awareness that racism exists, creating feelings of anxiety, guilt, and/or anger.
- *Reintegration.* Whites that experience this status typically try to lessen the anxiety experienced in the Disintegration status and demonstrate intolerance and anger toward those of different racial groups.
- *Pseudo-Independence.* Alternatively, Whites may move toward this status, whereas they address conflict by making a superficial commitment to racism issues. However, there are often discrepancies between attitudes and behaviors toward other racial groups: they do not "walk the talk."

- *Immersion/Emersion.* Whites in this status renew their efforts to address racism and redefine their "Whiteness." This status involves increased self-reflection and self-understanding of individuals' role in perpetuating racial privilege.
- *Autonomy.* This final status is one of advocacy for Whites: Whites strive to relinquish some of their White privilege and dismantle the racial status quo.

Helms (1995) also created the **racial interaction theory**, whereas she conceptualized how Whites and people of color, at various racial identity development statuses, might interact and if those interactions would be adaptive or maladaptive. There are three types of racial interactions according to her theory:

- *Parallel interactions.* Both individuals are at similar racial identity statuses, resulting in more harmonious race-based communications. In counseling, the counselor and client will either address or avoid racial discussions.
- *Regressive interactions.* One individual (typically the one with more social power [e.g., White]) is at a lower racial identity status than the other individual. This creates frustration and leads to early termination in a counseling setting.
- *Progressive interactions.* One individual of a higher social power exhibiting a more advanced racial identity status than the other individual. This creates an interaction whereby race and culture may be addressed in counseling, thereby facilitating the racial identity development process for both individuals.

Hardiman (1994) developed a model of White racial identity development that asserted that the general developmental issue for Whites is to integrate their "Whiteness" with other components of their cultural identities. The five-stage model is represented as follows:

- *Naiveté.* This initial stage is characterized by Whites categorizing others by racial groups and receiving and transmitting messages about power and privilege.
- *Acceptance.* Whites in this status believe that there is an equal opportunity for all racial groups, although they hold White values as the gold standard for others to follow.
- *Resistance.* Similar to Helms' (1995) Disintegration status, Whites in this status experience conflict and anxiety about their beliefs of equal opportunity, as they engage in significant and meaningful cross-racial interactions.
- *Redefinition.* This status involves a self-reflection process about Whites' ethnic identity membership (unlike Helms' model, which involves redefining Whiteness). Whites in this status increase their understanding of their ethnic identities independent of their attitudes toward other racial/ethnic groups.
- *Internalization.* In this final status, Whites define themselves independent of the anxiety and resistance of earlier stages.

2.4.1.3 BIRACIAL IDENTITY DEVELOPMENT With the increasing number of multiracial individuals in the United States,

Poston's (1990) model of biracial identity development is becoming more important to conceptualize the racial identity development process of those who identify with more than one race. You will notice that Poston conceptualizes "healthy" biracial (or multiracial) individuals as those who integrate aspects of all of their racial and ethnic identities within their self-definition. The five statuses of Poston's model include the following:

- *Personal Identity.* This status is common for younger individuals, who may not be aware of their multiracial characteristics—that is, similar to other initial statuses of aforementioned racial identity development models, race or ethnicity is not salient.
- *Choice of Group Categorization.* Multiracial individuals experience anxiety or conflict as they select one racial group over another.
- *Enmeshment/Denial.* This status represents increased anxiety based on chosen racial group, as individuals cannot fully express any of their racial group identities. Self-hatred and a sense of disloyalty may be present for these individuals.
- *Appreciation.* Multiracial individuals begin to accept and value their multiple identities.
- *Integration.* This status involves multiracial individuals experiencing an increased recognition and infusion of multiple racial identities into their self-concepts.

2.4.2 Gender Identity Development

Gender identity refers to the degree to which individuals endorse gender role expressions associated with their perceived gender. Gender identity most often (but not always) corresponds with biological sex. Thus, a biological female typically will identify as female and will endorse feminine characteristics. Gender identity development, then, is the process by which individuals come to terms with gender expression. A majority of the gender identity development research focuses on the identity process for females. Two gender identity development models are presented here: the Downing and Roush (1985) and the Hoffman (2006) feminist identity development models.

Downing and Roush (1985) developed a feminist identity development model to help explain how women come to know themselves in a sexist society. Gender identity, for women, involves addressing sexism according to this model. There are five stages:

- *Passive Acceptance.* This stage refers to women internalizing traditional gender roles and societal views of women. Women in this stage often do not interact with women who identify as feminist.
- *Revelation.* Women move into this stage if they experience an event of sexism so salient that it calls into their awareness that their development is hindered in some way. This event, or series of events, may lead to dualistic thinking (i.e., all women are good, all men are bad).
- *Embeddedness-Emanation.* This stage is best characterized by women developing a support network with other women to deal with negative feelings of the Revelation

stage. Toward the end of the stage, women remain guarded in their interactions with men.
- *Synthesis.* Women in this stage integrate evolving feminist principles with other personal and cultural values. Events deemed previously as solely caused by sexism are reexamined to consider other causes as well.
- *Active Commitment.* This stage involves women advocating for other women and working to eradicate sexism.

Hoffman (2006) developed a feminist identity development model that gives special attention to the concept of gender self-confidence. **Gender self-confidence** involves the degree to which an individual defines himself or herself according to traditional views of masculinity and femininity *and* accepts those views. There are four statuses in Hoffman's model:

- *Unexamined Female Identity.* This status is similar to Downing and Roush's (1985) Passive Acceptance stage. It involves the acceptance of traditional gender roles for women.
- *Crisis.* This stage is similar to Downing and Roush's (1985) Revelation stage in that women become aware of societal discrimination in the form of sexism. This usually occurs because of one or more events.
- *Moratorium/Equilibrium.* Women in this stage are actively committed to a feminist identity search.
- *Achieved Female Identity.* The final stage involves the synthesis of new feminist identity with other aspects of identity. Gender self-confidence occurs.

2.4.3 Sexual Identity Development

As previously noted, sexual identity refers to the process by which individuals become oriented in terms of sexuality, whether this is heterosexual, bisexual, or homosexual. Sexual identity development is viewed as a continual, developmental journey, whereas sexual orientation is conceptualized as a continuum. Three gay identity development models (i.e., Cass, 1979; McCarn & Fassinger, 1996; and Troiden, 1989), one bisexual identity development model (Weinberg, Williams, & Pryor, 1994), and one heterosexual identity development model (Worthington, Bielstein-Savoy, Dillion, & Vernaglia, 2002) are presented.

2.4.3.1 GAY IDENTITY DEVELOPMENT Cass (1979) was the first to publish a gay identity development model, and this model has been widely cited in the counseling literature. There are six stages to Cass's model:

- *Conscious Awareness.* Individuals in this stage feel different and note that they may not be heterosexual.
- *Identity Comparison.* This stage represents the initial attempts individuals may make as they accept or reject various aspects of a gay identity. Three possible responses might be rejecting a gay identity and seeking to be heterosexual, passing as heterosexual while working toward accepting a gay identity, or rejecting traditional societal views of being gay while still accepting a gay identity.
- *Identity Tolerance.* Similar to the Immersion/Emersion statuses of racial identity development models and the

Embeddedness/Emanation and Moratorium/Equilibrium stages of feminist identity development models, in this stage there is some movement to retreat into the culture. Specifically, individuals desire to connect with other sexual minorities and distance themselves from heterosexuals.

- *Identity Acceptance.* There is movement toward a more active commitment to the gay community, beyond simple tolerance of it.
- *Identity Pride.* This stage is marked by stronger commitment to an active gay identity with some activism.
- *Identity Synthesis.* A gay identity is integrated with other cultural identities.

Troiden (1989) developed a model that is similar to Cass's (1979) model, yet focuses more on how the social context creates a nonlinear gay identity development process. The four statuses are these:

- *Sensitization.* There is an awareness of same-sex attraction; the individual sees self as different from peers.
- *Identity Confusion.* This status is characterized by uncertainty about sexual orientation by the individual; there is an awareness of an incongruence between societal assumptions of heterosexual and gay identities.
- *Identity Assumption.* There is exploration within the gay community, and individuals present as gay ("come out").
- *Commitment.* Individuals in this status are fully active in the gay community and have a positive gay identity.

McCarn and Fassinger (1996) developed a gay identity development model, partly in response to a traditional focus in the literature on the experiences of White men. Although this model was initially created to address lesbian identity development, it has increasingly been used to explain gay identity development more comprehensively. This model contains two discrete yet parallel individual and group developmental processes. The four statuses are these:

- *Awareness.* At an individual level, the individual feels different. There is also acknowledgment at a group level of sexual orientations other than heterosexual.
- *Exploration.* Individuals begin to have strong same-sex attractions and seek to belong, on a group level, by seeking information about others who identify as gay.
- *Deepening Commitment.* Individuals in this status confirm their gay identity at an individual level and actively commit to a gay identity at a group level.
- *Identity Integration.* Individuals at this status internalize their gay identity and integrate it with other aspects of their identity. At a group level, there is synthesis of the gay culture into self-identity.

2.4.3.2 BISEXUAL IDENTITY DEVELOPMENT   Weinberg et al. (1994) outlined four stages of bisexual identity development:

- *Initial Confusion.* Individuals in this status may experience anxiety about their sexual identity. They are attracted to both sexes and display discomfort about selecting a gay or heterosexual identity.

- *Finding and Applying the Label of Bisexuality.* Individuals become more comfortable with being attracted to both sexes and select the "bisexual" label.
- *Settling into the Identity.* This status is characterized by individuals' increased acceptance of a bisexual identity.
- *Continued Uncertainty.* This final status may occur for some individuals and is characterized by individuals feeling intermittent uncertainty about their bisexual identity.

2.4.3.3 HETEROSEXUAL IDENTITY DEVELOPMENT
Worthington, Bielstein-Savoy, Dillion, and Vernaglia (2002) developed a five-status model that incorporates both individual and group identity development processes and is similar to McCarn and Fassinger's (1996) model. The heterosexual identity statuses are these:

- *Unexplored Commitment.* Individuals accept themselves as heterosexual without exploring this identity. They conform to heterosexual norms present in society.
- *Active Exploration.* This status involves a more active identification with heterosexuality and attention to heterosexual privilege (either positive or negative).
- *Diffusion.* This status represents a period of no commitment or exploration at the individual or group level.
- *Deepening and Commitment.* Individuals show a greater commitment to their heterosexuality and focus more attention on acknowledging heterosexual privilege and dismantling oppression.
- *Synthesis.* This final status involves the development of an overall sexual self-concept, which involves solidified attitudes toward self and others' sexual identities.

2.4.4 Spiritual Identity Development

Spiritual identity refers to the degree of connection individuals have with their spiritual force. Poll and Smith (2003) described a developmental process by which individuals become more personally connected with a higher power. Their model includes four stages:

- *Pre-Awareness.* Individuals in this status do not view spirituality as salient in their lives.
- *Awakening.* This status refers to the notion that individuals become aware of themselves as spiritual beings after a spiritual event or conflict.
- *Recognition.* Spirituality is integrated throughout life experiences. Individuals begin to develop spiritual practices.
- *Integration.* Spirituality is synthesized with the overall self-concept during this final status.

2.4.5 Practice Multiple-Choice Items: Cultural Identity Development

1. Which identity development model includes Encounter, Immersion-Emersion, and Internalization as some of its statuses?
   a. McCarn and Fassinger's lesbian/gay identity development model
   b. Cross's Nigrescence model

c. Hardiman's White racial identity development model

d. Helms' White racial identity development model

2. A racial interaction in which an individual of a lower racial identity status holds more social power over an individual would be considered a(n)

a. parallel interaction.

b. progressive interaction.

c. autonomous interaction.

d. regressive interaction.

3. Which of the following best describes the developmental issues of feminist identity development models?

a. Women must relinquish their gender privilege.

b. Men are to actively commit to support networks that include women.

c. Women are to accept traditional gender roles for men and women.

d. Women grow psychologically as they address sexism.

4. One of the most popular sexual identity development models that was often used in developing other identity development models was developed by

a. Troiden.

b. Coleman.

c. Cass.

d. Weinberg.

5. Mary becomes angry with God after the death of her close friend, and she questions herself as a spiritual person. What spiritual identity development status is Mary most likely in?

a. Recognition

b. Awakening

c. Pre-Awakening

d. Integration

Answer Key: 1. b; 2. d; 3. d; 4. c; 5. b.

2.5 COUNSELING RACIAL AND ETHNIC GROUPS

In this fifth section of Chapter 2, we cover six major racial and ethnic groups, including African Americans, Arab Americans, Asian Americans, European Americans, Latin Americans, and Native Americans.

2.5.1 African Americans

African Americans comprise approximately 12.3% (34.7 million) of the U.S. population (U.S. Census Bureau, 2001), primarily originating from areas including Africa, the Caribbean, the West Indies, Latin America, central Europe, and South America (Kent, 2007).

- African Americans have a unique "immigration" history in that beginning in the 1600s they have historically been enslaved and forced to migrate for indentured servitude. Colorism (see section 2.2.1) has been around since slavery and still exists today. Further, laws against racial mixing and interracial marriage existed for over three

centuries. These laws implied that being Black was unfortunate, and a **one drop rule** was put in place (i.e., a hierarchical social system that implied that possessing one drop of Black blood indicated you were Black and thus of a lower social status).

- After slavery ended in 1865, **Jim Crow laws** were enacted to maintain separate and unequal social and economic situations for Blacks.

- Depression, anxiety, posttraumatic stress, and schizophrenia are seen in the African American community at similar rates as in Whites. However, research has indicated that overdiagnosis may be prevalent. African Americans face environmental stressors that affect mental health, including poverty, higher unemployment rates, education and occupational barriers, higher rates of incarceration for Black men, higher rates of violence in urban communities, and often a single-parent family status and associated economic hardships.

- Common African American cultural values include the following, although these may be mediated by acculturation level and other individual experiences (Helm & James, 2010):

  - Emphasis on a kinship network and extended relative and nonrelative family relationships, especially to care for children and the elderly

  - Respect for the family, particularly adult figures, by children

  - Collectivism and interdependence

  - Spiritual and/or religious orientation

  - Harmony with nature

  - Egalitarian gender roles within the family and other interpersonal relationships

  - Educational attainment

  - Flexible time orientation

  - Racial socialization of children

  - Assertiveness and expressiveness in communication style

2.5.2 Arab Americans

Arab Americans comprise approximately 0.42% (1.2 million) of the U.S. population (U.S. Census Bureau, 2003) and originate from a 22-state League of Arab States that includes Gulf states, Greater Syria, and Northern Africa (Nassar-McMillan, Gonzales, & Mohamed, 2010).

- Geographically, Arabs are those with ties to the Saudi Arabian peninsula and historically have practiced Islam (Abudabbeh & Aseel, 1999). However, only about 80% of Arabs in the Middle East are Muslim, and the majority of the Muslims in the world reside outside of the Middle East. Thus, it is inaccurate to consider *Arab* and *Muslim* synonymous.

- Approximately 40% of Arab Americans identify as Lebanese, 20% as Arab, 12% as Egyptian, and 12% as Syrian (Nassar-McMillan, 2009).

- Nassar-McMillan et al. (2010) noted that Arab Americans migrated to the United States in four waves: (a) Individuals from Lebanon, Syria, Palestine, and Jordan arrived at the end of the 19th century and beginning of the 20th century to escape religious persecution; (b) those from Egypt, Syria, Jordan, Iraq, Yemen, and Lebanon (mostly educated Muslims with the means to leave) arrived after World War II to escape political tension; (c) Muslims, mainly from Palestine, migrated in the 1960s for economic opportunity; and (d) Iraqi refugees fled to the United States after the Persian Gulf War in the 1990s.

- Since the terrorist attacks against the United States on September 11, 2001, discrimination in the form of ethnic profiling and hate crimes has dramatically increased for Arab Americans, even those who do not fit stereotypical "Middle Eastern" images (e.g., religious fanatics, dictators, desert nomads) (Nassar-McMillan et al., 2010).
- Common Arab American cultural values include the following:
  - Collectivism: extended family, community oriented; decisions made by consulting others and considering what is best for family and community
  - Hierarchical family relationships
  - Duty and family honor
  - Religious diversity, including Catholic, Muslim, Orthodox, and Protestantism
  - Educational attainment
  - Use of nonverbal communication, comfort with touching, and use of high volume or repetition to elucidate main points

2.5.3 Asian Americans

Asian Americans make up approximately 4.2% of the U.S. population, and by 2050 Asian Americans will increase by 200% and constitute about 8% of the population (U.S. Census Bureau, 2004). In 2000 this group was labeled as one of the fastest-growing racial and ethnic groups (Reeves & Bennett, 2004).

- There are 43 distinct Asian groups from 24 countries of origin. These groups may be categorized into three primary groups: (a) East Asians (e.g., China, Taiwan, Philippines, Korea, and Japan); (b) South Asians (e.g., Pakistan, India, Nepal, Bhutan, Sri Lanka, and Bangladesh); and (c) Southeast Asians (e.g., Cambodia, Vietnam, Laos, and Hmong) (Tewari, Inman, & Sandhu, 2003).
- The influx of Asian immigrants and refugees to the United States is a recent phenomenon. Inman and Alvarez (2010) note that the history of Asians immigrating to the United States began in the mid-1800s, when Chinese laborers arrived in California and Hawaii to work on sugar plantations and in the gold mines, respectively. Since then, Asian immigrants have been drawn to the United States for economic opportunities or in some cases to escape political or social persecution, famine, or war.
- An important concept specific to Asian Americans is the **model minority myth**, which states that Asian Americans have excelled in U.S. society without confronting Whites, despite past experiences of discrimination from them. It further states that Asian Americans should serve as a "model minority" for other racial/ethnic minority groups to follow to achieve the American Dream. Unfortunately, this myth insinuates that all Asian Americans no longer experience discrimination and thus no longer need social services.
- Although a heterogeneous group, Asian Americans possess some similar cultural values (see Table 2.4). Degree of acculturation will affect how salient each of the values are for individual Asian Americans.

2.5.4 European Americans

European Americans are those individuals originating from Europe, also labeled as Whites or Anglo-Americans. European Americans are the predominant racial/ethnic group in the

---

TABLE 2.4 Asian American Cultural Values.

Family	Primary socialization unit; kinship network, patriarchal with traditional gender roles, authoritarian and directive parenting styles, **filial piety** (needs of individual often are secondary to those of the family, especially to parents and elders), **saving face** (an individual's behavior's are reflective of family and thus should protect the honor of the family).
Gender and sexuality	Traditional gender roles, with males as the primary decision makers and women having main roles as spouses and mothers; traditional and nondemonstrative of sexuality, youth not encouraged to date, homosexuality discouraged.
Harmony	Harmony with nature, harmonious interpersonal relationships (i.e., nondirective, nonconfrontational, humility).
Emotional restraint	Self-restraint and self-control is viewed as a strength.
Education	Education is highly valued and indicative of a "good family."
Religion	Various religions followed depending on geography, belief in fatalism and rebirth, mind-body-spirit connection.
Help-seeking	Mental health issues cited in research include racism, depression, PTSD, domestic violence, anxiety, and schizophrenia. Three times less likely than Whites to use mental health services, although college students are open to counseling for career-related concerns.

Source: Inman and Alvarez (2010).

TABLE 2.5   European American Cultural Values.

Individualism	Individual needs are most valued; independence, competitiveness, live the "American Dream," overcome obstacles
Religion	Judeo-Christian most prevalent, dedication to God and moral living
Time orientation	Future time orientation, everything is planned and scheduled
Family	Patriarchal family system, extended family not as valued as nuclear family
Relationship with nature	Mastery over nature, individuals have a right to exploit the environment
Scientific method	Values insight and reason, rationality
Status	Status and power necessary for survival
History	U.S. history constructed as European American history
Communication	Verbal communication

United States and constitute approximately 69.4% of the U.S. population (U.S. Census Bureau, 2004).

- Individuals identifying as White are from families that immigrated to the United States at some point (unlike Native Americans; see section 2.5.6). Immigration began in the late 15th century and included individuals primarily from Germany, France, Scotland, and England. These immigrants came to the United States for economic security and political freedom. The English had the most influence in the Americas in shaping European American (White) cultural values, as evidenced by the use of English as the primary language.
- European Americans have continued to immigrate to the United States over the past five centuries for economic, religious, and political reasons. Between 1820 and 1998, approximately 60% of documented immigrants were from Europe; this number has decreased to about 30% since 1998 (McMahon, Paisley, & Molina, 2010).
- European Americans throughout history have oppressed other racial and ethnic groups mentioned throughout this section. Having the most power and influence, they have been able to establish the dominant U.S. cultural values (see Table 2.5).

2.5.5   Latin Americans

Latin Americans make up over 15% (45.5 million) of the U.S. population (U.S. Census Bureau, 2008) and originate from approximately 20 countries. Latin Americans have also been labeled as "Hispanic" by the U.S. Census Bureau, a term originating from the Spanish word *Hispano*, indicating one of Spanish heritage. It is important to note that not all Latin Americans have a Spanish heritage. There are four major groups of Latin Americans (Latinos):

- *Mexicans* make up approximately 64% of Latinos (Pew Hispanic Center, 2006). A treaty signed at the end of the Mexican-American War in 1848 ceded Mexican territory to the United States, and most Mexican Americans can trace their roots to ancestors who were living in U.S. territory before then. Since the 1970s, there has been an increase in Mexican immigration for economic reasons.

- *Puerto Ricans* constitute 9% of all Latinos (Pew Hispanic Center, 2005). Since Puerto Rico is a U.S. territory, all are considered U.S. citizens.
- *Cubans* make up about 4% of Latin Americans (Pew Hispanic Center, 2005). Cubans have immigrated more recently (past 50 years), seeking economic security and political freedom from Communism.
- *Central Americans, South Americans, and Caribbeans* comprise a group including approximately 500,000 from each country in these regions (Pew Hispanic Center, 2005). This final group immigrated to the United States for economic and political reasons.

For Latin Americans as a whole, there seem to be fewer educational and economic opportunities as compared to Whites. Another barrier or stressor involves the immigration process. Latin Americans often experience **acculturative stress**, or cognitive and affective consequences associated with leaving one's own country and entering a host country (in this case, the United States). Individuals with acculturative stress have to adapt to a new culture and lose some of their cultural identity in the process. In fact, research shows an increase in mental health issues for those immigrants residing longer in the United States and, presumably, having higher acculturation levels. Some common Latin American cultural values include these:

- Language: Since about 72% are born outside the United States, many Latin Americans hold Spanish as their dominant language.
- Family: Often termed **familismo**, this value refers to the strong connection Latinos have to their extended families. Latin Americans comprise a collectivist culture that considers the needs of the family primary.
- Interpersonal relationships: **Personalismo** refers to having compassion and caring for those in their communities and families. This often coincides with **confianza**, or possessing trust and confidence in those with whom one is in relationship.
- Catholicism: Roman Catholicism is the predominant religion of Latin Americans. The Virgin Mary is revered, and women who emulate her characteristics are more valued.
- Gender: There are traditional gender roles, in which masculinity is termed **machismo** (traditional male traits such

as competitive, powerful, decision maker and breadwinner for the family) and femininity is termed **marianismo** (traditional female traits such as nurturing, emotional, and sexually pure).

2.5.6   Native Americans

Native Americans constitute about 2.4 million (1%) of the U.S. population (U.S. Census Bureau, 2001). Of this number 1.7 million are enrolled tribal members of 563 federally recognized tribes and nations. More than 200 tribes or nations are currently petitioning for federal status.

- Although not considered U.S. citizens until 1924, Native Americans were the first inhabitants of North America. Unfortunately, genocide and disease decimated this population, beginning in the late 1400s.
- Approximately 78% of Native Americans live in urban areas, with the remaining living in suburban or rural areas, or on one of 314 federally recognized or 46 state-recognized reservations (Garrett, 2010).
- The U.S. Bureau of Indian Affairs (1988) declared that a Native American is an individual enrolled in a tribe or nation with at least ¼ blood quantum. The U.S. Census Bureau relies on individuals self-identifying as Native American as "evidence" of their race/ethnicity.
- Garrett (2010) cited mental health and public health issues with which Native Americans struggle, including tuberculosis, alcoholism, diabetes, pneumonia, homicide, and suicide. In addition, only 52% of Native Americans finish high school, 75% earn less than $7,000 per year, 45% live below the poverty line, and the majority who live on reservations (and in other areas) reside in substandard housing.
- Table 2.6 notes some common Native American cultural values.

2.5.7   Practice Multiple-Choice Items: Counseling Racial and Ethnic Groups

1. _____ comprise the smallest percentage of the U.S. population.
   a. Native Americans
   b. Arab Americans
   c. Asian Americans
   d. European Americans

2. Filial piety regarding family applies most closely to which cultural group?
   a. Latin Americans
   b. African Americans
   c. Native Americans
   d. Asian Americans

3. _____ are considered the fastest-growing racial and ethnic group.
   a. African Americans
   b. Arab Americans
   c. Native Americans
   d. Asian Americans

4. The largest group making up what constitutes Latin Americans is
   a. Puerto Ricans.
   b. Muslims.
   c. Mexicans.
   d. Cubans.

5. _____ are mistakenly considered to be the model minority.
   a. African Americans
   b. Arab Americans
   c. Latin Americans
   d. Asian Americans

Answer Key: 1. b; 2. d; 3. b; 4. c; 5. d.

2.6   COUNSELING OTHER CULTURAL GROUPS

In addition to racial and ethnic groups, other cultural classifications are reflected in NCE and CPCE items. These cultural groups include sexual minority clients, transgender individuals, the elderly, adolescents, and international students.

2.6.1   Sexual Minority Clients

Sexual minority individuals include lesbian, gay, bisexual, queer, and those questioning their sexual orientation. This group also often includes transgender individuals (see section 2.6.2). These clients may experience the same issues that arise when counseling any other client. However, these clients may need additional services related to coming out and other identity development concerns as well as help coping with individual and institutional discrimination and violence that hinders physical and mental well-being.

TABLE 2.6   Native American Cultural Values.

Sharing	Group needs significant, emotional relationships valued, patience encouraged, sharing freely and keeping only needed materials important
Cooperation	Avoidance of competition, participation after observation, speaking softly and at a slower rate
Noninterference	Try to control self and not others, self-discipline, humility
Time orientation	Present-time focus; "Time is always with us"
Extended family orientation	Reliance on extended family
Harmony with nature	Explanation according to nature

Source: Garrett (2010).

- The sexual identity development process may be an important counseling consideration when working with this population. The **coming out process** involves recognizing oneself as a sexual minority and disclosing one's sexual identity to others. This process mostly occurs in the teenage years; however, some individuals hide their identity for years and even have opposite sex relationships. Aspects of the coming out process indicated in sexual identity development models (see section 2.4.3) include becoming aware of attraction to same sex; being sexually involved; becoming familiar with the sexual minority community; self-identifying as gay, lesbian, bisexual, or transgender; and coming out to others. Although this process seems linear, individuals can cycle through components of it and opt to come out to various individuals at different times.
- Counselor competency in counseling sexual minority clients includes dedication to the ideas set forth by the Multicultural Counseling Competencies by Sue, Arredondo, and McDavis (1992) and the Association for Lesbian, Gay, Bisexual, and Transgender Issues in Counseling (ALGBTIC) Competencies for Counseling Gay, Lesbian, Bisexual, and Transgendered Clients (Terndrup, Ritter, Barrett, Logan, & Mate, 1997).
- Counselor competency also includes knowing one's own ideas and biases about this population. In addition, counselors have a responsibility to understand current events that involve this group, the group's culture and community, and oppression against sexual minorities. Practitioners must also be aware of how their own spiritual and religious background may affect the client, while keeping in mind that some clients may have been ostracized by the religious community. Counselors should never impose their own values about sexual orientation and the intersection of gender onto a client (ACA, 2005). If a counselor deems that he or she cannot work with a client, it is an ethical requirement for the counselor to refer the client. Counselors must seek out educational opportunities, such as seminars and current literature, to maintain quality services for these clients.
- Mental health professional organizations reinforce the idea of acceptance of sexual minority clients, as opposed to working to change them. **Reparative therapy** or **conversion therapy**, or attempting to change one's sexual orientation, has not been supported by research or any professional organization, although many attempts have been made using shock therapy, pain therapy, hypnosis, medications, and religious counseling. The American Psychiatric Association not only announced the inefficacy of reparative therapy but also discussed how this form of treatment could further complicate the client's identity and reinforce negative feelings.

2.6.2 Transgender Individuals

Virginia Prince coined the term *transgender* to identify men who lived as women but did not have a sex change operation. Now, the term is used more broadly to describe persons who do have the biology or appearance of someone that is in line with traditional gender roles. Transgender is not sexual orientation but rather gender identification, a fact that is often confused. Transgender also includes the following categories:

- *Transsexuals.* Persons who choose to alter their biology to be more in line with their identified gender.
- *Crossdressers.* Persons who dress in clothing traditionally worn by the opposite sex. Most commonly seen as men in women's clothes, and may provide sexual pleasure. *Drag kings* (females dressing as males) and *drag queens* (males in female attire) are terms also used to describe individuals who cross-dress to entertain. About 1 person in every 50 is estimated to be a cross-dresser.
- *Transgenderist.* Persons who live the life of the opposite sex without biological intervention.
- *Intersexed.* Formerly known as hermaphrodites, these individuals possessed both male and female genitalia and hormones.
- *Genderqueer.* Persons who do not conform to traditional ideas of gender roles and sexual orientation.
- *Two-spirited.* A Native American term that identifies a person with the spirit of both a male and female. It is important to note, however, that individuals from the dominant culture would be disrespectful if they used this term to describe a Native American.
- *Gender dysphoria.* Persons who were born one gender, identify with another, and experience conflict about it. This occurs in an estimated 3% to 10% of the population.
- Accurate counts of transgendered persons are difficult to obtain.
- Much like sexual minority clients, transgender individuals will present with issues similar to those of other clients. However, they may also present with issues such as substance abuse, low self-worth, and an HIV/AIDS diagnosis. Counselors should discuss **transphobia**, or discrimination against this community due to their nonalignment with cultural expectations, and also take a **trans-affirmative approach**, which involves the counselor taking on the role of an advocate by being involved politically, teaching the client how to advocate, and rallying for equal community resources.

2.6.3 Gerontological Clients

Gerontological counseling is an area of counseling tailored for individuals 65 years of age and older, an age group that continues to increase as a percentage of the U.S. population. In the year 2000, for example, 35 million Americans were age 65 years or older, compared to 3 million in 1900. In 2060, the number is expected to grow to 90 million (U.S. Census Bureau, 2003). Gerontological counselors must have the special skill set put forth by the Association for Adult Development and Aging (AADA) in the Gerontological Competencies.

- There are unique counseling considerations for those over the age of 65 years. Clients may present with terminal illness, grief and loss issues, physical challenges, and caregiver issues. Clients may be living alone, having an identity crisis, or experiencing **ageism**, which is discrimination based on one's age. In particular, this population may also have changes in memory and decreases in speed, attention span, and vision/hearing.

- Counselors must be able to distinguish between depression symptoms and aging issues to make the proper diagnosis and also must assess this high risk population for suicidal intent. This population may have varying ideas regarding counseling, and the clinician should address them as needed.
- Counselors should respect the client, know diseases and normal aging processes, and be able to offer resources within the community to the client.

2.6.4 Adolescents

Adolescence occurs between 10 and 20 years of age and is a time of significant developmental transitions, including physical changes (e.g., hormonal changes and biological development affecting cognition and self-concept). In addition, the social self is also very important during this time, with increasing value on peer groups for solidifying self-concept.

- Issues that may present when counseling adolescents include eating disorders, substance abuse, depression, anxiety, and behavioral problems (including sexually risky behaviors).

2.6.5 International Students

International students are those who leave their home country to pursue higher education in the United States. Over the past three decades U.S. higher education has experienced a notable growth in enrollment numbers to over 600,000 (Institute of International Education, 2007).

- Counselors working with international students should be knowledgeable about difficulties in transitioning (e.g., language difficulties, discrimination, monetary issues, isolation, and cultural differences, culture shock, acculturation) and anything else that may hamper the efficacy of counseling. International students may suffer from depression, anxiety, and feeling powerless. Positive factors for these students include host family bonds, desire to learn the native language, family support, and institutional support.
- **Culture shock** involves having to transition to a foreign environment by adjusting to the new foods, customs, language, and so on. Four phases of culture shock have been proposed (Pedersen, 1995):
  - *Honeymoon Phase.* Involves hopefulness, excitement, and captivation of the new culture.
  - *Crisis or Disintegration Phase.* Involves the individual being frustrated or let down by cultural aspects that were at first fascinating.
  - *Reorientation and Reintegration Phase.* Involves reintegrating into the new culture by viewing both the good and bad of the culture.

- *Adaptation or Resolution Phase.* Feelings of belonging to multiple cultures and having a sense of well-being.
- As noted, acculturation occurs when an individual comes into contact with a new culture and experiences changes in their own beliefs or actions. Acculturative stress occurs when acculturation causes a person to decompensate either physically, mentally, or socially.
- Other stressors that international students might encounter include language differences that might affect academics and social functioning, racism, and lack of social support. Further, there may be additional stress toward the end of an academic career as individuals decide whether to remain in the host country on graduation.
- International students may not seek counseling for fear the government may find out about their issues and force the student to return home, may assume any somatic complaints are a physical problem only, or may perceive a stigma for seeking help.

2.6.6 Practice Multiple-Choice Items: Counseling Other Cultural Groups

1. Feelings of hopefulness and captivation of a new culture are part of the _____ phase of culture shock.
   a. Crisis
   b. Honeymoon
   c. Reorientation
   d. Resolution

2. A cultural group that typically deals with issues with eating disorders and sexually risky behaviors is
   a. international students.
   b. the elderly.
   c. transgender individuals.
   d. adolescents.

3. *Intersexed* is defined as an individual who
   a. is two-spirited.
   b. lives as the opposite sex without biological intervention.
   c. alters their biology.
   d. possesses both male and female genitalia

4. Some of the unique issues affecting _____ clients are grief, loss, physical challenges, and terminal illness.
   a. adolescent
   b. elderly
   c. transgender individuals
   d. international clients

5. Counselors should advocate for
   a. reparative therapy.
   b. acceptance of sexual minorities.
   c. pain therapy.
   d. conversion therapy.

Answer Key: 1. b; 2. d; 3. d; 4. b; 5. b.

2.7 CRISIS, TRAUMA, AND SPECIALIZED INTERVENTIONS

When a person experiences a crisis, the person is going through an intense time of distress when normal stress management and solution-finding skills are not adequate for the situation—that is, the perceived or actual stressors exceed perceived or actual resources. Although a crisis is considered short term, a **trauma** consists of a longer-term crisis for which there is no resolution or balance of stressors and available resources. This section highlights various crises and traumas, including aggression, child abuse, intimate partner violence, and divorce and separation. In addition, this section provides treatment information for crisis intervention, trauma counseling, suicide intervention, conflict resolution, peer mediation, and addictions counseling.

2.7.1 Aggression

Aggression involves actions taken with the goal of inflicting harm. Aggression can be verbal, physical, or relational. *Relational aggression*, or harm within the context of a social group, is receiving increased attention in the counseling literature. Examples of aggression include verbal insults, hate crimes, physical injury, gossiping, and bullying.

- A **microaggression** involves an aggressive act against a minority, such as men and women of color. These acts are not necessarily overtly violent but rather more insidious acts that build up and occur within everyday social interactions. Eventually, accumulated microaggressions lead individuals to feel they do not belong.
- **Violence** is a focused intent to cause harm. Violence may be premeditated or occur at the spur of the moment. It is thought that perpetrators of violence act out to deal with their feelings of anger, shame, and humiliation. Violence occurs in a series of steps, starting from the act of humiliation that causes an eventual perpetrator to feel disconnected from society around him, which leads to intense self-consciousness, then to destructive behaviors and ineffective boundaries.
- Warning signs of violence include (Thompson, 2004) feelings of rejection, history as a violence victim, disciplinary problems, fear of ridicule, academic problems, portrayal of violence in artwork or writing, serious threats of violence toward others, intolerance, gang membership, substance abuse, and access to a weapon.

2.7.2 Child Abuse

Although specific legal definitions range from state to state, the broad definition of **child abuse** involves harm to an individual under the age of 18 years, caused by either exploitation, neglect, or physical, sexual, or emotional abuse. The Child Abuse Prevention and Treatment Act (CAPTA) adds to the definitions list by including caregiver lack of action to combat and prevent possible or actual harm or death of one under the age of 18 years. Professional counselors are mandated to report suspected child abuse.

- **Neglect**, the most prevalent type of abuse, involves not taking care of a child's needs, either physically (e.g., food, housing, proper care/supervision), medically (e.g., not providing needed treatments), educationally (e.g., not supplying schooling or not enrolling a qualified student in special education), or emotionally (e.g., lack of affection, being around abuse and turmoil or substance abuse). An important distinction to note is that families who are financially unable to support themselves are distinguished from those who have the money but decide not to use it.
- **Physical abuse** involves causing injury and harm in the form of bruising, sprained muscles, bones being broken, burns, cuts, being shaken, hit, thrown, asphyxiation, and genital mutilation. This is the easiest type of abuse to show, and any injury caused to a child, regardless of motivation, is considered abuse.
- **Sexual abuse** involves any sexual activity with a child, even if there is no direct touching. This includes exposing oneself, exposing children to pornography, touching of genitalia (by adult to child or vice versa), intercourse, sexual assault, and sodomy. **Sexual exploitation** is defined as forcing a child into prostitution or pornography.
- Across abuse report types, there is approximately equal prevalence by gender, and approximately 55% of abuse victims are younger than 8 years old. Approximately 80% of known child abusers are parents (U.S. Dept. of Health and Human Services, 2007).

2.7.3 Intimate Partner Violence

Intimate partner violence (IPV), a predominant form of adult domestic violence, is defined as any behavior that is physically, emotionally, or sexually abusive in nature and used to gain authority over one's relationship with an intimate partner. Marriages, intimate relationships, families, and dating couples may experience domestic violence, as may heterosexual or same-sex couples. Women are victims more often than males.

- A cycle of violence may be noted in abusive relationships, including tension buildup, the actual abuse occurrence, and then the honeymoon phase, the last of which occurs less and less frequently in abusive relationships as they progress.
- A risk factor for IPV survivors is previous abuse, often occurring in childhood. Other risks include lack of healthy self-esteem, low educational level, isolation from social supports, and lack of friends, family, and neighbors. Relationships with violence may have certain characteristics, such as strife or fighting within the marriage, a dominant male, low healthy functioning within the family, fostering dependence emotionally, rigid adherence to traditional gender roles, and a need for control and authority. Inability to leave the situation may be due to fear for children and losing custody of them, intellectualizing abuser behavior, worry about employment, and lack of financial resources or shelter.

- Consequences of IPV for the survivor include physical injury, isolation, depression and anxiety symptoms, academic and occupational problems, risky behaviors (e.g., unprotected sexual activity, unwanted pregnancies, rape, and substance abuse), and eating disorders, to name a few.

2.7.4 Divorce and Separation

Separation is a legal process that allows couples to remain legally married while living separate lives. This often precedes **divorce**, which is the formal, legal termination of a marriage with no death of either individual involved. **Annulment** is the formal voiding of a marriage. Causes of divorce vary from extramarital affairs, irreconcilable differences, abuse, money, mood disturbances like depression or anxiety, and fighting to differences on how to raise the children, clashing personalities, ineffective communication, sexual incompatibility, and differing expectations of gender roles. Rich (2002) has defined four phases of divorce:

- *Shock and disbelief.* Counselors can help clients talk about issues and reality testing.
- *Initial adjustment.* Can include practical adjustments to the first set of changes triggered by divorce, such as moving, family changes, and legal proceedings.
- *Active reorganization.* Occurs after finalization of legal proceedings and involves connecting with new individuals for socialization, be it friends or perhaps a new romantic interest.
- *Life reformation.* Accepting and integrating one's former and current lives.

Children may be affected by divorce as well, and professional counselors should watch for changes in daily activities (e.g., eating, sleeping, interacting with others) and mental health issues (e.g., depression, suicidality, anxiety, academic difficulties, behavioral problems).

2.7.5 Crisis Intervention

Five forms of crises may warrant intervention from a professional counselor. These include (a) developmental crises (i.e., crises due to normal lifespan events such as childbirth, marriage, graduation, and aging); (b) environmental crises (i.e., those due to natural or human-made events such as an economic downturn, disease, natural disasters, famine, and fire); (c) existential crises (i.e., crises due to realizations concerning one's meaning and purpose in life that cause internal strife, conflict, or anxiety; (d) situational crises (i.e., those due to an unexpected circumstance outside of one's control, such as being fired, being a victim of a violent crime, or experiencing the death of a loved one); and (e) psychiatric crises (i.e., those due to substance abuse or issues with mental health). James and Gilliland (2005) outlined steps in crisis intervention:

- *Define the problem.* Discover how the client conceptualizes the event and to what extent it is perceived as a crisis and not simply an obstacle. Rely on Rogerian or microskills (see Chapter 5) and validate the client's point of view. Examine how serious the crisis is, the client's emotional state, any impairment to client behavior or cognitions, and any potential threats the client may exhibit to harm self or others.
- *Ensure client safety.* It is an ongoing process to ensure that both the client and individuals affiliated with the client are safe mentally and physically. Follow the ethical duty to report if harm to self or others is determined. Some basic universal actions that help ensure client safety are to be in touch with law enforcement, individuals in the medical field, and local child protective services (CPS) staff and to work toward creating a plan of action for the client to follow.
- *Provide support.* A counselor should provide support to the client in crisis regardless of what the actual event is or how the client's beliefs or worldview may differ from the counselor's. Use skills such as unconditional positive regard and empathy.
- *Examine alternatives.* Help the client to make decisions he or she may find overwhelming or unable to make at the present time. Work with clients on a list of different ways to manage a situation and help them to choose the most appropriate action while making sure to empower, and not railroad, the client.
- *Make plans.* Do this after examining the alternatives. Help the client to discover a support system (e.g., among family, friends, community, etc.) and to come up with uplifting behaviors (e.g., exercise, journaling, etc.). It is important for the client to establish a sense of control by being involved in devising these plans.
- *Obtain commitment.* Ensure that the client will stick to the plan and commit to a reasonable action that begins to get life back on track.

2.7.6 Trauma Counseling

Trauma may result from a one-time occurrence, such as a violent crime or natural disaster, or from being in a prolonged stressful situation, such as combat or a chronic illness. Experiencing a trauma overwhelms an individual and steals power and control, resulting in helplessness and questions of purpose.

- Posttraumatic stress disorder (PTSD) symptoms can present in the primary victim of a trauma but may also present vicariously in secondary victims, or those who were not directly involved or who were merely bystanders. The *Diagnostic and Statistical Manual of Mental Disorders, Fourth Edition (DSM-IV-TR;* American Psychiatric Association, 2000) specifies symptoms of PTSD as hypervigilance; change in sleep patterns; intrusive thoughts; flashbacks; numbness; memory issues; avoiding places, triggers, or people that remind the individual of the trauma; mood disturbance; and problems with focus. These symptoms present soon after the trauma and last longer than a month.

Judith Herman, author of *Trauma and Recovery* (1997), believes healing from a psychologically traumatic situation occurs in three phases that are ongoing and not necessarily ever completed but rather are integrated into one's life and sometimes reworked:

- **Establishment of safety.** Diagnosis, client empowerment to return control, and client opportunity for decision making are critical pieces of this first phase. Opportunities for prevention of symptom worsening and treatment of existing issues should occur. Complex PTSD may also present in this phase, often rooted in a repressed or long-lasting event, with symptomology including insomnia, eating disorders, interpersonal relationship issues, drug or alcohol abuse, and mood disturbances such as anxiety or depression. Reduction of isolation and ensuring the physical well-being of the survivor is important. Counselors should assess whether the threat of harm is past or still lurking in the future and come up with a safety plan. Counselors should also be aware of the need for a reduction in feelings of fear and should encourage the client to be aware that treatment for trauma is not a quick fix but rather a longer process requiring extended work. Every facet of an individual is affected by trauma, including behavior, cognition, physical presentation, social aspects, emotional aspects, and spiritual aspects. Crisis intervention, treatment of symptoms, and increasing client knowledge are keys in this phase.
- **Remembrance and mourning.** This phase involves the client working with a counselor to tell the story of the trauma, to remember the details and make it more reality oriented and less surreal. The client should always maintain control and monitor any bodily symptoms that occur during this draining process. Particular attention should be paid to proper techniques and possible medications that are effective for the various symptoms present following a trauma. Individuals may seek to get even with the perpetrator of the event or resist mourning. If the survivor focuses on the perpetrator, however, then the focus of the survivor is always on the one who inflicted harm.
- **Reconnection with ordinary life.** Individuals in this phase begin to reintegrate into a more regular existence and find purpose in the new normal. Survivors may benefit from participation in groups focused on interpersonal relationships and groups that focus on where they want to be in the future. Outreach and advocacy also may be desired activities for the client.

2.7.7 Suicide Intervention

Taking one's own life, whether intentional or not, is **suicide.** Unintentional suicides occur when a cry for help results in accidental death, such as when a person takes many pills in the hope that friends and family will intervene.

- Most suicides occur within either end of the spectrum of life, meaning 35 years and younger or 65 years and older. Males are four times more likely to commit suicide than are women, although women attempt suicide more often.

Whites and Native Americans are the most likely races/ethnicities to attempt and complete suicide (Centers for Disease Control, 2006).

Professional counselors should do the following for suicidal clients:

- Assess clients for risk and immediate danger to self that would warrant hospitalization without delay within the least restrictive environment. Factors to look for involving immediate suicide risk include suicidal intent that is specific and in place for a long duration, active planning, and a very fatal suicide plan.
- Remove the method of harm delivery (e.g., pills, gun) and access to method (e.g., hanging). Supply a safe environment for the client until the risk is over.
- If the risk is very high and the client is not cooperative, *involuntary hospitalization* may be needed. *Voluntary hospitalization* is possible when the client agrees to go into a care facility for treatment.
- For less severe cases with less serious intent, counselors may help clients to create a check-in system with members of their social network to keep isolation to a minimum and/or engage the client in a *no suicide contract,* which clients sign in agreement to call a suicide hotline or other support source in the event of increased suicidal ideation or pain. Professional counselors only engage in contracting with those who understand exactly what the contract entails and will follow through with their commitment.

2.7.8 Conflict Resolution

Conflict resolution is the way individuals seek resolution to interpersonal differences and usually involves negotiating, mediating, facilitating, and arbitrating. The goal is to keep the risk of violent acts to a minimum. *Win-win* situations are the ideal ending to conflicts, providing a benefit to both parties. Conflict resolution begins with a discussion of what each person believes is the root of the issue and takes several forms:

- **Negotiation** involves compromise by involved individuals. **Power negotiations** occur when individuals vie to have the strongest influence on the outcome and may involve deceitful tactics such as relaying false information and cheating. **Rights negotiations** involve the legality of what is right and uses norms, policies, and rules. **Interest-based negotiations** involve the process of finding a commonality between the individuals involved. **Transformation-based negotiations** deal with promoting empowerment and recognition of involved persons. Empowerment elevates people's sense of what they can do and their personal value. Recognition deals with being able to connect to the situation and engage in true listening.
- **Mediation** is the use of an objective, uninvolved person to help with conflict resolution with the goal of working toward determining specific desires and good solutions. This may be a voluntary process or mandated by a court. (section 2.7.9 provides more detail on peer mediation.)

- **Facilitation** is the use of counseling-related skills, especially in groups, to analyze the conflict, find compromise and solutions, and elicit commitment among individuals.
- **Arbitration** is the use of a third party to make decisions that resolve a conflict for the involved individuals. Arbitration may be binding, which means there is no extra legal action, or nonbinding, which warrants further action.
- **Med-arb** uses both mediation and arbitration. The objective individual listens to both sides, problem solves to incorporate mediation, and then lets individuals make the final decision. Often used for divorces or child custody cases, during which counselors may be called in to give their perceptions of the case.
- Not every form or technique will work for every client, so counselors should tailor their choices to each situation.

2.7.9 Peer Mediation

Peer mediation, used frequently in the school system, involves an objective third-party individual who helps individuals to negotiate, compromise, and problem solve when issues arise. Peer mediation attempts to instill better conflict resolution skills in students.

- The three stages of peer mediation include (a) making operational decisions, (b) introducing the program to stakeholders (e.g., faculty and staff), and (c) obtaining support for its use. Peer mediation is similar to mediation (see section 2.7.7), which is when individuals come together to lessen conflict between two parties.
- Steps to peer mediation are as follows:
  - Supply a safe environment for each party to talk about their perception of the issue.
  - Get all individuals to look at what they consider the main problem, then strive to reach some commonality.
  - With all parties, develop a few ways to solve the problem and explain why each way is needed.
  - Help individuals to see each other's side or perspective.
  - Help individuals to come up with a compromise solution to the problem, and get a commitment from all persons to see the solution through.

2.7.10 Addictions Counseling

Valente (2009) defines **addiction** as "a preoccupation and dependence on a drug or process, resulting in increased tolerance, withdrawal, and repeated patterns of relapse" (p. 4). Individuals may be addicted to substances, either illegal or legal, which can include pills, alcohol, cigarettes, or caffeine, or they may be addicted to a process, which can include eating, being online, having sex, or gambling.

- Regardless of the type of addiction, being addicted has certain characteristics, including increased tolerance to the substance or process of choice, withdrawal symptoms, an unjustifiable compulsion for acting on the addiction (e.g., pills taken when not medically necessary), and previous attempts to decrease involvement level or quit entirely that have not been met with success. A functioning impairment may occur economically, interpersonally, within the family, physically, on the job, and at school.

- Addictions counseling attempts to reduce the dependence of the person on the addiction by helping the person to stop engaging in addictive behaviors and then to reduce or eliminate relapses and impairment. Professional counselors may utilize various therapeutic techniques, provide coping skills, educate regarding addictions, and discuss a prevention plan concerning relapses with the client. This plan can include discussing the triggers that led up to the relapse and any emotions or environments that affected them. Twelve Step program attendance is typically encouraged in addictions counseling.

- Counselors also engage in **harm reduction**, which is the view that addiction is a health issue and that there are physical risks to abuse. Harm reduction and risk reduction are accomplished through education and managed use.

- Assessing an individual who is coming in for services requires taking a look at the client's willingness to change, access to medical and mental health services, current crises, and whether acute treatment such as detox or hospitalization in a psychiatric facility is needed. Biopsychosocial intake evaluations are often administered with a history of family, jobs, interpersonal relationships, schooling, medical needs, and so forth. Comorbidity, meaning the individual has an addiction plus another disorder (i.e., dual diagnosis), may be present. Domestic violence may be of concern as well, so proper steps must be taken to ensure safety of all individuals involved. As always, a counselor should never practice outside of his or her competency range and if needed should refer clients to practitioners with more expertise.

2.7.11 Practice Multiple-Choice Items: Crisis, Trauma, and Specialized Interventions

1. (A) _____ is an intense, generally short-term, time of distress in which a person's normal stress management skills are inadequate.
   a. Trauma
   b. Crisis
   c. Conflict
   d. Neglect

2. All of the following are considered forms of child abuse EXCEPT
   a. neglect.
   b. physical abuse.
   c. sexual abuse.
   d. separation.

3. Behavior that is used to gain authority over one's relationship with an intimate partner is
   a. neglect.
   b. trauma.
   c. sexual exploitation.
   d. intimate partner violence.

4. The use of an uninvolved person to help with conflict resolution is
   a. mediation.
   b. facilitation.
   c. negotiation.
   d. litigation.

5. Aggression can take the form of each of the following EXCEPT
   a. verbal abuse.
   b. hate crimes.
   c. bullying.
   d. alcoholism.

Answer Key: 1. b; 2. d; 3. d; 4. a; 5. d.

2.8 ADDITIONAL CONSIDERATIONS IN MULTICULTURAL COUNSELING PRACTICE

This final section of Chapter 2 highlights specialized theories that apply to cross-cultural populations: motivational interviewing, feminist theory, social identity theory, social influence model, and sociometry.

2.8.1 Motivational Interviewing

Contrary to the popular focus on pathology and a forceful confrontation-based model known as the **Minnesota Model (MM)**, **motivational interviewing (MI)** uses a more respectful person-centered, yet distinctly directive, approach used initially in addictions counseling. MI, heavily supported by research, contradicts MM, which has much less supporting research in two main areas. First, what had previously been seen as client resistance to be conquered is now seen as resistance as a working part of the therapeutic relationship. MI practitioners try to elicit awareness of incongruence between actions and goals (Lewis & Osborn, 2004).

- As MI is a briefer model focused on solutions, an acronym, **FRAMES**, was developed to guide timely and effective interventions (Lewis & Osborn, 2004):
  - *F: Feedback.* Give pertinent and immediate input on what is happening.
  - *R: Responsibility.* Clients are in charge of their modifications and should take ownership of the process.
  - *A: Advice.* Provide direction on client situations.
  - *M: Menu.* Offer a menu of various treatment opportunities.
  - *E: Empathy.* As MI is based on Rogerian principles (see Chapter 5), displaying this understanding is key.
  - *S: Self-Efficacy.* The client's perception of their ability to overcome challenges effectively is another important component of this model.
- Another acronym, which has its roots in MI, is **OARES**, which outlines MI techniques:
  - *O: Open-Ended Questions.* Open-ended questions will draw out more information from the client.
  - *A: Affirm.* Encourages client change behaviors.
  - *R: Reflective Listening.* Shows the counselor is tracking the client.

  - *E: Elicit Self-Motivational Statements.* To foster an environment in which the client can feel more comfortable changing and can make goals to move toward a desired behavior.
  - *S: Summarize.* Shows the counselor understands the client.
- When a client is leaning toward a decision to change, it is important that the professional counselor becomes more directive and proactive with the client.

2.8.2 Feminist Theory

Feminist theory, which began as a political movement, is generally concerned with equality of women. This theory is not heavily technique laden but rather promotes values taken from the areas of multiculturalism, politics, and social advocacy. Those who espouse a feminist viewpoint want equality for all individuals and are interested in eliminating sexism. Feminist theory practitioners are critical of classical theories that typically analyze individuals from only the male perspective, and feminist clinicians also find fault with "gendercentric" psychological developmental models that operate on the assumption that males and females advance differently.

- Practitioners of feminist theory should be well aware of their values and should be able to have a cooperative, empowering relationship with the client, viewing them as an important and capable person in the process. Feminist theory does not focus on the pathology in a person but examines the social and political environment within which a person operates.
- The main beliefs of feminist theory include the following:
  - Males and females are equal politically, socially, and economically.
  - The patriarchal male oppresses women in society.
  - At their base, people are political.
  - Rather than mental health issues and other difficulties being the result of pathology, the issues stem more from the skills a person uses to cope with their world.
  - Value-free therapy is not possible.
  - The counselor must establish a relationship that promotes equality between counselor and client.
- Several distinct phases exist within feminist doctrine:
  - *Liberal feminism.* This marks the beginning of the feminist movement in the 18th and 19th centuries when this view sprang to life in response to discrimination against women. Liberal feminism focuses on human rights and the desire to be treated, like men, as "rational" human beings. This movement touts accomplishments such as women's eventual participation in medical and mental health studies and also the incorporation of women into the voting population.
  - *Radical feminism.* Emerging in the 1960s and continuing through the 1980s, this particular phase focused on discrimination against women in capitalism, particularly white middle-class women, and was the building block for feminist therapy. A book written by author Betty Friedan (1963) entitled *The Feminine Mystique*

brought awareness to feminism and sparked discussions worldwide. Also during this time period, birth control pills were introduced, enabling women to choose for themselves their path either to or away from motherhood.

- *Cultural feminism.* Workplace environment, politics, sexual identity, and sexual harassment of women were the particular concentration of this movement, which began in the mid 1980s. In addition, females were studied to determine how their life experiences were distinct due merely to the fact that they are women. Cultural feminism looks at styles of management in the workplace as well, comparing them to male authority styles.
- *Women of color feminism.* Promotes embracing all women regardless of the color of their skin.
- *Black feminism.* Puts forth that African American women are the targets of both sexism and racism.
- *Social feminism.* Focuses on the whole of society, which pertains to particulars such as women's roles and careers, race, capitalism in a patriarchal context, socioeconomic status, ethnicity, culture, and the financial realm.
- *Ecofeminism.* The beliefs that women understand the balance between humans and nature better than men do and that men hurt both women and the environment.
- Feminist counseling is concerned with empowering women to become more aware of their place in society and the various means through which success has been impeded. Women are not seen as being pathological in nature. This holistic counseling theory focuses on raising the quality of life and looks at many issues, such as oppression, body image, abuse, independence, power discrepancies, roles, and sexual identity.

2.8.3 Social Identity Theory

Based on social psychology, **social identity theory** was created to understand discrimination within groups. This theory puts forth that people sort themselves into groups based on similar characteristics, such as ethnicity or gender. The basis for social identity is categorization, identification, and comparison. Categorization refers to how social groups are labeled and assessed according to group member characteristics. Prestige, or social value, is identified by comparing persons against other groups, and then persons choose a group to identify with based on social comparison results.

- **Self-categorization** is an important piece of social identity theory. The "self" is seen as an object to be classified into membership in a social group that gives worth to the person. People are categorized into groups as a result of birth characteristics (e.g., sex, race); however, some group memberships are chosen.
- The **in-group** is the group to which an individual feels similar, and the **out-group** is the group to which the person feels least similar. The in-group is viewed positively, and the out-group is viewed negatively and may be the object of discrimination.

- Theories similar to social identity theory include social identity theory of leadership, self-categorization theory, optimal distinctiveness theory, and social identity model of deindividuation.

2.8.4 Social Influence Model

The **social influence model** was created by Stanley Strong (1968) and encompassed two counselor pieces: (a) *credibility* or the expertise and trustworthiness of the counselor and (b) *interpersonal attractiveness,* or how the counselor shows the client that the counselor likes and has commonalities with him or her. Based on social psychology, this theory asserts that if counselors are viewed as having expertise and being attractive, they will have greater influence on the client.

- Increasing client perceptions of counselors' expertise can be done by showing proof of expertise by displaying credentials, behaving competently, and having a solid reputation.
- Trustworthiness can be increased by being honest and open. Attractiveness can be increased when the client feels commonalities exist between client and counselor, which is primarily accomplished through appropriate self-disclosure.

2.8.5 Sociometry

Sociometry gauges the extent of relationship among people or groups, or how people relate to one another, via a **sociogram**, which is a scientific, visual way to analyze and display these relationships. Sociometry was developed by Jacob Moreno.

- Two important principles for scientific testing of sociometry are spontaneity, which is the appropriate response to new situations, and creativity, which interfaces with spontaneity. Most persons have varying levels of these two factors; rarely are they equal.
- Methodology and technique in sociometry vary. Sociograms may be used to see connections or disconnections among individuals, using arrows and symbols, and can be reanalyzed to discover any progress.
- A *near-sociometric test* is conducted in a hypothetical situation and will have no action taken following the results. A **sociometric test** studies actual behavior, as opposed to *psychometric tests,* which infer ideas from similar behaviors. Researchers should know that reliability and validity of sociometric tests are not thought of in the traditional sense.

2.8.6 Practice Multiple-Choice Items: Additional Considerations in Multicultural Counseling Practice

1. The social influence model espouses that a counselor should have _____ for maximum influence.
   a. equity
   b. creativity
   c. spontaneity
   d. credibility

2. Two forms of feminism are women of color feminism and Black feminism. What is the difference between the two?
   a. There is no difference.
   b. Women of color feminism embraces all women, regardless of color, and Black feminism focuses mainly on the oppression of African American women.
   c. Women of color feminism embraces all women except Caucasians, and Black feminism was the main movement in the 1980s and focused on career.
   d. Women of color feminism focuses on the oppression of African American women, and Black feminism embraces all women, regardless of color.

3. Motivational interviewing is mainly based on a Rogerian counseling style, but
   a. is also directive.
   b. focuses heavily on transference and countertransference.
   c. is highly confrontational.
   d. focuses on the source of problems.

4. Each of the following is correct concerning the acronym OARES, from motivational interviewing, EXCEPT
   a. O = Open-Ended Questions.
   b. A = Action.
   c. R = Reflective Listening.
   d. S = Summarize.

5. Motivational interviewing has been primarily used in
   a. addictions counseling.
   b. feminist counseling.
   c. supervision.
   d. sociometry.

Answer Key: 1. d; 2. b; 3. a; 4. b; 5. a.

2.9 KEY POINTS FOR CHAPTER 2: SOCIAL AND CULTURAL DIVERSITY

- Social and cultural diversity, or multiculturalism, is an important consideration of the counseling relationship, as all counselor–client pairs are multicultural in some manner. The degree to which all counseling is considered multicultural depends on how broadly culture is defined.
- Multiculturalism is considered the fourth force of counseling, whereas social advocacy is considered the fifth force of counseling.
- Being familiar with the tripartite model of counseling and working to facilitate one's multicultural counseling competency is an ethical imperative.
- The three components of the tripartite model are counselor awareness of one's own cultural values and biases, counselor awareness of the client's worldview, and culturally appropriate intervention strategies. Each of these components is described in terms of attitudes and beliefs, knowledge and skills.
- Communication patterns are significant cultural considerations. Although traditional counseling theories and interventions rely heavily on verbal communication, nonverbal communication is the predominant form of communication across cultures. Counselors must be aware of types of nonverbal communication, including context communication, paralanguage, kinesics, chronemics, and proxemics.
- Worldview has been conceptualized primarily in two ways: (a) the intersection of locus of responsibility and locus of control and (b) the combinational features of views of human nature, relationship to nature, sense of time, activity, and social relationships.
- Each cultural group has an underlying power structure imbued with oppression experiences: racism for race, ethnocentrism for ethnicity, classism for socioeconomic status, sexism for gender, heterosexism for sexual orientation, ableism for ability status, and so forth.
- Several forms of racial prejudice can occur in multicultural counseling and include color blindness (ignoring race), color consciousness (focusing predominantly on race), and colorism (more favorable treatment of those with lighter skin).
- Research indicates that androgyny, or the combination of masculine and feminine characteristics, is the most psychologically ideal.
- The major types of world religions are Buddhism, Christianity, Confucianism, Hinduism, Islam, Judaism, and Taoism.
- Social justice involves the belief that individuals are to advocate for others to address issues of cultural privilege and oppression. It includes four components: equity, access, participation, and harmony.
- Individuals can be oppressed by having experiences or labels imposed on them or by being deprived of experiences or labels. Three levels of oppression are primary (individual acts of oppression), secondary (benefits individuals receive based on others' acts of oppression), and tertiary (internalized oppression).
- Racism can be overt or covert, intentional or unintentional, and occur at three levels: individual, institutional, and cultural.
- Resilience is an important characteristic to assess for and foster in individuals who experience oppression.
- For each cultural group that constitutes our identity, there is likely an identity development process. Identity development processes occur within social interactions with others who both identify with the cultural group membership and those outside of the membership.
- Individuals experiencing various identity development processes typically go through the following statuses: unawareness/denial, conflict/anxiety, retreat into own group and cautious interaction, integration of one's cultural identity with other identities and factors, and advocacy.
- Cross published the first racial identity development model, and Helms' White and people of color racial identity development models are the most widely cited.
- Gender identity development models tend to focus on women becoming aware of sexism and working to eliminate it in society.

- Cass's sexual identity development model is well known and has been expanded to examine social and environmental processes for individuals of all sexual orientations.

- The prominent racial/ethnic groups in the United States are (from largest to smallest) Whites/European Americans, Latin Americans, African Americans, Asian Americans, Native Americans, and Arab Americans.

- Some of the common cultural values across racial/ethnic groups involve the concepts of family, gender roles, time orientation, harmony with nature, communication patterns, and spirituality.

- International students face culture shock and acculturative stress, which affects their psychological and academic functioning.

- A crisis is an intense time of distress during which perceived resources are insufficient to deal with perceived or actual stressors. Some methods for intervening in crises include defining the problem, ensuring safety, providing support, examining alternative actions, making plans, and obtaining commitment from the client.

- A trauma seems to be more pervasive than a crisis, with long-term psychological consequences likely involving PTSD symptoms. The three stages associated with trauma recovery are (a) establishing safety for the sur-

vivor, (b) remembering the trauma and mourning associated losses, and (c) reconnecting and finding meaning.

- Child abuse and intimate partner violence are two prominent trauma experiences. Child abuse involves child neglect (e.g., not caring for a child's physical, educational, or emotional needs), physical abuse (e.g., physical injury, genital mutilation), and sexual abuse (e.g., direct touching, sexual exploitation, or exposure to sexually inappropriate material).

- Intimate partner violence tends to follow a cycle, beginning with tension building, the abuse or battering incident, and then the honeymoon phase.

- The five major forms of conflict resolution include negotiation, mediation, facilitation, arbitration, and mediation-arbitration (med-arb).

- Addictions counseling involves several interventions, including Twelve Step self-help groups, motivational interviewing, harm reduction methods, relapse prevention, and family and group counseling.

- Some of the primary principles of feminist theory are (a) personal matters are political endeavors that promote equity, particularly among genders, (b) sexism exists in society as evidenced in a patriarchal system, and (c) the counseling relationship should be collaborative and egalitarian.

CHAPTER 3

Human Growth and Development

3.1 FOUNDATIONAL ISSUES IN HUMAN GROWTH AND DEVELOPMENT

The topic of human growth and development covers the entire lifespan of human beings, from conception to death. Descriptive and theoretical approaches offer stage or task models to explain the complex processes of human development. The sheer breadth of this field makes it a fascinating and challenging area of study.

About 7.5% of the scored items (including trial questions that are not counted toward the overall score) on recent versions of the National Counselor Examination (NCE) have been directed at measuring understanding of human growth and development (rank = 7 of 8, the 2nd fewest of the eight domains). The average item difficulty index was .75 (rank = 3 of 8, the 3rd easiest content among the eight domains), meaning that the average item in this domain was correctly answered by 75% of test-takers.

The Counselor Preparation Comprehensive Exam (CPCE) generally includes 17 scored items designed to measure human growth and development, plus several trial items that do not count toward overall score. The average item difficulty index was .68, meaning that the average item in this domain was correctly answered by 68% of test-takers, making this set of items among the easier items on the examination.

The Council for Accreditation of Counseling and Related Educational Programs (CACREP, 2009) defined standards for human growth and development as the following:

Studies that provide an understanding of the nature and needs of individuals at all developmental levels, and in multicultural contexts including all of the following:

a. theories of individual and family development and transitions across the lifespan;
b. theories of learning and personality development, including current understandings about neurological behavior;
c. effects of crisis, trauma and disasters on individuals of all ages;
d. theories and models of individual, cultural, and community resilience;
e. a general framework for understanding exceptional abilities and strategies for differentiated interventions;
f. human behavior including an understanding of developmental crises, disability, psychopathology, and situational and environmental factors that affect both normal and abnormal behavior;
g. theories and etiology of addictions and addictive behaviors including strategies for prevention, intervention and treatment; and
h. strategies for facilitating optimum development and wellness over the lifespan. (p. 11)

The remainder of this first section of Chapter 3 discusses the stages of human development, types of aging, common methods for categorizing human developmental theories, and special designs used in human developmental research.

3.1.1 Stages of Human Development

Development involves the changes a human being undergoes between conception and death. Ordinarily, these changes are influenced by genetic and environmental conditions and are described within the physical, cognitive, moral, emotional, personality, and social development domains. Human development is often presented and analyzed according to developmental stages, which are socially, culturally, and historically constructed, for example:

- Prenatal period (conception to birth)
- Infancy (birth to 2 years)
- Toddlerhood (2–3 years)
- Early childhood (3–5 years)
- Middle childhood (6–12 years)
- Adolescence (13–19 years)
- Young adulthood (19–30 years)
- Middle adulthood (about 30–60 years)
- Late adulthood (about 60–75 years)
- Old age (about 75+ years)

3.1.2 Types of Aging

Aging, a set, predictable process involving growth and change in an organism over time, has been categorized as biological, psychological, and social. All three aspects are intertwined in the aging process.

- **Biological aging** involves how the body functions and changes over time. Biological changes rely heavily on metabolic changes, which are of two types: anabolism and catabolism.
  - *Anabolism* is the body building to peak potential and occurs from birth to an age that varies by individual. (Remember that anabolic steroids build physical muscle mass.)
  - *Catabolism* is the body's usually slow deterioration from peak through an individual's death.
- **Psychological aging** is one's perception of personal age. Given two people of the same age, one person may feel "old," whereas another may feel "young."
- **Social aging** is how one's chronological age is viewed within the societal or cultural context and is affected by vocation and socioeconomic status. For example, aged citizens in Eastern cultures are frequently regarded with greater respect as they age, whereas aged citizens in Western cultures frequently experience less respect as they age. Likewise, a 75-year-old wealthy doctor is often perceived quite differently from a retired blue-collar worker of the same age.

3.1.3 Categorizing Theories of Human Development

The theories of human development presented later in this chapter are frequently categorized as learning, cognitive, psychoanalytic (psychodynamic), humanistic, ethological, language, physical, and moral developmental. Such categorizations help us understand the complex and wide-ranging nature of human development. Theories can also be categorized according to nature vs. nurture, discontinuous vs. continuous, and active vs. reactive theories.

Nature vs. nurture is a controversial topic from developmental psychology and generally refers to the impact on human development of genetics and heredity versus environmental influences. In nearly all circumstances, human development is not exclusively one or the other. For example, in determining intelligence, most of the research concludes that genetic transmission accounts in most cases for the majority of one's intellect, but environmental influence certainly plays a role as well—that is, people are probably born with a range of potential intellectual ability (hereditary predisposition), but environmental circumstances will determine whether one achieves the high end (e.g., great nutrition, high intellectual stimulation) or low end (e.g., poor nutrition, low stimulation) of the potential range of intelligence. Most developmental theories (e.g., Freud, Erikson, Piaget) are interactionist or epigenetic: they acknowledge the relationship of nature and nurture.

Discontinuous development and continuous development pertain to the nature and degree of changes that occur over time. **Continuous development** emphasizes the small shifts or gradual, sequential, changes that occur over time and that are difficult to separate. For example, Skinner's operant conditioning portrayed developmental changes as a series of stimulus-response contingencies—that is, change occurs by strengthening a pattern of behavior over time. **Discontinuous development** portrays changes in behaviors and abilities as qualitatively different from previous or subsequent behaviors and abilities—that is, as abilities develop, an individual reaches a point where the abilities jump to qualitatively different and more advanced levels. Stage theories, such as Piaget's and Erikson's, are examples of discontinuous development. Individuals at more advanced stages are qualitatively superior to individuals at lower levels of development.

Active and reactive theories stress the roles that people play in determining their own development. **Active theories**, such as Erikson's psychosocial developmental theory, portray people as active in regulating or governing their behavior. In **reactive theories**, such as Skinner's operant conditioning, people are passive and react to environmental stimuli to accommodate to changes.

3.1.4 Special Designs in Human Development Research

Human development research is conducted using some specialized methodologies. Some of these methods are expanded on in Chapter 8: Research and Program Evaluation but are introduced here in the context of human development. These methods include case study, naturalistic, survey, correlational, cross-sectional, longitudinal, and time-lag (cohort sequential) studies (Erford, 2008).

A **case study** involves collecting data on a developmental change from a single individual, or a single group of individuals experiencing a similar developmental phenomenon. Case studies allow for in-depth study and analysis, but have the disadvantage of not being able to systematically compare differences across individuals. Also, the generalizations of the findings from one case are not automatically applicable to other cases. A **naturalistic study** is conducted in natural settings, usually through observation and interview and, as such, is oftentimes likened to qualitative research. Naturalistic inquiry yields rich, meaningful data that must be analyzed, synthesized, and interpreted by the researcher. Two primary disadvantages of this approach are that the presence of the observer will oftentimes influence the individuals being observed (observer effect) and that the causal reasons for the phenomenon being observed cannot be ascertained with certainty.

Survey research can be conducted via interviews or through administration of questionnaires and involves sampling a large pool of participants to assess and understand their thoughts, feelings, and perceptions regarding the stimuli under study. Large sample sizes (>100) are needed in survey research, and sampling bias can negatively affect generalizability of findings. **Correlational research design** allows researchers to study the relationship between two variables that exist but are not experimentally manipulated. The derived statistic—a correlation coefficient—describes the strength and direction of the relationship between the two variables but does not allow determination of whether one variable causes change in the other variable.

Cross-sectional design studies simultaneously examine several groups from differing levels of development (e.g., 5-year-olds, 10-year-olds, 15-year-olds). These studies are usually less expensive and require less time than longitudinal studies because data can be collected quickly and analyzed immediately. A major disadvantage of cross-sectional designs is the diffusion of individual changes because analyses are between groups—that is, there are different people of different developmental levels in the different groups. Thus, changes noticed among the groups could be due to the "cohort effect," meaning that people born during the same time may have similar lived experiences that make them qualitatively different from those born years earlier or years later, experiences that are unique to their age and lead to shared perspectives within the cohort.

Longitudinal design studies examine and re-examine the same group (cohort) of individuals of a specific developmental level as they mature and age, usually over a time frame of at least 10 years. These designs are usually more expensive to conduct in both time and money, and participant attrition/mortality is usually a problem. Data collection occurs at preplanned intervals, and thus a major advantage of longitudinal design studies is a legitimate display of developmental trends (changes across ages).

Time-lag studies, sometimes called cohort sequential studies, involve replications of previous studies on a modern-day cohort using the same parameters as the previous study. For example, a study of parental disciplining style conducted during the 1960s could be replicated on a sample of parents today to see if parental disciplining styles have changed since the initial study was conducted. As such, the time-lag design has elements of the cross-sectional approach and allows intergenerational comparisons.

3.1.5 Practice Multiple-Choice Items: Foundational Issues in Human Growth and Development

1. Aging is
   a. biological.
   b. social.
   c. psychological.
   d. All of the above.

2. Which of the following is NOT a true statement about biological aging?
   a. Biological aging depends on metabolic changes.
   b. Biological aging refers to people's perceptions of how old or young they feel.
   c. Biological aging involves anabolism.
   d. Biological aging involves catabolism.

3. Catabolism refers to
   a. the body's decline to death from its peak.
   b. the body's development from birth to its peak.
   c. the metabolic changes that occur in the elderly.
   d. None of the above.

4. Intelligence is accounted for mostly by a person's
   a. environment.
   b. genetics.
   c. genetics and environment in equal parts.
   d. educational level.

5. Epigenetic theorists emphasize the importance of
   a. nature.
   b. nurture.
   c. the combination of nature and nurture.
   d. None of the above.

Answer Key: 1. d; 2. b; 3. a; 4. b; 5. c.

3.2 THE CENTRAL NERVOUS SYSTEM

Human development relies heavily on cognitive and physical processes, thus making development and maturation of the central nervous system critical. This second section of Chapter 3 discusses development of the central nervous system and representative genetic disorders.

3.2.1 Development of the Central Nervous System

The nervous system is composed of the central nervous system and the peripheral nervous system. The **central nervous system** consists of the brain and spinal cord. The **peripheral nervous system** is the network of nerves that connects the central nervous system to the rest of the body (e.g., fingers, arms, toes, legs).

Growth of the brain involves not only the addition of new neurons but also an interconnectedness of these neurons and **myelination** (i.e., insulation of the neurons to enhance speed of neural transmissions). When a baby is born, the size of its brain is about 25% of its mature adult size and weight. But growth occurs rapidly, and the brain reaches approximately 60% of its adult weight by the end of the first year, 80% by the end of the second year, and its full adult size by age 16 years. By about age 30 years, the brain begins to shrink (lose neurons), and by the late 80s the brain has diminished to a weight about 20% less than that when it was 30 years old. As an individual approaches old age, blood flow to the brain decreases, as do levels of some neurotransmitters (i.e., any substance that transmits nerve impulses across neural synapses.)

The brain is divided into three parts: (a) the hindbrain (brain stem) and (b) the midbrain, both of which are highly developed at birth, and (c) the forebrain (cerebral cortex), which is mostly undeveloped at birth.

- The **hindbrain** is responsible for life maintenance and survival functions and includes the following:
  - *Medulla oblongata.* Regulates the heart and breathing.
  - *Cerebellum.* Regulates balance.
  - *Pons.* Connects the left and right cerebellum.
  - *Reticular activating system.* Regulates arousal and attention.
- The **midbrain** connects the hindbrain and forebrain, controls eye muscles, and relays auditory and visual information to the brain's centers for higher level thinking.
- The **forebrain** consists of the cerebral cortex, which is responsible for higher order behavior and conscious thought. Simplistically speaking, the cerebrum consists of the left and right hemispheres, corpus callosum, and cerebral cortex:
  - *Left hemisphere.* Controls the right side of the body and is responsible for language and writing abilities, and logical and systematic thought.
  - The *right hemisphere.* Controls the left side of the body and is responsible for muscle abilities, imagination, and emotional expression.
  - The *corpus callosum.* Is a bundle of nerve cells that connects the two hemispheres and allows them to integrate cognitive, emotional, and bodily functions.
  - The *cerebral cortex.* Covers the two cerebral hemispheres; is responsible for memory, concentration, problem-solving abilities, and muscle coordination; and is divided into four lobes:
    - *Occipital lobe.* Helps brain interpret sensory information through the eyes.
    - *Parietal lobe.* Controls spatial reasoning and sense of touch.
    - *Temporal lobe.* Responsible for hearing and storage of permanent memory.
    - *Frontal lobe.* Regulates the sense of smell, body control, and movement.

Other structures within the brain include the *thalamus*, which relays nerve impulses from sensory pathways to the cerebral cortex, and the *limbic system*, which is concerned with emotions and motivation. The limbic system contains the *hypothalamus* (the control center for pleasure and pain, regulates hunger, thirst, sexual functions, body temperature, etc., through release of hormones), the *amygdala* (influences behavior and activities, such as sexual interest, feeding, anger), and the *hippocampus* (influences memory and helps to recognize novel information or situations). Finally, *hemispheric specialization* or *lateralization* (i.e., right brain, left brain dominance) begins early in development but for many individuals occurs gradually through childhood.

3.2.2 Genetic Disorders

One should be familiar with three different classes of genetic disorders and some major examples of each: autosomal diseases, X-linked diseases, and sex chromosomal disorders. Genetic screening and counseling are growing in prominence.

- **Autosomal diseases** are genetic disorders that involve a chromosome other than the sex chromosome. Common examples include the following:
  - *Phenylketonuria.* A recessively transmitted disorder that occurs in about 1 in 8,000 births and involves an inability to neutralize the amino acid phenylalanine, which is found in many proteins. Failure to identify and treat the disorder leads to severe damage of the central nervous system. Prenatal diagnosis is possible, and special dietary precautions are needed.
  - *Sickle cell anemia.* A recessively transmitted disorder that occurs in about 1 in 500 African American births and causes an abnormal shaping of the red blood cells, usually shaped like a sickle or cylinder, leading to oxygen deprivation, pain, tissue damage, anemia, and pneumonia. Prenatal diagnosis is possible, and treatment ordinarily involves blood transfusions and painkillers. As many as 50% of those with sickle cell anemia die by their 20th birthday.
  - *Tay-Sachs disease.* A recessively transmitted disorder that occurs in about 1 in 3,500 births to Jews of European descent and involves an inability to metabolize fatty substances in neural tissues, leading to central nervous system degeneration. Prenatal diagnosis is possible, but no treatment is known, and death ordinarily occurs by age 4 years.
- **X-linked diseases** are passed on by the maternal X-chromosome to males. X-linked characteristics are numerous, male pattern baldness being one of the best known. Another example of an X-linked disease is *hemophilia,* a recessively transmitted disease that occurs in about 1 in 5,000 male births, and involves the failure of blood to clot, typically leading to severe bleeding and tissue damage. Prenatal diagnosis is possible, and treatment ordinarily involves prevention of injuries and blood transfusions, as necessary.
- **Sex chromosomal diseases** involve some genetic anomaly occurring on the sex-determining pair of chromosomes, usually affecting male or female characteristic displays or sexual reproduction. Common examples include the following:
  - *Turner syndrome (XO).* Occurs in about 1 in 5,000 female births in which all or part of the second X chromosome is missing. Individuals usually have undeveloped or underdeveloped ovaries and incomplete sexual development at puberty, are of short stature, have a webbed neck, and show impaired spatial intelligence. Treatment usually involves special education services to address learning disorders and hormone therapy to stimulate physical growth and sexual development.

- *Klinefelter's syndrome (XXY).* Occurs in about 1 in 1,000 male births and involves an extra X chromosome on the sex chromosomal pair (XY). Individuals are unusually tall, have higher amounts of body fat, have incomplete sex characteristics at puberty, and are usually sterile. Treatment involves hormone therapy at puberty to stimulate development of sex characteristics and special education services to help with verbal ability deficits.

3.2.3 Practice Multiple-Choice Items: The Central Nervous System

1. The brain usually reaches its adult weight by the time a person is
   a. 12 years old.
   b. 16 years old.
   c. 44 years old.
   d. 64 years old.

2. The most primitive part of the brain is the
   a. hindbrain.
   b. midbrain.
   c. forebrain.
   d. cerebral cortex.

3. The _____ is responsible for regulating arousal and attention.
   a. medulla oblongata
   b. cerebellum
   c. reticular activating system
   d. hypothalamus

4. Sickle cell anemia is
   a. an X-linked disease.
   b. a sex chromosomal disorder.
   c. an autosomal disorder.
   d. none of the above.

5. Males born with an extra X chromosome have
   a. Turner syndrome.
   b. Tay-Sachs disease.
   c. phenylketonuria.
   d. Klinefelter's syndrome.

Answer Key: 1. b; 2. a; 3. c; 4. c; 5. d.

3.3 LEARNING THEORIES

Learning is a relatively permanent change in behavior or thinking resulting from an individual's experiences. Learning theorists propose that individuals observe and react to their environment. Put simply, learning theories can be divided into *stimulus-response theories,* such as classical conditioning (e.g., Pavlov, Watson, Wolpe) and operant conditioning (e.g., Skinner, Thorndike), and *social learning theories* (e.g., Bandura, Rotter), which purport that learning occurs through observation and internalized motivational forces. Placement of some theorists within these categories was not universally accepted, so an additional category was added and includes the work of Dollard and Miller (section 3.3.4).

3.3.1 Classical Conditioning

3.3.1.1 IVAN PAVLOV   Ivan Pavlov was a Russian physiologist best known for his studies on the salivation of dogs when presented with food powder (Pavlov, 1960). He noticed that the dogs not only salivated when they could taste, see, or smell the food powder, but they also salivated when he entered the room or when the dogs entered the room where he was. In a series of well-controlled **classical conditioning** experiments, Pavlov demonstrated that pairing an *unconditioned stimulus* (US), such as meat powder, that automatically elicited the *unconditioned response* (UR), such as salivation, with a neutral, conditioned stimulus (CS), such as something that ordinarily would not elicit salivation (e.g., a tone, buzzer, or bell), would, after a number of pairings, result in the CS eliciting the UR, now called the *conditioned response* (CR). Thus, pairing the tone with the presentation of the food eventually led to the tone causing salivation whether the food was presented or not. This relationship is graphically represented in Figure 3.1. Note that the term *neutral stimulus* means that, ordinarily, the stimulus would not elicit the response—that is, dogs ordinarily do not salivate when they hear a buzzer; only after pairing the buzzer repeatedly with the food, will the dog salivate.

A number of factors are important in establishing a classically conditioned response:

- The temporal relationship between the US/CS is important. *Simultaneous conditioning* occurs when the US and CS are presented at the same instant. *Delayed conditioning* occurs when the CS begins first but overlaps presentation of the US; it is the most effective conditioning procedure. *Backward conditioning* means that the US is presented before the CS; it is only rarely effective in establishing a conditioned response.
- Once a US/CS pairing is accomplished, the repeated display of the CS without presentation of the UR/CR will lead to a weakening of the learning, known as **extinction**. **Spontaneous recovery** occurs when the CS/CR connection is reestablished, turning the weakened response very quickly into the formerly strong learned response. Thus, once a US/CS pairing is established, refresher events periodically may be needed to reinforce the learned response. This observation also led Pavlov to conclude that learning was never totally lost or forgotten, just inhibited and waiting to be revived.
- **Stimulus generalization** occurs when the participant's CS/CR connection is generalized to other stimuli similar to the original CS. For example, if a green light is the CS that leads the participant to respond (CR), and an experimenter

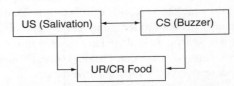

FIGURE 3.1 Pavlov's classically conditioned response.

uses a red light on a subsequent trial, the participant may generalize the response when the red light is lit. If the participant is reinforced for responding to the red light, generalization will occur; but if the response is not rewarded with the presentation of the CR, and the participant stops responding to the red light, **stimulus discrimination** is occurring—that is, the participant is discriminating between a green light, which will lead to a response, and a red light, which will not lead to a response.

3.3.1.2 JOHN B. WATSON
John B. Watson, sometimes called the "father of American behaviorism," campaigned for his idea that psychology should only deal with what can be observed and accurately measured—that is, if you can't observe it, it doesn't exist—which was a radical notion given the prominence of introspection as a method of psychological inquiry and understanding in the early part of the 20th century. Borrowing notions from Pavlov, Watson proposed that development involved learned associations between stimuli and responses. Watson is perhaps most remembered for the (in)famous Watson and Rayner (1920) experiment with "Little Albert," in which he attempted to condition a phobia into an 11-month-old infant (which he accomplished) and then attempted to decondition the phobia (which he did not accomplish). In doing so, he presented a white rat (CS), which elicited no adverse response, and paired the rat with presentation of a loud noise (US), which caused a startle response (UR). After several trials, Watson demonstrated that the presentation of the rat alone created a phobic response in Little Albert. Watson further demonstrated stimulus generalization, as Albert demonstrated fear of white rabbits and even balls of cotton. He was unable to decondition Little Albert's phobia. Watson further boasted that, given a dozen healthy infants, regardless of ability or talent, he could, through use of classical conditioning procedures, shape them into whatever occupation was required. Fortunately, he never had the opportunity to carry out this experiment.

3.3.1.3 JOSEPH WOLPE AND TECHNIQUES BASED ON CLASSICAL CONDITIONING
Joseph Wolpe (1958) applied classical conditioning procedures to psychotherapy. He wrote about the principle of **reciprocal inhibition**, which basically means that a person cannot engage in two mutually exclusive events simultaneously. Thus, a person cannot feel relaxed and anxious at the same time, think negative and self-affirming thoughts at the same time, visualize traumatic and relaxing scenes at the same time, or have muscles that are tense and relaxed at the same time. Reciprocal inhibition serves as the basis for many counseling interventions. Wolpe is perhaps best known for his treatment of phobias using **systematic desensitization**, which involves developing a fear hierarchy and progressively introducing each step on the hierarchy while the client attains a simultaneous state of relaxation. Thus, the fear is systematically deconditioned using reciprocal inhibition; the client cannot be fearful and relaxed at the same time.

Other techniques based on classical conditioning, but not necessarily developed by Wolpe, include these:

- *Counterconditioning.* A strong pleasant stimulus is paired with a weak aversive stimulus.

- *Aversive counterconditioning.* A noxious stimulus is applied when a maladaptive response is made. In a thought-stopping procedure, a rubber band is snapped on the wrist when clients experience the thoughts they are trying to suppress.
- *Flooding.* A stimulus that provokes anxiety is continuously presented until the client unlearns the response or becomes too fatigued to respond.

3.3.2 Operant Conditioning

3.3.2.1 EDWARD L. THORNDIKE
Edward L. Thorndike studied learning principles in animals (i.e., cats) even before Pavlov. Perhaps his most lasting contribution was his **Law of Effect** (Thorndike, 1911), which basically states that when a response (R) accompanying some stimulus (S) is followed by a satisfying reward, a connection is made and the response is likely to be repeated. The opposite is also true: if a satisfying reward does not follow a response, or if the consequence is unpleasant, the strength of the connection is diminished.

3.3.2.2 B. F. SKINNER
B. F. Skinner was influenced by Thorndike's research. The premise of Skinner's theory, which proposes that a response is either strengthened or diminished because of the consequence that follows, is very similar to Thorndike's Law of Effect. Skinner considered Pavlov's theory to involve respondent behaviors, so he only involved automatic reflexes (e.g., fear, anxiety). Skinner (1953) termed his theory **operant conditioning** because he viewed the vast majority of learning to occur either when an individual operates on the environment or when the environment controls the contingencies of reinforcement for the individual. According to Skinner, all learning was controlled by the contingencies surrounding the stimulus and response. Skinner's research produced numerous concepts and learning principles, including these:

- **Positive reinforcement**. Occurs when the addition of a stimulus (e.g., reward) immediately following the response increases the likelihood that the behavior will reoccur.
- **Negative reinforcement**. Occurs when the removal of a stimulus (e.g., loud noise) increases the likelihood that a behavior will reoccur.
- **Punishment**. The addition or removal of a stimulus that decreases the frequency of a given behavior. It is also commonly referred to as an aversive behavioral technique (e.g., spanking, extra chores, removing allowance or privileges).

The differences between positive reinforcement, negative reinforcement, and punishment depend on whether one is trying to increase or decrease a given behavior and whether one is applying (S+) or removing (S−) a stimulus, as demonstrated in Figure 3.2.

- **Reinforcers** can either be primary or secondary. **Primary reinforcers** satisfy a primary need (e.g., food, rest). **Secondary reinforcers** are anything that becomes associated with a primary need, such as money, which can be traded for food or comfort, or tokens, which can be exchanged for rewards.

Goal	Stimulus condition	
	Add stimulus (S+)	Remove stimulus (S–)
Increase behavior	Positive reinforcement	Negative reinforcement
Decrease behavior	Punishment (S+)	Punishment (S–)

FIGURE 3.2   The differences between reinforcement and punishment strategies.

- **Reinforcement schedules** dictate how frequently reinforcements are administered. Skinner described a continuous reinforcement schedule, during which a reinforcement is administered immediately following each response, and an intermittent reinforcement schedule, during which a reinforcement is not administered every time a response is made. Intermittent reinforcement schedules are of four types:
  - In *fixed ratio* (FR) schedules, a reinforcer is administered each time a participant makes a certain number of responses (e.g., every response [FR1], every 5th response [FR5], every 10th response [FR10]). FR schedules usually lead to the quickest acquisition of a response, particularly when the FR is low at the start. However, this schedule may lead to high quantity with low quality. For example, a factory worker who gets paid for every bundle of 10 products produced would likely reason that he would get paid more if he produces more bundles but that he would do so at the expense of quality.
  - In *variable ratio* (VR) schedules, reinforcements are presented periodically so that, on average, they occur every other, every 5th, or every 10th time. Thus, a participant on a VR10 schedule may be reinforced after 5, 8, 12, and 15 responses (with an average of 10 responses). Due to the lack of predictability, VR schedules produce high response rates and are more resistant to extinction, such as in the case of individuals who play slot machines.
  - In *fixed interval* (FI) schedules, reinforcements are presented after a fixed period of time (e.g., every 15 seconds, every hour). FI schedules produce low rates of responding since administration of the reinforcer is dependent on the passage of time rather than frequency of responding. For example, paying hourly wages in a work setting tends to produce minimal levels of work because an individual gets paid the same amount regardless of the amount of work produced.
  - In *variable interval* (VI) schedules, the time interval of the reinforcement administration is varied. Pop quizzes are an example of a VI schedule; one knows they are coming but not precisely when, which usually leads to maximal response rates.

Behavior is shaped through a process known as *successive approximations*, meaning that a rat may not automatically know to press a bar to obtain food but easily can be taught to do so by reinforcing the rat when it moves closer to the bar, then makes contact with the bar, then, eventually, presses the bar, obtaining the reward on demand. Many counseling strategies based on operant conditioning have been developed (e.g., contingency contracting, token economy, Premack principle, extinction, time out, response cost; Erford, Eaves, Bryant, & Young, 2010) and are reviewed in Chapter 5: Helping Relationships.

3.3.3 Social Learning

Social learning models view learning as more than simple stimulus-response connections and take into account both social and cognitive developmental factors. Social learning theorists believe we observe and learn from what we experience in the social context by considering new information, constructing meaning from it, and using it in future interactions, frequently without receiving any overt reinforcement.

3.3.3.1 ALBERT BANDURA   Albert Bandura (1977) developed **social learning theory**, which is based on the principle that people learn through observation, imitation, and modeling. An individual can observe a model perform some behavior, then imitate (i.e., duplicate exactly) that behavior without receiving any tangible reinforcement, thereby demonstrating new learning even in the absence of a contingency. **Observational (vicarious) learning**, then, is learning through passive observation, whereas **modeling** is demonstrating how a behavior is performed so that it may be learned and passed on. Bandura believed effective modeling has four components:

1. *Attention.*   Learners must attend to and perceive the modeled behavior accurately.
2. *Retention.*   Learners must process the modeled behavior and store it in memory either through visual imagery or verbal coding.
3. *Reproduction.*   Learners must accurately reproduce and practice/rehearse the behavior.
4. *Motivation.*   Internal reinforcement or external reinforcement increases an individual's motivation and the likelihood of mastery.

Bandura indicated that modeling can be made more effective if observers and models are of similar demographic characteristics (e.g., sex, age, race) or have positive interpersonal attributes (e.g., compassion, nurturance, warmth). Modeling can be performed live or covertly (i.e., via imagery). **Self-efficacy** is a term developed by Bandura and refers to an individual's confidence in his or her ability to perform a given behavior or accomplish a given task.

3.3.4   The Dollard and Miller Approach

John Dollard and Neal Miller were influenced by the psychoanalytic, behavioral, and social science concepts that preceded them. Dollard and Miller were considered "drive" or incentive theorists and believed that anxiety and psychological disturbances were learned from experiences. As people develop, they form *habits* (i.e., stable characterological patterns) that allow them to respond predictably to social and other stimuli. These habits help to reduce *primary drives*, which are innate (e.g., thirst, hunger), and *secondary drives*, which are learned (e.g., parental approval, peer acceptance). They identified three primary types of conflicts:

- *Approach-approach conflicts* occur when two positive choices are presented, but only one can be chosen, even though they may be equally appealing (e.g., a person who loves both chocolate licorice and granola bars).
- *Approach-avoidance conflicts* occur when a person wants something appealing but fears being punished or being negatively evaluated for obtaining it (e.g., asking an attractive person on a date but fearing rejection).
- *Avoidance-avoidance conflicts* occur when the person loses no matter which choice is made (e.g., a person wants to avoid conflict with her spouse but is very upset and embarrassed by the way he is behaving in public).

3.3.5   Practice Multiple-Choice Items: Learning Theories

1. In Ivan Pavlov's famous experiments with dogs, the conditioned stimulus was
   a. the salivation.
   b. the meat powder.
   c. the bell, buzzer, or tone.
   d. None of the above.

2. In classical conditioning, when people present a conditioned stimulus at the same time as the unconditioned stimulus, they are using
   a. backward conditioning.
   b. simultaneous conditioning.
   c. retroactive conditioning.
   d. delayed conditioning.

3. _____ is the most successful form of conditioning.
   a. Backward conditioning
   b. Simultaneous conditioning
   c. Retroactive conditioning
   d. Delayed conditioning

4. John B. Watson is most well-known for his experiments involving
   a. a rat.
   b. dogs.
   c. ducklings.
   d. cats.

5. _____ is best known for the theory of operant conditioning.
   a. Ivan Pavlov
   b. B. F. Skinner
   c. John B. Watson
   d. Albert Bandura

Answer Key: 1. c; 2. b; 3. d; 4. a; 5. b.

3.4   COGNITIVE DEVELOPMENT

Theories of cognitive development describe how individuals construct meaning from their experiences by using thought processes across various developmental levels—that is, cognitive complexity is strongly related to reasoning and behavior. Two theories to be aware of include the cognitive developmental approaches of both Piaget and Vygotsky. In addition, this fourth section of Chapter 3 reviews memory, cognition, and a number of other important concepts related to cognitive development.

3.4.1   Jean Piaget's Cognitive Developmental Theory

Jean Piaget (1963) rejected the notion that learning was primarily biologically or environmentally determined and presented the most influential and comprehensive model of cognitive development to date. He believed that growth in mental development depended on one's ability to order and classify new information, which he called **organization**. Piaget proposed that changes in cognitive structure occurred through **adaptation** (i.e., change necessitated by new information), which involved two complimentary processes:

- **Assimilation** occurs when an individual perceives and interprets new information in terms of a previously existing context—that is, adding a thought to an existing framework. For example, an individual who has no awareness that different breeds of dogs have different names will refer to every dog encountered as a dog—that is, all dogs are called "dogs."
- **Accommodation** occurs when an individual perceives and interprets new information in a way that causes a restructuring or change in mental organization so that new information or categories of information can be added to the existing cognitive framework—that is, a change in perspective. For example, an individual who becomes aware that dogs can be categorized according to different breeds that have different names will pay attention to and discern distinguishing features of each dog encountered, using this newly recognized information to make more refined distinctions. Thus, dogs are called "dogs" but are more specifically referred to as golden retrievers, Great Danes, beagles, poodles, and so on.
- A **schema** is a mental structure that processes or integrates experiences, information, or perceptions. Schemas sometimes change as new information is taken in and new insights are derived.
- Piaget believed that learning occurs when an individual experiences disequilibrium because of some conflict or

challenge to his or her way of thinking or understanding. Motivated people naturally attempt to make sense of the new information (adapting thoughts to reduce the conflict or disequilibrium) through a process known as **equilibration**, ordinarily accomplished through a combination of assimilation and accommodation.

Piaget's stages of cognitive development, and related concepts, include the following:

1. *Sensorimotor stage* **(birth to about 2 years).** Infants and toddlers use their senses (i.e., sight, sound, taste, touch, and smell) and developing motor abilities (e.g., crawling, walking, prehensile grasping) to learn about their environment and the people in it. They proceed from reflexes (sucking, hitting, grasping) to intentional and meaningful interaction (coordination of motor skills to obtain objects and solve problems). During this stage, children learn *cause-and-effect, trial-and-error problem solving,* and *object permanence* (i.e., objects do not vanish when out of sight), which mark a transition to symbolic or representational thought—a prerequisite to language development and formation of mental images.

2. *Preoperational stage* **(2 to 7 years).** Children develop *symbolic representations* that allow them to use language and engage in imitative play (e.g., going "on safari" in one's living room). *Egocentric thinking* also permeates this stage—that is, children are unable to take on the perspectives of others, except to receive some tangible benefit. For example, children frequently converse without regard to the responses or participation of others. *Centration*, or *centering*, also reflects egocentrism as children are only capable of focusing on one facet, rather than several facets, of a situation at the same time. *Animism* is the attribution of life or human characteristics to inanimate objects, making it possible for teapots to sing and trees to grab a princess in the forest. *Irreversibility* is observed in a child's lack of understanding that actions or circumstances can be undone, changed, or even reversed.

3. *Concrete operational stage* **(7 to 11 years).** Children can now readily use symbols to engage in mental operations involving logic, and they are able to classify, seriate, conserve (i.e., quantity remains constant regardless of the configuration), and understand concepts such as reversibility (i.e., capable of mentally reversing an object), reduced egocentrism (i.e., now able to take the perspective of another), and relational terms (e.g., bigger, yesterday, heavier). However, children at this stage are still unable to reason abstractly.

4. *Formal operational stage* **(11+ years).** Piaget proposed that during this final stage of cognitive development individuals are able to think abstractly, relativistically, engage in hypothetico-deductive reasoning (i.e., deducing a conclusion given a premise), and systematically prove/disprove multiple alternative explanations for observed occurrences to deduce a reasonable conclusion to a problem. Not everyone reaches the level of formal operations.

3.4.2 Lev Vygotsky's Cognitive Developmental Theory

Lev Vygotsky was a Russian psychologist who developed a constructionist, cognitive developmental theory that integrated language as well as social and cultural influences. Vygotsky (1978, 1997) believed that cognitive progress was facilitated by language development and occurred in a social context.

- *Zone of proximal development* refers to the gap between what children are able to learn on their own and what they are potentially able to learn with help.
- *Scaffolding* refers to the supports that must be put in place to help children learn in order to reach their potential. After children have reached their potential and are capable of performing the task independently and automatically, the scaffolding supports can be removed.

Vygotsky derived stages of language development to explain cognitive advances. He described children's speech during the first 3 years of life as social speech aimed at controlling the actions of others in the environment (e.g., shouting, laughing, crying, excitement). Around age 3 years, and aligned with Piaget's preoperational stage, he noticed that children's speech is very egocentric: children talk (think) out loud to themselves to guide their own actions and explain to themselves what they are doing. Vygotsky deduced that the reason children do this is because they have not yet developed the capacity for private speech. At about 7 years of age, children develop *private speech* (inner speech), internalized thoughts that help guide personal behavior and allow individuals to engage in higher mental processes.

3.4.3 Cognition and Memory

Mature cognition is dependent on memory. Memory is often categorized as follows:

- **Sensory memory (trace memory)** refers to all the environmental stimuli to which one is exposed at any given moment in time (e.g., what the teacher is saying, distracting noises made by other students, what interesting clothing other students are wearing, hum of equipment in the room, rain on the roof, shivers due to uncomfortable room temperature). This information is ordinarily retained for only a few seconds.
- **Short-term memory** is a temporary information storage system that allows information to be retained for seconds to minutes, if the information is focused on and received properly. Thus, if one were focused on the information conveyed by the teacher, one might be able to retain it long enough to make sense of it and write it down in a format meaningful to the listener. If not, one might only remember shivering or what the person across the room was wearing. *What* one focuses on at any given moment has a chance of making it into short-term storage. The normal limit of short-term recall is disputable, but probably is 7 ± 2 bits of information.
- **Long-term memory** enables a person to store a large amount of information for relatively permanent amounts

of time, depending on how efficiently the person learned the information.

The transfer from short-term to long-term memory is more efficient if the individual can **encode** (i.e., compact the information in a meaningful way so that it can be stored and retrieved efficiently) and *rehearses* (i.e., practices the information to memorize it) the information. Information can be placed in *echoic storage* (i.e., auditory information) or *iconic storage* (i.e., visual information).

Why do people forget? Three theories are commonly proposed to explain forgetting. **Retrieval theory** (or *poor retrieval theory*) purports that information is held in long-term storage forever but that we often have insufficient cues to retrieve the information. The tip-of-the-tongue phenomenon is often used as an example of poor retrieval theory; everyone has had an experience in which the answer to a question was just "on the tip of my tongue." Interestingly, the answer often emerges minutes to hours later, when some cue emerges that unlocks the storage container where the information was held. A second theory (**decay of memory theory**) suggests that traces of information held in memory simply decay over time and that the memory eventually disappears forever.

A third theory, called **interference theory**, proposes that learned information is inhibited by other learning experiences. **Retroactive inhibition** refers to a loss of memory that occurs when new information interferes with information learned previously (*retro* means "backward in time"). In classic experiments designed to test this theory, the control group participants were taught information (X), given a break, then asked to recall X; not surprisingly, they had little difficulty doing so. In contrast, the experimental group participants were taught information (X), then taught new information (Y), then asked to recall the first set of information (X). Interestingly, many of these participants had difficulty accurately recalling X, because the newly learned information (Y) interfered. **Proactive inhibition** refers to a loss of memory that occurs when old information interferes with newly learned information (*pro* means "forward in time"). In classic experiments designed to test this condition, the control group participants were given a rest break, taught information (Y), then asked to recall Y; not surprisingly, they had little difficulty doing so. In contrast, the experimental group participants were taught information (X), then taught new information (Y), then asked to recall the second set of information (Y). Interestingly, many of these participants had difficulty accurately recalling Y, because the previously learned information (X) interfered.

How can memory be improved? A number of suggestions have evolved:

- *Chunking* is a grouping of information into chunks so that a greater amount of information can be stored (and retrieved). For example, if short-term memory is able to hold 7 ± 2 bits of information, one may struggle recalling the following string of nine digits in sequence: 7-9-2-4-1-6-3-8-5. However, if one chunks the information into three groups of three (792, 416, 385), one has a better chance of recalling all nine digits in sequence.

- *Method of loci* is a guided visual imagery procedure in which an individual imagines objects or concepts to be remembered in a familiar environment and in a given sequence. When the information is needed, the individual visually returns to the image and recalls the information.

- Some find the use of *acronyms* helpful in recalling information. For example, Holland's hexagonal model (reviewed in Chapter 4) includes realistic, investigative, artistic, social, enterprising, and conventional. Some find this list of six dimensions difficult to remember. However, if one takes the first letter from each of these six dimensions and forms an acronym, RIASEC, the likelihood of recalling all six dimensions is substantially enhanced.

- *Eidetic memory*, sometimes referred to as photographic memory, uses visual images to recall visual information with clarity and detail.

Memory and performance are optimized when an individual attains a moderate state of arousal, as low and high states of arousal tend to suppress performance; this is known as the **Yerkes-Dodson law**. Also, as information is learned more thoroughly, retention is enhanced. Finally, *massed learning* (e.g., one 4-hour period to study for an exam) is not as efficient as *spaced learning* (e.g., four 1-hour periods to study for an exam).

3.4.4 Other Important Concepts in Cognitive Development

- **Cognitive dissonance** is a term coined by Leon Festinger (1957) used to explain the conflict or discomfort that an individual experiences when a discrepancy is noticed between what he or she already knows and new information being received. Ordinarily, a person either alters an existing notion and accommodates the new information or rejects the new information in favor of a previously held belief. Usually, the latter holds true. A related term is **confirmatory bias**, which refers to a person's likelihood of screening for information that confirms previously held beliefs (i.e., hearing what one wants to hear).

- **Attribution theory** was proposed by Fritz Heider (1967) and is used to explain why things happen. Thus, people assign attributes (reasons) to outcomes and events. Heider described three dimensions:
  - The dimension of *stability* attributes outcomes to stable causes (i.e., consistent over time) and frequently leads to hopelessness, whereas attributing outcomes to unstable causes (i.e., not consistent over time) ordinarily leads to persistence and hope.
  - The dimension of *locus* attributes outcomes to internal or external foci. Internal attributions lie within an individual and usually lead a person to claim responsibility for the outcome. External attributions lie outside the individual (e.g., outside force, event, agent).
  - The dimension of *control* attributes outcomes to controllable and uncontrollable facets. Controllable attributions allow the person some control over the

outcome or event, whereas an uncontrollable attribution is out of the person's hands.

- **Imaginary audience** is a construct proposed by David Elkind (1979) to describe the adolescent egocentric belief that everyone is watching and critically judging the adolescent. As an example, even though a teenager is completely alone in the hallway when he trips and falls, he believes that others have seen this and negatively evaluated him. According to Elkind, adolescence is a time for reemergence of substantial egocentrism.
- **Personal fable** is the adolescent belief of absolute uniqueness. Thus, an adolescent believes he can engage in reckless, dangerous acts because bad things only happen to others; likewise, a teenage girl believes she can have unprotected sex because, since she is unique and special, pregnancy and disease only happen to others, not her.
- *Intelligence* is a construct designed to describe one's ability to solve problems and learn new information. **Crystallized intelligence**, proposed by Raymond B. Cattell (1963), includes verbal and mathematical capabilities and experiences that are learned. Fluid intelligence, also proposed by Cattell, includes nonverbal problem solving and pattern recognition. Spearman (1927) referred to general intelligence as *g* and specialized abilities as *s*. It is important to realize that intelligence is not fixed at birth through genetics (although there is a strong genetic component) but develops through social and environmental interactions. (Chapter 7 has more information on intelligence and theories of intelligence.)
- *Creativity* involves *divergent thinking* (i.e., thinking of many possibilities) and *convergent thinking* (i.e., picking the best solution and focusing on the final product). In general, creative thinkers produce a greater number of ideas, from more qualitatively different categories, and provide greater elaboration or detail.
- Females differ very little from males in cognitive development, although some specific gender differences in cognitive abilities do exist. However, researchers are not sure whether these differences can be attributed to genetic or environmental influences. What is clear is that the differences within a gender group are larger than between the genders themselves—that is, the average differences between the sexes are actually quite small, but the differences, for example, that some women display compared with other women, are quite large. Between the ages of 10 and 12 years, females start to outperform males in verbal ability, whereas males start to outperform females in math. Again, these average differences are very small but are still statistically significant.
- Ordinarily, significant declines in cognitive abilities do not occur until about 70 years of age. Older adults have more difficulty learning new information and retrieving old information, and they perform more poorly on timed tests and tests requiring memorization.

3.4.5 Practice Multiple-Choice Items: Cognitive Development

1. According to Piaget, when people use their existing cognitive framework to understand new information, they are involved in the process of adaptation known as
   a. assimilation.
   b. accommodation.
   c. symbolic representation.
   d. All of the above.

2. Children learn object permanence in the _____ stage of Piaget's theory of cognitive development.
   a. sensorimotor
   b. preoperational
   c. concrete operational
   d. formal operational

3. Animism refers to
   a. only being able to focus on one aspect of a problem at a time.
   b. thinking that humans created everything in the world.
   c. giving life to lifeless objects.
   d. the belief that actions cannot be reversed.

4. Individuals can think logically and abstractly when they reach the _____ stage of Piaget's theory of cognitive development.
   a. sensorimotor
   b. preoperational
   c. concrete operational
   d. formal operational

5. Some teenagers drive over the speed limit without wearing seatbelts because they do not believe that they can be hurt. These teenagers
   a. have an imaginary audience.
   b. have created a personal fable.
   c. are engaged in magical thinking.
   d. are using divergent thinking.

Answer Key: 1. a; 2. a; 3. c; 4. d; 5. b.

3.5 LANGUAGE DEVELOPMENT

Humans have the innate capacity to develop and use language to communicate and solve problems. In this section of Chapter 3, we discuss important concepts and theories of language development as well as milestones humans achieve en route to mature language use. Finally, common communication disorders clients may present with are reviewed.

3.5.1 Theories of Language Development

Three categories of **language development** theories are presented in this section: learning theory approaches, nativist approach, and an interactionist approach. *Learning theory* approaches include social learning theory, in which children acquire language skills by observing and imitating others who are using language (e.g., parents, siblings, teachers, peers). Although imitation does certainly occur, social learning theory does not explain novel speech and language. The stimulus-response approach explains language development as a reinforcement of speech sounds that leads to successively closer and closer approximations of adult speech.

The *nativist* approach of Noam Chomsky (2006) proposes that the human brain is genetically programmed to enable people to create and understand language. Chomsky hypothesized that a *language acquisition device* existed in humans that allowed the production of speech sounds, grammar, and the invention of novel sentences. Thus, humans have the capacity to learn any language through exposure. (Note that language comprehension exceeds language production.) Chomsky proposed that sentences are generated using a system of rules made up of surface structures (i.e., rules specific to each language) and deep structures (i.e., rules that are innate and universal, such as letter sounds). Chomsky's theory is supported by observations that all children, regardless of culture, go through the same developmental stages and, by 5 to 6 years of age, typically master the basics of the spoken language. The *interactionist approach* proposes that a combination of learning and nativist approaches is responsible for language development through social and cultural influences.

3.5.2   Important Concepts in Language Development

- *Psycholinguistics* is the study of language development.
- *Speech* is the physical act of forming and sequencing sounds of oral language.
- *Language* refers to the system of grammatical rules and semantics that allows similar individuals to be understood by each other.
- *Semantics* is the study of word meanings.
- *Syntax* is the proper use of grammar.
- *Pragmatics* is how language is used in the social context (e.g., taking turns, pointing, incorporating facial and hand gestures).
- *Phonology* is what a language sounds like. A *phoneme* is a language's most basic sound element. English, for example, has 40 basic sounds.
- *Morphology* governs the rules of word formation. A *morpheme* is the smallest, meaningful language unit (e.g., "at" has one morpheme, "boys" has two: "boy" and "s").
- A *dialect* is a variation in language. Dialects vary by occupation, age, geographical region, and social class.
- Three areas of the brain are important in the context of language development:
  - *Broca's area* is related to speech production. Damage to Broca's area often results in motor aphasia (i.e., causes speech to be slow and labored).
  - *Wernicke's area* is related to speech comprehension. Damage to Wernicke's area can result in sensory aphasia (i.e., difficulty understanding language through sense organs).
  - The *arcuate fasciculus* is the bundle of nerve fibers that connects Broca's area and Wernicke's area.

3.5.3   Milestones in Early Language Development

Some important language milestones include the following:

3 months	Smiles when talked to
4 months	Responds to voice by turning head
5 months	Cooing
6 months	Babbling, which closely resembles speech
8 months	Repeats syllables (e.g., ma-ma)
1 year	Shows understanding of some words
1.5 years	Can produce about 50 one-word utterances (holophrases)
2.0 years	Uses some two-word phrases
2.5 years	A vocabulary of several hundred words; speaks in short sentences
3.0 years	A vocabulary of about 1,000 words
4.0 years	Basic rules of language consistently demonstrated

3.5.4   Communication Disorders

Normal language development involves both receptive and expressive language, and these facets of language development are closely related to learning and information processing. It is estimated that 2% to 5% of children have difficulty with receptive or expressive language (American Psychiatric Association, 2000). Four **Communication Disorders** are discussed in the *DSM-IV-TR* (in addition to Communication Disorder Not Otherwise Specified [NOS]):

- *Expressive Language Disorder* is diagnosed if a person's expressive language skills (as measured on a standardized test) are substantially lower than receptive language development and nonverbal intelligence. Symptoms include difficulty producing developmentally appropriate sentences and limited vocabulary.
- *Mixed Receptive-Expressive Language Disorder* is diagnosed if a person's expressive and receptive language skills (as measured on a battery of standardized tests) are both substantially lower than nonverbal intelligence. In addition to having difficulty producing developmentally appropriate sentences and limited vocabulary, individuals might also have difficulty understanding words or sentences,
- *Phonological Disorder* is the most commonly diagnosed of the communication disorders and involves difficulties in producing developmentally expected speech sounds (e.g., developmental misarticulations, sound substitutions).
- *Stuttering* is a disturbance in speech fluency and patterning (e.g., repeating syllables, prolongation of sounds, or pausing while in the middle of a word).

Adult onset communication disorders can usually be attributed to a stroke, dementia, or brain trauma, often resulting in *aphasia* (difficulty in naming objects) and *anomia* (word finding difficulties).

3.5.5 Practice Multiple-Choice Items: Language Development

1. Noam Chomsky's theory of language development is considered to be a(n)
   a. learning theory approach.
   b. nativist approach.
   c. interactionist approach.
   d. epigenetic approach.

2. Language rules that transcend specific languages and cultures are called
   a. surface structures.
   b. global structures.
   c. deep structures.
   d. intrinsic structures.

3. How many morphemes does the word "books" have?
   a. 1
   b. 2
   c. 3
   d. 4

4. The appropriate use of grammar is the definition of
   a. syntax.
   b. pragmatics.
   c. semantics.
   d. phonology.

5. When do babies become adept at holophrasing?
   a. Approximately 8 months of age
   b. Approximately 10 months of age
   c. Approximately 1 year of age
   d. Approximately 1½ years of age.

Answer Key: 1. b; 2. c; 3. b; 4. a; 5. d.

3.6 PERSONALITY DEVELOPMENT

Numerous approaches to understanding personality have been proposed, and each theory supplies some insight into a client's world. In this sixth section of Chapter 3, we discuss Freud's psychosexual theory; Erikson's psychosocial theory; Loevinger's ego development theory; Maslow's humanistic theory; and the ethological theories of Lorenz, Bowlby, Ainsworth, and Harlow. In addition, we present important areas of personality development, including identity development, sex role and gender development, social development, and adjustment to aging and death.

3.6.1 Psychosexual Theory of Sigmund Freud

According to **Sigmund Freud** (1925), personality develops through interaction of personal needs (drives) and the environment, and past experiences play an essential part in present behaviors. The *libido* represents a basic, instinctual life force. Personality development involves transforming these basic instincts into socially acceptable, rational behavior. Freud presented a tripartite structure of personality:

- The **id**, present at birth, contains the individual's basic instincts (libido; e.g., sex, aggression, survival, pleasure instincts) and operates on the *pleasure principle*, meaning that the id strives to reduce tension by seeking immediate gratification of needs, usually through unrealistic or irrational means.
- The **ego**, which Freud believed emerged during the first year of life, operates on the *reality principle*. The purpose of the ego is to make a socially acceptable, reality-based resolution to the urges of the id and demands of the superego. Failure to resolve issues may lead to use of defense mechanisms to lower anxiety.
- The **superego**, which operates on the *morality principle*, emerges at about 5 years of age and displays the moral values and standards internalized through social interactions and from societal rules and mores. The superego counterbalances the id by substituting morals-based responses for the id's impulsive urges.

If the ego is unable to reconcile the id's urges with the superego's moralized response, a conflict occurs, leading to anxiety and, eventually, pathology. Some defense mechanisms used to control anxiety include these:

- *Repression.* Pushing undesirable thoughts and feelings from consciousness.
- *Regression.* Return to an earlier, more comfortable (childlike) period in life.
- *Displacement.* Redirecting feelings onto a less threatening person or object.
- *Projection.* Placing personal feelings, thoughts, or motives on someone else.
- *Rationalization.* Justifying one's behavior with logical-sounding reasons, thus concealing the real reason for a behavior.
- *Compensation.* Substituting a successful experience for one that produced failure.
- *Denial.* Refusing to believe that something has occurred or exists.
- *Reaction formation.* Expressing the opposite motive than was originally intended in order to help prevent unwanted attitudes or feelings from becoming expressed.

Freud developed a **psychosexual theory** of personality development, basically proposing that people must resolve various conflicts resulting from the psychic or libidinal energy focused within different parts of the body as one matures. An inability to resolve an important conflict, either due to an overgratification or undergratification of a need in any stage, can lead to **fixation**. Freud's stages include these:

1. *Oral stage.* Birth to about 1 year old; primary source of pleasure is through the mouth—sucking or mouthing; a fixation through overgratification or undergratification will result in oral needs continuing to influence personality (e.g., dependence, passivity, gullibility, sarcasm) and habits (e.g., smoking, gum chewing, thumb sucking, overeating).
2. *Anal stage.* Ages 1 to 3 years; primary source of gratification is the anus and buttocks area; pleasure is attained through retention and expulsion of feces and urine; how parents handle toileting will influence future personality

development; fixation produces retentiveness (e.g., stinginess, obsessive thinking, compulsive behavior, cleanliness, orderliness) or expulsiveness (e.g., messiness, destructiveness, cruelty).

3. *Phallic stage.* Ages 3 to 5 years; primary source of gratification is the genitals; pleasure derived through manipulation of genitals, fondling and masturbation prevalent; *Oedipus complex* (i.e., a desire by a male child to eliminate the father to take the central position in the mother's life) and *Electra complex* (i.e., a desire by a female child to eliminate the mother to take the central position in the father's life) emerge (resolved through identification with same-sex parent); fixation can involve sexual exploitation of others; superego develops and is integrated into the personality structure.

4. *Latency stage.* Ages 6 to 11 years; sexual desires become dormant as the individual focuses on mastery of social skills, personal awareness, and ego refinement; children learn how to relieve anxiety through use of defense mechanisms.

5. *Genital stage.* Adolescence; puberty causes a reemergence of sexual impulses; individuals show interest in sex and emergence of the capability of real love; potential reemergence of Oedipus and Electra complexes, but successful development leads to sublimation of parental love and identification with nonparent primary love objects, sexual maturation, marriage, and child rearing.

3.6.2 Psychosocial Theory of Erik Erikson

The **theory of psychosocial development** proposed by **Erik Erikson** (1950) focused on an individual's learned social interactions within the environment as a key influence on ego development. Unlike Freud, Erikson, sometimes referred to as a neo-Freudian and a close follower of Freud, believed that personality continues to develop throughout one's life and that developmental problems are reversible. Indeed, Erikson believed that the ego develops through a series of psychosocial crises (i.e., Erikson's eight stages of development), resulting from an individual's societal interactions, which are developmentally encountered throughout the lifespan. Importantly, successfully resolving these crises at each stage holds the potential for positive growth. Erikson believed that personality continues to evolve throughout the lifespan and that people can reconstruct their personalities at any stage of the lifespan.

1. *Basic Trust v. Mistrust.* Birth to 1 or 2 years. The caretaker's responsibility is to create a trusting environment for, and positive relationship with, the infant. Parents are central characters in the infant's life and help nurture trust, predictability, optimism, and comfort. Mistrust occurs when infants are not comforted, encounter unpredictability, or are handled in an uncaring manner.

2. *Autonomy v. Shame and Doubt.* Ages 1 or 2 to 3 years. Toddlers use their developing motor and cognitive skills to decide for themselves. A battle of wills may ensue, and Erikson believed positive interactions with caretakers would lead the toddler to develop a sense of autonomy (a reasonable balance of freedom and control), rather than forcing the child to comply, resulting in feelings of shame or doubt over one's ability to operate on the social environment.

3. *Initiative v. Guilt.* Ages 3 to 5 years. Children display a sense of ambition and responsibility, and parents can help foster these characteristics by helping children set goals and carry out their plans without being too controlling, which could lead to feelings of guilt and inhibition. Family relationships (e.g., parents, siblings, extended) are key social interactions, and children must recognize and respect the rights of others.

4. *Industry v. Inferiority.* Ages 6 to 11 years. Productivity in work and play is emphasized, and children of all cultures strive for competence. Children must master social and academic tasks while learning to cooperate, or else they develop a sense of inferiority, incompetence, and failure. School and neighborhood social interactions become essential.

5. *Identity v. Role Confusion.* Adolescents recognize and integrate a sense of uniqueness, personal identity (i.e., "Who am I?"), and future direction (i.e., "Where do I fit in society?"). Peer group interactions become very important. Individuals choose goals and values to establish a personal identity. Adolescents who do not choose goals experience confusion and question their purpose and direction.

6. *Intimacy v. Isolation.* Young adults' main task is to establish intimate bonds of love and friendship, rather than isolation and self-absorption. Peer relationships continue to be central social supports. Individuals must learn to trust another and trade some independence for intimacy and love.

7. *Generativity v. Stagnation.* Individuals in middle adulthood consider family relations, partners, and intimate friendships to be of greatest importance, and people seek to enhance future generations through child rearing and nurturing others. Work productivity is also essential as people seek a peak in their personal abilities to generate performance. Negative outcomes reflect feelings of meaninglessness in one's accomplishments.

8. *Integrity v. Despair.* Individuals in old age come to terms with their own mortality and limitations in order to reflect on their life with a sense of pride, achievement, satisfaction, and integrity and to face death with dignity. Others may reflect on life with regret and despair. All of humankind is now the social focus.

Erikson's theory has been criticized as being ethnocentric and gender biased because of its focus on independence, rather than community.

3.6.3 Ego Development Theory of Jane Loevinger

Jane Loevinger (1979) proposed an ego development stage theory that explained human personality developmental progression and fixation:

1. *Presocial Stage.* Babies self-differentiate from an outer world.

2. *Symbiotic Stage.*   Differentiation of self from others.
3. *Impulsive Stage.*   Affirms separate identity; demanding.
4. *Self-Protective Stage.*   Self-control; rule-governed behavior.
5. *Conformist Stage.*   Obey group rules; strive for acceptance from family.
6. *Self-Awareness/Self-Conscious Stage.*   Strive for stability and maturity.
7. *Conscientious.*   Internalize rules, morality.
8. *Individualistic.*   Strive for individuality; awareness of inner conflict.
9. *Autonomous.*   Strive for self-fulfillment; cope with inner conflict.
10. *Integrated.*   Consolidated identity.

3.6.4 Humanistic Theory of Abraham Maslow

Humanistic theories are holistic (i.e., the whole is greater than the sum of its parts) and view humans as intrinsically good. Humanists espouse that people make choices about themselves based on self-perceptions and perceived circumstances. **Abraham Maslow** (1947) developed the **hierarchy of needs** to demonstrate that humans have an innate need for self-actualization, which can only be attained when lower order needs are met. The needs are listed from lower order to higher order here:

1. Physiological needs (e.g., food, water, rest)
2. Safety needs (e.g., shelter, warmth, physical security, emotional security)
3. Belongingness needs (e.g., loving relationships, sense of belonging)
4. Esteem needs (e.g., self-respect, self-confidence, feelings of success)
5. Self-actualization (e.g., sense of purpose)

Self-actualization needs are usually not met until middle adulthood (usually over 60 years old), if at all, and only after the lower order needs have been met. Characteristics of self-actualized individuals include acceptance of self and others, spontaneity, autonomy, creativeness, resistance to enculturation, problem centering, and continued freshness of appreciation.

3.6.5 Ethological Theories of Konrad Lorenz, John Bowlby, Mary Ainsworth, and Harry Harlow

Ethological theories emphasize the role of instinct (biological bases) in human development and use naturalistic observation—that is, people are born with innate capacities resulting from evolution that affect learning experiences.

Konrad Lorenz carried out a famous set of experiments on imprinting, the process by which a duck or gosling attaches to the first moving object it encounters shortly after hatching (e.g., its mother, a human, an inanimate object in the environment made to move by an experimenter). This *imprinting* is irreversible and is an example of his concept known as a *critical period* or *sensitive period*.

John Bowlby described infants as being born with an innate potential for attachment. Infants have the ability to form a natural bond with a caregiver, thus enabling the infant to explore the environment without fear of abandonment. A failure to attach to a caregiver early in life is believed to affect trust and intimacy in latter development. Bowlby (1988) described three stages that are readily observed in infants exposed to prolonged separations:

1. *Protest.*   The infant refuses to accept separation and cries.
2. *Despair.*   The infant seems to give up all hope of summoning the caretaker and becomes quiet, inactive, and withdrawn.
3. *Detachment.*   The infant begins to accept attention from others and seems less unhappy. Interestingly, when the caretaker reemerges, the infant often appears disinterested in the caretaker, almost seeming to "get even" for the perceived abandonment.

Mary Ainsworth (1989) described four patterns of attachment:

1. *Securely attached.*   Normal and secure relationships in which children explore the environment and protest separation.
2. *Avoidantly attached.*   Withdrawn behaviors in which children explore without regard for the caretaker, ignore separations, and avoid reunions when a caretaker reemerges.
3. *Ambivalently attached.*   Clinging behaviors in which the child refuses to explore the environment and protests separations quite vehemently.
4. *Disorganized attachment.*   Children show little emotion at separation and mostly confusion at reunion.

Another individual deserving mention is **Harry Harlow,** who described classic experiments with infant rhesus monkeys that were placed into cages with wire surrogate mothers, one with a bottle to provide food (oral gratification and sustenance) and another with a terrycloth covering (comfort and warmth). The infant monkeys would move to the wire monkey for food but preferred contact comfort with the terrycloth monkey, spending the vast majority of time with and running to the terrycloth monkey when frightened.

Ethological theory is helpful in explaining two normal developmental phenomena observed in human infants:

- **Stranger anxiety** occurs around 6 months of age when infants become fearful in the presence of strangers (even noncaretakers the infant had seen weeks earlier, such as grandparents). This phenomenon is probably due to enhanced visual acuity, onset of object permanence, and increasing cognitive awareness.
- **Separation anxiety** usually occurs in infants between the first and second birthdays and involves extreme distress when separation from a primary caregiver occurs. Usually, the anxiety is short lived after the disappearance of the caregiver (i.e., the child ordinarily adjusts quickly).

This developmental phenomenon differs from the clinical disorder known as Separation Anxiety Disorder, described in the final section of this chapter.

3.6.6 Identity Development

Erikson (1950) described the preeminent stage of adolescence to be identity v. role diffusion. **Identity** means an understanding of oneself as a separate, distinct individual and springs from a synthesis of successive identifications with other people into a consistent, coherent, and unique whole. Teenagers often try, and shift between, many different roles, constantly evaluating each and determining which role fits them. Common roles include student, athlete, peer/friend, and family member. Identity has been described in a number of ways:

- A *normative identity* is consistent with the values and expectations of society or culture (e.g., becoming a doctor, teacher, mother).
- A *deviant identity* is inconsistent with the values and expectations of society or culture, or, at least, not systematically reinforced (e.g., addiction to drugs/alcohol, criminal).
- An *achieved identity* has been earned through effort and ability (e.g., counselor, teacher, mother).
- An *ascribed identity* has been given by others or is the result of another's efforts and achievements (e.g., "You're just like your father/mother," spouse of an elected official).

Marcia (1966, 1980) used the concept of identity status to expand on Erikson's psychosocial crisis and identified four types of identity:

- *Identity Achievement.* Committing to goals and taking a course of action to achieve those goals.
- *Identity Moratorium.* Continuing to take in and analyze information without agreeing on goals or a course of action.
- *Identity Foreclosure.* Occurs when others (e.g., parents, friends) have determined the goals and the teen pursues the goals without question.
- *Identity Diffusion.* Occurs when teens procrastinate or become so confused that they are unable or unwilling to even take in and analyze identity-related information that could lead to goal setting.

3.6.7 Sex Role and Gender Role Development

Sexual identity refers to biological features as determined by chromosomal information (i.e., genetically determined). *Gender identity* refers to psychosocial awareness of one's maleness or femaleness and thus contains an environmental or cultural component. Gender identity ordinarily occurs by about age 3 years when children self-refer as a boy or girl, and children even younger than two years of age often show preferences for gender-specific toys. *Gender roles* are socially defined behaviors associated with a particular sex (e.g., girls wear dresses, boys wear a jacket and tie), as opposed to the concept of *androgyny*, which involves gender neutral concepts (e.g., everyone drives cars, cleans living areas, establishes a career). *Gender role conflict* occurs when an individual feels anxiety and dissonance as previously held gender expectations conflict with changing gender roles. (For further details on the terms cited in this paragraph, see Chapter 2.)

Four theories of gender role development predominate. *Social learning theory* proposes that children learn gender roles through observational learning and differential reinforcement of sex-typed behaviors from same-sexed caregivers and models. *Cognitive-developmental models* propose that as children develop high levels of cognition, they become more aware of their own gender identities. For example, Kohlberg (1969) observed that gender identity was ordinarily recognized by boys and girls by age 2 or 3 years, slightly older children realize that one's gender identity is stable over time, and by about age 7 years, children realize that one cannot change gender across situations, such as by altering one's appearance. *Biological theories* stress the role of hormones, observing that more aggressive females (sometimes referred to as "tomboys") and males have higher levels of testosterone than less aggressive peers. *Psychoanalytic theory* stresses the role of the Oedipus and Electra complexes and that children emulate their parents, thereby establishing gender role identification.

Gender role development is influenced by parents who differentially teach boys to be independent and aggressive while teaching girls to be gentle and affectionate or encourage children to play in different ways through activities or toy selections. Teachers may influence gender role differentiation through subtle stereotyping of behaviors and occupations. Peer interactions frequently encourage differential interactions as young boys are generally more active and engage in activities requiring greater use of gross motor activities, whereas young girls tend to engage in less active or quieter pursuits. In addition, it is difficult to assess or estimate the effects of media sources (e.g., TV, radio, Internet, music, books, magazines), as the portrayal of men and women through the media can lead to stereotypes that are difficult to undo.

3.6.8 Social Development

Childhood peer group experiences allow children to develop autonomy and competence by learning how to interact in social situations. To be accepted into a peer group, members must comply with patterns of interactions known as rituals and routines. Dominance hierarchies of leaders and followers are noticeable even in peer groups of very young children. **Prosocial behavior** involves sensitivity to the needs of others and, although it occurs in early childhood, is not consistently displayed until later childhood. Children learn about and experience the world through play. By 3 to 4 months, infants display both exploratory play and destructive play; both are normal. *Instrumental aggression* is aimed at acquiring territory, objects, or rewards. *Hostile aggression* is aimed at another person. On average, young boys are more aggressive than young girls, and aggressive children tend to be raised by aggressive parents. **Sociodramatic play** is the imitation of adult play and facilitates more mature social interactions among children. Parten (1933) described social play categories:

1. *Nonsocial activity.* Throughout the preschool years, children play by themselves, wander around, and observe

others but do not play with another child in the same activity.

2. *Parallel play.* Children play near each other, sometimes doing the same activity, but not *with* each other—that is, two children may be coloring pictures as they sit next to each other but not in a cooperative fashion.

3. *Associative play.* While engaged in separate activities, children talk and comment on each other's activities.

4. *Cooperative play.* Children play with each other in order to attain a common goal.

Among other specifics, social development also influences the development of self-concept. The general *self-concept* is stable and difficult to change, even if it is negative. After being formed, a self-concept becomes self-perpetuating, meaning that children, teenagers, and adults tend to focus only on what is consistent with their self-concepts. Ordinarily, it is more helpful to conceive of and focus change on more specific areas of self-concept, rather than on a general notion (e.g., academic self-concept, peer relations self-concept, family relations self-concept, emotional self-concept, and physical self-concept, such as appearance and athletic ability). When attempting to change self-concept, counselors should start with concrete experiences that a child can perform successfully, evaluate these experiences objectively, and build on success experiences.

3.6.9 Adjustment to Aging and Death

Successful aging depends on one's satisfaction with life, social roles, financial security, autonomy, physical functioning, mental health, and having a lifestyle consistent with one's personality. Two primary theories of aging have been proposed:

- *Disengagement theory* (detachment theory) proposes that withdrawal from the social system is a natural process precipitated by the need for reflection, self-preoccupation, and lower need for emotional connectedness with others.
- *Activity theory* suggests that as people age they prefer to remain socially active in order to resist self-preoccupation and maintain closer social relationships.

Atchley (1975) proposed four stages of retirement:

1. *Preretirement.* Making plans.
2. *Immediately after retirement.* A "honeymoon" phase when one enjoys newfound autonomy.
3. *Period of disenchantment.* Novelty of retirement wears off and individuals may realize their plans were unrealistic.
4. *Reorientation.* Putting together a satisfactory and realistic lifestyle.

Elisabeth Kübler-Ross (1969) proposed that anyone facing a loss, such as imminent death, loss of a loved one, or even an unexpected life transition, will experience *grief*, as characterized by the following stages:

1. *Shock and denial.* Disbelief or denial that an event has occurred.

2. *Anger.* A period of rage.
3. *Bargaining and guilt.* A feeling that one must have done something to deserve the loss, and bargaining to change what has happened.
4. *Hopelessness.* Loneliness and depressed feelings, a stage that becomes so uncomfortable that one becomes motivated to move on.
5. *Acceptance.* Moving on and readjusting to a new life situation.

When counseling clients in these circumstances, counselors should be aware of determinants of the intensity of grief (e.g., intensity of relationship, mode of loss, age and sex of mourner), obstacles to grieving (e.g., sudden loss, lack of finality, lack of support), and the potential for complicated grief.

3.6.10 Practice Multiple-Choice Items: Personality Development

1. Freud believed that fixation results from
   a. overgratification.
   b. undergratification.
   c. both overgratification and undergratification.
   d. None of the above.

2. Erikson would consider a normal 4-year-old child to be in the _____ stage of personality development.
   a. Initiative vs. Guilt
   b. Basic Trust vs. Mistrust
   c. Autonomy vs. Shame and Doubt
   d. Industry vs. Inferiority

3. A person who obeys group rules and seeks familial acceptance is in the _____ stage of Loevinger's ego development theory.
   a. integrated
   b. conformist
   c. self-awareness
   d. conscientious

4. According to Maslow, before people can meet their needs for esteem, they must meet their need for
   a. safety.
   b. belongingness.
   c. survival (physiological needs).
   d. All of the above.

5. Children who are clingy and react strongly to separation from their caretakers are considered by Mary Ainsworth to display
   a. secure attachment.
   b. avoidant attachment.
   c. ambivalent attachment.
   d. disorganized attachment.

Answer Key: 1. c; 2. a; 3. b; 4. d; 5. c.

3.7 MORAL DEVELOPMENT

Moral development involves an individual's growing ability to distinguish right from wrong and to act in accordance with those distinctions. Kohlberg's theory of moral development is the most influential but has been criticized for being too male centered. Gilligan's moral developmental theory focuses on the stages women progress through. Finally, several less influential approaches are briefly reviewed: Piaget's cognitive approach, Freud's psychoanalytic approach, the behavioral approach, and the social learning approach.

3.7.1 Lawrence Kohlberg

A cognitive developmental theory suggesting that cognitive developmental accomplishments lead to moral developmental accomplishments is the stage theory of moral development of **Lawrence Kohlberg**. Importantly, the ages associated with each stage vary widely, and not everyone necessarily reaches the highest levels of moral development. In fact, Kohlberg's own research indicated that as many as two thirds of adults do not reach his or her postconventional level (Kohlberg's highest level). Kohlberg also recognized that moral reasoning often differs from moral behavior; in other words, just because a person knows what moral behavior is does not mean that the individual will actually pursue that behavior. Kohlberg conducted some of his research using the Defining Issues Test, which presented participants with moral dilemmas and then a multiple-choice response format, with each choice aligning with one of his stages of moral development. Kohlberg's theory has three levels, and each level has two stages. Thus, the theory is sometimes referred to as a three-stage theory, other times as a six-stage theory.

Level I: Preconventional Level.   Individuals have little awareness of socially acceptable moral behavior and follow rules primarily to avoid punishment or reap rewards. Thus, judgments are made chiefly on the basis of anticipation of either rewards or punishments.

Stage 1: Obedience and Punishment.   A mentality that the weak must please or, at least, avoid displeasing the strong. Egocentric thinking dominates, so individuals focus on themselves and their own actions. Good acts have positive consequences, whereas bad acts have negative consequences.

Stage 2: Instrumental Hedonism.   Morality focuses on pleasure as a motivator, serving one's own self is paramount, and typically one does not interfere in the affairs of others. You do what you do to get what you want from others. You take into consideration the perspectives of others, so long as you still get what you want. People at this stage are less focused on avoiding punishment and more focused on satisfying personal needs.

Level II: Conventional Level.   During this level of moral development, familial or societal authority is recognized and people conform to rules in order to avoid social disapproval or avoid criticism by those in authority.

Stage 3: "Good Boy, Good Girl."   Individuals in this stage try to please everyone; the correct action is the one likely to receive the greatest approval by others. The focus is on maintaining a good relationship with, and the approval of, those immediately involved in judging their behavior. True empathy starts to develop, and justice is seen as reciprocal. Equality among individuals also begins to emerge. One desires to be seen as "good."

Stage 4: Law and Order.   The rules are the rules. Follow the rules. No examination is necessary. Follow the rules for their own sake. Societal order is very important in making judgments at this stage, and justice involves reciprocity between each individual and the social system—that is, individuals conform to rules to avoid censure by legitimate authority.

Level III: Postconventional Level.   In this highest level, people examine and select moral codes to live by, although these codes are not necessarily shared by most others in society. People at this level also behave in a way that respects the dignity of all people.

Stage 5: Social/Moral Contract and System of Laws.   Morality in this stage is defined in terms of general individual rights and standards that have been agreed on by society. However, because these rights have the group's support, they are arrived at democratically, allowing for the changing of laws if doing so is considered best for society. Thus, rules and values are relative and, as necessary, subjected to change.

Stage 6: Universal Ethical Principles.   Moral behavior is determined by individual decisions of consciousness, based on universal ethical principles. Individuals are accorded respect as an end, not as a means. Individuals may form their own principles and use them to guide their behavior and mitigate negative feelings or avoid guilt.

3.7.2 Carol Gilligan

Carol Gilligan (1982) is an American feminist, ethicist, and psychologist best known for her work with and against Lawrence Kohlberg on ethical community and ethical relationships, and certain subject-object problems in ethics. Gilligan pointed out that Kohlberg's theory of moral development was biased against females, whose moral judgments are often influenced by concerns for an ethic of caring, connectedness, responsibility for others, or compassion. An ethic of caring is in conflict with a male-dominated society, leading to an ongoing struggle between the woman's self and other orientations. Women struggle with the obligation to exercise care and avoid hurt, which serves as the basis for Gilligan's three-stage theory:

1. *Orientation to Individual Survival.*   The focus is on the self, and the goal is for individual survival. Transition to the next stage occurs when selfishness is transformed into a sense of responsibility for others.
2. *Goodness as Self-Sacrifice.*   Self-sacrifice equals goodness. Good is equated with doing for others and, the more

one sacrifices, the greater a person's perceived moral goodness. Transition to the final stage occurs when the individual realizes that she has personal needs while she still maintains an altruistic attitude.

3. *Morality of Nonviolence.*   The woman resolves the conflict between selfishness and responsibility by reaching equilibrium between individual needs and the social caring ideal. The core of this stage involves the realization that an individual will make choices so as not to harm herself or others.

3.7.3   Other Approaches to Understanding Moral Development

Jean Piaget believed morality was based on cognitive awareness and explored this developing awareness by presenting stories of children engaging in various behaviors and asking children to evaluate these behaviors. Piaget suggested a stage theory:

1. *Premoral stage.*   During the first several years of life, children display only a limited awareness of rules.
2. *Moral realism stage.*   At about 4 or 5 years of age, children begin to develop an awareness of rules as concrete objects and the notion that rules should be obeyed. They learn these rules from parents and others but often do not understand the reason for the rules. They believe that a person who creates more damage is more guilty than a person who creates less damage.
3. *Moral relativism stage.*   At about 7 years of age, children are aware not only that rules exist but are now capable of understanding the reasons behind the rules. They understand that rules can be changed cooperatively, by consensus, or unilaterally by authority—that is, there is no absolute right or wrong—and that the morality of an action is judged by one's intention, not by the consequences.

Sigmund Freud believed that morality resulted from unconscious, irrational motives perpetuated by the id, being reconciled by the superego, to keep antisocial urges from becoming conscious (the ego).

The behavioral approach places emphasis for morality on environmental influences and focuses on the rewards or punishments associated with moral actions. In this way, individuals who are rewarded for antisocial acts may actually conclude that these behaviors are acceptable, causing conflict with societal values. For example, a parent may demand that his or her child "not be pushed around" and, therefore, the child fights with children who pick on him at school. Such aggressive behavior conflicts with a zero-tolerance aggression policy at school. When the child gets into a fight at school and is punished by school officials, the parents react by rewarding the child at home, creating conflict as to what is acceptable behavior.

Social learning theory (Albert Bandura) focuses on the importance of imitation and vicarious learning in moral development. As such, children learn moral or socially acceptable behavior by observing others in similar situations. For example,

children can learn that stealing is sometimes an acceptable behavior when they observe a parent cheat on taxes or accept too much change when making a purchase.

3.7.4   Practice Multiple-Choice Items: Moral Development

1. Most adults are in the _____ level of Kohlberg's theory of moral development.
   a. preconventional
   b. conventional
   c. postconventional
   d. None of the above.

2. Individuals who adhere to moral standards to satisfy their own personal desires are in Kohlberg's _____ stage of moral development.
   a. instrumental hedonism
   b. "good boy, good girl"
   c. obedience and punishment
   d. law and order

3. People who are in the conventional stage of Kohlberg's theory of moral development may do all of the following EXCEPT
   a. follow the rules to avoid societal disapproval.
   b. follow the rules to avoid familial disapproval.
   c. follow the rules because they have been agreed on through a democratic process.
   d. follow the rules so that law and order can be maintained.

4. A woman who balances her personal needs with those of others is in the _____ stage of Gilligan's theory of moral development.
   a. goodness as self-sacrifice
   b. orientation to individual survival
   c. morality of nonviolence
   d. All of the above.

5. Children often do not understand the reasons behind rules when they are in the _____ stage of Piaget's theory of moral development.
   a. premoral
   b. moral realism
   c. moral relativism
   d. moral orientation

Answer Key: 1. b; 2. a; 3. c; 4. c; 5. b.

3.8   LIFESPAN THEORIES: INDIVIDUAL TASK DEVELOPMENT AND MILESTONES

A number of theorists have described development in humans as achieving certain milestones or tasks. As people achieve these tasks, they demonstrate maturity and progress to higher levels of development that require even more advanced milestone attainments. In this section of Chapter 3, we discuss the developmental approaches of Gesell, Havighurst, Gould, Peck, and Levinson and consider specific developmental issues for women and individuals from different generations.

3.8.1 The Developmental Milestone Approach of Arnold Gesell

Arnold Gesell, an American psychologist and pediatrician, believed that human development reflects a genetic unfolding of, and maturational readiness for, physical, cognitive, language, and social-emotional characteristics or milestones with only slight environmental influence. He developed a well-known set of assessments, known as the Gesell scales, and he and other researchers developed norms for numerous developmental milestones, some of which are listed below.

Birth to 6 months

Physical/cognitive. Sucking reflex; organized sleep cycle; can lift head, roll over, and reach objects; hearing and depth perception develop; repeats pleasurable behaviors, displays object permanence.

Language/personal-social. Differential crying; social smile and laughter; cooing and babbling; expresses most basic of emotions (e.g., happiness, sadness, surprise, fear, anger, interest); imitates adult expressions.

7 to 12 months

Physical/cognitive. Can sit up, crawl, and walk; pincer grasp; more advanced depth perception; goal-directed behavior; finds hidden objects; recall of people, places, and things.

Language/personal-social. Sounds of spoken language; gestures (pointing); stranger and separation anxiety; attachment to caregiver; more intense displays of emotions.

13 to 18 months

Physical/cognitive. Coordinated walking; scribbling; stacks cubes two to three high; trial-and-error experimentation; climbs stairs; throws objects.

Language/personal-social. Can play peek-a-boo and pat-a-cake; speaks first words; points to desired objects; recognizes self in mirror; signs of empathy and compliance; vocabulary may reach 50 words.

19 to 24 months

Physical/cognitive. Runs, jumps, and climbs; builds four- or five-block tower.

Language/personal-social. Vocabulary consists of approximately 200 words; three- to four-word sentences; parallel play; takes turns and cooperates; uses language for emotional self-regulation; begins to display self-control.

3 to 5 years

Physical/cognitive. Increasing skill in running, jumping, climbing, throwing, and catching; completely toilet trained; can stand on one foot.

Language/personal-social. Make-believe play; vocabulary of several thousand words; gender identity and self-concept developing; cooperative play emerges.

6 to 11 years

Physical/cognitive. Growth slows; gross motor skills and coordination improve substantially; handwriting becomes smaller and more legible; reaction time improves; thinking becomes more logical; attention is more focused and activity more deliberate; memory improves.

Language/personal-social. Dominance hierarchies become stable; vocabulary and grammar improve; awareness of double meanings leads to advances in humor and flexibility; emotional self-regulation; friendships and peer groups.

Adolescence

Physical/cognitive. Pubertal growth spurt and sexual maturation; secondary sex characteristics develop; complex problem solving; formal operational reasoning.

Language/personal-social. Use of abstract words; complex grammar and writing; increase time spent with peers; intimacy and loyalty in friendships; peer pressure to conform; cliques; identity and sexual behavior.

3.8.2 Robert Havighurst's Developmental Task Approach

Robert Havighurst (1972), an American professor, physicist, educator, and aging expert, proposed a series of developmental tasks that humans achieve as they grow and develop from infancy through late adulthood. As humans achieve these tasks, their sense of self and mastery improves. Although many of the earlier tasks have biological determinants, later tasks are socially and culturally determined.

I. Developmental Tasks of Infancy and Early Childhood
 1. Learning to walk
 2. Learning to take solid foods
 3. Learning to talk
 4. Learning to control the elimination of body wastes
 5. Learning sex differences and sexual modesty
 6. Forming concepts and learning language to describe social and physical reality
 7. Getting ready to read
 8. Learning to distinguish right and wrong and beginning to develop a conscience
II. Developmental Tasks of Middle Childhood
 1. Learning physical skills necessary for ordinary games
 2. Building wholesome attitudes toward oneself as a growing organism
 3. Learning to get along with age-mates
 4. Learning an appropriate masculine or feminine social role
 5. Developing fundamental skills in reading, writing, and calculating
 6. Developing concepts necessary for everyday living

7. Developing conscience, morality, and a scale of values
8. Achieving personal independence
9. Developing attitudes toward social groups and institutions

III. Developmental Tasks of Adolescence
1. Achieving new and more mature relations with age-mates of both sexes
2. Achieving a more masculine or feminine social role
3. Accepting one's physique and using the body effectively
4. Achieving emotional independence of parents and other adults
5. Preparing for marriage and family life
6. Preparing for an economic career
7. Acquiring a set of values and an ethical system as a guide to behavior—developing an ideology
8. Desiring and achieving socially responsible behavior

IV. Developmental Tasks of Early Adulthood
1. Selecting a mate
2. Learning to live with a marriage partner
3. Starting a family
4. Rearing children
5. Managing a home
6. Getting started in an occupation
7. Taking on civic responsibility
8. Finding a congenial social group

V. Developmental Tasks of Middle Age
1. Assisting teenage children to become responsible and happy adults
2. Achieving adult social and civic responsibility
3. Reaching and maintaining satisfactory performance in one's occupational career
4. Developing adult leisure-time activities
5. Relating oneself to one's spouse as a person
6. Accepting and adjusting to the physiological changes of middle age

VI. Developmental Tasks of Late Maturity
1. Adjusting to decreasing physical strength and health
2. Adjusting to retirement and reduced income
3. Adjusting to death of a spouse
4. Establishing an explicit affiliation with one's age group
5. Adopting and adapting social roles in a flexible way
6. Establishing satisfactory physical living arrangements

3.8.3 Roger Gould's Adult Developmental Theory

Roger Gould, an American writer and psychiatrist, studied more than 1,000 adults and discovered that they strove to eliminate false assumptions (protective devices), usually relating to parental dependency, that restricted young and middle adult development. He viewed adult development as a series of task resolutions that allowed adults to correct these false assumptions and ultimately take control of their lives.

I. Young Adulthood
   a. Leaving Our Parents' World (16–22 years): "Adults will always live with their parents."
   b. I'm Nobody's Baby Now (22–28 years): "My parents will always be there to help when things go wrong or not exactly as I want."
   c. Opening Up to What's Inside (29 years to low 30s): "My parents can always offer a simplified version and solution to complicated inner realities."

II. Midlife Decade (35–45 years)
   a. "Safety can last forever."
   b. "Death cannot happen to me or my loved ones."
   c. "It is impossible to live without a partner in the world."
   d. "No life or change exists beyond the family."

3.8.4 Robert Peck's Phase Theory of Adult Development

Robert Peck, whose research interests centered upon human development, coping skills, motivation, career competence, moral behavior, and teacher effectiveness, expanded on the final two stages (last 40–50 years) of Erikson's stages.

I. Phases of Middle Adult Psychological Changes
   a. *Valuing Wisdom v. Valuing Physical Powers.* A decrease in physical strength, stamina, and attractiveness leads individuals to value wisdom, the judgmental powers that emerge from successful lived experiences.
   b. *Socializing v. Sexualizing.* Sex is replaced by empathy, understanding, and compassion.
   c. *Cathetic Flexibility v. Cathetic Impoverishment.* Individuals must develop the capacity to shift emotional energies from one person or activity to another in order to deal with losses they will encounter in the future.

II. Phases of the Retirement Years Psychological Development
   a. *Ego Differentiation v. Work-Role Preoccupation.* Individuals must adapt and learn to define their personal worth in ways other than a full-time occupation. Thus, planning for retirement becomes crucial.
   b. *Body Transcendence v. Body Preoccupation.* Physical decline is experienced. Some may become preoccupied with symptoms, whereas others pursue satisfying relationships and creative mental activities.
   c. *Ego Transcendence v. Ego Preoccupation.* Individuals attempt to make life more secure and meaningful for those who survive them.

3.8.5 Daniel Levinson's Adult Male Development Theory

American-born **Daniel Levinson** (1978) studied adult male development and presented a combination task/stage theory. He observed that adult males created life structures (i.e., periods of stability and growth) alternated with transitional periods that helped the adult reach a more mature life structure level.

I. *Novice Phase*
a. *Early Adult Transition (17–22 years).* Terminate the adolescent life structure and develop job skills to live in the adult world.
b. *Entering the Adult World (22–28 years).* Test initial life structure and lifestyle while comparing personal values to adult societal values.
c. *Age 30 Transition.* Reassessment of the young adult life structure to make changes before fully joining the adult world.
II. *The Settling Down Phase*
a. *Early Settling Down.* Establishing a niche in society.
b. *Becoming One's Own Man* (BOOM). Men work at advancement and strive to succeed.
III. *Midlife Transition (40–45 years).* Men assess their successes and failures in meeting the goals set in the previous phase, experiencing satisfaction with successes while building motivation to use their remaining life wisely.
IV. *Entering Middle Adulthood (45–50 years).* Several polarities arise from individuation (i.e., a person's relationship to himself and the external world), including the young/old polarity, mortality/generativity polarity, and masculine/feminine polarity.
V. *Age 50 Transition.* More individuation occurs, and this transition can be an especially difficult one for those not conducting the necessary preparations.
VI. *Building a Second Middle Adult Structure (55–60 years).* Progress is made toward new goals and aspirations; a time of rejuvenation and enrichment.
VII. *Late Adult Transition (60–65 years).* Men experience changing physical and mental capacities and a sense of mortality as they experience decreasing physical vitality and experience losses.
VIII. *Late Adulthood (65+ years)* Pursuit of enjoyable and rewarding past times in retirement, preparation for own death, concern over the fate of family and humanity, and reaching ultimate involvement with self.

3.8.6 Women's Development

Theories of human development have been criticized for being gender specific, male-centric, and anti-feminine. A number of scholars have provided diverse perspectives on women's development, although none have developed a comprehensive theory that has gained widespread support.

- Carol Tavris (1992) wrote *The Mismeasure of Woman*, proposing that women are judged based on how well they fit into a male-dominated world and that American society pathologizes women.
- Carol Gilligan (1982) wrote *In a Different Voice*. She observed that communication patterns displayed by women differ from men and that women are socialized to be dependent and caretakers, rather than independent, as men are.
- Gail Sheehy (1976) wrote *Passages: Predictable Crises in Adult Life*, proposing that women face crises as they pass through developmental transitional periods, resulting in constructive changes.

3.8.7 Generational Considerations in Human Development

A generation is a group of individuals aggregated according to birth years and location in history; generations form cohorts whose shared experiences form peer personalities. As many as 18 generations have been documented in U.S. history, beginning with the Puritans from 1588–1617. Following is a summary of living generations in the United States according to their dates of birth (Strauss & Howe, 1991):

- General Issue (GI) Generation: 1891–1924
- Silent Generation: 1925–1942
- Baby Boomer Generation: 1943–1960
- Generation X: 1961–1981
- Millennials (Generation Y): 1982–2000

3.8.8 Practice Multiple-Choice Items: Lifespan Theories

1. According to Gesell, human development is PRIMARILY due to
   a. genetics.
   b. nurture.
   c. the environment.
   d. None of the above.

2. Havighurst believes that relating to one's spouse as a person is a developmental task of
   a. young adulthood.
   b. middle age.
   c. late maturity.
   d. All of the above.

3. In Havighurst's model of human development, many of the earlier (childhood) tasks are
   a. biologically determined.
   b. socially determined.
   c. culturally determined.
   d. psychologically determined.

4. In Gould's theory of adult development, adults must do all of the following EXCEPT

a. refute false assumptions.
b. decrease parental dependency.
c. increase spousal dependency.
d. increase self-reliance.

5. Peck's theory of adult development is an expansion of
   a. Erikson's psychosocial theory.
   b. Freud's psychosexual theory.
   c. Havighurst's developmental task approach.
   d. Gould's adult development theory.

Answer Key: 1. a; 2. b; 3. a; 4. c; 5. a.

3.9 FAMILY DEVELOPMENT AND ISSUES

Like individuals, family development often follows a predictable pattern, although at times the diversity of modern-day family structures and sociocultural issues leads to substantial variations and differences. In this section we discuss the stages of family development, parenting influences, divorce and remarriage, maternal employment, and effects of abuse on family development.

3.9.1 Family Development

Family development can be thought of as occurring in stages and determined by key life decisions and events that lead to greater responsibilities (Carter & McGoldrick, 1998).

I. *Leaving Home.* Single young adults accept the financial and emotional responsibilities of caring for themselves. The timing of this stage often determines when, how, and whether the person will marry, and in turn determines the timing for subsequent stages of family development. Key tasks are the development of intimate peer relations, differentiation of self from the family of origin, and establishment of an individual identity.

II. *Joining Families Through Marriage.* Adults commit to establishing a new family system that merges two previously independent families, leading to a realignment of relationships to integrate the spouse into the extended family.

III. *Welcoming Children into the Family.* The couple brings children into the new family structure and in the process adjusts the marital dyad; shares financial, household, and child-rearing tasks; and incorporates the extended family to accommodate new roles for grandparents.

IV. *Raising Adolescents.* Family boundaries become more flexible to allow adolescent children to move in and out of the family structure. Couples also shift to caring for the older generations and refocus on career and marital issues as they transition through midlife. About 50% of married couples divorce, so great diversity exists in how families handle these stages and the family structures that result.

V. *Launching.* Families must adjust to the multiple exits of adult children and entries into the system of children's spouses. Couples must renegotiate the marital dyad to accommodate the multiple system changes, while dealing effectively with the care of parents (death and disability). Parents also must establish adult-to-adult relationships with their children and welcome children's partners, in-laws, and grandchildren.

VI. *Later Family Life.* The couple needs to accept the shifting roles necessitated by generational changes. Couples need to flexibly explore new family and social roles while adjusting to physical deterioration and supporting the growing role of their children in family leadership. Older adults must also value the experiences and wisdom of their aged parents in a supportive manner without overfunctioning for them. Finally, adults may have to deal with the loss of a spouse, siblings, peers, and eventually their own lives.

3.9.2 Parenting Influences

Parents play important roles in the social development of children, which become reflected in parent personality. **Parenting styles** are frequently categorized along two continua: permissive/controlling and warm/hostile. Parental styles include the following:

• *Authoritarian* (called *autocratic* in the extreme manifestation) parents are restrictive and lack outward expressions of warmth. They exert control over children, often through physical punishment, and require adherence to absolute standards of behavior and life choices. Children reared by authoritarian parents are often either submissive or rebellious and, typically, have lower levels of achievement and responsibility.

• *Authoritative* (sometimes called *democratic* or *egalitarian*) parents display moderate control and explain the reasoning behind their decisions in order to help children understand the important factors that go into governing behavior and decision making. These children tend to have the best outcomes, becoming independent, assertive, and responsible.

• *Permissive* (sometimes called *laissez-faire*) parents display little control and, at most, moderate warmth. Usually, children reared by these parents are self-centered, aggressive, low-achieving, and lack social responsibility.

• *Uninvolved* (sometimes called *unengaged*) parents show little if any interest in their children and are indifferent or rejecting toward them. In the extreme, uninvolved parenting constitutes neglect and should be reported to Child Protective Services. Children reared by uninvolved parents fare the worst of all parental styles; with no support or guidance, children are left to essentially raise themselves.

3.9.3 Divorce and Remarriage

About 50% of first marriages end in divorce. Most divorced adults remarry (75–80%), although about 60% of second marriages, 70% of third marriages, and virtually all of subsequent marriages that are not ended by the death of a spouse also end in divorce. In general, women perceive divorce to be more stressful than men but end up adjusting psychologically better to divorce. Interestingly, prior to 1970, most divorces were blamed on abuse, alcoholism/drug abuse, or nonsupport; in recent years though, separation is more likely to be blamed on incompatibility, poor communication, and unfulfilled life goals.

About 85% of single parent households are headed by females. Financial problems are frequently cited as a primary stressor in single parent families. Single parents often have less time and patience for parenting and display less consistent, more punitive discipline styles. Noncustodial fathers are frequently more overindulgent and permissive, but after maintaining normal visitation over the first few months after the divorce, frequently fail to make visitation arrangements and child support payments. Although children of divorce experience a complex array of difficulties, problems experienced by children of divorce are minimized if parents are cooperative, psychologically healthy, empathic, and openly communicative with the children. Recent research has indicated that the negative results of divorce are similar to those experienced by children in high-conflict families of parents who are not divorced, leading some to conclude that the single parent family structure is less responsible for negative outcomes than ongoing parental conflict.

3.9.4 Maternal Employment

Women account for about 45% of the U.S. workforce but are frequently confined to lower status jobs because of child-rearing responsibilities. Women still frequently receive lower pay for the same job as compared to men, although women who have forgone childbearing usually receive pay equivalent to their male counterparts. Mothers who work tend to be more satisfied with their lives, less stressed, and less depressed than women who do not work, although they worry more about time away from family and childrearing. No differences in marital satisfaction are apparent between working and nonworking mothers, unless the spouse is opposed to maternal employment. The effect of maternal employment on children indicates that quality day care likely ameliorates any negative outcomes and may even have some advantages for children in terms of socialization and intellectual growth.

3.9.5 Abuse

Physical abuse occurs most frequently with very young children during early childhood, primarily because of stressors experienced by parents (e.g., caring for young children, alcoholism, finances, work) and the child's inability to verbally express needs and defend oneself. Parents who have been abused are more likely to abuse their children, often due to the lack of an effective disciplinarian role model.

Sexual abuse includes incest (i.e., sexual intercourse with a close relative), sexual assault, and fondling of minor children. Girls are most frequently the victims of incest, with fathers being the most frequent perpetrators, whereas boys are more often the victims of nonfamily sexual abuse. Victims of sexual abuse frequently report strange feelings of guilt over their roles

in the abuse and rarely self-refer. Counselors have a duty to protect vulnerable children suspected of experiencing abuse and are required by law to report abuse orally and in writing. Counselors cannot be held liable for making an unsubstantiated report unless the report is made with malicious intent.

3.9.6 Practice Multiple-Choice Items: Family Development and Issues

1. What percentage of first marriages end in divorce?
    a. ~30%
    b. ~40%
    c. ~50%
    d. ~60%

2. During the _____ stage of family development, it is most important for boundaries to become more flexible.
    a. welcoming children into the family
    b. raising adolescents
    c. launching
    d. later family life

3. Children of permissive parents often become all of the following EXCEPT
    a. rebellious.
    b. aggressive.
    c. self-centered.
    d. irresponsible.

4. Parents who enforce a set standard of conduct and frequently use physical punishment to control their children are
    a. authoritative.
    b. authoritarian.
    c. uninvolved.
    d. permissive.

5. Today, a couple's divorce is most commonly blamed on
    a. domestic abuse.
    b. substance abuse.
    c. incompatibility.
    d. All of the above.

Answer Key: 1. c; 2. b; 3. a; 4. b; 5. c.

3.10 CRISIS, RESILIENCE, AND WELLNESS

The counseling profession promotes developmental and preventive approaches to intrapersonal and interpersonal human events. Although the medical model is widely used for diagnosis of mental disorders in clinical practice, much research exists to underscore the importance of using facets of client resiliency and wellness when helping clients cope with and compensate for psychosocial challenges. In addition, as mental health professionals, counselors are trained to intervene in individual client and larger scale societal crises.

3.10.1 Crisis and Crisis Management

A *crisis* is a time-limited period of disequilibrium caused by a precipitating event (stressor) that temporarily affects an individual's normal coping abilities, rendering him or her inadequate in dealing with the circumstances. Importantly, crises have the potential for both negative outcomes and positive growth potential. **Eric Lindemann** was a pioneer in the development of crisis models, having treated and studied survivors of the famous Cocoanut Grove Nightclub fire of 1942 during which 493 people perished (Lindemann, 1944). Lindemann observed that mental health professionals can help those people affected by traumatic events to grieve and mourn properly, thereby preventing further mental health complications. His colleague, **Gerard Caplan**, expanded Lindemann's work by applying public health and preventative psychiatry principles.

Five types of crises have been described: (a) *developmental crises* are caused by normal life experiences (e.g., career change, birth of a child); (b) *environmental crises* are caused by natural or human-caused events affecting multiple people in the affected environment (e.g., hurricanes, war); (c) *existential crises* are caused by realizations of personal purpose and meaning (e.g., questioning the meaning of career, life, existence); (d) *situational crises* are caused by a precipitating event that is shocking and traumatic (e.g., rape, accident, loss of a loved one); and (e) *psychiatric crises* are caused by mental health and/or substance use problems (e.g., psychosis, drug abuse).

James and Gilliland (2005) proposed a 6-step model for assessing client needs during a crisis: (1) Defining the problem, (2) Ensuring client safety, (3) Providing support, (4) Examining alternatives, (5) Making plans, and (6) Obtaining commitment.

Hill (1949) proposed the **ABC-X model of family crisis and stress** through his observations of families experiencing separation and reunification during and after World War II: (A) provoking stressor/event; (B) family resources; (C) meaning attached to the stressor/event; and (X) the crisis, which is an acute state of family disequilibrium/immobilization.

Several other terms are important in the context of crisis management:

- **Transcrisis** occurs when the traumatic event of an initial crisis is not fully dealt with and becomes submerged into a client's subconscious. Subsequent similar events then trigger these subconscious feelings.
- **Burnout** is exhaustion stemming from repeated exposure to stressful circumstances that results in emotional exhaustion, depersonalization, and reduced personal accomplishment. Crisis counselors repeatedly encounter stressful client circumstances and normal counselor coping mechanisms may not serve as persistent protective factors.
- **Compassion fatigue**, sometimes called secondary traumatic stress reaction, occurs in helping professionals who experience overwhelming feelings after being exposed to client crisis states (pain and suffering). Professionals may experience hopelessness, a decrease in pleasure, constant stress and anxiety, and a pervasive negative attitude.
- **Vicarious trauma** is a stress reaction resulting from exposure to client disclosures of traumatic events. While also leading to a secondary traumatic reaction, it can also affect the crisis counselor's worldview and sense of self. Thus, counselors experiencing vicarious trauma experience long-term and pervasive attitudinal shifts.

Suicide is the act of taking one's own life and is a crisis situation most counselors will encounter during their careers. When working with potentially suicidal clients, professional counselors must exercise an expected *standard of care*, which involves reliable and appropriate interventions and precautions that a prudent professional would exercise under similar circumstances. Counselors must also exercise *foreseeability*, which involves discernment of likely client actions based on a comprehensive assessment of risk. Counselors who do not engage in comprehensive assessment of client suicidal tendencies fall below the expected standard of care. The American Association of Suicidology (2006) provides a mnemonic method to remember the warning signs of suicide, **IS PATH WARM**: Ideation, Substance abuse, Purposelessness, Anxiety, Trapped, Hopelessness, Withdrawal, Anger, Recklessness, and Mood change. A second helpful acronym to remind counselors of the major areas covered during a suicide risk assessment is **SLAP**: Specific details, Lethality of plan, Availability of method, and Proximity to obtaining help. Many helpful standardized assessments are available for clinical use, but counselors must understand that clients who complete the assessments in an untruthful manner may not report a level of clinical threat, even though they are truly in danger of harming themselves.

3.10.2 Risk and Resiliency Factors

Risk factors are characteristics of students and clients that place them at higher risk of developing mental disorders, academic problems, or personal-social difficulties. It is important to realize that a single risk factor leads to only a slight increase in risk, whereas multiple factors exponentially increase one's risk status. Although risk factors are sometimes helpful when implementing prevention or early intervention models, **resiliency factors** are ordinarily more important to assess, because resilience involves characteristics that allow an individual to rebound from adversity or to maintain equilibrium of positive functioning when exposed to traumatic events or environmental stressors. The Search Institute (2005) published a list of 40 developmental assets helpful to counselors using a resilience-based or wellness approach to counseling, broken into eight organizing categories.

I. Support: (1) family support, (2) positive family communications, (3) other adult relationships, (4) caring neighborhood, (5) caring school climate, (6) parent involvement in schooling;
II. Empowerment: (7) community values youth, (8) youth as resources, (9) service to others, (10) safety;
III. Boundaries and Expectations: (11) family boundaries, (12) school boundaries, (13) neighborhood boundaries, (14) adult role models, (15) positive peer influence, (16) high expectations;
IV. Constructive Use of Time: (17) creative activities, (18) youth programs, (19) religious community, (20) time at home;

V. Commitment to Learning: (21) achievement motivation, (22) school engagement, (23) homework, (24) bonding to school, (25) reading for pleasure;

VI. Positive Values: (26) caring, (27) equality and social justice, (28) integrity, (29) honesty, (30) responsibility, (31) restraint;

VII. Social Competence: (32) planning and decision making, (33) interpersonal competence, (34) cultural competence, (35) resistance skills, (36) peaceful conflict resolution;

VIII. Positive Identity: (37) personal power, (38) self-esteem, (39) sense of purpose, (40) positive view of personal future.

3.10.3 Wellness

Wellness refers to an integration of mind, body and spirit resulting in positive well-being. Counselors frequently approach counseling using a wellness perspective across a continuum— that is, these counselors do not portray clients as mentally ill seeking help to get better but view clients as searching for a healthier lifestyle through a more balanced integration of the mind, body and spirit. Myers and Sweeney (2005a, 2005b) proposed an evidence-based model of wellness known as the Indivisible Self. They proposed five dimensions of wellness, each with multiple facets:

I. Physical: exercise, nutrition.

II. Essential: spirituality, gender identity, cultural identity, self-care.

III. Social: friendship, love.

IV. Coping: leisure, stress management, self-worth, realistic beliefs.

V. Creative: thinking, emotions, control, work, positive humor.

3.10.4 Practice Multiple-Choice Items: Crisis, Resilience, and Wellness

1. The death of a child is a
   a. developmental crisis.
   b. psychiatric crisis.
   c. existential crisis.
   d. situational crisis.

2. All of the following are developmental crises EXCEPT
   a. the birth of a child.
   b. moving to a new state.
   c. a car accident.
   d. changing jobs.

3. Counselors who become emotionally affected after exposure to crisis victims are experiencing
   a. compassion fatigue.
   b. vicarious trauma.
   c. burnout.
   d. transcrisis.

4. Counselors should assess _____ when they believe a client might be suicidal

   a. whether the client has a plan
   b. whether the client has a means for carrying out the plan
   c. whether the plan is specific, detailed, and plausible
   d. All of the above.

5. According to the Indivisible Self wellness model, the following is NOT part of the essential self:
   a. gender identity
   b. nutrition
   c. spirituality
   d. self-care

Answer Key: 1. d; 2. c; 3. a; 4. d; 5. b.

3.11   DIAGNOSIS OF MENTAL DISORDERS

Professional counselors in clinical practice often have the responsibility to diagnose and treat mental disorders. All counselors should be aware of diagnostic classification systems used by mental health professionals and the diagnostic categories most commonly displayed by the populations the counselor serves. The remainder of this final section of Chapter 3 reviews basic information about the *DSM-IV-TR* and mental disorders professional counselors may encounter in clinical practice.

3.11.1   Using the *DSM-IV-TR*

The American Psychiatric Association periodically publishes a revised edition of the *Diagnostic and Statistical Manual of Mental Disorders* (*DSM*). The current edition is the *DSM-IV-TR* (*Fourth Edition, Text Revision*)(APA, 2000). [*Note:* The American Psychiatric Association expects to release the *DSM-V* after 2010.] The *DSM-IV*-TR is the most common nosological system used by mental health practitioners in the United States. The *DSM-IV-TR* defines mental disorders and describes symptoms of each condition. Importantly, the manual is atheoretical, meaning that diagnoses are not defined through the lens of a counseling theory, and etiology (causation) is only provided for diagnostic categories that are caused by specific factors (e.g., Acute Stress Disorder, Posttraumatic Stress Disorder).

In the *DSM-IV*, **mental disorder** is defined as a

clinically significant behavioral or psychological syndrome or pattern that occurs in an individual and that is associated with present distress (e.g., a painful symptom) or disability (i.e., impairment in one or more important areas of functioning) or with a significantly increased risk of suffering death, pain, disability, or an important loss of freedom. In addition, this syndrome or pattern must not be merely an expectable and culturally sanctioned response to a particular event, for example, the death of a loved one. (APA, 2000, p. xxxi)

For most disorders, a client must experience symptoms to an extent that impairment or distress in academic, occupational, social, or some other important area of functioning is evident. The *DSM-IV-TR* uses a *multiaxial system* (multidimensional) to describe a client's condition:

> *Axis I* specifies Clinical Disorders and Other Conditions That May be the Focus of Clinical Attention (e.g., Attention-Deficit/Hyperactivity Disorder [AD/HD], Generalized Anxiety Disorder, Dementia).
>
> *Axis II* specifies Personality Disorders and Mental Retardation (e.g., Antisocial Personality Disorder, Schizoid Personality Disorder).
>
> *Axis III* specifies General Medical Conditions, knowledge of which may be helpful in treating mental disorders (e.g., infectious diseases, hearing or vision problems, cancer).
>
> *Axis IV* specifies Psychosocial and Environmental Problems, stressors that may influence the client's diagnosis or treatment (e.g., unemployment, homelessness, financial problems).
>
> *Axis V* specifies the client's Global Assessment of Functioning (GAF) scale, a numerical rating from 0 (Inadequate Information) or 1 (Persistent Danger of Harm, Serious Suicidal Act) on the low end and 100 (Superior Functioning, No Symptoms) on the high end. The GAF is usually reported for current functioning and the highest level evident within the past year (e.g., GAF = 45 [current]; 75 [highest level past year]).

Thus, mental disorders are coded on Axis I and Axis II. Information related to differential diagnosis is provided to help differentiate the diagnosis of each disorder from other conditions that share similar features and may supersede the suspected condition. For example, although both are Mood Disorders, Dysthymic Disorder is differentiated from Major Depressive Disorder because Dysthymic Disorder is a pervasive condition prevalent for more than two years. Finally, the *DSM-IV-TR* addresses culture-bound syndromes that are only found in certain parts of the world and, by extension, helps clinicians understand that diagnosis of mental disorders always occurs within a cultural context.

Important Note: Diagnosis of mental disorders is a huge content area and not a major focus on the NCE or CPCE. Thus, the summary information presented below is just the names of *selected* disorders and the essential diagnostic features of each. For further, in-depth information on any of these disorders, please consult the *DSM-IV-TR* (APA, 2000). Also, the diagnostic labels and descriptions in the remainder of this section are all referenced from the *DSM-IV-TR*.

3.11.2 Disorders Usually First Diagnosed in Infancy, Childhood, or Adolescence

The disorders reviewed in this category ordinarily are diagnosed prior to adulthood, although some may have been apparent during childhood but went undiagnosed until after age 18 years. (Communication Disorders were reviewed earlier in this chapter within the discussion of language development.)

- *Mental Retardation* is a developmental disorder defined as significant subaverage intellectual ability (IQ = 70) and adaptive functioning that is prevalent prior to 18 years of age. Intellectual ability is ordinarily obtained using a standardized, individual test of intelligence (IQ = 70), whereas adaptive functioning is obtained through an assessment of age-appropriate independent living skills. Four subtypes, based on degree of intellectual impairment exist: mild, moderate, severe, and profound.
- *Learning Disorders* are diagnosed when a client's academic achievement (as measured using standardized tests) is below expected levels given the client's age and intellectual ability.
  - *Reading Disorder.* Reading achievement (comprehension, word identification, oral reading fluency) is significantly below expected levels for age and intellectual ability and significantly affects academic performance.
  - *Mathematics Disorder.* Math achievement (calculation, problem solving) is significantly below expected levels for age and intellectual ability and significantly affects academic performance.
  - *Disorder of Written Expression.* Writing achievement (ability to express ideas in writing, proper mechanics when constructing text) is significantly below expected levels for age and intellectual ability and significantly affects academic performance.
- *Motor Skills Disorder* has only one primary category. *Developmental Coordination Disorder* involves significant impairment in gross or fine motor coordination skills.
- *Pervasive Developmental Disorders* involve pervasive, severe impairment in more than one area of development and include:
  - *Autistic Disorder.* Abnormal communication, social interactions, and restricted (repetitive, stereotyped) range of interests and behaviors; four to five times more prevalent in males than females; overall prevalence rate of about 5 in 10,000 individuals.
  - *Asperger's Disorder.* Deficiencies in social interaction and restricted (repetitive, stereotyped) range of interests and behaviors without a clinically significant delay in cognitive abilities or language development.
- *Attention-Deficit and Disruptive Behavior Disorders:*
  - *Attention-Deficit/Hyperactivity Disorder* involves a significant pattern of inattention and/or hyperactivity/impulsivity that begins prior to age 5 years. Prevalence is 3% to 7% of a school-age population and is two to nine times more likely to be diagnosed in males. Three subtypes exist: Predominantly Inattentive Type, Predominantly Hyperactive-Impulsive Type, and Combined Type.
  - *Oppositional Defiant Disorder* involves a recurrent pattern of defiant, disobedient, hostile, and negative behaviors toward authority figures. Individuals with

Conduct Disorder cannot be simultaneously diagnosed with Oppositional Defiant Disorder.

- *Conduct Disorder* involves a persistent pattern of behaviors that violate the rights of others or social rules (e.g., cruelty, stealing, bullying, fighting, rape) in an individual under the age of 18 years.
- *Tic Disorders* involve "sudden, rapid, recurrent, non-rhythmic, stereotyped motor movement or vocalization" (APA, 2000, p. 108).
  - *Tourette's Disorder* involves a combination of at least one vocal tic and multiple motor tics occurring a number of times per day over at least a year. Tourette's also onsets prior to age 18 years.
  - *Chronic Motor or Vocal Tic Disorder* involves the presence of vocal or motor tics, but not both, differentiating it from Tourette's Disorder, occurring a number of times per day over at least a year.
  - *Transient Tic Disorder* involves the presence of vocal and/or motor tics occurring a number of times per day for at least a month but for less than a year. Thus, Transient Tic Disorder is often diagnosed in individuals prior to the other more chronic and severe tic disorders.
- *Elimination Disorders* involve difficulties controlling bowel and urinary functions not due to a general medical condition.
  - *Encopresis* is the (usually involuntary) depositing of feces in inappropriate places (e.g., floor, clothing, furniture).
  - *Enuresis* is (usually involuntary) urination in inappropriate places (e.g., bedding, clothing), either during nighttime sleep (nocturnal) or during the day (diurnal).
- *Other Disorders of Infancy, Childhood, or Adolescence* is a mixed category that includes Separation Anxiety Disorder (described below), Selective Mutism, Reactive Attachment Disorder, and Stereotypic Movement Disorder.
  - *Separation Anxiety Disorder* involves excessive anxiety when separated from an attachment figure (e.g., mother), lasting at least 4 weeks, beginning before 18 years of age, and causing significant impairment in academic or social functioning.

3.11.3 Delirium, Dementia, and Amnestic and Other Cognitive Disorders

This cluster of conditions involves changes in cognitive abilities from previously higher levels of functioning to present deficiencies because of a general medical condition or substance use.

- *Delirium* involves a disturbance in consciousness (e.g., awareness of environment) and cognition (e.g., disorientation, memory problems), due either to a general medical condition or substance use. Ordinarily, Delirium develops over the course of several hours and fluctuates in severity throughout the day.
- *Dementia* involves memory impairment and at least one other cognitive deficiency (e.g., language, motor, executive functioning), either due to a general medical condition

(e.g., Alzheimer's type, Vascular Dementia, HIV) or substance use.

- *Amnestic Disorders* involve a disturbance in memory (e.g., learning new information, unable to recall previously learned information) due to a general medical condition or substance use but not due to Delirium or Dementia.

3.11.4 Mental Disorders Due to a General Medical Condition Not Elsewhere Classified

The disorders presented in this section of the *DSM-IV-TR* involve symptoms (i.e., catatonic, personality change, mental disorder NOS) that cannot be classified as a mental disorder elsewhere but are the direct physiological result of a general medical condition. These disorders share three criteria (APA, 2000, pp. 182–184):

> There is evidence from the history, physical examination, or laboratory findings that the disturbance is the direct physiological consequence of a general medical condition [and]. . . . The disturbance is not better accounted for by another mental disorder [and]. . . . The disturbance does not occur exclusively during the course of a delirium.

3.11.5 Substance-Related Disorders

A substance is a drug of abuse, medication, or toxin. *Substance-Related Disorders* are categorized as *Substance Use Disorders* (including dependence and abuse) and *Substance-Induced Disorders* (including intoxication and withdrawal). Eleven classes of substances are described: alcohol; amphetamine; caffeine; cannabis; cocaine; hallucinogen; inhalant; nicotine; opioid; phencyclidine; and sedative, hypnotic, or anxiolytic. Also, a diagnosis of polysubstance or unknown substance is permitted.

- *Substance Abuse* involves a pattern of maladaptive substance use that interferes with major role obligations, is physically hazardous, results in legal problems, or causes persistent interpersonal problems.
- *Substance Dependence* involves continued use of a substance in spite of noticeable impairment (e.g., tolerance, withdrawal, desire to "cut down" on the substance, reduction in other activities because of substance use).
- *Substance Intoxication* occurs after ingesting a substance that leads to maladaptive behavior (e.g., mood lability, impaired judgment, impaired social or occupational functioning).

3.11.6 Schizophrenia and Other Psychotic Disorders

The disorders in this section all feature one or more psychotic symptoms (e.g., hallucinations, delusions, disorganized thoughts/speech, catatonic/disorganized behavior, or negative symptoms [flattened affect, alogia]).

- *Schizophrenia* involves two or more of the psychotic symptoms listed above occurring for most of the time during an active phase period of at least 1 month out of at least a 6-month disturbance period during which social or occupational functioning is significantly impaired. APA (2000) lists five subtypes: *Paranoid Type* (i.e., frequent delusions or auditory hallucinations of persecution), *Disorganized Type* (i.e., disorganized speech, disorganized behavior, and flat/inappropriate affect), *Catatonic Type* (e.g., motoric immobility or stupor, extreme negativism, bizarre posturing), *Undifferentiated Type*, and *Residual Type* (absence of psychotic symptoms after an active phase). Schizophrenia usually exhibits onset in late adolescence through young adulthood.

- *Schizophreniform Disorder* symptoms are similar to those of Schizophrenia, except that the duration is less than 6 months (with a 1-month active phase) and social or occupational functioning may not occur. At times, the diagnosis of Schizophreniform Disorder is given provisionally until the 6-month time period has been reached when a diagnosis of Schizophrenia can be made.
- *Schizoaffective Disorder* includes an uninterrupted period during which concurrent symptoms of active-phase Schizophrenia (2 or more weeks of hallucinations and delusions) and a Mood Disorder (e.g., depression, mania) occur.
- *Delusional Disorder* involves nonbizarre delusions (e.g., being followed, deceived by a spouse) occurring for at least 1 month without concurrent prominent Schizophrenia or mood symptoms.
- *Brief Psychotic Disorder* involves a psychotic symptom (e.g., hallucinations, delusions, disorganized speech, catatonic/disorganized behavior) present for at least 1 day but less than 1 month.

3.11.7 Mood Disorders

Mood Disorders all share the common characteristic of having one or more of the following: (a) Major Depressive Episode, (b) Manic Episode, (c) Hypomanic Episode, and/or (d) Mixed Episodes.

1. A *Major Depressive Episode* includes 2 or more weeks with at least five of the following symptoms: depressed mood, diminished interest/pleasure, significant weight loss or gain, insomnia/hypersomnia, fatigue, lack of concentration, feelings of worthlessness/guilt, or suicidal ideation.
2. A *Manic Episode* includes 1 week of an elevated, expansive or irritable mood with at least three of the following symptoms: inflated esteem/grandiosity, decreased sleep, excessive talkativeness, racing thoughts, distractibility, increased goal-directed activity, or excessive pleasurable activities with potential negative consequences (e.g., promiscuity, spending sprees).
3. A *Hypomanic Episode* is similar to a Manic Episode but is of shorter duration (at least 4 days) and does not result in marked impairment or hospitalization.
4. A *Mixed Episode* includes meeting the criteria for both a Manic Episode and Major Depressive Episode nearly every day for 1 week.

Mood Disorders include the following:

- *Major Depressive Disorder* involves one or more Major Depressive Episodes in the absence of a Manic, Hypomanic, or Mixed Episode. This disorder is diagnosed in females twice as frequently as in males.
- *Dysthymic Disorder* involves a chronically depressed mood occurring most days for a minimum of 2 years (1 year in children and adolescents). Many of the symptoms resemble those of Major Depressive Episode, but the individual does not experience the classic 2-week acute marked impairment; rather the symptom display is less severe and more chronic. This disorder is often diagnosed prior to adulthood.
- *Bipolar I Disorder* involves one or more Manic or Mixed Episodes, with no history of Major Depressive Episode. Bipolar I Disorder is genetically transmitted and occurs equally in males and females.
- *Bipolar II Disorder* involves the presence of at least one Major Depressive Episode and Hypomanic Episode and is more commonly diagnosed in females than males.
- *Cyclothymic Disorder* is characterized by numerous periods of depression interspersed with periods of hypomania lasting for at least 2 years in adults (1 year in children or adolescents).

3.11.8 Anxiety Disorders

Anxiety Disorders involve conditions in which clients present with significant anxiousness and avoidance that affect major life activities.

- *Panic Attack* is not a codable disorder on its own but can occur in conjunction with Anxiety Disorders and other mental disorders (e.g., Mood Disorder, Substance-Related Disorder) and involves a period of intense fear peaking in 10 minutes or less and involving (at least four) symptoms such as palpitations, sweating, shaking, shortness of breath, chest pain, nausea, numbness, chills, fear of death, and fear of losing control.
- *Agoraphobia* is not a codable disorder on its own but can occur in the context of a Panic Disorder. Criteria for Agoraphobia (loosely translated as meaning "fear of the marketplace") include intense anxiety over being in situations in which escape may be difficult and embarrassment may occur should a Panic Attack ensue. Agoraphobia may occur with or without the occurrence of a Panic Attack.
- *Panic Disorder* involves recurrent Panic Attacks either with or without Agoraphobia.
- *Specific Phobia* is a marked, persistent fear of a specific situation or object (e.g., flying, animals, insects, enclosed spaces).
- *Social Phobia* is a marked, persistent fear of performance or social situations in which humiliation or embarrassment may occur as a result of scrutiny by others (athletic performance, bullying, making a speech in public).
- *Obsessive-Compulsive Disorder* involves recurrent obsessions (i.e., thoughts, impulses, images) that cause

marked distress, that are not simply excessive worries about life situations, that the person has great difficulty suppressing, and that are recognized as the product of one's own mind. Likewise, compulsions are recurrent behaviors or mental acts (e.g., counting, praying) aimed at reducing distress but not connected to what they are designed to prevent.

- *Posttraumatic Stress Disorder (PTSD)* involves development of symptoms following exposure to a traumatic stressor or event involving actual or threatened death or serious injury and during which the person responded in horror or helplessness. The individual must persistently reexperience the event, persistently avoid associated stimuli, and experience persistent symptoms of arousal/stress not present prior to the trauma. Importantly, PTSD is not diagnosed until 1 month has elapsed after the trauma
- *Acute Stress Disorder* has characteristics similar to PTSD but is only diagnosed within 1 month after the traumatic event. Thus, at times an individual may be diagnosed with Acute Stress Disorder immediately after a traumatic event, then that diagnosis may change to PTSD should the symptoms not ameliorate within a 1-month period.
- *Generalized Anxiety Disorder* involves excessive anxiety occurring most days over at least a 6-month period, accompanied by at least three of the following symptoms: restlessness, fatigue, difficulty concentrating, irritability, muscle tension, and difficulties sleeping. The symptoms of anxiety cannot be due to some other Anxiety Disorder or other Axis I disorder.

3.11.9 Somatoform Disorders

Somatoform Disorders involve physical symptoms resembling a general medical condition but cannot be fully explained by a medical condition, substance use, or other mental disorder. These disorders are not intentionally produced and cause marked distress or impairment.

- *Somatization Disorder* involves a history of physical complaints occurring over several years, beginning before age 30 years, and causing significant impairment. Symptoms must include complaints of pain in at least four areas of the body (e.g., head, back, joints, chest), two gastrointestinal complaints (e.g., nausea, diarrhea), one sexual complaint (e.g., erectile dysfunction), and one pseudoneurological complaint (e.g., impaired coordination, deafness, blindness). Importantly, the complaints are not the result of a general medical condition or are far in excess of such a condition.
- *Conversion Disorder* involves symptoms/deficits in voluntary motor or sensory functions, preceded by stressors or psychological conflicts, which are not the result of a general medical condition or substance use. Importantly, the symptoms are judged not to be intentionally produced.
- *Pain Disorder* involves pain in at least one part of the body judged to be caused by psychological factors and not due to a general medical condition, substance use, some other mental disorder, or intentionally produced.

- *Hypochondriasis* involves a preoccupation (greater than 6 months) with a perceived somatic disease due to a misinterpretation of bodily symptoms and despite appropriate medical reassurances and evaluations. This disorder is not better accounted for by a general medical condition, substance use, or some other mental disorder and does not rise to the level of a delusion.
- *Body Dysmorphic Disorder* involves a preoccupation with an imagined appearance defect, or an exaggeration of a slight defect, that is not better accounted for by another mental disorder (e.g., Anorexia Nervosa).

3.11.10 Factitious Disorder

Factitious Disorder involves the intentional feigning of physical or psychological symptoms in order to assume the "sick role." Importantly, no external reward is sought (e.g., economic gain, avoiding legal responsibilities), which differentiates this disorder from malingering.

3.11.11 Dissociative Disorders

Dissociative Disorders involve a disruption in normal integrated functions of consciousness, memory, identity, or perception. Onset of these disorders may be sudden or gradual; the duration may be transient or chronic; and they are not due to another mental disorder, substance, or general medical condition. The Dissociative Disorders include the following:

- *Dissociative Amnesia* is an inability to recall important (and usually traumatic) information that is beyond ordinary forgetfulness.
- *Dissociative Fugue* is sudden, unexpected travel away from home or work and an inability to recall one's past, including confusion about personal identity.
- *Dissociative Identity Disorder* (formerly Multiple Personality Disorder) is the presence of two or more distinct identities or personalities recurrently taking control of the person's behavior, along with an inability to recall important personal information.
- *Depersonalization Disorder.* encompasses feelings of detachment from one's mental processes or body (e.g., dreamlike state), without loss of contact with reality.

3.11.12 Sexual and Gender Identity Disorders

The various Sexual Disorders and Gender Identity Disorders are numerous so they are presented in clusters:

- *Sexual Dysfunctions* involve disturbances in the sexual response cycle or pain associated with intercourse. Examples include Male Erectile Disorder, Male or Female Orgasmic Disorder, Premature Ejaculation, and Vaginismus.
- *Paraphilias* involve intense sexually arousing fantasies, urges, or behaviors usually involving nonhuman objects, humiliation of one's partner, or children. Examples include Exhibitionism, Fetishism, Frotteurism, Pedophilia, Sexual Masochism, Sexual Sadism, and Voyeurism.

- *Gender Identity Disorder* involves a persistent cross-gender identification and discomfort with one's sex or sex-role.

3.11.13   Eating Disorders

Eating Disorders involve extreme disturbances in eating behaviors. (Childhood feeding disorders are presented in section 3.11.2.) Obesity is not considered a mental disorder unless it is caused by psychological reasons; in such cases it is V-coded (see section 3.11.17). There are two primary Eating Disorders:

- *Anorexia Nervosa* involves a refusal to maintain a normal body weight for age and height, usually defined as less than 85% of normal expected weight. Furthermore, clients display an intense fear of gaining weight, disturbance in body image, and (in postmenarchal females) the absence of at least three consecutive menstrual cycles.
- *Bulimia Nervosa* involves recurrent binge eating episodes in which an individual ingests a significantly large amount of food over a 2-hour or shorter time period, perceives a lack of control to stop eating during this period, then engages in some compensatory action to prevent weight gain (e.g., laxatives, vomiting, excessive exercise). The binging-compensation cycle occurs at least three times per week for at least 3 months, and clients experience a disturbed body image.

3.11.14   Sleep Disorders

Sleep Disorders are ordinarily categorized as primary or due to another mental disorder or a general medical condition. Primary Sleep Disorders are comprised of Dyssomnias and Parasomnias.

- *Dyssomnias* are characterized by excessive sleepiness or difficulties initiating or maintaining sleep (amount, quality, or timing of sleep). Dyssomnias include Primary Insomnias, Primary Hypersomnia, Narcolepsy, Breathing-Related Sleep Disorder, and Circadian Rhythm Sleep Disorder.
- *Parasomnias* are characterized by abnormal behaviors (activation of physiological systems) associated with sleep, stages of sleep, or the sleep-wake transition. Parasomnias include Nightmare Disorder, Sleep Terror Disorder, and Sleepwalking Disorder.

Sleep Disorders can also be caused by another mental disorder or a general medical condition or substance use, and they should be coded accordingly.

3.11.15   Impulse-Control Disorders Not Elsewhere Classified

Although many mental disorders recognize an impulsive component, they are frequently better classified in another category of the *DSM* (e.g., AD/HD, Paraphilias, Substance-Related Disorders). The Impulse Disorders included in this section are not better classified elsewhere (so they have been included in this separate section); cause significant impairment in a major area of functioning; and are not better accounted for by another mental disorder, general medical condition, or substance use.

- ***Intermittent Explosive Disorder.***   Distinct episodes of aggressive impulses, significantly disproportional to the social context, resulting in serious assault or destruction of property.
- ***Kleptomania.***   Theft of objects not needed for personal use or monetary value, accompanied by feelings of tension preceding the theft, and pleasure or satisfaction at the time the theft is committed. Importantly, the stealing is not an expression of anger.
- ***Pyromania.***   Intentional fire setting accompanied by a fixation or fascination with fire, accompanied by feelings of tension preceding the fire setting and pleasure or satisfaction at the time the fire is set. Importantly, the fires are not set for personal or political gain.
- ***Pathological Gambling.***   Recurrent maladaptive gambling behaviors, not occurring during a Manic Episode. Symptoms include preoccupation with gambling, escalation of amount of money to achieve excitement, attempts made to cut back, and use as a way to escape problems.
- ***Trichotillomania.***   Repeated hair pulling resulting in noticeable hair loss, accompanied by feelings of tension preceding the hair pulling and pleasure or satisfaction at the time the hair is pulled.

3.11.16   Adjustment Disorders

Adjustment Disorders involve psychological responses to identifiable stressors. Symptoms must begin within 3 months after the stressful event, and a more significant impairment than would ordinarily be expected must result. Ordinarily, adjustment to the stressor is expected within 6 months after the precipitating event, unless the stressor is chronic. Adjustment Disorders are coded according to subtype:

- With Depressed Mood (tearfulness, feelings of hopelessness)
- With Anxiety (nervousness, worry)
- With Mixed Anxiety and Depressed Mood
- With Disturbance of Conduct (violation of rules and rights of others)
- With Mixed Disturbance of Emotions and Conduct
- Unspecified

3.11.17   Personality Disorders

Personality Disorders are enduring patterns of behavior and internalized experiences that are significantly different from societal/cultural expectations. Personality Disorders are pervasive across settings, are stable over time, have onset in adolescence or adulthood, and cause significant impairment. Personality Disorders are presented in the *DSM-IV-TR* in three clusters.

Cluster A Personality Disorders
- ***Paranoid Personality Disorder.***   Pattern of suspicion and distrust resulting in attributions of malevolence to the motives of others.

- *Schizoid Personality Disorder.* Pattern of social detachment and restricted expression of emotions.
- *Schizotypal Personality Disorder.* Pattern of relational discomfort, perceptual distortion, and behavioral eccentricities.

Cluster B Personality Disorders

- *Antisocial Personality Disorder.* Pattern of violations and disregard of others' rights.
- *Borderline Personality Disorder.* Pattern of unstable relationships, self-image, and affect, and impulsive behaviors.
- *Histrionic Personality Disorder.* Pattern of excessive attention seeking and emotional reactivity.
- *Narcissistic Personality Disorder.* Pattern of grandiose behaviors, need for admiration, and reduced empathy for others.

Cluster C Personality Disorders

- *Avoidant Personality Disorder.* Pattern of social avoidance, inadequacy, oversensitivity to negative evaluations.
- *Dependent Personality Disorder.* Pattern of submissiveness and an excessive need to be cared for.
- *Obsessive-Compulsive Personality Disorder.* Pattern of perfectionism, control, and orderliness.

3.11.18 Other Conditions That May Be a Focus of Clinical Attention

Many other psychological conditions require attention but do not rise to the level of a diagnosable mental disorder. These disorders are presented here in clusters and are all coded on Axis I, except for Borderline Intellectual Functioning.

- *Psychological Factors Affecting Medical Condition.* Presence of one or more behavioral or psychological factors that adversely affects a patient's general medical condition (e.g., Mental Disorder Affecting Medical Condition, Stress-Related Physiological Response Affecting Medical Condition).
- *Medication-Induced Movement Disorders.* Movement disorders related to the use of some medications to treat a general medical condition or mental disorder (e.g., Neuroleptic-Induced Parkinsonism, Medication-Induced Postural Tremor).
- *Relational Problems.* Patterns or interaction that cause significant impairment to an individual or relational unit (e.g., couple, family)(e.g., Parent-Child Relational Problem, Partner Relational Problem, Sibling Relational Problem).
- *Problems Related to Abuse or Neglect.* Involves severe mistreatment (i.e., physical abuse, sexual abuse, neglect) of one individual by another.
- *Additional Conditions That May Be a Focus of Clinical Attention.* A catchall category (e.g., Noncompliance with Treatment, Malingering, Academic Problem, Bereavement).

3.11.19 Practice Multiple-Choice Items: Diagnosis of Mental Disorders

1. General medical conditions are noted on which *DSM-IV-TR* axis?
   a. Axis V
   b. Axis IV
   c. Axis III
   d. Axis II

2. All of the following would be listed under Axis I of the *DSM-IV-TR* EXCEPT
   a. Posttraumatic Stress Disorder.
   b. Antisocial Personality Disorder.
   c. Dementia.
   d. Oppositional Defiant Disorder.

3. Individuals with Conduct Disorder cannot simultaneously be diagnosed with
   a. Oppositional Defiant Disorder.
   b. Attention-Deficit/Hyperactivity Disorder.
   c. Separation Anxiety Disorder.
   d. Learning Disorder.

4. A person who experiences a depressed mood more often than not for at least 2 years would likely be diagnosed with
   a. Major Depressive Disorder.
   b. Cyclothymic Disorder.
   c. Bipolar I Disorder.
   d. Dysthymic Disorder.

5. _____ has been translated to mean "fear of the marketplace."
   a. Agoraphobia
   b. Factitious Disorder
   c. Paraphilia
   d. Hypochondriasis

Answer Key: 1. c; 2. b; 3. a; 4. d; 5. a.

3.12 KEY POINTS FROM CHAPTER 3: HUMAN GROWTH AND DEVELOPMENT

- Human development relies on the interplay between genetic and environmental conditions.
- Human development is frequently conceptualized based on socially constructed developmental stages that span from conception until death.
- The aging process involves biological aging, psychological aging, and social aging.
- Autosomal diseases are carried on any chromosome except the sex chromosome; X-linked diseases are transmitted by mothers to sons on the X chromosome.
- Classical conditioning is achieved by pairing a neutral stimulus with an unconditioned stimulus.
- Operant conditioning posits that people learn to behave in certain ways based on whether their actions are reinforced or punished.

- Social learning theory asserts that people learn to behave based on observing, imitating, and modeling other people.
- Assimilation occurs when people interpret new information based on their current cognitive framework; accommodation occurs when people restructure their cognitive framework to make sense of new information.
- People possess three different types of memory: sensory memory, short-term memory, and long-term memory.
- People must rehearse or encode information to transfer it from their short-term memory to long-term memory.
- Freud's psychosexual theory suggests that personality development depends on the interchange between the id, ego, and superego. Erikson's psychosocial theory contends that healthy personality development depends on the successful resolution of crises at various stages of the life cycle.
- There are four types of identity: identity achievement, identity moratorium, identity foreclosure, and identity diffusion. Identities can also be classified as achieved or ascribed, deviant or normative.
- Caregivers, school personnel, peers, and the media influence gender role development.
- Kohlberg's theory asserts that moral development is dependent on cognitive development.
- Families progress through a series of developmental stages just as each individual passes through developmental stages.
- Parenting styles (i.e., authoritarian, authoritative, permissive, uninvolved) influence the personal, social, cognitive, and moral development of children.
- Conflictual, intact families are more harmful to children's psychosocial development than low conflict single-parent families.
- There are five types of crises: developmental, environmental, existential, situational, and psychiatric.
- The *Diagnostic and Statistical Manual of Mental Disorders* (*DSM*) uses a multiaxial system and is the most commonly used manual for diagnosing mental disorders.

CHAPTER 4

Lifestyle and Career Development

Career development is a process that refers to how individuals manage their careers throughout their lifetime. Engaging in the career development process can increase current job performance and satisfaction and assist individuals in taking advantage of future vocational opportunities. As career plays a critical role in people's lives and often intersects personal issues, career development is recognized as a core area of counselor preparation. Specifically this chapter includes important historical events in career development, key terms and people in career development, career theories and related assessments, labor force and occupational information, and career development program planning.

Over the past several years, administrations of the National Counselor Examination (NCE) have included 20 (of the 160 total, or 12.5% of the) scored items (plus some trial items that do not count) designed to measure career development (rank = 3.5 of 8; an average number of items from the eight domains). The average item difficulty index was .68 (rank = 7 of 8; 2nd most challenging domain of item content), meaning that the average item in this domain was correctly answered by 68% of test-takers.

Over the past several years, administrations of the Counselor Preparation Comprehensive Exam (CPCE) have included 17 scored items designed to measure career development, plus several trial items that do not count in your score. The average item difficulty index was .53, meaning that the average item in this domain was correctly answered by only 53% of test-takers, making this set of items by far the most challenging on the examination.

The Council for Accreditation of Counseling and Related Educational Programs (CACREP, 2009, p. 11) defined standards for Career Development as

studies that provide an understanding of career development and related life factors, including all of the following:

a. career development theories and decision-making models;
b. career, avocational, educational, occupational and labor market information resources, and career information systems;
c. career development program planning, organization, implementation, administration, and evaluation;
d. interrelationships among and between work, family, and other life roles and factors, including the role of multicultural issues in career development;
e. career and educational planning, placement, follow-up, and evaluation;
f. assessment instruments and techniques relevant to career planning and decision making; and
g. career counseling processes, techniques, and resources, including those applicable to specific populations in a global economy.

In this chapter we discuss key introductory information and concepts in career development, trait and type career theories, lifespan and developmental career theories, special focus career theories, career assessment, labor market and sources of occupational information, career counseling and intervention, and career development program planning, implementation, and evaluation.

4.1 INTRODUCTION TO CAREER DEVELOPMENT

In this first section of Chapter 4, we discuss: (a) how key historical events such as the Industrial Revolution, the development of professional organizations, and 20th-century developments shaped the field of career counseling; (b) the key people in career development and their individual contributions to the field; (c) the ethical guidelines of the National Career Development Association (NCDA) for career professionals and the ethical use of the Internet in career services; and (d) the federal and state laws and regulations that affect the field of career development.

4.1.1 Key Historical Events in Career Development

Several clusters of key historical events influencing the field of career development include the Industrial Revolution, the rise of professional organizations, and legislative initiatives.

4.1.1.1 INDUSTRIAL REVOLUTION The U.S. career-guidance movement was initiated in the late 1800s with the start of the Industrial Revolution. The **Industrial Revolution** transformed America's agriculturally based economy into an industrial and manufacturing economy. This transformation brought both increased standards of living and job opportunities. However, it created urban slums, deplorable working conditions, the exploitation of child labor, and labor unrest and violence. Efforts to ameliorate these alarming social conditions led to the establishment of the Boston Vocational Bureau in 1908 by Frank Parsons (see section 4.1.2 for more information). The bureau worked to develop a system of vocational guidance in Boston public schools that could offer vocational assistance to youth needing to make a career choice. The work of the bureau highlighted the need for vocational guidance in the schools, and by 1918 more than 900 vocational guidance programs were instituted in high schools around the nation.

4.1.1.2 CAREER DEVELOPMENT PROFESSIONAL ORGANIZATIONS The career-guidance movement was further facilitated by the development of professional organizations that strove to promote nationwide career assistance and guidance. In 1913, the **National Vocational Guidance Association (NVGA)** was founded. The NVGA was the first career-guidance organization, and it worked to legitimize and increase the number of guidance counselors by offering credentialing. In 1951, NVGA was one of the founding divisions of the **American Personnel and Guidance Association (APGA)**, which today is known as the **American Counseling Association (ACA).**

- In 1985, the NVGA changed its name to the NCDA, a division of ACA. NCDA's mission is to promote individuals' career development throughout the lifespan. NCDA offers professional development activities, publications, research, public information, professional standards, and advocacy to the public and professionals who deliver career services.

4.1.1.3 CAREER DEVELOPMENT LEGISLATIVE INITIATIVES IN THE 20TH CENTURY During the 20th century, the career-guidance movement was shaped by several legal and political events. In 1913, the U.S. Department of Labor was established to promote the welfare of American workers, job seekers, and retirees by administering federal labor laws concerning worker safety, wages, working conditions, employment discrimination, and unemployment benefits.

- The Smith-Hughes National Vocational Education Act of 1917 promoted vocational education through the provision of federal funds and called for the isolation of vocational education from the rest of the academic curriculum.
- In 1939, the U.S. Employment Service was created through the Wagner-Peyser Act of 1933. The U.S. Employment Service offers job search and placement assistance to job seekers and recruitment services to employers with job openings. In 1998 the Wagner-Peyser Act was amended to include the U.S. Employment Service under the **One-Stop delivery system**, which provides a variety of labor exchange services under one roof in easy-to-find locations.
- The nation experienced a severe shortage in job opportunities during the Great Depression of the 1930s and created the need to provide vocational assistance to dislocated workers. In response to this need, D. G. Patterson developed special aptitude tests and personality inventories to assist workers in gaining employment. Also, Roosevelt's New Deal, a series of economic programs enacted between 1933 and 1936, led to the creation of millions of jobs through public works projects.
- With involvement of the United States in World War II came the need to accurately and efficiently assess military recruits for armed forces occupations. As a result, formal inventories and tests were developed to evaluate individual characteristics, such as intelligence and aptitude. These assessments provided standardized assessment materials to the field of career guidance.
- The last half of the 20th century saw the introduction of career development theories (see section 4.3 for more information on career development theories) and increased federal and state government support.
  - In 1958, the **National Defense Education Act (NDEA) of 1958** was passed in response to the Soviet Union's launching of *Sputnik*. In regard to career counseling, the NDEA sought to expand K–12 counselor education programs by offering reimbursement to programs that offered counselor training institutes and stipends to graduate students. The government's initiative for increasing the number of trained counselors in secondary schools was to raise the number of students enrolled in higher education that were pursuing math and science careers.
  - During the 1960s and 1970s the U.S. Department of Education became instrumental in the development of career education programs. The department mandated

all public schools to include career education programs in their curricula. Career education programs were further expanded by the **Vocational Education Act of 1963** to include career services for elementary schools, technical institutions, and public community colleges.

- In the 1980s the government sought to address the needs of disadvantaged students, technical education programs, and unemployed workers through the **Job Training Partnership Act (JTPA) of 1982** and the **Carl D. Perkins Vocational and Technical Education Act of 1984**.

- In the nineties, career development was influenced by the School-to-Work Act and the Americans with Disabilities Act. The **School-to-Work Act of 1994** provides all students with equal opportunities to participate in programs that combine academic and occupational education, combine school-based learning with work-based learning, and prepare students for postsecondary education. The **Americans with Disabilities Act (ADA) of 1990** provides protection against employment discrimination (see section 4.1.4 for more information on the ADA).

4.1.2 Key People in Career Development

A number of individuals served key roles in the rise of career and vocational development in the field of counseling.

- **George A. Merrill** was a pioneer and forerunner in career guidance. He developed a curriculum that combined academic instruction with technical and vocational training.

- **Frank Parsons** was considered the "father" of career guidance and the counseling profession. He established the Boston Vocational Bureau, where he developed the Trait and Factor approach (see section 4.3 for more information) to vocational guidance. This approach, which assisted individuals in choosing a career, involved a three-step framework:
  - Gaining self-understanding (e.g., your abilities, attitudes, interests, limitations)
  - Understanding the world of work (e.g., requirements for success, compensation, opportunities in different lines of work)
  - True reasoning (the ability to combine an understanding of self with knowledge about the world of work to make a career decision)

- Parsons authored 14 books during his lifetime; the most well-known was *Choosing a Vocation* (Parsons, 1909).

- **Edmund Williamson** was best known for his contribution to the **Minnesota point of view**, a career guidance theory that was derived from the work of Frank Parsons. Williamson believed that counselors should share their wisdom with clients to help them reach a career decision. Consequently, the Minnesota point of view is considered a directive counseling approach. Williamson (1939) outlined five steps for counselors to follow:
  - Assessing the problem and obtaining/reviewing client records and testing results

- Organizing and synthesizing the client information gathered to fully understand the problem
- Interpreting the problem
- Providing counseling to assist the client in reaching a solution
- Following up with the client after a solution is reached

- **Donald Super** developed the lifespan, life-space career theory, a developmental approach to career counseling (see section 4.3 for more information about the lifespan, life-space career theory). Super's theory involved five life stages and numerous developmental career tasks. He also proposed a career rainbow that represented the many roles an individual has throughout life. Super also developed several career inventories: work values inventory, career development inventory, and adult career concerns inventory.

- **John Crites** was known as one of the leading vocational psychologists of the 20th century. He was a leading researcher in the area of career maturity and developed the career maturity inventory (see section 4.6 for more information). He also developed the first objective taxonomy for classifying career decision-making problems and endorsed comprehensive career counseling, which emphasizes that all aspects of life functioning are interrelated (Crites, 1981).

- **John Holland** was known for developing the theory of vocational choice, which involves matching persons to work environments (see section 4.3 for more information on the theory of vocational choice). Holland proposed six personality and work environment types: realistic, investigative, artistic, social, enterprising, and conventional. This typology is used in the Strong Interest Inventory (SII) and the Armed Services Vocational Aptitude Battery (ASVAB). Holland is best known for developing the Self-Directed Search, a self-administered and self-scored career inventory (see section 4.4 for more information).

- **John Krumboltz** developed the social learning theory of career counseling. Krumboltz espoused that individuals' learned experiences lead them to develop specific career beliefs. These beliefs then influence career decision making. Krumboltz has published over 90 articles on career beliefs and their influence on career choice.

- **Joanne Harris-Bowlsbey** developed computerized vocational systems such as CVIS, DISCOVER, and VISIONS (see section 7.2.2 for more information about computerized vocational systems). Harris-Bowlsbey is also known for her work in training career development facilitators internationally and for writing print-based career curriculum for high school and college-age students.

4.1.3 Ethical Issues in Career Development

This section provides information on several important ethical issues in career development and counseling, including the applicable ethical codes of the ACA, National Board for Certified Counselors (NBCC), and NCDA, differentiation between the types of services usually offered, and use of the Internet when providing career counseling services.

4.1.3.1 ETHICAL CODES When faced with an ethical dilemma, professional career counselors can turn to the American Counseling Association's (ACA) *Code of Ethics* or the National Board for Certified Counselors' (NBCC) *Code of Ethics* (see Chapter 1). In addition to ACA and NBCC, the NCDA provides ethical guidelines for career practitioners. The NCDA's *Code of Ethics* (2007) was developed specifically for career counseling professionals. It is adapted from ACA's 2005 *Code of Ethics*, so considerable overlap between the two codes exists. Both codes address client welfare, boundaries of the counseling relationship, confidentiality, professional responsibilities, appropriate use of assessment tools, counselor education and supervision, and research. The NCDA's ethical guidelines do differ from the ACA's codes in that they address differences between career services provided and the use of technology in career counseling.

4.1.3.2 DIFFERENTIATION BETWEEN TYPES OF SERVICES Career planning services are distinct from career counseling services; career planning services involve the active provision of information (i.e., resume review, job search assistance, administering career assessments) to assist a client with a specific need, whereas career counseling services involve the establishment of a counseling relationship to assist clients with career and personal developmental concerns.

- Whether providing career planning or career counseling services, career professionals should offer only the services that are within the boundaries of their professional competence and qualifications.

4.1.3.3 USE OF THE INTERNET IN THE PROVISION OF CAREER SERVICES

Benefits and Limitations

- Career professionals inform clients of the benefits and limitations associated with using career technology.
- Career professionals assess the client's intellectual, emotional, and physical ability to benefit from the use of career technology.
- Career technology is defined as, but not limited to, computer hardware and software, telephones, the Internet, online assessment instruments, and other communication devices.

Technology Applications

- Technology can be used in four ways to provide career services: (a) provide career information (e.g., occupations, the world of work, career planning, job searching), (b) vocational assessments, (c) integrative career services, and (d) databases of job openings.
- When it is determined that the use of career technology will not benefit the client, the career professional must provide appropriate alternatives.
- When providing career technology assistance to clients, the career professional ensures reasonable access to computer applications.

- Career professionals discuss with clients their credentials, fees, legal rights, and verification of identity as related to the use of career technology.
- Career professionals inform clients of the issues and limitations related to maintaining confidentiality when using career technology.

Qualifications of the Developer or Provider

- All career technology services should be developed with content input from career professionals. In addition, the qualifications and credentials of these developers should be readily available.

Access and Understanding of Environment

- Career professionals should work to ensure that lack of financial resources is not a barrier to accessing online career resources.

Content of Career Services on the Internet

- The content of a Web site of other online career services should be appropriate to client needs.
- Career professionals regularly maintain career Web sites.

Ongoing Client Support

- Career professionals regularly monitor client progress when providing career technology services.

Internet Job Posting and Searching

- Online job postings should represent valid openings and appropriate employer contact information.

Unacceptable Behaviors on the Internet

- Career professionals do not use a false e-mail identity when corresponding with clients and other professionals.
- Career professionals do not provide services to a client who refuses to self-identify.
- Career professionals do not use technology (e.g., chat rooms, mass e-mails, blogs, Web communities) to advertise and offer career services when these services have not been solicited.

4.1.4 Key Legal Issues in Career Development

When providing career services, professional counselors must be attentive to all federal and state laws and regulations that impact the field of career development. The following is a summary of important public laws concerning career development practices.

- *Fair Labor Standards Act (FLSA) of 1938.* Established a national minimum wage, provided minimum standards for overtime entitlement, and prohibited the employment of minors. Today, FLSA remains the primary legislation for enforcing and protecting the rights and wages of employees.
- *Occupational Safety and Health Act of 1970.* Ensured safe and healthful working conditions for employees through the creation of the Occupational Safety and Health Administration (OSHA). OSHA works to prevent work-related injuries, illnesses, and death by issuing and enforcing workplace safety and health standards.

- *Section 504 of the Rehabilitation Act of 1973.* Prohibits discrimination against an individual with a disability in programs sponsored by federal agencies or receiving federal financial assistance, in federal employment and federal contracting employment.
- *Americans with Disabilities Act (ADA) of 1990.* Prohibits employers from discriminating against a qualified individual who has a mental or physical disability. Discrimination may include denying employment opportunities to qualified workers; failing to advance, demoting, or firing employees because of a disability; and not providing reasonable accommodations for employees with disabilities.
- *Family and Medical Leave Act of 1993.* Allows employees to take up to 12 weeks of unpaid leave when an employee is unable to perform his or her job, to care for a sick family member, or to provide care to a child (including birth, adoption, or foster care). The act ensures that employees will not be terminated or forced into a lower position on returning from the unpaid leave.
- *Individual with Disabilities Education Improvement Act (IDEA) of 2004.* Ensures that children with disabilities receive special education and related services that are designed to meet their individual needs and prepare them for further education, employment, and independent living. It also mandates that individuals with disabilities receive transition services to facilitate their move from school to employment or further education.

4.1.5 Practice Multiple-Choice Items: Introduction to Career Development

1. _____ is considered the forerunner of career guidance.
   a. Frank Parsons
   b. George Merrill
   c. Donald Super
   d. Mark Savickas

2. The _____ is a division of ACA that strives to promote individuals' career development throughout the lifespan.
   a. National Vocational Guidance Association (NVGA)
   b. American Personnel and Guidance Association (APGA)
   c. National Career Development Association (NCDA)
   d. National Employment Counseling Association (NECA)

3. According to the NCDA *Code of Ethics*, which of the following behaviors is considered unacceptable when using the Internet?
   a. Providing services to clients who refuse to self-identify
   b. Referring a client to an online job posting site that lists valid openings and appropriate employer contact information
   c. Informing clients of the issues and limitations related to maintaining confidentiality when using career technology
   d. None of the above

4. The _____ allows employees to take up to 12 weeks of unpaid leave when they are unable to perform their job, need to care for a sick family member, or need to provide care to a child.
   a. Fair Labor Standards Act (FLSA) of 1938
   b. Occupational Safety and Health Act of 1970
   c. Section 504 of the Rehabilitation Act of 1973
   d. Family and Medical Leave Act of 1993

5. _____ developed computerized vocational systems such as CVIS, DISCOVER, and VISIONS.
   a. John Holland
   b. Frank Parsons
   c. John Krumboltz
   d. Joanne Harris-Bowlsbey

Answer Key: 1. b; 2. c; 3. a; 4. d; 5. d.

4.2 KEY CONCEPTS IN CAREER DEVELOPMENT

How would you explain the difference between a job, an occupation, and a career to your client? As with most areas of counseling, professional counselors must be aware of several concepts and terms used in career development to provide effective services. This section of Chapter 4 provides an overview of key career development concepts widely used in the field but not necessarily related to one specific career development theory.

4.2.1 Career

The term *career* is often broadly defined, encompassing all the roles people play over their lifetime (e.g., student, parent, employee, retiree; see section 4.2.2 for more information on roles). However, the NCDA's definition of career is more narrowly defined to include only a person's work and leisure roles. Regardless of the definition's scope, it is imperative that professional counselors understand that an individual's career encompasses more than that person's occupation.

- It is also important that professional counselors be able to differentiate between the terms *job*, *occupation*, and *career*.
  - **Job** refers to positions that require a specific skill set and are within an organization or company.
  - **Occupation** is defined as the primary activity that engages one's time. An occupation includes similar jobs found in many organizations. Occupations exist regardless of whether or not individuals are employed in them.
  - **Career** refers to the lifetime pursuits of an individual, whereas *jobs* and *occupations* center more on organizational needs and the industry.
- The terms *work* and *leisure* are commonly used in career development. **Work** refers to activities that serve as one's regular source of livelihood and is commonly associated with a job position. **Leisure**, on the other hand, refers to engaging in activities as a means of passing time. Leisure activities are those that a person does for fun (i.e., hobbies). Leisure is viewed as an important part of one's lifetime career and is incorporated into many career and vocational theories (see section 4.3 for more information on career and vocational theory).

- **Career choice** involves decisions individuals make at any point in their career about which work and leisure activities to pursue. At times, people may struggle to make a career decision (e.g., what major to pursue, whether to quit work and be a stay-at-home parent). As a result, several career theories and vocational assessments specifically address career choice and decision making.

4.2.2 Roles

Roles are an important concept in understanding career development. The term **role** broadly refers to a set of interconnected behaviors, rights, and obligations that are associated with a particular social situation. Individuals play a number of different roles throughout their lifetime (e.g., student, parent, employee, spouse, friend). Because life demands that we play multiple roles in our day-to-day life, individuals are vulnerable to role overload, role conflict, and role spillover.

- *Role overload* occurs when expectations associated with multiple roles exceed an individual's time and energy and ability to perform the role adequately.
- *Role conflict* involves how the demands and expectations of an individual's multiple roles conflict with each other. Role conflict often occurs when one takes on two different and incompatible roles at the same time (e.g., work and family).
- *Role spillover* is the carryover of one role's demands and expectations into another role. A common example of role spillover is to continue to worry over work issues while you are at home. Role spillover can have negative and positive consequences.

4.2.3 Career Salience

Career salience refers to the significance an individual places on the role of career in relationship to other life roles. Career salience involves three factors:

- Participation: spending time and energy in a work role
- Commitment: an emotional attachment to the work role
- Value expectation: the satisfaction gained from the vocational decisions and actions one makes throughout the course of one's lifespan

4.2.4 Work Values

Values can be defined as beliefs that guide an individual's behavior and emotional responses (Brown, 2002). Three major types of values exist:

- *Lifestyle values* refer to the beliefs that guide an individual's behavior outside of work (e.g., family, leisure).
- *Cultural values* refer to cultural beliefs and norms that shape the behaviors of an individual. These values often involve beliefs regarding human nature, time orientation, rules of emotional expression, and the value of community/social relationships.
- *Work values* reflect needs that a work environment must reinforce to ensure an individual's work satisfaction and

success. In other words, to attain job satisfaction and success people will pursue occupations and jobs that are congruent with their work values. There are two types of work values:

- *Intrinsic values* relate to the rewards received, or values satisfied, from performing the work itself (e.g., help others, express creativity, better society). To truly feel satisfied with their work, most individuals must find intrinsic value in the job.
- *Extrinsic values,* on the other hand, refer to the rewards received, or values satisfied, as a result of completing the work (e.g., salary, job security, social status). Importantly, extrinsic rewards do not necessarily establish intrinsic motivation.
- Brown (2002) espouses that cultural and work values are the primary values that affect an individual's occupational decision.

4.2.5 Career Interests

Career interests are defined as preferences for particular life activities and are thought to play a key role in career decision making and choice. Three types of career interests are typically distinguished:

- *Expressed interests* are those interests that are verbally reported. When a college student states, "I would like to work as a financial analyst," he or she is providing an example of an expressed interest. A career counselor can assess expressed interests by asking a client what his or her career interests are or administering an interest inventory (see section 4.6.1 for more information on interest inventories).
- *Manifest interests* refer to the activities in which people engage. For example, an individual who enjoys music may manifest this interest by playing piano. Manifest interests can be assessed through observation (which assumes that individuals engage in activities they find interesting) or client self-report methods.
- *Tested interests* are reflected in an individual's knowledge of a specific topic and measured by objective tests. For example, an individual who has an interest in auto mechanics might score high on the Technical Test Battery (TTB2), a mechanical aptitude test. Measuring tested interests rests on the assumption that people are motivated to gain knowledge and information on activities in which they take an interest.

4.2.6 Career Adaptability

In today's postindustrial economy, the days of stable and reliable employment have been replaced by a constantly changing and unpredictable job market. This churning of the job market has led to an increased number of job vacancies, unannounced and unexpected job layoffs, increased part-time and temporary employment, and a highly competitive work environment. As a result, it is increasingly important that individuals demonstrate the ability to adjust and adapt to changing conditions.

- Donald Super (1953) was the first to consider how adult workers managed their careers amid an unstable job market. In doing so, he introduced the term *career adaptability*. **Career adaptability** refers to an individual's readiness and available resources for coping with changing work and employment conditions. It involves the ability to cope with predictable career development tasks (e.g., preparing and locating a job) and a future orientation that permits individuals to continually capitalize on their skills and abilities. Savickas (2005) describes four global dimensions that characterize adaptable individuals from those floundering in their careers:
  - Concern for future work life
  - Control over future career
  - Curiosity for exploring career possibilities
  - Confidence to pursue career goals

4.2.7 Career Adjustment

Career adjustment is concerned with the relationships of workers and their environments. It refers to the ability to adapt or adjust to one's work environment. Three career theories/theorists have shaped our current understanding of career adjustment:

- The theory of work adjustment (TWA) proposes that individuals must be able to adjust their skills to perform the required job tasks and achieve job satisfaction (see section 4.3 for more information of work adjustment theory).
- John Crites (1981) found that employees who thrived in the workplace were able to adjust to their job tasks, develop sufficient workplace relationships, and consider future career goals.
- Donald Super (1953) proposed that career adjustment includes adapting to workplace changes, learning different skills, and acquiring an awareness of sources of workplace stress.

4.2.8 Job Satisfaction

The term **job satisfaction** describes how content individuals are with their jobs. Job satisfaction is said to result from a match between individuals' self-concept and the characteristics of their work environments. A number of factors influence job satisfaction: quality of work environment, relationship with co-workers and supervisor, degree of fulfillment obtained from work, pay and benefits, job mobility, and degree of employee autonomy. Low levels of job satisfaction have been linked to an increase in physical and psychological symptoms: anxiety, depression, burnout, and increased susceptibility to disease.

4.2.9 Self-Efficacy

Self-efficacy (also see Chapter 3) refers to the belief that one is capable of performing specific behaviors to attain a certain goal. A person's self-efficacy beliefs determine whether they will engage in a behavior and the amount of energy and persistence that will be expended (Bandura, 1986). In short, persons will be more likely to engage in a behavior or task if they believe they can succeed. Self-efficacy beliefs play a role in career performance and career decision making:

- In regard to career performance, persons with high self-efficacy tend to perform at higher levels than those with low self-efficacy.
- The term **career decision-making self-efficacy** has been used to describe the role self-efficacy plays in career decision making. Specifically, career decision-making self-efficacy refers to the degree to which individuals feel competent in their ability to make a career decision. Persons with high career decision-making self-efficacy will readily engage in career decision-making behaviors (e.g., exploration of the self and work environment), whereas those with low career decision-making self-efficacy may give up easily if they run into barriers or avoid engaging altogether in these behaviors.
- It is important to make the distinction that *self-efficacy beliefs may or may not correspond with actual abilities*. Individuals with low self-efficacy may underestimate their actual abilities.

4.2.10 Occupational Stress

Occupational stress is defined as the chronic physiological and psychological strain that results from ongoing job-related stressors. A number of harmful physical and emotional symptoms can result from occupational stress, including increased anxiety, irritability, anger, fatigue, difficulty concentrating, tearfulness, decreases in immune system functioning, hypertension, heart disease, stroke, kidney disease, increase in self-medicating behaviors (e.g., illicit substance use, increased consumption of alcohol, overeating) and an increase in risky behaviors.

- The experience of ongoing occupational stress can lead to a phenomenon known as burnout. *Burnout* (also see Chapter 3) is a type of work-related strain that results in emotional exhaustion, depersonalization, and reduced personal accomplishment (Maslach, 1982).
  - *Emotional exhaustion* is the first stage of burnout and involves the depletion of one's emotional resources.
  - *Depersonalization* occurs in response to emotional exhaustion and involves a detachment from the job and the development of cynicism and indifference.
  - *Reduced personal accomplishment* characterizes the last stage of burnout and involves a decrease in one's self-efficacy regarding one's ability to do the job. This final stage leads to failure to be successful in the job.
- Burnout, like occupational stress, has been linked to a mirage of mental (e.g., increased anxiety, anger, apathy guilt, hopelessness, depression), behavioral (e.g., decreased effectiveness and work performance, absenteeism, low productivity, workplace aggression, sabotage, theft, alcohol and illicit drug abuse), and physical symptoms (e.g., heart attacks, chronic fatigue, insomnia, nausea, dizziness, breathing difficulties, skin problems, muscle aches, headaches, gastrointestinal disturbances, infections, recurrent flu, back pain, poor concentration).

TABLE 4.1 Factors Influencing the Experience of Occupational Stress and Burnout.

Personality Factors

Type A personality characteristics (e.g., perfectionist, compulsive, competitive)

- Neuroticism: the tendency to experience negative emotional states such as anxiety, anger, guilt
- Orientation to achievement
- Low self-esteem
- External locus of control

Organizational Factors

- Work overload
- Lack of employee autonomy
- Insufficient reward
- Absence of fairness
- Conflicting employee and organizational values
- Poor communication
- Lack of clarity regarding one's role in the organization

- Occupational stress can also adversely affect organizations. Specifically, occupational stress is associated with low productivity, reduced organizational commitment, and increased absenteeism (Wright, 2004). Therefore, organizations may see a decline in organizational efficiency, high rates of staff turnover, and a drop in the quality of their services.
- Occupational stress and burnout are thought to be mediated by a combination of individual (Grosch & Olson, 1994) and organizational factors (Maslach & Leiter, 1997). Table 4.1 lists the factors that are thought to increase the experience of occupational stress and burnout.

4.2.11 Practice Multiple-Choice Items: Key Concepts in Career Development

1. _____ refers to the significance an individual places on the role of career in relationship to other life roles.
   a. Career salience
   b. Role spillover
   c. Career adaptability
   d. Career adjustment

2. Expressed interests refer to
   a. the activities in which people engage.
   b. interests that are verbally reported.
   c. an individual's knowledge of a specific topic and measured by objective tests.
   d. activities individuals hurry to complete.

3. Low levels of job satisfaction have been linked to
   a. higher levels of anxiety and depression.
   b. burnout.
   c. increased susceptibility to disease.
   d. All of the above.

4. Which of the following is NOT true regarding self-efficacy?
   a. People will be more likely to engage in a work behavior or task if they believe they can succeed.
   b. Persons with high self-efficacy tend to perform at higher levels than those with low self-efficacy.
   c. Individuals with low self-efficacy may overestimate their actual abilities.
   d. Persons with low self-efficacy may avoid making career decisions.

5. Salary, benefits, and job security are three examples of
   a. lifestyle values.
   b. extrinsic work values.
   c. cultural values.
   d. intrinsic work values.

Answer Key: 1. a; 2. b; 3. d; 4. c; 5. b.

4.3 TRAIT AND TYPE CAREER THEORIES

Trait and type career theories, sometimes referred to as person-environment fit theories, were the first career development theories to emerge. These theories stem from Frank Parsons' work in vocational guidance. In his book *Choosing a Vocation*, Parsons (1909) proposed that individuals must (a) have a clear understanding of their attitudes, abilities, interests, and resources, (b) knowledge concerning job requirements, conditions of success, compensation, and opportunity, and (c) true reasoning to understand the relationship between (a) and (b).

- Generally speaking, trait and type theories adhere to Parsons' ideas by assessing the traits or characteristics of individuals in order to "match" them with an occupation that has similar characteristics. This section describes theories falling under the trait and type classification: trait and factor theory, theory of work adjustment, Holland's theory of types, and Myers-Briggs type theory.

4.3.1 Trait and Factor Theory

Trait and factor theory has been heavily influenced by the work of both Frank Parsons and Edmund G. Williamson. This theory is rooted in three basic assumptions: (a) every person has a unique set of traits; (b) every occupation requires a person to have a specific set of traits to be successful in that occupation; and (c) choice of an occupation involves matching the traits of a person with those required of an occupation. Consequently, an individual must gain self-understanding, acquire knowledge about the world of work, and integrate this information (i.e., self-understanding and world of work) in order to choose an occupation in which he or she will be successful and derive satisfaction.

4.3.1.1 STEP 1: GAINING SELF-UNDERSTANDING Self-understanding is derived from assessing five basic individual traits and factors:

- *Aptitude* refers to an individual's innate abilities (e.g., mathematical abilities, artistic abilities). In career counseling, aptitudes are measured through the use of aptitude tests, which assess an individual's capability to learn and potential for future occupational success. Commonly used aptitude tests in trait and factor counseling include the Differential Aptitude Test (DAT), U.S. Employment Services General Aptitude Test Battery (GATB), and the Armed Services Vocational Aptitude Battery (ASVAB). These tests measure various aptitudes: verbal, numerical, clerical, mechanical reasoning, spelling, spatial, hand-eye coordination, and abstract reasoning (see Chapter 7 for more information regarding aptitude testing).

- *Interests* refer to the activities and tasks people enjoy doing. Vocational interests are usually assessed through the administration of interest inventories such as the Kuder Career Search (KCS), Strong Interest Inventory (SII), Basic Interest Scales, and the California Occupational Preference Survey (COPS). (See section 4.6.1 for more information on interest inventories.)

- *Values* are the ideals and beliefs that shape a person's behavior and emotions and define what is important to that individual. Trait and factor theory is concerned with both general values (e.g., political, social, economic, religious) and work-related values (e.g., prestige, risk, altruism, achievement). Although the assessment of values can play a vital role in career decision making, it is a difficult and elusive concept to measure. Consequently, very few reliable and valid value inventories exist; instead, career counselors often use informal assessment measures (e.g., checklists, interviews, guided imagery) to assess a client's values (see section 4.6.3 for more information on value inventories).

- *Personality* involves aspects of an individual's character (i.e., behaviors, thoughts, and feelings) that remain stable throughout his or her lifetime. Trait and factor theory is primarily concerned with normal personality characteristics and uses personality inventories that assess nonpathological traits (e.g., independence, flexibility, sociability, tolerance). Two commonly used personality inventories include the California Psychological Inventory (CPI) and the Sixteen Personality Factors Questionnaire (16PF).

- *Achievement* is a wide range of activities that individuals participate in and accomplish throughout their lifetime. Trait and factor theory recognizes three types of achievement: academic (e.g., high grades, awards), work (e.g., above average employee evaluations, promotions), and tests for certification or entry into the workforce (e.g., NCE, CPCE). Achievement can be measured quantitatively through tests or client self-report.

4.3.1.2 STEP 2: OBTAINING KNOWLEDGE ABOUT THE WORLD OF WORK
An understanding of the world of work is most often obtained through occupational information (e.g., government Web sites, career books and magazines). To locate occupational sources and derive useful information from these sources, one must have an understanding of the following:

- *Quality and content* of occupational information. At minimum all occupational information should include a description of the occupation, qualifications for entry, education requirements, working conditions, salary, and employment outlook. Career counselors can use the NCDA's guidelines to assess the quality of the occupational information they use (see section 4.7 for more information)

- *Classification systems* used. Due to the overwhelming amount of career information that is housed in career resources, classification systems are used to organize the information and enhance client usability. However, each occupational source uses its own classification system (e.g., the U.S. government has three separate classification systems alone), making it important for career counselors and clients alike to have an understanding of how each system works (see section 4.7)

- *Trait and factor requirements* To "match" individual traits with specific occupations, clients must have access to occupational information that contains information about required aptitudes, interests, values, personality, and achievements.

4.3.1.3 STEP 3: INTEGRATING SELF-UNDERSTANDING WITH KNOWLEDGE OF THE WORK ENVIRONMENT
According to trait and factor theory, career satisfaction is achieved when an individual is able to "match" personal traits with traits required by an occupation. Although it can be difficult to integrate such a large amount of information, several career tests and inventories provide information regarding occupations that align with specific aptitudes, interests, values, and personality characteristics to assist individuals in the matching process.

4.3.2 Theory of Work Adjustment

The **theory of work adjustment (TWA)**, which developed out of the work of Dawis and Lofquist (1984), is another well-known trait and type theory. The theory was originally designed for vocational rehabilitation clients, but its application has been broadened to include adults facing career decisions and work adjustment problems. TWA describes the relationship between, and several core assumptions regarding, individuals and their work environments. Table 4.2 outlines these assumptions, which are demonstrated in Case 4.1.

TABLE 4.2 Core Assumptions of the Theory of Work Adjustment.

Individual Assumptions

- Individuals have needs that have to be met through their work environment.
- Individuals have capabilities that enable them to meet these needs through the work environment.
- Much of an individual's behavior in interacting with the work environment is concerned with meeting his or her needs.

Work Environment Assumptions

- Work environments have needs that have to be met.
- Work environments have capabilities that enable them to meet these needs.

CASE 4.1
Case of Mark

Mark, a master's-level mental health counselor, began working at a community service board (CSB) 5 years ago (i.e., tenure). He was initially hired as a substance abuse counselor because his expertise and skill set matched the job requirements. Three years later, Mark's manager was so pleased with Mark's work that she offered him a promotion to manager of the substance abuse department (i.e., satisfactoriness). Mark accepted the position because he enjoyed working for the CSB and received a pay raise (i.e., satisfaction). For the next 2 years, Mark fulfilled the company's needs as a manager, and the job provided him with annual pay raises and personal fulfillment (i.e., correspondence). Two weeks ago, the CSB revised the job requirements for department managers and now requires that all managers be licensed professional counselors (LPCs). Mark, who is not an LPC, is no longer qualified to be a manager. As a result, an adjustment is required to restore satisfaction and satisfactoriness. One adjustment involves Mark obtaining licensure (i.e., reactiveness). Another adjustment involves Mark making an effort to change the CSB's new job requirements by speaking with his boss and board members (i.e., activeness). Regardless of which action Mark chooses, failing to adjust to the work environment's new requirements will result in the loss of his current position.

4.3.2.1 KEY CONCEPTS ASSOCIATED WITH THEORY OF WORK ADJUSTMENT *Work* is defined as the interaction between an individual and a work environment.

- Individuals and work environments are considered to be complementary. The work environment requires that tasks be performed, and the individual possesses the skills needed to perform these tasks. In turn, the individual is reciprocated for performance (e.g., compensation, job security).
- A high level of **correspondence**, the degree to which the individual and work environment continue to meet each other's needs, must be maintained.
- **Work adjustment** refers to the continuous process by which an individual achieves and maintains correspondence with the work environment.
- Satisfaction and satisfactoriness are predictors of work adjustment. **Satisfaction** refers to an employee's contentment with the work environment. **Satisfactoriness** describes the employer's satisfaction with an individual's job performance.
- The degree of satisfaction and degree of satisfactoriness determine **tenure**, how long an individual will remain with a company. Tenure is said to be the principal indicator of work adjustment.
- When individuals are dissatisfied with the work environment, they will make adjustments to increase correspondence. Two such adjustments include *activeness* (i.e., making changes to the work environment) or *reactiveness* (i.e., making changes in themselves).
  - *Flexibility* refers to an individual's ability to tolerate problematic and dissatisfying aspects of the job. *Perseverance* is defined as how long an individual will endure unfavorable work conditions before changing jobs.
  - It is also important to remember that, unlike a lot of other career theories, TWA is concerned with *actual performance* on the job.

4.3.2.2 THEORY OF WORK ADJUSTMENT CASE STUDY The above case study has been provided to assist you to better understand work adjustment theory and the related concepts.

4.3.3 Holland's Theory of Types

Another career theory that adheres to the tenets of trait and type theory is **Holland's theory of types**. John Holland (1966) proposed that career choice and satisfaction were a product of personality characteristics. Consequently, he felt individuals should "match" their personality type with the work environment. Holland proposed that there are six personality and work environment types: Realistic (R), Investigative (I), Artistic (A), Social (S), Enterprising (E), and Conventional (C). Table 4.3 describes each of the six types. Obviously, no one person or work environment is purely one type but rather is a combination of types. Holland maintained that individual and work environments were dominated by two or three different types. Therefore, a three-letter code, known as the *Holland code*, is used to characterize individuals and work environments. For example, the code of a person who is realistic, artistic, and investigative, in respective degree, receives the code RAI.

4.3.3.1 THEORY CONSTRUCTS There are three constructs that are important in understanding and using Holland's theory:

- **Congruence** is concerned with the relationship between an individual's personality and the work environment. The more similar an individual's personality traits are to the work environment characteristics, the more congruent the relationship. Therefore, using Holland's three-letter code, an SEC personality is most congruent with an SEC work environment and less congruent with an SEA environment, and it is very incongruent with an IRA environment. As you can see, congruence increases as the similarity between the three-letter code of the personality and work environment increases. Congruence between personality and work types leads to satisfaction, whereas incongruence can create frustration and disappointment.

TABLE 4.3 Holland's Six Personality and Work Environment Types.

Realistic (R)

Work environment: Includes tools, machinery, or animals that the worker has to manipulate, physically demanding, workers need to have technical competencies (e.g., repair electronic equipment, operate machinery). Examples of realistic occupations include construction worker.

Personality type: Enjoys working with hands, tools, machinery; practical; mechanically inclined.

Investigative (I)

Work environment: Requires workers to solve problems using complex and abstract thinking. Examples of investigative occupations include computer programmer, physician, and biologist.

Personality type: Enjoy working with theory and information; analytical; intellectual; scientific; explorative.

Artistic (A)

Work environment: Encourages creativity, personal expression, freedom, and unconventionality. Examples of artistic occupations include musicians, artists.

Personality type: Enjoy self-expression; value originality and independence; they are nonconforming and creative.

Social (S)

Work environment: Involves working with and assisting people; emphasizes values such as kindness, friendliness, and generosity. Examples of social occupations include teaching, counseling, social work.

Personality type: Desire to help others, enjoy solving problems through discussion and teamwork; they are cooperative, supportive and nurturing.

Enterprising (E)

Work environment: Requires workers to manage and/or persuade others to achieve organizational or personal goals; workers often take risks to attain larger rewards; value promotion, leadership, and power. Examples of enterprising occupations include restaurant management, politics, business management, selling.

Personality type: Enjoy persuading and leading people, tend to be assertive, competitive, and value wealth.

Conventional (C)

Work environment: Entails organization and planning; requires employees to keep records, file, organize reports, and make calculations. Examples of conventional occupations include executive assistant and clerk.

Personality type: Prefer to follow rules and instructions, be in control of situations; detail-oriented, enjoy organizing, possess clerical skills and numerical ability, are dependable.

- **Differentiation** refers to the level of distinctiveness between each of the six Holland types. In other words, a differentiated individual strongly resembles one or two Holland types (e.g., an individual likes creativity and art but dislikes working with machinery), whereas an

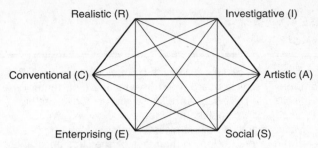

FIGURE 4.1 Holland's hexagon.

undifferentiated individual identifies with each of the six types (e.g., an individual enjoys doing all kinds of activities and does them well). Differentiation is calculated by subtracting the lowest score of any type from the highest score of any type on Holland's Self Directed Search (SDS) or Vocational Preference Inventory (VPI). A low score indicates undifferentiation and a high score differentiation. Because undifferentiated individuals have many interests and abilities, they often have difficulty making a career choice. Work environments also vary in terms of differentiation. Some environments are undifferentiated and embody several Holland types (e.g., a counselor sees clients [S] maintains records [C], and develops creative techniques [A]). Other work environments are highly differentiated and only include one Holland type (e.g., an assembly line worker may only engage in realistic [R] work).

- **Consistency** is defined as the degree of similarity between the six different Holland types. Certain types have more in common with some types than others. To illustrate this concept, Holland used a hexagon (see Figure 4.1); the closer types are to each other, the more consistent (i.e., similar) they are. For example, a social person is likely to have more in common with an artistic person than a realistic individual. The same is true of work environments; investigative work environments are similar to realistic environments but have little in common with enterprising environments. Generally speaking, very few occupations have inconsistent Holland codes. Therefore, individuals with inconsistent Holland codes may have difficulty finding a satisfying occupation.

4.3.4 Myers-Briggs Type Theory

The Myers-Briggs type theory was not originally intended to be a career development theory; however, many career counselors use it to assist clients in making career decisions. Therefore, it is imperative that you understand the theoretical concepts associated with the theory. The **Myers-Briggs type theory** is considered to be a psychological (personality) theory that was derived from the work of Carl Jung (1971) by Katharine Briggs, a psychologist, and her daughter, Isabel Myers. Specifically, the theory exerts that four dichotomous dimensions shape what individuals pay attention to in the world and how they make decisions about what they see. Table 4.4 summarizes these four bipolar dimensions. Within the scope of career development, the Myers-Briggs is classified as a trait and type theory and describes personality type.

TABLE 4.4 The Four Dimensions of the Myers-Briggs Type Theory

Introversion v. Extraversion

- This dimension refers to how one prefers to relate to the world.
- *Introverts:* interested in one's inner world, concepts and ideas are important, draw energy from personal reflection, thought oriented, seek depth.
- *Extraverts:* interested in the outer world, concerned with other people and objects, draw energy from action, prefer interaction.

Sensing v. Intuition

- This dimension reflects how people perceive (i.e., take in information) events in their world.
- *Sensing:* use five senses (i.e., vision, hearing, smell, taste, and touch) to take in information and make meaning. Sensing types focus on and trust information that is in the present, tangible and concrete; prefer to look for details and facts.
- *Intuition:* use insight to make meaning of the information around them, have a future orientation are abstract, imaginative, and creative; relate sensory information to theory.

Thinking v. Feeling

- This dimension describes how individuals make decisions with the data they have received from their information-gathering styles (sensing or intuition).
- *Thinking:* use logic and analysis to make decisions, concerned with making reasonable and consistent decisions.
- *Feeling:* make value-based decisions; concerned with the impact of the decision and, therefore, consider the needs of those involved; strive to attain harmony.

Judging v. Perceiving

- This dimension identifies individuals' preference for using the judging function (thinking, feeling) or the perceiving function (sensing, intuition) when relating to the outer world.
- *Judging:* make decisions based on few facts, have a sense of order in their life.
- *Perception:* need to weigh many facts before reaching a decision, have difficulty making decisions, like to keep their options open.

4.3.4.1 THE MYERS-BRIGGS TYPOLOGY The four dichotomous dimensions yield a total of 16 different psychological types. These different types are denoted by an abbreviation of four letters (i.e., the first letter of every type with the exception of intuition [N]). For example, a typology of introverted, intuition, feeling, and perceiving is referred to as INFP. No typology is "better" or "worse" than any other, but Briggs and Myers believed that individuals usually prefer one over another. Each psychological typology coincides with specific occupations. Therefore, individuals can "match" their personality type with a compatible occupation. Briggs and Myers developed the Myers-Briggs Type Indicator (MBTI) to assess each individual's psychological typology (see Chapter 7 for more information regarding the MBTI).

4.3.4.2 DOMINANT AND AUXILIARY PROCESSES The last concepts important to understanding the Myers-Briggs type theory are dominant and auxiliary processes. Briggs and Myers theorized that for each of the 16 psychological types, one guiding or *dominant function* usually develops as does an *auxiliary function*. To determine which functions are dominant and auxiliary, the last typology letter is used.

- If P is the last letter, then intuition or sensing is a key function.
- If J is the last letter, then thinking or feeling is a key function.

To determine which specific functions are dominant and auxiliary, the first typology letter is used.

- For extraverts, the last letter (J or P) indicates the dominant process.
- For introverts, the last letter (J or P) indicates the auxiliary process.

Therefore, for an INFJ:

- The dominant function is introverted intuition
- The auxiliary function is extraverted feeling.

For an ESTP:

- The dominant function is extraverted sensing.
- The auxiliary function is introverted thinking.

4.3.5 Practice Multiple-Choice Items: Trait and Type Career Theories

1. According to career trait and factor theory, self-understanding is derived from assessing
   a. personality.
   b. ability.
   c. values.
   d. All of the above.

2. _____ refers to an employee's contentment with the work environment. _____ describes the employer's satisfaction with an individual's job performance.
   a. Tenure; Satisfaction
   b. Satisfaction; Satisfactoriness
   c. Satisfaction; Tenure
   d. Satisfactoriness; Satisfaction

3. According to Holland's theory of types, the personality type IAS is most congruent with which of the following work environments?
   a. IRE
   b. ECS
   c. IAR
   d. IES

4. According to the Myers-Briggs type theory, an individual who uses logic and analysis to make decisions uses which information-gathering style?
   a. Feeling
   b. Sensing
   c. Intuition
   d. Thinking

5. For a person with the Myers-Briggs typology INTP, _____ indicates the dominant function.

    a. T

    b. N

    c. P

    d. I

Answer Key: 1. d; 2. b; 3. c; 4. d; 5. a.

4.4 LIFESPAN AND DEVELOPMENTAL CAREER THEORIES

Lifespan theory, as it relates to career development, is concerned with how growth and maturation affect the way individuals handle career issues throughout their entire lifespan. This group of theories outlines chronological stages that correspond to several diverse theories of career development tasks. Individuals move through these stages as they age. This section provides an overview of theories falling under the lifespan classification: Gottfredson's theory of circumscription, compromise, and self-creation; Ginzberg's career development theory; lifespan, life-space career theory; Schlossberg's transition theory; and Hopson and Adams' model of adult transitions.

4.4.1 Gottfredson's Theory of Circumscription, Compromise, and Self-Creation

Linda **Gottfredson's theory of circumscription, compromise, and self-creation** (1981) is a lifespan theory that outlines the career development process of children and adolescents. The theory is concerned with how the development of self-concept (i.e., how people see themselves privately and publicly in society) affects vocational choices and outcomes. Specifically, Gottfredson emphasizes the role that gender and prestige play in making career decisions.

4.4.1.1 CIRCUMSCRIPTION *Circumscription* refers to the process by which individuals eliminate career alternatives they believe are not compatible with their self-concept. Gottfredson proposed that as children begin to recognize distinctions between jobs they must rule out occupations that they deem socially unacceptable. This process of elimination entails stages of circumscription and is heavily influenced by a child's ideas regarding gender, social class, and prestige. These stages are outlined in Table 4.5.

4.4.1.2 COMPROMISE *Compromise* refers to the process by which adolescents give up highly preferred career alternatives for those that are less compatible but more accessible. Accessibility is influenced by external barriers such as family obligations or limited educational opportunities. Regarding compromise, Gottfredson (1981) believes:

- Individuals will settle for a "good enough" career because they are unwilling or unable to thoroughly examine their interests, values, and abilities.
- Sometimes there is not a "good enough" career choice and individuals must delay the decision-making process and search for more alternatives.

TABLE 4.5   The Stages of Circumscription.

1. *Orientation to size and power* (3–5 years old): Children classify their world in simple terms (e.g., big-small; strong-weak). They identify occupations with adult roles (e.g., Mom is big and strong so she goes to work, but I am small so I cannot work).

2. *Orientation to sex roles* (6–8 years old): Children begin to gain an awareness of gender roles and are likely to choose occupations that are congruent with their own gender (e.g., girls desire to be nurses, and boys want to be firefighters).

3. *Orientation to social valuation* (9–13 years old): Children become aware of distinctions in social class and are sensitive to social evaluation. In this stage children choose occupations that align with familial expectations and their social class (e.g., a child from a wealthy background is not likely to consider factory work as a viable occupation).

4. *Orientation to the internal unique self* (14 years and older): Up until now, children have eliminated occupations based on their self-concept and have acceptable career alternatives. As they move into adolescence, career choices are based on accessibility and personal preferences (i.e., occupations that match their values, abilities, family needs, and personality).

- When the compromise is small, individuals will give highest priority to satisfying their interests.
- When the compromise is moderate, individuals will sacrifice interest before prestige or gender role.
- When the compromise is severe, individuals will sacrifice interest and prestige before gender role.

4.4.1.3 SELF-CREATION Gottfredson (1981) asserted that individuals have the capability to improve their career options and integrate their self-concept into the career decision-making process. However, biological and environmental factors mediate an individual's ability to execute the compromise process.

4.4.2 Ginzberg and Associates: Career Development Theory

Career development theory, a lifespan theory, focuses on the career decision-making process. The development of this theory was a collaborative effort between Ginzberg, an economist; Ginsburg, a psychiatrist; Axelrad, a sociologist; and Herma, a psychologist. Although Ginzberg and his associates (1951) recognized that the career decision-making process extended into adulthood; their theory focuses on child and adolescent development. They differentiated three developmental stages in the career selection process.

Ginzberg's Developmental Stages

- *Fantasy Stage (up to 11 years of age).* Ideas regarding future careers are influenced by play and imagination.
- *Tentative Stage (11–17 years of age).* Adolescents pass through four substages that influence their career decisions: *Interests* (career decisions are based on likes and dislikes); *Capacity* (individuals are able to assess and consider their capabilities in relation to career aspirations);

Value (personal goals and values are incorporated into the decision-making process); and *Transition* (availability, demand, and benefits of certain careers are taken into account).

- *Realistic Stage (17–early 20s).* Young adults begin to make realistic career choices as they progress through three substages: *Exploration* (narrow down career choices); *Crystallization* (commit to a specific career field); and *Specification* (selection of jobs or education and training).

    Early in the theory's formulation, Ginzberg proposed the career decision-making process was irreversible, meaning that individuals cannot return psychologically or chronologically to previous stages. However, in his later writings, Ginzberg modified his views, stating that the process was somewhat reversible. However, he still maintained that changes in career decisions could have many implications and even impede an individual's career development.

4.4.3 Lifespan, Life-space Career Theory

The **lifespan, life-space career theory** was developed by Donald Super (1953) and is somewhat similar to other developmental theories. Super suggested that career development involved a series of successive stages and developmental tasks. He also proposed that a person's career continues to unfold past early adulthood and that individuals engage in a lifelong process of career development. As a result, Super's developmental stages extend from birth to death, including five developmental stages and 16 substages. These stages are described in Table 4.6.

Key Concepts of Super's Lifespan, Life-Space Theory

- *Self-Concept.* One of Super's most notable contributions to the field of career development was his emphasis on the role self-concept plays in a person's career. He defined self-concept as an individual's perception of his or her personality characteristics, abilities, and preferences. The self-concept changes and develops over time as individuals acquire experiences and learn how they differ from others. Super saw career choices as reflections of self-concept. Specifically, he believed the self-concept influences an individual's ideas regarding suitable occupations.
- *Life Roles.* Super emphasized the importance of the roles individuals play throughout their lifetime. He described six major roles: child, student, leisurite, citizen, worker, and homemaker. Super developed the **life-career rainbow** to illustrate how these roles can vary over a person's lifetime. For example, a new professional is likely to be focused on the worker role; however, an individual nearing retirement may place more emphasis on the leisurite role.
- *Role Salience.* Super believed the importance individuals assign to each life role varies throughout their lifetime. He proposed three indicators of **role salience**: participation (e.g., being active, spending time on something, improving performance), commitment (e.g., desire to be involved, feeling proud), and values expectations (e.g.,

---

TABLE 4.6 Super's Five Life Stages.

Growth (birth–14 years of age): During this stage, children do not make a deliberate effort to advance their career development. Rather they reach developmental milestones that later guide the career process, such as gaining control over their behaviors, developing a time perspective, and gaining self-awareness,.

Substages

- Curiosity: Use natural curiosity to gain information about work
- Fantasy: Use imagination and role-play to learn about work
- Interest: Develop likes and dislikes; begin to express interest in certain occupations

Exploration (15–24 years of age): Career development becomes more intentional and individuals begin to gather occupational information, choose career alternatives and decisions, and begin to gain work experience.

Substages

- Crystallizing: Involves the clarification of different types of careers that are of interest to an individual
- Specifying: The process of moving from a tentative career plan to a more specific occupational choice
- Implementing: The process of actively pursuing a career choice through vocational training, higher education, and/or work experiences

Establishment (25–45 years of age): Individuals begin to establish themselves in their work by starting in a chosen job or occupation.

Substages

- Stabilizing: Settling down in a job and meeting the job requirements. Individuals find out if their career decisions were appropriate
- Consolidating: Becoming competent, productive employees and gaining a positive reputation
- Advancing: Moving into a position with added responsibilities and an increase in pay and status

Maintenance (45–65 years of age): Individuals focus on maintaining their status at work by adjusting to changes and innovations in the field.

Substages

- Holding: Maintaining the success and status one has attained
- Updating: To hold onto a position, updating one's knowledge by learning new skills to stay competitive, participating in continuing education, and/or attending professional meetings
- Innovating: Contributing to the progress of the field through new developments

Disengagement (65 years of age and above): Individuals begin to disengage from work and turn their energy toward retirement.

Substages

- Decelerating: A decreased interest in work, leading to a slowing down of workplace responsibilities
- Retirement planning: Formulation of plans for retirement (e.g., financial planning, establish retirement activities)
- Retirement living: Implementation of retirement plans; leisure, home, family, community services activities more important

persons may feel a sense of achievement, gain economic rewards, utilize their creativity).

- **Career maturity** refers to an individual's readiness to make good career choices. Super (1953) believed that career maturity entailed the following:
  - *Career planning.* Knowledge about the various aspects of work due to active engagement in information-seeking activities.
  - *Career exploration.* Willingness to explore and use career-related resources.
  - *Decision making.* The ability to use the knowledge gained from career exploration activities to make career plans.
  - *World-of-work information.* Knowledge of job duties, education requirements, salary, and so on for a few selected occupations.
  - *Knowledge of preferred occupational group.* Understanding of preferred occupations and ability to judge one's own capability to be successful in these occupations.
  - *Realism.* An individual's vocational choice is realistic.
- **Recycling.** Although Super's theory outlines a relatively linear career development process, he recognized that individuals can recycle through the various stages during their lifetime. **Recycling** refers to people entering a stage that they have been through before. Take, for instance, a high school math teacher with 20 years of teaching experience who returns to school to pursue a career in engineering. It is likely that this teacher was in the maintenance phase of career development before leaving his or her job. It is also likely that he or she recycled through the exploration phase to decide to switch careers and return to school. Lastly, we can assume that at some point in the future, this teacher will recycle through the establishment phase.

4.4.4 Career Transition Theories

Transition refers to a move from one developmental stage to the next. A **career transition** can be smooth and seamless (e.g., a job promotion; move from the establishment to maintenance stage) or chaotic and disruptive (e.g., being fired; move from the maintenance to exploration stage). Transitions that create significant disruption and cause one to develop new methods of dealing with a career issue are referred to as a *crisis*. Several theories have been developed to describe how individuals cope with career transitions and crises.

4.4.4.1 SCHLOSSBERG'S TRANSITION THEORY APPLIED TO CAREER TRANSITIONS Nancy **Schlossberg's transition theory** (1984) proposed four different types of transitions: anticipated, unanticipated, chronic hassles, and nonevents. *Anticipated transitions* are those that will happen for most individuals over their lifespan (e.g., getting a job, retirement). *Unanticipated transitions* refer to those career events that are not expected (e.g., being laid off). *Chronic hassles*

are characterized by their continuous and pervasive nature (e.g., a long commute to work). *Nonevents* are transitions that never happen despite an individual's desire for such events to occur (e.g., a job promotion that never happens). Schlossberg proposed that an individual's willingness and ability to deal with transitions depends on the situation (e.g., concurrent events, the trigger, timing, meaning of transition), self (e.g., demographic and personality characteristics), support (e.g., available help), and strategies (e.g., change the situation, change the meaning of situation, manage stress that results from the transition).

4.4.4.2 HOPSON AND ADAMS' MODEL OF ADULT TRANSITION Hopson and Adams (1977) introduced two other types of transition: voluntary (e.g., decision to leave a job) and involuntary (e.g., being fired). They proposed that crises are usually unanticipated and involuntary. To conceptualize how individuals handle crises, Hopson and Adams proposed the **model of adult transitions**. This model outlines seven developmental stages: *Immobilization* (initial shock, overwhelmed, and unable to make plans); *Minimization* (desire to minimize crisis, denial); *Self-Doubt* (doubt about one's ability to solve the problem, feelings of anxiousness); *Letting Go* (detachment from original crisis, looking to future); *Testing Out* (feeling of being able to handle the situation); *Searching for Meaning* (seeking understanding of situation); and *Internationalization* (i.e., change in values and lifestyle).

4.4.5 Practice Multiple-Choice Items: Lifespan and Developmental Career Theories

1. Gottfredson emphasizes the role that _____ play in making career decisions.
   - **a.** transitions and crises
   - **b.** gender and prestige
   - **c.** self-concept and life roles
   - **d.** accessibility and race

2. Ann was promoted to a senior analyst position a year ago. This past year, she attended several continuing education workshops to update her skills and stay abreast of the new developments in the field. According to Super's lifespan, life-space career theory, in what developmental stage is Ann?
   - **a.** Growth
   - **b.** Establishment
   - **c.** Maintenance
   - **d.** Implementing

3. Super recognized that individuals can recycle through the various stages during their lifetime, reentering a stage that they have been through before. Which of the following scenarios is an example of recycling?
   - **a.** An employee is promoted to vice president of his company and has to learn new skills.
   - **b.** An employee retires after 30 years of working in the health care industry.
   - **c.** A recent college graduate enters the workforce and begins working in the education field.

    d. An employee loses her job in construction after 15 years and begins taking classes at the local college to pursue a career in architecture.

4. Hopson and Adams' model of adult transitions proposes that crises are usually

    a. voluntary and involuntary.

    b. unanticipated and involuntary.

    c. voluntary and anticipated.

    d. situational and unanticipated.

5. Early in their theory's formulation, Ginzberg and colleagues proposed that the career decision-making process was

    a. irreversible.

    b. influenced by gender and social class.

    c. cyclic.

    d. reversible.

Answer Key: 1. b; 2. c; 3. d; 4. b; 5. a.

4.5 SPECIAL FOCUS CAREER THEORIES

A number of theories have been developed to describe the career development process. Each of these theories endorses a different approach to viewing career selection, decision making, and development. This section provides an overview of theories within the special focus theories classification: career decision-making theories, social learning theory, relational approaches, constructivist and narrative approaches, and career construction theory.

4.5.1 Career Decision-Making Theories

Career decision-making theories focus on the career decision-making process and are less concerned with careers people actually choose. The two categories of career decision-making models are prescriptive and descriptive. *Prescriptive* theories describe ideal approaches to decision making; whereas, *descriptive* theories explain how individuals actually make vocational choices. The following sections cover the career decision-making approaches with which you must be familiar.

4.5.1.1 TIEDEMAN AND O'HARA: THEORY OF CAREER DECISION MAKING
Tiedeman and O'Hara's (1963) **theory of career decision making** is a descriptive approach that proposes two stages of career decision making. The first stage, *anticipating a choice*, describes the process of making a career choice and has four phases: *Exploration*—individuals try out new behaviors and fantasize about different careers; *Crystallization*—individuals evaluate the advantages and disadvantages of potential alternatives, which leads to vocational clarification; *Choice*—a choice is made and individuals may feel confident or unsure about the decision; and *Specification*—individuals reassess their decision and clarify options. The second stage, *adjusting to the choice*, describes the process of implementing the decision chosen in stage one. This stage involves three phases: *Induction*—implementation of career choice; *Reformation*—as a result of implementing the career

decision, individuals must adjust to new situations and people; and *Integration*—occurs as individuals become comfortable and familiar with the new environment.

4.5.1.2 JANIS AND MANN'S CONFLICT MODEL OF DECISION MAKING
This theory is largely a descriptive decision-making approach as it describes how individuals handle conflicts when making career choices; however, the theory does outline strategies for improving the quality of career decision making. **Janis and Mann's conflict model of decision making** (1977) rests on the assumption that stress significantly contributes to the quality of the decision that is made; high levels of stress can lead to a "defective" career decision. The theory proposes five patterns people use to cope with this stress: *unconflicted adherence* (i.e., the person ignores the potential risk associated with a particular decision); *unconflicted change* (i.e., the person accepts career options that are suggested or provided without questioning); *defensive avoidance* (i.e., the person escapes the conflict by putting decision-making responsibilities on others, procrastinating or rationalizing); *hypervigilance* (i.e., the person impulsively chooses a decision that will bring immediate relief); and *vigilance* (i.e., the person weighs the costs and benefits of each alternative before making a decision). In addition, the theory outlines three antecedent conditions, whose presence or absence determines which of the five coping patterns an individual will use. These include (a) awareness of serious risks associated with preferred alternatives (absence of this condition leads to unconflicted adherence or change), (b) hope for finding a better alternative (absence of this condition leads to defensive avoidance), and (c) belief that one has adequate time to search and evaluate alternatives (absence of this condition leads to hypervigilance).

4.5.1.3 GELATT'S DECISION-MAKING MODEL
Gelatt's decision-making model (1962) is prescriptive. The model exerts that all decisions have similar qualities in that a choice, which has two or more possible courses of action, must be made and an individual must rationally analyze information to accurately predict the outcome of his or her choice. Given these qualities, Gelatt proposed that the decision-making process consists of: (a) recognizing that a decision needs to be made; (b) collecting data and surveying possible courses of action; (c) determining possible outcomes and applying a prediction and value system to analyze possible outcomes; and (d) making a choice, which could be terminal (i.e., a final decision) or investigatory (i.e., call for additional information). Lastly, Gelatt suggested that the nature of decision making is continuous and cyclical.

4.5.2 Social Learning Theory

Application of social learning theory to the career domain stems from the work of John Krumboltz (1976). This theory focuses on the learning process and emphasizes the role of behavior (i.e., actions) and cognitions (i.e., knowing and thinking) in career decision making. Unlike other theories of career development, social learning theory is concerned with teaching clients how to implement career decision-making techniques in their own life.

4.5.2.1 DETERMINANTS OF CAREER CHOICE Krumboltz (1976) proposed there four determinants influenced peoples' career choices.

- *Genetic endowment* refers to those aspects of an individual that are inherited (e.g., race, sex, physical characteristics). This factor also includes innate special abilities (e.g., musical talent, artistic ability, intelligence).
- *Environmental conditions and events* refer to conditions or events that happen outside of an individual's control (e.g., social, educational, political, and economic factors).
- *Instrumental and associative learning experiences:* Instrumental learning experiences occur when a person's behavior leads to a consequence such as reward or punishment. Associative learning refers to observational learning (e.g., desiring to be a news anchor after watching the local news on TV) or classical conditioning experiences.
- *Task approach skills* refer to how an individual approaches and deals with a task, problem, or challenge. Task approach skills that play an important role in career decision making include goal setting, clarifying values, predicting future events, generating alternatives, and seeking occupational information. Krumboltz suggested that career outcomes (e.g., obtaining a job) are affected by task approach skills (e.g., searching for position openings, sending out resumés).
- The interaction of these four determinants of career choice is mediated by three factors: self-observation and worldview generalizations, task approach skills, and action.

4.5.2.2 PLANNED HAPPENSTANCE A third component of social learning theory recognizes the role chance events play in career development. Mitchell, Levin, and Krumboltz (1999) suggested that individuals need to take advantage of unpredictable social, educational, and occupational conditions; capitalizing on such conditions is referred to as **planned happenstance**. Planned happenstance can lead to open-mindedness and an increase in career options and opportunities. Mitchell, Levin, and Krumboltz maintained that counselors should encourage clients in the following ways to implement planned happenstance:

- Normalizing planned happenstance in the client's history
- Assisting clients to transform curiosity into opportunities for learning and exploration
- Teaching clients to produce desirable chance events
- Teaching clients to overcome blocks to action

4.5.3 Relational Approaches to Career Development

Relational approaches propose that relationships play an important role in the career development and decision-making processes of children and adolescents. Theories falling under the relational approach umbrella have attended to how parents, siblings, extended family, friends, teachers, and many others influence career choice and development.

4.5.3.1 ROE'S PERSONALITY DEVELOPMENT AND OCCUPATIONAL CLASSIFICATION Roe's (1957) theory was concerned with predicting occupational choices based on biological, sociological, and psychological differences. The theory, which was rooted in the work of Sigmund Freud, proposed that occupational selection was heavily influenced by the psychological needs that develop from interactions between children and their parents. Ultimately, Roe desired to show that individuals in certain occupations have commonalities in the way they were raised. Her theory involves the classification of parental attitudes and occupations.

4.5.3.1.1 Parental Attitudes

Concentration on the Child

- *Overprotection.* Parent encourages the child to be dependent by restricting the child's curiosity and exploration.
- *Overdemanding.* Parent expects perfection from the child, setting high standards.

Avoidance of the Child

- *Rejection.* Parent criticizes or punishes the child, showing no love or affection.
- *Neglect.* Parent ignores the child.

Acceptance of the Child

- *Casual acceptance.* Parent is permissive of child's behavior but offers minimal love.
- *Loving acceptance.* Parent encourages autonomy while providing love and support.

4.5.3.1.2 Occupational Classification System
Roe and Lunneborg's (1990) **Occupational Classification System** is a two-dimensional classification system that comprises eight *Groups* (i.e., classify the primary focus of activity involved in each occupation) and six *Levels* (i.e., classify the amount of responsibility and ability required by the occupation). The eight occupational groups are service; business contact; organization; technology; outdoor; science; general cultural; and arts and entertainment. The six occupational levels are professional and managerial 1, professional and managerial 2, semiprofessional and small business, skilled, semiskilled, and unskilled.

4.5.4 Constructivist and Narrative Approaches to Career Development

Constructivist and narrative approaches to career development have been derived from constructivism. **Constructivism** is a psychological perspective that proposes individuals construct their own realities and truths. Proponents of constructivism do not endorse the existence of an absolute truth and, therefore, focus on the meaning clients assign to their problems. Counselors need to be familiar with two different approaches to constructivist career counseling: Personal Construct Psychology and Cochran's Narrative Career Counseling Approach.

4.5.4.1 PERSONAL CONSTRUCT PSYCHOLOGY Personal **construct psychology** is based on the work of George Kelly (1955). The theory states that individuals develop *constructs* (i.e., theories) to understand how the world works and to anticipate events. Constructs are comprised of two bipolar points (i.e., happy versus sad); individuals place events and people at either extreme or a point in between. Constructs can also be grouped into themes and applied to similar events. Kelly proposed that the group of vocational constructs (i.e., the **vocational construct system**) assists individuals in finding purpose at work, evaluating career decisions and tasks, and developing a sense of identity through work. Three vocational assessments are commonly used in career counseling to assist individuals in specifying and understanding their vocational constructs: Vocational Reptest, Laddering Techniques, and Vocational Card Sort.

4.5.4.2 NARRATIVE CAREER COUNSELING

Narrative career counseling focuses on the stories of individuals' lives rather than their personal construct system. From this perspective, career is seen as a story that includes an individual's past, present, and future career development (Cochran, 1997). The narrator of the story is referred to as the *agent*; there is a *setting* (or settings) in which the story occurs, an *action* that is designed to reach a goal, and an *instrument* (e.g., personal abilities, employer, family) that the agent uses to reach the goal. Problems in the career story arise when: (a) the instruments and goals do not match, (b) the actions and goals do not match, or (c) the agent and goals do not match. In narrative career counseling, the client and the counselor learn from the narration of the client's story. The story begins with a description of the problem. The middle of the story is characterized by a description of the obstacles and instruments that can be used to reach the client's goal. The end portion of the story involves the counselor and client working collaboratively to develop solutions to reach client goals.

4.5.4.3 CAREER CONSTRUCTION THEORY

Savickas' (2005) **career construction theory** is another postmodern, narrative approach to career counseling. The theory maintains that individuals construct their careers by imposing meaning on vocational behaviors. Savickas uses recurring vocational themes to help individuals identify and reconstruct their life stories. Specifically, this approach emphasizes individual personality types, life themes, and career adaptability.

- *Personality types* are socially constructed clusters of attitudes and skills that have no truth or value apart from the social constructions of time, place, and culture. Personality types are viewed as strategies for adapting to work and securing an employee's reputation among coworkers. Accordingly, the theory focuses on how an individual's personality evolves through work, rather than personality type, before entering the workforce.
- *Life themes* are stories of personal meaning that relay important factors in an individual's life story. Life themes provide individuals with meaning and purpose in their vocational work. They also clarify key components of the life story that guide an individual's career choices.
- In terms of *career adaptability,* according to Savickas, life themes guide the expression of the vocational personality, whereas the career adaptation process manages this expression.

For more information regarding the career adaptation process see section 4.2.

4.5.5 Practice Multiple-Choice Items: Special Focus Career Theories

1. Which career theory emphasizes the role of behavior (i.e., actions) and cognitions (i.e., knowing and thinking) in career decision making?
   a. Roe's relational theory
   b. Gelatt's decision-making model
   c. Social learning theory
   d. Janis and Mann's conflict model of decision making

2. What parental style encourages autonomy while providing love and support?
   a. Rejecting
   b. Loving acceptance
   c. Overprotection
   d. Casual acceptance

3. Jenna is a second-semester sophomore and needs to declare her major by the end of the semester, but she remains undecided. Her academic advisor has suggested that she research career and major information to help her reach a decision. However, Jenna has been putting off this task for several months and still has not made a decision. Jenna is displaying
   a. unconflicted change.
   b. defensive avoidance.
   c. hypervigilance.
   d. vigilance.

4. Kelly (1955) proposed that individuals develop _____ that assist them in finding purpose at work, evaluating career decisions and tasks, and developing a sense of identity through work.
   a. career narratives
   b. task approach skills
   c. mentoring relationships
   d. vocational constructs

5. Which of the following is an example of an occupational group, according to Roe?
   a. Professional and managerial
   b. Business contact
   c. Semiskilled
   d. Social

Answer Key: 1. c; 2. b; 3. b; 4. d; 5. b.

4.6 CAREER ASSESSMENT

Career assessment refers to a broad process of systematically collecting career-related information using multiple methods. Career assessment results can provide an individual with information concerning career options, career-planning courses, personality type, aptitudes, career-related beliefs, interests,

TABLE 4.7   Commonly Used Interest Inventories.

Strong Interest Inventory (SII)®

Purpose: Measures self-reported interests

Intended population: Persons 16 years of age and older

Test format and administration: 291 items, each of which asks the examinee to indicate a preference from three responses. Can be administered individually or in a group setting.

Scales: Five interpretive scales:

- General Occupational themes: Offers a three-letter Holland code
- Basic Interest scales: Scores 25 broad interest areas
- Strong Occupational scales: Indicate similarity between respondent's interests and people, with high job-satisfaction, working in 211 occupations
- Personal Style scales: Assess respondent's learning, working, leadership, and risk-taking style
- Total Response index: Scores three administrative scales that are used to identify test errors or unusual profiles (e.g., depression or apathy)

Campbell Interest and Skill Survey (CISS)

Purpose: Measures self-reported vocational interests and skills

Intended population: Individuals 15 years and older

Test format and administration: 320 total items written at a 6th-grade reading level; 200 interest items ask respondent to rate level of interest on a 6-point scale (from *strongly like* to *strongly dislike*); 120 skill items ask respondent to rate level of skill on a 6-point scale (*expert* to *no skill*) to indicate level of confidence.

Scales: Seven (7) orientation scales (Influencing, Organizing, Helping, Creating, Analyzing, Producing, Adventuring), which closely resemble Holland's codes; 25 basic scales represent areas of interest and skill sets within each of the 7 orientation scales; 60 occupational scales.

Forms: Paper-and-pencil or Computer/Internet administration

COPSystem

- Contains three instruments that can be administered individually or together.
- The instruments measure interest, abilities, and values.

Career Occupational Preference System Interest Inventory (COPS)

Purpose: Measures career interests

Intended population: Individuals ages 14 years and older

Test format and administration: 168 items, respondents are asked to rate each item activity according to how much the person likes or dislikes doing it.

Scales: 14 COP system career clusters (professional science, skilled science, professional technology, skilled technology, consumer economics, outdoor, professional business, skilled business, clerical, communication, professional arts, skilled arts, professional service, and skilled service)

Career Ability Placement Survey (CAPS)

Purpose: Designed to measure how the respondent's abilities correlate with the entry requirements for each of the COPS 14 occupational clusters.

Intended population: Individuals ages 14 years and older

Scales: Eight subtests (mechanical reasoning, spatial relations, verbal reasoning, language use, work knowledge, perceptual speed and accuracy, manual speed and dexterity, and mathematical ability)

Career Orientation Placement and Evaluation Survey (COPES)

Purpose: Measure values that are relevant to occupational selection and job satisfaction

Intended population: High school or college students

Scales: Eight dichotomous poles (Investigative vs. Accepting, Orderliness vs. Flexibility, Practical vs. Carefree, Recognition vs. Privacy, Independence vs. Conformity, Aesthetic vs. Realistic, Leadership vs. Supportive, and Social vs. Reserved)

Self-Directed Search (SDS)

Purpose: Based on Holland's hexagon model (see section 4.3) and primarily measures career interests but also includes self-estimates of abilities and competencies

Intended population: High school students, college students, and adults

Test format and administration: 228 total items (66 Activities, 66 Competencies, 84 Occupations, 12 Self-Estimated Work Abilities). Respondents rate their like or dislike for each item. As the name suggests, the SDS can be self-administered, self-scored, and self-interpreted.

TABLE 4.7 (*Continued*)

Scales: Four subsections (Activities, Competencies, Occupations, and Self-Estimates); each subsection measures Holland's six personality types (realistic, investigative, artistic, social, enterprising, and conventional).

Scoring and interpretation: The test is scored by adding the raw personality type scores from each subsection. The three highest totaled scores indicated the respondent's Holland code. The respondent can then match his or her Holland code to occupations found in the Occupational Finder.

Forms: Form R (Regular); Form E (Easy-to-Read; written at a fourth-grade reading level); Form CE (Career Explorer; designed for middle school students); Form CP (Career Planning; designed for professional level employees).

Transition-to-Work Inventory

Purpose: Match respondents' interests to occupational options by assessing leisure activities. Particularly useful for those with limited work experience, those who are seeking a new career, or those who are engaging in retirement planning.

Intended population: High school students and adults

Test format and administration: Uses a 6-point scale that allows respondents to rate their degree of interest in 84 nonwork activity statements; can be self-administered and self-scored.

Scales: Assess an individual's patterns of nonwork interest in 14 career interest groups (Arts, Entertainment, and Media; Science, Math, and Engineering; Plants and Animals; Law, Law Enforcement, and Public Safety; Mechanics, Installers, and Repairers; Construction, Mining, and Drilling; Transportation; Industrial Production; Business Detail; Sales and Marketing; Recreation, Travel, and Other Personal Services; Education and Social Service; General Management and Support; Medical and Health Services)

Forms: Paper-and-pencil or online

Kuder Career Search (KCS)

Purpose: Matches respondents' top vocational interests with occupational clusters. Particularly useful for those with limited work experience, those who are seeking a new career, or those who are engaging in retirement planning.

Intended population: Middle school students to adults

Test format and administration: 180 items, consisting of a verb and object (e.g., take a counseling class); items are presented in the form of 60 forced-choice triads (i.e., most, next most, and least); items are written at a sixth-grade reading level; can be administered individually or in a group setting.

Scales: Activity Preference Scales and six Career Clusters (Outdoor/Mechanical, Science/Technical, Arts/Communication, Social/Personal Services, Sales/Management, and Business Operations)

Forms: Pencil-and-paper version, which is scored and profiled by the user; pencil-and-paper version, which is mailed back to the publisher for scoring; and an Internet-based inventory.

---

work values, career-development stage, and career barriers. Three common methods are used in career assessment: interviewing, formal testing, and self-assessment. *Interviewing* can uncover career-related information that concerns a client's employment history, academic background, career goals, interests, and perceived employment barriers. *Formal testing* refers to the use of standardized career-related assessments to evaluate a client's vocational situation. *Self-assessments*, on the other hand, involve the use of nonstandardized inventories and facilitate career exploration and self-discovery. Career assessments commonly assess the following domains: interests, achievement, aptitude, values, personality, and career development stages. In this section of Chapter 4, we discuss frequently used formal career assessments that measure interests, personality, values, and career-development stages.

4.6.1 Interest Inventories

Interest inventories identify an individual's work-related interests. Interest inventories often reveal what an individual finds enjoyable and motivating but do not necessarily correlate with ability or job success. Interest inventories solicit an individual's preferences and have no right or wrong answers. Table 4.7 outlines commonly used interest inventories.

4.6.2 Personality Inventories

Personality inventories identify a person's unique characteristics and styles of relating to others, tasks, and situations. They are frequently administered in career counseling to facilitate the vocational decision-making process. Similar to interest inventories, measures of personality are concerned with a person's preferences and have no right or wrong answers. Table 4.8 summarizes personality inventories commonly used in career counseling.

4.6.3 Values Inventories

Values inventories assist individuals in identifying what they value in a career or specific job. In addition to values clarification, these inventories are usually designed to help individuals prioritize their work values. Values inventories can serve as a blueprint for the career decision-making process. Table 4.9 provides an overview of the most commonly used value inventories.

4.6.4 Career Development Inventories

Career development inventories identify personal factors that may impede an individual's career development process. Typically these inventories measure factors related to faulty

TABLE 4.8 Commonly Used Personality Inventories.

Vocational Preference Inventory (VPI)

Purpose: Assesses an individual's personality orientation and career interests; based on Holland's hexagonal model

Intended population: High school students, college students, and adults

Test format and administration: 160 occupations to which the respondent replies yes (i.e., interesting or appealing), no (i.e., dislike or uninteresting), or no response.

Scales: 11 total scales. Six Holland Personality Types (Realistic, Investigative, Artistic, Social, Enterprising, and Conventional), Self-Control, Masculinity, Status, and two response set scales (Infrequency and Acquiescence).

Scoring and interpretation: Unlike the SDS, the administrator scores the VPI. Raw RIASEC scores can be used with the Occupational Finder to assist the client in career exploration.

Keirsey Temperament Sorter II (KTS-II)

Purpose: Assesses personality type with the intention of facilitating self-understanding and awareness. The KTS-II is closely associated with the Myers-Briggs types.

Intended population: High school students, college students, and adults

Test format and administration: 70 forced-choice items (a or b)

Scales: Four temperaments (Artisan, Guardian, Rational, Idealist); the temperaments are broken down into eight subcategories (Operators, Entertainers, Administrators, Conservators, Mentors, Advocates, Coordinators, Engineers).

Scoring and Interpretation: Produces four score reports: Corporate Temperament Report (leadership style, workplace preferences) Career Temperament Report (provides career options, communication tips, how to navigate job market based on personality type), Classic Temperament Report (provides in-depth introduction to temperament and ways to improve interpersonal skills), and Learning Styles Temperament Report (provides learning style and provides tips for studying and test taking).

Myers-Briggs Type Indicator

(See Chapter 7.)

TABLE 4.9 Commonly Used Values Inventories.

Work Values Inventory

Purpose: Assesses the importance of 15 work values

Intended population: Seventh-grade students to adults

Test format and administration: 45 items; respondents use a 5-point Likert-type scale to rate each item's degree of importance in relation to future job satisfaction.

Scales: 15 work value scales (creativity, management, achievement, surroundings, supervisory relations, way of life, security, associates, esthetics, prestige, independence, variety, economic return, altruism, and intellectual stimulation)

Work Orientation and Values Survey (WOVS)

Purpose: Assesses respondent's values and beliefs concerning work

Intended population: High school students and adults who are unhappy at their current job and/or are seeking a more satisfying job

Test format and administration: 32 total statements; respondents use a 5-point Likert-type scale to rate how important the statement is to them.

Scales: Eight work value categories (earnings and benefits, working conditions, time orientation, task orientation, mission orientation, co-worker relations, supervisor relations, and managing others)

Career Orientation Placement and Evaluation Survey (COPES)

(See Table 4.7.)

---

career beliefs, anxiety, career maturity, and career barriers. Table 4.10 summarizes commonly used career development inventories in career counseling.

4.6.5 Practice Multiple-Choice Items: Career Assessment

1. If a client is administered My Vocational Situation (MVS) and receives a low score on the Barriers scale, he or she may
   a. have a high need for educational information.
   b. be having difficulty obtaining needed education and/or training.
   c. not have a clear and stable view of personal vocational goals.
   d. face few vocational barriers.

2. Which of the following assessments is based on Holland's hexagon model and is self-administered, self-scored, and self-interpreted?

   a. Self-Directed Search
   b. Vocational Preference Inventory
   c. My Vocational Situation
   d. Career Development Inventory

3. Which inventory would you administer to determine whether a client is experiencing decision-making confusion, commitment anxiety, and/or external conflict in regard to vocational decision making?
   a. Career Beliefs Inventory
   b. Work Values Inventory
   c. Career Thoughts Inventory
   d. Myers-Briggs Type Indicator

4. _____ inventories reveal what an individual finds enjoyable and motivating but do not necessarily correlate with ability or job success.
   a. Interest
   b. Personality
   c. Values
   d. Career development

5. _____ is NOT one of the four temperaments included in the Keirsey Temperament Sorter.
   a. Artisan
   b. Guardian
   c. Scientist
   d. Idealist

Answer Key: 1. b; 2. a; 3. c; 4. a; 5. c.

TABLE 4.10   Commonly Used Career Development Inventories.

My Vocational Situation (MVS)

Purpose: Diagnoses difficulties in vocational decision making

Intended population: High school students, college students, and adults

Test format and administration: 26 total items (18 Vocational Identity items, 4 Need for Information items, and 4 Barrier items)

Scales: 3 scales

- *Identity:* degree to which an individual has a clear and stable view of his or her goals, interests, and talents
- *Need for information:* need for educational, training, and employment information
- *Barriers:* Problems with funding/finishing education/training or lack of approval from an important person

Scoring and interpretation: Lower scores indicate a problem.

Career Thoughts Inventory (CTI)

Purpose: To improve the quality of an individual's career decisions by measuring and identifying negative/dysfunctional career thoughts

Intended population: High school students, college students, and adults

Test format and administration: 48 total items, a 4-point scale

Scales: 3 construct scales

- *Decision-making confusion:* difficulty in initiating or sustaining the career decision-making process
- *Commitment anxiety:* anxiety or fear that accompanies difficulty in implementing a career decision
- *External conflict:* difficulty balancing own views and vocational desires with other's input

Scoring and interpretation: The total score identifies individuals who are likely to experience difficulties in career decision making due to dysfunctional/negative career thoughts. The CTI is accompanied by a workbook that assists examinees in challenging and altering their negative thoughts.

Career Beliefs Inventory (CBI)

Purpose: Developed by Krumboltz (1976) to assess an individual's career beliefs and identify faulty beliefs that may interfere with the career decision-making process

Intended population: Eighth-grade students to adults

Test format and administration: 96 total items, 5-point rating scale

Scales: 25 scales organized into 5 categories (My Current Career Situation; What Seems Necessary for My Happiness; Factors That Influence My Decision; Chances I Am Willing to Take; and Effort I Am Willing to Initiate)

Career Transitions Inventory

Purpose: Assesses the psychological barriers that adults may face during a career transition as well as the resources individuals possess to make a successful transition

Intended population: Adults

Test format and administration: 40 total items, 6-point rating scale

Scales: 5 subscales

- *Readiness:* individual's motivation to make a career transition
- *Confidence:* self-efficacy in terms of making a successful career transition
- *Control:* degree to which individuals feel in control of their own vocational decisions
- *Perceived support:* degree of social support individuals feel they receive
- *Decision independence:* extent to which individuals make decisions based on own needs vs. others' requests and desires

Career Development Inventory

Purpose: Based on Super's career maturity concept; measures an individual's readiness to make educational and vocational choices

Intended population: High school and college students

Test format and administration: 120 items

Scales: 8 scales

- Career Planning (CP), Career Exploration (CE), Decision Making (DM), World of Work Information (WW), Knowledge of Preferred Occupation (PO), Career Development Attitudes (CDA), Career Development Knowledge and Skills (CDK), and Career Orientation Total (COT)

Alternate forms:

- The School form: designed for students in grades 8–12
- The College and University form: designed for students attending higher education institutions

TABLE 4.10   (Continued)

Career Maturity Inventory-Revised (CMI-R)

Purpose: Assesses career choice attitudes and competence

Intended population: Adolescents and young adults

Test format and administration: Attitude scale of 25 items; competence test of 25 brief narrative items; agree (A) or disagree (D) response format

Scales:

- *Attitude scale:* measures attitudes toward decision making, including decisiveness, involvement, orientation to work, independence, and compromise
- *Competence test:* measures comprehension and problem-solving abilities that are vital to vocational decision making

Career Decision Scale

Purpose: Designed to measure degree of vocational indecision and identifies career decision-making difficulties

Intended population: High school and college students

Test format and administration: 19 items; 18 items use a 4-point Likert-type response continuum of Like Me to Not Like Me, and the last item is an open-ended question.

Scales: 2 subscales (Certainty Scale and Indecision Scale)

4.7   LABOR MARKET AND SOURCES OF OCCUPATIONAL INFORMATION

In addition to facilitating client self-awareness (e.g., interests, values, abilities, and personality) and career decision-making processes, professional career counselors need to provide labor market and occupational information. However, in a world where the labor market and occupational information are constantly evolving, it can be nearly impossible to supply clients with the latest facts. So what is a counselor to do? The responsibility of obtaining up-to-date career information lies with the client, but a counselor needs a basic understanding of the labor market and must be able to refer the client to sources that provide current occupational information. In this section, we discuss factors that influence the labor market, labor market projections, electronic sources of occupational information, computer-assisted career guidance systems, and how to evaluate occupational information.

4.7.1   The U.S. Labor Market

The U.S. **labor market** comprises two main groups: the employer and worker. The worker group, which is commonly referred to as the **workforce**, includes employed individuals and those seeking gainful employment. Labor markets function through the interactions of the employer and worker. Specifically, the employers and workers negotiate fair wages and **employment rates**. The following is a list of common labor market terms with which you should be familiar:

- *Employment rate.*   The number of currently employed individuals divided by the total number of individuals who are of working age (i.e., 16 years of age and older).
- *Unemployment rate.*   The level of unemployment (i.e., workforce minus the number of currently employed individuals) divided by the workforce.
- *Nonlabor force.*   The number of individuals who are not actively seeking employment. This includes institutionalized individuals (e.g., those in prisons or psychi-

atric hospitals), stay-at-home spouses, children, and those serving in the military.

4.7.1.1   OCCUPATIONAL PROJECTIONS   To effectively assist clients in making informed career decisions, professional counselors must be future oriented with regard to the labor market. In other words, they must have knowledge about projections concerning the growth and availability of specific occupations. Occupational projections are usually obtained by examining growth and replacement needs. **Growth needs** occur when the demand for workers exceeds the number of existing workers and requires more workers to be added to the workforce. **Replacement needs** occur when workers are needed to replace those who have left the workforce due to retirement, returning to school, assuming household and child-raising duties, or choosing not to work. It is estimated that 60% of all job openings between 2002 and 2012 will be the result of replacement needs. Table 4.11 presents an overview of the U.S. Department of Labor's (2005) occupational and industry projections through the year 2014.

4.7.1.2   FACTORS INFLUENCING OCCUPATIONAL PROJECTIONS   To understand and provide occupational projections, professional counselors must be familiar with the factors that affect employment. The U.S. Department of Labor recognizes three factors that impact employment:

- *Population factors.*   Changes in population influence the size and demographic composition of the workforce. Population growth generates the need for more goods and services, which in turn creates the need for more workers. A decline in population growth leads to a decrease in the workforce; there will be fewer people to employ and fewer people in need of goods and services.
- *Economic factors.*   The United States is involved in the global economy, which means its economy is both affected and influenced by other countries. As a result, the need for unskilled laborers in the United States is rapidly

TABLE 4.11   U.S. Department of Labor (2005) Occupational and Industry Projections.

Occupational Projections

- *Professional occupations* will grow faster than any other occupational group. Jobs included in this occupational group are computer and mathematician occupations, health-care practitioners, and education and library occupations.
- Other occupations that are expected to grow include *Service Occupations; Management, Business, and Financial Occupations; Construction and Extraction Occupations; Installation, Maintenance, and Repair Occupations; Transportation and Material Moving Occupations; Sales Occupations; and Office and Administrative Support Occupations.*
- Occupations that are expected to decline include *Farming, Fishing, and Forestry Occupations, and Production Occupations*

Industry Projections

- *Education and Health Services* are expected to add more jobs to the labor market than any other industry.
- Other industries that are expected to grow include *Professional and Business Services; Information, Leisure and Hospitality; Trade, Transportation, and Utilities; Financial Activities;* and *Government* (more growth will occur at the state and local government levels than at the federal level).
- Industries that are expected to decline include *Construction, Manufacturing, Agriculture, Forestry, and Mining.*

declining. This has resulted in the need for a better-educated and skilled workforce.

- *Technological factors.*   With increases in technology comes the future automation of several occupations. In other words, the worker becomes replaced by a computer or machine. Such advances in technology will require that workers upgrade to occupations that require more skills and training.

4.7.2   Occupational Information

Occupational information refers to facts about a position, job task, career field, or industry and is used to assist clients in making decisions regarding future employment. Occupational information commonly includes, but is not limited to, duties and nature of work, work settings and conditions, education and training, methods of entry, salary and benefits, advancement opportunities, and employment outlook. Sources for occupational information can be formal (e.g., literature, electronic resources and databases, computer-based systems, audio/video tapes, webinars, professional associations, career centers) or informal (e.g., direct observation, parents and advisors, employers). Exploring, gathering, and analyzing occupational information is a critical component of the career planning process. Therefore, professional counselors must be familiar with a variety of occupational sources.

4.7.2.1   PRINT AND ELECTRONIC SOURCES OF OCCUPATIONAL INFORMATION

- **Occupational Outlook Handbook (OOH)** is a nationally recognized source of career information. It is published by the Bureau of Labor Statistics, a division of the U.S. Department of Labor, and revised every 2 years. The OOH is available in print or electronically (http://www.bls.gov/oco/ocos067.htm). It provides occupational information on 270 broad occupations that are grouped into 11 different career clusters. These career clusters include Management, Professional and Related Occupations, Service, Sales, Administrative Support, Farming, Construction, Installation, Production, Transportation, and Armed Forces. For each occupation, the OOH pro-

vides information regarding the nature of the work, working conditions, employment, training, other qualifications, advancement, job outlook, earnings, related occupations, and sources of additional information. The OOH also offers job search tips and links to state-specific job market information.

- **Occupational Information Network (O*NET)** is an electronic source for occupational information published by the U.S. Department of Labor and updated semiannually. It was developed to replace its predecessor, the *Dictionary of Occupational Titles.* The O*NET database provides one of the most comprehensive occupational listings, housing current information and skill requirements for 1,170 occupations. Specifically, the O*NET supplies information regarding the tasks, knowledge, skills, abilities, work activities, work context, job zone, interests, work values, work needs, related occupations, and wages for each occupation listed in the database. Occupational titles are organized and classified using the **Standard Occupational Classification (SOC) System**. The SOC system uses a six-digit code to classify occupations into four levels: major group, minor group, broad occupation, and detailed occupation. For example, a postsecondary computer science teacher has a code of 25-1021.
- The first and second digits indicate the major group. In our example, 25 indicates that the occupation falls under the major group: education, training, and library occupations.
- The third digit indicates the minor group. Therefore, 1 indicates that the occupation falls under the minor group of postsecondary teachers.
- The fourth and fifth digits indicate the broad occupation. As a result, 02 indicates that the example occupation falls under the broad occupation of math and computer teachers.
- The sixth digit indicates the detailed occupation. The 1 indicates that the occupation is a computer teacher instead of a math teacher.

In addition to the occupational database, the O*NET system provides O*NET OnLine, which provides easy access to information contained in the database (http://online.onetcenter.org), and the O*NET Career Exploration Tools.

- The **Guide for Occupational Exploration (GOE)** is currently published by JIST Works, though it was originally issued by the U.S. Department of Labor. The GOE, which is now in its fourth edition, is only available in print. This occupational resource offers information regarding compensation, projected growth rate, education and/or training needed, values, skills, and working conditions on over 900 occupations. Occupations are classified into 14 interest categories and 83 work groups.

4.7.2.2 COMPUTER-ASSISTED CAREER GUIDANCE SYSTEMS
Computer-Assisted Career Guidance (CACG) Systems offer individuals the opportunity to move through the basic steps of the vocational decision-making process using a computer. Such systems provide assessments that foster an individual's self-awareness, occupational and educational information, and career-planning tools. Commonly used CACG systems include DISCOVER, SIGI PLUS, Choices, and Guidance Information Service.

- *DISCOVER* is published by ACT. This system employs a trait-and-factor method, matching an individual's self-assessment results to occupational information. It is available in two versions: a middle school version (Grades 5–9) and an adult version (Grades 9–adult). DISCOVER includes research-based assessments that measure an individual's interests, abilities, and work values and databases that offer information on occupations, college majors, higher education and training institutions, financial aid/scholarships, and military options. The system also includes information pertaining to job search strategies (e.g., resumé and cover letter writing, interviewing skills).
- *System of Interactive Guidance and Information (SIGI PLUS)* is a CACG system that integrates self-assessment information with in-depth and current occupational information. Recently, SIGI PLUS was replaced by a new version, *SIGI 3*. This system can be used to assist high school students, college students, and adults with vocational decision making and career planning. SIGI 3 assists individuals in evaluating their skills, interests, and work values, acquiring up-to-date information on hundreds of occupations, determining the education and training requirements needed for each occupation, and putting a career plan into action.
- *Choices* is a computer-guided system that provides career assistance to high school and postsecondary individuals. The system offers a variety of inventories (Basic Skills Survey, Interest Profiler, and Work Importance Locator) and information on colleges, technical schools, graduate schools, and occupations. It also provides a financial aid search, electronic portfolio, and job search information. A middle school version, *Choices Explorer*, is available.
- *Guidance Information Service (GIS)* provides information regarding occupations, military careers, higher education, and financial aid to high school and college students.

4.7.2.3 INFORMATIONAL INTERVIEWING
Informational interviewing is an informal method of obtaining occupational information that affords a client the opportunity to interview people who are currently employed in a career field of interest. Informational interviewing is *not* a job interview. Whereas the goal of a job interview is to obtain a position, an informational interview occurs prior to the job search process and is a tool used to assist clients in exploring occupations. By conducting an informational interview, a client can gain a better understanding of an occupation and access up-to-date career information. Specifically, the client may obtain the information needed to choose or refine a career path, to learn how to break into the field, and to understand what it takes to succeed in a given occupation. In addition, informational interviews help clients to build their confidence and identify their professional strengths and weaknesses.

4.7.2.4 JOB SHADOWING
Job shadowing is another informal source of occupational information and involves observing a work environment. By shadowing a competent worker, clients can decide whether or not they may enjoy certain jobs. Typically, a job shadowing experience is temporary and unpaid.

4.7.3 Evaluating Occupational Information

In addition to being familiar with a variety of occupational resources, professional counselors are also responsible for providing their clients with high quality career information. The following are guidelines established by the NCDA concerning the evaluation of career and occupational information literature:

- Occupational information should be accurate, current, and free from self-serving biases and sex stereotyping.
- This information should be revised at least every 3 to 4 years. Resources 5 years and older should be avoided.
- The name of the publisher, consultants, sponsors, and sources of any statistical data should be credited in sources of occupational information.
- Occupational information should specify the intended purpose, target audience, and potential use of the information.
- The information included in the occupational source should be clear, consistent, and organized. It should also be presented in a concise and interesting manner.
- Bias and stereotyping against the gender, race, ethnicity, religion, age, social status, sexual orientation, or disability status of a person should be eliminated from sources of occupational information.

4.7.4 Practice Multiple-Choice Items: Labor Market and Sources of Occupational Information

1. According to the U.S. Department of Labor's 2005 Occupational Projections, _____ occupations are expected to decline.
   a. Construction and Extraction
   b. Office and Administrative Support
   c. Transportation and Material Moving
   d. Farming, Fishing, and Forestry

2. _____ refers to the number of individuals who are not actively seeking employment.
   a. Nonlabor force
   b. Employment rate
   c. Workforce
   d. Unemployment rate

3. Using the Standard Occupational Classification System, the fourth and fifth digits of the six-digit code represent the
   a. broad occupation.
   b. detailed occupation.
   c. minor group.
   d. major group.

4. The *Occupational Outlook Handbook* (OOH) provides occupational information on
   a. 1,170 broad occupations.
   b. 270 broad occupations.
   c. 110 broad occupations.
   d. 890 broad occupations.

5. _____ is NOT a Computer-Assisted Career Guidance System.
   a. System of Interactive Guidance and Information (SIGI 3)
   b. Choices
   c. DISCOVER
   d. Occupational Information Network (O*NET)

Answer Key: 1. d; 2. a; 3. a; 4. b; 5. d.

4.8 CAREER COUNSELING AND INTERVENTIONS

4.8.1 Career Counseling Defined

The NCDA defines **career counseling** as the process by which professional counselors facilitate an individual's development of a life career; specifically, counselors focus on assisting clients with defining their role as a worker and understanding how that role interacts with their other life roles. As this definition suggests, clients' career issues often intersect with their personal lives; therefore, career counseling is, in many ways, very similar to personal counseling. Career counselors often employ the basic helping skills (e.g., attending, paraphrasing, reflecting, questioning) to establish a therapeutic alliance and obtain a deeper understanding of the client's situation. Despite these similarities, career counseling differs from personal counseling in that clients' work and career-related issues remain central throughout the counseling process. Consequently, common goals for career counseling include the selection of an occupation or adjustment to an occupation. Read Case 4.2 and keep James in mind as you peruse the remainder of this section.

4.8.2 Career Counseling Competencies

Given the unique nature of career counseling, the NCDA has developed a set of professional competency statements to guide the work of professional career counselors. The NCDA's Career Counseling Competencies (1997) specify the minimum skills and knowledge needed to perform effectively as a career counselor. The needed skills and knowledge cover 11 content areas, which include the following:

- Career development theory
- Individual and group counseling skills
- Individual/group assessment
- Information/resources
- Program promotion, management, and implementation
- Coaching, consultation, and performance improvement
- Diverse populations
- Supervision
- Ethical/legal issues
- Research/evaluation
- Technology

4.8.3 The Structure of Career Counseling

Career counseling, like personal counseling, can be organized into a framework that involves client progression through different phases. Although several frameworks have been used to conceptualize career counseling, the process typically involves a beginning, middle, and end phase. These stages are outlined here in further detail. It is important to remember that although these stages are listed sequentially, career counseling involves a back-and-forth flow between stages. At times, it may be necessary to return to a previous stage before moving forward.

- *The Beginning Phase of Career Counseling.* This phase includes the establishment of a therapeutic alliance between the counselor and the client; gathering information about the client's worldview, family, and significant work and life experiences; and a discussion of preliminary

---

CASE 4.2
Case of James

James is a 17-year-old, African American high school student who has been referred to counseling for truancy. During his initial counseling session, James reveals that his father recently suffered a stroke and is now permanently disabled and unable to work. Because his father can no longer work, James has been working nearly 40 hours a week at a local grocery store to support his mother, father, and two sisters. James also shares that his dreams of attending college and becoming an elementary school teacher are no longer possible as he now must work to support his family. As a counselor, this scenario may bring to mind all sorts of questions. Are James' career issues related to his personal circumstances? If so, would he benefit most from career counseling or personal counseling or both? Is there even a difference between career and personal counseling in his case? What types of interventions would be most helpful to James?

goals. During this phase, counselors use career development theory to conceptualize the information gathered from clients.

- **The Middle Phase of Career Counseling.** This phase is often referred to as the "working" stage and includes deeper exploration of the client's concerns, goal setting, and the development of a specific plan of action. Counselors also propose and implement several interventions that address the client's concerns.
- **The End Phase of Career Counseling.** During this phase, the counselor assesses client progress by comparing the client's current status with initial counseling goals. If the client's goals have been met, the counselor prepares the client for termination by reviewing the client's progress and preparing for future challenges.

4.8.4 Career Counseling Interventions

During the middle or working phase of career counseling, a counselor will typically implement career interventions. A **career intervention** is an intentional act that is meant to facilitate clients' career development processes and the attainment of their counseling goals. Career counseling interventions can be implemented in an individual or group session. Specific interventions will vary with regard to the counselor's theoretical approach, the client's vocational issue, and the goals for counseling. Interventions can be designed to address career exploration, vocational decision making, vocational transitions, initiating an employment campaign, adjusting to a chosen occupation, and coping with losing a job. Table 4.12 provides an overview of commonly used career counseling interventions.

In addition to individual and group counseling interventions, individuals can also seek career assistance from mentors, career placement services, career coaching, and/or career education services.

- **Mentoring.** A more experienced and skilled worker facilitates an individual's career development through modeling, teaching, and coaching. Mentors also provide the mentee with support and encouragement.
- **Career placement services.** These services can assist individuals with identifying career opportunities, obtaining current job market/occupational information, and developing the job search skills needed to secure a position. These services are usually provided by public and private agencies, institutions of higher education, and online sources (e.g., monster.com, careerbuilder.com). Career placement services can also include outplacement services, which assist workers who have been recently terminated.
- **Career coaching.** Career coaches have expertise in identifying vocational barriers and devising strategies to help individuals overcome these barriers. Although career coaching is similar to career counseling in that the ultimate goal is to facilitate a client's career development, career coaching does not require any education, training, or special certification.
- **Career education services.** Such services integrate career-related information and activities into educational curricula. For example, a school may invite guest speakers from different career fields to come speak to classrooms or may require that students complete an internship before graduating.

4.8.5 Career Counseling for Diverse Populations

By the end of the 20th century, non-Whites, women, and immigrants represented more than half of the new entrants into the U.S. workforce. However, the majority of career interventions used in the United States are driven by five basic tenets that reflect a European-American perspective: (a) individualism, (b) affluence, (c) opportunity open to all, (d) work as a salient aspect of people's lives, and (e) a linear progression of career development (Gysbers, Heppner, & Johnston, 2003). Given that the number of minorities in the workforce is expected to increase,

---

TABLE 4.12 Interventions Commonly Used in Career Counseling.

- *Guided imagery*: Uses the power of the imagination to help clients gain insight into their vocational interests, personal strengths, and decision-making skills.
- *Career genograms*: A pictorial display of the client's family relationships can help the counselor and client to understand family influences on career development and enable occupational decisions.
- *Vocational card sorts*: Often used in the initial stages of career exploration to help clients expand their vocational options; understand how their interests, values, and skills apply to occupational choices; link past experiences to current vocational goals; and clarify their current vocational situation.
- *Checklists*: Assist the client with assessing and prioritizing their work-related interests and values.
- *Career assessments:* See section 4.6.
- *Job shadowing:* Assist a client in vocational decision making by allowing them to gain insight into a particular work environment through observing a competent worker. (For more information see section 4.7.)
- *Informational interviewing:* Provides the client an opportunity to gain information about the world of work by interviewing people who are currently employed in a career field of interest. (For more information see section 4.7.)
- *Job search strategies:* To assist the client with gaining employment, counselors can help clients prepare job search documents (e.g., cover letter, resumé), develop networking skills, learn job interviewing strategies, and understand how to effectively negotiate a job offer.

it is imperative that professional counselors employ multiculturally sensitive career interventions. Two approaches underlying the provision of multicultural interventions are etic and emic.

- *Etic* perspectives suggest that career interventions used for the majority population are appropriate to use with minority populations and maintain that current career theories and techniques are sufficient enough to have universal applicability.
- *Emic* perspectives, on the other hand, maintain that career interventions should be tailored to the client's culture.

4.8.6 Practice Multiple-Choice Items: Career Counseling and Interventions

1. Career assistance can include
   a. mentoring.
   b. career coaching.
   c. career counseling.
   d. All of the above.

2. In the middle phase of career counseling, the counselor
   a. establishes the therapeutic alliance.
   b. reviews the client's progress and prepares the client for future challenges.
   c. develops an action plan and provides interventions to address the client's concerns.
   d. gathers information about the client's significant work and life experiences.

3. _____ perspectives maintain that career interventions used for the majority population are appropriate to use with minority populations.
   a. Etic
   b. Emic
   c. Culturally competent
   d. Culturally sensitive

4. In career counseling, interventions
   a. are employed in the termination phase of counseling.
   b. can only be implemented in a group setting.
   c. can address issues related to career exploration, vocational decision making, and career transitions.
   d. are not driven by one particular theoretical approach.

5. _____ uses the power of the imagination to help clients gain insight into their vocational interests.
   a. Guided imagery
   b. Career genogram
   c. Therapeutic journaling
   d. Vocational card sort

Answer Key: 1. d; 2. c; 3. a; 4. c; 5. a.

4.9 CAREER DEVELOPMENT PROGRAM PLANNING, IMPLEMENTATION, AND EVALUATION

School and mental health counselors often have large caseloads, making it difficult and cost ineffective to provide one-on-one career interventions. As a result, it is imperative that professional counselors be able to provide career development programming that provides maximum benefit to clients at the lowest cost. Although career development programming can be time and cost effective, it should not be thrown together haphazardly. Quality career development programming requires the implementation of thoughtful and intentional designs that strive to positively affect participants and the larger community. Such effective programming employs prudent planning, strategic implementation, and systematic evaluation. In this section, we discuss the steps for planning, implementing, and evaluating career interventions programs.

4.9.1 Steps for Career Development Program Planning

- *Define the target population.* This step involves obtaining a clear picture of the population that will be served by the program. Population descriptors at this stage may include demographics such as age, race, ethnicity, socioeconomic status (SES), gender, geographic location, educational level, grade level, employment status, and occupation. This information can be obtained by reviewing agency, school, or company records or by administering a questionnaire to randomly selected members of the target population.
- *Conduct a needs assessment.* Once the target population has been defined, a needs assessment should be conducted. A **needs assessment** is the systematic process for identifying gaps between "what is" and "what should be." It allows the professional counselor to explore the target population's perception of the problem and determine whether or not client needs are currently being met by an existing program. Several methods can be used to conduct a needs assessment; these include reviewing historical data, surveying the target group, conducting focus group interviews, and hiring consultants.
- *Establish program goals and objectives.* Following the needs assessment, professional counselors must translate the target population's needs into program goals and objectives. **Program goals** are broad statements that indicate how the career intervention program will respond to the population's needs. **Program objectives** include specific, measurable, action-oriented steps that must be attained to accomplish a particular program goal.
- *Design a program.* The last step in program planning involves designing the career development program. Specifically, the counselor must determine the program's content, methods for delivery (e.g., workshop, courses, software, curriculum, self-help materials), and needed resources.

4.9.2 Steps for Career Development Program Implementation

- *Marketing and promotion.* Once the career intervention program has been designed, counselors should direct their attention toward successfully marketing their program to the target population. When marketing the program, it is important to describe the program's features and benefits, cost to participate, and location (Family Business Institute Inc., 2004).

- *Delivering the program.* After successfully marketing the career intervention program, counselors can finally deliver the program to the target population. At this stage of implementation, it is imperative that the program be delivered as originally planned. To determine whether or not the program is being implemented as planned, Dane and Schneider (1998) recommend assessing the program's adherence, exposure, quality of delivery, and participant responsiveness.
  - *Adherence* considers if the program being delivered adheres to the original design.
  - *Exposure* examines the total number of sessions delivered, the length of sessions, and the occurrence of program strategies.
  - *Program quality* assesses the counselor's skill, preparedness, and attitude with regard to implementing the program.
  - *Participant responsiveness* determines the extent to which participants were engaged in the program's content and activities.

4.9.3 Steps for Career Development Program Evaluation

Program evaluation is essential to the development and implementation of a successful career intervention program. It can document the program's progress, assess the effectiveness of the program in meeting its goals and objectives, and facilitate change in the program's direction and content. Program evaluation steps include the following:

- *Determine goals and objectives to be evaluated.* Program evaluators must decide which of the program's goals and objectives are going to be evaluated. In addition, the type of program evaluation (e.g., summative, formative, both) the evaluator will employ should be determined.
- *Determine the behaviors, skills, attitudes, and/or knowledge to be evaluated.* For example, evaluators can evaluate program participants' readiness to make a career decision, job interviewing skills, or number of employer contacts. It is important that these measured behaviors, skills, attitudes, and knowledge are directly related to the program goals and objectives being evaluated.
- *Determine data sources.* Several sources can be used to collect program evaluation data. Common data sources include program participants, trained observers, hired consultants, program or agency records, budgets, and follow-up studies.
- *Determine data collection tools.* Tools for collecting program evaluation include anecdotal records, expert review checklists, focus group interviews, questionnaires, and individual interviews.
- *Determine how data will be analyzed, interpreted, and used.*

4.9.4 Practice Multiple-Choice Items: Career Development Program Planning, Implementation, and Evaluation

1. Broad statements that indicate how the career intervention program will respond to a population's needs are referred to as
   a. program objectives.
   b. program goals.
   c. program evaluation.
   d. program mission statement.

2. _____ are NOT a data collection tool for program evaluation.
   a. Focus groups
   b. Questionnaires
   c. Individual interviews
   d. Trained observers

3. _____ is NOT included in the program planning phase.
   a. Conducting a needs assessment
   b. Defining the target population
   c. Marketing and promoting the program
   d. Establishing program goals and objectives

4. When defining a target population, counselors should
   a. consider demographics such as age, race, SES, and gender.
   b. explore the population's perception of the problem.
   c. determine whether or not the population's needs are being met by an existing program.
   d. determine the community's need for a career development program.

5. Program evaluation can
   a. document the program's process.
   b. assess the effectiveness of the program in meeting its goals and objectives.
   c. facilitate change in the program's direction and content.
   d. All of the above.

Answer Key: 1. b; 2. d; 3. c; 4. a; 5. d.

4.10 KEY POINTS FOR CHAPTER 4: LIFESTYLE & CAREER DEVELOPMENT

- Frank Parsons is known as the father of the career guidance and counseling profession. He wrote *Choosing a Vocation*, which proposed that persons must have (a) a clear understanding of his or her attitudes, abilities, interests, and resources, (b) knowledge concerning job requirements, conditions of success, compensation, and opportunity, and (c) true reasoning to understand the relationship between the two.
- The NCDA is a branch of the ACA and strives to promote individuals' career development throughout the lifespan. This professional organization also provides a code of ethics for career counseling professionals.
- Career is defined broadly as the lifetime pursuits of an individual and encompasses all the roles people play over

their lifetime. An occupation is defined as the primary activity in which one engages (e.g., professional counselor). A job is defined as a specific position within an organization or company (e.g., Crisis Counselor Level IV). Leisure includes activities that individuals engage in to pass time (e.g., hobbies).

- Trait and type theories assess an individual's traits (e.g., interests, skills, abilities, values, personality) to "match" them with occupational characteristics. Trait and type theories include trait and factor theory, theory of work adjustment, Holland's theory of types, and Myers-Briggs type theory.

- Lifespan theory outlines stages of career development that extend throughout an individual's lifespan. Lifespan theories include Gottfredson's theory of circumscription, compromise, and self-creation; career development theory; lifespan, life-space career theory; and career transition theories.

- Special focus theories include career decision-making theories, social learning theory, relational approaches, and constructivist approaches. Decision-making theories focus on how individuals make career decisions; social learning theories emphasize the roles behavior and cognition play in an individual's vocational situation; relational approaches are concerned with the effect of relationships on the career development process; and constructivist approaches propose that individuals construct their own vocational meaning.

- Career assessments are used to systematically gather career-related information from clients presenting with vocational concerns. Career assessments can measure an individual's work-related interests, personality characteris-

tics, values, and personal factors that may hinder the career development process.

- Occupational information typically includes information related to job duties and the nature of work, work settings and conditions, education and training, methods of entry, salary and benefits, advancement opportunities, and employment outlook. Sources for occupational information include the print and electronic resources (e.g., *Occupational Outlook Handbook* (OOH), Occupational Information Network (O*NET), *Guide for Occupational Exploration* (GOE), and computer-assisted career guidance systems (e.g., DISCOVER, SIGI PLUS, Choices, and Guidance Information Service).

- The career counseling process can be divided into three different phases. The beginning phase consists of building the therapeutic relationship and gathering information related to the client's current situation. The middle phase of counseling involves a deeper examination of client concerns, mutual goal setting, and the development of an action plan. The end phase includes an assessment of client progress and preparation for termination.

- Career-development program planning involves defining the target population, conducting a needs assessment, establishing program goals and objectives, and designing the program. Career program implementation involves marketing and promoting the program and delivering the program in a way that adheres to the original design. Career program evaluation should document the program's progress, assess the effectiveness of the program in meeting its goals and objectives, and facilitate change in the program's direction and content.

CHAPTER 5

Helping Relationships

5.1 INTRODUCTION TO HELPING RELATIONSHIPS

This content area covers the key concepts, theories, skills, and interventions that make up the core of the counseling profession and, in particular, the helping relationship. The National Counselor Examination (NCE) and Counselor Preparation Comprehensive Exam (CPCE) use this information to ensure that you fully understand and can apply the concepts and theories discussed. Specifically, it is important to know about the basic counseling skills, psychodynamic theories and interventions, cognitive-behavioral theories and interventions, humanistic-existential theories and interventions, multicultural theories and interventions, and family theories and interventions.

Over the past several years, administrations of the NCE have included 36 of the 160 total, or 22.5% of the scored items (plus some trial items that do not count) designed to measure helping relationships (rank = 1 of 8; the most items of any of the eight domains). The average item difficulty index was .73 (rank = 4 of 8; 4th easiest domain of item content), meaning that the average item in this domain was correctly answered by 73% of test-takers.

Over the past several years, administrations of the CPCE have included 17 scored items designed to measure helping relationships, plus several trial items that do not count in a score. The average item difficulty index was .71, meaning that the average item in this domain was correctly answered by 71% of test-takers, making this set of items among the easiest on the examination.

The Council for Accreditation of Counseling and Related Educational Programs (CACREP, 2009, p. 11) defined standards for Helping Relationships as

> studies that provide an understanding of the counseling process in a multicultural society, including all of the following:
>
> a. an orientation to wellness and prevention as desired counseling goals;
> b. counselor characteristics and behaviors that influence helping processes;
> c. essential interviewing and counseling skills;
> d. counseling theories that provide the student with models to conceptualize client presentation and that help the student select appropriate counseling interventions. Students will be exposed to models of counseling that are consistent with current professional research and practice in the field so they begin to develop a personal model of counseling;
> e. a systems perspective that provides an understanding of family and other systems theories and major models of family and related interventions;
> f. a general framework for understanding and practicing consultation; and
> g. crisis intervention and suicide prevention models, including the use of psychological first aid strategies.

The remainder of this first section of Chapter 5 contains an overview of some of counseling's overarching concepts and building blocks, including: wellness, the therapeutic alliance, resistance, the five factor model of personality, the stages of counseling, models of consultation, and psychological first aid strategies.

5.1.1 Wellness

Wellness is a holistic concept that refers to a person's overall healthy state of being. Wellness means being not only physically healthy but also mentally, psychologically, and spiritually healthy. Wellness is a philosophy that arose out of a desire by some health and mental health professionals to view health as a "state of positive well-being rather than an absence of illness" (Tanigoshi, Kontos, & Remley Jr., 2008, p. 65). Wellness models emphasize the lifestyle (way of living) choices people make that either contribute to or hinder their general well-being.

- The *Indivisible Self* is one empirically based wellness model that is used by clinicians to support clients in improving their state of wellness. The Indivisible Self is based on the *wheel of wellness model*, inspired by Alfred Adler's theory of individual psychology (Myers & Sweeney, 2005a).
- The Indivisible Self model encourages wellness throughout the duration of people's lives (Myers & Sweeney, 2005a). In this model, wellness is characterized as one overarching factor that is composed of 17 wellness dimensions within five second-order factors. The second-order factors include the *Essential Self* (includes four dimensions: spirituality, self-care, gender identity, and cultural identity), *Social Self* (includes two dimensions: friendship and love), *Creative Self* (includes five dimensions: thinking, emotions, control, positive humor, and work), *Physical Self* (includes two dimensions: exercise and nutrition), and *Coping Self* (includes four dimensions: realistic beliefs, stress management, self-worth, and leisure).

To counsel individuals from a wellness model, clinicians normally introduce and explain the model, assess the client in terms of the model, implement interventions to help the client improve his or her overall state of well-being based on assessment results, and then continually evaluate client progress and growth.

5.1.2 Therapeutic Alliance

The **therapeutic alliance** between counselors and clients is considered to be one of the most important predictors of whether clients will benefit from counseling, regardless of the theoretical orientation of the counselor (Young, 2005). Research has indicated that successful client outcomes are more dependent on the counseling relationship than the techniques employed by the counselor.

The therapeutic alliance depends largely on the counselor's ability to express warmth and **empathy** (the counselor's ability to understand and effectively communicate back a client's thoughts, feelings, and worldview), confront when necessary, make accurate interpretations and reflections, listen actively, work with clients to set goals, and recognize and reinforce client successes. According to Carl Rogers, if the counselor is able to create a safe, trusting environment for clients, progress and growth will occur (Young, 2005). However, the ability to establish a positive therapeutic alliance also depends on client readiness and motivation. The basic counseling skills that help counselors foster a positive therapeutic alliance are covered in section 5.2.

5.1.3 Resistance

Resistance is characterized by clients' unwillingness to work on their problems and initiate changes in their lives (Otani, 1989). Although it is difficult to work with resistant clients, it is vital that counselors learn how to work through resistance because it is an issue that is likely to manifest itself with *all* clients at one point or another. Because client resistance can affect the counseling relationship and client progress, counselors must explore with the client any resistant behaviors that occur. A few theoretical models address why clients are resistant, three of which are briefly discussed in this section: anxiety control, noncompliance, and negative social influence.

5.1.3.1 ANXIETY CONTROL Proposed by Sigmund Freud, this theory asserts that resistance is due to clients' attempts to repress unsavory, anxiety-causing memories that are part of their unconscious (Otani, 1989). These clients may repress disturbing memories to preserve their self-concept or ability to function in their lives.

5.1.3.2 NONCOMPLIANCE The idea of noncompliance is the behavioral framework for conceptualizing resistance (Otani, 1989). According to behaviorists, resistance is displayed when clients do not complete their behavioral homework. The three common reasons for noncompliance are "(a) the lack of necessary skills or knowledge of the client to follow behavioral assignments, (b) negative expectations or cognition of the client about therapeutic outcome or process, and (c) undesirable environmental conditions" (p. 459).

5.1.3.3 NEGATIVE SOCIAL INFLUENCE In this model, resistance is caused by the presence of a negative dynamic in the counselor–client relationship or a client's desire for power or control within the counseling relationship (Otani, 1989). Resistance in clients can manifest itself in many ways, including silence, minimal self-disclosure, intellectualizing, missing appointments, and excessive small talk. All clients will likely show signs of resistance, but it only becomes an issue when these resistant behaviors become habitual. Thus, counselors must carefully monitor clients' resistant behaviors and their own behavior to help determine the root cause and how to best address the issue.

5.1.4 The Five Factor Model

The **five factor model** is an evidence-based model of personality (frequently referred to as the "Big Five") that is considered to be one of the most important, influential, and comprehensive explorations into personality ever developed (Costa & McCrae, 1992). The model breaks down the construct of personality into five factors: openness, conscientiousness, extraversion, agreeableness, and neuroticism. The acronym OCEAN is helpful for remembering these five factors.

- People with high degrees of *openness* often have rich imaginations, a strong awareness of their emotions, intellectual curiosity, and the desire to seek out new experiences and ideas. People who are not very open are considered to be *closed* or more conventional.

- People with high degrees of *conscientiousness* often plan carefully, act responsibly, strive for achievement, and are adept at self-regulating their behavior. People with low degrees of conscientiousness are more spontaneous and often considered to be risk-takers.
- People with high degrees of *extraversion* are often social, outgoing, and energetic. Introverts characterize the other end of the spectrum, preferring to spend more time alone and engaged in quieter activities.
- People with high degrees of *agreeableness* are often friendly, easy to get along with, interested in other people, sympathetic, compassionate, and trusting. Conversely, disagreeable individuals care less about other people's feelings and more about achieving their own wants and needs.
- People with high degrees of *neuroticism* are often emotionally imbalanced, anxious, or depressed. They frequently have trouble coping with stress and experience negative moods. People with low degrees of neuroticism are typically more stable and better able to regulate their emotions.

More often than not, people will possess moderate degrees of each of these five factors, rather than being at one end of either extreme. The **NEO Personality Inventory–Revised (NEO-PI-R;** Costa & McCrae, 1992) is commonly used to measure these factors in clients, and clinicians can use the results to help formulate useful interventions to help clients improve the quality of their lives.

5.1.5 Stages of Counseling

Although stage theory approaches to counseling are many, the counseling process generally consists of three key stages: relationship-building (beginning stage), action/intervention (middle stage), and termination (end stage). In each stage, the counselor has different tasks to accomplish with the client.

- In the *relationship-building stage*, it is essential that the counselor establish an open, trusting, and collaborative relationship with the client. In addition, the counselor must explain the concept of informed consent, discuss the counseling process, and clarify the roles and responsibilities of both the counselor and client.
- Next, in the *action/intervention stage*, the counselor works with the client to target the issues to be addressed during counseling and establish meaningful goals. Goals should be specific, attainable, observable, and relevant (Young, 2005). At this point, the counselor often conducts an assessment, either directly or indirectly. For example, the counselor may observe the client's nonverbal communication and appearance, create a genogram to better understand the client's background, administer psychological tests, or use strategic questioning to elicit information about a client's affective, behavioral, and cognitive strengths and weaknesses. Once assessment and goal setting have been

accomplished, the counselor begins using techniques and interventions to help the client work toward goals. Continual evaluation of progress should be observed throughout this process to efficiently address any obstacles or client resistance that occurs.

- During the *termination stage*, it is the professional counselor's responsibility to effectively end the counseling relationship (Young, 2005). Termination is usually initiated after clients have achieved their goals. At this stage, it is crucial that the counselor help clients process their emotions about ending the counseling relationship, highlight client successes and progress, encourage future progress, and summarize the entire experience. Termination may also be initiated when it is evident that the client is not making progress or if the counselor decides he or she does not have the adequate skills to help the client. In these circumstances, it is the ethical duty of the counselor to make a referral to another counselor.

5.1.6 Consultation

Consultation in counseling is the formal process by which individuals meet to solve a problem. In this section, three primary models of consultation are reviewed, along with the process of consultation.

5.1.6.1 TRIADIC-DEPENDENT MODEL The most familiar form of consultation is the *triadic-dependent model*, consisting of a consultant, a consultee, and a client. Generally, the consultee seeks advice from an expert (i.e., the consultant) about a third party (i.e., the client; Erford, 2011). The client may be an individual, a group, a family, or an organization. In this model, the consultee relies on the consultant for help in resolving the client's problem. However, it is the consultee who actually puts the consultant's recommendations into action. For example, a professional counselor who is having trouble helping a certain client may consult with her supervisor. Based on the supervisor's comments and suggestions, the counselor then applies the advice to improve her client's functioning.

5.1.6.2 COLLABORATIVE-DEPENDENT MODEL In the *collaborative-dependent model*, the consultee still relies on the consultant for help while both parties contribute their unique background and skills to resolve the problem (Erford, 2011). For example, a teacher may approach a school counselor about a student who has been disrupting class. Although the teacher is counting on the school counselor for advice, the school counselor draws on the teacher's familiarity with the student, as well as information about the teacher's teaching style and strategies that have not worked, to formulate a plan and potential solution. In this way, the consultee and consultant must collaborate to help the client because they both possess distinctive abilities and information that are critical to reaching a resolution.

5.1.6.3 COLLABORATIVE-INTERDEPENDENT MODEL The *collaborative-interdependent model* is ideal for addressing problems that are intricate and involve the larger society (Erford, 2011). No "expert" is part of this model. Everyone who participates in the consultation process holds equal authority and depends on the others for their specialized knowledge, making it necessary for each member to contribute to the problem-solving process. For example, this model could be used to approach a problem such as how to reduce the number of homeless youth. Participants would include a counselor but also parents, students, social workers, and community members, and everyone would be responsible for sharing their ideas and working cooperatively and collaboratively to brainstorm and implement potential solutions.

5.1.6.4 THE CONSULTATION PROCESS

The **consultation process** is fairly straightforward. First the consultant establishes rapport with the consultee, explains the consultation process, and defines the responsibilities of each member. Next, the consultant works with the consultee to assess and define the problem in clear, specific terms, and set a goal related to the identified problem. Once a goal has been set, solutions are brainstormed, evaluated, selected, and implemented. After an intervention has been executed, the consultant and consultee determine its effectiveness and whether it makes sense to terminate the consultative relationship because the goal has been achieved or to return to the drawing board to devise and try another strategy. This process continues until the overarching objective has been met.

5.1.7 Psychological First Aid

This section briefly summarizes the purpose of psychological first aid. For an overview of crisis intervention and suicide prevention models, please refer to section 3.10.1 of this study guide.

Psychological first aid (PFA) is an evidence-based approach used to respond to individuals who have experienced a disaster, terrorist attack, or other disturbing event (National Child Traumatic Stress Network and National Center for PTSD, 2006). Professional counselors who would like to offer their assistance in such circumstances are encouraged to follow specific guidelines and seek training in PFA.

In the immediate aftermath of a disaster, counselors should assess the needs of individuals and aid them in getting their most basic needs met (i.e., food, water, clothing, shelter). Then they should provide victims with a comfortable environment and accurate, developmentally appropriate information about the situation to clear up any confusion or misconceptions. Once people's immediate needs have been met, the counselor should help connect survivors to family and friends to help support them and to community organizations to assist them in any fulfilling additional needs they may have (e.g., housing, employment, medical evaluation, ongoing psychological support). It is important throughout this process to respect each individual's desires and not to coerce people into talking if they are not ready or interested. Simply being available to those who wish to talk can be enormously beneficial. For those who would like to talk, the counselor should be there to listen, comfort, provide hope and information, and offer emotional support. For a more detailed explanation of PFA, along with further suggestions and best practice guidelines for working with survivors of traumatic events, visit http://www.ptsd.va.gov/professional/manuals/psych-first-aid.asp.

5.1.8 Practice Multiple-Choice Items: Introduction to Helping Relationships

1. Wellness is a state of
   a. physical well-being.
   b. spiritual well-being.
   c. psychological well-being.
   d. All of the above.

2. The indivisible self model of wellness is based on _____ psychological theory.
   a. Sigmund Freud's
   b. Alfred Adler's
   c. Carl Rogers'
   d. Albert Ellis'

3. A person who loves to travel to new destinations and, once there, enjoys exploring cultural epicenters and experiencing new types of food probably has a high score on the _____ factor of the Five Factor model.
   a. adventurous
   b. openness
   c. agreeableness
   d. intellectual

4. _____ is NOT one of the five factors in the Five Factor model.
   a. Conscientiousness
   b. Neuroticism
   c. Introversion
   d. Agreeableness

5. A counselor collaborates with clients to set goals in the _____ stage of counseling.
   a. initial
   b. action
   c. termination
   d. All of the above.

Answer Key: 1. d; 2. b; 3. b; 4. c; 5. b.

5.2 COUNSELING SKILLS

Effective professional counselors must master a number of basic counseling skills. These are skills that all counselors learn and practice during their training programs and continue to hone and refine as professionals. This second section of Chapter 5 summarizes the skills needed, along with a brief description of their purpose and examples.

5.2.1 Basic Counseling Skills

This section provides a review of the counseling skills deemed to be fundamental to all counselors: attending, questioning, reflecting, paraphrasing, summarizing, confronting, interpreting, self-disclosure, feedback, and giving information (Ivey & Ivey, 2007). The ability to masterfully use these skills enables professional counselors to effectively help clients grow and shows them that they are heard and understood.

- **Attending.** Verbal and nonverbal behaviors are used by the counselor to convey to the client that the counselor is actively listening and interested in the client's self-disclosures. Nonverbal attending behaviors could include making appropriate eye contact, facing the client in an "open" stance, head nodding, gesturing, and using silence (Young, 2005). Verbal attending behaviors include **encouragers**, which encourage the client to speak. There are two types of encourager: door openers and minimal encouragers. A **door opener** invites the client to talk (e.g., "Tell me more about that," "What can we talk about today that would be helpful for you?"). **Minimal encouragers** are one or two-word responses made by the counselor that show the client the counselor is listening (e.g., "Uh huh," "I see," "Okay," "Right," "I hear you").
- **Questioning.** Using open- and closed-ended questions to elicit further information from clients, often for clarification or to encourage deeper explorations of topics. *Open-ended questions* invite the client to elaborate on a topic and cannot be answered with a simple "yes" or "no" response (Young, 2005). An example of an open-ended question is. "How did you feel when your husband yelled at you?" *Closed-ended questions* are used to gather factual or specific information and can usually be answered with a few words or, sometimes, a "yes" or "no." An example of a closed-ended question is "When was the last time that you spoke with your mother?"
- **Reflecting.** Verbal responses to clients that indicate that the professional counselor understands their emotions, thoughts, or the meaning behind their disclosures (Young, 2005). Accurate reflections require the counselor to listen attentively to clients and observe not only their verbal communication but also their nonverbal communication. Reflecting allows counselors to express empathy and encourages further discussion. Reflecting also gives clients the opportunity to clarify their thoughts or feelings if the counselor does not accurately reflect client thoughts or feelings, providing the counselor with a better understanding of the client. An example of a reflection is. "You feel hurt because your friend chose to hang out with Jennifer instead of you."
- **Paraphrasing.** Repeating back the essence of what a client has said in the counselor's own words (Young, 2005). Paraphrasing is used to convey understanding, check the accuracy of the counselor's comprehension, and summarize the significant elements that have been disclosed by the client. An example of a paraphrase is. "You want to romantically reconnect with your wife, but you are unsure if she will reciprocate your feelings. Is that correct?"
- **Summarizing.** Condensing the important aspects discussed over a substantial period of time into a succinct

synopsis. Summarizing is often used at the end of a session to recap the important topics that were discussed, but it also can be used at the beginning and middle of a session to tie together important themes, patterns, feelings, facts, and plans (Young, 2005). An example of a summary is "We have talked about a lot of important things in this session. You mentioned that you would like to go back to school, but you would feel guilty about the financial toll it would have on your family. However, once you earn your degree, you would have much higher earning potential. You are conflicted about how to proceed. This sounds like something that might be useful to discuss in more depth in our next session. What do you think?"
- **Confronting.** Informing clients about discrepancies in their words, behaviors, feelings, or nonverbal communication in order to increase clients' self-awareness so they can become more congruent. An example of a confrontation is. "You say you want to spend more time with your parents, but over the past few weeks you have not made any attempts to see them, and when they suggest an activity, you decline."
- **Interpreting.** Suggesting possible reasons for client behavior, thoughts, or feelings or helping clients recognize hidden meaning in their actions. An example of an interpretation is. "It sounds like you spend all your time in the company of others because you are afraid of what you might have to deal with if you are alone with your thoughts."
- **Self-disclosure.** Sharing personal information with clients. Self-disclosure can be used to help connect with the client, give feedback, or provide the client with alternative perspectives or ideas (Young, 2005). However, it is important that self-disclosure be used appropriately. It should benefit the client, not the counselor. In other words, there should be sound therapeutic reasons when counselors choose to reveal information about themselves. An example of a self-disclosure is. "I, too, have experienced a difficult breakup, and I can relate to your feelings of loss and loneliness."
- **Feedback.** Sharing thoughts, feelings, and impressions about the client directly with the client. Giving feedback helps clients gain increased self-awareness so that clients can "confront inconsistencies in their own attitudes and to know how they are affecting others" (Young, 2005, p. 177). Feedback also can be used to reinforce client progress. Counselors should ask permission before giving feedback, and the feedback should be given using an "I" statement. An example of feedback is. "I think you have made real progress on your goal of making friends with some of your co-workers. I noticed that although you said it was hard, you were able to invite one co-worker out to lunch this week."
- **Giving information.** Providing clients with information to help them achieve their goals. For example, a counselor might provide a client applying to colleges with information about financial aid and admissions criteria for schools

in which the client is interested. Or a counselor might give a client looking for jobs a referral to a career counselor.

5.2.2 Practice Multiple-Choice Items: Counseling Skills

1. _____ is NOT a minimal encourager.
    a. "Hmm"
    b. "I'm with you"
    c. "Tell me more about that"
    d. "I've got you"

2. Which of the following is a closed-ended question?
    a. "How does it feel when your husband is gone for weeks at a time?"
    b. "Tell me more about how your family has solved conflicts in the past year."
    c. "When was the last time you fought with your daughter?"
    d. All of the above.

3. "You say you want to get better grades, but you have not completed any homework in the last week." This is an example of
    a. a reflection.
    b. a confrontation.
    c. giving feedback.
    d. a paraphrase.

4. Summaries are used by counselors to
    a. begin sessions.
    b. end sessions.
    c. highlight important themes.
    d. All of the above.

5. Repeating a client's statement back to them in different words is called
    a. paraphrasing.
    b. reflecting.
    c. summarizing.
    d. attending.

Answer Key: 1. c; 2. c; 3. b; 4. d; 5. a.

5.3 PSYCHODYNAMIC THEORIES AND INTERVENTIONS

Psychodynamic theories, often referred to as the "first force" in counseling, are concerned with explaining the psychological forces that drive human behavior, in particular the interaction between people's conscious and unconscious motivations. Although the theories in this section all fall under the umbrella of psychodynamic theories, they diverge in many important ways. For example, Freud's psychoanalytic theory revolves around the belief in **determinism**, which contends that people's actions are predetermined by forces of which they are unaware. Adler's theory of individual psychology asserts that humans have free will. This third section of Chapter 5 will review the following theories and interventions: psychoanalysis, neo-Freudian approaches, Individual Psychology, and Jungian psychology.

5.3.1 Psychoanalysis

Sigmund Freud (1856–1939) is considered the father of psychoanalysis. Developed over a hundred years ago, psychoanalysis was the first psychological theory to be widely accepted in Europe and North America and influenced the work of innumerable therapists around the world. Psychoanalysis is based on Freud's belief that psychological disorders stem from people's unconscious conflicts and repressed desires. Thus, one of the chief goals of psychoanalysis is to help clients make the unconscious conscious. In other words, Freud assisted people in making the unknown known. Beyond increasing clients' awareness of their unconscious motivations, psychoanalytic theories also aim to help clients address unresolved psychosexual developmental stages (see section 3.6.1), learn effective coping mechanisms, and become more insightful about themselves. Many of the goals of psychoanalysis require a restructuring of clients' personalities, which makes the process long term and quite expensive. Clients receiving psychoanalysis often see their therapists a few times each week for years. In this section, techniques are reviewed, along with the following concepts: **consciousness**, personality development, transference, and countertransference.

5.3.1.1 CONSCIOUSNESS Freud believed that each person has a conscious mind, a preconscious mind, and an unconscious mind:

- The **conscious mind** is aware of everything occurring in the present.
- The **preconscious mind** combines characteristics of both the conscious and unconscious minds. For example, although the preconscious mind contains forgotten memories and vast stores of knowledge and information, with assistance or cues, they can easily be recalled.
- The **unconscious mind** is the most nebulous part of a person's mind. It contains memories, instincts, and drives that are exceedingly difficult to bring to a person's conscious awareness.

5.3.1.2 PERSONALITY DEVELOPMENT Freud believed that each individual's personality is based on the interplay between three main elements: the id, ego, and superego (also see Chapter 3).

- The **id** is present from the time of birth and operates on the pleasure principle (Gladding, 2005). Residing in a person's unconscious, the id is considered the unprincipled, selfish part of the personality. The id is impetuous, ruled by primitive drives (e.g., food, sex, aggression), and concerned solely with achieving pleasure, no matter what the consequences.
- The **ego** operates on the reality principle and balances the id and the superego. Found mainly in the conscious part of the mind, the ego exists to "keep the person from being either too self-indulgent or too morally restrained, the ego moderates the wishes and desires of the id and the

superego" (Gladding, 2005, p.18). Essentially, the ego is the logical, rational part of the personality that allows the person to function effectively in society.

- In contrast to the id, the **superego** operates on the morality principle. Like the id, the superego also exists in the unconscious. The superego is a person's conscience: the inner voice that urges the person to do the right thing and always expects perfection. Children develop the superego based on interactions with their parents and societal norms, through which a sense of morality is engrained. When people fail to follow their conscience, the result is often a sense of guilt.

5.3.1.3 TRANSFERENCE AND COUNTERTRANSFERENCE
In psychoanalysis, transference is encouraged because it gives clients an emotional release and allows the psychoanalyst to interpret the behavior and raise the clients' self-awareness.

- **Transference** occurs when a client brings feelings from a past relationship into the counseling relationship, often transferring those feelings onto the clinician (Young, 2005). For example, a client who is upset about her relationship with her mother may take those feelings out on a therapist who reminds her of her mother.
- **Countertransference** is the reverse of transference: It occurs when clinicians transfer feelings from past relationships onto clients.

5.3.1.4 PSYCHOANALYTIC TECHNIQUES Freud used techniques such as free association, dream analysis, interpretation, and analysis of resistance and transference to help clients uncover their unconscious thoughts, desires, and forgotten memories (Gladding, 2005).

- Psychoanalysts use **free association** to help clients decrease their self-censorship, which they think helps the clients come closer to exploring the unconscious drives in their id. Thus, clients are encouraged to speak about early life memories without thinking. They are asked to say anything that occurs to them, no matter how absurd.
- In **dream analysis**, clients are asked to pay attention to and remember their dreams. Then, during sessions, the psychoanalyst interprets the client's dreams, looking for both manifest and latent content. **Manifest content** is the symbolism in dreams with meaning that is easily perceived. **Latent content** is the symbolism in dreams that is harder to understand and interpret. Dreams are highly important in psychoanalysis: Freud considered them to be the "royal road to the unconscious." Freud also believed that dreams represent unmet wishes and desires.
- **Interpretation** plays a critical role in psychoanalysis. Psychoanalysts interpret the meaning of clients' thoughts, emotions, behavior, and dreams to increase their self-awareness and understanding of their unconscious desires.
- Not only do psychoanalysts analyze transference (as discussed above), but they also analyze any client resistance that is observed. If client resistance is not addressed, it is thought that clients will fail to gain necessary insight into

their behavior, and the counseling process will not move forward effectively.

5.3.2 Neo-Freudian Approaches

Neo-Freudian approaches are modifications of Freud's theory of psychoanalysis and psychosexual development. Some examples of established neo-Freudian theories include ego psychology, interpersonal psychoanalysis, object relations, and self-psychology.

- **Ego psychology** is based on Freud's concepts of the id, ego, and superego. Unlike Freud, Heinz Hartmann believed that the ego could act independently (free from the id and superego) under favorable conditions. For example, children who grow up with a caring, responsive parent are thought to develop healthy egos. However, children in less-than-ideal home situations often develop conflicted egos. Thus, ego psychologists help people whose egos have become conflicted by drives and desires adapt to their environment through resolving these conflicts, leading to a more autonomous ego. Beyond Hartmann, major contributors to ego psychology are Anna Freud, Edith Jacobson, and Margaret Mahler.
- **Interpersonal psychoanalysis**, developed by Henry Stack Sullivan, contends that people's mental disorders stem from dysfunctional patterns of interpersonal interactions. Analysts help clients by exploring their interpersonal relationships and their relationship with the analyst in the hopes of finding explanations for their disorder. Unlike psychoanalysis, interpersonal psychoanalysis is more focused on present client interactional patterns, rather than events from the past.
- **Object relations** theory maintains that people's personalities are developed through early parent-child interactions. Therefore, healthy personality development is dependent on satisfying interpersonal relationships. In object relations theory, objects are people or things that meet a child's need (e.g., mother, father, mother's breast, etc.), and object relations theorists are concerned with how children represent and relate to the objects in their environment. When babies are born, they are unable to differentiate themselves from external objects (like their parents). As they get older, they begin to recognize themselves as distinct and separate from these objects. However, they form internal mental representations of these external objects, which may or may not be accurate but play a pivotal role in their relationships and personality development. For example, if children encounter **splitting** (seeing objects "in black and white," such as all good or all bad) and are unable to move past these polarities to integrate the complexity of human behavior, their psychological health and ability to form relationships will be negatively affected. Major contributors to this theory are W. R. D. Fairbairn, Otto Kernberg, Melanie Klein, Margaret Mahler, and D. W. Winnicott.
- **Self-psychology**, developed by Heinz Kohut, asserts that psychological disorders result from unsatisfied

developmental needs (e.g., a lack of empathy in the caregiver-child relationship). Diverging from Freud, Kohut believed that clients benefit more from analyst empathy than interpretation.

5.3.3 Individual Psychology

Alfred Adler (1870–1937) developed the theory of individual psychology (also known as Adlerian psychology), which is based around the core belief that healthy individuals have social interest and compassion for other people (Gladding, 2005). Adler's view of human nature is highly optimistic and holistic. He believed that all individuals "strive to become successful" and "that each person strives for growth" (p. 35). As part of the counseling process, Adler often examined clients' lifestyles, cognitive fictions, and family constellations to help them develop insight into their lives and change their lifestyles to one that promoted greater growth and wholeness. The ultimate goals of counseling are to help clients increase their social interest and reduce feelings of inferiority. Adlerian counselors achieve these objectives by developing a trusting, egalitarian relationship with clients, assessing their lifestyles, and using teaching and interpretation to help clients learn new ways of living. In this section, the following Adlerian concepts are reviewed: inferiority complex, birth order, lifestyle, fictions, and techniques.

5.3.3.1 INFERIORITY COMPLEX   Adler contended that all individuals have the propensity for feeling inferior to others (Gladding, 2005). When people are unable to move beyond these feelings of inferiority, they develop an **inferiority complex**, which affects their ability to live healthy, socially interested, and goal-directed lives. In some individuals, feelings of inferiority lead to overcompensation, resulting in a **superiority complex**. Most individuals develop inferiority/superiority complexes because of early parent-child relationships involving an overly critical parent, physical limitations or disabilities, mental limitations or disabilities, or socioeconomic barriers.

5.3.3.2 BIRTH ORDER   To help understand clients' thoughts and behavior, Adler examined their family constellations, and birth order in particular. Adler believed that where a person falls in their family **birth order** influences personality development.

- *Firstborns* are often the leaders of the family—the "reigning monarchs" (Gladding, 2005, p. 36) before the second child arrives—and take over familial responsibility should a parent be impaired or unavailable.
- *Second children* strive to differentiate themselves from the firstborn and, thus, may become competitive. They are often more relaxed and easygoing than firstborns but expend more energy seeking their parents' attention.
- *Middle children* often feel left out and that they do not receive adequate parental attention, but they are the children best able to adapt to new situations.
- *Youngest children* are sometimes pampered or spoiled and, thus, may have a hard time later in life acting independently. They usually receive the same amount of attention as firstborns and benefit from the examples set by their siblings.
- *Only children* are often not as socially adept as other children. It is not uncommon for only children also to be spoiled and perpetually placed in the center of attention, making it hard for them to adjust when they do not get what they want from others. However, only children often excel in their pursuits.

5.3.3.3 LIFESTYLE   According to Adler, a person's lifestyle is established by the time they are 5 years old as a result of early life experiences and interactions with the family unit. However, Adler had a **phenomenological philosophy**, asserting that it was not merely these early events that influenced a person's lifestyle but rather that person's *perception* of those events.

- People with healthy lifestyles help others, are involved in society, work cooperatively, and live courageously. Courage is defined as "a willingness to take risks without knowing what the consequences may be" (Gladding, 2005, p. 37).

5.3.3.4 FICTIONS   Fictions are people's beliefs about themselves and others that are false. People who are defined by fictions often lead unhealthy lifestyles. Fictions can lead to behaviors such as an excessive need for success, the need to gratify and be liked by everyone, low self-concept, and overgeneralization (Gladding, 2005).

5.3.3.5 ADLERIAN TECHNIQUES   When working with clients, Adler used a host of techniques. The most recognized Adlerian techniques are discussed in this section: lifestyle analysis, encouragement, acting "as if," asking the question, spitting in the client's soup, catching oneself, and the pushbutton technique.

- Adlerian therapists often conduct a lifestyle analysis during the first few sessions with a client. A **lifestyle analysis** entails interviewing clients about early life memories (prior to the age of 10 years), their perceptions of their relationships with their parents and siblings, family dynamics, their experiences in school and society, and their beliefs about themselves. This information allows the clinician to formulate a theory of the client's basic lifestyle, which is then shared with the client to help promote personal insight and awareness.
- **Encouragement** is a technique whereby the counselor conveys to clients his or her belief and conviction that the client can make important lifestyle changes.
- To help clients practice new behaviors, Adlerian counselors often encourage **acting "as if"** the client is the person he or she hopes to be someday. For example, insecure clients may be encouraged to act as if they are confident in themselves. However, counselors usually start with small tasks for their clients and work up to larger ones. A person who is shy may first be urged to act is if he or she had the ability to make steady eye contact while talking

to a new acquaintance. If the client is successful, the counselor can then move on to a more daunting task. This technique helps clients realize that they are capable of changing and being the person they want to be.

- **Asking the question** "How would your life be different if you were well?" is a technique often used with clients in Adlerian psychology. Many variations of this question are used, with the primary goals being to help clients think about the possibility of no longer having their problem and to show clients that they have the ability to change their lives. This question also helps counselors gain a clearer picture of what the client would like to change and whether the problem is physiological or psychological.

- Counselors sometimes use **spitting in the client's soup**, a technique that points out certain client behaviors so that the behavior no longer seems as desirable to the client (Gladding, 2005). For example, a counselor may tell a client that she seems to disparage her sister to feel better about herself. In the future, the client is less likely to feel better when making these belittling comments to her sister, thus reducing the likelihood that the behavior will be continued.

- Adlerian counselors encourage clients to use the technique of **catching oneself** when they are engaging in the behaviors that are perpetuating their presenting problem (Gladding, 2005). This technique helps clients gain an awareness of their self-defeating thoughts and behaviors and gives them responsibility for creating change in their lives.

- The **pushbutton technique** is used to teach clients that they play a role in maintaining their problems. Specifically, clients are instructed that they have control over how they respond to, perceive, and recollect people and events. Clients are shown that they have the ability to pay attention to either negative or positive thoughts, memories, and experiences. By focusing on the positive, they learn that positive feelings result and, thus, are encouraged to push the positive pushbutton rather than the negative pushbutton. Like cognitive theories, the pushbutton technique teaches clients the relationship between their thoughts and emotions.

5.3.4 Jungian Psychology

Carl Gustav Jung (1875–1961) was a follower of Freud but eventually broke ties with Freud after disagreements over some of the central tenets of Freud's psychoanalytic theory. Jung went on to develop **Jungian Analytic Psychology**, which focuses on the role of the larger culture, spirituality, dreams, and symbolism in understanding the human psyche. Jung believed that through exploring the unconscious, people's psychological health could be improved. Thus, the goal of analytic psychology is to help people develop appropriate contact with their unconscious so that they are neither overwhelmed by it nor completely unaware of its forces. Clients are helped to encounter their unconscious through their dreams, spirituality, and culture. Through recognizing dream symbolism and the role of

religion and culture in their lives, acknowledging their shadow, and reconciling various archetypes, people are able to undergo the process of **individuation**, the process of discovering one's true, inner self (i.e., psychological growth). Jung believed that as individuals move through life they lose touch with important parts of themselves; therefore, he suggested, through listening to the messages of dreams and waking imagination, individuals can reestablish contact with these different parts. Individuation is seen as a life goal and is thought to have a holistic, healing effect on individuals, which is the ultimate goal of analytic psychology. In this section, the following Jungian concepts are reviewed: the unconscious, archetypes, complexes, personality types, and Jungian techniques.

5.3.4.1 UNCONSCIOUS According to Jung, people possess both a personal unconscious and a collective unconscious.

- The **personal unconscious** is a Jungian term that is synonymous with Freud's unconscious. It is unique to the individual and includes information (e.g., memories, desires, drives) that, at one time, has been conscious but has been forgotten or repressed. The person can become familiar with this information through dream analysis.

- The **collective unconscious**, on the other hand, is a much more complex concept. Jung contended that all human beings have a collective unconscious, which is not unique to each individual but, rather, shared by the entire human race. Residing within the collective unconscious are archetypes, or overarching human tendencies, which are important for each person to become aware of so that they can become whole and individuated. These archetypes can be understood through studying philosophy, art, religion, mythology, and dreams.

5.3.4.2 ARCHETYPES Archetypes are inherent templates for human thought and behavior. They also can be thought of as patterns of human experience that have existed since the dawn of humanity. Some of the most prominent archetypes found within the collective unconscious are The Self, The Persona, The Shadow, and The Anima and The Animus. However, a multitude of other archetypes exist, such as The Child, The Mother, The Father, The Family, The Wise Old Man, The Trickster, and The Hero.

- *The Self* contains the conscious and unconscious aspects of a person and is the primary archetype.

- *The Persona* can be thought of as the psychological masks that all humans wear. The persona allows people to be like chameleons—that is, it allows people to change their behavior depending on the social situation. For example, a father may have a persona that he puts on while he is at work, which may be very different from the way he acts and behaves when he is with his family. Ultimately, personas enable people to disguise their true selves to adapt to new situations and function appropriately in society.

- *The Shadow* is characterized as the repressed or unknown aspects of each person. It is the part of The Self that a person does not want to acknowledge or accept. For example, people who put up a hard, tough exterior may not want to accept that they also have a softer, more vulnerable side to them. People's shadows can be destructive or constructive. Essentially, the shadow can contain both positive and negative aspects of a person and both positive and negative influences. Jung thought that it was crucial that people become aware of their shadows so that they do not project them onto other people in their lives.

- *The Anima* comprises female traits that exist in the collective unconscious of men, and *The Animus* comprises male traits that exist in the collective unconscious of women. Jung asserted that The Anima represents irrationality and The Animus represents rational thought. The Anima and The Animus exist in all people and, as with their shadows, people must reconcile and connect with them to avoid projecting them onto others. For example, a woman who has connected with her animus might be strong and assertive and a man in touch with his anima might be more nurturing and emotional. According to Jung, love at first sight is explained by people's recognition of their anima or animus in another person.

5.3.4.3 COMPLEXES

People develop a **complex**, or more than one complex, as a result of repressed thoughts and desires amalgamating in the unconscious. According to Jung, complexes revolve around an archetype. For example, a person may have a "mother complex." These complexes symbolize issues that a person needs to resolve.

5.3.4.4 PERSONALITY TYPES

Jung created a **personality typology** that consists of two attitudes (introversion and extraversion) and four functions comprised of two pairs (sensation/intuition and thinking/feeling). Although people usually have one dominant attitude and two dominant functions (one from each pair), each person possesses each attitude and function to some degree. The popular **Myers-Briggs Type Indicator (MBTI)** is based on Jung's personality theory and informs people about their preferences for thinking and acting.

- People with a preference for *introversion* are reflective and energized by their internal world of thoughts and ideas.
- People with a preference for *extraversion* are outgoing and energized by the external world of people, action, and objects.
- Sensation and intuition are the information-gathering functions. People with a preference for *sensation* take in information through their senses and rely on concrete, factual information, whereas people with a preference for *intuition* trust their instincts and hunches and are interested in abstract ideas and theories.
- Thinking and feeling are the decision-making functions. People with a preference for *thinking* make decisions objectively; they look at all angles of a problem and follow a logical process to reach a conclusion. People with a preference for *feeling*, on the other hand, involve emotion in their decision making; they consider all the people involved in the situation and how each will be affected by a given course of action.

5.3.4.5 JUNGIAN TECHNIQUES

Jung most commonly employed dream interpretation to help clients resolve their problems and begin the process of individuation. To interpret dreams, Jung used the techniques of explication, amplification, and active imagination.

- Jung believed that archetypes from the collective unconscious often reveal themselves in dreams, and he used **dream interpretation** to help clients understand the personal meaning behind their dreams.
- **Explication** is a technique used to help clients determine the reason why certain objects appeared in their dreams. Jung did not believe, as Freud did, that images in dreams have hidden symbolism. Rather, he believed that an object in a dream is exactly what it appears to be but that it is important to discover *why* the unconscious chose that specific object as opposed to other, similar objects.
- Jung also used the technique of **amplification** to help understand images in dreams. To amplify an image, Jung compared the dreamer's image to stories or images in myths, fairy tales, literature, art, and folklore. Amplification helps the analyst identify central archetypes and possible meanings behind dreams.
- The technique of **active imagination** requires clients to actively talk to the characters in their dreams. For example, the client might be asked to talk to characters in the dream and ask them why they used a certain object or engaged in a particular action. Through this technique, it is thought that clients can connect with their unconscious.

5.3.5 Practice Multiple-Choice Items: Psychodynamic Theories and Interventions

1. The _____ operates according to the reality principle.
   - **a.** id
   - **b.** ego
   - **c.** superego
   - **d.** None of the above.

2. Images and tendencies that are inherent in all human beings are contained in the
   - **a.** preconscious.
   - **b.** unconscious.
   - **c.** collective unconscious.
   - **d.** subconscious.

3. This Adlerian technique can help reduce the desirability of unhealthy client behaviors.
   - **a.** Asking the question
   - **b.** The pushbutton
   - **c.** Catching oneself
   - **d.** Spitting in the client's soup

4. According to Adler, _____ tend to be bright but are often spoiled and lack social skills comparable to those of other children.
   a. only children
   b. youngest children
   c. firstborns
   d. second children

5. Which Jungian archetype is said to contain the parts of the self that a person does not want to acknowledge?
   a. The self
   b. The anima
   c. The shadow
   d. The persona

Answer Key: 1. b; 2. c; 3. d; 4. a; 5. c.

5.4 COGNITIVE-BEHAVIORAL THEORIES AND INTERVENTIONS

Cognitive theories focus on how people's thoughts influence their emotions and behavior; *behavioral theories* emphasize the importance of changing people's behaviors to change the quality of their lives; and **cognitive-behavioral theories** work to alter both the thoughts *and* actions of clients. This group of theories comprises the "second force" of counseling. In this section, the following theories and concepts are reviewed: behavioral counseling techniques, cognitive-behavior modification, cognitive therapy and cognitive-behavioral therapy, rational emotive behavior therapy, and reality therapy. For a detailed review of behavioral theories, including classical conditioning and operant conditioning, see section 3.3.

5.4.1 Behavioral Counseling Techniques

Behaviorism is a scientific, research-based theory of counseling that aims to modify clients' maladaptive behaviors. In general, behaviorists concern themselves with what can be observed and seen in clients, rather than focusing on the indeterminate, mysterious workings of the mind, which are the focus of psychodynamic therapists. As such, behaviorists use concrete techniques to help clients change their behavior rather than trying to delve into clients' childhood experiences or interpret their behavior. In essence, behaviorists believe that all behavior is learned and, therefore, can be unlearned. Although the primary behavioral theories and several behavioral techniques are discussed in section 3.3 of this study guide, a selection of additional techniques is presented here.

- **Shaping** is a technique that reinforces successive approximations of a desired behavior. Thus, a difficult, anxiety-provoking, or new task is broken down into smaller steps, with the successful accomplishment of each step being reinforced, gradually building up to the performance of the target behavior. For example, a client who is afraid of flying would first be encouraged to just spend time in an airport, and the counselor would praise the successful completion of that task. Then the client would be encouraged to complete a series of more difficult tasks until eventually he or she is able to fly in a plane without excessive anxiety.

- **Maintenance** is a term that refers to clients' ability to perform desired behaviors without continual reinforcement or help from others.

- **Extinction** is the termination of a behavior by withholding reinforcement. For example, a child who discovers that she can get her teacher's attention by standing on her chair would reduce that behavior when the teacher no longer pays attention to her behavior. However, the undesired behavior would likely increase in frequency and intensity at the onset of this technique, a phenomenon that is known as the *extinction burst*.

- When clients are learning new behaviors, the counselor might engage the client in **behavioral rehearsal** or **role-playing**. Just as the name implies, clients practice or rehearse new behaviors in a safe environment until they feel confident enough to try the new behaviors outside of the counseling environment. During behavioral rehearsal, the counselor provides clients with feedback to help them improve performance of the behavior. In role-playing, clients try out the new behaviors in dynamic situations, with the counselor or another group member playing a complementary role.

- **Environmental planning** involves having clients rearrange their environments to encourage or discourage certain behaviors. For example, a client who has a problem with eating too much junk food would be encouraged to organize his kitchen so that unhealthy foods are not present or available.

- **Assertiveness training** teaches clients the distinction between aggression, passivity, and assertiveness. Through the use of shaping, modeling, and behavioral rehearsal, clients learn to speak up for themselves in an appropriate manner.

- **Contingency contracts** are often presented in the form of a chart or table that lists desired behaviors, provides a space for noting whether the desired behaviors were achieved, and describes the conditions that must be met for the individual to be rewarded. Contingency contracts are most commonly used with children. For example, many parents use contingency contracts to keep track of and encourage their children's regular completion of chores.

- A **token economy** is most commonly used with children (usually in a classroom setting) and provides clients with rewards for demonstrating desired behavior. Generally, teachers give tokens (i.e., secondary reinforcers) to students when they behave appropriately. The tokens can then be traded in for primary reinforcers (rewards, e.g., privileges, candy, toys). To implement a token economy, a goal that details the desired behavior must first be set. Then the teacher or parent must establish a schedule for reinforcing the behavior (for a discussion of reinforcement schedules, refer to section 3.3.2.2). For example, the teacher might decide to give Johnny a token every two times he waits to be called on before speaking. At the end of the day, he can trade the tokens in for a reward. As Johnny demonstrates the desired behavior more frequently, the number of times he is reinforced and given a token will decrease until he is able to maintain the behavior without reinforcement.

- **Response cost** reduces undesirable behaviors by removing a positive reinforcement (e.g., removing a token if a child calls out before being called on to speak). Response cost is often used in conjunction with a token economy. For example, Johnny may be given a token for every two times he waits to be called on before speaking; however, he may also have a token removed if he speaks out without first being called on.
- **Implosion or implosive therapy** involves having clients imagine hypothetical scenarios that would cause them severe anxiety until they become desensitized to them.
- **Time-out** is an aversive behavioral technique (i.e., punishment) that removes a child so that he or she is no longer able to receive any kind of positive reinforcement.
- **Overcorrection**, also an aversive behavioral technique, requires the client to return the environment to its original condition prior to the undesirable behavior and then to make the environment better. For example, a child who throws a temper tantrum and throws toys everywhere may be required not only to put the toys back in their appropriate places but also to sweep the floor. Often, overcorrection is done repeatedly to serve as a deterrent to future misbehavior. For example, a child who does not hang up his coat is made to practice hanging up his coat 10 times, or a child who runs in the hallway at school is made to practice walking the length of the hallway five times.

5.4.2 Cognitive-Behavior Modification

Cognitive-behavior modification, created by Donald Meichenbaum (1996), is a cognitive-behavioral approach that trains clients to alter their internal cognitions, also known as **self-talk** or *self-statements*, in order to change the way they react and respond to situations. The assumption underlying this approach is that faulty self-statements lead to deleterious behavior and negative emotions.

- **Cognitive restructuring** is a technique used to help clients adjust their self-talk. The process involves targeting the client self-statements that result in problematic behaviors or feelings and replacing the self-statements with new statements that are more rational, logical, and positive. Once the new, more helpful self-statements have been created, the counselor models by using them in a hypothetical situation that would be stressful for the client. Finally, the client is encouraged to imagine a stressful situation and discuss out loud the statements she would use to help herself through the situation. Once the client has mastered the new self-talk, the counselor asks the client to begin practicing these new skills outside the counseling relationship.
- **Self-instructional training** teaches clients how to alter their thoughts and behavior. First, counselors demonstrate appropriate behaviors and thoughts to clients, explaining out loud the reasons for what they are doing. Then clients are asked to demonstrate the same behavior and repeat the instructions aloud to themselves. Clients continue practicing by speaking out loud or in whispers to themselves until they have mastered the task and need only to repeat the instructions to themselves silently. Outside of the counseling sessions, it is hoped that clients can use these self-instructions to change their thoughts and behaviors to improve the quality of their lives.
- **Stress Inoculation Training (SIT)** combines cognitive and behavioral techniques to help clients learn how to cope with stress (Meichenbaum, 1996). The process has three phases: conceptualization, skills acquisition and rehearsal, and application and follow through. During the *conceptualization* phase, clients are encouraged to identify their stressors; their cognitive, behavioral, affective, and physiological reactions to stress; and the aspects of stress that they can modify. In the *skills acquisition and rehearsal* phase, counselors teach clients skills to help them cope with stress (e.g., cognitive restructuring, relaxation training, problem solving, etc.), and then the clients practice these new skills. Finally, in the *application and follow-through* phase, clients begin to use these skills while imagining stressful situations and to apply them in real-life situations that trigger stress.

5.4.3 Cognitive Therapy

Cognitive therapy, developed by Aaron Beck, posits that peoples' emotions and behaviors are a direct result of their cognitions (Gladding, 2005). Accordingly, if clients can change their cognitions, they also can change their negative or harmful feelings and actions. Cognitive therapists are particularly interested in discerning and then restructuring clients' **automatic thoughts**, which are immediate, unhealthy internal cognitions. In this section, the types of distorted thinking and cognitive-behavior techniques are reviewed.

5.4.3.1 TYPES OF DISTORTED THINKING Once professional counselors are able to identify clients' patterns of **distorted thinking**—that is, inaccurate thoughts or ideas that maintain dysfunctional thinking and negative emotions—counselors can help challenge clients' logic and replace clients' harmful cognitions with more realistic, health-promoting self-statements. Specific types of distorted thinking include dichotomous thinking, selective abstraction, overgeneralization, magnification/minimization, labeling, mind reading, and negative predictions (Gladding, 2005).

- *Dichotomous thinking* is also known as all-or-nothing thinking. This occurs when people evaluate themselves according to extreme categories. For example, a mother who believes that good mothers never yell at their children may determine that she is a failure or a horrible mother after she yells at her child. In essence, she thinks that if she is not the perfect mother, then she is a failure. There is no middle ground.

- *Selective abstraction* occurs when people focus on only the negative aspects of a situation to support their distorted thinking rather than examining the bigger picture or context. For example, a hardworking man who is respected by his boss and co-workers may determine that he is bad at his job or incompetent if he makes a mistake.
- *Overgeneralization* occurs when clients reach a conclusion based on limited information or experience. For example, a woman may decide that all men are uncaring and insensitive based on a negative experience with an ex-boyfriend.
- *Magnification* occurs when people *catastrophize*—that is, they exaggerate personal flaws or situations. For example, a teenage boy who thinks it is the end of the world when he does not make the football team is catastrophizing. Conversely, *minimization* or *discounting* occurs when people fail to recognize or take ownership of their successes.
- *Labeling* occurs when people define themselves based on perceived imperfections (e.g., people who label themselves as stupid, mean, worthless, ugly).
- *Mind reading* occurs when people believe that they know what others are thinking about them without any evidence. For example, a teenage girl may convince herself that everyone thinks she is dumb, so she may avoid speaking during class.
- *Negative predictions* or *fortune telling* occurs when people anticipate, without any evidence, that something bad will happen and then alter their behaviors accordingly. For example, if a person determines that her relationship is going to end in failure, then she may inadvertently act in certain ways that bring about that failure, turning it into a self-fulfilling prophecy.

5.4.3.2 COGNITIVE THERAPY TECHNIQUES While working with clients, cognitive counselors take on the role of expert, collaborator, and educator (Gladding, 2005). They also use the Socratic method to help clients reach their own conclusions about the impact and rationality of their automatic thoughts and thinking patterns. Cognitive counselors employ a host of techniques to help their clients restructure or alter their thinking processes, a few of which are reviewed here.

- The primary goal of cognitive therapy is to assist clients in identifying their automatic thoughts so that they can be challenged and changed.
- **Cognitive rehearsal** helps clients practice using their new thoughts before implementing them in an actual situation. Counselors may ask clients to imagine certain scenarios and describe the positive self-statements they would use to promote healthy behavior, emotions, and interpersonal interactions.
- Cognitive therapists give clients **homework (directives)** to reinforce learning and skill acquisition outside of counseling sessions. For example, clients might be asked to practice their new self-statements in certain real-life situations.

- When clients engage in **scriptotherapy**, or therapeutic writing, they write down their thoughts, which helps to clarify and enhance them.
- **Thought stopping** is a technique that teaches clients how to interrupt a pattern of negative self-statements or thinking, and it usually involves the substitution of one thought for another. For example, clients may be asked to yell "Stop!" in their heads until their self-defeating thoughts end. Or they may be encouraged to create healthy thoughts to repeat to themselves whenever certain negative thoughts arise. In this way, clients gain control over their thinking.

5.4.4 Rational Emotive Behavior Therapy

Rational emotive behavior therapy (REBT), formerly known as rational-emotive therapy (RET), was created from the belief of **Albert Ellis** that other psychological theories were not adequately addressing the salient relationship between thinking and emotion. Although other theories tended to accept that a favorable event leads a person to feel positive emotions and an unfavorable event leads a person to feel negative emotions, Ellis argued that those theorists were making quite a leap (Ellis & Harper, 1975). Ellis proposed that events, in and of themselves, are neither good nor bad; therefore, a person's feelings are not a direct result of an event. Rather, somewhere between the activating event and the emotional consequence, people engage in self-talk, either rational or irrational, that triggers certain emotions (Ellis, 1996; Ellis & Blau, 1998; Ellis & Harper). These rational beliefs (rBs) or irrational beliefs (iBs) are what produce people's emotional responses to any given event. Essentially, people experience emotions because they judge events to be either positive or negative in relationship to their personal objectives (Ellis & Harper). Thus, people who possess irrational thinking patterns need only learn how to think more rationally in order to vastly increase their quality of life. Appropriate feelings help people work toward their goals of survival and enjoyment. Inappropriate feelings, on the other hand, impede people from feeling happy or satisfied and cause unnecessary pain and suffering (Ellis, 1996). In this section, the following concepts are reviewed: irrational thoughts, the ABCDEs of REBT, and REBT techniques.

5.4.4.1 IRRATIONAL THOUGHTS Any time people use the words *must, should, have to,* or *supposed to,* they place extraordinary demands on themselves that usually lead to emotional consequences (Ellis, 1996). One of the primary goals of REBT is to dispute people's irrational beliefs and help them change their musts and shoulds and wants and wishes. Desires are much more advantageous than demands, encouraging people to change rather than become hopeless and helpless.

5.4.4.2 THE ABCDEs OF REBT The **ABCDEs** of REBT explain the core beliefs of the theory and help clients understand the root of their emotions. The activating event (A) is any event or experience that elicits negativity or unease (Ellis, 1996). People's belief systems (B) can be either rational or irrational in response to (A) and are what result in an emotional consequence (C) that is either beneficial or detrimental. By delineating this idea to clients, they can see that (C) actually results from (B) and not (A), as is often thought by clients. Next, irrational beliefs must be disputed (D) with the goal of developing an effective new philosophy (E) that allows people to replace their irrational beliefs with rational beliefs.

5.4.4.3 REBT TECHNIQUES The role of the counselor in REBT is to pay close attention to a client's disclosures to unearth any irrational ideas or statements. Once irrational thoughts have been identified, it is the counselor's job to be active and teach the client how to dispute those irrational thoughts and replace them with increasingly rational ones. It is also necessary for REBT counselors to be tenacious in showing the clients how unreasonable and self-defeating their thoughts are. The following are some of the most common REBT techniques:

- **Reverse role-playing** can be used to show clients how to dispute their iBs. Usually, the counselor pretends to be the client and holds dearly to the client's iBs while the client plays the counselor and attempts to persuade the "client" to think in a more rational manner (Ellis, 1996). In this way, clients can actively practice **disputing irrational beliefs**.
- **Rational emotive imagery** is an uncomfortable, yet potent, technique sometimes used in REBT (Ellis & Blau, 1998). In rational emotive imagery, the client is asked to imagine the anxiety-provoking situation, whatever that may be. Next, the counselor asks the client to stay with the difficult, painful emotions that surface. The client is then urged to allow himself to be flooded with all of his iBs. Once the client has done this for a few minutes, the counselor asks the client to construct his new rational belief and then repeat this new rational belief over and over until he can palpably feel a shift from his "dysfunctional" emotion to a "self-helping" emotion. Once this has been accomplished, the client can apply this skill in his everyday life and generalize the technique to new experiences that arise.
- Clients often must be continually encouraged to think in a rational manner, which is why REBT counselors assign homework to help clients reinforce the ABCDEs of REBT outside of the counseling relationship and practice new behaviors. For example, the counselor might recommend that clients practice disputing their iBs for 10 minutes each day for a specified period of time (Ellis & Blau, 1998).
- Counselors also can give clients **emotional control cards** to help reinforce the disputation of iBs outside of the counseling sessions (Gladding, 2005). These cards list appropriate and inappropriate feelings, which can serve as reminders to clients who are having a difficult time.
- When clients have an iB that interferes with their ability to engage in certain activities, they may be assigned a **shame attack exercise**. These exercises ask clients to participate

in an activity that normally creates anxiety to help them realize that the outcomes are not nearly as embarrassing or devastating as they imagine (Gladding, 2005).

5.4.5 Reality Therapy

William Glasser developed the therapeutic approach known as reality therapy. **Reality therapy** is based on the underlying theory known as choice theory, an approach that is frequently used to work with children in educational settings. The basic premise of reality therapy is that people make choices to meet their five basic needs: survival (e.g., food, water, shelter, breathing), belonging (e.g., friends, family, relationships, love), power (e.g., self-respect, achievement, success, competence), freedom (e.g., independence, control, autonomy), and fun (e.g., hobbies, leisure activities, enjoyment, satisfaction) (Gladding, 2005). According to Glasser, people can make decisions that result in healthy, positive lives or they can make decisions that result in self-destructive, unhappy lives. In this section, the following concepts are reviewed: criteria for healthy behavior, planning, and reality therapy techniques.

5.4.5.1 CRITERIA FOR HEALTHY BEHAVIOR Unlike Freud, who believed that people were motivated by unconscious drives, Glasser emphasized that people are self-determining and have control over their behavior. Thus, the role of counselors is to serve as educators and models, helping clients understand that they are in control of their actions and encouraging them to assess whether their current behaviors are meeting their needs in a constructive, health-promoting way. If not, clients work with the counselor to develop alternative ways to meet their needs without harming themselves or other people. Past behaviors are deemed unimportant because they cannot be changed. Healthy behavior should meet the following standards:

1. The behavior is noncompetitive.
2. The behavior is easily completed without a great deal of mental effort.
3. The behavior can be done by oneself.
4. The behavior has value for the person.
5. The client believes that improvements in lifestyle will result from the behavior.
6. The client can practice the behavior without being self-critical. (Gladding, 2005, p. 95)

By examining these criteria, clients can determine whether their current actions are helping them meet their needs or, conversely, preventing them from meeting their needs.

5.4.5.2 PLANNING An important part of reality therapy is collaborating with clients to help them develop a plausible plan for how to fulfill their wants and needs in a beneficial manner (Gladding, 2005). Plans are usually written out as contracts and list many alternatives for how clients can successfully meet their needs. In this way, clients learn that there are many different choices that they can make that will lead to favorable outcomes. If clients fail to follow the contract, the counselor and client work together to create a new plan with which the client feels more comfortable. Clients are not allowed to give excuses for failing to carry through on a plan; likewise, counselors do not penalize or condemn clients who do not uphold the plan. Consequently, clients must take full responsibility for themselves and their choices.

5.4.5.3 REALITY THERAPY TECHNIQUES Reality therapists teach clients better ways of behaving to meet their needs and they also confront when necessary. Confrontation is used to help clients think critically about their present behavior and whether it is truly meeting their needs in the best possible manner. The predominant technique used by reality therapists is the **WDEP system** (Wubbolding, 2004). W stands for *wants*: counselors ascertain what clients want and need and what actions they have been taking to fulfill their needs. D stands for *doing*: counselors examine clients' actions, thoughts, and feelings. E stands for *evaluation*: counselors encourage clients to evaluate their current behavior and whether it is healthy and responsible, often through the use of questioning. P stands for *plan*: clients come up with a plan for meeting their needs in new ways. Plans should be specific, realistic, and measurable, and clients should express their resolution to carry out the plan. It is the counselor's job to continually support and encourage clients throughout this process and help them work through any failures or setbacks.

5.4.6 Practice Multiple-Choice Items: Cognitive-Behavioral Theories and Interventions

1. All of the following behavioral techniques are most commonly used with children, EXCEPT
   a. token economy.
   b. contingency contract.
   c. behavioral rehearsal.
   d. response cost.

2. Reinforcing clients' accomplishment of successive approximations of a desired behavior is known as
   a. maintenance.
   b. shaping.
   c. overcorrection.
   d. extinction.

3. In the WDEP system of reality therapy, the P stands for
   a. practice.
   b. purpose.
   c. power.
   d. plan.

4. The theory most concerned with irrational thoughts is
   a. Gestalt therapy.
   b. reality therapy.
   c. rational emotive behavior therapy.
   d. cognitive therapy.

5. A woman volunteers at a child-care center. During one of her visits, two of the children get upset with her when she tells them it's time to clean up and start kicking her. The woman quits volunteering because she concludes that all

children are violent. The type of distorted thinking that best describes this example is
   a. magnification.
   b. overgeneralization.
   c. labeling.
   d. selective abstraction.

Answer Key: 1. c; 2. b; 3. d; 4. c; 5. b.

5.5 HUMANISTIC-EXISTENTIAL THEORIES AND INTERVENTIONS

Humanistic-existential theories represent the "third force" of counseling. Underlying **humanistic counseling** theories is a shared philosophy. In general, humanistic counselors believe in human goodness and the ability of all individuals to strive toward self-actualization given the proper environment. **Existential counseling** assists clients in addressing universal questions about life, death, and freedom and helps them find meaning in their lives. Both approaches stress the importance of showing clients unconditional positive regard and allowing the client to direct the sessions. Humanistic-existential counselors do not attempt to analyze clients, nor do they spend time focusing on the past. Counselors trust that clients have the ability to make important changes in their lives without being directed; rather, they believe that if counselors provide clients with a safe, trusting environment, clients will naturally move toward personal growth. Famous humanistic-existential theorists include Carl Rogers, Abraham Maslow, Fritz Perls, Victor Frankl, Rollo May, and Virginia Satir. In this section of Chapter 5, client-centered counseling, existential counseling, and Gestalt therapy approaches are reviewed.

5.5.1 Client-Centered Counseling

Carl Rogers developed **client-centered counseling**, also known as **person-centered therapy**. Although almost all counselors today use this theory to some extent, at the time of its inception it was considered quite unorthodox. The prevailing theories at that time focused on the role of the counselor in controlling sessions and were focused predominantly on clients' problems or issues. Rogers, however, believed that it was not necessary for therapists to be directive for client change to occur. He thought that clients would set the pace of counseling and determine the focus of each session. Rogers also downplayed the use of techniques, instead focusing on the development of a trusting, genuine, and accepting therapeutic relationship to facilitate change. In this section, the following concepts are reviewed: phenomenology, core conditions of counseling, and client-centered techniques

5.5.1.1 PHENOMENOLOGY Client-centered counselors approach clients from a **phenomenological perspective**, meaning that counselors focus on how clients *perceive* an event rather than the event itself (Gladding, 2005). The ultimate goal for counselors is to help clients resolve any disparities between their beliefs about themselves and reality. In other words, clients must reconcile "their *ideal self* (i.e., what they are striving to become) and their *real self* (i.e., what they are)" (p. 65) to become psychologically adjusted and healthy.

5.5.1.2 CORE CONDITIONS OF COUNSELING

Rogers believed that counselors must embody the **core counseling conditions** (i.e., genuineness/congruence, respect/unconditional positive regard, and empathy) to promote client change, growth, and self-actualization. Not only must counselors be genuine, respectful, and empathic, but clients must also *regard* counselors as genuine, respectful, and empathic.

- *Genuine* counselors are authentic. They are honest with their clients and ensure that counselor verbal and nonverbal communication is *congruent*. Being genuine helps to build trust in the counselor-client relationship.
- Client-centered counselors strive to show *respect*, *acceptance*, and *unconditional positive regard* for their clients. Counselors may not agree with everything that a client does, but they must continue to communicate their acceptance of the client as a person. The importance of this condition is paramount. Rogers believed that many people do not experience unconditional regard from friends and family, which undermines their sense of self. Therefore, he believed it was critical for counselors to accept and prize clients no matter what, freeing them to develop a more congruent and integrated identity.
- *Empathic* counselors successfully enter the client's worldview and are able to convey their understanding of a client's thoughts, feelings, and actions.

5.5.1.3 CLIENT-CENTERED TECHNIQUES

As mentioned, client-centered therapists de-emphasize the use of specific techniques, focusing more on the development of a therapeutic alliance that incorporates the core conditions of counseling. However, the counseling skills discussed in section 5.2 are commonly employed by client-centered counselors to facilitate the counseling process; in particular, reflecting skills, invitational skills, confronting, and summarizing are used.

5.5.2 Existential Counseling

Existential counseling, pioneered by **Victor Frankl** and **Rollo May**, is concerned with helping clients to find meaning and value in their lives and to explore philosophical concepts, such as life, death, freedom, and responsibility (Gladding, 2005). Existentialists believe that people have **free will** (i.e., self-determination) and maintain that everyone has the ability to change their lives and their actions to create a healthy, meaningful life. The role of the existential counselor is to encourage clients to take responsibility for their lives, seek and find meaning in their existence, reflect on and assess their choices, and improve their relationships with others. Existential counselors accomplish these goals by being honest and congruent and establishing meaningful relationships with clients. In addition, clients are urged to address what they are currently experiencing in their lives rather than past issues or concerns. The following concepts are reviewed in this section: logotherapy, anxiety, and existential techniques.

5.5.2.1 LOGOTHERAPY

Logotherapy is an approach created by Victor Frankl that focuses on individuals' search for meaning in their lives. According to Frankl, meaning can be found in everything, even the worst of circumstances. He contended that people find meaning in their lives through achievement or creation, suffering, and experiencing and appreciating people and the world around them (Gladding, 2005). Without meaning, clients experience an **existential vacuum** (i.e., meaninglessness). Thus, logotherapy is the process of helping clients identify or seek meaning in their lives. Frankl's renowned book *Man's Search for Meaning* discusses his internment in a concentration camp during the Holocaust and the meaning he derived from his experience.

5.5.2.2 ANXIETY

Rollo May studied the concept of anxiety in-depth. *Anxiety* often interferes with people's ability to accomplish goals, and May believed that whereas it is beneficial to experience moderate amounts of anxiety, too much anxiety causes people to avoid certain activities and actions. Thus, one goal of counseling is to explore clients' anxiety, find meaning in it, and help them work through it so that they can make decisions that bring them closer to their life goals.

5.5.2.3 EXISTENTIAL TECHNIQUES

Similar to client-centered counseling, existential counseling does not have an array of techniques specific to the theory. Existential counselors do not believe in a one-size-fits-all style of counseling. Rather, existential counselors draw techniques from a wide range of theories, depending on the needs of their clients (Gladding, 2005). In general, existential counselors believe it is essential to form a strong bond with clients and to confront clients when necessary to help them become aware of the role they play in shaping their own lives. Although not many techniques are specific to existential counseling, Frankl did develop a technique called paradoxical intention, which is used by counselors from a variety of theoretical backgrounds.

- **Paradoxical intention** involves prescribing the symptom. For example, if a client laments about how she cannot seem to stop crying, the counselor might tell her to try to cry all day. Or a client with insomnia might be told to try to stay up all night. In this way, the fear or anxiety accompanying the symptom is removed, and clients are able to recognize that they have some control over expression of the symptom.

5.5.3 Gestalt Therapy

Fritz Perls created Gestalt therapy to fill a void in the field of psychology. At a time when many psychologists subscribed to the psychodynamic approaches of Freud, Jung, and Adler, Perls was convinced that these psychodynamic theorists could not fully attend to the goal of improving people's lives because the approaches were not taking the "whole" person into consideration (Perls, 1973).

Gestalt psychology comprises a handful of beliefs that form the bedrock of its philosophy. To begin, it is important to define the German word *gestalt*. A gestalt, in relation to human nature is "the organization of facts, perceptions, behavior or phenomena, and not the individual items of which they are composed, that defines them and gives them their specific and particular meaning" (Perls, 1973, p. 2). To neglect these gestalts, or patterns, that every person has is to not fully understand that person. Moreover, if counselors do not adequately understand their clients and the organizations of thought and action under which they operate, it is unlikely that they will be able to help their clients understand their own problems and work to improve their lives. In this section on Gestalt therapy, the following concepts are reviewed: homeostasis, the holistic doctrine, contact boundary, and Gestalt techniques.

5.5.3.1 HOMEOSTASIS

One of the important premises of Gestalt psychology is that human beings seek to maintain a state of balance, called **homeostasis**. People are continually taking inventory of their needs, prioritizing, and tending to their needs so as to maintain health and well-being. Perls (1973) proposed that homeostasis is not merely physiological but also psychological. For example, when people are hungry, their equilibrium is thrown off, so they eat to return to a state of balance. Likewise, if someone is lonely, their psychological equilibrium is thrown off, and they seek social contact to mollify that need. Accordingly, when a person is chronically unable to recognize, prioritize, and find ways to successfully alleviate their needs, they fall into a neurotic state. Gestalt psychology attempts to help these people with neuroses by facilitating an awareness of their most important needs and what they must do to allay these needs. When a need is satisfied, a gestalt is closed, and the client can move on to the next most pressing need.

5.5.3.2 THE HOLISTIC DOCTRINE

Perls (1973) strongly opposed theorists who viewed the mind and the body as separate entities. In Gestalt psychology, the mind-body connection is heralded as a powerful way to heighten clients' awareness. The mind-body connection is paramount in this approach and is key to clients' improvement and self-understanding. By alerting clients to physical movements they unwittingly make, Gestalt therapists hope that they will become increasingly aware of their body language as it relates to their unexpressed emotions. A client's physical movement, tic, or mannerism that a client has may be connected to something that is occurring mentally and emotionally. Thus, the mind and body must be viewed as interconnected and equally relevant.

Similarly, it is believed that thinking and doing are inextricably linked. How a person processes problems mentally can help to explain how that person behaves and vice versa. Perls (1973) used the idea of fantasy to exemplify this idea: "I anticipate in fantasy what will happen in reality, and although the correspondence between my fantasy anticipation and the actual situation may not be absolute, it is close enough for me to base my actions upon it" (p. 12). In this way, people are able to formulate and fantasize about solutions to their problems before acting them out in real life. Gestalt therapists put this belief to work in their use of psychodrama, which helps clients move from fantasizing about certain actions or behaviors, to practicing them, to using them in reality, when appropriate.

5.5.3.3 CONTACT BOUNDARY

Another basic premise of Gestalt psychology is the supposition that how a person makes contact and interacts with his or her environment, or field, is essential to the understanding of that person. By environment, Perls (1973) referred to the environment as any social interaction or contact with the community. However, Perls was careful to point out that people are not victims of their environment and that the environment is not a victim of people. Rather, people make either healthy or unhealthy contact with their environment, or healthy or unhealthy withdrawal from their environment. A psychologically healthy person has the ability to make positive contact with the environment and positive withdrawals from the environment and to decide which one is appropriate in any given situation. People with neuroses, on the other hand, are so overwhelmingly preoccupied with the unfinished business in their lives that they are unable to judge when contact or withdrawal with their environment would be necessary or beneficial.

Perls (1973, p. 57) described **unfinished business** as "the past which remains in the present." The purpose of Gestalt psychology is to help individuals with neuroses become integrated and self-supportive through resolving their unfinished business. When that goal is accomplished, clients will be able to interact with their environment in a way that satisfies their needs without infringing on the field.

5.5.3.4 GESTALT TECHNIQUES

In the Gestalt approach, techniques are often experiential and experimental. **Experiments** are conducted spontaneously, whereas **exercises** are preplanned. Exercises used by Gestalt therapists often include psychodrama, role-playing, and the empty chair technique.

- **Here and now therapy** encourages clients to discuss only what is bothering them in the present moment (Perls, 1973). To accomplish this task, the counselor may begin a counseling session by asking the client to finish the statement, "Now I am aware. . . ." Not only does that sentence urge clients to speak in the present tense but, through the use of the word *I*, they are also asked to take responsibility for their thoughts. Through this technique, clients become aware of how they are thinking and feeling at every moment, which helps them define their most pressing problems and seek solutions. Once clients are able to solve a problem they are more self-supportive and better able to solve future problems in a healthy manner.

- **Psychodrama** is used in Gestalt therapy to help clients understand their internal conflicts. This can be achieved by having clients play a variety of roles simultaneously, which allows them to engage in discussion with conflicting parts of their personalities (Perls, 1973). Clients may also be asked to talk to someone with whom they are in conflict, often characterized by an **empty chair**, which facilities a dialogue between the client and the other individual.

- The role of a Gestalt counselor is as a facilitator; however, the counselor must also be willing to *frustrate* and *confront* clients when it is determined that clients are not being genuine or taking responsibility for themselves

(Perls, 1973). It is only through challenging that clients are able to see the thought and behavior patterns contributing to their neuroses.

5.5.4 Practice Multiple-Choice Items: Humanistic-Existential Theories and Interventions

1. The core condition of counseling known as unconditional positive regard is also referred to as all of the following EXCEPT
   a. respect.
   b. empathy.
   c. acceptance.
   d. prizing.

2. Logotherapy is an approach that helps clients
   a. work through anxiety.
   b. come to terms with death.
   c. find meaning in their lives.
   d. accept their personal freedom.

3. A counselor who suggests that a depressed client spend at least 2 hours a day being depressed is using what technique?
   a. Paradoxical intention
   b. Reverse psychology
   c. Logotherapy
   d. Confrontation

4. Humanistic counselors are
   a. directive.
   b. problem focused.
   c. person focused.
   d. All of the above.

5. According to Rollo May, healthy people
   a. should not experience anxiety.
   b. should experience moderate levels of anxiety.
   c. should experience high levels of anxiety because it is motivational.
   d. None of the above.

Answer Key: 1. b; 2. c; 3. a; 4. c; 5. b.

5.6 MULTICULTURAL THEORIES AND INTERVENTIONS

Multicultural theories represent the "fourth force" of counseling and are some of the newest counseling theories to gain recognition in the field. The emphasis in multicultural theories is on viewing clients within the context of their culture (Gladding, 2005). Inspired by **social constructionism**, multicultural counselors strive to determine how clients *construct* their lives and their realities. Once dysfunctional patterns of behavior are identified, counselors can work with clients to help them reconstruct their lives to be more health enhancing. Most important, multicultural counselors approach clients from a **strengths-based perspective** rather than a deficits-based perspective. Instead of focusing on clients' problems and

weaknesses, multicultural counselors hone in and build on clients' strengths and successes to initiate change. In this section, the following multicultural theories are reviewed: narrative therapy and solution-focused brief therapy.

5.6.1 Narrative Therapy

Created by **Michael White** and **David Epston, narrative therapy** is concerned with how individuals reauthor their lives. Narrative therapists believe that people construct stories about themselves and their lives, referred to as **self-narratives**, which help clients develop a consistent identity (Goldenberg & Goldenberg, 2008). In so doing, some people create self-narratives that are harmful and detrimental to their well-being. These narratives are referred to as **problem-saturated stories**. Therefore, the goal of narrative therapy is to help clients who are experiencing difficulties in their lives to reauthor their self-narratives to promote greater wellness. Clients are viewed as the experts in narrative therapy, and it is the counselor's responsibility to assist them in deconstructing and reconstructing their life stories. Beyond self-narratives, counselors also work with clients to reauthor any **dominant narratives**—that is, cultural customs—that adversely affect their lives (e.g., sexism, racism, ageism). The following concepts are important in narrative approaches: thin/thick descriptions, problem externalization, unique outcomes, and narrative techniques.

5.6.1.1 THIN/THICK DESCRIPTIONS One objective of narrative therapy is to help clients who possess thin self-narratives create thick self-narratives (Goldenberg & Goldenberg, 2008). A **thin description**, or self-narrative, is one that is imposed on a person by others (e.g., society) that the individual then internalizes. For example, a teenage girl thinks she is fat because of her society's preference for thin women. Conversely, a **thick description** is more complex and detailed and involves clients' interpretations of themselves, and the labels that are put on them by others. It is through the therapeutic process of creating alternative narratives that clients develop thick descriptions.

5.6.1.2 PROBLEM EXTERNALIZATION A key component of this modality is **problem externalization** of clients' problems. Many clients view their problems as innate and hard to alter. Thus, narrative therapists strive to help clients distance themselves from their problems, reconstruct their stories, and rid themselves of undesirable narratives. Counselors accomplish this feat through the use of *externalizing questions*. For example, a client who is angry might be asked, "How has anger been ruling your life these past few months?" By naming the problem and separating it from the client, blame is taken out of the equation, and the client is given control over the problem. Questions often seek to ascertain what clients are going through and how the problem is affecting their lives.

5.6.1.3 UNIQUE OUTCOMES Similar to solution-focused brief therapy (discussed in section 5.6.2), narrative therapists help clients **seek unique outcomes** by asking clients to identify times when their problems were not present or were less pronounced (Goldenberg & Goldenberg, 2008). For example, counselors might ask clients to tell them about a time when they were not controlled by their problems (e.g., "Tell me about a time when melancholy did not stop you from socializing with your friends."). These unique outcomes help clients begin the process of creating *alternative self-narratives*. Once clients have constructed new self-narratives, counselors urge them to recount their stories repeatedly, and in considerable detail, to help them thicken and internalize these fresh narratives.

5.6.1.4 NARRATIVE TECHNIQUES Although the core methodologies of narrative therapy have been summarized in previous sections, some counselors employ a couple of additional techniques to assist their clients in reauthoring their life stories. These include bringing in outside witnesses and writing therapeutic letters.

- **Outside witnesses** are sometimes brought into counseling sessions to help clients gain an outside perspective on themselves, or to meet people who share a similar concern. Outside witnesses are frequently family members, friends, or some of the counselors' previous clients. Witnesses usually observe a session and then talk about what they heard, what they connected with, and what affected them. Then the client is given the opportunity to discuss what it was like hearing from the witness. This process helps clients solidify their new self-narratives. Other times, clients tell their new stories to an audience of outside witnesses, called a **definitional ceremony**. Once the telling is completed, the witnesses are given the opportunity to comment on what they heard. This technique helps clients thicken their stories.
- Narrative therapists frequently write **therapeutic letters** to clients following sessions. These letters review what was discussed in the session and highlight important moments. The ultimate goal of these letters is to keep the work that occurred during the session going long after the session has ended. In addition, letter writing can assist clients to internalize new self-narratives.

5.6.2 Solution-Focused Brief Therapy

Solution-focused brief therapy (SFBT), developed by **Steve deShazer**, is based on the assumption that all individuals possess the ability and resources to solve their problems (Goldenberg & Goldenberg, 2008). In essence, SFBT maintains that people become immobilized by unsuccessful attempts to solve problems and that they need only to find new solutions to achieve change and progress. Counselors working from this perspective believe that clients are the experts and that the counselor's role is to collaborate with clients to help them unearth these potential solutions. SFBT is not concerned about the history of a problem or seeking insight into why a problem has arisen; the primary goal is client change and instilling hope in clients that change will happen. SFBT, as its name suggests, is short term, usually lasting no more than 10 sessions (Gladding, 2005).

Keeping with its social constructionism roots, language plays a key role in this theory. Counselors pay special attention to

how clients view and talk about their situations and goals, and they use this information to help clients restructure their stories (Goldenberg & Goldenberg, 2008). SFBT counselors believe that if clients can change their thoughts about situations, they will be able to change their behavior. In relation to change, SFBT counselors do not expect that enormous changes will occur as a result of their work. Rather, they contend that if clients can make a baby step toward their goal, that small change will increase their expectation for future changes and will motivate them to keep trying new behaviors and solutions. In this section, the following concepts are discussed: core beliefs; visitors, complainants, and customers; and SFBT techniques.

5.6.2.1 CORE BELIEFS In general, the foundation of SFBT counseling is based on these three beliefs: (a) if clients are already doing something that works, they should continue doing it; (b) if clients try something that does not work, they should stop doing it and try something else; and, (c) if clients try something that works, they should do more of it.

5.6.2.2 VISITORS, COMPLAINANTS, AND CUSTOMERS SFBT counselors sometimes categorize clients based on their willingness and readiness to change. **Visitors** are clients who are not at all ready or willing to change; they do not recognize that a problem exists (Gladding, 2005). **Complainants** are clients who recognize the existence of a problem and can define it but have yet to commit to solving it. **Customers** are the most ideal clients; such clients recognize that a problem needs to be fixed and are committed to finding a solution. Until clients become customers, it is difficult to help them effectively improve their lives.

5.6.2.3 SFBT TECHNIQUES SFBT comprises a host of specific techniques that counselors use strategically to encourage clients to begin to change and think about their situations in a new, hopeful light.

- Although SFBT counselors focus predominantly on solutions and using "solution-talk," they also take the time to *acknowledge* and *validate* clients' thoughts and emotions related to their problem (Goldenberg & Goldenberg, 2008). It is this acknowledgment that sets the stage for a collaborative and trusting counselor-client relationship, in which clients feel listened to and understood. Through the combination of acknowledgment and solution-talk, SFBT counselors assist clients in rewriting their stories and creating a more beneficial, multilayered story.
- One way that SFBT counselors help clients find possible solutions is by asking them exception questions, which target times when the problem was not present in their lives or when they were able to circumvent an issue that had been plaguing them, even if only briefly (Goldenberg & Goldenberg, 2008). Using these exceptions, counselors can encourage clients to explore how they were able to avoid a problem or temporarily alleviate the problem in the hope that these experiences will provide clues to possible solutions.

- The **miracle question** is used in SFBT to help clients begin to think about how to solve their problems. Usually, the question is some variation of "If a miracle happened and you woke up to find that your problem was solved, what would be different?"
- **Scaling questions** are used to keep track of clients' progress and help them continue making small changes. An example of a scaling question is "On a scale of 1 to 10 (with 10 meaning that your problem is solved), how close are you to meeting your goal?" If a client says that he is a 7, the counselor can them ask him what he would need to do to reach an 8, and so on.
- Counselors often give clients very general assignments that ask clients to behave in a new manner or keep track of the times when their problem does not seem to be present. These tasks, although generic, can help clients begin the process of trying alternative methods for working through a problem. Before introducing an assignment, counselors may give clients *compliments* (planned in advance) to acknowledge their successes and encourage them to keep up the good work (Gladding, 2005).
- **Positive blame** is used to reinforce clients' capabilities when they successfully make a change or engage in a behavior that brings them closer to their goal. For example, if a client who has trouble talking with her husband without getting into a fight is able to hold a calm, pleasant conversation with him, the counselor might ask her, "How did you do that? What did you do that prevented the conversation from turning into a fight?"
- **Skeleton keys** are techniques that "have worked before and have universal application" (Gladding, 2005, p. 215). Asking clients to do something different or to behave in a new manner are examples of skeleton keys because clients can use them to improve many different situations and concerns.

5.6.3 Practice Multiple-Choice Items: Multicultural Counseling Theories and Interventions

1. A client comes to counseling and admits that she has a problem with alcohol abuse but does not seem committed to making any changes in her life. This client is most likely a
   a. visitor.
   b. complainant.
   c. customer.
   d. None of the above.

2. Therapeutic letters are written by
   a. clients.
   b. therapists.
   c. outside witnesses.
   d. All of the above.

3. Thick descriptions are all of the following EXCEPT
   a. detailed.
   b. multilayered.
   c. based primarily on outsider labels.
   d. complex.

4. A dominant narrative is one constructed by
   a. the client.
   b. the client's family of origin.
   c. the counselor.
   d. society.

5. Which of the following is NOT an example of an externalizing question?
   a. How long have you been sad?
   b. How has depression affected your personal life?
   c. When have you been able to ignore anxiety?
   d. How have your academics been affected by compulsiveness?

Answer Key: 1. b; 2. b; 3. c; 4. d; 5. a.

5.7 FAMILY THEORIES AND INTERVENTIONS

Family theories of counseling provide practitioners with a systemic way of conceptualizing problems within a family. These systems theories aim to ameliorate the functioning of entire family units, rather than the one "symptomatic" individual within the family. It is believed that when a family *as a whole* develops healthier patterns of interaction, each individual member's psychological state will also improve. One of the earliest theories of family counseling was the **psychodynamic model**, which was developed by Nathan Ackerman and based on some of the key concepts of Freud's psychoanalytic theory (Goldenberg & Goldenberg, 2008). In particular, psychodynamic family therapists explored the role of anxiety, defense mechanisms, and unconscious conflicts and desires in the functioning of individuals and families. Since that time, additional family theories based largely on systems theory have emerged. The widely used family theories and concepts that are reviewed in this section of Chapter 5 include general systems theory, Bowen family systems therapy, experiential family counseling, Milan systemic family counseling, strategic family therapy, and structural family counseling. For an overview of the stages of family development, refer to section 3.9.1.

5.7.1 General Systems Theory

Developed by Ludwig von Bertalanffy, **general systems theory** provides a basic framework for understanding the interactions and issues that occur within family systems. Bertalanffy suggested that it is more helpful to examine family relationships and transactions between members than to scrutinize the personalities or actions of any one family member in isolation (Goldenberg & Goldenberg, 2008). Families are viewed as complex, organized systems, with each member influencing and being influenced by other members, a concept known as **circular causality**. In essence, there is no discrete cause-and-effect phenomenon in families: "A does not cause B, nor does B cause A; both cause each other" (p. 18). In this section, the ways in which family members organize themselves and their relationships are discussed, including a review of family rules, homeostasis, boundaries, and open and closed systems.

5.7.1.1 FAMILY RULES

Every family has **rules** that members abide by. Some of these rules are overtly stated (e.g., no one starts eating dinner until everyone has been served), whereas others are more subtle and unspoken (e.g., the family does not disclose dad's drug addiction to outsiders). The purpose of these rules is to establish a template of expected family behavior and to provide members with predictability and a foundation for interacting with each other (Goldenberg & Goldenberg, 2008). Some rules preserve and enhance family functioning, whereas others do the opposite. Therefore, it is essential for professional counselors to ascertain and reveal each family's rules because they provide insight into how the family functions, expose possible reasons for dysfunction, and may point to rules that must be revised or discarded.

5.7.1.2 HOMEOSTASIS

Homeostasis is the tendency for families to sustain their normal functioning and patterns of interaction unless someone or something intervenes (Goldenberg & Goldenberg, 2008). Regaining homeostasis after a change requires families to either find a way to revert to their previous level of functioning or use the change as a catalyst to find new and better ways of maintaining stability. Most current counselors attend to the latter, helping families foster growth while also maintaining security.

5.7.1.3 BOUNDARIES

Boundaries help to separate the family system from outsiders and define roles and responsibilities within a family unit (Goldenberg & Goldenberg, 2008). Families often develop certain boundaries that help delineate what is and is not acceptable or allowable in various family **subsystems** (i.e., spousal, parental, sibling). For example, the parental subsystem might set up a boundary whereby the parents make all of the final decisions in the family. However, the oldest child may be allowed to take on that parental authority in their absence and with their permission. Depending on the family, boundaries can be either rigid or flexible. It is important that boundaries be well established, known, and understood by all members because "if boundaries are too blurred or too rigid, they invite confusion or inflexibility, increasing the family's risk of instability and ultimate dysfunction" (p. 90).

5.7.1.4 OPEN AND CLOSED SYSTEMS

Open family systems have flexible boundaries, are open to change, and have ongoing interaction and involvement with their communities (Goldenberg & Goldenberg, 2008). *Closed family systems* have rigid boundaries, are averse to change, and cordon themselves off from the outside world. Ideally, families strike a healthy balance between these two extremes, establishing clear boundaries with outsiders, while also allowing for exchange and interaction with them.

5.7.2 Bowen Family Systems Therapy

Developed by **Murray Bowen**, **Bowen family systems therapy** is one of the most prominent theories of family counseling. Several of Bowen's ideas stemmed from his own relationship with his **family of origin (FOO)**, which is the family in which a person grows up. Essentially, Bowen maintains that people are affected by their family of origin and that they must resolve any issues from their childhood to keep from repeating dysfunctional patterns of interaction in future relationships (Gladding, 2005). Bowen's theory encourages professional counselors to examine what he considered to be the eight elements influencing a family's operation, all of which are discussed in this section: differentiation of self, triangles, nuclear family emotional system, family projection process, multigenerational transmission process, emotional cutoff, sibling position, and societal regression.

5.7.2.1 DIFFERENTIATION OF SELF

Differentiation of self refers to people's ability to separate themselves from their family of origin without cutting themselves off from their families. Someone who is adequately differentiated is able to remain connected with her family without becoming **fused** (i.e., enmeshed) with any family members or situations. A differentiated person is able to encounter emotionally charged family situations and balance her emotions with logic and rationality (Goldenberg & Goldenberg, 2008). On the other hand, an undifferentiated person is highly dependent on the family and easily affected by family conflicts and emotional tension.

5.7.2.2 TRIANGLES

A **triangle** is a relationship system comprised of three people. It is considered to be more stable than a dyad because stress and tension can be spread out among the three different relationships (Goldenberg & Goldenberg, 2008). A family creates a triangle when two members (usually the parental subsystem) who are experiencing an uncomfortable amount of stress in their relationship draw in a third member (usually a child) to help release emotional tension. The more differentiated a person is, the less likely he or she will need to triangulate to reduce the pressure of a relationship. It is also important to note that any family member with a low level of differentiation is more likely than other members to be pulled into a triangle.

5.7.2.3 NUCLEAR FAMILY EMOTIONAL SYSTEM

A **nuclear family emotional system** is formed based on the parental subsystem's degree of differentiation. Bowen asserted that individuals are normally attracted to partners who have the same level of differentiation as they do (Goldenberg & Goldenberg, 2008). Thus, one undifferentiated person is likely to marry another undifferentiated person and create a fused family emotional system that eventually results in physical or emotional impairment in one of the spouses, marital discord, or a child with psychological issues. To resolve these problems, the undifferentiated members must work to become more differentiated from their families of origin, which will result in changes in the marital dyad and the nuclear family emotional system.

5.7.2.4 FAMILY PROJECTION PROCESS

The **family projection process** occurs when undifferentiated parents project their tension and anxiety onto their most susceptible or sensitive child. As a result of this triangulation, the child often becomes symptomatic and the parents focus on the child as the source of the problem, rather than on themselves. Ultimately, through this process, the child ends up with the same low level of differentiation as the parents.

5.7.2.5 MULTIGENERATIONAL TRANSMISSION PROCESS
When considering the concepts of the nuclear family emotional system and the family projection process, it becomes clear how low levels of differentiation can be passed on through a **multigenerational transmission process** (Goldenberg & Goldenberg, 2008). If undifferentiated parents create undifferentiated children, it is likely that those children will find similarly undifferentiated marriage partners and begin the transmission process all over again.

5.7.2.6 EMOTIONAL CUTOFF
Children who are highly fused with their families and affected by the family projection process may try to emotionally cut themselves off (i.e., **emotional cutoff**) from their family of origin to try and improve or maintain their well-being (Goldenberg & Goldenberg, 2008). These individuals may try to emotionally cut themselves off in a variety of ways: moving, refusing to talk to family members, or only interacting with family members on a surface level. Although these individuals believe they are solving their problems, Bowen would argue that until they truly resolve their issues with their family and increase their level of differentiation, they will still remain fused to their family of origin and that fusion will manifest itself in their marital relationship and family system.

5.7.2.7 SIBLING POSITION
Bowen believed that people's birth order or *sibling position* substantially affects the personality traits they develop (Goldenberg & Goldenberg, 2008). He concluded that marriages work out best when spousal roles match the partners' sibling positions from their families of origin. For example, Bowen would assert that an oldest child and a youngest child would be well suited for each other because they both would be able to continue in the roles they carried out in childhood. In addition, both spouses would be accustomed to their own roles and the role of his or her partner.

5.7.2.8 SOCIETAL REGRESSION
Societal regression occurs when a society that is experiencing too much stress regresses in its level of differentiation (Goldenberg & Goldenberg, 2008). Like families, Bowen thought that societies, too, could be either differentiated or undifferentiated.

5.7.2.9 BOWEN FAMILY SYSTEMS TECHNIQUES
In the process of Bowen family systems therapy, a variety of techniques are used as necessary. In particular, the counselor *asks questions* to facilitate clients' awareness and insight into their patterns of interaction. The techniques include genograms, back home visits, and detriangulation.

- Bowen created **genograms** with clients, which are visual representations of approximately three generations of a family (Goldenberg & Goldenberg, 2008). Genograms include information such as members' names, ages, marriage dates, divorce dates, dates of deaths, important events, and symbols to describe relationship patterns, fusion, and emotional cutoff. These genograms can help professional counselors and families become aware of patterns of interaction that have occurred throughout a family's history and work to resolve any dysfunction that becomes apparent.
- **Back home visits** are recommended for clients who have unresolved issues with their family of origin (Gladding, 2005). The ultimate goal of these visits is to increase the client's differentiation. Prior to the visit, the counselor works with the client to prepare for the visits home and to achieve a beneficial outcome.
- Back home visits also can help some clients with **detriangulation** (i.e., learning how to avoid becoming involved in triangles and how to avoid triangulating others).

5.7.3 Experiential Family Counseling

Similar to the humanistic-existential theories of counseling, **experiential family counseling** is less concerned with techniques and more concerned with establishing a genuine relationship with clients and helping them bring their problems into the here and now. Experiential counselors approach each family in a different way because no two families are the same. Nonetheless, they all strive to be honest and open and allow themselves to come in close contact with families, implementing creative interventions to encourage client development and insight (Goldenberg & Goldenberg, 2008). The goal of counseling is to help family members become more aware of their emotions, become more self-actualizing, and increase their ability to interact with each other and give and receive love and affection in a more authentic and spontaneous manner. Two prominent experiential models are Whitaker's symbolic-experiential family therapy and Satir's human validation process model, both of which are reviewed in this section.

5.7.3.1 SYMBOLIC-EXPERIENTIAL FAMILY THERAPY
Symbolic-experiential family therapy is an approach developed by **Carl Whitaker** to help families strike a balance between independence and togetherness and learn how to interact with each other in a meaningful and natural way, while moving away from the tendency to behave in the same monotonous patterns that led to the dysfunction (Goldenberg & Goldenberg, 2008). Symbolic-experiential counselors encourage clients to engage with one another and solve problems creatively instead of relying on previous habits. Ideally, counselors aim to involve several generations of a family in counseling, where they are better able to study patterns of family interaction that have occurred in multiple generations. Throughout the counseling process, counselors search for and bring to the family's attention the hidden symbolism and impulses that underlie their interactions. In general, counselors using this approach serve as facilitators, helping the family discover and

apply their skills and abilities to solve their problem. This, of course, requires that family members be willing to take responsibility for the entire family's growth.

5.7.3.2 HUMAN VALIDATION PROCESS MODEL Virginia Satir (1916–1988), who created the **human validation process model**, believed in the innate goodness of humans, their desire to grow and learn, and their ability to change (Goldenberg & Goldenberg, 2008), much like Carl Rogers did. Accordingly, her goal in counseling families was to create a safe, warm, and welcoming environment in which they would feel comfortable exploring their issues and beginning the process of change. In this approach, symptoms are viewed as ways to preserve the family's homeostasis and as obstructions to growth. Thus, these blockages must be unclogged to allow development to occur.

Satir focused much of her attention on how family members communicate with one another. She identified four types of dysfunctional communication patterns that family members often adopt: placater, blamer, intellectualizer/super-reasonable, and distracters/irrelevants (Goldenberg & Goldenberg, 2008).

- *Placaters* agree with and try to please everyone; they also mollify people, are unsure of themselves, and often lack self-confidence.
- *Blamers* are critical of other people, charge others with wrongdoing, and fail to take any responsibility for their actions.
- *Intellectualizers* or *super-reasonables* approach situations in a detached manner, rationalizing everything and never allowing their emotions to be shown.
- *Distracters* want to avoid dealing with situations, so they distract others by introducing unrelated, irrelevant topics.

Satir worked with family members to replace these toxic styles of communication with a more health-enhancing one, the *congruent* communicator, who sends clear messages and verbal comments matching his or her nonverbal behavior and internal thoughts and feelings. To help facilitate this process, Satir modeled congruence in her counseling.

In summary, Satir's model of family counseling emphasizes the positive and endeavors to make use of the resources families already possess to enact change. Satir thought the therapeutic alliance was the most important characteristic in the change process, which included conveying to families her belief in their ability to change and grow.

5.7.3.3 FAMILY SCULPTING Although not many techniques are unique to experiential family counseling because counselors following this model prefer to design their own interventions based on the particular needs of the family, one technique is worth mentioning: family sculpting. In general, techniques used by experiential counselors can run the gamut from the use of art, music, and body movements to psychodrama, reframing, and role playing.

- **Family sculpting** is a technique used to help the counselor and the family more fully understand one family

member's impression of family relationships (Goldenberg & Goldenberg, 2008). To implement this technique, the counselor asks a family member to physically arrange the entire family in the room. The end result can be quite telling: Were certain family members put close to one another? Were others placed far away from each other? Were some sitting and others standing? All these details can provide insight into family dynamics and functioning.

5.7.4 Strategic Family Therapy

Strategic family therapy, like behavioral approaches to counseling, emphasize altering behavior rather than helping clients gain insight and personal awareness (Gladding, 2005). Using directive strategies tailored to each family, strategic family therapists aim to resolve the problem as quickly as possible; consequently, this type of family counseling is generally short term in nature. Strategic family therapists are active during sessions and strive to quickly identify the presenting problem and enact a strategy to help the family begin to resolve it. This process involves four steps: (a) defining the problem, (b) asking family members to discuss what they have done to try to solve the problem themselves, (c) establishing the goal of counseling for the family, and (d) developing a strategy to help the family reach its goal. It is also important to note that strategic family therapists, like multicultural theorists, strive to reframe client problems in a positive and constructive light, giving the family hope and control over their situation.

Milton Erickson developed the main tenets of strategic family therapy (Gladding, 2005). However, many other individuals have contributed significantly to this theory of family counseling and expanded on his work. **Jay Haley**, who helped found the Bateson Group, the Mental Research Institute (MRI), and the Family Research Institute, is one such theorist. The MRI has created its own approach to strategic family therapy, known as **MRI Interactional Family Therapy** (Goldenberg & Goldenberg, 2008).

Although strategic family therapy has many unique techniques, the theory itself adheres to the basic principles of general systems theory (i.e., family rules, homeostasis, and circular causality). However, a few additional concepts integral to this theory are discussed here: quid pro quo, the redundancy principle, punctuation, and symmetrical relationships/complementary relationships.

5.7.4.1 QUID PRO QUO Quid pro quo refers to the propensity of individuals to treat others like they are treated (Gladding, 2005). For example, one family member does something (e.g., "a favor") to get something from another family member. This "reciprocal behavior" is common between marriage partners. Quid pro quo behavior is present in all families, and often it is unspoken.

5.7.4.2 THE REDUNDANCY PRINCIPLE Family members tend to interact with each other in the same way, and it is unusual for those patterns of behavior to change or expand. This is what is known as the **redundancy principle**.

5.7.4.3 PUNCTUATION **Punctuation** refers to the conviction by individuals that their verbal communication, especially during a conflict, occurs in reaction to someone else (Goldenberg & Goldenberg, 2008). In an argument between two people, what one person says is not *caused* by what the other person says. Strategic family theorists assert that people punctuate conversations in this way, but in reality there is no straightforward cause-and-effect relationship in communications between people.

5.7.4.4 SYMMETRICAL RELATIONSHIPS/COMPLEMENTARY RELATIONSHIPS **Symmetrical relationships** are relationships in a family between equals (Goldenberg & Goldenberg, 2008). These types of relationships may become competitive because there is not a dominant member. **Complementary relationships** are relationships in a family between unequals, where one member is "one down" and the other is "one up." Although this description appears negative, complementary relationships are not necessarily objectionable. For example, a family member who asks for help from another family member would be involved in a complementary relationship, with the person asking for help being "one down" and the person helping being "one up."

5.7.4.5 STRATEGIC FAMILY THERAPY TECHNIQUES Strategic family therapy is propelled by techniques and, as mentioned, these techniques are usually designed or customized for the specific family to best help them reach their goals (Gladding, 2005). The techniques that are reviewed in this section are relabeling/reframing, the use of paradox, directives, ordeals, and the pretend technique.

- **Relabeling/reframing** involves interpreting a family's situation in a new way to encourage family members to view their problem in a more favorable light (Gladding, 2005). It is particularly important that the counselor reframe the problems in a way that increases the family's willingness to change their behavior and give them confidence that they have the ability to solve their problem. Using this technique, a teenager who is rebellious may be relabeled as a person who is seeking independence or trying to become more autonomous. Thus, the behavior can be perceived by family members as more understandable and may give them new ideas about how to handle the situation.
- The use of **paradoxical intention**, also called **prescribing the symptom**, in strategic family therapy helps to lower client resistance to change (Goldenberg & Goldenberg, 2008). Essentially, the counselor tells clients to keep engaging in their troublesome behavior. For clients who are resistant to change, this assignment seems simple and nonthreatening. For example, a couple who argues a lot might be asked to argue for at least a half hour each day. Besides decreasing resistance, this technique also can show clients that they have control over behavior they thought was uncontrollable. By following the counselor's advice, they recognize that they are *choosing* to perpetuate the problem.

- Strategic family therapists often give **directives** (i.e., homework assignments) for clients to complete between sessions (Goldenberg & Goldenberg, 2008). These directives encourage clients, either directly or subtly (through paradox), to participate in new behaviors.
- Counselors sometimes ask clients to engage in an **ordeal**, which is a paradoxical technique that asks them to complete an undesirable but health-promoting task before participating in their worrisome behavior (e.g., fighting, excessive crying; Gladding, 2005). For example, a counselor might tell a client that she must run for 30 minutes on the treadmill before she can start crying. Ideally, the woman will stop crying as often so that she does not have to run on the treadmill all the time.
- In the **pretend technique**, clients are encouraged to simulate their symptoms (Gladding, 2005). In this way, they realize that they are able to exert some control over what they say and do, as well as over the outcome of the situation.

5.7.5 Milan Systemic Family Counseling

Milan systemic family counseling, developed by the Milan group in Italy, is a departure from the strategic family therapy model discussed in the previous section. Instead of examining patterns of interaction among family members and developing strategies to change them, this approach focuses more on exploring family members' *perceptions* of each other and their interactional patterns, as well as asking questions to increase their awareness of unhealthy family behaviors (Goldenberg & Goldenberg, 2008). Unlike strategic family therapy, where the counselor is the expert who is responsible for enacting change and creating strategies, in this model the counselor collaborates with clients to set goals, and it is the family's responsibility to either work toward change or remain in their current style of functioning. In this section, the following aspects of this model are discussed: long brief therapy, positive connotations, paradox, and techniques.

5.7.5.1 LONG BRIEF THERAPY The Milan approach is sometimes referred to as *long brief therapy* because counselors only meet with families once per month (Goldenberg & Goldenberg, 2008). However, they meet with the family for up to 12 months. Milan counselors structure therapy sessions to allow substantial time to elapse between sessions, which gives their interventions ample time to take hold. As such, counselors do not comply with family requests to meet more frequently or hold emergency sessions because they believe these are covert attempts to undermine the interventions and perpetuate the family "games" and patterns that are causing problems.

Another unique characteristic of this approach is that counselors try to work in teams, with two counselors involved in each session and additional counselors observing behind a one-way mirror (Goldenberg & Goldenberg, 2008). The team behind the mirror often interrupts sessions to share comments and suggestions with the counselors, help move the session in a new direction, or implement a paradoxical technique.

5.7.5.2 POSITIVE CONNOTATIONS

Although Milan systemic family counseling diverges from strategic family therapy in important ways, the two also share some similarities. For example, the Milan approach encourages counselors to use **positive connotations** when working with a family, a concept similar to relabeling/reframing. Essentially, counselors attach positive motives to a family member's problematic behavior (Goldenberg & Goldenberg, 2008). For example, a certain behavior may be explained as a way for that member to sustain family equilibrium.

5.7.5.3 PARADOX

Another similarity between this model and the strategic model is the use of paradoxical intention. *Paradox* is used in this model to interfere with games that family members play to exert control over one another; it is also used to address the family paradox of coming to therapy for help but then not wanting to make any changes (Goldenberg & Goldenberg, 2008). Thus, paradox is an artful way of stimulating change without the family's knowledge. **Counterparadox**, which asks family members not to change too quickly and helps the family avoid resistance, is also used.

5.7.5.4 Milan Techniques

In this section, some Milan techniques are briefly reviewed: circular questioning, hypothesizing, neutrality, and ritual prescriptions.

- Counselors use **circular questioning** to ascertain family members' differences in perspective about the family's situation, particular events, and relationships within the family. Questions often ask one family member to comment on other family members (e.g., "Who fights more with your mom: your sister or your brother?"). This questioning provides family members with an awareness of not only their own perceptions but other members' perceptions, as well. These questions are a way to help a family member understand that not everyone shares the same beliefs about the family as he or she does. In addition, responses to these questions allow counselors to form hypotheses that then generate additional questions. Ultimately, this style of questioning serves to give members a clearer and more global understanding of the family's problem and themselves, which often leads to change.
- **Hypothesizing** is fundamental to the Milan model of family counseling. Counselors begin formulating hypotheses from their very first contact with family and often arrive at sessions with hypotheses already conceived and ready to be confirmed or denied. As counselors learn more about the family, new hypotheses take form or old ones are refined for better accuracy. The objective of hypotheses is to help family members change and gain more insight into their behavior; they are not supposed to be accepted as absolute truths.
- **Neutrality** refers to the objective position that counselors adhere to when working with families. Simply put, neutrality means that the counselor does not take sides with any family members. Rather, all members' perceptions and beliefs are deemed valid and are used to provide the counselor with helpful information to guide questioning and develop hypotheses. It is believed that if counselors fail to be neutral, they will become involved in the family's game or will be viewed as partial to certain family members and prejudiced against others, both of which impede change.
- **Ritual prescriptions** are usually paradoxical assignments that indicate certain actions to be taken on specific days and times by particular family members. The goal of rituals is to help families try new ways of behaving and interacting.

5.7.6 Structural Family Counseling

Developed by **Salvador Minuchin**, **structural family counseling** incorporates many of the general systems theory concepts discussed in section 5.7.1. As implied by its name, this model of family counseling is concerned with examining and changing the structure and organization of families, including their hierarchies and subsystems (Goldenberg & Goldenberg, 2008). It is believed that dysfunction results from faulty organization. In this approach, the counselor is responsible for restructuring the family's organization to bring about improved functioning. Techniques are reviewed in this section, along with the following concepts: structure; subsystems; boundaries; alignments, power, and coalitions.

5.7.6.1 STRUCTURE

Structure refers to how a family organizes itself (Goldenberg & Goldenberg, 2008). For example, a family's structure involves elements such as how members interact with one another, family rules and rituals, who exerts authority, how permeable the boundaries are, and what subsystems exist. Ideally, Minuchin believed that a family's structure should have an internal hierarchy whereby the parents serve as the main sources of authority. In addition, he thought it was essential for older children to have more duties and freedoms than younger children. Structural family counselors also emphasize complementarity of roles, believing that parents should be allies and work together to meet the needs of the family system using each one's skills.

5.7.6.2 SUBSYSTEMS

There are a host of subsystems that can be found within a family, with the most important ones being the spousal subsystem (i.e., husband and wife, partners), the parental subsystem (i.e., mother and father, partners), and the sibling subsystem (Goldenberg & Goldenberg, 2008). Each subsystem has unique patterns of interaction, rules, and tasks that are integral to the overall functioning of the family. For couples with children, it is thought that the stronger the spousal subsystem, the stronger the parental subsystem and, therefore, the better the functioning of the entire family. As mentioned in the previous section, it is critical for the parental subsystem to exert ultimate authority and nurture the sibling subsystem.

5.7.6.3 BOUNDARIES

Boundaries between the various family subsystems should be semi-permeable and clearly delineated, allowing for a balance between autonomy and involvement with the family unit (Goldenberg & Goldenberg, 2008). Rigid, impermeable boundaries, characterized by too much subsystem independence and separation (i.e., disengagement), and diffuse, permeable boundaries, characterized by enmeshment (i.e., overinvolvement) and dependence, often lead to dysfunction.

5.7.6.4 ALIGNMENTS, POWER, AND COALITIONS

Alignments refer to alliances between family members, and **power** refers to who exerts authority in a family in different situations (Goldenberg & Goldenberg, 2008). **Coalitions** occur when some family members form an alignment against another family member.

5.7.6.5 STRUCTURAL FAMILY COUNSELING TECHNIQUES

The following structural family counseling techniques are reviewed in this section: joining, structural maps, enactment, reframing, and restructuring.

- When structural family counselors first meet with a family, they engage in **joining** the family "by imitating the manner, style, affective range, or content of its communications in order to solidify the therapeutic alliance with them" (Goldenberg & Goldenberg, 2008, p. 249). This mimicry helps facilitate the family's comfort in the therapeutic process.
- **Structural maps** are visual representations of a family's coalitions, alignments, boundaries, and conflicts. Counselors use these maps to help assess the family's strengths, weaknesses, and needs.
- **Enactment** is the deliberate process by which the counselor encourages the family to play out its problem in the session. While family members interact with each other, the counselor observes; notes any alignments, coalitions, and structural problems; and begins to formulate a plan to address them. This technique provides the counselor with an opportunity to observe a family's issues and patterns of interaction firsthand.
- *Reframing*, a concept discussed in several of the family theories outlined in previous sections, occurs when counselors reframe a problem to sound more positive, understandable, or controllable, making families more confident in their ability to solve it and change their behavior.
- *Restructuring* is an intervention that involves actively working to change the structure of a family system. **Unbalancing** is a technique used to better establish a proper family hierarchy. For example, the counselor might help parents learn how to be more authoritative instead of allowing their children to make decisions and control them, thus reaffirming the parental subsystem's power. The counselor might also work with the family to create clearer boundaries, especially when there is evidence of enmeshment or disengagement. For example, the counselor might work to create more separation between certain members or, conversely, create more closeness between certain members.

5.7.7 Practice Multiple-Choice Items: Family Theories and Interventions

1. Long brief therapy is another name for
   a. Milan systemic family counseling.
   b. structural family counseling.
   c. strategic family therapy.
   d. Bowen family systems therapy.

2. All of the following words could describe someone who is a super-reasonable communicator EXCEPT
   a. detached.
   b. intellectual.
   c. self-deprecating.
   d. flat.

3. Which of the following couples would Bowen consider well matched?
   a. An oldest child and another oldest child
   b. An oldest child and a youngest child
   c. A youngest child and another youngest child
   d. A middle child and another middle child

4. A counselor encourages a couple to argue in the counseling session about how to discipline their children, a fight that frequently occurs outside of the counseling session. This technique is referred to as
   a. family sculpting.
   b. an enactment.
   c. an ordeal.
   d. unbalancing.

5. A counselor tells a family that it should not try to change too soon. The counselor is using
   a. a ritual.
   b. the pretend technique.
   c. positive connotation.
   d. paradox.

Answer Key: 1. a; 2. c; 3. b; 4. b; 5. d.

5.8 OTHER COUNSELING THEORIES AND INTERVENTIONS

This final section of Chapter 5 highlights some additional counseling approaches of importance that are less easily categorized. These theories are eclectic counseling, multimodal therapy, eye movement desensitization and reprocessing (EMDR), play therapy, transactional analysis, and feminist therapy.

5.8.1 Eclectic Counseling

Eclectic counseling refers to professional counselors who draw from an assortment of theories in their work with clients (Gladding, 2005). **Frederick Thorne** was an early proponent of this type of counseling because of his belief that no single counseling theory encompasses all the elements necessary to effectively help a client. Instead of approaching clients from one primary theoretical perspective, eclectic counselors use numerous theories to attempt to improve their clients' functioning.

Two main types of eclecticism, also known as *integration,* are *technical eclecticism,* in which counselors use just the techniques from a wide range of theories, and *theoretical integration*, in which counselors strive to combine at least two theories into a unified whole.

Although eclecticism may certainly benefit many clients because it focuses on clients' unique needs, it can become problematic when counselors use theories and techniques they are unable to implement adeptly or by which they randomly use a diverse range of techniques without giving sufficient thought to why they are using them or how they will work together, a phenomenon known as **syncretism** (Gladding, 2005). Thus, it is essential that counselors refrain from eclecticism unless they have the appropriate training in the theory's techniques, in-depth knowledge of the theory, a sound rationale for why each theory should be used with a particular client, and a vision for how the theories will synergize to achieve a successful outcome.

5.8.2 Multimodal Therapy

Created by **Arnold Lazarus**, **multimodal therapy** is a form of technical eclecticism. Using this model, clients are assessed in seven domains, which can be easily remembered by the acronym **BASIC ID**: behavior, affect, sensations, imagery, cognitions, interpersonal relationships, and drugs/biological functions/nutrition/exercise. By determining which domains clients think they need the most assistance with, counselors develop a multimodal treatment plan that draws techniques and interventions from myriad theories to target the concerns in each domain.

During the assessment process, the counselor also determines from which domain (also known as a *modality*) the client prefers to operate. For example, if counselors know that their client prefers the affective domain, they might approach counseling from a humanistic, client-centered approach. Likewise, if the client indicates a preference for functioning in the behavior domain, the counselor might start the counseling process with a behavioral approach to strengthen the therapeutic alliance and increase the client's comfort with the counseling process. This technique is called **bridging**.

Another technique specific to multimodal therapy is called the **firing sequence**. Essentially, when a client indicates a stressor, the counselor works with the client to determine the chain of events that led to the stressor affecting the client's life in a maladaptive way. For instance, through this process the counselor can help the client determine that negative cognitions (C) led to negative imagery (I), which led to negative affect (A) and a negative behavioral response (B) and, ultimately, distress. Knowing this firing sequence, the counselor can implement techniques that address the client's needs related to cognition, imagery, affect, and behavior.

Multimodal therapy has been effectively implemented with a wide variety of clients and presenting problems. In addition, **Donald Keat** has adapted the BASIC ID for use with children using the acronym HELPING (Health, Emotions, Learning, Personal, Imagery, Need to Know, Guidance of ABCs) to indicate the same seven modalities as the BASIC ID.

5.8.3 Eye Movement Desensitization and Reprocessing (EMDR)

Eye movement desensitization and reprocessing (EMDR) is a therapy approach developed by Francine Shapiro (2001) that uses the concepts of **adaptive information processing (AIP)** theory and bilateral stimulation to enhance the brain's adaptive capabilities. AIP theory holds that the brain is capable of adapting and learning from the events in our life. Pathology develops when this adaptive process has not occurred or has not been completed around a traumatic or stressful event. Highly recommended for single event trauma, the most frequent application of EMDR is to process heretofore unprocessed disturbing memories. The therapist helps the client access a troubling memory (target). Once the target has been chosen, the therapist helps the client name the emotions and physiological sensations experienced with the memory. Then the client and therapist identify a cognitive distortion (negative belief) created because of the incomplete processing and a positive belief that will replace the negative belief. After this assessment phase, the therapist applies bilateral stimulation, activating both hemispheres of the brain, to process the memory (desensitization and reprocessing). Bilateral stimulation was first done by guiding clients to move their eyes back and forth; hence, the term *eye movement*. Currently, practitioners use tactile and aural techniques in addition to eye movements to activate both hemispheres. The bilateral stimulation continues until the client has successfully processed the event. Success means there is no remaining affective disturbance or unwanted physiological sensations and that the positive cognition has replaced the negative belief and feels very close to 100% true for the client. This technique is particularly beneficial for clients with posttraumatic stress disorder (PTSD). A simplified explanation of EMDR has been presented here; many other steps are involved in the total EMDR procedure, and interested individuals should review related literature for further information.

5.8.4 Play Therapy

The Association for Play Therapy describes **play therapy** as "the systematic use of a theoretical model to establish an interpersonal process wherein trained play therapists use the therapeutic powers of play to help clients prevent or resolve psychosocial difficulties and achieve optimal growth and development" (2009). Importantly, play therapy is actually a methodology and not a theory of counseling. Most theoretical orientations discussed thus far in Chapter 5 use play therapy in a manner consistent with the theoretical tenets of that approach. Play therapy is most commonly used with children, who naturally express themselves through play. This approach allows many children to give voice to and work through their concerns with the assistance of the counselor. It may be particularly useful for young children who have trouble communicating verbally. Some play therapists select the toys and activities for the client to engage in (i.e., *directive play therapy*), whereas other counselors allow the child to choose the toys and guide the play (i.e., *nondirective play therapy*); many counselors include both directive and nondirective components in their sessions.

5.8.5 Transactional Analysis

Transactional analysis (TA), developed by **Eric Berne**, is a cognitive theory with roots in psychoanalysis (Gladding, 2005). The focus of TA is on examining how clients interact with others. It is believed that if clients can change their styles of interaction, the result will be improved functioning. According to Berne, people operate from three common ego states in their interactions: parent, adult, or child. The *parent ego state* is characterized by either criticism or nurturance of others and is often based on people's experiences with their parents when they were growing up and what they learned about how people should and should not behave. The *adult ego state* is characterized by rational thought and the absence of emotions in decision making. The *child ego state* is characterized by youthful behavior and qualities such as playfulness and spontaneity, called the *natural child*, and obedience and inhibition, called the *adapted child*. Most people switch between these three ego states as dictated by the particular situation. Problems arise when someone lacks versatility and approaches others from only one ego state in all situations. Thus, one of the goals of TA is to help people learn how to function from all of their ego states.

Transactions between people can be complementary, crossed, or covert (Gladding 2005). *Complementary transactions* occur when two people interact with each other using the same, or complementary, ego state (e.g., adult to adult or parent to child). *Crossed transactions* occur when someone functions from an ego state that is undesirable or unsuitable for the others' wants or needs (e.g., a wife wanting an adult to adult interaction with her husband and instead finding herself involved in an adult to natural child interaction). *Ulterior transactions* occur when people seemingly operate from one ego state but are actually just concealing their true ego state (e.g., an adult ego state covering up a child ego state). Many ulterior transactions lead to **games**, which are described as "ulteriorly motivated transactions that appear complementary on the surface but end up in bad feelings" (p. 157). TA counselors work with clients to help them avoid becoming involved in games and instead learn how to express their feelings and needs to others in a positive, healthy manner.

Another concept of TA that is important is the life script. Berne asserted that all individuals develop a **life script** at a young age based on their interactions with others, particularly parents, which forms a blueprint for future interactions with people (Gladding, 2005). Children who frequently receive *positive strokes* (i.e., feedback) from others usually develop healthy life scripts. However, children who receive *negative strokes* and messages sometimes develop self-perpetuating, harmful life scripts that interfere with their abilities to connect and interact well with others as adults. For those with maladaptive life scripts, counselors using the TA approach help these clients become aware of their unhealthy life script and work toward reconstructing them.

5.8.6 Feminist Therapy

Feminist therapy, pioneered by Carol Gilligan (also see Chapter 2), aims to help clients become more aware of the affect of gender on their lives and to empower them to improve their lives and the lives of others (Gladding, 2005). Feminist therapists contend that women have been oppressed and put at a disadvantage by society; therefore, they encourage clients to become social change agents. When working with clients, counselors strive to create an egalitarian relationship and educate women about how many common problems are related to the way women are treated in society. Interventions often involve helping clients identify and analyze gender-role messages they have received throughout their lives, reframe their problems, and become more assertive.

5.8.7 Practice Multiple-Choice Items: Other Counseling Theories and Interventions

1. All of the following words describe the adapted child ego state EXCEPT
   a. compliant.
   b. reserved.
   c. creative.
   d. docile.

2. Which of the following four options represents the least complementary transaction?
   a. Parent to child
   b. Adult to natural child
   c. Adult to adult
   d. Child to child

3. A professional counselor uses techniques from a variety of theories but does not actually embrace all the theories from which these interventions come. This is an example of
   a. technical eclecticism.
   b. traditional integration.
   c. theoretical integration.
   d. syncretism.

4. The two I's in BASIC ID stand for
   a. interpersonal relationships and imagination.
   b. imagery and interpersonal relationships.
   c. insight and imagination.
   d. interests and imagery.

5. A multimodal counselor who approaches clients from their preferred domain/modality, is using the technique known as
   a. connecting.
   b. firing sequence.
   c. positive strokes.
   d. bridging.

Answer Key: 1. c; 2. b; 3. a; 4. b; 5. d.

5.9 KEY POINTS FOR CHAPTER 5: HELPING RELATIONSHIPS

- Wellness is a state of optimal health and well-being.
- The therapeutic alliance is the single best predictor of whether clients will benefit from counseling, regardless of the theoretical orientation of the counselor.

- Counselors should explore any client resistance that emerges during counseling and help the client work through it.
- The counseling process has three stages: the relationship-building stage, the action/intervention stage, and the termination stage.
- Consultation is the process by which individuals meet to resolve a problem.
- Attending, questioning, reflecting, paraphrasing, summarizing, confronting, interpreting, self-disclosing, giving feedback, and giving information are all essential counseling skills.
- Psychodynamic theories represent the first force of counseling, behavioral and cognitive-behavioral theories represent the second force of counseling, humanistic-existential theories represent the third force of counseling, and multicultural theories of counseling represent the fourth force of counseling.
- Determinism is the belief that forces separate from people's wills determine their actions; self-determination is the belief that people have free will and can act without being driven by an external force. Many psychodynamic theorists believe in determinism.

- Psychodynamic theories examine how clients' unconscious impulses, drives, and desires affect their psychological health and personality.
- Cognitive theories focus on how people's thoughts influence their emotions and behavior, behavioral theories emphasize the importance of changing people's behaviors to change the quality of their lives, and cognitive-behavioral theories work to alter both the thoughts and actions of clients.
- Humanistic counselors believe in human goodness and the tendency of all individuals to strive toward self-actualization.
- Existential counseling assists clients in addressing universal questions about life, death, and freedom and helps them find meaning in their lives.
- Multicultural theories of counseling take the impact of culture into consideration when working with clients and focus on clients' strengths rather than their weaknesses.
- Family theories approach problems from a systems perspective, conceptualizing problems as caused by a complex system rather than the result of one symptomatic individual.
- Eclectic counselors use a variety of theories and techniques in their work to best match the needs of their clients.

CHAPTER 6

Group Work

6.1 FOUNDATIONAL ISSUES IN GROUP WORK

Group work is the application of knowledge and skill in group facilitation to assist members in reaching mutual goals (Gladding, 2008). In this chapter, the facilitator of group process is referred to as the leader, and clients or students are referred to as members.

Over the past several years, administrations of the National Counselor Examination (NCE) have included 16 (of the 160 total, or 10% of the) scored items (plus some trial items) designed to measure group work (rank = 5.5 of 8; slightly fewer than the average number of items for the eight domains). The average item difficulty index was .79 (rank = 1 of 8; the easiest domain of item content), meaning that the average item in this domain was correctly answered by 79% of test-takers.

Over the past several years, administrations of the Counselor Preparation Comprehensive Exam (CPCE) have included 17 scored items designed to measure group work, plus several trial items that do not count in your score. The average item difficulty index was .68, meaning that the average item in this domain was correctly answered by 68% of test-takers, making this set of items among the easiest on the examination.

The Council for Accreditation of Counseling and Related Educational Programs (CACREP) defined standards for Group Work as

> studies that provide both theoretical and experiential understandings of group purpose, development, dynamics, theories, methods, skills, and other group approaches in a multicultural society, including all of the following:
>
> **a.** principles of group dynamics, including group process components, developmental stage theories, group members' roles and behaviors, and therapeutic factors of group work;
> **b.** group leadership or facilitation styles and approaches, including characteristics of various types of group leaders and leadership styles;
> **c.** theories of group counseling, including commonalities, distinguishing characteristics, and pertinent research and literature;
> **d.** group counseling methods, including group counselor orientations and behaviors, appropriate selection criteria and methods, and methods of evaluation of effectiveness; and
> **e.** direct experiences in which students participate as group members in a small group activity, approved by the program, for a minimum of 10 clock hours over the course of one academic term. (CACREP, 2009, p. 12)

In this chapter the following topics are covered: foundational issues in group work; types of group work; group leadership; group member roles; planning for groups; stages/process of group work; techniques of group work; assessment and evaluation in group work; and theoretical approaches to group work.

In this first section of Chapter 6 on the basic, foundational issues of group work, we review group work history, advantages and challenges of group work, goals of group work, curative factors, key group work organizations, ethical and legal issues in group work, Association for Specialists in

Group Work (ASGW): Best Practices Guidelines, ASGW training standards, and ASGW multicultural and diversity principles.

6.1.1 Group Work History

Many events and persons have contributed to the current state of group work knowledge and practice, including the following (Erford, 2010):

- Joseph Pratt is credited with establishing the first group experience that was not intended specifically for psychoeducational or occupational purposes. An internist, Pratt used groups to save time in educating and supporting patients with tuberculosis.
- Jesse Davis, a school principal in Grand Rapids, Michigan, introduced group work in a school setting in 1907. Davis' groups were intended to provide students with effective tools for making educational, vocational, and moral decisions (Herr & Erford, 2011). Davis emphasized the use of the group as an effective environment for teaching life skills and values.
- Frank Parsons, often cited as the founder of the vocational guidance and counseling profession, used groups to facilitate career and vocational development.
- During World War I (and later in WWII), soldiers were tested and instructed in groups, and teamwork was emphasized. Groups were also used on occasion to treat combat fatigue, known today as posttraumatic stress disorder (PTSD).
- During the 1920s and 1930s, Alfred Adler emphasized the innate social nature of human beings to support a group treatment model and conducted groups in the 1920s that investigated the relationship between children's problems and family experiences (Gazda, Ginter, & Horne, 2008).
- In the 1920s, **J. L. Moreno** created the Theater of Spontaneity, the earliest form of psychodrama. Psychodrama was a technique developed to bring about mental and emotional catharsis for the purpose of tension relief. Moreno wrote prolifically, organized the first society of group therapists (the American Society for Group Psychotherapy) and psychodrama, and first coined the term *group psychotherapy*.
- In the 1920s, Lewis Wender articulated the first guidelines for group therapeutic factors (e.g., factors that promote effectiveness of group work with members) after examining the many difficulties associated with facilitating successful psychotherapeutic interventions with inpatient populations.
- **S. R. Slavson** founded the American Group Psychotherapy Association in 1942. He offered activity therapy groups for children and reported that group activity sessions were equally as effective as individual counseling for stimulating change, catalyzing significant increases in the use of group treatment procedures for children and adolescents, resulting in the introduction of group counseling in schools.

- A significant event of the 1930s was the founding of the first major self-help group in America, **Alcoholics Anonymous**.
- **Kurt Lewin** studied group dynamics and has been credited with the invention of training groups (or T-groups), which gave rise to the encounter and sensitivity groups of the 1960s and 1970s. His research resulted in the identification of predictable stages of group work and specific change markers for individual clients.
- In the late 1940s, Wilfred Bion, a member of the Tavistock Institute of Human Relations in Great Britain, studied group cohesiveness and stated that group dynamics often differ greatly from the dynamics of a family unit (Gladding, 2008).
- School counseling rose to prominence after the Soviet launch of *Sputnik I* in 1957 and the creation of the National Defense Education Act of 1958. By the end of the 1950s and throughout the 1960s, classroom guidance—a psychoeducational group work approach—was largely replaced by group counseling (although it is still used quite often to achieve educational and career development goals) with the goal or bringing about behaviorally based changes in educational environments.
- The application of group work to family counseling settings increased considerably during the 1950s. Rudolph Dreikurs used Adler's counseling theory to set up and work with parent groups.
- The popularity of groups flourished during the 1960s, largely due to the social climate of that era. The power of groups to create change became evident in light of such historical events as the Vietnam War and the "hippie movement." Interestingly, group therapy research decreased from 1960 to 1980 (Gazda et al., 2008).
- During the 1960s and 1970s, Fritz Perls developed Gestalt therapy, based on Gestalt psychology, and demonstrated its use in a group setting through workshops conducted at the Esalen Institute in California.
- During the 1960s and 1970s, Eric Berne highlighted his transactional analysis approach to therapy in group settings.
- During the 1960s and 1970s, Carl Rogers initiated encounter groups, also known as sensitivity training groups, to encourage and assist the pursuit of individual growth and development.
- The **marathon group** also came into prominence during this era. As the title suggests, marathon group members met together for extended periods of time, usually between 24 and 48 hours, throughout which members were expected to become more authentic and engage in true self-disclosure.
- The exploitation of group therapy was sensationalized by journalists during the 1960s and beyond, especially because many participants with emotional disturbances were harmed by membership in groups that functioned without adequate prescreening.
- The ASGW, a division of the American Counseling Association (ACA), was founded in 1973 for the advancement of professionalism in group work.

- Self-help groups, frequently led by group members rather than professionals, but still falling under the group counseling functional model, became particularly prevalent with between 2,000 and 3,000 self-help groups in existence during the 1980s (Gladding, 2008), some hosted by schools and school–community partnerships.
- CACREP revised its standards in 1994 (and again in 2001 and 2009) to include specific group work specialist preparation guidelines for graduate-level degrees.
- Group work proliferated in schools during the 1990s as an effective means for improving student academics and social skills.
- During the 1990s, the ASGW converged on a preferred language, featuring the term *group work*, and specified four types of group work: task groups, psychoeducational groups, counseling groups, and psychotherapy groups.

6.1.2 Advantages and Challenges of Group Work

The group work literature has identified numerous advantages and challenges in conducting group work (Erford, 2010). Strengths of group work include the following:

- *Time efficiency for the leader.* Meeting with several members simultaneously for a common purpose (e.g., advising, problem solving, strengthening social support, aiding in personal development) can save substantial time and effort, especially when a counselor's caseload is large.
- *Less costly per individual.* Lower cost is generally associated with group work, as compared with individual counseling; all other things being equal, a counselor seeing 5 to 10 members at a time is 5 to 10 times more time and cost efficient.
- *Greater resources.* Group members often have access to a greater variety of resources (e.g., concrete information, problem-solving tools, abstract viewpoints and values) from multiple members within a group than a member in a one-on-one counseling relationship.
- *Feeling of safety.* Interpersonal safety can be achieved in groups. Member relationships are developed with a controlled intimacy, which makes it possible for individuals to open up and share their true emotions without the contingent obligations that often arise with this type of self-disclosure in personal relationships.
- *Experiencing a sense of belonging.* Most humans have a powerful need to belong. Working with a group of individuals in a therapeutic setting allows members to exchange ideas and feel greater self-confidence and a sense of belonging.
- *Replication of the everyday world.* The group is essentially a microcosm of society. Conflicts that arise in group settings are often similar in nature to those that are experienced in the outside world, especially if the group's membership is diverse and true-to-life issues are addressed.
- *It is safe to practice new skills and receive feedback.* Members can use the group as a sounding board for trying out alternative problem-solving techniques and

consequently can assess the likelihood that they will be successful when using those techniques in their everyday lives.
- *Commitment.* Group settings often enhance a member's motivation to follow through with commitments that are made during group sessions. The support that members feel from others, and the desire to live up to their expectations so as not to let anyone down, are powerful forces that affect individual change.
- *Power of the peer group.* The influence of various groups on an individual's life is almost inevitable and can affect member development in diverse ways, especially in terms of conformity, identity, reward and punishment, and social controls.
- *Interpersonal power.* In group settings, members not only have the opportunity to receive help but are empowered to help others.

Challenges of group work may include the following:

- *Pressure to conform.* The power of the group can be problematic if it leads members to actively pursue unrealistic goals, take actions that are detrimental to their well-being, or conform to behaviors that go against their beliefs, to be accepted by other members.
- *Reality distortion.* **Reality distortion** (Trotzer, 1999) occurs when the group provides an example of social reality that is not achievable in the outside world.
- *Avoidance.* Certain group members may not reap adequate benefits from group work if they are less comfortable participating openly or are not given enough attention. Individual members are sometimes able to avoid confronting their problems if they blend in with the group (e.g., camouflage) or if the group setting becomes so safe and accepting that the individual members do not feel compelled to take risks or action toward addressing the issues for which they sought counseling in the first place.
- *Confidentiality.* Confidentiality cannot be guaranteed in group settings. Since numerous individuals are participating in each session, the risk is greater that information will be shared with others outside of the group.
- *Unhealthy attachments.* The counseling group is transitional, not a permanent social outlet. Members who lack a feeling of acceptance from others in their everyday lives can rely too heavily on relationships formed in groups. Experiencing a sense of belonging is only valuable if it facilitates the achievement of a better life outside the group.
- *Institutional barriers.* Some institutions have systemic barriers in place that inhibit effective group work (e.g., parental permission, personnel not realizing the value of group work versus other activities, scheduling challenges, finding space in the buildings to run groups).

6.1.3 Goals of Group Work

Numerous goals of group work exist, but these goals are typically classified as individual member goals, which are goals that a single member may be interested in achieving, and group goals, which are committed to by all group members. These goals normally are overt and agreed to during the beginning stages of group experiences. Examples of individual member goals include developing a more interpersonally intimate relationship with one's spouse, communicating more openly with one's parent, or becoming more interpersonally assertive when meeting a potential dating partner. Whole group goals are also agreed to by all members of the group and include the following:

- Understand the universality of member problems.
- Learn to trust and appropriately self-disclose.
- Display sensitivity to the needs of others and support for member goals.
- Experience the acceptance and support of other members.
- Put newly learned knowledge and skills into practice.

6.1.4 Curative Factors

In group work, a **therapeutic factor**, or *curative factor*, is an element, generally created by the group leader or relationships with other members, that improves a member's overall condition. Yalom (Yalom & Leszcz, 2005) developed what is now considered the landmark classification of curative factors:

- *Instillation of hope* provides members with a sense of assurance that the treatment will work.
- *Universality* is the awareness of the similar concerns of others. As members interact, they come to realize that other members are going through similar situations and, so, feel much less alone and isolated, creating a sense of unity.
- *Imparting of information* about healthy living is important to the growth of members and their ability to function more effectively. Leaders may provide information about helpful techniques such as those that aid in socialization, whereas members learn about how to deal with academic, career, personal/social, mental health, mental illness, and other real-life problems.
- *Altruism* is exemplified by members giving of themselves and working for the common good.
- *Family reenactment* helps re-create early childhood dynamics so that members are able to relive early family conflicts and effectively resolve them. Psychotherapy (and sometimes counseling) groups can create a caring family environment in which issues of trauma can be safely aired and confronted.
- *Development of socialization techniques* is necessary for members to function successfully in their everyday lives. Group work allows members to give and receive personal feedback that facilitates learning about the desirability of one's behaviors.
- *Imitative behavior* occurs when members have an opportunity to observe the behaviors of other members and witness the positive or negative responses elicited by their actions.
- *Interpersonal learning* occurs through member interactions with others. Members affect each other in much the same way that they affect the people they interact with in

their everyday lives, and members receive feedback on their conduct and can learn new ways of being while feeling safe and supported.

- *Group cohesiveness* is similar to a feeling of unity and a sense of being bonded together. Cohesiveness indicates that effective therapy is occurring because it facilitates trust and a willingness to take risks.
- *Catharsis* is the expression of strong and often hidden emotions by an individual. Instead of masking one's true feelings, group work provides a forum for releasing tension and venting about whatever a member has kept inside.
- *Existential factors* are realized when members are encouraged to consider important and sometimes painful truths about life, including an awareness of one's own mortality and the unpredictability of existence.

6.1.5 Key Group Work Organizations

The following are several key group work organizations:

- The ASGW, a division of ACA, promotes training, practice, and research in group facilitation. ASGW has established best practice guidelines, training standards, and multicultural and diversity competencies (see sections 6.1.7, 6.1.8, and 6.1.9, respectively).
- The **American Group Psychotherapy Association (AGPA)** is an interdisciplinary organization promoting research and practice in group psychotherapy for individuals with mental disorders.
- The **American Society of Group Psychotherapy and Psychodrama (ASGPP)** was founded by J. L. Moreno and promotes standards in training, research, and practice in psychodrama, sociometry, and group psychotherapy.
- The **National Training Laboratory (NTL)** uses Lewin's approach to organizational leadership and change. The NTL offers certificate programs for business professionals and a master's degree in organizational development.
- The **Tavistok Institute** promotes interdisciplinary training in group dynamics and leadership coaching for businesses.
- The **Esalen Institute** uses a humanistic approach to enrich and explore human potential through multidisciplinary workshops, forums, and retreats.

6.1.6 Ethical and Legal Issues in Group Work

Ethical and legal issues of general counseling were presented in Chapter 1, and certain sections of the ACA *Code of Ethics* (2005), especially A and B, address important group work issues. The purpose of this section is to highlight several essential ethical and legal issues specifically applied to group work.

- *Informed consent* allows members to understand their rights and responsibilities prior to beginning group work. Members are free to end treatment at any time and should be made aware of any general group planning in order to decide if the group will meet their needs.
- *Confidentiality* in group work is desirable and required of the group leader, but because more than one client is

present at a time, confidentiality cannot be guaranteed—that is, there is no ethical requirement that clients will maintain confidentiality, just that counselors will. Whereas leaders stress the importance of confidentiality, members must understand that confidentiality from other members is not guaranteed.

- **Group member screening** must be conducted by the leader(s) to ensure the appropriateness of member and group fit.
- Leaders adhere to their *scope of practice* and only provide services for which they are qualified by training and experience.

6.1.7 Association for Specialists in Group Work: Best Practices Guidelines

You are strongly encouraged to review the ASGW Best Practices Guidelines (2007). The guidelines were designed to address leaders' responsibilities when planning and conducting groups and contain important information for study purposes.

6.1.8 Association for Specialists in Group Work: Training Standards

You are strongly encouraged to review the ASGW Professional Standards for the Training of Group Workers (2000). These standards were designed to outline the core and specialization guidelines for group worker training and contain critical information for study purposes.

6.1.9 Association for Specialists in Group Work: Multicultural and Diversity Issues in Group Work

You are strongly encouraged to review the ASGW Principles of Diversity Competent Group Workers (1998). These principles were designed to educate group workers about the awareness, skills, and knowledge necessary to engage in multiculturally competent group work.

6.1.10 Practice Multiple-Choice Items: Foundational Issues in Group Work

1. _____ introduced group work to schools.
   a. Frank Parsons
   b. Jesse Davis
   c. Lewis Wender
   d. Joseph Pratt

2. Which of the following is NOT a true statement about marathon groups?
   a. Marathon groups can last up to 48 hours.
   b. Members of marathon groups are encouraged to be authentic with each other.
   c. Marathon groups became popular during the 1980s.
   d. Self-disclosure is an integral part of marathon groups.

3. A _____ group is NOT one of the four primary types of group work.
   a. psychoeducational

   b. task
   c. growth
   d. psychotherapy

4. Reality distortion occurs when
   a. the social environment in the group is radically dissimilar to the outside world.
   b. group members view their problems through rose-colored glasses.
   c. members engage in avoidance behaviors.
   d. All of the above.

5. The first form of psychodrama was called
   a. role playing.
   b. psychological improvisation.
   c. dramatic reenacting.
   d. the Theater of Spontaneity.

Answer Key: 1. b; 2. c; 3. c; 4. a; 5. d.

6.2   TYPES OF GROUP WORK

Until recently, numerous types of group work had been identified. During the 1990s, the ASGW developed a typology of functional group models, but the previous categorizations (e.g., self-help, personal growth, T-groups) still exist in the literature. The ASGW (2007) categorized various functional types of group work experiences as task groups, psychoeducational groups, counseling groups, and psychotherapy groups.

- **Task groups** are designed around accomplishing a specific goal. Principles of group dynamics and such methods as collaboration, problem solving, and team building exercises are used to reach goals. The focus is not on changing people but on completing the task at hand in an efficient and effective manner. For example, committee work is often task oriented with a designated leader and members working collaboratively to accomplish some agreed-on goal.
- **Psychoeducational groups** are more structured than counseling or psychotherapy groups, emphasizing skill development through various nonthreatening skill-building exercises but at the same time encouraging discussion, sharing, and feedback among members (Corey, Corey, Callahan, & Russell, 2004). The goal of psychoeducational group work is to prevent psychological disturbance by increasing self-awareness, knowledge, and skills about specific developmentally relevant issues. The fact that a psychoeducational group can be preventive, growth oriented, or remedial makes it a very versatile type of group model. The psychoeducational group model is commonly used in PK–12 comprehensive developmental school counseling programs, whether in small groups to address study or social skills or in large group classroom guidance to address educational planning or career developmental goals.
- **Counseling groups** are designed to help members work on interpersonal problems and promote behavioral changes related to these problems. Counseling groups are

typically problem oriented, helping members explore their problems and seek resolution, but counseling groups also can be preventive, growth oriented, or remedial. Counseling groups are relatively short in length, focusing on adjustment issues for individuals who function relatively normally. People usually come to group counseling because they are experiencing some sort of problem, such as dealing with family issues, difficult relationships, or stress-related problems.

- **Psychotherapy groups** are designed to treat those who may be experiencing severe or chronic problems in their lives. Ordinarily, members in psychotherapy groups display more dysfunctional behavior and typically carry a psychiatric (i.e., *DSM*) diagnosis. Psychotherapy groups are typically offered by agencies and in residential treatment settings but are increasingly being offered in alternative schools or full-service schools that may offer school-based mental health services.

6.2.1 Practice Multiple-Choice Items: Types of Group Work

1. Psychoeducational groups are
   a. remedial.
   b. preventative.
   c. growth oriented.
   d. All of the above.

2. _____ groups focus heavily on skill-building.
   a. Psychoeducational
   b. Psychotherapy
   c. Task
   d. Counseling

3. Counseling groups are more _____ than psychoeducational groups.
   a. structured
   b. problem oriented
   c. pedagogic
   d. None of the above.

4. _____ groups are for members who have severe psychiatric problems.
   a. Counseling
   b. Psychoeducational
   c. Psychotherapy
   d. Task

5. Which of the following is a FALSE statement about task groups?
   a. The primary goal is completing a task.
   b. Leaders work to change and improve member behavior.
   c. Task groups are run using principles of group dynamics.
   d. Collaboration is used to facilitate goal achievement.

Answer Key: 1. d; 2. a; 3. b; 4. c; 5. b.

6.3 GROUP LEADERSHIP

This section of Chapter 6 reviews the role of the leader, standards for training, group leadership styles, traits, and techniques.

Special leadership issues include managing conflict within the group and co-leadership.

6.3.1 Leadership Tasks

Even though a leader's theoretical orientation (e.g., humanistic, cognitive-behavioral, integrative) will influence one's approach to group leadership, leadership style and tasks are important group process considerations. Leaders use the strengths inherent in their personality and monitor those aspects of their personality that may contribute to problems in a group process. Whereas leaders ordinarily demonstrate the core conditions of therapeutic change (i.e., genuineness, empathy, unconditional positive regard), leaders often must challenge or confront members to help them gain insights and accomplish constructive affective, cognitive, or behavioral changes. The primary tasks of leaders are threefold:

- *Executive functions.* Leaders are responsible for planning for and creating the group, convening the sessions, and maintaining the organizational integrity of continued meetings, including establishing effective boundaries that will allow members to grow and develop from the experience (e.g., safe environment, stability of membership).
- *Building a group culture.* Groups are therapeutic social systems that operate on norms for social interactions. Leaders help group members establish norms that facilitate occurrence of curative factors.
- *Bringing members into the here-and-now.* As social entities, groups offer members the opportunity to deal with real-life, present-day issues. Although often encouraged to gain insights into past life events and make future plans, members are primarily encouraged to process current life events and immediate interactions with other group members, thus making possible the generalization of in-group experiences into real-world interactions outside of the group. In the here and now, members must focus on their feelings toward others in the group, self-disclose, and provide feedback to others. Members also must examine and understand the process issues occurring within the group.

Leaders usually are more directive and active in the earlier stages of groups in order to create a safe environment and structure for accomplishing group tasks. Members often begin a group experience expecting the leader, rather than the group interaction, to provide "the cure," then become angry or disillusioned with the leader when it becomes clearer that members bear the responsibility for progress. As the group matures and begins to enter the working stage, leaders transfer more and more power and responsibility to group members and become less active and directive.

6.3.2 Group Leader Training Standards

The ASGW published three essential documents for group work training purposes; each can be located under the Standards and Practices tab at http//:www.asgw.org. These include (a) Professional Standards for the Training of Group Workers (ASGW, 2000); (b) Best Practice Guidelines (ASGW,

2007); and (c) Principles for Diversity-Competent Group Workers (ASGW, 1998). You should review these brief documents in some detail to become familiar with current standards for training and practice in group work.

6.3.3 Leader Styles

Leader style is the approach the leader takes when leading a group and is influenced by the leader's personality, group type, stage of group process, setting, membership, and theoretical orientation. Leadership styles have been categorized as follows:

- **Authoritarian.** Takes control of and responsibility for the group; sets the agenda, goals, and rules; serves as the conduit for member interaction (i.e., discussion occurs through the leader).
- **Democratic.** Facilitates member interactions; with leader guidance, members make decisions, take responsibility, set agenda, goals, and rules; sets norms encouraging member interaction, self-disclosure, and feedback.
- **Laissez-faire.** Assumes little or no leadership or responsibility for group agenda, goals, or rules; assumes members all have abilities to make changes and take responsibility for the group on their own; lacks structure and directedness.

Each style has pros and cons, depending on the purpose and structure of the group. Lewin (1943) referred to authoritarian, democratic, and laissez-faire leadership styles as Theory X, Theory Y, and Theory Z, respectively.

6.3.4 Leader Traits

Much has been written about effective leader traits. Yalom and Leszcz (2005) identified four primary leader goals: (a) provide a caring attitude, (b) provide meaning attribution (i.e., rational explanations for observed member changes), (c) model appropriate self-disclosure and confrontation (i.e., emotional stimulation), and (d) provide limits, rules, and structure (i.e., executive function). Under normal circumstances, effective leaders use moderate amounts of emotional stimulation and executive functioning along with frequent/consistent use of caring and meaning attribution. Under most circumstances, ineffective leaders use low or high amounts of emotional stimulation and executive function along with low displays of caring and meaning attribution. Again, these are generalizations, as the optimal level of each trait is dependent on group type, purpose, member needs, and leader personality.

Other effective leader traits described in various group work literature include self-awareness, flexibility, self-confidence, responsibility, honesty, trustworthiness, genuineness, empathy, compassion, respect, objectivity, creativity, spontaneity, humor, enthusiasm, and charisma.

6.3.5 Leader Techniques

Specific leader skills and techniques have been described that help members achieve goals and create an effective group work environment (Erford, 2010).

- *Initiating.* Provide direction for members by initiating group topics or activities, thereby allowing members to focus energy and achieve desired outcomes.
- **Active listening.** Attend to nonverbal and verbal behaviors of members to show that the leader is paying attention, and creating an environment that encourages self-disclosure.
- **Clarifying.** Help the leader check his or her understanding of what a member has said.
- **Questioning.** Use questions to elicit information from members and help them focus their comments on core issues and concerns.
- *Provide feedback.* Model how to give and receive feedback to help members develop greater degrees of self-awareness and insight.
- **Empathizing.** Communicate understanding to promote trust and cohesion.
- **Linking.** Connect member themes, issues, and similarities to facilitate shared perspectives, commonalities, and goals.
- *Blocking (cutting off).* Stop a counterproductive member behavior in order to protect other members from potentially damaging interactions.
- *Confronting.* Promote member self-awareness by pointing out inconsistencies between or among member statements and actions.
- *Instruction.* Teach members various information or skills.
- *Self-disclosure.* Reveal a personal experience or feeling in the here-and-now context.
- *Modeling.* Demonstrate a particular skill or behavior so that members may learn through watching.
- *Role playing.* Demonstrate and practice (leader and members) skills and applications in a safe environment so that members gain experience and feedback that will allow them to apply the skills and behaviors in out-of-group situations.
- **Tracking.** Verbally clarify to keep up with and clarify for members the content and process of group interactions.
- *Interpreting.* Offer explanations or hypotheses for why events, behaviors, or interactions may have occurred as they did both inside and outside of group.
- *Summarizing.* Review the important element of conversation in order to transition to another phase of group process (e.g., ending of the session, next topic, focus on an important point).
- **Evaluating.** Monitor and assess group progress, process, and outcomes.
- **Setting tone.** Provide structure; the leader sets a style of interaction for group members to follow.
- **Drawing out.** Interact directly with a member to get the member to contribute to a discussion topic or activity. Used with shy members and members the leader believes have something pertinent to contribute.
- **Pairing.** Form smaller groups within the larger group to engage in activities or focused sharing.
- **Making the rounds.** Have group members take turns sharing their perspectives on a given focused topic; so

named because the sharing usually proceeds in the direction of chairs positioned in a circle.

- **Pacing.**   Facilitate the pace or rate at which the group process moves. At times, leaders will speed up the pace, and at other times the leader will slow the pace to allow group members to focus on a particularly relevant topic.

6.3.6 Handling Group Conflict and Resistance

Conflict (e.g., disagreement, friction, hostility) and resistance are common occurrences in groups, serve protective functions, and should be dealt with directly. Resistance may take the form of absences, tardiness, silence, excessive talkativeness (monopolizing), rescuing behaviors, or distracting the group from pursuing goals. Conflicts often occur when members blame other members, gossip, express anger toward or grievances against other members, intimidate, or display intolerant attitudes (e.g., prejudices). Ordinarily, leaders should confront resistive behaviors and conflict when they occur, albeit in a supportive and caring manner that will help to build group cohesiveness and move the group closer to attaining agreed-on goals. Resistance and conflict are frequently observed during the transition stage of counseling and psychotherapy groups, or the beginning stages of task and psychoeducational groups.

6.3.7 Co-Leadership

Co-leadership occurs when more than one leader shares or helps to facilitate the group process. Advantages of co-leadership include (a) creation of a team model or (if co-leaders are male and female) parental model for dealing with family-of-origin issues; (b) help in handling difficult issues that may arise; (c) insights provided by multiple leaders; (d) leaders can give feedback to each other; (e) different leader reactions can enrich the group process; (f) more experienced leaders can train less experienced leaders; (g) sharing of responsibilities; (h) ability to continue the group in the event of leader illness, vacation, or incapacity; (i) better support for lower functioning members; and (j) efficient use of leader modeling and role play. Disadvantages may include (a) potential competition/rivalry between leaders; (b) inconsistency in pacing; (c) lack of consistency in approach as leaders alternate; (d) excessive focus on the leaders; and (e) appearance of collusion.

Co-leaders are usually paired in one of three ways: (a) Experience with Experience—allows well-trained individuals to equitably share leader tasks and functions; (b) Experience with Inexperience—allows a mentoring relationship to emerge as the experienced leader models skills for and supervises the inexperienced leader; or (c) Inexperience with Inexperience—which sometimes occurs in training programs with some type of supervisory support provided by a third, more experienced leader between sessions.

6.3.8 Practice Multiple-Choice Items: Group Leadership

1. In the beginning stage of a group, a leader is generally more _____ than in later stages.
    a. laissez-faire
    b. directive
    c. democratic
    d. passive

2. _____ is NOT an executive function of a group leader.
    a. Establishing boundaries
    b. Beginning and ending group sessions
    c. Establishing norms
    d. Planning group sessions

3. Each of the following are examples of ways to bring members into the here and now EXCEPT
    a. processing members' current situations.
    b. discussing immediate interactions between group members.
    c. helping members make future plans.
    d. encouraging members to provide feedback to other members.

4. A group in which the members take almost full responsibility for the group sessions and process most likely have a(n) _____ leader.
    a. laissez-faire
    b. democratic
    c. authoritarian
    d. uninvolved

5. Group conflict usually occurs during the _____ stage of a counseling group.
    a. initial
    b. working
    c. final
    d. transition

Answer Key: 1. b; 2. c; 3. c; 4. a; 5. d.

6.4 GROUP MEMBER ROLES

Although leaders certainly have an important part to play in groups, it is equally important to understand the roles and responsibilities of members. This section will review group member roles, strategies for facilitating member development, and dealing with challenging group members.

6.4.1 Types of Group Member Roles

Group member roles describe the various positions group members may adopt during group work. These roles involve expected patterns of behavior by an individual within the social context, and they often complement or conflict with other roles served by other group members. *Formal roles* are specific roles assigned to a group member; for example, many task groups have a chair and someone who records minutes of the meeting. *Informal roles* are not specified but are developed through interactions with other group members, such as an advice giver or aggressor. Roles define one's relationship to the group and can change over time but ordinarily result from self-expectations, personality characteristics, group leader characteristics, and group characteristics. As members begin to adopt different roles within the group, **role differentiation** is said to occur. **Role conflict** occurs when members experience conflicting demands of various roles, such as when a member who prefers to avoid emotional expression is encouraged to self-disclose reactions to emotionally laden group content and process—that is, the roles a member plays come into conflict with each other. Finally, **role ambiguity** emerges when a member is not sure of the role expectations or behavior requirements he or she should fulfill. Much has been written about problematic member behaviors and their effects on group process. These challenging member roles are discussed in section 6.4.3, but first we review the positive role expectations for effective group members.

6.4.2 Facilitating Member Development

A pro-developmental approach to group work focuses on what members should do in group to help facilitate the group process and goal attainment. Leaders often play a vital role in helping members to understand how members can facilitate group progress. At the core, all members must engage in two essential tasks: self-disclosure and feedback.

- *Self-disclosure* requires members to take risks, share information, and describe their internal thoughts and feelings with the group. In this way, members share their reactions to other group members and content, rather than stating what they would do or giving advice on what the other member should do to solve a problem. Self-disclosure ordinarily promotes cohesion and other curative group factors, but understanding when and how much information to self-disclose is a premier challenge for group members.
- Often, leaders help members understand appropriate levels of self-disclosure and interpersonal behavior by using the **Johari window** (Luft, 1984). Members are helped to realize that internal information the member is aware of can be presented to others (self-disclosure) or kept to oneself (private information). At the same time, the member is always unaware of some information, some of which is evident to others and some of which is unknown by anyone, including the member. Human interaction and self-disclosure in interpersonal relationships affect the amount of information relegated to each of these areas. In Figure 6.1, note that a change in one quadrant affects the dimensions of the other three quadrants, so as one self-discloses private information (thus shrinking quadrant II), public information becomes larger (i.e., quadrant I

increases). Safety and cohesion must be present within the group for quadrant II to shrink and quadrant I to grow.
- *Feedback* is shared by members when they notice and comment on group member interactions. It is an essential characteristic of effective groups. Good feedback is solicited, specific, descriptive, clear, and well timed. Returning to Figure 6.1, note that as other members provide feedback, a member may gain insights about information to which they were previously blind (thus shrinking quadrant III) or perhaps that was even unknown or unconscious (thus shrinking quadrant IV), thereby growing either the public (quadrant I) or private (quadrant II) windows, depending on whether the insights occurred publicly or privately, respectively. Procedures for effective feedback can be taught through the use of *I-messages* (When I see/hear _____, I feel _____, and I want to _____). Advice giving should be avoided.

6.4.3 Dealing with Challenging Group Member Roles

All group members and leaders get anxious. Some harness the anxiety and assume facilitative roles, whereas others assume challenging or problematic roles, usually to address a personal issue related to identity, control/power, individual needs, or acceptance/intimacy (Schein, 1969). Following are examples of various group member behaviors; some are facilitative or building roles, some are task or maintenance roles, and others are more individual centered. Note that in some texts, individuals displaying these behaviors are often labeled (e.g., one who monopolizes group time is called a "monopolizer"). We have chosen to address group member behavior without the label, and we thereby avoid pathologizing member behavior.

- *Facilitation* by group members helps promote group process and cohesion. Those who self-disclose and even attempt to identify group process variables or speak on behalf of the group when summarizing are using facilitation.
- *Encouragement* of others' ideas helps promote cohesiveness and group member comfort.
- **Compromise** helps group members detach their ideas from their egos in order to promote group goals and enhance the group process.
- **Gatekeeping** occurs when group members and leaders insist on adherence to the established group norms.

	Known to others	Unknown to others
Known to self	**Quadrant I** Public/open (e.g., sex, clothing)	**Quadrant II** Private/hidden (e.g., fear of failure, inadequacy)
Unknown to self	**Quadrant III** Blind (e.g., facial expressions)	**Quadrant IV** Unknown/unconscious (e.g., family-of-origin issues)

FIGURE 6.1 The Johari Window.
Source: From B. T. Erford, (Ed.). (2010). *Group work in the schools* (p. 51). Columbus, OH: Pearson Merrill.

- **Initiation** occurs when group members make suggestions or take action to move the group toward goals.
- **Information seeking** occurs when group members ask for clarification or help promote self-disclosure in self or other group members.
- **Opinion seeking** involves self- or other-disclosure of group member values in relation to a group task. Often, group members want to know what others believe or value to gain insights into others' worldviews.
- **Evaluation** includes the sharing of insights or judgments about whether a group is accomplishing agreed on goals.
- **Observation** includes member and leader feedback to the group.
- **Aggressiveness** is displayed as frequent disagreement with, and forceful attempt to impose ideas upon, the group leader and other members. Leaders should avoid negative confrontation and encourage the member to be specific about personal feelings. Leaders may also want to ask for a private conference to share feelings and ask for cooperation and point out the harmful effects on others.
- **Attention-seeking behaviors** call attention to the member and away from other members. Leaders should respond to member's feelings of insecurity if present, avoid eye contact, and refrain from responding to off-task comments/behavior.
- *Hostility* or fighting can serve to disrupt the group's focus, particularly when explosive reactions occur. Leaders should avoid negative confrontation, observe nonverbal behavior, and set limits firmly but not angrily. Often, by turning the task back to the group, group members can effectively process the hostile actions and explain the effects the reactions have on the group, leading to support, feedback, and self-disclosure.
- *Giving advice* helps to prevent disclosure and keeps feedback on a superficial level. Leaders should observe the reaction to the advice on the member who receives it and encourage self-disclosure on the part of the advice giver, while avoiding reinforcing the advice giver's inappropriate advice.
- **Blocking**, or resisting, behaviors, when performed by a group member, impede group cohesion and progress, usually by not fully participating in exercises or discussions, thus keeping the group from progressing to a working stage. The resistance may be demonstrated as silence or nonparticipation. Leaders may find it helpful to interpret the member behavior, have others self-disclose the effects on them, and invite the resistant member to fully participate. (*Note:* Blocking, in the context of a member role, is counterproductive because it impedes group progress. This is distinguished from the use of blocking as a leadership skill, discussed in section 6.3.5. As a leadership skill, blocking is an appropriate technique that protects group members and facilitates group progress.)
- **Informing** occurs when a member talks about other members outside group. Leaders should remind all members that what happens in group stays in group and underscore the importance of confidentiality to group work success and goal accomplishment.
- **Monopolizing** behaviors usually involve underlying anxieties demonstrated by neediness, demandingness, excessive talkativeness, and control through a focus on self. Leaders should confront and interpret the behavior, pointing to the effects it has on group process. Future attempts to monopolize could be handled using the blocking, or cutting off, technique.
- **Manipulation** ordinarily stems from the need for control and anger and promotes group tension and conflict. Leaders should block manipulative behavior or confront it. Concurrent individual therapy is often indicated.
- **Sarcasm** is an attempt to mask and not express anger. A leader may want to interpret the sarcastic behavior, seek feedback from other group members, and encourage members to be emotionally honest in the here and now.
- **Focusing on others** is often an attempt to avoid self-focus and self-disclosure. Leaders should encourage self-disclosure and self-focus or group focus. In the end, the purpose of the group is to meet group goals and individual goals.

Corey and Corey (2006) provide a number of helpful suggestions for nondefensive leader responses when dealing with group member behaviors:

- Do not dismiss members.
- Express your difficulty with a member without denigrating the character of the person.
- Avoid responding to sarcasm with sarcasm.
- Educate members about how the group works.
- Leaders are honest with members rather than mystifying the process.
- Encourage members to explore their defensiveness rather than demanding they give up their way of protecting themselves.
- Avoid labeling and instead describe the behavior of the member.
- State observations and hunches in a tentative way, as opposed to being dogmatic.
- Demonstrate sensitivity to a member's culture and avoid stereotyping the individual.
- Avoid using the leadership role to intimidate members.
- Monitor your own countertransference reactions.
- Challenge members in a caring and respectful way to do things that may be painful and difficult.
- Do not retreat from conflict.
- Provide a balance between support and challenge.
- Do not take member reactions in an overly personal way.
- Facilitate a more focused exploration of the problem rather than offering simple solutions.
- Do not meet your own needs at the expense of members' needs.
- Invite members to state how they are personally affected by problematic behaviors of other members while blocking judgments, evaluations, and criticisms. (p. 193)

6.4.4 Practice Multiple-Choice Items: Group Member Roles

1. A group member is anxious and uneasy because she is unsure of how she is supposed to behave in group counseling. This individual is experiencing
   a. role overload.
   b. role ambiguity.
   c. role conflict.
   d. role dissonance.

2. _____ is one of the two most essential group member tasks.
   a. Modeling
   b. Active listening
   c. Providing feedback
   d. Confronting

3. Information that is known to self but unknown to others is found in which quadrant of the Johari window?
   a. Public/open quadrant
   b. Private/hidden quadrant
   c. Blind quadrant
   d. Unknown/unconscious quadrant

4. Group members sometimes take on challenging roles to address a personal need or issue related to each of the following EXCEPT
   a. attachment.
   b. acceptance.
   c. identity.
   d. power.

5. _____ can be a challenging group member behavior.
   a. Opinion seeking
   b. Gatekeeping
   c. Evaluation
   d. Advice giving

Answer Key: 1. b; 2. c; 3. b; 4. a; 5. d.

6.5 PLANNING FOR GROUPS

Planning by the group leader is critical to group success. In this section of Chapter 6, information pertaining to group formation and member preparation prior to the initial session of a group are discussed. Readers are urged to review the ASGW (2007) Best Practice Guidelines or Erford (2010) for excellent authoritative summaries of group planning.

6.5.1 Planning for Group Work

Before beginning a group work experience, leaders should be sure they have the knowledge and expertise related to the type of group work (e.g., group counseling, psychoeducational group) and content/topic of the group (e.g., divorce, chronic illness). Effective planning gives a group focus and allows for intentional intervention. In this section, components of effective planning are reviewed, including purpose, planned v. spontaneous groups, homogeneous v. heterogeneous group membership, open v. closed groups, group size, and duration.

6.5.1.1 PURPOSE Most groups have a certain theme or purpose, such as to learn more about a given topic (e.g., depression, domestic violence), enhance intrapersonal and interpersonal awareness, and learn more effective ways of coping with social situations and problems. Members frequently join groups to reduce their social isolation and explore the resolution of problems with others who share similar problems.

6.5.1.2 PLANNED V. SPONTANEOUS GROUPS Some groups are planned around a content theme and focus on helping members resolve problem areas. Membership in a **planned theme group** is restricted to individuals with a demonstrated need in this themed area. Examples include social skills groups for children and adolescents, domestic violence for adults, parenting skills, and addiction groups for adolescents and adults. **Spontaneous content groups** do not have planned content themes and are designed to provide personal growth and support. Membership in a spontaneous group is generally dictated by the need for general development and member characteristics, such as age or severity of issues. For example, in a men's personal growth group, middle-age men may meet every 2 weeks to share and discuss challenges they encounter, give feedback, and experience support and empowerment for personal growth and development.

6.5.1.3 HOMOGENEOUS V. HETEROGENEOUS GROUPS A **homogeneous group** consists of members with similar characteristics (e.g., sex, age, sexual orientation, race, physical ability) and concerns (e.g., a planned theme group). For example, a group run in an elementary school may include only second- and third-grade boys whose parents are considering a divorce. Homogeneous grouping may lead to quicker identification, better attendance, decreased resistance, and better insight. **A heterogeneous group** consists of members with diverse characteristics and concerns. For example, a group for adults may consist of members with diverse age, gender, race, socioeconomic, and sexual orientation characteristics, and members also may have diverse presenting problems (e.g., divorce, domestic abuse, career issues, depression, substance abuse). Heterogeneous grouping may lead to better reality testing, deeper learning, and better transference. Culturally diverse members with heterogeneous issues add a richness to therapeutic relationships and provide real-life experiences encountered in the real world outside of group, thus facilitating generalizability of learning. However, group members who are too heterogeneous may have difficulty relating to each other.

6.5.1.4 OPEN V. CLOSED GROUPS Leaders of **open groups** allow members to enter and leave at various points while continuing a primary group focus. For example, in psychiatric hospitals, patients' lengths of stay vary, and many engage in group therapy during their stay. In this example, leaders do not have much control over when a member begins or terminates the member's group participation. **Closed groups** allow a set number of members to participate from the group's beginning to termination, and leaders expect consistent attendance throughout the group experience. Allowing members to enter and exit the group can provide continuous energy and enthusiasm but also limits group cohesion, trust, and process. Thus, closed groups are ordinarily preferred to promote group process, goals, and purpose, whereas open groups are utilized to advantage when discontinuity of individual member participation is anticipated.

6.5.1.5 LARGE V. SMALL GROUPS Group size is an essential planning consideration for task, psychoeducational, counseling, and psychotherapy groups. Size varies depending on the model, purpose, member age, and intensity of planned interactions. Task groups ordinarily function best when membership includes at least four or five individuals. The maximum number depends on the complexity and scope of the expected group outcomes; simple decisions or products ordinarily require fewer members, whereas complex decisions or products ordinarily require more input and expanded manpower. The purpose and planned intensity of interaction of the psychoeducational group often determines group size (Erford, 2010). Informational presentations to parents or students often can be accomplished in groups of 50 or more, whereas interaction-based interventions (e.g., social skills, grief groups, divorce groups) often involve 6 to 12 members, or fewer if the members are younger than 8 years of age. Counseling groups require greater attention to process and ordinarily involve 6 to 12 members, whereas psychotherapy groups require smaller group sizes because of more serious member conditions and greater expectations for member interaction and feedback, usually 4 to 5 members at a minimum and up to about 8 to 10 members as a maximum.

Importantly, if co-leaders are used, group membership usually can be increased by about 50% to 75%. Also, young children, disruptive members, or members with serious psychological conditions require smaller group sizes. Under normal circumstances, about 8 members is considered optimal for counseling, psychotherapy, or interaction-focused psychoeducational groups.

6.5.1.6 DURATION Group duration refers to two components: duration of a single session and duration of an entire group experience (Erford, 2010). Optimal duration of a single session varies depending on the group purpose, age of members, and expected intensity of interactions. In general, the younger the member, the shorter the session duration should be. That said, it is widely regarded that a minimum of 60 minutes is ordinarily required for a group to warm up, address the session theme, process the session, and terminate the session. Most psychotherapy group sessions last 90 minutes, and many experienced leaders believe that little is gained when groups run longer than 120 minutes. Many groups with very young children last only 30 minutes, with most groups with school-age children lasting about 45 to 60 minutes.

In terms of duration of the entire group experience, wide variation is expected. In a task group, the group continues until the task has been completed or the group has disbanded. Psychoeducational groups tend to be time limited and run until the required information has been conveyed or set of skills

mastered. Counseling groups and psychotherapy groups tend to be run for longer durations. It is not unusual for counseling groups to be planned to run between 8 and 30 sessions. On the other hand, psychotherapy groups frequently run for a minimum of 15 sessions and up to several years.

6.5.2 Preparing Members

Selecting and preparing members for group often is as critical as the other leader functions in group work. Indications that members may be a good fit for group work include a need for peer support, responsiveness to peer feedback, problems that are interactional in nature, and ineffective social skills. Counterindications to group work include a client crisis state, disruptive needs for attention, social phobia or fear of speaking/sharing in the presence of others, and severe/extreme psychological disturbance. This section briefly explores why members join groups, why some drop out prematurely, and how to conduct a pregroup interview to prepare members for the group experience, thus minimizing member dropouts.

6.5.2.1 WHY MEMBERS JOIN GROUPS Groups meet basic human needs. Members are often referred to groups by counselors, friends, or family members, but whether people choose to participate in group work is often determined by whether members believe the group will help meet basic therapeutic needs, such as skill development, information sharing, affiliation with like-minded members, learning better ways to socially interact with peers, experiencing social and emotional support, and re-experiencing or re-creating experiences from one's family of origin in order to more successfully resolve the events. Often, groups serve to fulfill an existential need for individuals seeking insight and meaning into life events or a bolstering of their self-concept. These are more global or general needs; often, members have more specific needs related to personal presenting problems or conditions.

6.5.2.2 WHY MEMBERS DROP OUT OF GROUPS Premature termination occurs for numerous reasons and affects not only the member who drops out of the group but also the group process and cohesion of the remaining members. Members who drop out of groups prematurely are likely to have one or more of the following characteristics: low motivation, lower socioeconomic status, lower IQ, high levels of problem denial, poor social skills, poor self-disclosure skills, unrealistic demands, lack of motivation to change, and lack of insight or interpersonal sensitivity. Poor leader skill or an incompatible leadership style may also contribute to a member's decision to terminate prematurely. Of course, members may also terminate because of external factors, such as moving or significant disruptions in work and family circumstances.

6.5.2.3 THE PREGROUP INTERVIEW When members are selected to participate in a group, leaders should prepare members for what to expect and how to maximally benefit from the group experience. Usually this preparation occurs individually and sometimes over a period of several weeks before the group sessions begin. The pregroup interview is used for counseling and psychotherapy groups, and sometimes for psychoeducational groups to give both the leader and member the opportunity to decide if the group is right for the member. Leaders should address the goals and purpose of the group, leadership style, leader's role, and member roles. Leaders should present basic ground rules (e.g., attendance, payments, confidentiality). Attendance is particularly important to address as it is a good indicator of group cohesion and performance. Absences may suggest anxiety, dissatisfaction, and premature termination, and absences should be addressed with the member during the group session whenever possible.

Leaders should assess member motivations for joining the group to be sure it matches the group theme and goals and determine the potential member's previous experiences with group work and the results. This is also a good time to assess the potential for scheduling problems and potential member comfort with group characteristics (e.g., open v. closed, voluntary v. involuntary).

In addition, the member should be presented with an informed consent agreement that outlines the pros and cons, risks, confidentiality, release of information, fee arrangements, goals, group history, and so on. Pregroup meetings help leaders better understand each group member and assess the member's fit within the group. It also gives group members the opportunity to meet the group leader and better understand the needs of the other group members prior to finally committing to the group experience.

6.5.3 Practice Multiple-Choice Items: Planning for Groups

1. A _____ is an example of a spontaneous content group.
   a. social skills group
   b. young women's personal growth group
   c. divorce group for children
   d. grief group

2. _____ is NOT a potential benefit of a homogeneous group.
   a. Better insight
   b. Better attendance
   c. Better skill generalization
   d. Less resistance

3. Heterogeneous groups may have
   a. members with diverse presenting problems.
   b. members with diverse demographics.
   c. cohesion difficulties if members are too dissimilar.
   d. All of the above.

4. Open groups are most appropriate in
   a. school settings.
   b. private practice.
   c. psychiatric hospitals.
   d. All of the above.

5. The ideal size for counseling groups and psychotherapy groups is about
   a. 6 members.
   b. 8 members.
   c. 10 members.
   d. 12 members.

Answer Key: 1. b; 2. c; 3. d; 4. c; 5. b.

6.6 STAGES/PROCESS OF GROUP WORK

Effective group workers must be aware of process dynamics and developmental issues that contribute to successes and challenges. Process dynamics refers to the forces that create positive and detrimental movement in groups, such as member cohesion and member resistance. These process dynamics are often viewed as developmental, occurring naturally as group members progress through recognized phases or stages of group work, including the forming and orienting stage, transition stage, working stage, and termination.

6.6.1 Group Dynamics: Content and Process Issues

This section reviews elements of group dynamics, such as content and process balance, group cohesion, group norms, power, transference and countertransference, resistance, and resolving conflict/aggression.

6.6.1.1 GROUP CONTENT AND GROUP PROCESS/DYNAMICS Group dynamics create movement between and among group members through the development and interaction of forces. These dynamic forces result in a continuum from socially acceptable behaviors to socially unacceptable behaviors. At the extreme end of socially unacceptable behaviors are detrimental and destructive behaviors. Many factors contribute to group dynamics, including group structure, content, and process.

- *Structure issues* include group size, function (i.e., task, psychoeducational, counseling, psychotherapy), voluntary/involuntary, and open/closed groups and were discussed earlier in this chapter.
- *Content issues* involve the "what" or actual subject under discussion by the group members. Sometimes this content or topic is agreed on at the outset of group formation (e.g., a changing family group will discuss topics related to parent separation/divorce), whereas at other times the content may be unstructured and involve a very recent topic or event that was not agreed on during the group's formation (e.g., an event that just occurred in a member's life yesterday).
- *Group process issues* involve the interplay of forces or dynamics between and among members and leaders—or "how" the interaction is occurring in the here and now. Group process and group dynamics are often used interchangeably. Focus on group process leads to affective learning and understanding and to development of trust and group cohesion. Numerous forces have been identified as potential group process or dynamic issues, including norms (what is expected), cohesiveness, safety and trust, expression of feelings, catharsis, leadership patterns, reality testing, identification, power, conflict, and

resistance. Several of these important process issues are explained in more detail in the remainder of this section. Leaders must be skilled in processing group issues and modeling these processing skills for group members.

6.6.1.2 GROUP COHESION **Group cohesion** refers to feelings of belonging and inclusion that members and leaders experience through group interactions. Cohesion is an important determiner of group effectiveness, attendance, and self-disclosure.

- Smaller groups tend to reach higher levels of cohesion more quickly because of fewer communication problems and higher member satisfaction.
- As groups become larger, subgroupings (cliques) and alienation are more likely to occur.
- Group members from similar backgrounds (e.g., race, socioeconomic status) and with similar characteristics and attitudes tend to reach higher levels of cohesion more quickly.
- When a cohesive group is challenged or attacked, greater cohesion usually results; challenges to low cohesion groups may lead to higher or lower degrees of group cohesion.
- Cohesiveness is enhanced when members set personal and group goals and when members are dependent on the group to meet those goals.
- Cohesion is enhanced when group membership is stable and frequent. Thus, closed groups that meet frequently (one or two times per week) tend to be more cohesive than open groups with sporadic, transitory attendance.
- Yalom (Yalom & Leszcz, 2005) identified three primary factors of cohesion, each with various facets:
  - *Interpersonal* (i.e., attractiveness of members, homogeneity of members, interdependence, and atmosphere)
  - *Group factors* (i.e., size, goals, activity, history and leadership)
  - *Group environment* (i.e., intergroup conflict, and group status)
- Cohesiveness is usually strongest during the working stage of group development as members are able to take on tasks, deal efficiently with conflicts, and embrace diverse member perspectives on the way to addressing important group issues. Cohesion binds members to each other and to the task undertaken.
- Leaders must be aware that cohesiveness may lead to development of member **alliances** or subgroupings. Alliances can be beneficial or destructive. Positive alliances can provide sources of support and strength and lead to high levels of group performance and cohesion, serving much the same intimacy function as friendships and families. However, alliances that are exclusionary can prevent members from forming productive relationships and achieving individual and group goals.
- *Sociograms* are graphical representations of group member interaction patterns and have been used to display member relationships and educate group members about the intricacies of group dynamics.

6.6.1.3 GROUP NORMS **Norms** are the rules for individual member and group behavior, communicating to members what is and is not socially acceptable within the group environment. Norms bring order and organization to the group process by defining permissible behaviors and the tolerable range of behaviors acceptable to the group. In other words, norms set standards for group behavior and interaction, and members may actually feel included or excluded depending on adherence to these norms.

- Norms may be formal or informal, spoken or unspoken, conscious or unconscious, and may even be different from the rules or norms people adhere to outside of the group. For example, in many work settings, self-disclosure may be discouraged (formally or informally), but in a group, self-disclosure is an essential process variable; without self-disclosure, group cohesion, growth, and understanding are less likely to occur.
- Like families, groups define acceptable behaviors and sanctions for unacceptable behaviors, thus maintaining a group's equilibrium. Thus, norms help to stabilize and bring order to group interactions.
- Conformity to group norms is influenced by the degree to which members helped to establish the norms (or at least consented), the cohesiveness of group members, and member status (e.g., low status members have less to lose by not conforming to group norms; high status members have less to lose by deviating from the norms; low status members who desire a higher status are more likely to conform to norms).
- Norms may facilitate member growth or stifle it. Functional norms include work on your problems, everyone participates, show respect to the leader and other members, appropriately self-disclose, and be supportive of other member efforts. Dysfunctional norms include showing disrespect for the leader, refusing to self-disclose, and engaging in aggression/conflict with other members or a leader.
- Group leaders often point out the group process issues occurring around group norms as they evolve to influence the development of group norms and address member hesitancies that inhibit group processes and performance. For example, a leader may ask, "What is keeping members from sharing their feelings about this issue?" "How can the group help all members feel respected for their contributions?" or "What are the group's expectations for who is responsible for guiding the exploration of these emotional issues—the leader or the members?"

6.6.1.4 POWER In the group context, *power* is viewed as having control over the resources the group values or desires (e.g., materials, role/position, information, ability, punishment/reward). Power may involve one's ability to exert control over group process or content (i.e., to control others and events) or to defend oneself against some other power within the group.

- French and Raven (1968) proposed six sources of power in groups: (a) *reward power* (e.g., dispensing rewards);

(b) *coercive power* (e.g., dispensing punishment or sanction); (c) *legitimate power* (e.g., belief that it is one's duty to follow the leader's directions); (d) *referent power* (e.g., respect and attraction for the leader or a model member); (e) *expert power* (e.g., a member has expertise or ability that the group relies on); and (f) *informational power* (e.g., a member has the knowledge to accomplish a goal or task).

6.6.1.5 TRANSFERENCE AND COUNTERTRANSFERENCE

One of the therapeutic factors discussed in section 6.1.4 was the ability of the group to re-create the dynamics evident in important relationships in the lives of members, such as between the member and a parent, sibling, or spouse. Transference and countertransference are constructs from psychoanalytic theory used to explain how these re-created interactions are played out in relationships that serve as extensions of the original relationship.

- *Transference* occurs when the member's previous relationship is manifest in the relationship with another group member. For example, an adolescent male who rebels against his authoritarian father may attempt to rebel against the male leader, thus re-creating the reenactment dynamic of the father–son relationship by transferring his emotional reaction onto the leader. This presents the opportunity for the leader and member to reprocess the interaction and father–son dynamic, helping the member to gain new insights into the relationship and new ways of interacting and coping to achieve a more satisfying result.

- *Countertransference* occurs when the interactions with a group member influence the leader's unconscious emotional state. Thus, the rebellious son (group member) may unconsciously re-create in the group leader a previously lived experience (perhaps a dynamic relationship with the leader's own rebellious son), and the leader experiences an emotional reaction (e.g., feeling his authority threatened, need to control) when engaging the rebellious youth.

- Leaders must constantly self-monitor and self-evaluate instances of transference and countertransference as they tend to reoccur and can inhibit productive group processes. Importantly, transference can work to the advantage of the group as previous positive interactions and relationships also can be played out, leading to quickly established rapport and respect. As leaders and members interact, transferences are frequently resolved because members come to see leaders as multifaceted humans quite different from the previous relationships.

6.6.1.6 RESISTANCE

Resistance in group members ordinarily stems from content or processes the member finds anxiety producing, threatening, or sensitive. Members frequently feel that they must defend against (i.e., resist) this anxiety and use a variety of strategies (defenses) to accomplish this resistance. At the core, resistance is a covert attempt to prevent or resist change.

- Resistance can occur in individual members, several members, or the entire group. Examples of resistances include acting as an assistant to the leader to avoid personal emotional vulnerabilities, retelling of childhood events or episodes without an attempt to resolve the issues and move forward, engaging in lengthy silences, distracting the group from an emotionally sensitive topic, dependency on the leader for support and advice, and attacks on the leader to avoid emotional content.

- Leaders should deal proactively with resistance, although opinions are mixed over whether leaders should attempt to overtly interpret the resistance to the group members directly because such an approach could make the group more cohesive around the resistance. Trivial resistances (i.e., those not impeding the group process) should be ignored, but when resistance is impeding the group process and relationships, the issue must be addressed.

- Because resistance is a covert attempt to prevent change, the leader should bring the issues into the open for discussion and processing in the here and now and in a nondefensive manner. Focus should be on what the resistance means, rather than on the actual behavior. Leaders who openly discuss the resistance and model appropriate coping allow for the free expression of feelings and the correction of any misunderstandings that members or leaders may have. Some leaders have success by reframing resistance behaviors, highlighting the protective functions served, and minimizing the member's need for self-protection. In extreme cases, open confrontation of seriously resistant behaviors may become necessary to make the covert overt and to give the resistant members the choice of making constructive changes or admitting the lack of intention for working toward agreed-on group or individual goals.

6.6.1.7 RESOLVING CONFLICT/AGGRESSION

Conflict within a group often reveals group members' anxieties or primary needs. Conflict is a natural part of any interpersonal relationship and usually stems from member efforts to redistribute power. Although more passive members often readily cede any claim to power, more aggressive members often move to influence discussions and solutions to group problems.

- Conflict can lead to deeper self-understanding and greater cohesiveness, resulting in a more productive group, but sometimes conflict inhibits group process and requires intervention by the group leader.

- In general, mild and moderate conflicts can help groups grow, whereas aggressive and hostile attacks require leader or group intervention.

- *Aggression* may include verbal attacks, physical attacks, or relational aggression (e.g., spreading rumors or innuendo to destroy the relationships a person has with others). Aggression may be directed at the leader or other group members.

- Aggression is more common in some populations (e.g., delinquent youth, incarcerated prisoners) than others, although it can occur among any population.

- Leaders must understand that aggression usually stems from unmet needs and anxieties unrelated to the group process (e.g., members who are habitually easily frustrated, easily provoked, resent authority). Once the underlying reasons are understood, the leader and other group members can empathically help the aggressive member deal with the causes and effect, both within the group context and during real-world experiences.
- Effectively dealing with aggressive members and group conflict allows leaders to model appropriate problem-solving and conflict-resolution skills and allows the group to process the dynamics that underlie conflicts so members can generalize the experiences to out-of-group contexts.

6.6.2 Stages of Group Development

Most groups develop through an orderly sequence of stages. In the process, groups become more organized, cooperative, and interdependent. Understanding this orderly group progression is critical to understanding and predicting the group processes and dynamics that will occur throughout the group experience. Many authors have named and described the sequence of stages, but the commonalities shared by all is that all groups experience some initial phase in which the group forms and is oriented to the expectations and goals of the group work. This is followed by a phase of transition in which members experience anxiety and some degree of conflict as they struggle to organize themselves to accomplish the goals of the group. As group members establish trust and cohesion, they enter a productive phase when the group goals are pursued in earnest and personal and group achievements become evident. In addition, members consolidate their gains, strive for generalizability of these gains to out-of-group experiences, and prepare to end the group experience. Although different authors call these stages by different names (e.g., Tuckman: forming, storming, norming, performing, and adjourning [Tuckman & Jensen, 1977]; Yalom: orientation, conflict, cohesion, and termination [Yalom & Leszcz, 2005]; Corey: orientation and exploration, transition, working, and consolidation and termination [Corey & Corey, 2006)]). For organizational convenience, the remainder of this section uses the designations proposed by Erford (2010): (a) the forming and orienting stage; (b) the transition stage ; (c) the working stage; and (d) the termination stage.

6.6.2.1 THE FORMING AND ORIENTING STAGE   Much of the success in the forming and orienting stage is presaged by efficient group planning (see section 6.5). Prior to the first group meeting, the leader has screened the members for inclusion, established preliminary rapport, discussed potential goals and expectations for group performance, addressed informed consent, and answered member questions about the upcoming group experience. Some leaders will even conduct pregroup trainings to bolster member communication skills (e.g., reflecting feelings, I-messages), and basic group process issues. During the first session, and sometimes the first several sessions, group members and leaders begin the work of the group.

The following characterizes the **forming and orienting stage**:

- Anxiety, discomfort, insecurity, and preoccupation with personal issues as members cautiously test the leader and group members to see if the group will yield a trusting, safe, and secure environment. At the same time, hope for the group's possibilities emerges (e.g., acceptance, shared issues), leading to an approach-avoidance response to the group work.
- Initial communications oriented toward the leader. However, effective leaders soon establish the group norm that communication should be oriented toward each other, not through the leader.
- Agreements on group rules (norms) and personal and mutual goals.
- A group leader who is didactic and directive early on, and less so as group members become more active and responsible for group process.
- A group leader who models honesty, openness, spontaneity, genuineness, positive communication, and social skills to shape group norms.
- Development of social relationships among all participants to create an inclusive group environment and inspire members to self-disclose and work together to accomplish goals. **Inclusion** is the sense of connectedness a member has to the group.
- Group members testing out potential activity levels and identities within the group to understand how they can best belong and fit into an emerging group identity. Finding one's identity involves figuring out who one is in the group in relation to others.
- Member awareness of participation fundamentals, group expectations, and need for risk, self-disclosure, and feedback.
- Superficial social acceptance and communications to "test the waters."
- Dependence on the leader and avoidance of conflict among members.
- An expectation by members that the group leader will take control and solve all their problems.
- Member determination as to whether they are "in or out" (i.e., whether the group will be worth it and whether the member should return for the next session). Essentially, members must make a commitment to the group and to accomplishing personal and group goals.
- Emphasizing member similarities and avoiding rejection.

Basically, in the forming and orienting stage, leaders must review group goals, help members establish personal goals, specify group rules, model facilitative group behavior, assist members in expressing their apprehensions, establish and maintain trust, promote positive interchanges among members, teach members basic interpersonal skills, instill hope, and resolve possible group problems (Erford, 2010).

6.6.2.2 THE TRANSITION STAGE   The **transition stage**, similar to the adolescent phase in human development, is a

time of testing boundaries and power structures that can range from subtle testing to full-blown rebellion and conflict. Professional counselors must understand the dynamics of this stage in great detail to help more challenging groups through this developmental transition. Group work authors have referred to this stage as storming, conflict, resistance, and power and control; the transition stage involves all these and more. Research suggests that the dynamics of the transition stage are driven by anxiety and fear, which result in resistance, defensiveness, and conflict around the issues of control and power (Billow, 2003). These dynamics can be understood through developmental or systems theory models (see section 5.7; Connors & Caple, 2005).

The transition stage is characterized by the following:

- Members testing each other to see if the environment is safe for self-disclosure and what the potential is for relationships within the group.
- Members competing for status (rank) and individuality.
- Attempts to create factions, pairs, and subgroups (depending on group size) for support and protection.
- Attrition in cases where group conflict is too intense or when an individual does not feel included.
- Members testing the leader to see if they can trust the leader to keep them safe or comfortable.
- Members targeting the leader to express their inner feelings of anxiety and anger/hostility.
- Dependence on the leader to make the group anxiety free, for solutions to their problems, or for understanding their problems without ever explaining out loud what their issues are.
- Developing cohesiveness and intimacy through use of self-disclosure, feedback, and confrontation.
- Feedback that can either be change provoking or change resisting.
- A leader who effectively demonstrates empathy, caring, reinforcement, and confrontation.
- Members receiving support and respect for taking risks.
- The discovery that difficulties can be resolved with sensitivity and support and without negative judgments.
- Increasingly supportive, open, and direct communication.
- An emerging degree of order and appropriate behavioral norms.

In general, during the transition stage, the group proceeds from superficial discussions to deeper levels of affective commitment and self-understanding by developing intimacy and trust. In doing so, the group is transitioning into the working stage when personal and group goals can be accomplished.

6.6.2.3 THE WORKING STAGE The **working stage** is a time when committed members work to accomplish personal and group goals and help other members to do so by giving feedback, working as a cooperative team, and facilitating a supportive environment of positive change. The working stage is characterized by the following:

- Productive exploration of problems and solutions.
- Members who openly share issues, provide feedback to others, and challenge/support member change.

- A focus on accomplishing personal and shared goals.
- Deepening levels of trust and self-disclosure, along with more intimate relationships.
- Greater self- and other-acceptance.
- More spontaneous and open expression.
- Less resistance to the views and suggestions of others.
- Efficient use of group resources and time.
- Less dependence on the group leader.
- Leaders who provide linkages between members and issues, reinforcement, effective modeling of problem solving, and facilitation of the transformation of insight into action.

An efficient group in the working stage focuses on the goals of the group and behaves in a supportive manner to help members accomplish personal goals. As goals are met, the leader begins to prepare the group for the eventual termination of group meetings.

6.6.2.4 THE TERMINATION STAGE The final stage in a developmental group process is called termination. Interestingly, recent conceptualizations of the **termination stage** have expanded it to include more than the end of group. Termination issues also occur at the end of an individual session or when a member or leader leaves the group prematurely for some reason.

The termination stage at the end of a group experience is characterized by the following:

- Closure of group process and the relationships members have established throughout the group experience.
- Expression of member and leader feelings about termination, separation, unfinished business, and generalizability of what was accomplished within the group to the outside world.
- Leaders helping members make postgroup plans.
- Leaders reaffirming the importance of confidentiality after the group ends.
- Consolidation, summarization, and integration of learning.
- Development of future goals and plans for having member needs met in the real world.
- Evaluation of the total group experience (see section 6.7).

When a group member desires to prematurely terminate the group experience, the leader should attempt to hold a termination session for that member so that the member and other group members have an opportunity to bring closure to their relationship. Oftentimes, on receiving supportive feedback from other members the terminating member will reconsider leaving the group. Alternatively, the session can help all members consolidate their learning up to that point in time and discuss how to generalize the learning to the outside world.

6.6.3 Practice Multiple-Choice Items: Stages/Process of Group Work

1. _____ issues are NOT primary contributors to group dynamics.
   a. Content
   b. Structural

   c. Leader style
   d. Process

2. Discussing a conflict that arises in a group with all group members would be an example of addressing a
   a. content issue.
   b. structural issue.
   c. leader style issue.
   d. process issue.

3. Group cohesion normally is highest in the
   a. forming/orienting stage.
   b. transition stage.
   c. working stage.
   d. termination stage.

4. Norms can best be described as
   a. roles.
   b. rules.
   c. attitudes.
   d. All of the above.

5. The transition stage is referred to by some as the
   a. storming stage.
   b. forming stage.
   c. norming stage.
   d. performing stage.

Answer Key: 1. c; 2. d; 3. c; 4. b; 5. a.

6.7 ASSESSMENT AND EVALUATION IN GROUP WORK

Groups can be evaluated using methods and procedures similar to those discussed in Chapter 8: Research and Program Evaluation, and members can be assessed using methods and procedures similar to those discussed in Chapter 7: Assessment. This section contains information specifically tailored to the application of assessment and evaluation in group work.

6.7.1 Evaluating Groups

Program evaluation is discussed in greater detail in Chapter 8. This section covers specific applications of process evaluation, outcome evaluation, and member satisfaction, as each pertains to group work evaluation. Each can be applied to the four functional group models (i.e., task, psychoeducational, counseling, and psychotherapy groups) and conducted at the beginning, during, or at the end of a group using formal or informal methods.

6.7.1.1 PROCESS EVALUATION Process evaluation refers to assessment of the group dynamics and interaction processes occurring within the group sessions, usually related to the leader, members, and the interactions between the leader and members. Understanding the group dynamics helps to improve the efficiency and effectiveness of the interactions. Several resources are available that provide ideas for conducting process evaluations. The *Handbook of Group Psychotherapy: An Empirical and Clinical Synthesis*, edited by Fuhriman and Burlingame (1994), identifies numerous measures and methods for evaluating group process and outcomes, as has DeLucia-Waack (1997, 1999) and DeLucia-Waack, Gerrity, Kalodner, & Riva (2004).

Some interaction and process evaluation instruments used in the past include the Hill Interaction Matrix (Hill, 1966), Bales' (1950) Interaction Analysis scale, and Simon and Agazarian's (1974) Sequential Analysis of Verbal Interaction (SAVI). In addition to standardized measures, process evaluation can be conducted through a variety of other methods, including peer/supervisor observation, informal member evaluation, and evaluation of videotapes. Colleagues with expertise in group work can observe sessions and provide feedback in an informal or formal supervisory relationship. Although this is sometimes requested by the group leader when a group is at an impasse or not moving in an appropriate direction, observation by a colleague may provide helpful feedback at any point in a group counseling process.

Informal member evaluations should be conducted during each session to help the leader understand how group members are progressing and perceiving the group process. Members frequently give helpful feedback and make suggestions for improvement when presented with basic questions such as the following:

- What did you like most (or least) about this session?
- What did and did not work well or go well in this session?
- How could the session have been improved?
- What could the leader or members have done differently to make the session more successful?
- What was the most important gain or insight you realized in today's session?

Alternatively, members can journal about their session experiences and insights to communicate similar thoughts, feelings, and behaviors. Leaders should always keep in mind that some members may give inaccurate negative feedback, inaccurate positive feedback, or say what they believe the leader wants to hear (i.e., social desirability).

Videotapes have the advantage of being an actual record of real-life events that can be reviewed at the leisure of the group leader, a consulting colleague, or a supervisor. It is difficult to dispute the advantages of actually seeing and hearing oneself, repeatedly if need be, engaging in the actual group process. Comments, sequences, and interchanges can be broken down and analyzed so that strengths can be identified and areas in need of improvement targeted. Videotaping is used extensively in training programs and less frequently in clinical practice. Videotaped sessions are among the most effective process evaluation tools available.

6.7.1.2 OUTCOME EVALUATION Outcome evaluation (often called results evaluation) assesses how members are different because of the group work. Many leaders view outcome evaluation as a discrete component, but it is actually an integrated part of a continuous process for program improvement. All accountability procedures must have the institution's mission in mind because the institutional values and needs will determine the focus of study. Questions of worth and effectiveness are derived from a confluence of values, needs, goals, and mission, and these questions lead to the determination of what evidence must be collected. Evidence may exist in many places, but typically it is derived using preplanned measures or from the performances or products clients produce during program activities. Once information has been gathered, it must then be interpreted, and conclusions must be drawn from it regarding the worth, strengths, and weaknesses of the program or activity. In addition, the interpretations and conclusions must be used to improve the program or parts of the program. As assessment information is used to prompt programmatic changes, goal setting and the posing of new questions about the revised program are revised. Chapter 8 provides in-depth exploration of outcomes research methodology.

6.7.1.3 MEMBER SATISFACTION
Leaders frequently assess the general satisfaction of members with the total group experience near the end of a group experience and sometimes assess member satisfaction with specific facets of group activities and process during the ongoing sessions. Member satisfaction varies greatly and is affected by numerous factors, including the particular group's stage of group process. For example, satisfaction tends to be high in the working and termination stages and substantially lower during the transition stage. Attendance also affects satisfaction. Mandatory (e.g., court ordered) attendance usually leads to lower levels of member satisfaction, whereas members whose attendance is voluntary usually experience higher general satisfaction. Some standardized measures have been created for assessing member satisfaction both in session and at termination, but many leaders construct informal assessment instruments tailored to the specific group purpose.

6.7.2 Assessment in Group Work

Assessment instruments used in group work usually involve five facets: (a) screening and selection, (b) leadership skills, (c) therapeutic factors, (d) group climate, and (e) in-session behavior. **Screening and selection measures** help leaders assess potential member attitudes toward groups, assess prosocial attitudes and problematic group member interpersonal behaviors, and select group members. Assessment of leadership skills helps leaders understand the affects of their behaviors on creating effective group process. Critical feedback can be provided by members, supervisors, and co-leaders. Although *assessment of leadership skills* is almost always done during training experiences for new leaders, such feedback is helpful at any level of expertise, often providing valuable insights to leader skill improvement and how to help a struggling group progress in the group experience. As described in section 6.1.4, therapeutic factors are the elements and processes experienced by members that make group work helpful and effective. *Assessment of therapeutic factors* gives leaders and members insight into how the group process is progressing (e.g., cohesion, universality) and which factors need more attention in the process to help the group function more efficiently. **Group climate**

measures can help assess which stage of group process the members have entered and provide leaders with member perceptions of group climate. In-session behavioral assessments can be conducted via video recordings, transcripts, and inventories and help leaders recognize patterns of interactions across group sessions or within a single session. By integrating the use of these five assessment facets, comprehensive understandings of group dynamics and progress can be attained, improving not only the effectiveness of a given group's experience but also the level of leader expertise and experience. Table 6.1 includes a listing of inventories commonly used in group assessment.

TABLE 6.1 Process and Outcome Measures Used in Group Work.

Screening/Selection Measures

Elements (Schutz, 1992)

Group Psychotherapy Evaluation Scale (Van Dyck, 1980)

Group Therapy Survey (Slocum, 1987)

Hill Interaction Matrix (Hill, 1965, 1973)

Leader Behaviors/Skills Measures

Corrective Feedback Self-Efficacy Instrument (Page & Hulse-Killacky, 1999)

Group Counselor Behavior Rating Form (Corey & Corey, 1987)

Group Leadership Self-Efficacy Instrument (Page, Pietrzak, & Lewis, 2001)

Leadership Characteristics Inventory (Makuch, 1997)

Skilled Group Counseling Scale (Smaby, Maddux, Torres-Rivera, & Zimmick, 1999)

Trainer Behavior Scale (Bolman, 1971)

Group Climate Measures

Group Climate Questionnaire–Short (MacKenzie, 1983, 1990)

Group Environment Scale (Moos, 1986)

Therapeutic Factors Measures

Critical Incidents Questionnaire (Kivlighan & Goldfine, 1991)

Curative Factors Scale–Revised (Stone, Lewis, & Beck, 1994)

Therapeutic Factors Inventory (Lese & McNair-Semands, 2000)

Therapeutic Factors Scale (Yalom, Tinklenberg, & Gilula, 1968)

Member Behavior Measures

Group Cohesiveness Scale (Budman & Gurman, 1988)

Group Observer Form (Romano & Sullivan, 2000)

Group Sessions Rating Scale (Cooney, Kadden, Litt, & Getter, 1991)

Hill Interaction Matrix (Hill, 1965, 1973)

Individual Group Member Interpersonal Process Scale (Soldz, Budman, Davis, & Demby, 1993)

Interaction Process Analysis (Bales, 1950)

Systems for Multiple Level Observation of Groups (SYMLOG) (Bales, Cohen & Williams, 1979)

Source: From B. T. Erford, (Ed.). (2010). *Group work in the schools* (p. 298). Columbus, OH: Pearson Merrill.

6.7.3 Practice Multiple-Choice Items: Assessment and Evaluation in Group Work

1. _____ could be used for process evaluation purposes in group work.
   a. Standardized instruments
   b. Evaluation of videotapes
   c. Observations
   d. All of the above

2. Which question does outcome evaluation answer?
   a. "What did members like about group work?"
   b. "How are members different because of group work?"
   c. "How many individuals received the benefit of group work?"
   d. All of the above.

3. Outcome evaluation can be used for all of the following purposes EXCEPT to
   a. demonstrate accountability.
   b. process group dynamics.
   c. improve the program.
   d. determine whether the program met its goals.

4. _____ is NOT a characteristic that usually leads to higher member satisfaction.
   a. Mandatory attendance
   b. Being in the working stage
   c. Voluntary attendance
   d. Being in the termination stage

5. The Hill Interaction Matrix is a measure of
   a. group climate.
   b. therapeutic factors.
   c. screening/selection.
   d. leader behaviors/skills.

Answer Key: 1. d; 2. b; 3. b; 4. a; 5. c.

6.8 THEORETICAL APPROACHES TO GROUP WORK

Theoretical approaches to group work mirror individual counseling approaches, so the reader is advised to review Chapter 5: Helping Relationships for an excellent overview of theoretical approaches to counseling. In particular, when reviewing Chapter 5, readers should consider any applications or modifications of these individual approaches to group work, including, where applicable, group stages, important concepts, and facets leaders should attend to when operating from these theoretical perspectives. Questions on the NCE and CPCE seldom require the specific application of an individual approach to the group work context, but examinees should be prepared nonetheless. NCE and CPCE questions ordinarily address the content reviewed in sections 6.1 to 6.7 in this chapter.

6.9 KEY POINTS FOR CHAPTER 6: GROUP WORK

- The ASGW is the ACA division devoted to group work.
- Self-help groups became prevalent in the 1980s. They differ from other types of groups in that members rather than leaders run them. Alcoholics Anonymous is one of the most well-known self-help groups.
- Benefits of group work include time efficiency for the leader, less cost per individual, greater sources, feelings of safety, a sense of belonging, replication of the everyday world, and a safe place to practice new behaviors.
- Challenges of group work include reality distortions, avoidance, limitations to confidentiality, unhealthy attachments, and institutional barriers.
- Leaders should ensure that group goals and individual member goals are set.
- The following are curative factors in group work: instillation of hope, universality, imparting information, altruism, family reenactment, development of socialization techniques, imitative behaviors, interpersonal learning, group cohesiveness, catharsis, and existential factors.
- Confidentiality cannot be guaranteed in group work.
- Leaders must screen group members prior to conducting a group to ensure that each member is appropriate for the group.
- There are four primary types of groups: task groups, psychoeducational groups, counseling groups, and psychotherapy groups. Task groups are formed to accomplish a specific goal. Psychoeducational groups are structured and emphasize skill development. Counseling groups are designed to help members work on interpersonal problems and promote behavioral change. Psychotherapy groups are created for individuals who are experiencing severe or chronic problems.
- Group leaders have three main tasks: executive functions, building a group culture, and bringing the group into the here and now. Leadership styles are categorized as authoritarian, democratic, or laissez-faire.
- Conflicts in groups are normal and should be addressed within the group whenever possible.
- Planning is critical to group success. The planning process involves deciding whether the group will be planned or spontaneous, homogeneous or heterogeneous, open or closed, large or small, and for how long the group will run.
- The four stages of group work are the forming and orienting stage, the transition stage, the working stage, and the termination stage.
- Group cohesion plays a significant role in determining group effectiveness, attendance, and level of self-disclosure.
- Process evaluation is the assessment of group dynamics and interaction processes; outcome evaluation is the assessment of the worth and effectiveness of a group.

Assessment

7.1 INTRODUCTION TO ASSESSMENT

Assessment refers to the systematic process of gathering and documenting information regarding a client's knowledge, skills, attitudes, and/or beliefs. Assessment is a core area of counselor preparation and involves the professional counselor's review, selection, administration, and interpretation of evaluative procedures. Thus, this chapter includes topics such as the formal assessment of ability, personality, and intelligence and informal methods of assessment. In addition, Chapter 7 covers topics related to test construction and interpretation and considers ethical, professional, and cultural issues in assessment.

Over the past several years, administrations of the National Counselor Examination (NCE) have included 20 (of the 160, or 12.5% of the) scored items (plus some trial items) designed to measure assessment (rank = 3.5 of 8; the average number of items for the eight domains). The average item difficulty index was .71 (rank = 5 of 8; 5th easiest or 4th most difficult domain of item content), meaning that the average item in this domain was correctly answered by 71% of test-takers. Thus, on the NCE, the Assessment domain is represented by an average number of items, and the items are of average difficulty, overall.

Over the past several years, administrations of the Counselor Preparation Comprehensive Exam (CPCE) have included 17 scored items designed to measure assessment, plus several trial items that do not count in your score. The average item difficulty index was .62, meaning that the average item in this domain was correctly answered by 62% of test-takers, making this set of items among the more challenging item sets on the examination.

The Council for Accreditation of Counseling and Related Educational Programs (CACREP, 2009) defines standards for Assessment as studies that provide an understanding of individual and group approaches to assessment and evaluation in a multicultural society, including all of the following:

a. historical perspectives concerning the nature and meaning of assessment;
b. basic concepts of standardized and nonstandardized testing and other assessment techniques, including norm-referenced and criterion-referenced assessment, environmental assessment, performance assessment, individual and group test and inventory methods, psychological testing, and behavioral observations;
c. statistical concepts, including scales of measurement, measures of central tendency, indices of variability, shapes and types of distributions, and correlations;
d. reliability (i.e., theory of measurement error, models of reliability, and the use of reliability information);
e. validity (i.e., evidence of validity, types of validity, and the relationship between reliability and validity);
f. social and cultural factors related to the assessment and evaluation of individuals, groups, and specific populations; and
g. ethical strategies for selecting, administering, and interpreting assessment and evaluation instruments and techniques in counseling. (pp. 12–13)

A broad range of assessment tools exists; Table 7.1 lists the evaluative procedures that are typically used. It is good practice to use multiple evaluative procedures when making decisions regarding client treatment.

TABLE 7.1 Evaluative Procedures Used in Counseling.

Clinical interviewing	Structured, semi-structured, unstructured
Informal assessment	Observation of behavior, rating scales, classification techniques, records, personal documents
Personality assessment	Standardized tests (e.g., MMPI), projective tests (e.g., TAT), interest inventories (e.g., Strong Interest Inventory)
Ability assessment	Achievement tests (e.g., WRAT), aptitude tests (e.g., SAT), intelligence tests (e.g., WISC)

In the remainder of this first section of Chapter 7, we discuss the history of assessment and key events critical to understanding the field of modern assessment, primary functions of and terminology used in assessment, ethical and legal issues associated with assessment, and sources that provide information on a wide variety of assessment tools.

7.1.1 Key Historical Events in Assessment

The ancient Chinese are given credit for developing the first widely used tests around 2300 B.C.E. The Chinese government used grueling, and often brutal, physical fitness tests to screen candidates for government civil service positions.

- Several major developments in the 19th century shaped modern-day assessment (Erford, 2007). Table 7.2 lists the early pioneers whose work significantly affected today's assessment practices.

TABLE 7.2 19th-Century Pioneers.

Jean Esquirol (1772–1840) used language development to identify varying levels of intelligence. His work is considered a forerunner of verbal IQ. He is credited with recognizing that mental retardation was related to developmental deficiencies rather than mental illness.

Edouard Seguin (1812–1880) developed the form board, which improved the motor skills of individuals with mental retardation. The form board is considered a predecessor to performance IQ testing.

Sir Francis Galton (1822–1911) was a biologist credited with launching the testing movement and developing the first test of intelligence. He pioneered the use of rating-scale and questionnaire methods and developed the correlation coefficient through his work in examining the relationship between reaction time, grip strength, and intelligence.

William Wundt (1832–1920) founded one of the first psychological laboratories to conduct experimental research.

James Cattell (1860–1944) was one of the first to apply statistical concepts to psychological assessment. Cattell popularized the term *mental test*.

Hermann Ebbinghaus (1850–1909) studied human memory and is well known for his work on the forgetting curve. He administered mental tests to school-age children and was able to show that his sentence completion test was related to scholastic achievement.

- The 20th century saw a growing interest in scientifically measuring human ability; more specifically, scientists were concerned with individual intelligence. As the popularity of intelligence testing exploded, it became apparent that these tests failed to consider and measure the diversity of human intelligence. Consequently, tests that assessed aptitude, personality, and interests emerged. Table 7.3 lists

TABLE 7.3 20th-Century Developments in Assessment.

Alfred Binet (1875–1911) developed the first modern intelligence test, the Binet-Simon scale, with Theophile Simon.

Lewis Terman (1877–1956) revised the Binet-Simon scale, naming the enhanced version the Stanford-Binet Intelligence Test. The Stanford-Binet was the first intelligence test to incorporate the *intelligence quotient* (ratio IQ), which is chronological age divided by mental age.

Arthur Otis (1886–1964) devised the first scientifically reliable measure for testing the intelligence of individuals in groups. The assessment was called the Otis Group Intelligence Scale.

Robert Yerkes (1876–1956) used Otis' group intelligence instrument to develop the Army Alpha and Army Beta group intelligence tests. The **Army Alpha** was designed to screen the cognitive ability of military recruits. The intelligence measure was eventually revised for civilian use. The **Army Beta** is the language-free version of the test designed for recruits who could not read or were foreign born.

Charles Spearman (1863–1945) and *L. L. Thurston* (1887–1955) developed a statistical test known as factor analysis, which led to the development of multiple aptitude testing.

James Bryant Conant (1893–1978), in conjunction with the Educational Testing Service (ETS), developed the Scholastic Aptitude Test (SAT). Conant believed his test would decrease disparity among social classes and create equal opportunities in education.

Edward Thorndike (1874–1949) developed the first achievement test battery, the Stanford Achievement Test (SAT), which provided an objective measure of academic performance and could be administered to large groups of students.

Robert Sessions Woodworth (1896–1962) developed Woodworth's Personal Data Sheet, an emotional stability-screening test for World War I military recruits. It was the first standardized personality inventory.

Starke Hathaway (1903–1984) and *J. Charnley McKinley* (1891–1950) developed the Minnesota Multiphasic Personality Inventory (MMPI), an objective measure of personality structure. The second version, MMPI-2, is now the personality test most widely used to identify and diagnosis psychopathology.

Carl Jung (1875–1961), *Herman Rorschach* (1884–1922), and *Henry Murray* (1893–1988) developed projective techniques (Jung's word associations, Rorschach's inkblots, and Murray's Thematic Apperception Test, respectively) to assess personality.

Frank Parsons (1854–1908) was the father of vocational guidance and counseling. His work gave birth to the development of vocational and interest inventories.

Edward Strong (1884–1963) devised the Strong Vocational Interest Blank, which is known today as the Strong Interest Inventory. The Strong Interest Inventory remains the most widely used and researched vocational measure in career counseling.

the individuals who significantly contributed to modern-day assessment through developments in intelligence, ability, personality, and interest testing.

7.1.2 Assessment Terminology in Counseling

Measurement, in counseling, is the process of defining and estimating the magnitude of human attributes and behavioral expressions. The use of measurement rests on three fundamental assumptions:

1. All human attributes and behavioral expressions are distinct enough to be objectively defined and quantified.
2. All human attributes and behavioral expressions are present in all people.
3. The presence or absence of specific attributes and behavioral expressions in certain situations indicates normalcy or deficiency.

The act of measuring involves the use of a measurement instrument, such as a test, survey, or inventory.

- The terms *assessment* and *test* are commonly misused and mistakably interchanged. Remember, *assessment* is a broad term that involves the systematic process of gathering and documenting client information. A **test** is a subset of assessment and is used to yield data regarding an examinee's responses to test items.
- *Interpretation* is part of the assessment process wherein the professional counselor assigns meaning to the data yielded by evaluative procedures. Meaning can be derived from the data by comparing an individual to his or her peer group, using a predetermined standard or set criteria, or through a professional counselor's judgment.
- **Evaluation** refers to making a determination of worth or significance based on the result of a measurement. For example, a professional counselor can examine a client's monthly scores on the Beck Depression Inventory to evaluate the client's progress in counseling. Professional counselors use evaluation to assess client progress or to determine the effectiveness of interventions, programs, and services on client change.

7.1.2.1 TYPES OF ASSESSMENTS
Assessments are often designed to prevent test-takers from attaining perfect scores so that differences between individuals taking the test can be recognized (Erford, 2007).

- **Power tests** limit perfect scores by including difficult test items that few individuals can answer correctly. These tests measure how well the test-taker can perform given items of varying difficulty regardless of time or speed of response.
- **Speed tests** use limited testing time to prevent perfect scores. Typically, these tests have easy questions but include too many items to answer in the allotted time. Speed tests assess how quickly the test-taker can understand the question and choose the right answer.
- Maximal and typical performance refers to the intention of the assessment. If a professional counselor would

like information regarding the client's best attainable score/performance then the counselor would use a **maximal performance test**. Achievement and aptitude tests are measures used to test maximal performance. A **typical performance test**, on the other hand, is concerned with one's characteristic or normal performance. For example, personality measurements assess a client's typical personality characteristics.

- **Standardized tests** are designed to ensure the conditions for administration, test content, scoring procedures, and interpretations are consistent. They use predetermined administration instructions and scoring methods. Because standardized tests undergo rigorous empirical validation measures, they have some degree of validity and reliability. As a result, an individual's test score can be compared to a norm group. The Scholastic Aptitude Test (SAT) and Graduate Record Examination (GRE) are examples of standardized tests.
- **Nonstandardized tests** allow for variability and adaptation in test administration, scoring, and interpretation. These tests do not permit an individual's score to be compared to a norm group; consequently, the professional counselor must rely on one's judgment to interpret the data. Projective personality measures, such as the Rorschach inkblot test and the Thematic Apperception Test, are nonstandardized tests.
- **Individual tests** require that a test be administered to one examinee at a time. Individual tests allow professional counselors to establish rapport with the examinee and closely monitor the factors that influence examinee performance (e.g., fatigue, anxiety). However, individual testing is time consuming for the practitioner and costly to the client.
- **Group tests** are administered to two or more test-takers at a time. Group tests typically use objective scoring methods and have established norms. Group tests are economical and simplify test administration and scoring for the examiner. However, client responses are more restricted, and test administration lacks flexibility.
- **Objective tests** provide consistency in administration and scoring to ensure freedom from the examiner's own beliefs or biases. Objective tests include questions that have a correct answer (e.g., multiple-choice, true/false, matching).
- **Subjective tests**, on the other hand, are sensitive to rater and examinee beliefs. They employ open-ended questions, which have more than one correct answer or way of expressing the correct answer (e.g., essay questions).

7.1.3 The Purpose of Assessment in Counseling

Suppose you are working with a client who presents with depression symptoms. You decide to administer the Beck Depression Inventory. What will you do with the results? The use of client assessment in counseling has four primary functions (Erford, 2007):

- *Diagnosis and Treatment Planning:* As a professional counselor, it is necessary to determine if a client needs services and, if so, what type. Because this decision relies on making an accurate diagnosis, professional counselors use assessment instruments to assist in gathering accurate information about a client's personality structure and the presence of psychological symptoms/disorders. The Beck Depression Inventory, for example, may assist counselors in diagnosing a mood disorder and recommending treatment based on the severity of the disorder.

- *Placement Services:* Once a client is diagnosed, professional counselors may use additional assessment procedures to determine the type of program/service in which the client should be placed. For example, a school counselor on a child study team may use classroom behavioral records, observation, and achievement test scores (e.g., Wide Range Achievement Test [WRAT]) to determine whether a child should be placed in a mainstream classroom.
- *Admission:* Assessment procedures are often used to determine admission into an educational institution. Aptitude tests such as the GRE are considered for entrance into most postgraduate educational programs.
- *Selection:* Assessments are also used to select candidates for a special program or job position. For example, an auto mechanic may be asked to complete a battery of mechanical aptitude tests when applying for a mechanic position. The information yielded by these assessments will assist the employer in determining the candidate's suitability for the position.

As a professional counselor, it is important to remember that assessment and evaluation procedures focus on client strengths, wellness characteristics, and areas of growth.

7.1.4 Key Ethical Issues in Assessment

Imagine you are working with a 4½-year-old client who has demonstrated some developmental delays. You have talked with the parents about testing before the client begins public school. Even though you have discussed the importance of establishing an Individualized Education Program (IEP), the parents are reluctant to "label" their child and have not given consent to administer an intelligence test. Your clinical judgment tells you that the child will not succeed in a mainstream classroom without the provision of proper support through an IEP. You realize that failing to give the intelligence test is neglectful and does not promote client welfare. However, administering the intelligence test without parental consent violates a client's right to informed consent. What should you do?

7.1.4.1 ETHICAL CODES FOR PROFESSIONAL COUNSELORS
As you can see, the use of psychological testing in counseling creates a number of situations in which ethical principles must be applied. Luckily, a number of ethical codes are available to guide helping professionals through ethical issues that arise in testing and assessment. The American Counseling Association (ACA, 2005) and the National Board for Certified Counselors

(NBCC, 2005) outline principles dealing specifically with psychological testing in their respective ethical codes. These principles include the following:

- *Competence to Use and Interpret Assessment Instruments:* Professional counselors should use only the assessment instruments they have been trained in and are competent to administer and interpret.
- *Informed Consent:* Professional counselors are obligated to inform the client of the nature and purposes of an assessment instrument prior to administration and the intended purpose of the assessment results.
- *Release of Results to Qualified Professionals:* Assessment results are released only to persons who are qualified to interpret the test data. To include identifying client information with the release of test results, a professional counselor must secure client consent.
- *Instrument Selection:* When selecting assessment instruments, professional counselors should consider a measure's validity, reliability, psychometric limitations, and multicultural appropriateness.
- *Conditions of Assessment Administration:* All assessments should be administered under conditions that facilitate optimal results.
- *Scoring and Interpretation of Assessments:* When reporting results, professional counselors should indicate any concerns regarding the validity and reliability of the assessment results due to the testing conditions or inappropriateness of the norms for the person tested.
- *Obsolete Assessments and Outdated Results:* Professional counselors should refrain from using assessment instruments or results that are outdated for the present need.
- *Assessment Construction:* Professional counselors are to use established scientific methodology and current professional knowledge when developing psychological and educational measures.

7.1.4.2 STANDARDS OF PRACTICE FOR ASSESSMENT IN COUNSELING
To assist professional counselors, several professional organizations have established standards for psychological assessment development and use. These standards expand on the ethical codes and address the responsible use of tests. You should be familiar with the following sets of standards:

- **Standards for Educational and Psychological Testing** were developed through collaboration between the American Educational Research Association (AERA), American Psychological Association (APA), and the National Council on Measurement in Education (NCME; 1999). These standards promote the appropriate and ethical use of tests and provide professionals with a set of guidelines for test development, evaluation, and use. The most recent revision in 1999 includes standards for testing individuals with disabilities and those from diverse linguistic backgrounds. Table 7.4 provides an overview of the organization and content of the 1999 Standards for Educational and Psychological Testing.

TABLE 7.4 Overview of the 1999 Standards for Education and Psychological Testing.

Part I: Test Construction, Evaluation, and Documentation

1. Validity
2. Reliability and Errors of Measurement
3. Test Development and Revision
4. Scales, Norms, and Score Comparability
5. Test Administration, Scoring, and Reporting
6. Supporting Documentation for Tests

Part II: Fairness in Testing

7. Fairness in Testing and Test Use
8. The Rights and Responsibilities of Test Takers
9. Testing Individuals of Diverse Linguistic Backgrounds
10. Testing Individuals with Disabilities

Part III: Testing Applications

11. The Responsibilities of Test Users
12. Psychological Testing and Assessment
13. Educational Testing and Assessment
14. Testing in Employment and Credentialing
15. Testing in Program Evaluation and Public Policy

- **Responsibilities of Users of Standardized Tests (RUST)** (3rd edition) is a policy statement published by the Association for Assessment in Counseling and Education (AACE, 2003), a division of the ACA. The intent of RUST is to ensure that ACA members use standardized tests with clients in an accurate, fair, and responsible manner. RUST test-user responsibilities involve the following:
  - *Qualifications of Test-Users:* Test-users are responsible for obtaining and demonstrating appropriate education, training, and experience in standardized test selection, administration, scoring, interpretation, reporting, and communication of results.
  - *Technical Knowledge:* Test-users should be able to demonstrate technical knowledge related to the validity of test results, reliability, error of measurement, and scores and norms.
  - *Test Selection:* Test-users must provide a purpose for administering the selected test and demonstrate that the chosen assessment aligns with that purpose. During test selection, users should also consider the test-taker, accuracy of scoring procedures, norming and standardization procedures, modifications, and fairness.
  - *Test Administration:* Test administrators follow standard procedures to ensure that the test is employed in the manner specified by the test developers. In an effort to ensure optimal test results, test-users provide test-takers with the most favorable test environments to maximize optimal test-taker results.
  - *Test Scoring:* Test-users must demonstrate that assessments are scored in an accurate and consistent manner. In addition, scoring procedures should be regularly audited.

- *Interpreting Test Results.* Test-users should be knowledgeable regarding the technical aspects of the test, the test results, and its limitations. Test-users must consider the psychometric, test-taker, and contextual factors that influence the legitimacy and usefulness of test results.
- *Communicating Test Results.* Test-users must be familiar with test interpretation and the particular test being used. They are to convey test results in a way that the client understands, discuss how the test results can be interpreted, explain the limitations of those interpretations.

- The **Joint Committee on Testing Practices (JCTP)** was established in 1985 by a collaborative effort between AERA, APA, and NCME and included a number of other organizations, including the ACA. The committee published several documents concerning testing standards in educational, psychological, and counseling fields. The JCTP disbanded in 2007. The most notable of the JCTP's publications include *Rights and Responsibilities of Test Takers, Test User Qualifications*, and the *Code for Fair Testing Practices in Education*.
  - *Rights and Responsibilities of Test Takers* (JCTP, 1998) outlines 10 rights and 10 responsibilities of test-takers during the testing process. For example, test-takers have the right to know the purpose of testing, how the test will be used, and who will have access to test results; but test-takers also are responsible for asking questions related to test administration and scoring, following test instructions, and being familiar with the consequences of not taking the test.
  - The JCTP introduced a 143-page technical report entitled *Test User Qualifications* (2000). The report established guidelines that informed test-users of the qualifications needed to responsibly use psychological tests. The JCTP further delineated test-user qualifications in specific contexts, which include employment, education, career-counseling, health care, and forensics.
  - The *Code of Fair Testing Practices in Education* (JCTP, 2004) seeks to ensure that fair testing is provided to all test-takers, regardless of age, gender, disability, race, ethnicity, national origin, religion, sexual orientation, linguistic background, or other personal characteristics. The code offers guidance to test developers and test-users in four areas: developing and selecting tests, administering and scoring tests, reporting and interpreting tests, and informing test-takers.

7.1.5 Key Legal Issues in Assessment

In addition to the ethical guidelines and testing standards developed by professional organizations, the field of assessment is affected by public law. It is imperative that counselors be aware of and adhere to the federal and state laws and regulations that affect assessment practices. The following summarizes important public laws concerning testing practices.

- *Civil Rights Act of 1964 and the 1972, 1978, and 1991 Amendments:* Assessments used to determine employability must relate strictly to the duties outlined in the job description and cannot discriminate based on race, color, religion, pregnancy, gender, or origin.
- *Family Educational Rights and Privacy Act of 1974 (FERPA):* Ensures the confidentiality of student test records by restricting access to scores. At the same time, this law affirms the rights of both student and parent to view student records.
- *Individuals with Disabilities Education Improvement Act of 2004 (IDEA):* Confirms the right of students, believed to have a disability, to receive testing at the expense of the public school system. The act further mandates that students with disabilities receive an IEP that specifies the accommodations a student will must optimize learning.
- *The Vocational and Technical Education Act of 1984:* Also known as the Carl D. Perkins Act, this law provides access to vocational assessment, counseling, and placement services for the economically disadvantaged, those with disabilities, individuals entering nontraditional occupations, adults in need of vocational training, single parents, those with limited English proficiency, and incarcerated individuals.
- *Americans with Disabilities Act of 1990 (ADA):* Employment testing must accurately measure a person's ability to perform pertinent job tasks without confounding the assessment results with a disability. In addition, the act ensures that persons with disabilities receive appropriate accommodations during test administration (e.g., more time to take the assessment, special equipment).
- **Health Insurance Portability and Accountability Act (HIPAA)** of 1996: Secures the privacy of client records by requiring agencies to obtain client consent before releasing records to others. HIPAA also grants clients access to their records.
- **No Child Left Behind (NCLB) Act of 2001:** The act aims to improve the quality of U.S. primary and secondary schools by increasing the accountability standards of states, school districts, and schools. As a result, No Child Left Behind requires states to develop and administer assessments in basic skills to all students.

In addition to the public laws that govern testing practices, several legal guidelines that affect assessment and current testing practices have been established by court cases.

- *Larry P. v. Riles (1974, 1979, 1984):* Ruled that schools had used biased intelligence tests, which led to an overrepresentation of African American children in programs for students with educable mental retardation. As a result, professional counselors must provide written documentation that demonstrates the use of nondiscriminatory and valid assessment tools.
- *Diana v. California State Board of Education (1973, 1979):* This case was settled out of court and requires that schools provide tests to students in their first language as well as in English to limit linguistic bias. As a result,

professional counselors must provide testing information in the client's first language.
- *Sharif v. New York State Educational Department (1989):* Ruled that SAT scores alone could not be used to determine scholarship awards.
- *Griggs v. Duke Power Company (1971):* Ruled that assessments used in the job hiring and promotion process must be job related.
- *Bakke v. California (1978):* Barred the use of quota systems for minority admissions procedures in U.S. colleges and universities.

7.1.6 Sources of Information on Assessments

As the number of available assessments and new tests increases, how does a professional counselor successfully choose, administer, and interpret an assessment instrument? Several sources provide information related to assessment purposes and procedures.

- **Mental Measurements Yearbook (MMY):** The best source for information regarding commercially available assessment instruments in the English language is the MMY, published by the Buros Institute of Mental Measurements every 2 to 8 years. Each entry in the MMY offers pertinent assessment information, including the test name, acronym, test author and publisher, copyright date, purpose, intended test population, administration time, forms, and prices. The MMY also contains information related to test reliability and validity, norming data, scoring and reporting services, and available foreign language versions. The majority of entries include test critiques by experts in the testing and assessment field; these reviews provide an additional measure of credibility to the assessment instruments.
- **Tests in Print (TIP):** *Tests in Print* (TIP) is published by the Buros Institute of Mental Measurements every 3 to 13 years as a companion to the MMY. It offers a comprehensive listing of all published and commercially available tests in psychology and education. TIP provides information regarding the test title, intended population, publication date, acronym (if applicable), author, publisher, foreign adaptations, and references. Unlike the MMY, TIP does not provide critical reviews or psychometric information on the assessment instrument.
- **Tests:** *Tests* is published by Pro-Ed, Inc. and contains information on thousands of assessment instruments in the psychology, education, and business industries. *Tests* provides quick access to concise instrument descriptions that include the test title, author, publisher, intended test population, purpose, major features, administration time, scoring method, cost, and availability. This resource does not provide assessment critiques or information regarding test norms, validity, or reliability.
- **Test Critiques:** *Test Critiques*, also published by Pro-Ed, is designed to be a companion text to *Tests*. Each entry in *Test Critiques* contains an overview of the assessment, practical applications (e.g., intended population, administration, scoring, and interpretation procedures), and

information regarding the instrument's reliability and validity. In addition, *Test Critiques* offers comprehensive reviews of psychological assessments from testing experts; the reviews average eight pages in length. The text is designed to be a user-friendly resource and is written not only for professionals but also for persons unfamiliar with assessment jargon. *Test Critiques* is updated annually.

7.1.7 Practice Multiple-Choice Items. Introduction to Assessment

1. Developed by Robert Yerkes, the _____ is a language-free test that was designed for individuals who could not read or were foreign born.
   a. Army Alpha
   b. Stanford-Binet
   c. Minnesota Multiphasic Personality Inventory
   d. Army Beta

2. If a professional school counselor wants to know if a student is ready to move to the next grade level, she should administer a(n)
   a. maximal performance test.
   b. speed test.
   c. objective test.
   d. typical performance test.

3. The Vocational and Technical Education Act of 1984 (Carl D. Perkins Act)
   a. ensures the confidentiality of student test records by restricting access to scores.
   b. mandates that students with disabilities receive an Individualized Education Plan (IEP).
   c. provides disadvantaged populations access to vocational assessment, counseling, and placement services.
   d. secures the privacy of client records.

4. A professional counselor releases a client's test results to a bachelor's-level case manager who has no training in testing and assessment. What ethical guideline was violated?
   a. Informed consent
   b. Release of results to qualified professionals
   c. Communicating test results
   d. None of the above.

5. Which source is designed to provide the layperson with understandable assessment information?
   a. *Mental Measurements Yearbook*
   b. *Tests in Print*
   c. *Tests*
   d. *Test Critiques*

Answer Key: 1. d; 2. a; 3. c; 4. b; 5. d.

7.2 KEY PRINCIPLES OF TEST CONSTRUCTION

Why is it important that professional counselors have an understanding of test construction? Suppose you are planning to administer an assessment that will measure an adult client's level of depression. How do you choose an instrument that will accurately measure depression and provide a consistent depression score for your client? Better yet, how do you assure your client that the chosen instrument is a credible measure? In this second section of Chapter 7, we discuss the role validity and reliability play in test construction; how to verify that a test enhances decisions made by the professional counselor; the relationship between SEM and reliability; item analysis as it relates to test item discrimination and degree of difficulty; the theory underlying test development; and the types of scales commonly used on assessments.

7.2.1 Validity

Validity refers to how accurately an instrument measures a given construct. Validity is concerned with what an instrument measures, how well it does so, and the extent to which meaningful inferences can be made from the instrument's results. It is important to note that an instrument does not have high or low validity. Instead, validity is a property of the scores obtained using a given instrument and will vary according to the purpose and intended test-taker population. For example, scores using an instrument that measures anxiety in adults may have low validity when administered to disruptive children but may have high validity when given to anxious adults. Therefore, validity should always be reported in terms of the specific test purpose and target population.

7.2.1.1 TYPES OF VALIDITY

- *Content validity* is the extent to which an instrument's content is appropriate to its intended purpose. To establish content validity, test items must reflect all major content areas covered by the domain (i.e., a clearly defined body of knowledge). For example, if you decide to develop an instrument to measure client depression and survey the domain content, you may find depression is composed of physical (e.g., sleep problems, weight loss/gain), psychological (e.g., sadness, loss of interest, irritability), and cognitive factors (e.g., guilt, suicidal thoughts, worthlessness). To establish content validity, your instrument must contain items measuring the physical, psychological, and cognitive factors. Also, the number of test items covering each content area must represent the importance of the content in the domain (i.e., more items represent more important areas of the domain). Therefore, if psychological factors were found to be more important in detecting depression than physical or cognitive factors, then your instrument must contain more items related to sadness, loss of interest, and irritability than to guilt, suicidal thoughts, and worthlessness.
- *Criterion validity* indicates the effectiveness of an instrument in predicting an individual's performance on a specific criterion. Criterion validity is empirically established by examining the relationship between data collected from the instrument and the criterion. The two types of criterion validity are concurrent and predictive validity.

- *Concurrent validity* is concerned with the relationship between an instrument's results and another currently obtainable criterion. To determine concurrent validity, instrument results and criterion performance scores must be collected at the same time. For example, to establish concurrent validity for your depression instrument, you may give the instrument to a group of adults and, at the same time, collect data from hospital records on the number of times each adult had been admitted for suicidal ideation in the past 6 months. When comparing the relationship between depression scores and hospital admissions, you would expect to see hospital admissions increase as depression scores increased. If such a relationship were not found, the concurrent validity of your instrument would be questionable.

- *Predictive validity* examines the relationship between an instrument's results collected now and a criterion collected in the future. By establishing predictive validity, a test developer uses an instrument to try to predict performance on a future criterion measure. Therefore, a client's criterion performance scores are collected some time after the instrument results. To establish predictive validity for the depression instrument, client scores on the depression instrument would be compared to the number of times the client was hospitalized for suicidal ideation in a 6-month period occurring 2 years after taking the assessment. If the relationship is positive between client scores and the number of times hospitalized in the future, one could say that the instrument predicts the future occurrence of hospitalization.

- *Construct validity* is the extent to which an instrument measures a theoretical construct (i.e., idea or concept). It is especially important to establish construct validity when an instrument measures an abstract construct such as personality characteristics. Construct validity is determined by using experimental designs, factor analysis, convergence with other similar measures, and discrimination with other dissimilar measures.

- *Experimental design validity* refers to the implementation of experimental design to show that an instrument measures a specific construct. For example, to show that the depression instrument actually measures depression, you may develop a pretest/posttest experimental design that asks a professional counselor to administer your instrument to clients diagnosed with depression before they begin therapy and once again at therapy termination. Ordinarily, the treatment is standardized and becomes the study's independent variable. You hypothesize that if the instrument measures the depression construct, client posttest scores on the measure will be lower than client pretest scores. If the experimental results confirm your hypothesis, then the instrument measures depression. If the hypothesis is not supported, you must decide if you have an inaccurate instrument, flawed design, or ineffective treatment.

- **Factor analysis** is a statistical technique that analyzes the interrelationships of an instrument's items, thus revealing predicted latent (hidden) traits or dimensions called factors. To demonstrate construct validity, a factor analysis must show that the instrument's subscales are statistically related to each other and the larger construct. Therefore, on the depression instrument, the items reflecting the subscales (e.g., sadness, loss of interest, irritability, suicidal thoughts, and worthlessness) must be related to the larger construct of depression. Also, the subscales must be somewhat related to each other, but not too closely related, as each subscale is supposed to measure a different facet of depression (for more information regarding factor analysis, see section 8.6).

- *Convergent validity* is established when measures of constructs that theoretically should be related are actually observed to be related to each other. In other words, convergent validity shows that the assessment is related to what, theoretically, it should be. For example, if you correlate a new depression test with the Beck Depression Inventory II (BDI-II)—a similar instrument that has already been established to measure depression—and find a significantly positive relationship, there is evidence of convergent validity.

- *Discriminant validity* is established when measures of constructs that are not theoretically related are observed to have no relationship. Therefore, to demonstrate discriminant validity, you would must show that scores from the depression measure are not related to scores from an achievement instrument.

- *Face validity* is not a type of validity, although it is often falsely referenced as one, thus deserving a brief caveat here. **Face validity** is a superficial measure that is concerned with whether an instrument looks valid or credible. Therefore, your depression test would have face validity if it simply "looked like" it measured client depression.

- Remember that establishing the existence of multiple types of validity provides stronger evidence for the credibility of the instrument.

7.2.1.2 REPORTING VALIDITY In test reports and manuals, validity is expressed as a correlation coefficient (For more information regarding correlation coefficients see section 8.6.1). The **validity coefficient** is a correlation between a test score and the criterion measure. Validity also can be reported as a regression equation. A regression equation can be used to predict an individual's future score on a specific criterion based on his or her current test score. For example, college admission counselors may use a regression equation to predict an applicant's future GPA from a current SAT score. Unfortunately, some degree of error is always present in prediction, and we are never able to say that our predictions are 100% accurate. Consequently, the standard error of estimate must be calculated and reported when predicting criterion scores. The **standard error of estimate** is a statistic that indicates the expected margin of error in a predicted criterion score due to the imperfect validity of the test. The standard error of estimate is calculated by the following equation where s_{est} is the standard error of the estimate, Y is an actual score, Y' is a predicted score, and N is the number of pairs of scores. The numerator is the sum of squared differences between the actual scores and the predicted scores.

$$\sigma_{est} = \sqrt{\frac{\sum (Y - Y')^2}{N}} \qquad (7.1)$$

7.2.1.3 DECISION ACCURACY The work of a professional counselor involves making decisions regarding client diagnosis, treatment, and placement. Professional counselors often use psychological tests to enhance the accuracy of their decisions. For example, a professional counselor may notice that a client is demonstrating depressive symptoms but may consider administering a depression inventory to augment observations and subsequent diagnosis. Before administering the depression inventory, the professional counselor will want to assess the instrument's decision accuracy. **Decision accuracy** assesses the accuracy of instruments in supporting counselor decisions. Table 7.5 provides an overview of the terms commonly associated with decision accuracy.

7.2.2 Reliability

Reliability refers to the consistency of scores attained by the same person on different administrations of the same test. Ideally, we expect a person to receive the same score on multiple administrations of the same test. However, all test administrations are subject to some degree of error. This error may be attributed to instrument characteristics (e.g., poorly worded

---

TABLE 7.5 Terms Commonly Associated with Decision Accuracy.

Sensitivity: The instrument's ability to accurately identify the presence of a phenomenon.

Example: The depression inventory results indicate that a depressed client has depressive symptoms.

Specificity: The instrument's ability to accurately identify the absence of a phenomenon.

Example: The depression inventory results indicate that a non-depressed client does not have depressive symptoms.

False positive error: An instrument inaccurately identifies the presence of a phenomenon.

Example: The depression inventory would indicate that a non-depressed client has depressive symptoms.

False negative error: An instrument inaccurately identifies the absence of a phenomenon.

Example: The depression inventory would indicate that a depressed client has no depressive symptoms.

Efficiency: The ratio of total correct decisions divided by the total number of decisions.

Incremental validity: Concerned with the extent to which an instrument enhances the accuracy of prediction of a specific criterion (e.g., job performance, college GPA).

---

questions or directions), the test-taker (e.g., anxiety), or testing environment (e.g., distraction in the testing room). The presence of error in testing makes it difficult for a person to obtain the same score when reexamined on the same test. Consequently, it can be said that an individual has a true score and an observed score. A person's observed score (X) is equal to his or her true score (T) plus the amount of error (e) present during test administration:

$$X = T + e \qquad (7.2)$$

- Reliability is concerned with the error found in instruments. Researchers figure that when measurement error is known, the degree to which personal and environmental conditions play a role in an individual's obtained score can be estimated. Therefore, when seeking to estimate reliability, researchers are seeking to determine an instrument's degree of freedom from measurement error. Reliability can be approximated through a variety of methods, which include test-retest reliability, alternate form reliability, and internal consistency.

7.2.2.1 TYPES OF RELIABILITY

- *Test-retest reliability*, also known as *temporal stability*, determines the relationship between the scores obtained from two different administrations of the same test. This type of reliability evaluates the consistency of scores across time. Participant memory and practice effects can influence the accuracy of the test-retest method. Also, the correlation between scores tends to decrease as the time interval between test administrations increases. The test-retest form of reliability is most effective when the instrument assesses stable characteristics (e.g., intelligence).
- *Alternate form reliability*, also referred to as *parallel form reliability*, or *equivalent form reliability*, compares the consistency of scores from two alternate, but equivalent, forms of the same test. To establish reliability, two tests that measure the same content and are equal in difficulty are administered to the same group of individuals within a short period of time, and the scores from each test are correlated. Administering parallel forms of the same test eliminates the concern of memory and practice effects. However, it is difficult to find truly equivalent forms of the same test.
- *Internal consistency* measures the consistency of responses from one test item to the next during a single administration of the instrument. For example, if a depressed client agreed with the test items "I feel sad," "I feel sad and can't seem to get over it," and "I feel unhappy," the instrument would have good internal consistency.
  - *Split-half reliability* is a type of internal consistency that correlates one half of a test against the other. Using split-half reliability can be challenging because tests can rarely be divided into comparable halves. Another drawback to using split-half reliability is that it shortens the test by splitting it into two halves. All things being equal, a shorter test yields less reliable scores

than longer tests. To compensate mathematically for the shorter length, the *Spearman-Brown Prophecy Formula* can be used to estimate reliability:

$$\text{Spearman-Brown Prophecy Formula} = \frac{2r_{hh}}{1 + r_{hh}} \quad \textbf{(7.3)}$$

with r_{hh} representing the split-half reliability estimate.

- *Interitem consistency* is a measure of internal consistency that compares individual test item responses with one another and the total test score. Reliability is estimated through the use of mathematical formulas that correlate all of the possible split-half combinations present in a test. One such formula is the *Kuder-Richardson Formula 20*, which is used when test items are dichotomous (e.g., scored as right or wrong, true or false, yes or no). Another formula, *Cronbach's Coefficient Alpha*, is used when test items result in multipoint responses (e.g., Likert-type rating scales with a 4-point response format).
- *Inter-scorer reliability*, sometimes called *inter-rater reliability*, is used to calculate the degree of consistency of ratings between two or more persons observing the same behavior or assessing an individual through observational or interview methods. This type of reliability is important to establish when an assessment requires scorer judgment (e.g., subjective responses). For example, if a client were administered a test of open-ended questions regarding depression, you would need to establish inter-scorer reliability by having two or more clinicians independently score the test.

7.2.2.2 REPORTING RELIABILITY In test reports and manuals, reliability is expressed as a correlation, which is referred to as a **reliability coefficient**. The closer a reliability coefficient is to 1.00, the more reliable the scores generated by the instrument. Any reliability coefficient less than 1.00 indicates the presence of error in test scores. Reliability coefficients typically range from .80 to .95; however, an acceptable reliability coefficient depends on the purpose of the test. For example, nationally normed achievement and aptitude tests, such as the GRE, are expected to have reliability coefficients above .90, whereas reliability coefficients for personality inventories can be lower than .90, and the instrument is still considered to yield reliable scores.

7.2.2.3 STANDARD ERROR OF MEASUREMENT Suppose you administered a math exam to a student on five separate occasions, and he scored a 95, 91, 98, 86, and 89, respectively. How do you know which score best reflects his understanding of the material (i.e., which is his true score)? Recall from the previous discussion of reliability that all measurement instruments have some degree of error. Consequently, it is unlikely that repeated administrations of an instrument would yield the same scores for a given person. Since an individual's true score is always unknown, the **standard error of measurement (SEM)** is used to estimate how scores from repeated administrations of the same instrument to the same individual are distributed around the

true score. The SEM is computed using the standard deviation (SD) and reliability coefficient of the test instrument:

$$\text{SEM} = \text{SD}\sqrt{1 - r_{tt}} \quad \textbf{(7.4)}$$

- Simply stated, the SEM is the standard deviation of an individual's repeated test scores when administered the same instrument multiple times. The SEM is inversely related to reliability in that the larger the SEM, the lower the reliability of a test; thus, if the reliability coefficient is 1.00, the SEM = 0. Therefore, the reliability of a test can be expressed in terms of the SEM. The SEM is often reported in terms of confidence intervals, which define the range of scores where the true score is thought to lie. For example, let's say you give a student the same math test 100 times. The distribution of her observed scores would form a curve when graphed, where the mean is defined as her true score and the standard deviation represents the SEM. Suppose that the mean was 93 and the SEM was 2. As 68% of all scores fall between ±1 SEM, we can conclude that 68% of the time her observed scores will fall between 91 and 95 when given the same math test 100 times. At the 95% level of confidence (±2 SEM), 95% of her observed scores would fall within the range of 89–97, given 100 administrations of the test.

7.2.2.4 FACTORS THAT INFLUENCE RELIABILITY At least five influences on reliability of test scores have been noted:

- *Test Length:* Longer tests are generally more reliable than shorter tests.
- *Homogeneity of Test Items:* Lower reliability estimates are reported when test items vary greatly in content.
- *Range Restriction:* The reliability of test scores will be lowered by a restriction in the range of test scores.
- *Heterogeneity of Test Group:* Test-takers who are heterogeneous on the characteristic being measured yield higher reliability estimates.
- *Speed Tests:* These yield spuriously high reliability coefficients because nearly every test-taker gets nearly every item correct.

7.2.2.5 THE RELATIONSHIP BETWEEN VALIDITY AND RELIABILITY Although scores produced by instruments must have both reliability and validity to be considered credible, test scores can be reliable but not valid. However, valid test scores are always reliable.

7.2.3 Item Analysis

Item analysis is a procedure that involves statistically examining test-taker responses to individual test items with the intent to assess the quality of test items and the test as a whole. Item analysis is frequently used to eliminate confusing, easy, and difficult items from a test that will be used again.

- **Item difficulty** refers to the percentage of test-takers who answer a test item correctly. Test authors compute item difficulty to ensure that items provide an appropriate level of difficulty and to increase the variability of scores. Item difficulty is calculated by dividing the number of individuals who correctly answered the item by the total number of test-takers. The calculation is expressed as a decimal point called the *p* value. The reported *p* value ranges from 0 to 1.0, with higher values indicating an easier test item. For example, a test item with a 0.9 *p* value is interpreted as easy because 90% of the test-takers answered the question correctly. In general, test authors look for items to have an average *p* value of 0.50; as half of the test-takers will miss this item, this *p* value yields the most variation in a test score distribution.

- **Item discrimination** is the degree to which a test item is able to correctly differentiate test-takers who vary according to the construct measured by the test. For example, items on a depression inventory need to discriminate between test-takers who are depressed and those who are not depressed. Item discrimination is calculated by subtracting the performance of the top quarter of total scores from the bottom quarter of total scores on a given test item. Most test developers consider a test item to be a good discriminator when increasingly higher numbers of upper group members answer the question correctly than lower group members (i.e., positive item discrimination). Items with zero and negative item discrimination are generally considered poor items.

7.2.4 Test Theory

Test theory expects that test constructs, in order to be considered empirical, must have the ability to be measured for quality and quantity to be considered empirical (Erford, 2007). Consequently, test theory strives to reduce test error and enhance construct reliability and validity. Professional counselors must be familiar with the following types of test theory.

- *Classical test theory* has been the most influential psychometric theory. It postulates that an individual's observed score is the sum of the true score and the amount of error present during test administration. The central aim of classical test theory is to increase reliability of test scores.
- *Item response theory*, also referred to as *modern test theory*, refers to applying mathematical models to the data collected from assessments. Test developers use item response theory to evaluate how well individual test items and the test as a whole work. Specifically, item response theory can be used to detect item bias (e.g., whether an item behaves differently for males and females), equating scores from two different tests, and tailoring test items to the individual test-taker.

7.2.5 The Development of Instrument Scales

A **scale** refers to a collection of items or questions that combine to form a composite score on a single variable. Scales can measure discrete or continuous variables and can describe the data quantitatively or qualitatively. Quantitative data are numerical, whereas data presented qualitatively use forms other than numbers (e.g., check yes or no)

7.2.5.1 SCALES OF MEASUREMENT A thorough understanding of the scales of measurement is imperative to the development of instrument scales. *Scales of measurement* provide a method for classifying or measuring specific qualities or characteristics. Four different scales of measurement exist: nominal, ordinal, interval, and ratio (Erford, 2007).

- A **nominal scale** is the simplest measurement scale as it is only concerned with classifying data without respect for order or equal interval units. An example of a measure occurring on a nominal scale is gender. By assigning the label *male* or *female*, only a classification is being made. Magnitude cannot be assigned to gender (e.g., females are greater than males). Arbitrary labels, such as *numbers*, can be allocated to nominal data (e.g., males = 0; females = 1).
- An **ordinal scale** classifies and assigns rank-order to data. Likert-type scales, which often rank degrees of satisfaction toward a particular issue, are an example of an ordinal scale measure. Ordinal scales designate order, but the intervals between the numbers are not necessarily equal. For example, it can be said that student A, who rates satisfaction with a counseling course as 4, is more satisfied than student B, who gave a rating of 3.
- An **interval scale** includes all ordinal scale qualities and has equivalent intervals—that is, interval scale measures have an equal distance between each point on the scale. Therefore, the difference between 32 degrees and 31 degrees Fahrenheit is the same as the difference between 67 degrees and 66 degrees Fahrenheit. Interval scales do not have an absolute zero point. For example, 0 degrees Fahrenheit does not mean there is no temperature. As a result, it cannot be said that 60 degrees Fahrenheit is twice as warm as 30 degrees Fahrenheit. Educational and psychological testing data are usually interval scale measurements.
- A **ratio scale** is the most advanced scale of measurement as it preserves the qualities of nominal, ordinal, and interval scales and has an absolute zero point. As a result, difference between values can be quantified in absolute terms. Height is an excellent example of a measure occurring on a ratio scale, and it can be said that a 6-foot-tall person is twice as tall as a 3-foot-tall person. Physical measurements used in the natural sciences often are ratio scaled data (e.g., length, weight, time).

7.2.5.2 TYPES OF SCALES

- A **Likert scale**, sometimes called a Likert-type scale, is commonly used when developing instruments that assess attitudes or opinions. The item format employed by a Likert scale includes a statement regarding the concept in question followed by answer choices that range from strongly agree to strongly disagree. For example:

GRE scores accurately predict future graduate school performance.

1	2	3	4	5
Strongly Disagree	Disagree	Neutral	Agree	Strongly Agree

- **Semantic differential**, also referred to as *self-anchored scales*, refers to a scaling technique that is rooted in the belief that people think dichotomously. Although there are several varieties of this scale, the most common form involves the statement of an affective question followed by a scale that asks test-takers to place a mark between two dichotomous adjectives.

  How do you feel about your NCE scores?

  Bad _ Good

- A **Thurstone scale** measures multiple dimensions of an attitude by asking respondents to express their beliefs through agreeing or disagreeing with item statements. The Thurstone scale has equal-appearing, successive intervals and employs a paired comparison method.

	Agree	Disagree
I feel lonely all the time.	[ ]	[ ]
It is difficult to carry out my daily tasks.	[ ]	[ ]
I am sleeping more than usual.	[ ]	[ ]
I have frequent thoughts of death and suicide.	[ ]	[ ]

- A **Guttman scale** measures the intensity of a variable being measured. Items are presented in a progressive order so that a respondent, who agrees with an extreme test item, will also agree with all previous, less extreme items.

  Please place a check next to each statement that you agree with.

  _____Are you willing to permit gay students to attend your university?

  _____Are you willing to permit gay students to live in the university dorms?

  _____Are you willing to permit gay students to live in your dorm?

  _____Are you willing to permit gay students to live next door to you?

  _____Are you willing to have a gay student as a roommate?

7.2.6   Practice Multiple-Choice Items: Key Principles of Test Construction

1. Which of the following is NOT true about test validity?
   a. Validity should always be reported in terms of test purpose and intended population.
   b. Test scores do not have to be valid to be reliable.
   c. A validity coefficient of .25 is high.
   d. False positive errors contribute to a lack of test score validity.

2. What formula would you use to measure the interitem consistency of a test with a Likert-type scale?
   a. Cronbach's coefficient alpha
   b. Spearman-Brown prophecy formula
   c. Standard error of estimate
   d. Kuder-Richardson formula 20

3. If a math test item has positive item discrimination, it can be said that
   a. more students who knew the material answered the question correctly than students who did not know the material well.
   b. more students, who did not know the material well, answered the question correctly than students who knew the material.
   c. all students answered the question correctly.
   d. 50% of all students answered the question correctly.

4. Which type of instrument scale is based on the belief that people think dichotomously?
   a. Guttman
   b. Semantic differential
   c. Likert-type
   d. Thurstone

5. Item response theory can be used to
   a. detect equivalence in an item that is written in different languages.
   b. detect item bias in the same test given to an African American and a Latino American.
   c. determine if an SAT score of 1,000 is equivalent to an IQ score of 114.
   d. give a bright student an exam with more difficult items.

Answer Key: 1. c; 2. a; 3. a; 4. b; 5. b.

7.3   DERIVED SCORES

Suppose a student, Ivan, scored a 67 on a test; did he do well? If we assume the score is 67 out of 100, then the score may not be so good. But what if the highest possible score on the test is 70? Then the score is probably really good. The bottom line is that a **raw score** (original data that have not been converted into a derived score) lacks sufficient meaning and interpretive value. To interpret and understand Ivan's raw score, it must be converted to a derived score or compared to some criterion. A **derived score** is a converted raw score that gives meaning to a test score by comparing an individual's score with those of a norm group. In the remainder of this third section of Chapter 7, we discuss the characteristics of a normal distribution, the relationship between normal distribution and derived test scores, the purpose of norm-referenced assessments, and how to calculate and interpret percentile ranks, standard scores, and developmental scores. For examples throughout this chapter, we use the raw scores provided in Table 7.6.

Table 7.6   Student Raw Scores on a College Math Exam.

This table lists the individual raw scores of students who took a 100-item college math exam.

Ivan	67	Alexis	75	David	65	John	61
Mary	58	Leah	60	Myra	72	Chris	67
Jen	63	Matt	55	Lorie	68	Amy	61

Note: This data set is used throughout this chapter to illustrate the important concepts related to derived scores.

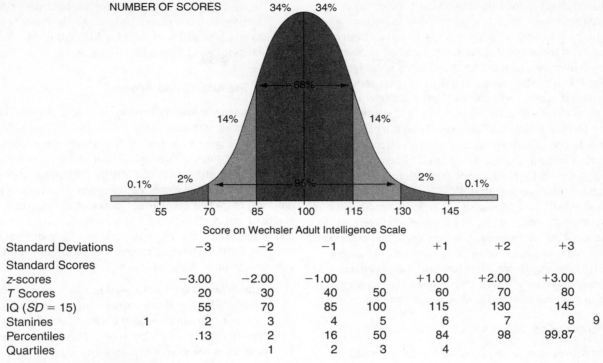

FIGURE 7.1 The Normal Curve.

From B. T. Erford (2011). *Transforming the school counseling profession*, 2nd ed. (p. 241). Upper Saddle River, NJ: Merrill Prentice Hall. Reprinted with permission.

7.3.1 The Normal Distribution

In a **normal distribution**, nearly all scores fall close to average and very few scores fall toward either extreme of the distribution. Normal distributions are a product of the laws of nature and probability. As a result, most psychological and physical measurements (e.g., height and intelligence) are approximately normally distributed. Normal distributions have important characteristics that are useful to the field of assessment.

7.3.1.1 CHARACTERISTICS OF NORMAL DISTRIBUTIONS
A normal distribution forms a bell-shaped curve when graphed. This graph is commonly referred to as a **normal curve (bell curve)**. (See Figure 7.1.) The normal curve is symmetrical, with the highest point occurring at the graph's center. The lowest points lie on either side of the graph. The curve is also *asymptotic*, meaning that the tail approaches the horizontal axis without ever touching it. Normal distributions are also characterized by their measures of central tendency and variability (For more information on central tendency and variability, see section 8.5.)

7.3.1.2 THE RELATIONSHIP BETWEEN NORMAL DISTRIBUTIONS AND TEST SCORES
Normal distributions are the foundation on which derived scores are built. The mathematical relationships found in a normal distribution permit comparisons to be made between clients' scores on the same test or between the same client's scores on multiple tests. As a result, many derived scores (e.g., percentiles, normal curve

equivalents, stanines, z-scores, and T scores) originate from the unique characteristics of a normal distribution.

7.3.2 Norm-Referenced Assessment

Derived scores are frequently used with norm-referenced assessments. **Norms** refer to the typical score/performance against which all other test scores are evaluated. In a **norm-referenced assessment**, an individual's score is compared to the average score (i.e., the mean) of the test-taking group. Knowing the relative position of a person's score in comparison to his or her norm group provides us with information regarding how that individual has performed. Table 7.7 lists examples of commonly used norm-referenced assessments.

Let us return to Ivan and his peers for a moment. By comparing Ivan against the average score on the math test ($M = 63$), we can now say that his score was slightly above average. Although we have a little more information concerning Ivan's score, to gain more insight into his performance the raw score must still be converted into a derived score. In the next few sections we discuss specific types of derived scores: percentiles, standard scores, and developmental scores.

TABLE 7.7 Examples of Norm-Referenced Assessments.

College admissions exams	GRE, SAT, ACT, MCAT, GMAT
Intelligence testing	Stanford-Binet, Wechsler
Personality inventories	MBTI, CPI

- Although the rest of this subsection focuses on norm-referenced assessments, there are other important ways to give raw scores meaning. One is to use a **criterion-referenced assessment**. Criterion-referenced assessments provide information about an individual's score by comparing it to a predetermined standard or set criterion. For example, if Ivan's instructor decided that 90 to 100 was an A, 80 to 89 was a B, 70 to 79 was a C, and 60 to 69 was a D, then Ivan would receive a D on the math exam. Examples of criterion-referenced assessments include driver's licensing exams, professional licensure testing (such as the NCE), high school graduation examinations, and exit exams (such as the CPCE).

- An individual's test score also can be compared against a previous test score. This type of comparison is referred to as an **ipsative assessment**. Whereas norm and criterion-referenced assessments use an external frame of reference, ipsative assessments are self-referenced and use an internal frame of reference. Ipsative assessments are commonly used in physical education classes or in computer games.

7.3.3   Percentiles

Percentage scores are easily confused with percentiles. A **percentage score** is simply the raw score (i.e., the number correct items) divided by the total number of test items. Consider Ivan's percentage score; he got 67 items correct on his math test, and the total number of items on the test was 100. Therefore, Ivan's percentage score is 67% (67/100). As you can see, the percentage score tells us the number of items Ivan answered correctly. Although the percentage score calculation is straightforward, it must be compared to some criterion or norm to give it interpretive meaning.

- **Percentile rank**, which is also referred to as a percentile, is a commonly used calculation that allows a comparison to be made between a person's raw score and norm group. A percentile rank indicates the percentage of scores falling at or below a given score. Percentile ranks range from less than 1 to greater than 99 and have a mean of 50. A percentile rank cannot be 0 or 100 because percentiles represent the percentage of scores below a given score. (Remember, a normal curve is asymptotic, so it goes to infinity in both directions). Percentile ranks are not equal units of measurement, meaning that the scale is inclined to exaggerate differences in percentiles near the mean and minimize differences at the tails.

- Considering the test data found in Table 7.6, what would Ivan's percentile rank be? First, we must calculate the mean and standard deviation of the data set. Using the calculations found in section 8.5, the mean is 63.0 and the standard deviation is 4. We then must determine how many standard deviations Ivan's score is from the mean. This can be determined by subtracting Ivan's score from the mean (i.e., 67 − 63 = 4). Because Ivan is 4 points above the mean and the standard deviation is 4, we know that he is one standard deviation above the mean. Ivan's percentile rank at +1 standard deviations (sd) can be de-

termined by consulting a score transformation table or by adding the known area underneath the curve (i.e., −3 sd to μ is 50% and μ to +1 sd is 34%, 50 + 34 = 84). Both methods yield a percentile score of 84.

7.3.4   Standardized Scores

In assessment, **standardization** relates to the conversion of raw scores to standard scores. Specifically, standardization refers to the process of finding the typical score attained by a group of test-takers. The typical score then acts as a standard reference point for future test results. Therefore, once a test is standardized, a score can be compared to the scores of the standard group. When comparing scores, it is important that the standard group reflects the test-takers who will be taking the test in the future. For example, you would want to compare a third-grader to a standard group of third-graders rather than a standard group of fifth-graders.

- Standardized scores are used in norm-referenced assessments. **Standardized scores** compare individual scores to a norm group through the use of formulas that convert the raw score to a new score. The standardized score specifies the number of standard deviations a score is above or below the mean. By converting a raw score into a standard score, we can compare an individual's scores on different types of tests. Common types of standardized scores include z-scores, T scores, deviation IQ, stanine scores, and normal curve equivalents scores.

7.3.4.1   Z-SCORES   The z-score is the most basic type of standard score. A **z-score** distribution has a mean of 0 and a standard deviation of 1. It simply represents the number of standard deviation units above or below the mean at which a given score falls. Z-scores are derived by subtracting the sample mean from the individual's raw score and then dividing the difference by the sample standard deviation.

$$z = \frac{X - M}{SD} \qquad (7.5)$$

- In the preceding equation, X is an individual's *raw score,* M represents the *sample mean*, and SD is the *sample's standard deviation*. You must know the sample's mean and standard deviation to convert an individual's raw score into a z-score. Consider the data set found in Table 7.6. Ivan's raw score on the math exam was 67, therefore his z-score is

$$z = \frac{67 - 63}{4} = +1.00$$

- A z-score represents an individual's raw score in standard deviation units. Therefore, we can tell if an individual's score is above or below the mean and where it falls on the normal curve. For example, Ivan's z-score of +1 tells us that he is above the mean (i.e., positive z-scores indicate a raw score is above the mean, whereas negative z-score indicate a raw score is below the mean). And we can see that he falls exactly one standard deviation above the mean on the bell curve or at the 84th percentile rank (i.e., 84% of Ivan's peers score at or below his score).

- Using the mean and standard deviation from the data set found in Table 7.6, what is Jen's z-score? What can you say about Jen's raw score using the converted z-score?

    If you found Jen's z-score to be 0, you are correct! If you said that she scored at the mean and at the 50th percentile, you really know your z-scores.

- It is important to remember that z-scores are the first step in analyzing a raw score because almost any other type of derived score can be found using the z-score formula.

7.3.4.2 T SCORES
A **T score** is a type of standard score that has an adjusted mean of 50 and a standard deviation of 10. These scores are commonly used when reporting the results of personality, interest, and aptitude measures. T scores are easily derived from z-scores by multiplying an individual's z-score by the T score standard deviation (i.e., 10) and adding it to the T score mean (i.e., 50):

$$T = 10\,(z) + 50 \qquad (7.6)$$

Using the preceding equation, Ivan's T score is

$$T = 10\,(+1) + 50 = 60$$

- T scores are interpreted similarly to z-scores, meaning that a T score above 50 represents a raw score that is above the mean, and a T score below 50 represents a raw score that is below the mean. Based on Ivan's T score (60), his raw score is above the mean; and since a T score has a standard deviation of 10, we know that he falls exactly one standard deviation above the mean on a normal curve.
- Using the data from Table 7.6, how would you find Matt's T score?

1. Start with the information you know: Matt's raw score is 55; the mean of the test scores is 63; the standard deviation is 4.
2. As we do not have a z-score for Matt, it must be calculated first.

$$z = \frac{55 - 63}{4} = -2.00$$

3. Now that we have a z-score, we can find the T score.

$$T = 10\,(-2) + 50 = 30$$

4. What can you say about Matt's score from his T score? It is two standard deviations below the mean and is equivalent to a percentile rank of 2.

7.3.4.3 DEVIATION IQ OR STANDARD SCORE
Deviation IQ scores are used in intelligence testing. Although deviation IQs are a type of standardized score, they are often referred to simply as standard scores (SS) because they are commonly used to interpret scores from achievement and aptitude tests, and it makes little sense to say "Johnny's reading score was a deviation IQ of . . . ." Deviation IQs have a mean of 100 and standard deviation of 15 and are derived by multiplying an indi-

vidual's z-score by the deviation IQ standard deviation (15) and adding it to the deviation IQ mean (100).

$$SS = 15\,(z) + 100 \qquad (7.7)$$

Deviation IQ scores are interpreted similarly to z-scores and T scores, meaning that a score above 100 represents a raw score that is above the mean, and a score below 100 represents a raw score that is below the mean.

7.3.4.4 STANINES
A **stanine**, which stands for "standard nine," is a type of standard score used on achievement tests. This standard score divides the normal distribution into nine intervals. Intervals 2 through 8 have a width of one half of a standard deviation, with the 5th stanine splitting the mean (i.e., −0.25 to +0.24 z-score range; see Figure 7.1). Stanine scores represent a range of z-scores and percentiles. For example a stanine score of 4 represents the z-score range of −.75 to −.26 and a percentile range of 23 to 40. Stanines have a mean of 5, with the mean falling at approximately the center of the 5th interval, a standard deviation of 2, and a range of 1 to 9. Stanine scores are obtained by multiplying the stanine standard deviation (2) by an individual's z-score and adding it to the stanine mean (5). Stanines are only expressed in whole numbers; therefore, scores must be rounded to the nearest whole number.

$$Staine = 2\,(z) + 5 \qquad (7.8)$$

- Consider the data set found in Table 7.6. Mary's raw score on the math exam was 58. What was her stanine score? We must first calculate Mary's z-score.

$$z = \frac{58 - 63}{4} =$$

Now that we have the z-score, we can convert this score into a stanine: $2\,(-1.25) + 5 = 2.5$ Although the preceding calculation yields a score of 2.5, stanines are expressed in whole numbers, so Mary's actual stanine score is 3. Stanines are interpreted similarly to z-scores in that a score below 5 is below the mean and a score above 5 is above the mean. Therefore, Mary's stanine score is around one standard deviation below the mean. She scored between the 11th and 23rd percentile.

7.3.4.5 NORMAL CURVE EQUIVALENTS
The **normal curve equivalent (NCE)** was developed for the U.S. Department of Education and is used by the educational community to measure student achievement. NCEs are similar to percentile ranks in that the range is from 1 to 99 and they indicate how an individual ranked in relationship to peers. Unlike percentile ranks, NCEs divide the normal curve into 100 equal parts (see Figure 7.1). NCEs have a mean of 50 and a standard deviation of 21.06. They can be converted from a z-score by multiplying the NCE standard deviation (SD = 21.06) by an individual's z-score and adding the NCE mean (M = 50).

$$NCE = 21.06\,(z) + 50 \qquad (7.9)$$

Using the NCE equation, Mary's NCE score would be 23.68. This means that roughly 23% of Mary's peers scored at or below her score, whereas roughly 77% of her peers scored above her score.

7.3.5 Developmental Scores

Developmental scores place an individual's raw score along a developmental continuum to derive meaning from the score. Unlike standard scores, which transform raw scores into scores with a new mean and standard deviation, developmental scores describe an individual's location on a developmental continuum. In doing so, developmental scores can directly evaluate an individual's score against the scores of those of the same age or grade level. Developmental scores are typically used when assessing children and young adolescents.

- *Age-equivalent scores* are a type of developmental score that compares an individual's score with the average score of those of the same age. Age-equivalents are reported in chronological years and months. Thus, we could say that a 7-year-5-month-old child with an age-equivalent score of 8.2 in height is the average height of a child age 8 years 2 months.

- *Grade-equivalent scores* are a type of developmental score that compares an individual's score with the average score of those at the same grade level. Grade equivalents are reported as a decimal number that describes performance in terms of grade level and months in grade. Thus, a grade equivalent score of 5.6 means the individual scored the average score of a student who has completed 6 months of the fifth-grade year.

- If a first-grader, who has completed 2 months of first grade, scored a grade equivalent score of 1.2 in reading, what can we say about her performance? If you said she was performing at the mean for her grade-mates, you have an understanding of how to interpret grade equivalent scores!

- Although grade equivalents are somewhat useful in measuring individual growth from year to year, they do *not* indicate that an individual is ready for a higher grade or should be moved back to a lower grade. A seventh-grader who obtains a grade-equivalent of 10.2 on a math test should not be moved into 10th-grade math. Grade-equivalent scores simply identify where an individual's score falls on the distribution of scores for individuals at the same grade level; they are not an analysis of skills. As this student was never compared to 10th-grade students, it is not accurate to say he is performing at the 10.2 grade level. What we can say is that the student probably is performing higher in math than most students in his grade.

7.3.6 Practice Multiple-Choice Items: Derived Scores

1. If a student scored 45 on a difficult English test, what can be said about her performance?
   a. The student performed poorly on the test.
   b. The student performed a little below average on the test.
   c. The student performed better than most of her classmates.
   d. There is not enough information to know how the student performed.

2. If a set of test scores with a mean of 74 and a standard deviation of 10 is normally distributed, what is the median?
   a. 64
   b. 84
   c. 74
   d. 104

3. In a normal distribution, _____ of scores falls between −1 and +2 standard deviations?
   a. 68%
   b. 2.25%
   c. 81.5%
   d. 97.5%

4. If the mean of an achievement test is 31 and the standard deviation is 3, what is the percentile rank of a student who scored a 37 on that test?
   a. 97.5%
   b. 50%
   c. 83.7%
   d. 99.75%

5. An individual with a z-score of −1.3 has a stanine score of
   a. 2.4
   b. 37
   c. 2
   d. 22.62

Answer Key: 1. d; 2. c; 3. c; 4. a; 5. c.

7.4 ASSESSMENT OF ABILITY

Ability assessment refers to a broad category of assessment instruments that measure the cognitive domain. The cognitive domain often includes knowledge, comprehension, application, analysis, synthesis, and evaluation of information. Assessment of ability includes tests that measure achievement and ability. In the remainder of this fourth section of Chapter 7, we discuss the characteristics of achievement tests and the different types of standardized achievement tests, the characteristics of aptitude testing and how it differs from achievement testing, commonly used cognitive ability tests and vocational aptitude testing, theories of intelligence and the characteristics of today's most widely used intelligence tests, and the key features of high stakes testing.

7.4.1 Achievement Tests

Achievement tests are designed to assess what one has learned at the time of testing. Specifically, they measure the knowledge and skills an individual has acquired in a particular area due to instruction or training experiences. Achievement tests are most frequently employed in educational settings and used for selection, classification, placement, or instruction purposes.

TABLE 7.8 Overview of Commonly Administered Survey Achievement Batteries.

Stanford Achievement Test (SAT 10)
- *Purpose:* To measure academic knowledge.
- *Intended population:* Elementary and secondary school students.
- *Test format:* Multiple-choice, short answer, and extended response (i.e., five or six sentence response) questions. Thirteen levels of the test are offered. Each level corresponds to the students' respective grade level.
- *Subsections:* Reading comprehension, mathematics, spelling, science, and writing.
- One of the oldest academic survey batteries.

Iowa Test of Basic Skills
- *Purpose:* To measure the basic educational skills needed to progress satisfactorily through school.
- *Intended population:* Students in Grades K through 8.
- *Subtests:* The test contains several subtests, which include content areas such as vocabulary, reading comprehension, spelling, grammar, mathematics, listening, and word analysis for the early grades. Social studies and science content areas are added for the upper grades.
- *Additional form:* Iowa Test of Educational Development (designed for high school students).

Metropolitan Achievement Test (MAT8)
- *Purpose:* Designed to assess students' knowledge over a broad range of subjects.
- *Intended population:* Students in Grades K–12.
- *Test format:* Test questions include multiple-choice and open-ended items.
- *Subtests:* Includes subtests that assess achievement in subject areas ranging from reading, language arts and mathematics to science and social studies.

TerraNova Tests
- *Purpose:* Designed to assess broad-based student achievement.
- *Intended population:* Students in Grades K–12.
- *Test format:* Multiple-choice and student-constructed response items.
- *Subtests:* Reading, language arts, mathematics, science, and social studies.
- *Alternate forms:* TerraNova Comprehensive Tests of Basic Skills, TerraNova CAT, and a Spanish edition (SUPERA).

Assessment of achievement can include standardized norm-referenced tests and teacher-constructed criterion-referenced tests. Standardized achievement tests can measure student academic growth, identify academically at-risk students, and provide accountability data for educational program evaluation.

Acceptable reliability coefficients for standardized achievement tests range begin at .80 and range higher. Achievement tests are written and evaluated on the basis of content validity, the extent to which the test includes content individuals are expected to have experienced. Standardized achievement testing includes survey batteries, diagnostic tests, and readiness tests.

7.4.1.1 SURVEY BATTERIES Survey batteries refer to a collection of tests that measure individuals' knowledge across broad content areas. These tests must cover material from multiple subject areas and, as a result, do not assess any one subject in great depth. Survey batteries are usually administered in school settings and are used to assess academic progress. Table 7.8 presents an overview of the most commonly administered survey batteries.

7.4.1.2 DIAGNOSTIC TESTS Diagnostic tests are designed to identify learning disabilities or specific learning difficulties in a

given academic area. In contrast to survey batteries, diagnostic tests provide in-depth analysis of student skill competency. As a result, these tests yield information regarding a student's specific strengths and weaknesses in an academic area. Table 7.9 includes an overview of commonly administered diagnostic tests.

7.4.1.3 READINESS TESTING Readiness tests refer to a group of criterion-referenced achievement assessments that indicate the minimum level of skills needed to move from one grade level to the next. These achievements tests are frequently used in high stakes testing (see section 7.4.4 for more information on high stakes testing). Readiness tests have been criticized for their cultural and language biases. Students from lower socioeconomic status (SES) groups, minority groups, and homes where English is not the primary language often have lower scores regardless of their actual educational ability level.

7.4.2 Aptitude Tests

When students prepare for the GRE, they often wonder how solving a math problem is related to counseling. Although the two seem to have little in common, the GRE is designed to measure aptitude. **Aptitude tests**, such as the GRE and SAT, assess what a person is capable of learning. Unlike an achievement test, which measures an individual's current knowledge, aptitude

TABLE 7.9 Overview of Commonly Administered Individual Diagnostic Achievement Tests.

Wide Range Achievement Test (WRAT4)

- *Purpose:* Measures the basic reading, spelling, and mathematical skills needed for effective learning and thinking. The WRAT4 attempts to eliminate the effects of reading comprehension on an individual's score.
- *Intended population:* Persons from ages 5 to 75 years.
- *Test format:* Examinees are asked to pronounce/read words, spell words, and figure out math problems. The test is available in two levels; level I can be administered to children ages 5 to 11 years and level II to children and adults ages 12 to 75 years.
- *Subtests:* Reading, spelling, mathematical skills, and a recently added sentence completion subtest.
- *Alternate forms:* Two equivalent forms, "blue" and "tan"

Key Math Diagnostic Test (Key Math 3)

- *Purpose:* Comprehensively assess math-related learning disabilities.
- *Intended population:* Children ages 4 to 21 years.
- *Test format:* 372 short-answer questions.
- *Subtests:* There are 10 subtests and 3 broad content areas: basic concepts, operations, and applications (i.e., problem solving).
- *Alternate forms:* Two forms, Form A and Form B.

Woodcock Johnson III-Tests of Achievement (WJ III ACH)

- *Purpose:* Measures academic achievement to identify and describe an individual's current strengths and weaknesses.
- *Intended population:* Persons from ages 2 to 90+ years.
- *Test format:* Includes a variety of items that require examinees to identify and read letters/words, comprehend sentences, calculate math problems, spell words, formulate and write simple sentences, and pronounce words. Uses basal and ceiling rules to establish the beginning and end of the battery.
- *Subtests:* Divided into two test batteries, Standard and Extended. These test batteries include subtests that directly parallel the IDEA areas: oral expression, listening comprehension, written expression, basic reading skills, reading comprehension, reading fluency, math calculation skills, and math reasoning.
- *Alternate forms:* Two forms, Form A and Form B. Form B includes Canadian pages for use in Canada.

Peabody Individual Achievement Test-Revised

- *Purpose:* Screen for learning disabilities related to reading, mathematics, and spelling.
- *Intended population:* Students in Grades K–12.
- *Test format:* Multiple choice.
- *Subtests:* Content areas covered include general information, reading recognition, reading comprehension, mathematics, spelling, and written expression.

Test of Adult Basic Education

- *Purpose:* Assesses the basic skills adults must master to participate fully in society.
- *Intended population:* Adult learners ages 16 years and older who are not enrolled in school and who want to improve their basic skills.
- *Test format:* Multiple-choice and open-response items. The five test levels range from limited literacy to advanced.
- *Subtests:* Basic skills include vocabulary, reading, language, language mechanics, mathematics, and spelling.
- *Alternative formats:* Two alternate forms.

---

tests attempt to predict how well that individual will perform in the future. Therefore, the GRE does not test your knowledge but rather your future performance in graduate school. Aptitude testing includes measures that assess intelligence, educational cognitive ability, and vocational aptitude. As a discussion on intelligence testing involves the inclusion of several broad topics on intelligence, it is covered in the following subsection, and the rest of this subsection is devoted to cognitive ability and vocational aptitude testing.

7.4.2.1 COGNITIVE ABILITY TESTS Cognitive ability tests make predictions about an individual's ability to perform in future grade levels, colleges, and graduate schools. Cognitive ability tests assess broad aptitude areas such as verbal, math, and analytical ability. Table 7.10 presents an overview of common cognitive ability tests.

7.4.2.2 VOCATIONAL APTITUDE TESTING Vocational aptitude testing refers to a set of predictive tests that are designed to measure one's potential for occupational success (Erford, 2007). These tests are useful to employers and potential employees. For the employer, test results assist in the process of screening for competent, well-suited employees. For the potential employee, test results can offer career guidance. Vocational aptitude testing includes multiple aptitude tests and special aptitude tests.

TABLE 7.10 Overview of Commonly Administered Cognitive Ability Tests.

The Cognitive Ability Test (CogAT Form 6)
- *Purpose:* To assess children's verbal, quantitative, and nonverbal reasoning abilities.
- *Intended population:* Students in grades K–12.
- *Test format:* Multiple choice.
- *Subtests:* The test has test batteries verbal, quantitative, and nonverbal and 9 different subtests: verbal classifications, sentence completion, verbal analogies, quantitative relationships, number series, equation building, figure classification, figure analogies, and figure analysis.

Otis-Lennon School Ability Test (OLSAT8)
- *Purpose:* Measures children's abstract thinking and reasoning abilities.
- *Intended population:* Students in Grades K–12.
- *Test format:* Multiple choice.
- *Subtests:* The test has five sections: verbal comprehension, verbal reasoning, pictorial reasoning, figural reasoning, and qualitative reasoning.

ACT Assessment
- *Purpose:* Undergraduate college admission exam that measures an individual's ability to complete college-level work.
- *Intended population:* Persons seeking to gain undergraduate admission into a college or university.
- *Test format:* 215 multiple-choice items.
- *Subtests:* Covers four skill areas (English, math, reading, and science ability).
- *Scoring:* Test scores range from 1 to 36, with the average score for college-bound students being 21.

SAT Reasoning Test
- *Purpose:* Undergraduate college admission exam that assesses the critical thinking skills needed to achieve academic success at the college level.
- *Intended population:* Persons seeking to gain undergraduate admission into a college or university.
- *Test format:* Multiple-choice questions, grid-in questions, and a brief essay.
- *Subtests:* Contains three subsections (critical reading, math reasoning, and writing).
- *Scoring:* On each of the three sections, individuals receive a standard score ranging from 200 to 800, which converts to a percentile score.

GRE General Test
- *Purpose:* Predicts success in graduate school.
- *Intended population:* Persons seeking to gain graduate admission into a college or university.
- *Test format:* Multiple choice and two essays.
- *Subtests:* Three sections (verbal reasoning, quantitative reasoning, and analytical writing).
- *Scoring:* Scores on quantitative and verbal sections range from 200 to 800, with writing scores ranging from 0 to 6. Uses a scaled score with a mean and standard deviation that change over time.

Miller Analogies Test (MAT)
- *Purpose:* Predicts graduate school success through the use of analogies. Measures analytical reasoning by assessing one's ability to identify analogous relationships.
- *Intended population:* Persons seeking to gain graduate admission into a college or university.
- *Test format:* 120 analogies.
- *Scoring:* Scores range from 200 to 600.

Law School Admission Test (LSAT)
- *Purpose:* Predicts academic success in law school.
- *Intended population:* Persons seeking to gain admission into law school.
- *Test format:* Multiple-choice format and an essay.
- *Subtests:* Sections include logical reasoning, reading comprehension, analytical reasoning, and writing.
- *Scoring:* Scores range from 120 to 180 with a mean of 150.

(Continued)

TABLE 7.10 Overview of Commonly Administered Cognitive Ability Tests. (*Continued*)

Medical College Admission Test (MCAT)

- *Purpose:* Predicts academic success in medical school by assessing problem solving, critical thinking, written analysis, and writing skills, as well as knowledge of scientific principles.
- *Intended population:* Persons seeking to gain admission into medical school.
- *Test format:* Multiple-choice format and two essays.
- *Subtests:* Four sections (physical sciences, biological sciences, verbal reasoning, and writing ability).
- *Scoring:* Scores for the physical science, biological science, and verbal reasoning sections range from 1 to 15. Scores for the writing sample range alphabetically from J (lowest) to T (highest).

- *Multiple aptitude tests* assess several distinct aspects of ability at one time. They are used to predict success in several occupations.
  - The *Armed Services Vocational Aptitude Battery* (ASVAB) is the most widely used multiple aptitude test in the world. Although it was originally developed for the military, the ASVAB now measures the abilities required for a variety of military and civilian jobs. The ASVAB includes eight ability tests: general science, arithmetic reasoning, word knowledge, paragraph comprehension, mathematics knowledge, electronics information, auto shop information, and mechanical comprehension.
  - The *Differential Aptitude Test* (DAT) is a multiple aptitude measure for students in Grades 7 through 12. Similar to the ASVAB, the DAT has eight separate tests that assess verbal reasoning, numerical reasoning, abstract reasoning, perceptual speed and accuracy, mechanical reasoning, space relations, spelling and language usage. The DAT also includes a Career Interest Inventory (CII) that assesses student vocational strengths and determines possible careers that might interest the student.

- *Special aptitude tests* assess one homogenous area of aptitude and are used to predict success in a specific vocational area. Table 7.11 lists several commonly used special aptitude tests.

TABLE 7.11 Commonly Used Special Aptitude Tests.

Clerical Aptitude Tests
- U.S. Postal Service's 470 Battery Examination
- Clerical Test Battery (CTB2)

Mechanical Aptitude Tests
- Wiesen Test of Mechanical Aptitude
- SkillsProfiler Series
- Technical Test Battery (TTB2)

Artistic and Musical Aptitude Tests
- Meir Art Test
- Graves Design Judgment Test
- Music Aptitude Profile
- Iowa Test of Music Literacy

7.4.3 Intelligence Tests

Intelligence tests broadly assess an individual's cognitive abilities. Because it is a type of aptitude testing, intelligence testing measures what one is capable of doing. These tests characteristically yield a single summary score, commonly called an IQ (intelligence quotient). Intelligence tests are often used to detect giftedness and learning disabilities and to identify and classify mental retardation.

7.4.3.1 THEORIES OF INTELLIGENCE What is intelligence? Is it related to a person's spatial and verbal aptitude? Or a person's music ability? Intelligence is difficult to measure and define because it is not an overt construct. As a result, experts continue to argue over the definition of intelligence. Several theories of intelligence exist, and each one strives to define the construct (Erford, 2007). Table 7.12 provides an overview of intelligence theories with which you must be familiar.

7.4.3.2 INTELLIGENCE TESTS Not surprisingly, the intelligence tests we use today are based on the preceding theories of intelligence. The majority of these tests are based on constructs such as the "g" and "s" factors and crystallized and fluid intelligence. Table 7.13 provides an overview of today's commonly used intelligence tests.

7.4.4 High Stakes Testing

High stakes testing refers to the use of standardized test outcomes to make a major educational decision concerning promotion, retention, educational placement, and entrance into college (Erford, 2007). The results of high stakes testing can have serious consequences for the students being tested. For example, a student who scores high may receive a college scholarship, whereas a low-scoring student may have his high school diploma withheld. Criterion-referenced assessments are typically used in high stakes testing. High stakes testing has received a lot of criticism. Specifically, critics argue that a single test is not representative of a student's abilities and, therefore, should not be the only factor considered when making an important educational decision. In addition, the standardized tests used in high stakes testing may fail to account for diverse factors influencing minority students' performance, which widens the achievement gap between

TABLE 7.12   Intelligence Theories.

Francis Galton	• Developed first intelligence theory. • Emphasized heritability and eugenics. • Theorized that perceptual abilities were critical to the development of intelligence.
Alfred Binet and Theodore Simon	• Developed first formal measure of intelligence: the Binet-Simon scale.
Lewis Terman	• Revised and translated the Binet-Simon scale and renamed the enhanced version the Stanford-Binet.
William Stern	• Developed the ratio intelligence quotient, which is calculated by dividing one's mental age by chronological age.
Charles Spearman's two-factor approach	• Defined intelligence as a single unit, which he termed "g" (i.e., general factor). • Acknowledged the existence of "s" or specific factors that referred to the skills acquired in a specific area as a result of training.
Louis Thurston's multifactor approach	• Instead of a "g" factor, Thurston recognized seven primary mental abilities: verbal comprehension, word fluency, number ability, spatial ability, associative memory, perceptual speed, and reasoning.
Phillip Vernon's hierarchical model of intelligence	• Postulated that intelligence is comprised of factors and skills that are arranged hierarchically into four levels.
J. P. Guilford's multi-dimensional model	• Intelligence is composed of 180 factors and involves three types of cognitive ability: operations, content, and products. • His model is shaped as a cube.
Raymond Cattell's fluid and crystallized intelligence model	• Proposed two distinct intelligences: fluid and crystallized • Fluid intelligence refers to innate ability that is not influenced by experience and education. Consists of reasoning ability, memory capacity, and speed of information processing. • Crystallized intelligence is gained through learning and is greatly affected by life experiences and culture. • Crystallized intelligence will increase with age, whereas fluid intelligence declines as we age.
Robert Sternberg's triarchic theory of intelligence	• Componential (the person's internal world); experiential (the person's external world and adaptation to novelty); and contextual (the person's external world and environmental adaptation or creation).
Howard Gardner's theory of multiple intelligences	• Proposed eight primary intelligences: linguistic, logical-mathematical, musical, spatial, bodily-kinesthetic, intrapersonal, interpersonal, and naturalistic.
Cattell-Horn-Carroll (CHC) theory of cognitive abilities	• Recognized as the most empirically validated theoretical model of intelligence. • Proposes that intelligence is hierarchical and comprised of three strata: general intelligence "g," broad cognitive abilities, and narrow cognitive abilities.

TABLE 7.13   Overview of Commonly Administered Intelligence Tests.

Stanford-Binet 5
- *Intended population:* Persons ages 2 to 90 years.
- *Format:* Uses basal and ceiling levels to determine starting and stopping points.
- *Subtests:* Measures verbal and nonverbal intelligence across five factors (fluid reasoning, knowledge, quantitative reasoning, visual-spatial processing, and working memory). This creates 10 subtests.
- *Scoring:* Uses a mean of 100 and a standard deviation of 15. Raw scores are based on the number of items answered correctly and are converted into a standard score based upon age norms.

Wechsler Scales
- Most widely used intelligence tests.
- Has three different tests for various age groups.
- Scores have a mean of 100 and an SD of 15.

Wechsler Adult Intelligence Scale–Fourth Edition (WAIS-IV)
- *Intended population:* Individuals ages 16 to 89 years.
- *Subtests:* Contains 15 subtests (symbol search, coding, arithmetic, digit span, matrix reasoning, picture completion, block design, visual puzzles, future weights, comprehension, similarities, vocabulary, and information).
- *Scoring:* Subtests generate a full-scale score and four composite scores (verbal comprehension, perceptual reasoning, processing speed, working memory).

(Continued)

TABLE 7.13   Overview of Commonly Administered Intelligence Tests. (*Continued*)

Wechsler Intelligence Scale for Children—Fourth Edition (WISC-IV)

- *Intended population:* Individuals ages 6 to 16 years.
- *Subtests:* Contains 10 core subtests (symbol search, coding, letter-number sequencing, digit span, matrix reasoning, picture concepts, block design, comprehension, similarities, and vocabulary). In addition to the 10 subtests, there are five supplemental tests (information, word reasoning, picture completion, arithmetic, and cancellation).
- *Scoring:* Subtests generate a full-scale score and four composite scores (verbal comprehension, perceptual reasoning, processing speed, and working memory).

Wechsler Preschool and Primary Scales of Intelligence—Third Edition (WPPSI-III)

- *Intended population:* Individual ages 2 years and 6 months to 7 years and 3 months
- *Subtests:* Composed of 14 subtests (matrix reasoning, vocabulary, picture concepts, symbol search, word reasoning, coding, comprehension, picture completion, similarities, receptive vocabulary, object assembly, picture naming).
- *Scoring:* Provides a verbal and performance IQ score and a full-scale IQ score.

Kaufman Assessment Battery for Children (KABC-II)

- *Purpose:* Designed to evaluate preschoolers, minority groups, and children with learning disabilities. Provides information about nonverbal intellectual abilities.
- *Intended population:* Children ages 3 to 18 years.
- *Subtests:* 5 subtests (simultaneous, sequential, planning, learning, and knowledge). Has a broad theoretical base that allows the test administrator to use the Luria neuropsychological model and the Cattell/Horn/Carroll (CHC) approach to interpret the subtests.
- *Scoring:* Yields 4 global scores (sequential processing, simultaneous processing, achievement, and mental processing composite). Uses a mean of 100 and a standard deviation of 15.

TABLE 7.14   Examples of High Stakes Testing.

- Standardized tests administered to measure school progress under No Child Left Behind (NCLB)
- Advanced placement exams
- High school exit exam
- Driver's license tests
- Professional licensure and certification examinations

higher and lower performing groups. Table 7.14 provides examples of high stakes testing.

- Key features of a high stakes test include the following:
  - A single defined assessment is the sole determining factor for making a decision.
  - A clear line is drawn between those who pass and those who fail.
  - Test results (i.e., passing or failing) have a direct consequence.

7.4.5 Practice Multiple-Choice Items: Assessment of Ability

1. Achievement testing includes
   a. standardized norm-referenced tests.
   b. teacher-constructed criterion-referenced tests.
   c. standardized high stakes tests.
   d. All of the above.

2. John, a third-grade student, is having trouble in math. The teacher suspects that John has a learning disability in math. Which of the following achievement tests should be used to determine whether John has a learning disability in math?
   a. Iowa Test of Basic Skills
   b. Stanford Achievement Test
   c. Graduate Record Exam
   d. Key Math Diagnostic Test

3. Which one of the following is NOT an example of an aptitude test?
   a. GRE general test
   b. Clerical Test Battery
   c. Test of Adult Basic Education
   d. Stanford-Binet 5

4. The _____ measures several distinct aspects of vocational ability, and the _____ measures one homogenous area of vocational ability.
   a. Skills Profiler Series; Armed Services Vocational Aptitude Battery (ASVAB)
   b. Differential Aptitude Test (DAT); Wiesen Test of Mechanical Aptitude
   c. Miller Analogies Test (MAT); Music Aptitude Profile
   d. Differential Aptitude Test (DAT); Otis-Lennon School Ability Test (OLSAT8)

5. William Stern's ratio intelligence quotient, popularized on early versions of the Stanford-Binet Intelligence Scales, was calculated
   a. by dividing one's mental age by chronological age.
   b. by dividing one's broad cognitive abilities by narrow cognitive abilities.
   c. by dividing one's chronological age by one's mental age.
   d. by dividing one's narrow cognitive abilities by broad cognitive abilities.

Answer Key: 1. d; 2. d; 3. c; 4. b; 5. a.

7.5 CLINICAL ASSESSMENT

Clinical assessment can be thought of as the "whole person assessment." It refers to the process of assessing clients through multiple methods such as personality testing, observation, interviewing, and performance. Clinical assessments may increase a client's self-awareness or assist the professional counselor in client conceptualization and treatment planning. In the remainder of this fifth section of Chapter 7, we discuss how to assess a person's affective realm using both objective and projective personality tests; the different types of objective and projective personality tests; informal assessment techniques such as observation, clinical interviewing, rating scales, and classification systems; the differences between direct vs. indirect observations; the three different approaches to clinical interviewing; other types of assessments such as the Mental Status Exam and the Performance Assessment; and suicide assessment, the risk factors associated with suicide, and how to gauge suicide lethality.

7.5.1 Assessment of Personality

Personality tests assess a person's affective realm. Specifically, personality tests describe the facets of a person's character that remain stable through adulthood (e.g., temperament, patterns in behavior). Several distinctive tests that emerged in the 20th century attempted to assess both individual personality characteristics and the personality as a whole. Today, these tests are classified as either objective or projective personality tests.

7.5.1.1 OBJECTIVE PERSONALITY TESTS Objective personality tests are standardized, self-report instruments that often use multiple-choice or true/false formats to assess various aspects of personality. The aims of objective personality tests are to identify personality types, personality traits, personality states, and self-concept. In addition, these tests can identify psychopathology and assist in treatment planning. Table 7.15 presents an overview of the most commonly administered objective personality tests.

TABLE 7.15 Overview of Commonly Administered Objective Personality Tests.

Minnesota Multiphasic Personality Inventory-2 (MMPI-2)

Purpose: To identify *DSM-IV-TR* Axis I psychopathology.

Intended population: Adults.

Test format: 567 true/false items written at an eighth-grade reading level.

Scales: 10 basic or clinical scales (hypochondriasis, depression, conversion hysteria, psychopathic deviant, masculinity-femininity, paranoia, psychasthenia, schizophrenia, hypomania, and social introversion). Plus validity scales, including the following:

- *Lie scale* (L)—detects the selection of an unusually large percentage of unusual or infrequent responses.
- *Correction scale* (K)—detects tendency to downplay psychological symptoms.
- *Infrequency scale* (F)—measures degree to which examinee is willing to report psychological symptoms.
- *Alternative forms:* An adolescent version (MMPI-A) is available.

Millon Clinical Multiaxial Inventory, Third Edition

Purpose: To assess *DSM-IV-TR* Axis II personality disorders and clinical symptomatology.

Intended population: Persons 18 years and older.

Test format: 175 true/false items written at an eighth-grade reading level.

Scales: Six major scales that allow for a differential diagnosis (clinical personality pattern scales, severe personality pathology scales, clinical syndrome scales, severe clinical syndrome scales, modifying indices, and validity index).

Alternative forms: Millon Adolescent Clinical Inventory (MACI).

Myers-Briggs Type Indicator

Purpose: Measures psychological preferences based on Carl Jung's psychological types. Can be used to help clients deepen self-awareness, understand similarities and differences in workplace or family personalities, and to help individuals in career counseling to match their personality to a career.

Intended population: Individuals 14 years and older.

Test format: 93 items, written at a seventh-grade reading level.

Scales: Eight scales representing four related dimensions:

- Extraversion vs. Introversion: Where your energy is directed?
- Sensing vs. Intuition: How do you perceive the world around you?
- Thinking vs. Feeling: How do you make decisions?
- Judging vs. Perceiving: How do you deal with the external world?

Alternative forms: Form Q, has 144 items and is administered to adults 18 years and older.

(Continued)

TABLE 7.15 Overview of Commonly Administered Objective Personality Tests. (*Continued*)

California Psychological Inventory, Form 434 (CPI 434)

Purpose: Describes basic personality traits of nonpathological, well-adjusted individuals. May be used to increase client insight and predict success in many vocational areas.

Intended population: Individuals 13 years and older.

Test format: 434 items, half of the items are drawn from the MMPI.

Scales: 20 folk-concept scales (dominance, capacity for status, sociability, social presence, self-acceptance, independence, empathy, responsibility, socialization, self-control, good impression, communality, well-being, tolerance, achievement via conformance, achievement via independence, intellectual efficiency, psychological mindedness, flexibility, femininity/masculinity).

Three Vector Scales (externality-internality, norm-favoring vs. norm questioning, self-realization).

13 Special-Purpose Scales (management potential, work orientation, creative temperament, masculinity and femininity scales, anxiety, social desirability, acquiescence, leadership, amicability, law enforcement orientation, tough-mindedness, narcissism).

The Sixteen Personality Factors Questionnaire (16PF)

Purpose: Measures the 16 basic personality traits of normal people as defined by Raymond Cattell.

Intended population: Individuals 16 years and older.

Test format: 185 multiple-choice items written at a fourth-grade reading level.

Scales: 16 primary scales (five global scales and three validity scales). The primary scales are dichotomous (e.g., relaxed vs. tense), with both high and low scores representing a particular personality characteristic.

Alternative forms: High School Personality Questionnaire, Children's Personality Questionnaire.

The NEO Personality Inventory–Revised (NEO PI-R)

Purpose: To obtain a detailed assessment of normal personality based on the Big Five personality factors: neuroticism, extroversion, openness to experience, agreeableness, and conscientiousness.

Intended population: Individuals 17 years and older.

Test format: 240 personality items answered on a 5-point agree-disagree continuum and 3 validity items.

Scales: Five scales that correspond with each of the Big Five personality factors.

Coopersmith Self-Esteem Inventories (SEI)

Purpose: Designed to measure children's self-esteem.

Intended population: Children ages 8 to 15 years.

Test format: 58 statements in which the test-taker answers "like me" or "unlike me."

Scales: Four subscales that measure self-esteem in regard to peers, parents, school, and personal interests. One lie scale that measures defensiveness.

Alternative forms: Adult Form.

7.5.1.2 PROJECTIVE PERSONALITY TESTS Projective personality tests assess personality factors by interpreting a client's response to ambiguous stimuli. These personality tests are rooted in psychoanalytic psychology and exert that the ambiguity of the presented stimuli will tap into the unconscious attitudes and motivations of the client. Projective tests are used to identify psychopathology and assist in treatment planning. Table 7.16 presents an overview of the most commonly administered objective personality tests.

7.5.2 Informal Assessments

Informal assessments refer to subjective assessment techniques that are developed for specific needs. Unlike formal, standardized tests, the intention of an informal assessment is not to provide a comparison to a broader group; rather, informal assessments seek to identify the strengths and needs of clients. Types of informal assessment include observation, clinical interviewing, rating scales, and classification systems.

7.5.2.1 OBSERVATION *Observation* is a broad term that refers to the systematic observation and recording of an individual's overt behaviors. Because the behavior is believed to serve a function in a particular environment, the antecedents and consequences are also recorded to ascertain the "why" behind the behavior. Behavioral assessments can be conducted by gathering data from direct or indirect observation.

- **Direct observation** assesses an individual's behavior in real time and usually occurs in a naturalistic setting. Table 7.17 presents an overview of commonly used direct observation procedures.
- **Indirect observation** assesses an individual's behavior through self-report or the use of informants such as family, friends, or teachers. Indirect observation methods include the use of behavioral interviewing, checklists, and rating scales.

7.5.2.2 CLINICAL INTERVIEWING Clinical interviewing is the most commonly used assessment technique in counseling.

TABLE 7.16   Overview of Commonly Administered Projective Personality Tests.

Rorschach Inkblot Test
- Consists of 10 inkblot cards. The client is asked to talk about what he or she sees on each card.
- Scoring of the response uses three components: the location of the portion the client responds to, the determinants that the client used to describe what he or she saw, and the content of the client's response.

Thematic Apperception Test (TAT)
- Consists of 31 cards that display vague pictures. The client is asked to create a story about the picture on the card with a beginning, middle, and end.
- The TAT lacks an agreed-on scoring system.

House-Tree-Person (HTP)
- A projective drawing technique that asks the client to draw a house, a tree, and a person. Drawing characteristics are then interpreted; guidelines for interpretation are available.

Sentence Completion Tests
- Ask the client to complete a statement such as "I am happy when...." There is no objective scoring method.
- Common sentence completion tests include Sentence Completion Series, the EPS Sentence Completion Technique, and the Rotter Incomplete Sentence Blank.

TABLE 7.17   Direct Observation Procedures.

Narrative	• Written description of all behavior as it occurs in the environment.
	• Provides descriptive and sequential data.
ABC	• Records events preceding behavior (A), target behavior (B), and events following the behavior (C).
Event	• Provides a frequency count for how many times the targeted behavior occurs within a specific time frame.
Duration	• Records the duration of the targeted behavior from beginning to end.
Partial interval	• Records the number of times a client engaged in the targeted behavior during a predetermined time interval.
Whole interval	• Records if the behavior occurs throughout the entire time interval.

Interviewing refers to the process by which a professional counselor uses clinical skills to obtain from a client information that will facilitate the course of counseling. Typically, clinical interviews are used to gather information concerning a client's demographic characteristics, presenting problems, current life situation, family, educational status, occupational background, physical health, and mental health history (Erford, 2006). Many different types of interviews exist, and they can all be classified as structured, semi-structured, or unstructured.

- **Structured interviews** use a series of preestablished questions that the professional counselor presents in the same order during each interview. The structured interview tends to be detailed and exhaustive as it covers a broad area of topics. Because the questions are predetermined and asked in a sequential manner, structured interviews provide consistency across different clients, counselors, and time periods. However, they do not provide the flexibility to ask follow-up questions or explore client issues more in depth.
- **Semi-structured interviews** use preestablished questions and topic areas to be addressed; however, the professional counselor can customize the interview by modifying questions, altering the interview sequence, or adding follow-up questions. Although semi-structured

interviews allow for more flexibility, they are more prone to interviewer error and bias. Therefore, they are considered to be less reliable than structured interviews.

- **Unstructured interviews** do not use preestablished questions and tend to rely on the client's lead to determine a focus for the interview. Typically, professional counselors rely on open-ended questioning and reflective skills when conducting an unstructured interview. This type of interview provides the most flexibility and adaptability but is the least reliable and most subject to interviewer error.

7.5.2.3 RATING SCALES Rating scales typically evaluate the quantity of an attribute. The following is an example of a common rating scale question:

I feel sad.

1	2	3	4	5
Hardly at All	Somewhat	Moderately So	Very Much	Extremely

- Rating scales are highly subjective as they often rely on the rater's perception of the behavior. Nonetheless, rating scales provide an efficient way to measure a client's functioning in terms of behavior, personality, social skills, and emotions.

- Rating scales vary in type and scope of information assessed. Some scales assess a broad array of behaviors, whereas others measure specific behaviors and the conditions in which they occur. *Broad-band behavioral rating scales* evaluate a broad range of behavioral domains. *Narrow-band behavioral rating scales* evaluate a specific dimension of the targeted behaviors. Often, a broad-band behavioral rating scale will be administered to identify the problematic behavior, and a narrow-band behavioral rating scale will be subsequently administered to provide detailed information about the problematic behavior.

7.5.2.4 CLASSIFICATION SYSTEMS Classification systems

are used to assess the presence or absence of an attribute. Three commonly used classification systems include the following:

- *Behavior and Feeling Word Checklists:* Allow the professional counselor or client to identify the words that best describe the client's feelings or behaviors.
- *Sociometric Instruments:* Assess the social dynamics within a group, organization, or institution.
- *Situational Tests:* Involve asking the client to role-play a situation to determine how he or she may respond in real life.

7.5.3 Other Types of Assessments

Other forms of assessments often used in counseling include the mental status exam, performance assessment, and suicide assessment.

7.5.3.1 MENTAL STATUS EXAM The **Mental Status Exam**

(MSE) is used by professional counselors to obtain a snapshot of a client's mental symptoms and psychological state. When information yielded from the MSE is combined with client biographical and historical information, the professional counselor can formulate an accurate diagnosis and treatment plan. The MSE addresses several key areas:

- *Appearance:* Refers to the physical aspects of a client, such as apparent age, height, weight, and manner of dress and grooming. Bizarre dress, odors, and body modifications are noted.
- *Attitude:* Refers to how the client interacts with the professional counselor during the interview.
- *Movement and Behavior:* Observation of client's abnormal movements, level of activity, eye contact, facial expressions, gestures, and gait.
- *Mood and Affect:* Mood refers to the way a client feels most of the time (e.g., depressed, angry). Affect refers to the external expression of a client's mood (flat, silly) and can change frequently. The professional counselor notes quality and intensity of affect and congruence with mood.
- *Thought Content:* Refers to abnormalities in thought content such as suicidal/homicidal ideation, delusions, obsessions, paranoia, and thought broadcasting/insertion.

- *Perceptions:* Refers to any sensory experience. There are three types of perceptual disturbance: hallucinations, derealizations, and illusions.
- *Thought Processes:* Refers to the connections between client thoughts and how they relate to the current conversation. Thought can be logical or illogical, coherent or incoherent, or flight of ideas, loose.
- *Judgment and Insight:* Judgment pertains to the client's ability to make decisions, and insight refers to the client's understanding of his or her current situation.
- *Intellectual Functioning and Memory:* Assesses client's level of intellect, current knowledge, and ability to perform calculations and think abstractly.

7.5.3.2 PERFORMANCE ASSESSMENT Performance as-

sessments are a nonverbal form of assessment that entails minimal verbal communication to measure broad attributes. The client is required to perform a task rather than answer questions using pencil-and-paper methods. Performance assessments are advantageous when working with clients who speak a foreign language, have physical or hearing disabilities, or have limited verbal abilities. Examples of intelligence performance tests include the Porteus Maze, Draw-a-Man Test, Bayley Scales, Cattell Culture Fair Intelligence Tests, and Test of Non-Verbal Intelligence (TONI). The Gesell developmental scales is an example of a developmental performance test.

7.5.3.3 SUICIDE ASSESSMENT Suicide assessment refers

to determining a client's potential for committing suicide. Specifically, the professional counselor must make a clinical judgment concerning the client's suicide lethality. **Suicide lethality** is defined as the likelihood that a client will die as a result of suicidal thoughts and behaviors. Lethality exists on a continuum from low to high as displayed in Table 7.18.

- Professional counselors often use the clinical interview to systematically assess for lethality. A thorough suicide assessment includes gathering information related to client demographics (e.g., gender, age, relationship status, ethnicity), psychosocial situation, history, existing

TABLE 7.18 Levels of Suicidal Lethality.

Low lethality	• The client is not suicidal at the time of the assessment.
Low–moderate lethality	• The client is somewhat suicidal but does not have any risk factors associated with suicide.
Moderate lethality	• The client is suicidal and has several risk factors.
Moderate–high lethality	• The client is determined to die and may commit suicide within the next 72 hours unless an intervention occurs.
High lethality	• The client is currently in the process of committing suicide (e.g., already swallowed pills) and needs immediate hospitalization.

TABLE 7.19 Suicide Risk Factors.

Demographics
- Male, single, divorced, widowed, White, risk increases with age.

Psychosocial
- Lack of social support.
- Unemployed/drop in socioeconomic level.

Psychiatric Diagnosis
- Those associated with increased risk of suicide are mood disorders, anxiety disorders, schizophrenia, substance abuse disorders, borderline personality disorder, antisocial personality disorder, and narcissistic personality disorder.

Psychological Dimensions
- Five key suicidal emotions: hopelessness, helplessness, worthlessness, loneliness, and depression.

History
- Family history of suicide, abuse, or mental illness.
- Client's previous suicide attempts.

Individual Factors
- Inability to problem solve.
- Current alcohol or drug use.
- Low tolerance for psychological pain.

Suicidality and Symptoms
- Past and present suicidal ideation, plans, behaviors, intent.
- Report no reason for living.
- Homicidal ideation.

TABLE 7.20 Standardized Assessments Used to Gauge Suicide Lethality.

Specific Suicide Assessments
- Beck Scale for Suicide Ideation
- Suicidal Ideation Scale
- Suicidal Ideation Questionnaire

Reasons-for-Living Inventories
- Reasons-for-Living Inventory
- College Student Reasons for Living Inventory
- Brief Reasons for Living

Standardized Personality Tests
- Minnesota Multiphasic Personality Inventory (MMPI)
- Millon Clinical Multiaxial Inventory-III

Projective Personality Techniques
- Thematic Apperception Test
- Rotter Incomplete Sentence Blank
- Rorschach inkblot method

---

psychiatric diagnosis, suicidality and symptoms (e.g., intent, plans, ideation), and individual strengths and weaknesses. Several assessment acronyms exist that can help professional counselors structure their suicide assessment. Two of the most common include PIMP (Plan, Intent, Means, and Prior attempts) and SAD PERSONS (Sex, Age, Depression, Previous attempt, Ethanol abuse, Rational thought loss, Social supports lacking, Organized plan, No spouse, Sickness).

- When using the clinical interview to assess suicide lethality, you should be familiar with the risk factors associated with committing suicide. Table 7.19 provides an overview of these risk factors.

In addition to the clinical interview, several standardized tests can be used to assess suicide lethality. Table 7.20 presents standardized assessments most commonly used to assess for suicide lethality.

7.5.4 Practice Multiple-Choice Items: Clinical Assessment

1. Which objective personality test is designed to identify *DSM-IV-TR* Axis II personality disorders?
   a. California Psychological Inventory (CPI)
   b. Millon Clinical Multiaxial Inventory (MCM-III)
   c. Myers-Briggs Type Indicator (MBTI)
   d. Minnesota Multiphasic Personality Inventory-2 (MMPI-2)

2. The Myers-Briggs Type Indicator uses four dichotomous scales to measure personality. What specific aspect of personality does the sensing vs. intuition scale measure?
   a. How you perceive the world around you
   b. How you make decisions
   c. Where your energy is directed
   d. How you deal with the external world

3. Which one of the following is NOT true?
   a. Rating scales usually evaluate the quantity of an attribute.
   b. Rating scales are highly subjective because they rely on the rater's perception of the behavior.
   c. Rating scales are used to assess the presence or absence of an attribute.
   d. Rating scales often assess a broad range of behaviors.

4. Performance assessments
   a. require examinees to complete a paper-and-pencil test.
   b. require examinees to perform a task.
   c. are advantageous when working with highly verbal clients.
   d. All of the above.

5. Based on the risk factors associated with committing suicide, which client is MOST likely to commit suicide?
   a. An 18-year-old, African American male with a family history of suicide
   b. A 78-year-old, widowed Caucasian female who is depressed
   c. A 40-year-old, Hispanic woman with a diagnosed anxiety disorder and a history of alcohol abuse
   d. A 67-year-old, divorced Caucasian male who recently lost his job and reports feelings of hopelessness

Answer Key: 1. b; 2. a; 3. c; 4. b; 5. d.

7.6 SPECIAL ISSUES IN ASSESSMENT

As the field of assessment continues to expand, it is important for professional counselors to know how diversity in culture and technology affect the assessment process. In the remainder of this sixth section of Chapter 7, we discuss assessment bias and the different types of biases that can occur during the assessment process; the ACA and NBCC ethical guidelines for reducing assessment bias; the differences between test translation and test adaptation; the use of test adaptation and the International Test Commission (ITC) guidelines for adapting assessments; and the advantages and disadvantageous associated with computer-based testing.

7.6.1 Bias in Assessment

Bias in assessment is a broad term that refers to an individual or group being deprived of the opportunity to demonstrate their true skills, knowledge, abilities, and personalities on a given assessment. Bias can result from the test itself, the examinee, the examiner, the testing context, or global systems that affect the examinee. For example, suppose you are a college counselor working with an international student who presents with depression. Given that this student recently arrived in the United States from an impoverished area in West Africa, what types of biases might occur when using assessments with this client?

7.6.1.1 TYPES OF BIAS IN ASSESSMENT Test bias occurs when the properties of a test cause an individual or particular group of individuals to score lower (negative bias) or higher (positive bias) on the test than the average score for the total population. This disparity in scores is due to factors that are not related to the true attribute being measured. Test bias frequently occurs when tests contain items that favor one group over another. For example, an item on a verbal analogies test that includes the word *bobsled* might tend to favor people living in northern regions over those who live in the south. Test bias also can occur when tests include the language or values of a distinct cultural group. For example, an international student may not understand test questions on an assessment written in English. Due to the language barriers, the assessment score does not represent her true ability.

- *Examiner bias* occurs when the examiner's beliefs or behavior influence test administration. For example, a professional counselor may believe that the international student does not understand English very well. Therefore, during a semi-structured interview, the counselor reads the questions slowly and follows up with lots of probes to ensure he fully understands the international student's situation. However, when conducting a semi-structured interview with American-born students, the counselor moves quickly through the questions, with minimal probing.
- *Interpretive bias* occurs when the examiner's interpretation of the test results provides unfair advantage or disadvantage to the client. For example, the professional counselor is aware that international students often experience distress while adjusting to American culture. As a result, the counselor immediately looks for signs of emotional distress when interpreting the international student's Rorschach inkblot test.
- *Response bias* occurs when clients use a response set (e.g., all yes or no) to answer test questions. For example, the international student may be embarrassed that he does not understand certain items on an assessment due to differences in culture. Therefore, she decides to answer yes to all of the questions she does not know.
- *Situational bias* occurs when testing conditions or situations differentially affect the performance of individuals from a particular group. For example, persons who are not from Western culture may not rely on a numerical concept of time. Therefore, the international student from West Africa may perform differently on a timed assessment than an American student would.
- *Ecological bias* occurs when global systems prevent members of a particular group of individuals from demonstrating their true skills, knowledge, abilities, and personalities on a given assessment. For example, ecological bias may occur if the college counseling center mandates that all students take the same Western-based career assessments. Because these assessments are written in English and endorse Western career theories and notions, the scores of the international student from West Africa may not be a true reflection of her abilities and personality.

7.6.1.2 REDUCING BIAS IN ASSESSMENT According to ethical codes outlined by the ACA and the NBCC, professional counselors must do the following:

- Choose assessments that are appropriate to use with multicultural populations.
- Use instruments that provide norms for the specific client population that is being assessed.
- Provide assessment instruments that use the most clear and understandable language for the client population.
- Consider how age, color, culture, disability, ethnic group, gender, language, religion, sexual orientation, and socioeconomic status affect test administration and interpretation.

In addition to following the ethical guidelines, professional counselors can reduce test bias in these ways:

- Understand the client's worldview to determine appropriate assessment methods.
- Consider a client's level of acculturation (i.e., number of generations in a new culture, language preferred, extent to which client socializes or comes in contact with those outside his or her own cultural group).
- Be knowledgeable about the culture of the client being assessed.
- Avoid relying solely on cultural stereotypes.

7.6.2 Test Translation and Test Adaptation

Test translation refers to a process by which test items are translated into the language spoken by examinees. Although test translation attempts to reduce cultural bias in testing, it has been heavily criticized for assuming equivalence in content and values across cultures. Because the translation of a test into a test-taker's native language is not enough to reduce test bias, test translation has been replaced by test adaptation.

Test adaptation involves the process of altering a test for a population that differs significantly from the original test population in terms of cultural background and language. The process includes translating language as well as empirically evaluating the cultural equivalence of the adapted test. The goal of test adaptation, then, is to develop two or more versions of the test that will elicit the same responses from test-takers regardless of the examinee's cultural or linguistic backgrounds. The ITC has developed guidelines for the adaptation of psychological and educational tests. Table 7.21 highlights the ITC guidelines.

TABLE 7.21   Overview of the ITC Test Adaptation Guidelines.

Context
- The effects of cultural differences should be minimized to the maximum extent possible.
- The degree to which the instrument's constructs overlap with the population of interest should be assessed.

Test Development and Adaptation
- The linguistic and cultural differences of the population for whom the adapted instrument is intended should be taken into account.
- The language used in the instrument's directions, rubrics, and test items should be appropriate for the intended population.
- The testing techniques, item formats, test convention, and procedures should be familiar to the intended population.
- The item content must be familiar to the intended population.
- Test developers and publishers must provide information concerning the adapted instrument's validity as well as content and linguistic equivalence of all test questions.

Administration
- Test administrators should anticipate problems that could arise during test administration and should take appropriate actions to remedy these issues.
- Test administrators should be aware of and sensitive to the factors related to stimulus materials, administration procedures, and response modes that can influence scores.
- The instructions used during test administration should be in the target language of the intended population.

Documentation/Scoreinterpretations
- When a test is adapted, test developers should provide documentation of these changes as well as evidence of equivalence.
- Test developers must provide information regarding the ways in which sociocultural and ecological contexts can affect test performance.

7.6.3 Computer-Based Testing

Computer-based testing (CBT), also known as *computer-based assessment* (CBA), refers to a method for administering, analyzing, and interpreting tests through the use of computer technology, software programs, or Internet sites. Computer-based testing is available for a variety of personality, intelligence, ability, and career development assessments. As with pencil-and-paper tests, computer-based testing has many benefits and some disadvantages.

Benefits Associated with Computer-Based Testing
- Administration time and cost are reduced.
- Scoring accuracy is greater.
- Feedback concerning client performance is quick, sometimes immediate.
- Standardization of test administration procedures is enhanced.
- Clients prefer tests administered via the computer when responding to sensitive topics.
- Reports are computer generated.

Disadvantages Associated with Computer-Based Testing
- Electronic equipment needed to administer the test can be expensive.
- Widely used assessments may not by compatible with computer-based testing.
- A lack of standards exists for obtaining and administering computer-based tests.
- It minimizes human contact and involvement.
- Computer-based tests may not have appropriate normative data.

7.6.3.1 COMPUTER-ADAPTIVE TESTING   Some computer-based tests have the ability to adapt the test structure and items to the examinee's ability level. This is known as **computer-adaptive testing**. The GRE is an example of a commonly used computer-adaptive test. Computer-adaptive tests provide precise scores and quickly assess the examinee's ability level. As a result, test administration is reduced without sacrificing score accuracy.

7.6.4 Practice Multiple-Choice Items: Special Issues in Assessment

1. Requiring minority students to take standardized college admission exams that were designed for Caucasian, middle-class students constitutes _____ bias.
   a. interpretive
   b. situational
   c. ecological
   d. test

2. According to the ACA and NBCC codes of ethics, professional counselors
   a. must rely on cultural stereotypes when assessing multicultural populations.
   b. do not need to be knowledgeable about the client's culture if using a multiculturally appropriate assessment.

    c. use instruments that provide norms for the specific client population that is being assessed.

    d. All of the above.

3. Test adaptation

    a. has been replaced by test translation.

    b. strives to elicit the same responses from test-takers regardless of the examinee's cultural or linguistic backgrounds.

    c. has been heavily criticized for assuming equivalence in content and values across cultures.

    d. provides linguistic equivalence but not content equivalence.

4. Which one of the following is NOT an advantage associated with computer-based testing?

    a. Greater scoring accuracy

    b. Can provide immediate feedback concerning client performance

    c. Clients prefer test administration via the computer when responding to sensitive topics

    d. Minimizes human contact and involvement in the testing process

5. A test that has the ability to modify the test structure and items to the examinee's ability level is known as a(n)

    a. computer-adaptive test.

    b. intelligent test.

    c. computer-based test.

    d. ethical test.

Answer Key: 1. c; 2. c; 3. b; 4. d; 5. a.

7.7 KEY POINTS FOR CHAPTER 7: ASSESSMENT

- Modern-day assessment has been shaped by the work of 19th-century scientists such as William Wundt, James Cattell, and Sir Francis Galton and 20th-century developments in intelligence, ability, personality, and interest testing.

- Assessment in counseling is used in diagnosing and treatment planning, client placement, admission decisions, and the selection of candidates into special programming or job positions.

- The ACA and the NBCC provide guidelines that outline the ethical use of assessments. These guidelines include counselor competence, obtaining client informed consent, releasing results only to qualified professionals, selecting appropriate assessment instruments, indicating concerns regarding test validity and reliability when providing assessment results, administering assessments under conditions that facilitate optimal results, not using outdated assessments, and using scientific methodology to develop new assessments.

- Several federal and state laws and legal guidelines established by court cases affect assessment practices.

- Several sources that provide information related to assessment purposes and procedures are available to the professional counselor. Popular sources include the *Mental Measurements Yearbook, Tests in Print, Tests,* and *Test Critiques*.

- Validity refers to how accurately scores from an instrument measure a given construct. Three types of validity are used in test construction: content validity, criterion validity, and construct validity.

- Reliability refers to the consistency of scores attained by the same person on different administrations of the same test. The four types of validity used in test construction are test-retest, alternate form, internal consistency, and inter-rater reliability.

- Assessments can be reliable but not valid; however, valid tests are always reliable. However, keep in mind that assessment measures have to have *both* validity and reliability to be considered credible.

- Test theory, which strives to reduce test error and enhance construct reliability and validity, affect test construction. Two influential test theories include classical test theory and item response theory.

- Raw scores are meaningless and must be converted into derived scores. Derived scores give meaning to raw test scores by comparing an individual's score with those of the norm group.

- Normal distributions are the foundation on which derived scores are built. In a normal distribution the majority of test scores fall close to the mean with very few scores falling to either extreme. As a result, a normal distribution forms a bell curve when graphed, where the mean, median, and mode fall in the center.

- Norm-referenced assessments make meaning from raw scores by comparing an individual's score to the norm group. Criterion-referenced assessments, on the other hand, compare an individual's score to a predetermined standard.

- Commonly used derived scores include z-scores, T scores, percentiles, normal curve equivalents, stanines, and deviation IQs.

- Achievement tests are an assessment of ability and are designed to assess what one has learned at the time of testing. Achievement tests include survey batteries, diagnostic tests, and readiness tests.

- Aptitude tests also evaluate ability and are designed to assess what a person is capable of learning. Aptitude tests include cognitive ability tests, intelligence tests, and vocational aptitude testing.

- Intelligence is a difficult construct to define because it is not covert. Throughout the past few centuries, several theorists have developed theories that attempt to identify and describe intelligence. Modern-day intelligence testing has been heavily influenced by these theories.

- The Wechsler scales are the most widely used intelligence test. The three versions of this test accommodate different age groups: Wechsler Adult Intelligence Scale WAIS-IV), Wechsler Intelligence Scale for Children (WISC-IV), and Wechsler Preschool and Primary Scale of Intelligence (WPPSI-III).

- Ability assessments are often used in high stakes testing to make major educational decisions concerning student promotion, retention, educational placement, and entrance into college.
- Objective personality assessment refers to the use of standardized, self-report instruments to assess a person's affective realm. Projective personality assessments, on the other hand, assess personality by interpreting a client's response to ambiguous stimuli.
- Informal assessments use subjective techniques to identify a client's specific strengths and needs. These techniques include observation, clinical interviewing, rating scales, and classification systems.
- The Mental Status Exam (MSE) is commonly used by professional counselors to obtain a comprehensive overview of a client's mental health. The MSE assesses a client's appearance, attitude, movement and behavior, mood, thought content, perceptions, thought processes, judgment and insight, and intellectual functioning and memory.
- When conducting suicide assessments, the professional counselor evaluates the client's suicide lethality. Specific risk factors are associated with committing suicide, and professional counselors must be familiar with and assess for these factors.
- Bias in assessment occurs when individuals are deprived of the opportunity to demonstrate their true skills, knowledge, abilities, and personalities on a given assessment. Specific types of bias include test bias, examiner bias, interpretive bias, response bias, situational bias, and ecological bias.
- Test adaptation refers to the process of altering a test for a population that is culturally different from the original test population. Test adaptation is concerned with developing an adapted test that demonstrates linguistic and conceptual equivalence.
- Computer-based testing involves the administration, analysis, and interpretation of tests via computer technology, software programs, and Internet sites. Although computer-based testing is cost effective and provides greater scoring accuracy, no standards have been developed for administering these tests, and human involvement in the testing process is minimized.

CHAPTER 8

Research and Program Evaluation

8.1 INTRODUCTION TO RESEARCH AND PROGRAM EVALUATION

Research and program evaluation as a core area in counselor preparation covers a broad range of theoretical and technical issues regarding planning and evaluating counseling interventions, assessing individuals' attitudes and knowledge about various phenomena, and developing statistically based counseling models. This area includes topics such as quantitative, qualitative, mixed-method, and single-subject research design, statistics, and program evaluation, as well as ethical, professional, and cultural issues in research.

Over the past several years, administrations of the National Counselor Examination (NCE) have included 16 (of the 160 total, or 10% of the) scored items (plus some trial items) designed to measure research and program evaluation (rank = 5.5 of 8; slightly below the average number of items for the eight domains). The average item difficulty index was .60 (rank = 8 of 8; the most difficult domain of item content), meaning that the average item in this domain was correctly answered by 60% of test-takers.

Over the past several years, administrations of the Counselor Preparation Comprehensive Exam (CPCE) have included 17 scored items designed to measure research and program evaluation, plus several trial items that do not count toward one's overall score. The average item difficulty index was .62, meaning that the average item in this domain was correctly answered by 62% of test-takers, making this set of items among the most difficult on the examination.

The Council for Accreditation of Counseling and Related Educational Programs (CACREP, 2009) defines standards for research and program evaluation as studies that provide an understanding of research methods, statistical analysis, needs assessment, and program evaluation, including all of the following:

   a. the importance of research in advancing the counseling profession;
   b. research methods such as qualitative, quantitative, single-case designs, action research, and outcome-based research;
   c. statistical methods used in conducting research and program evaluation;
   d. principles, models, and applications of needs assessment, program evaluation, and the use of findings to effect program modifications;
   e. the use of research to inform evidence-based practice; and
   f. ethical and culturally relevant strategies for interpreting and reporting the results of research and/or program evaluation studies. (p. 13)

Before addressing these objectives more specifically, it is valuable to note important historical, ethical, legal, and professional considerations in research and program evaluation. In this first section of Chapter 8 we discuss key paradigms in research and program evaluation; ethical considerations and important research studies in developing ethical standards; and legal considerations in research and program evaluation.

8.1.1 Key Paradigms in Research and Program Evaluation

Several research paradigms have shaped modern research design and practice. **Positivism** is one such paradigm and was formally developed in the early years (late 17th century) of the Age of Enlightenment.

Positivism states that an objective truth exists and can only be understood if directly observable. That is, truth must be directly measurable. Positivism has been closely tied to quantitative research (the use of measurement and statistics to answer research questions).

- Although it shares many of the characteristics of positivism, such as the idea that there is a universal truth, **post-positivism** departs by saying that this truth can only be approximated because of inherent errors present when measuring reality. The concept of measurement error in terms of validity and reliability is emphasized (see Chapter 7). Post-positivism tends to be more prevalent in quantitative research designs.
- *Constructivism* (sometimes referred to as *interpretivism*) differs from both positivism and post-positivism because this paradigm contends that there are multiple realities or perspectives for any given phenomenon. Truth differs for individuals and is an internal manifestation, as opposed to positivism and post-positivism, which exert that truth is external to the individual. Many of today's qualitative research methods find their foundation in constructivism.
- The last of the main paradigms is the **critical/ideological paradigm**, which centers on researchers taking a proactive role and confronting the social structure and conditions facing oppressed or underprivileged groups. This paradigm is also heavily tied to qualitative research design.

8.1.2 Key Ethical Considerations in Research and Program Evaluation

Ethics play an important role in counseling research. Ethics help guide the researcher in designing and conducting the study and reaching a decision regarding the methods used for collection of data. The Office of Research Integrity (a U. S. government organization) and the American Counseling Association (ACA) both provide guidance when it comes to research ethics. Before such organizations provided guidelines concerning the ethical practice of research, countless unethical studies were conducted.

During the height of World War II, Nazi Germany conducted experiments on human subjects that defied any moral standards and made it necessary to provide some boundaries that defined ethical practices in research studies. These studies, labeled the **Nazi Medical War Crimes**, involved exploiting and deceiving prisoners to understand how the human body would react to various conditions. This paved the way for the **Nuremberg Code** in 1948. However, unethical research continued, and not until 1979 with the advent of the **Belmont Report**, were all researchers held to standards that we would consider ethical today. In addition to the Nazi Medical War Crime studies, other important studies include these:

- **Milgram obedience study:** Stanley Milgram sought to investigate blind obedience and the use of deception without debriefing. Participants were deceived into thinking the study involved investigating memory and learning. Through a series of shocks (15–450 volts), "learners" (who were part of Milgram's team) pretended to be shocked by "teachers" (participants) when responding with incorrect answers. Although most participants showed signs of internal struggle, 65% "shocked" learners at the maximum level. There was no debriefing of the study.
- **Tuskegee syphilis study:** Physicians studying the long-term effects of syphilis (i.e., data from autopsies) told 400 African American males with syphilis they were receiving treatment for "bad blood." The study began in 1932 and lasted well into the 1970s. Participants were never informed of their actual diagnosis and, even when penicillin was discovered as a treatment in the 1940s, the participants never received the drug. This study, more than any other, led to construction of the Belmont Report and hastened the call for informed consent, right to withdraw, and guidelines for use of deception.
- **Jewish Chronic Disease Hospital study:** Both healthy and unhealthy patients were injected with live cancer cells so that researchers could better understand the impact of cancer based on health status. Participants never gave informed consent and were not told they were being injected with cancer cells.
- **Willowbrook study:** Willowbrook, a school for children with mental disabilities, became the setting for researchers interested in studying the effects of hepatitis in a controlled setting. Parents who wanted to enroll their children in the school signed an informed consent to allow their children to be injected with the hepatitis virus. Parents were never informed of their right to decline the injections for their children, nor were they told the long-term effects of hepatitis.

In 2005, the **ACA** *Code of Ethics* further solidified ethical and unethical behaviors with regard to counseling research (see http//www.counseling.org/ethics). ACA also addressed reporting false data, researcher/participant relationships, and source credit for published works, including works from other researchers.

8.1.3 Key Legal Considerations in Research and Program Evaluation

To protect participants, legal standards also have been developed. These standards protect participants while giving clear direction as to the use, collection methods, disclosure of personal information, and evaluation procedures in biomedical and behavior-modifying research.

- Much of the information regarding legal policies can be found in Title 45: Public Health Part 46: Protection of Human Subjects of the *Code of Federal Regulations* (45 CFR 46). Subpart A, or the **Common Rule**, outlines policies that guide researchers who use human subjects. It requires these studies to be approved by an institutional review board (see section 8.1.3.1). Other subparts protect the rights of those who may be more vulnerable to abuse, such as children, fetuses, and those with mental disabilities.

- In 1996, the U.S. Department of Health and Human Services established very specific guidelines on the use of participants' private health information. These guidelines are known as the Health Insurance Portability and Accountability Act (HIPAA) of 1996.

8.1.3.1 INSTITUTIONAL REVIEW BOARD As part of the 45 CFR mandates, any institution receiving federal funding must go through an **institutional review board (IRB)** to conduct research with human subjects. Even though studies are conducted at institutions without federal funding, it is still best to have research proposals reviewed by an IRB since legal interpretations of these stipulations have come to mean that if one study is conducted by the institution, then all research at that institution should be IRB approved.

- Although institutions support their own IRBs, they typically operate under the same general guidelines. Proposals must typically outline who the participants will be, how they will be sought, what risks participants may face, how those risks will be mitigated, and compliance with informed consent practices.
- The board is made up of at least five members. The makeup of the members includes those who have had some experience with research at the institution, members who are not researchers, and at least one representative from the community. The IRB, not the researcher, has the ability to decide if the research study should be exempt from federal oversight, should include some modifications to mitigate risks, or should be denied the use of human subjects all together.

8.1.4 Practice Multiple-Choice Items: Introduction to Research and Program Evaluation

1. A professional counselor is interested in developing an affirmative policy after investigating the treatment of gay, lesbian, and bisexual individuals in a community program. This study is represented best by which paradigm?
   a. Interpretivism
   b. Post-positivism
   c. Positivism
   d. Critical

2. The paradigm characterized most by the notion that with enough research we can gain knowledge of a universal truth is
   a. interpretivism.
   b. post-positivism.
   c. positivism.
   d. critical.

3. The _____ study failed the most to outline participants' voluntariness.
   a. Belmont
   b. Milgram's Obedience
   c. Jewish Chronic Disease Hospital
   d. Willowbrook

4. _____ outlines research participants' rights and researchers' responsibilities in conducting research.
   a. HIPAA
   b. 45 CRF 46
   c. Nuremberg Code
   d. Proposition 16

5. _____ outlines the privacy rights of participants pertaining to health information.
   a. HIPAA
   b. 45 CFR 46
   c. Nuremberg Code
   d. Proposition 16

Answer Key: 1. d; 2. c; 3. d; 4. b; 5. a.

8.2 KEY CONCEPTS IN RESEARCH AND PROGRAM EVALUATION

This second section of Chapter 8 will discuss some of the foundational aspects and key concepts in research and program evaluation, including types of variables, research questions, hypotheses and hypothesis testing, and sampling considerations.

8.2.1 Variables

A **variable** is a construct that has at least two levels or categories and, therefore, can vary. Variables might include such specifics as intelligence, anxiety, achievement, self-esteem, program type, spiritual affiliation, gender, and so forth. The basic requirement is that the construct must be multidimensional. Counselors should be aware of the three primary types of variables:

- An *independent variable* (IV) is a construct that is manipulated or controlled in some way by the professional counselor. For example, sex (i.e., male, female) and treatment condition (e.g., treatment group, wait-list control group) may be variables under the control of the researcher, and each may be expected to influence performance on some dependent variable.
- A *dependent variable* (DV) is the outcome variable that is influenced by an independent variable. For example, if a professional counselor wants to measure the time it takes various children to put together a certain object from identical pieces, a dependent variable would be the amount of time (in minutes or seconds) it takes for each child to put together the object correctly.
- Other variables that could affect the dependent variable are referred to as *extraneous variables* and should be closely monitored. A *confounding variable* is a special case of extraneous variables that the experimenter has not controlled for in the research design (i.e., it is not designated to be an independent variable) but that also affects the dependent variable—that is, at least two variables (i.e., an independent variable and a confounding variable) may create change at the same time. For example, if an experimenter allows participants to exercise at different rates (the independent variable or treatment) but does not control how much the participants eat (e.g., a potential confounding

In the Sample	In the Population	
	H_o False	H_o True
H_o is rejected	Correct hit $(1-\beta)$ (i.e., power)	Type I error (α)
H_o is retained	Type II error (β)	Correct hit $(1-\alpha)$

FIGURE 8.1 Decision making using the null hypothesis.

variable) and then measures weight loss (i.e., the dependent variable), the experimenter cannot tell if the weight loss is due to diet or exercise because the amount one eats could confound the ultimate weight of the participant.

8.2.2 Research Questions

A **research question** is a statement that identifies what a research study hopes to examine. There are three major types of research questions.

- *Relational research questions* examine the relationship between variables. An example is "What is the relationship between gender and preference for child discipline methods?"
- *Descriptive research questions* examine and describe what already exists. An example is "How many individuals are involved in motor vehicle accidents each year?"
- *Causal research questions* attempt to determine the cause-and-effect relationship among variables. An example is "Do commercials broadcast during the Super Bowl lead to greater product sales?"

8.2.3 Research Hypotheses and Hypothesis Testing

The three types of hypotheses are research hypothesis, null hypothesis, and alternative hypothesis.

- A **research hypothesis** is a testable, concise statement involving the expected relationship between two or more variables. Research hypotheses can be a *nondirectional hypothesis* (i.e., "There is a significant relationship between amount of sleep and career satisfaction") or a *directional hypothesis* (i.e., "There is a significant *positive* relationship between amount of sleep and career satisfaction").
- A **null hypothesis** (H_o) is a statement that "There is no relationship" between an IV and DV. Although the professional counselor really believes there is some significant relationship between variables, a null hypothesis is examined via statistics and will provide information about the likelihood (i.e., probability, or *p* value) that the actual findings could be obtained if the null hypothesis were true. Thus, by rejecting a null hypothesis, you are supporting the theory that generated the research hypothesis.
- A plausible **alternative hypothesis** (H_1) is developed in order to be eliminated and addresses the question "What else could be causing the results?" Alternative hypotheses usually involve outlining potential extraneous variables. For the aforementioned research hypotheses, examples of alternative hypotheses might be "There is a significant

positive relationship among job mentorship and career satisfaction" and "There is a significant interaction effect between gender and tutoring opportunities for achievement."

Hypothesis testing involves the decision-making process of determining if the null hypothesis is to be accepted or rejected (see Figure 8.1).

- Two important concepts in hypothesis testing include significance level and statistical significance. **Significance level** is a threshold for rejecting the null hypothesis, with values associated with α (alpha) (typically .001, .01, or .05). **Statistical significance** refers to the cutoff point (i.e., critical value); any value that exceeds the cutoff point will be noted as statistically significant. For example, if the significance level is set at .05, a *p* value of less than .05 would indicate significant results.
- Two types of errors are associated with hypothesis testing, or testing for statistical significance. A **Type I error** (alpha, α) occurs when a decision is made to reject a null hypothesis when that null hypothesis is in fact true. A **Type II error** (beta, β) occurs when a decision is made to retain the null hypothesis that should have been rejected because the null hypothesis was indeed false.
- **Power**, a term related to errors in hypothesis testing, refers to the likelihood of detecting a significant relationship between variables when one is really there. Thus, power is avoiding a Type II error ($1-\beta$). Power can be increased by increasing alpha (α), increasing sample size, increasing effect size, minimizing error, using a one-tailed test, or using a parametric statistic (see section 8.6).

8.2.4 Sampling Considerations

Researchers usually cannot access and study an entire population (i.e., all clients with depression), so they must sample willing participants (e.g., patients with depression who present at a clinic for treatment and volunteer for a study). How the sample of participants is selected is a very important research consideration. Quantitative sampling can be classified as probability and nonprobability sampling. **Probability sampling** involves sampling a known population. In other words, a professional counselor can sample just a small percentage of the population using randomization. **Nonprobability sampling** is more common in counseling research and typically involves accessing samples of convenience.

Probability sampling methods include (moving from most to least representative of a population) the following:

- *Simple random sampling:* Every member of the population has an equal chance of being selected. Typically, professional counselors use a table of random digits to select large samples.

- *Systematic sampling:*   Every *n*th element is chosen. For example, every 10th person on a national registry of school counselors would be selected.
- *Stratified random sampling:*   A population is divided into subgroups based on important characteristics (e.g., gender, race, marital status), and the professional counselor draws randomly from the subgroups. The degree of sampling per subgroup can be reflective of actual percentages in a population or may be the same sample size per subgroup.
- *Cluster sampling:*   The professional counselor identifies existing subgroups and not individual participants. This method is typically less representative than other probability sampling methods.
  - *Multi-stage sampling* is common in cluster sampling procedures that provide better selection controls. This might include a two-stage random sample (e.g., randomly select 60 schools and then 20 classes from those schools), three-stage random sample (e.g., randomly selecting 200 school districts, then 20 schools from each district, and then 10 classes per school), and so forth.

Nonprobability sampling methods include the following:

- *Convenience sampling:*   This is the most common sampling method. A professional counselor selects an easily accessible population that most likely does not fully represent the population of interest. For example, in order to assess the relationship between ethnicity and spiritual values, a professional counselor may survey clients who are willing to participate.
- *Purposeful sampling:*   A professional counselor selects a sample from a population based on who will be most informative about a topic of interest. Participants are selected because they represent needed characteristics.
- *Quota sampling:*   This method is similar to cluster and stratified sampling. However, there is no randomization. The professional counselor simply draws the needed number of participants with the needed characteristic (e.g., gender, race) from the convenience sample.

An important concept related to sampling method is randomization. *Randomization* helps to maximize the credibility and generalizability of a study's findings. It involves either or both random selection and random assignment.

- **Random selection** involves selecting participants from a population so that every member of the population has an equal chance of being selected. Random selection is closely related to external validity (see section 8.2.7).
- **Random assignment** involves randomly assigning participants to different groups, such as a treatment or control group. Random assignment helps to ensure that groups are equal and that any systematic group differences (common with nonprobability sampling) are due to chance. To this end, random assignment is closely related to internal validity.

8.2.5   Experimental and Control Conditions

In experimental designs, participants may be randomly assigned to experimental (treatment) conditions or control group conditions. A *treatment group* or experimental group is the group of participants receiving the active treatment under study. A **control group** comprises those participants in a study who share very similar attributes with the experimental group but who do not receive treatment. This group is critical in validating the results of an experimental treatment or otherwise untested theory. Three types of control groups are commonly used in the counseling literature: (a) a *wait list control group* (i.e., individuals who are awaiting treatment, but not receiving any treatment at all); (b) a *placebo control group* (sometimes call the "active placebo"; i.e., individuals who receive some "treatment" that will not affect the dependent variable, e.g., sugar pill); and (c) a *treatment as usual* (TAU) *control group* (i.e., individuals receive whatever treatment they would ordinarily receive if they sought treatment but do not receive the special treatment under study).

Another important consideration involves how the treatment and control conditions are administered. For example, in a **blind study**, the participants are not aware of the condition (treatment or control group) to which they have been assigned. In a **double blind study**, neither the researcher nor the participant knows if the participant belongs to the experimental group or the control group. A double blind study helps to combat subjective bias by both the researcher and the participant in the study. Randomly assigning participants to either the experimental group or control group greatly reduces the influences of the placebo effect or researcher bias. The **placebo effect** refers to the positive effects of a treatment felt by participants even though no treatment was actually administered. The famous example of the placebo effect involves individuals who, previously feeling ill, reported feeling better when given simple sugar pills. It is not unusual for 20 to 30% of participants in a placebo group to report substantial symptom reduction, even though they are not receiving an active treatment.

8.2.6   Internal Validity

Internal validity may be defined as the notion that changes in the DV are due to the effects of the IV(s). The degree to which extraneous variables can be controlled strengthens the study's internal validity. Several threats to internal validity are possible in counseling research (see Table 8.1 for examples of each). These threats include:

- *History:*   Extraneous incidents occur during the research. These events may occur within or outside the study. The longer the research study, the more likely history threats will occur.
- *Selection:*   Group differences exist before the intervention due to a lack of random assignment. Selection threats are common when participants are initially chosen based on group membership (e.g., gender, third-grade classes).
- *Statistical regression:*   Scores of participants who were selected because of their extreme score on a dependent

TABLE 8.1 Examples of Internal Validity Threats.

History	A group of students being treated for depression have a classmate commit suicide.
Selection	Two counseling agencies receive funding and a professional counselor wants to examine if increased funding yields more client participation. Differences between agencies independent to funding may have more of an effect on client participation.
Statistical regression	Participants who are selected because they are highly anxious on pretest scores "improve" (i.e., become significantly less anxious) over time (even though the treatment was not effective).
Testing	Second-graders take a spelling test at the beginning of a class and perform well on the same spelling test a few weeks later.
Instrumentation	The meaning associated with rubrics that professional counselors use to observe clients' changes over time.
Attrition	Most females drop out of a 6-month study on achievement motivation.
Maturation	A participant becomes tired while answering a 60-minute survey packet and begins to respond randomly.
Diffusion of treatment	Two counseling groups at the same agency discuss the treatments each is receiving.
Experimenter effects	The school counselor rates a high-achieving student referred to counseling as nonaggressive.
Subject effects	Members in a control group not receiving an incentive in a study investigating the effect of incentives in community service become resistant and refuse to engage in community work.

variable (e.g., severely depressed, low achievement, low self-efficacy) are affected. Those with extremely high or low scores will likely "regress toward the mean" when retested due to statistical regression. Thus, improvements in a participant's score on the dependent variable may be more of a result of a statistical phenomenon than any intervention.

- *Testing:* The test itself has an impact on individuals, particularly when pretests are involved. **Practice effects (memory effects)** are common (i.e., participants know what to expect and learn something from a pretest that helps to improve their performance on future tests). Testing effects are always to be considered when pretests are involved.
- *Instrumentation:* Changes in the instrument (e.g., paper-pencil, computerized, mechanized device, evaluator) affect results. Instrumentation may change meaning over the course of a study.
- *Attrition:* Participants drop out of a research study. Attrition (mortality) is an issue when individuals systematically drop out of a study. The risk for attrition is especially high for longitudinal studies.
- *Maturation:* Changes in a participant over time affect the DV. These tend to be normal developmental changes (e.g., cognitive ability changes, increased stress, boredom, fatigue, mental disability issues).
- *Diffusion of treatment:* The effects of an intervention are felt by those in another group. This is particularly a threat when participant groups are in close proximity to, or have contact with, one another.
- *Experimenter effects:* Bias of the investigator influences participant responses. Some of the well-known effects include the **halo effect** (i.e., the professional counselor's subjective, usually positive and initial, perceptions of the participant are generalized to other traits and characteristics) and the **Hawthorne effect** (i.e., the presence of the investigator affects participant re-

sponses independent of any intervention), sometimes called *reactivity*.
- *Subject effects:* Participants change their behaviors or attitudes based on their understanding of their role as participants. Participants will pick up cues, known as **demand characteristics**, from the researcher or research setting that motivate them in certain ways.

8.2.7 External Validity

External validity refers to the ability to generalize the results of a study to a larger group. The two types of external validity are *population external validity* (i.e., involves the population to which one can generalize) and *ecological external validity* (i.e., involves the conditions or settings to which one can generalize). For both forms of external validity, the professional counselor must sufficiently describe the participants, variables, study procedures, and settings so that readers can ascertain the degree of external validity of a particular study. Several threats are associated with external validity. In general, the more a professional counselor controls for these threats, the more likely internal validity threats will increase and vice versa. Some of these threats include the following:

- *Novelty effect:* A new treatment produces positive results just because it is novel to participants.
- *Experimenter effect:* (See description in section 8.2.6.)
- *History by treatment effect:* An experiment is conducted in a particular time period replete with contextual factors that cannot be duplicated easily in another setting.
- *Measurement of the dependent variable:* Similar to the instrumentation threat described in 8.2.6, the effectiveness of a program may depend on the type of measurement used in the study.
- *Time of measurement by treatment effect:* Timing of the administration of a posttest may influence the posttest results.

8.2.8 Practice Multiple-Choice Items: Key Concepts in Research and Evaluation

1. The type of counseling program a client selects would most likely be an example of a(n)
   a. independent variable.
   b. dependent variable.
   c. null variable.
   d. extraneous variable.

2. A(n) _____ variable can create an uncontrolled effect in a study's outcome.
   a. independent
   b. dependent
   c. null
   d. extraneous

3. Detecting a significant relationship when one is present is known as
   a. alpha.
   b. beta.
   c. effect size.
   d. power.

4. Randomly identifying a counseling agency that serves clients with attention-deficit/hyperactivity disorder (AD/HD) and sampling its entire staff is an example of a _____ sampling method.
   a. simple random
   b. cluster
   c. quota
   d. systematic

5. Which of the following internal validity threats is LEAST likely related to a repeated measures study for a group of sixth-graders?
   a. History
   b. Maturation
   c. Attrition
   d. Diffusion of treatment

Answer Key: 1. a; 2. d; 3. d; 4. b; 5. d.

8.3 BROAD TYPES OF RESEARCH

Research designs are categorized in several ways, yet typically include four key, broad categories: quantitative, qualitative, mixed-method, and single subject. These four types of research designs are described in more detail later in this section of Chapter 8. Additional, more specific forms of research that may be classified as one or more of these four types of research include descriptive research, longitudinal and cross-sectional designs, survey research, and action research.

Quantitative research attempts to capture the relationship between two things that can be measured numerically. In other words, experimenters weigh quantitative properties against each other to find a connection between the two. Typically, professional counselors test a hypothesis by looking at a descriptive or causal relationship among variables. Results usually involve numbers that are typically displayed in a statistically significant manner. This is often contrasted with qualitative research or referenced when qualitative research and quantitative research are integrated as in mixed-method research designs. Some examples of quantitative research include the following:

- Determining waiting room wait times
- Experimental drug studies with two groups, one being given a placebo and the other the actual drug
- Survey based studies on voter preferences

Quantitative research is explained in greater detail in section 8.4.

Qualitative research attempts to answer questions about *how* a behavior or phenomenon occurs. Data are typically represented in words rather than numbers and usually take the form of interview transcripts, field notes, pictures, video, or artifacts. The sampling is usually not randomized like that of a quantitative study, and the research can be more exploratory, meaning a hypothesis is not being tested. There is also greater subjectivity as the professional counselor plays a key role in the research. Qualitative research is useful in exploring policy or evaluating research itself. Some examples of qualitative research studies include the following:

- Observing and interviewing children to understand differences in the ways boys and girls play
- Studying a subculture to understand mores
- Case study research
- Policy evaluation

Qualitative research is explained in greater detail in section 8.7.

Mixed-method research blends or mixes qualities from quantitative and qualitative research. The most important characteristic of mixed-method research is that it can strengthen what quantitative or qualitative research methods can provide separately. It also can be applied to a broader range of inquiry because it is not confined to a single method. Mixed-method research also allows for results that apply more generally than if just using quantitative or qualitative methods. This type of research by its very nature can consume a great deal more time than using a quantitative or qualitative method alone. Generally two types of mixed-method research designs are considered (Creswell, 2003):

- *Concurrent design:* Quantitative and qualitative data are collected at the same time. This design is also known as *triangulation*.
- *Sequential design:* Either quantitative or qualitative data first is collected first. When professional counselors employ qualitative research strategies first, they are using an *exploratory* design. When they introduce a study with quantitative research strategies, they are using an *explanatory* design.

Some examples of mixed-method research design include the following:

- First conducting an experiment, and then following this up with questionnaires or interviews of the participants regarding their impressions of the results of the experiment.
- Conducting interviews and developing an instrument based on qualitative data.
- Observing a support group's nonverbal behaviors as the group completes a survey on religious values.

Single-subject research designs (SSRD) are those that measure how either receiving treatment or not receiving treatment affects a single subject (client) or group of subjects (clients) who can be treated as a single unit. This type of (usually quantitative) research is ordinarily applied to studies in which behavior is being modified or to examine the changes in a behavior. SSRDs are discussed in more detail in section 8.4.

8.3.1 Specialized Types of Research Designs

A number of more specialized types of research fall under the broad categories of both quantitative and qualitative research, including descriptive, longitudinal, cross-sectional, survey, and action research.

Descriptive research is used to describe a phenomenon and does not involve an intervention (treatment). Market researchers use it extensively to capture, for example, the buying habits of potential customers. This type of research can only present what is and how often something occurs; it cannot capture the reason a particular situation is occurring. Often descriptive research is conducted as either a precursor or in conjunction with other research methods—that is, before you look at relationships, you must be able to describe and summarize your data. Showing that children watch, on average, three hours of television a day would be an example of data collected from a descriptive research study.

Longitudinal research involves data collection for a particular group over time. Studying a group of children as they grow older would be an example of longitudinal design. Repeated assessments occur over time to track the pattern or development of a behavior. Limitations such as evaluation costs, cohort effects (i.e., effects shaped by individuals who share a common experience), or participant attrition (i.e., mortality) make this design more cumbersome than others.

Cross-sectional research examines different groups or cohorts at a particular point in time, with differences in experience being compared. Studying different age groups of children and how watching TV has affected their performance scores on tests at a certain time of day would be an example of a cross-sectional design. Although a cross-sectional design does not suffer the time or cost issues of a longitudinal design it has its own host of challenges. The comparisons made can only be inferred, since the same individuals are not being studied, and the developmental changes observed may in fact not be real change at all. Cohort effects also can still manifest themselves in this design. Longitudinal and cross-sectional designs are discussed in further detail in section 8.4.

Survey research is a method of collecting quantitative and qualitative data. A researcher selects a sample of participants and administers a series of questions to them. These questions can take the form of a written or verbal questionnaire, a survey, an interview, or a written statement from participants. The sample group can be small or large. The U.S. Census would be an example of a very large survey. Surveys are only as good as their design; choice of words, sentences, and format should all be considered when developing a survey. Also, the capabilities of those being surveyed must be taken into consideration. After all, giving a written survey to a group of participants with poor reading skills, or who may have difficulty understanding the questions, would make the results highly suspect.

Action research refers to research that is typically carried out by professional counselors in an effort to improve their own practice or organizational efficiency. It is site specific with results that can be applied to one's school or agency. Action research is a means to test new approaches, theories, or ideas and reflect on one's own teachings in an effort to enhance effectiveness. Some examples of action research include the following:

- Conducting a needs assessment among middle-school students to see what resources they need
- Interviewing adolescents about their experiences in a residential facility
- Presenting test scores to parents and school administrators to warrant intervention

In addition, although not a type of research, per se, the use of pilot studies is commonplace in research and serves an important function. A **pilot study** is smaller than a full-scale study and is designed to assess the feasibility of expanding a study to a much larger scale. For example, a pilot study might include the development and administration of a questionnaire to a focus group of 20 people to determine the effectiveness of the questionnaire before administering it to a group of 1,000 people. Pilot studies help to test run a study before it is carried out on a larger scale, and it also helps to ensure a greater likelihood of success for the full study. If the questionnaire in this example did not capture the expected responses because the questions were misleading, it would give the researcher an opportunity to revise the questions before conducting the full-scale study. Pilot studies are invaluable in identifying areas where the main study could fail.

8.3.2 Practice Multiple-Choice Items: Broad Types of Research

1. Conducting qualitative research followed by quantitative research is known as a(n)
   a. concurrent design.
   b. exploratory design.
   c. cross-sectional design.
   d. All of the above.

2. Analyzing digital recordings of patients with schizophrenia to determine the quality of their social interactions would most likely be an example of
   a. quantitative research.
   b. qualitative research.
   c. mixed-methods research.
   d. single-subject research design (SSRD).

3. Providing an overall picture of community crime statistics would most likely be an example of
   a. pilot research.
   b. survey research.
   c. descriptive research.
   d. single-subject research design (SSRD).

4. Pilot studies are useful for each of the following reasons EXCEPT
   a. they confirm post hoc a larger study's findings.
   b. they assist in revising data collection methods.
   c. they help to find potential limitations of a planned larger study.
   d. All of the above are useful aspects of pilot studies.

5. Which of the following is an example of a cross-sectional design?
   a. Studying children with reactive attachment disorder over their lives
   b. Examining participant attrition issues in a 10-year study
   c. Developing a needs assessment to investigate necessary policy changes
   d. Comparing the impact of a bullying incident across grade levels

Answer Key: 1. b; 2. b; 3. c; 4. a; 5. d.

8.4 QUANTITATIVE RESEARCH DESIGN

Quantitative research designs can be categorized as nonexperimental or experimental research designs. Table 8.2 provides examples of each type of quantitative research design.

- **Nonexperimental research designs** are those that are *exploratory* and *descriptive*. No intervention is involved, and thus no variables or conditions are manipulated. The goal of nonexperimental research designs is to observe and outline the properties of a variable.
- **Experimental research designs** involve an *intervention* whereby a counselor *manipulates conditions and variables*. The goal of experimental research is to assess cause-and-effect relationships among variables. In addition, random assignment is necessary for most experimental research designs. Experimental research designs may involve a single group, the comparison between a treatment and control group, or the comparison between two treatment groups.
- Although they may contain qualitative design components, SSRDs are primarily considered examples of quantitative research design. SSRDs involve the measurement of

behavioral and/or attitudinal changes across time for an individual or a few individuals. SSRDs are discussed in more detail in section 8.4.4.

In the remainder of this fourth section of Chapter 8, we discuss types of nonexperimental research designs, initial considerations in experimental research designs, types of experimental research designs, and characteristics and forms of SSRDs.

8.4.1 Nonexperimental Research Designs

The four types of nonexperimental research designs are descriptive, comparative, correlational, and ex post facto designs.

- A **descriptive design** is the most prevalent category of nonexperimental research design that includes thoroughly describing a variable at one time (simple descriptive design) or over time (longitudinal design).
  - *Simple descriptive designs* are one-shot surveys of a variable. For example, a simple descriptive study might involve exploring the average number of counseling sessions couples in a particular city attended. A special type of simple descriptive design is a cross-sectional design. *Cross-sectional designs* involve different groups of participants studied at the same time (e.g., the degree of financial support given to a university from alumni who graduated 1 year, 5 years, 10 years, and 20 years ago).
  - *Longitudinal designs* can be categorized further as trend, cohort, or panel studies. A **trend study** involves assessing the general population over time, with new individuals sampled each time data are collected. A **cohort study** refers to assessing the same population over time. A **panel study** involves studying the same individuals over time.
- A **comparative design** investigates group differences for a particular variable. This simplistic design allows the researcher to say there is a difference between groups but that it does not allow a causative inference. Some examples include examining racial and ethnic differences in the use of mental health services, gender differences in math achievement scores, and amount of change in career self-efficacy scores between two data collection times.

TABLE 8.2 Examples of Nonexperimental and Experimental Research Designs.

Nonexperimental Research Designs	Experimental Research Designs
Mental health prevalence among the elderly population over a 10-year period	The effectiveness of a study skills program for a class of third-graders
High school students' perspectives on school climate	A grief group in comparison to a study skills group in relieving grief symptoms
The relationship between amount of study time and test scores	A randomized trial of the impact of a mentoring program for students in alternative schools
Substance use among sixth-, seventh-, and eighth-graders	Comparing instructional strategies in two elementary classrooms
Predicting job performance based on rehabilitation services	Introducing incentives to one of two career counseling courses and measuring satisfaction

- A *correlational research design* describes the relationship between two variables. The function of this design is to compute a correlation coefficient that describes the strength and direction of a relationship. (Correlation coefficients are described in more detail in section 8.6.)
  - Counselors using a correlational design are interested in computing the shared variance of two variables (derived from the correlation coefficient). Consider a study assessing the relationship between severity of eating disorder symptoms and depression among adolescent females. If the relationship is $r = .50$, then there is a positive, moderately strong relationship between the number of eating disorder symptoms and level of depression. In addition, the amount of shared variance between the two variables (i.e., **coefficient of determination**) could be computed by squaring the correlational coefficient (i.e., $[.50]^2 = .25$, or 25% shared variance).
- An **ex post facto research design**, also known as a *causal-comparative design*, involves examining how an independent variable affects a dependent variable by assessing whether one or more pre-existing conditions possibly caused differences in groups. An ex post facto design is the nonexperimental design most closely resembling an experimental design because the counselor is interested in examining cause-and-effect relationships. Unfortunately, independent variables or conditions cannot be manipulated as the data have already been collected. Therefore, randomization is not possible. Ex post facto designs, therefore, involve looking at potential causes of a dependent variable after the fact (after data have been collected).
  - Consider the following example of an ex post facto design: You are interested in understanding factors related to the high number of high school dropouts in your school district. In brainstorming potential causes, you consider the role substance abuse might play in these rates. Using archival data, you use groups of matched characteristics with the exception of substance abuse. To this end, you may create three groups: those students denying substance use (Group A), those reporting occasional substance use—that is, once every few months (Group B), and those reporting heavy substance use—that is, at least once per week (Group C). Then you analyze the association between substance use and dropout rates. Of course, you could add additional independent variables, as long as groups are matched on characteristics with the exception of those variables in which you are interested.

8.4.2 Considerations in Experimental Research Designs

If one is interested in studying the effects of an intervention using one of the three types of experimental designs (discussed in section 8.4.3), the three general categories of experimental designs (i.e., within-subject designs, between-group designs,

and split-plot designs) should be considered in preparing for experimental research.

- A **within-subject design** involves assessing changes that occur within the participants in a group as they experience some intervention. The change that counselors are interested in measuring could be the change in a dependent variable before and after an intervention (repeated measures), or several interventions could be serially introduced to a group and outcomes assessed across time to determine the more effective interventions for a particular group. Thus, one or more treatments may be measured across time for a group.
- A **between-groups design** refers to exploring the effects of a treatment or intervention between two groups or among more than two groups. Each group involves a separate sample, and either group serves as a control (i.e., receives no treatment or intervention) or receives a distinct treatment.
- A **split-plot design** involves assessing a general intervention on the whole plot and assessing other treatments to subplots within the whole plot. Split-plot designs are appropriate for counseling research. Consider the example of the impact of a mentoring club for international students interested in preparing for careers after college graduation (i.e., whole plot). You are interested in what components of the club are effective in career preparation. You divide some of the students into smaller groups (i.e., subplots); these groups are designed to either focus on resume writing, job shadowing, or interviewing skills.

8.4.3 Experimental Research Designs

The three types of experimental research designs are pre-experimental, true-experimental and quasi-experimental designs. Table 8.3 presents each of these designs graphically. Some counselors categorize SSRDs as experimental designs, whereas others present them as a separate quantitative design. This guide takes the latter position and presents a discussion on SSRDs in section 8.4.4.

Pre-experimental designs do not use random assignment. Thus, they are not considered true experimental designs because they fail to control for internal validity threats. The following are the three types of pre-experimental designs:

- *One-group posttest-only design.* A group receives an intervention and change is measured. (Example: Depression symptoms are assessed after attending a structured counseling intervention.)
- *One-group pretest-posttest design.* A group is evaluated before and after an intervention. (Example: Depression symptoms are assessed before and after attending a structured counseling intervention to assess change in depression.)
- *Nonequivalent groups posttest-only design.* No attempt is made to begin the study with equivalent groups of participants. One group receives an intervention, and change is measured. Another group serves as a control and receives no intervention yet is assessed at the same

TABLE 8.3   Graphical Representations of Experimental Designs.

Pre-Experimental Designs

1. One-group posttest-only design	A: X → O
2. One-group pretest-posttest design	A: O → X → O
3. Nonequivalent groups posttest-only design	A: X → O
	B: n/a → O

True Experimental Designs

4. Randomized pretest-posttest control group design	(R) A: O → X → O
	(R) B: O → n/a → O
5. Randomized pretest-posttest comparison group design	(R) A: O → X → O
	(R) B: O → Y → O
	(R) C: O → Z → O
6. Randomized posttest-only control group design	(R) A: X → O
	(R) B: n/a → O
7. Randomized posttest-only comparison group design	(R) A: X → O
	(R) B: Y → O
8. Solomon four-group design	(R) A: O → X → O
	(R) B: O → n/a → O
	(R) C: n/a → X → O
	(R) D: n/a → n/a → O

Quasi-experimental Designs

9. Nonequivalent groups pretest-posttest control group designs	A: O → X → O
	B: O → n/a → O
10. Nonequivalent groups pretest-posttest comparison group designs	A: O → X → O
	B: O → Y → O
	C: O → Z → O
11. Time series designs	
A) One-group interrupted series design	A: O → O → O → X → O → O → O
B) Control group interrupted time series design	A: O → O → O → X → O → O → O
	B: O → O → O → n/a → O → O → O

Note. A, B, and C = groups; O = observation; X, Y, Z = interventions; (R) = random assignment; n/a = control group (no intervention or observation)

time as the other group. (Example. One group attends counseling while another group does not receive treatment. Depression symptoms are then measured for both groups after the counseling intervention.)

True experimental designs, also known as *randomized experimental designs*, are the gold standard for experimental designs in that they involve at least two groups for comparison and random assignment. Indeed, random assignment is usually what differentiates a true experimental design from a quasiexperimental design. The following are the five types of true experimental designs:

• *Randomized pretest-posttest control group design.* Participants are assigned to two groups (one group serves as the control), and both groups are measured before and after an intervention.
• *Randomized pretest-posttest comparison group design.* Participants are assigned to at least two groups, and each group receives a distinct intervention. The effectiveness of interventions is compared through the use of pre- and posttests.

• The following two designs challenge the need for the use of pretests when random assignment of participants occurs.
• *Randomized posttest-only control group design* involves the random assignment of participants to a treatment or control group, and administration of an intervention to one group, and then measurement of the outcome.
• A *randomized posttest-only comparison group design* is similar to a randomized posttest-only control group design but with at least two groups for comparison and no control group.
• The *Solomon four-group design* is a comprehensive true experimental design. Using four randomly assigned groups, the presence of a pretest and the presence of an intervention can be assessed more rigorously. In fact, the Solomon four-group design is a combination of the randomized pretest-posttest control group design and the randomized posttest-only control group design. Specifically:
• Group 1 receives a pretest, intervention, and posttest.
• Group 2 receives a pretest and posttest, but no intervention.

- Group 3 receives an intervention and posttest but no pretest.
- Group 4 receives a posttest only (no pretest or intervention).

Quasi-experimental designs are useful when it is impossible or inappropriate to randomly assign participants to groups. Quasi-experimental designs are often used with nested data (e.g., classrooms, counseling groups) or naturally occurring groups (e.g., males, African Americans, adolescents). There are two types of quasi-experimental designs:

- *Nonequivalent groups pretest-posttest control or comparison group designs:* The counselor keeps groups intact, administers a pretest, administers treatment to one group (control group design) or to at least two groups (comparison group designs), and then gives the groups a posttest.
- A *time series design* involves repeatedly measuring before and after an intervention for one group (*one group interrupted time series design*) or including a control group for comparison (*control group interrupted time series design*). In time series designs, observations should be made at equal time intervals with the same testing procedures, and the treatment or intervention should interrupt the baseline (i.e., be distinctive to the environment).

8.4.4 Single-Subject Research Designs

SSRDs allow for repeated measures of a target behavior over time for an individual or a select group of individuals. SSRDs are useful for counselors because they often provide concrete assessments of the effectiveness of programs for specific clients. In SSRD, A means a baseline data collection phase (without treatment), and B means a treatment data collection phase. The following are the three types of SSRDs (see Table 8.4 for specific examples):

- A *within-series design* examines the effectiveness of one intervention or program. Examples of within-series designs are (a) *single phase changes* (A-B designs; similar to a posttest only design), (b) *A-B-C designs* (examining the interaction among treatment components), (c) *changing-criterion designs* (the criterion for "success" for the target behavior becomes more restrictive to assess how much incentive is needed to achieve a maximum level of performance), and (d) *parametric designs* (treatments are compared across phases).
- A *between-series design* compares the effectiveness of two or more interventions for a single variable.
- *Multiple-baseline designs* assess data for a particular target behavior across various individuals, environments, or behaviors. For example, a counselor may want to initiate a response-cost intervention with Juan, Billy, and Tamika but not simultaneously. Therefore, the counselor collects the baseline (A) phase data for all three individuals, then implements the response-cost treatment (B) with Juan while continuing to collect baseline (A) phase data on Billy and Tamika. After a significant effect is noted in Juan's response to the intervention (B), the counselor continues Juan in the intervention phase (B) and implements the response-cost intervention (B) with Billy while continuing Tamika in the baseline (A) phase. Finally, when Billy's behavior has improved, the counselor moves all three individuals into the treatment (B) phase. The same process can be used for the same individual across three different environments (e.g., home, school, sports practice) or three different behaviors for the same individual (e.g., raising hand before calling out, staying in seat, keeping hands to self).

8.4.5 Practice Multiple-Choice Items: Quantitative Research Design

1. The question "How do students differ in their degree of involvement in college activities?" would be addressed best by a _____ design.
   a. causal-comparative
   b. correlational

TABLE 8.4 Examples of Single-Subject Research Designs.

Within-series designs	• Recording rates of aggression for a 1-hour period after a child has received counseling (A-B design)
	• Developing a narrative recording describing changes in aggressive behaviors after counseling and then again after adding a service learning component (A-B-C design)
	• Assessing success of an intervention for reducing aggressive behavior by changing the criterion from 10 aggressive acts per day to 6 aggressive acts per day (changing-criterion design)
	• Recording rates of aggression to assess the effectiveness of counseling for two time periods (parametric design)
Between-series designs	• Recording rates of aggression to compare the effectiveness of counseling and a service learning project
Multiple baseline designs	• Assessing aggression rates at school and home (multiple situations)
	• Assessing aggression rates among several children in the same classroom (multiple individuals)
	• Evaluating aggression and attentiveness for one child (multiple behaviors)

Note. The target behavior (aggression) is defined as the number of times a child physically harms another person (e.g., hitting, punching, poking, biting, pushing). The target behavior (attention) is defined as the number of times a child gets up from his or her seat. A = baseline data; B and C = treatment components.

c. comparative
d. longitudinal

2. Evaluating the impact of a smoking cessation program for a sample of 150 clients using repeated measures is an example of a
   a. time series design.
   b. single subject research design.
   c. single group posttest design.
   d. nonexperimental design.

3. "What is the relationship between driving speed and gas prices?" is an example of a question best addressed by a _____ design.
   a. causal-comparative
   b. correlational
   c. comparative
   d. ex post facto

4. Which of the following research designs requires random assignment?
   a. Pre-experimental
   b. True experimental
   c. Quasi-experimental
   d. Single subject

5. The amount of shared variance among the variables of depression and anxiety ($r = .30$) is
   a. .30.
   b. .70.
   c. .09.
   d. It depends on the validity of the instruments.

Answer Key: 1. c; 2. a; 3. b; 4. b; 5. c.

8.5 DESCRIPTIVE STATISTICS

Descriptive statistics organize and summarize data—that is, they describe the data set. Oftentimes, descriptive statistics are calculated as an initial method for interpreting a data set, after which organized and summarized data are studied for how they compare to a population. Thus, once we know what our data set is like, we can explore the question "How do our findings generalize to the population of interest?" (This latter question is known as inferential statistics and is described further in section 8.6.) In this fifth section of Chapter 8, we discuss using tables and graphs to present raw data sets or data distribution, methods for determining the typical score for a data distribution, indicators of variability of a data set, characteristics of data distributions, and shapes of data distributions.

8.5.1 Presenting the Data Set

Table 8.5 provides raw score data with the variable being number of beers consumed on average per week by each participant. The data in Table 8.5 are used to demonstrate how to describe the data set.

8.5.1.1 FREQUENCY DISTRIBUTION A **frequency distribution** is a tabulation of the number of observations (or number

TABLE 8.5 High School Seniors' Frequency of Alcohol Use.

Students responded to an Alcohol Use Survey. One of the items was "How many beers on average do you drink each week?" Here are the raw data for 30 respondents:

0	7	2	2	1
5	3	3	10	25
0	0	4	3	4
2	5	2	1	9
6	6	8	1	12
10	6	4	2	2

of participants) per distinct response for a particular variable. It is presented in a table format with rows indicating each distinct response and columns presenting the frequency for which that response occurred. Table 8.6 contains the frequency distribution for the example data presented in Table 8.5. The first column of a frequency distribution indicates the possible data points, or it may represent intervals or clusters of data points (grouped frequency distributions). One note on data intervals: Intervals should be equally sized, and ordinarily each frequency distribution should have an average of 5 to 15 intervals per frequency distribution. From the frequency distribution in Table 8.6, we can ascertain the following:

- Participants reportedly drank between 0 and 25 beers, on average, per week.
- The 30 students provided 13 different responses (i.e., 0 to 10, 12, and 25).
- The Frequency column indicates the number of participants who drank each amount. For example, two students reported drinking an average of 5 beers per week.
- We can visually estimate which were the most "popular" responses. In this data set, six students reported they drank 2 beers, on average, per week. Thus, 2 was the most popular response.
- We also can visually estimate how varied the responses are.
- By examining the Cumulative Percent column, we can assess what percentage of the 30 students drank a particular amount (or provided a particular response). For example, 80% of the respondents reportedly drank 7 beers or less on average per week.

8.5.1.2 FREQUENCY POLYGON The **frequency polygon** is a line graph of the frequency distribution. The X-axis typically indicates the possible values, and the Y-axis typically represents the frequency count for each of those values. A frequency polygon is used to visually display data that are ordinal, interval, or ratio. Figure 8.2 demonstrates what the frequency polygon would look like for the data set in Table 8.5

8.5.1.3 HISTOGRAM A **histogram** is a graph of connecting bars that shows the frequency of scores for a variable. Taller bars indicate greater frequency or number of responses. Histograms are used with quantitative and continuous variables

TABLE 8.6 Frequency Distribution for Alcohol Consumption Raw Score Data Provided in Table 8.5.

Valid	Frequency	Percent	Valid Percent	Cumulative Percent
0	3	10.0	10.0	10.0
1	3	10.0	10.0	20.0
2	6	20.0	20.0	40.0
3	3	10.0	10.0	50.0
4	3	10.0	10.0	60.0
5	2	6.7	6.7	66.7
6	3	10.0	10.0	76.7
7	1	3.3	3.3	80.0
8	1	3.3	3.3	83.3
9	1	3.3	3.3	86.7
10	2	6.7	6.7	93.3
12	1	3.3	3.3	96.7
25	1	3.3	3.3	100.0
Total	30	100.0	100.0	

(ordinal, interval, or ratio). Figure 8.3 provides the histogram for the Table 8.5 data set. Note that the histogram uses grouped frequency data (e.g., the first bar is the cumulative frequency of raw scores 0, 1, and 2; the second bar is the cumulative frequency of raw scores 3 and 4; the third bar is the cumulative frequency of raw scores 5 and 6; etc.).

8.5.1.4 BAR GRAPHS Although it may look similar to a histogram, a **bar graph** displays nominal data. Each bar represents a distinct (noncontinuous) response, and the height of the bar indicates the frequency of that response. Figure 8.4 provides an example of a bar graph based on participants' gender for the alcohol consumption example. As you can see from the bar graph, the majority of the participants are female (i.e., 20 of the 30 participants).

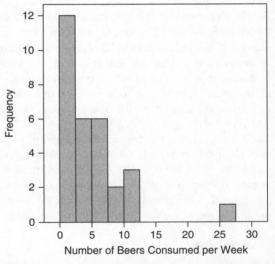

FIGURE 8.3 Histogram for the raw score data provided in Table 8.5.

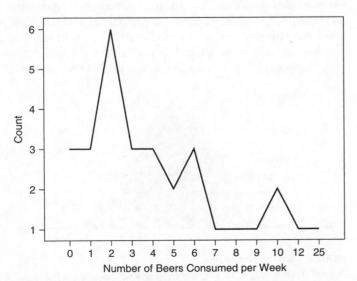

FIGURE 8.2 Frequency polygon for the raw score data provided in Table 8.5.

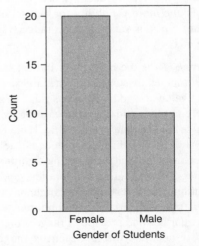

FIGURE 8.4 Bar graph by gender of participants in a study.

8.5.2 Measures of Central Tendency

Measures of **central tendency** relate to the question "What is the *typical* score?" In Table 8.5, what is the typical amount of beer high school students are reporting to consume? The three measures of central tendency, or three ways to assess the typical score, are the mean, median, and mode.

- The **mean** is the arithmetic average of a set of scores. It is computed by summing the values of all the data points and dividing by the total number of participants. An important concept in computing the mean is the presence of an outlier. An **outlier** is an extreme data point that distorts the mean (i.e., it inflates or deflates the typical score). In the example in Table 8.5, the mean is 5.0. Because this data set has an outlier score (i.e., 25), the mean would be considered inflated. If the outlier were removed from analysis, the mean would be 4.14.

- The **median** is the middlemost score when the scores are ordered from smallest to largest, or largest to smallest. When the number of scores is even, one takes the average of the two middlemost scores (i.e., interpolates them). For the example in Table 8.5, the median is 3.5 because the middle of the distribution of raw scores falls between 3 and 4. If the outlier score of 25 is removed, then only 29 scores remain and the median is now 3, the 15th score in the ascending order of the 29 remaining scores in the distribution. A median is often used when outliers are present in the data set or the distribution is skewed (see section 8.5.4).

- The **mode** is the most frequently occurring score. If a data set has two most frequently occurring scores, it is said to be *bimodal*. If a data set has more than two frequently occurring scores, it is *multimodal*. For the example in Table 8.5, the mode is 2.0 because the score of 2.0 occurs six times, more often than any other score.

8.5.3 Variability

Variability answers the question "How *dispersed* are scores from a measure of central tendency?" It is the amount of spread in a distribution of scores or data points. The more dispersed the data points, the more variability for that set of data points. The three main types of variability are range, standard deviation, and variance.

- The **range** (R) is the most basic indicator of variability and is computed by subtracting the largest value from the smallest value and adding 1 place value (e.g., in the case of whole number add 1, in the case of tenths add 0.1). The range for the data presented in Table 8.5 is 26 (i.e., $25 - 0 + 1 = 26$). The range does not tell the professional counselor much, as it can be significantly affected by outliers. When dealing with outliers, and thus skewed distributions, the **interquartile range** may be a more accurate estimate of variability as it eliminates the top and bottom quartiles and provides a range around the median score. To calculate the interquartile range, divide the range of scores into four equal parts. Then, subtract the

score that is one quarter from the bottom from the score that is three quarters from the bottom. Divide this number by 2, and this becomes the plus or minus range for the interquartile range. For the example in Table 8.1, the interquartile range would be $(6 - 2)/2 = 2$; the median = 4, so the interquartile range is 4 ± 2.

- The **standard deviation** (*s, sd, SD*) is the most frequently reported indicator of variability for interval or ratio data. The standard deviation of a known population is indicated by σ. Each data point is determined to be a certain number of units away from the central or average score. The larger the standard deviation, the greater the variability in scores.

- SPSS is ordinarily used to calculate the standard deviation, but the formula for standard deviation (corrected for attenuation) is $s = \sqrt{\dfrac{SS}{N-1}}$; that is, the standard deviation is the square root of the sum of squares (SS) divided by the sample size (N)—1 (a correction for attenuation due to small sample size). The **sum of squares (SS)** refers to sum of the squared deviation scores and is computed by subtracting the mean from each score (deviation scores), squaring each deviation score, and adding them together $[\Sigma X - M]^2$. The standard deviation for the example in Table 8.5 is 4.99.

- In the normal curve (see section 7.3), the standard deviation divides the normal distribution into approximately six parts, as displayed in Figure 8.5.

- **Variance** is the final form of variability, and it is the standard deviation squared. Because variance is stated in units that are squared, standard deviation is more frequently used to explain the concept of variability. The variance for the example in Table 8.5 is 24.9 (or 4.99^2).

8.5.4 Skewness

Recall from the discussion on the normal curve in section 7.3 that the two characteristics of a distribution of scores are symmetry and skewness. The normal curve is a perfectly symmetrical and nonskewed distribution—that is, each half of the distribution is a "mirror image" of the other half (i.e., bilaterally symmetrical). **Skewness** refers to an asymmetrical distribution with data

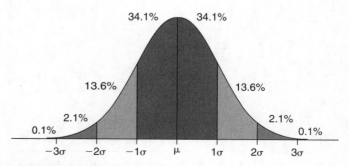

FIGURE 8.5   The normal curve.
From B. T. Erford, (2011). *Transforming the school counseling profession,* 2nd ed. (p. 241). Upper Saddle River, NJ: Merrill Prentice Hall. Reprinted with permission.

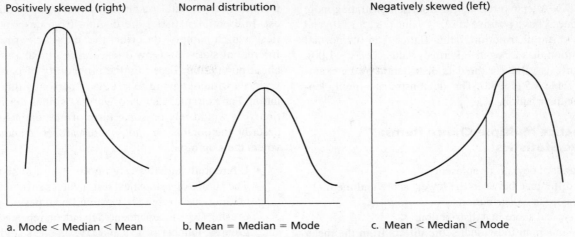

a. Mode < Median < Mean   b. Mean = Median = Mode   c. Mean < Median < Mode

FIGURE 8.6 Relationship of mean, median, and mode in normal and skewed distributions.

points that do not cluster symmetrically around a mean; some distributions may have scores or data points that cluster toward the lower end (i.e., a greater number of lower scores than higher scores) or the higher end of the distribution (i.e., a greater number of higher scores than lower scores). These are known, respectively, as a *positively skewed distribution* and a *negatively skewed distribution* (see Figure 8.6).

- Skewness is directly related to measures of central tendency. That is, by examining the order or sequence of values for mean, median, and mode, you can determine the degree to which your data distribution is skewed:

  Positively Skewed   Mode < Median < Mean
  Symmetrical   Mean = Median = Mode
    (Normal Curve)
  Negatively Skewed   Mean < Median < Mode

- In SPSS output, a positive valence (+) in front of the skewness value indicates a positively skewed distribution, and a negative valence (−) in front of the skewness value indicates a negatively skewed distribution. Ordinarily, a skewness index of −1.00 to +1.00 indicates a nonskewed distribution.

- The data distribution for the example in Table 8.5 has a skewness of +2.0, meaning the distribution is positively skewed (i.e., more data points lie at the lower end of the data distribution). Thus, as a collective sample, most high school seniors are drinking few beers on average per week.

8.5.5 Kurtosis

Kurtosis is another indicator of the shape of a data distribution. It is derived from a Greek word referring to "peakedness." When examining a distribution, the height of the distribution provides one with a lot of information about how data points are clustered. The more data points or scores are clustered around a mean, the more peaked the distribution (i.e., there is more area around the mean). The further scores are dispersed from the mean, the flatter the distribution.

- The three general shapes of distributions (see Figure 8.7) are *mesokurtic* (normal curve), *leptokurtic* (tall and thin), and *platykurtic* (flat and wide).
- Kurtosis is represented by numeric values, which can be easily derived from SPSS. A mesokurtic, or normal, distribution has a kurtosis value of 0 (technically from −1.00

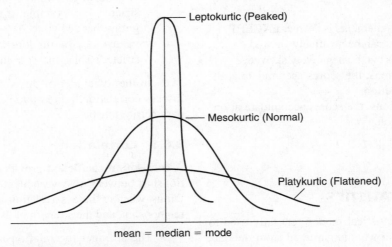

FIGURE 8.7 Examples of kurtosis.

to +1.00). A leptokurtic distribution, demonstrating more peakedness, has a positive kurtosis value (i.e., > 1.00), and a platykurtic distribution, being flatter than the normal distribution, has a negative kurtosis value (i.e., < −1.00).

- The kurtosis value for the data distribution of the example in Table 8.5 is +8.0. This demonstrates a highly leptokurtic distribution.

8.5.6 Practice Multiple-Choice Items: Descriptive Statistics

1. The standard deviation represents
   a. the difference between the lowest score and the highest score in a distribution.
   b. the typical score in a distribution.
   c. how much an individual score differs from the mean score in a distribution.
   d. the height of a distribution of scores.

2. Each of the following statements is true EXCEPT
   a. skewness can be identified if the values of the mean and median are known.
   b. the mean is influenced by extremely high or low scores.
   c. the median is influenced by the position of scores.
   d. the mode is influenced by extreme scores.

3. On a set of geography test results, the instructor informed the class that almost everyone had scored within one standard deviation of the mean. Results like these would be depicted by a(n) _____ distribution.
   a. platykurtic
   b. inverted
   c. mesokurtic
   d. leptokurtic

4. If you are trying to determine the typical salary for real estate professionals and your data includes $30,000, $32,000, $25,000, $38,000, and $249,000, using a _____ would be the most appropriate measure of central tendency.
   a. mean
   b. median
   c. mode
   d. All of the above.

5. Each of the following statements is correct EXCEPT
   a. skewed distributions can be positively skewed.
   b. skewed distributions can be negatively skewed.
   c. in skewed distributions, the scores accumulate at the center of the distribution.
   d. in skewed distributions, the scores accumulate at one end of the distribution.

Answer Key: 1. c; 2. d; 3. d; 4. b; 5. c.

8.6   INFERENTIAL STATISTICS

Inferential statistics is a statistical model generally used to try to describe results beyond what is garnered from the data alone. In other words, the inferential model attempts to infer from the sample data conclusions about a population of interest. Inferential statistics are distinct from descriptive statistics, which simply describe the data (see section 8.5). Inferential statistics allow a researcher to make assessments about populations based on the probability of particular differences without having to test every person within the population. For example, a study of voter positions during an election year would rely on some form of inferential statistics to describe the population, unless a researcher intends to ask all voters their opinion.

- Inferential statistics rely on the use of statistical tests. The choice of a statistical test involves several factors, including one's research question, the types of groups one is using (e.g., independent, dependent, repeated measures groups), number of IVs and DVs in one's study, scale of measurement (see section 7.2), and the ability to meet several statistical assumptions, including the following:
  - Data for the dependent variable(s) are approximately normally distributed.
  - Samples were randomly selected and/or assigned.
  - An interval or ratio scale of measurement was used for each of the variables involved in the study.
- If statistical assumptions are met, parametric statistics are used (see section 8.6.3). If these statistical assumptions are not met, nonparametric statistics are used (see section 8.6.4). Often, though, statistical assumptions are not met and researchers will use parametric statistics anyway because parametric statistics tend to be robust in spite of assumption violations.
- An important concept often noted in inferential statistics is degrees of freedom. **Degrees of freedom (df)** refers to the number of scores, or categories of a variable, "free to vary." The df value is important in most inferential statistics formulas, and computing df depends on the statistical test used. It is equal to the number of scores or variable categories minus the number of parameters (generally represented as $n - 1$). Typically, the more degrees of freedom, the greater the certainty that the sample is representative of the population.
  - A good way to think of degrees of freedom is as a restrictor. For example, if one has three variable categories that add up to 20 ($a + b + c = 20$), the first two values may be random numbers, but the third is restricted. Thus, the df in this case would be $3 - 1 = 2$.

In the remainder of this sixth section of Chapter 8, we discuss correlation, regression, parametric statistics, and nonparametric statistics.

8.6.1   Correlation

A **correlation coefficient** provides information about the relationship between two variables. Correlations indicate three things: whether there is a relationship at all, the direction of that relationship, and the strength of the relationship.

- The stronger the relationship, the higher the absolute value of the correlation is (e.g., −.87, +.63).

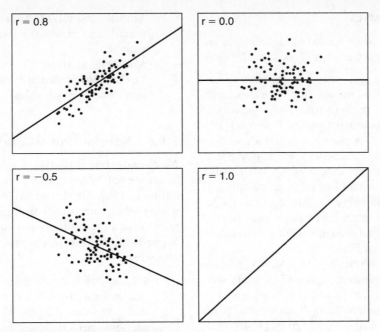

FIGURE 8.8 **Examples of scatterplots.**

- The valence (+ or −) that preceded the value indicates the direction of the relationship. A positive relationship involves variables that move in the same direction. For example, the relationship between height and weight is typically a positive relationship in that as height increases, so does weight. A negative relationship indicates that as one variable increases in value, the other variable decreases in value. For example, wealth and violent crime may have a negative relationship: As wealth increases, violent crime decreases.

- Correlation values range from −1.00 and +1.00, and are typically represented by the Pearson product moment correlation coefficient (commonly referred to as Pearson r). A correlation of +1.00 indicates a perfect positive relationship, and a −1.00 indicates a perfect negative relationship. Other types of correlation coefficients are Spearman r (for comparing rank-order variables), *biserial* correlation coefficients (comparing one continuous and one artificially dichotomous or dummy coded variable), and *point biserial* correlation coefficients (relating one continuous and one true dichotomous variable).

- It is important to note that correlations only indicate relationships between variables and do not indicate causation. For example, we can say that X is related to Y, but we cannot say X causes Y or Y causes X. In addition, other variables may mediate or moderate the relationship between X and Y.

- Correlations often are presented with scatterplots. Some examples are presented in Figure 8.8.

- When a correlation overrepresents or underrepresents the actual relationship, it is referred to as a **spurious correlation**.

  - Overestimation occurs when a common variable is part of both the independent variable and dependent variable

(overlap) or when a third unmeasured variable is common to both variables (such as age for reading achievement and body weight).

- Correlations may be misleading if measures are unreliable in that they may show a lower relationship between the two variables (known as **attenuation**).

- Restriction of range, or having a sample that is not representative of the population (either too heterogeneous or too homogenous), will result in inaccurate relationships.

- It is easy to confuse the decimals of correlations as percentages. We square correlation values to understand the percent of variance shared among variables (i.e., coefficient of determination, r^2).

8.6.2 Regression

Prediction studies are extensions of correlational studies and are known as **regression studies**. If professional counselors know that two variables have a high correlation, they have opportunities to predict outcomes (although we cannot also explain outcomes as we can in experimental designs). The following are the three types of regression:

- *Bivariate regression.* How well scores from an independent variable (predictor variable) predict scores on the dependent variable (criterion variable).

- *Multiple regression.* Involves more than one predictor variable; each predictor variable is weighted (*beta weights*) in a regression equation to determine the contribution of each variable to the criterion variable. Generally, the more predictor variables, the stronger the prediction that can be made.

- *Logistic regression.* Dependent variable is dichotomous. This form of regression may be similar to a bivariate or multiple regression.

8.6.3 Parametric Statistics

Parametric statistics are used when statistical assumptions are met. Several tests in this category exist, and some of the more common ones include these:

- **T-test.** Comparing two means for one variable. *Independent t-tests* involve comparing two independent groups (with participants usually assigned randomly) on one dependent variable. An example of an independent t-test would be gender differences in achievement. *Dependent t-tests* (repeated measures t-tests) involve similar groups paired or matched in some meaningful way, or the same group tested twice. An example of a dependent t-test would be changes in test scores for the same group of high school students from a pretest to a posttest. T-tests provide a *t* ratio.
- **Analysis of variance (ANOVA):** An ANOVA involves having at least one independent variable in a study with three or more groups or levels. For example, an independent variable such as household income (with categories of "Below $20,000," "$20,001–$40,000." "$40,001–$60,000," and "Above $60,000") would have four groups or levels. An ANOVA is an extension of the t-test used to minimize Type I error (i.e., rejecting a null hypothesis when it is true); it provides an *F ratio*, which tells one if two or more of the group means are statistically different. **Post hoc analysis** allows one to examine every possible pairing of groups for a particular independent variable after one has concluded there are *main effects* (i.e., significant difference among two or more groups comprising a single independent variable).
- When there is more than one independent variable, a *factorial ANOVA* is used. Factorial ANOVAs yield both main effects and *interaction effects* (i.e., significant differences among groups across two or more independent variables)—for example, if two treatments (e.g., cognitive-behavioral therapy [CBT] and interpersonal therapy [IPT]) are compared for effectiveness on males and females and different treatments were significantly more effective with different genders, such as CBT worked significantly better for males than females, although IPT worked significantly better for females than males). Post hoc analysis would determine the existence and direction of these interactions.
- **Analysis of covariance (ANCOVA).** This test includes an independent variable as a *covariate*, or a variable that needs to be statistically adjusted and controlled in order to look at the relationship of *other* independent variables and the dependent variable. (If one is also interested in the independent variable designated as a covariate, one would simply conduct a factorial ANOVA instead.) An example of an ANCOVA might be examining the relationship between household income and work satisfaction, with gender as a covariate—that is, the statistical effects of gender are removed from the analysis to control for any effects gender might have on work satisfaction.

- **Multiple analysis of variance (MANOVA).** A MANOVA is similar to an ANOVA, but involves multiple dependent variables.
- **Multiple analysis of covariance (MANCOVA).** A MANCOVA is similar to an ANCOVA but involves multiple dependent variables.

8.6.4 Nonparametric Statistics

Nonparametric statistics are used when professional counselors are only able to make a few assumptions about the distribution of scores in the underlying population. They are suggested when nominal or ordinal data are involved or when interval or ratio data are not distributed normally (i.e., are skewed). Some common nonparametric statistics include the following:

- **Chi-square test.** Used with two or more categorical or nominal variables, where each variable contains at least two categories. All scores must be independent—that is, the same person cannot be in multiple categories of the same variable.
  - The professional counselor forms the categories and then counts the frequency of observations or categories. Then, the reported (or observed) frequencies are compared statistically with theoretical or expected frequencies.
  - An example of a study suitable for this statistic might be investigating the relationship between the decision to terminate counseling (yes, no) and the gender of the professional counselor (male, female). A chi-square would test whether the tallies for the decision to quit counseling by gender of counselor are significantly different from those expected in the population.
- **Mann-Whitney U test.** Analogous to a parametric independent t-test, except the Mann-Whitney U test uses ordinal data instead of interval or ratio data. This test compares the ranks from two groups. For example, a professional counselor might use this test to compare students in Grades 9 through 12 with education aspiration (i.e., high school, 2-year degree, 4-year degree, graduate degree) as a dependent variable.
- **Kolmogorov-Smirnov Z procedure.** Similar to the Mann-Whitney U test but more appropriate to use when samples are smaller than 25 participants.
- **Kruskal-Wallis test.** Analogous to an ANOVA. This test is an extension of the Mann-Whitney U test when there are three or more groups per independent variable.
- **Wilcoxon's signed-ranks test.** Equivalent to a dependent t-test. This test involves ranking the amount and direction of change for each pair of scores. For example, this test would be appropriate for assessing changes in perceived level of competency before and after a training program.
- **Friedman's rank test.** Similar to Wilcoxon's signed-ranks test in that it is designed for repeated measures. In addition, it may be used with more than two comparison groups.

8.6.5 Factor Analysis

The purpose of a **factor analysis** is to reduce a larger number of variables (often items on an assessment) to a smaller number of factors (groups or factors). Factors are hypothetical constructs that explain covariation among variables; each factor explains a certain percentage of variance (i.e., strength of the association between variables and a factor). The two forms of factor analysis are exploratory factor analysis and confirmatory factor analysis.

Exploratory factor analysis (EFA) involves an initial examination of potential models (or factor structures) that best categorize the variables. EFA involves two steps: (a) extraction of factors and (b) rotation and interpretation of those factors. These two steps can be thought of as analogous to mining for precious metals. Let's say one is mining a forest comprised of several precious metals along with various other materials, such as stones, debris, rocks, and plants (variables or items). One further believes that various metals (gold, silver) are present and could be categorized as precious metals (factor) in that they all share something in common (common variance) even though each has unique aspects (unique variance). *Factor extraction* would consist of pulling out those various metals to clump them as precious metals, and *factor rotation* would consist of cleaning them up to see them better in order to ensure they are, in fact, precious metals.

- Three common types of factor extractions include (a) *principal axis factoring* (i.e., analysis of the common variance among variables or items, also referred to as *communality*); (b) *principal components analysis* (i.e., analysis of both the common and unique variance of variables to find as many linear combinations [principal components] as possible to explain as much information as possible about the variables); and (c) *maximum likelihood method* (i.e., likelihood that a correlation matrix representing the variables is similar to that derived from a population correlation matrix).
- *Factor rotation* involves changing the reference point for variables for easier interpretation. Rotation does not change the relationship among variables, just the perspective. The decision of what type of rotation to use is based on theoretical notions regarding whether or not the factors are correlated or uncorrelated. The two types of factor rotation are *orthogonal* (when factors are uncorrelated) and *oblique* (when factors are correlated).

Confirmatory factor analysis (CFA) refers to confirming the EFA results. The most common method is the maximum likelihood method (described above). After attaining a factor solution, one tests how the overall model fits the data using a *fit index*. Some fit indices include chi-square statistic, Tucker-Lewis Index, comparative fit index, standardized root mean-squared residual, and root mean squared error of approximation.

8.6.6 Meta-Analysis

Although the results of a single study are often helpful, similar studies often yield disparate or even contradictory results. Which results do you believe? Can the results be combined somehow to indicate what would happen on average? A **meta-analysis** allows a researcher to combine and synthesize the results of numerous similar studies for particular outcome or dependent variables. Examples of outcome variables might include depression symptoms, grade point averages, high school dropout rates, and so forth. Meta-analysis has been popular in counseling for several decades due to a desire to show what works in counseling, for whom, and under what conditions. Two seminal meta-analyses in psychotherapy (i.e., Eysenck, 1952; Smith & Glass, 1977) have sparked interest in determining the effectiveness of counseling (or psychotherapy, as they labeled it) and discussing limitations of conducting meta-analyses in counseling in general. Steps in conducting a meta-analysis include the following:

- Establish criteria for including a study based on operational definitions (e.g., psychotherapy, counseling).
- Locate empirical studies based on criteria. Include dissertations and theses as appropriate.
- Consider and code variables that could be independent variables (e.g., length of treatment, counselor training, rigor of research design).
- The dependent variable in a meta-analysis is the **effect size** (i.e., a measure of the strength of the relationship between two variables in a population) of the outcome. Calculate an effect size on any outcome variable in the study. Thus, there may be several effect sizes per study.
- Effect sizes are compared and combined across studies and grouped according to independent variables of interest.

Smith and Glass's (1977) study serves as an example.

- The term *psychotherapy* was operationalized, and studies were located that pertained to psychotherapy.
- In 375 psychotherapy studies, 833 effect sizes were computed. These effect sizes represented outcome variables such as self-esteem, anxiety, achievement, and stress.
- The effect sizes for the 375 studies became the DV, and 16 IVs were identified across the studies. Some IVs included duration of therapy in hours, age of the clients, and number of years' experience of the therapist.
- *Interrater reliability* (discussed in section 7.2) was computed to ensure that researchers were coding the IVs correctly across the studies.
- One of the findings was that the average study showed a .68 standard deviation superiority of the treatment over the control group. What this meant was that the average client who received treatment improved to the 75th percentile of the control group distribution (.68 standard deviations above the mean on a normal distribution is located at about the 75th percentile). This had a moderate treatment effect.

8.6.7 Practice Multiple-Choice Items: Inferential Statistics

1. Which of the following is most likely an example of restriction of range?
   a. Women in a particular community and depression levels
   b. Prediction of graduate school grades among students scoring > 1400 on the Graduate Record Examination

c. Elementary school children and depression levels

d. Clients at a psychiatric facility and depression levels

2. What is the key difference between a t-test and an ANOVA?

a. Number of dependent variables

b. Number of groups for an independent variable

c. The use of ratio data

d. The use of a continuous dependent variable

3. What is the key difference between an ANOVA and a MANOVA?

a. Number of dependent variables

b. Number of groups for an independent variable

c. The use of ratio data

d. The use of a continuous dependent variable

4. A professional counselor wants to examine the relationship between education level and the decision to participate in a continuing education program. Which statistical test would likely be appropriate?

a. ANOVA

b. ANCOVA

c. Chi-square

d. Wilcoxon's signed-ranks test

5. Answer the following analogy: An independent t-test is to a Kolmogorov-Smirnov Z procedure as a dependent t-test is to a(n)

a. ANOVA.

b. ANCOVA.

c. chi-square.

d. Wilcoxon's signed-ranks test.

Answer Key: 1. b; 2. b; 3. a; 4. c; 5. d.

8.7 QUALITATIVE RESEARCH DESIGN

Qualitative research involves the study of processes, participants' meaning of phenomena, or both. The phenomena studied can be exploratory (e.g., little research is available; the counselor wants to understand it from the perspectives of a group whose voice has been minimal on the topic). Often, counselors are intimately involved in the inquiry and conduct qualitative research on phenomena in a natural setting. Some important reflections for counselors conducting qualitative research include these:

- How do individuals within a particular context describe a phenomenon?
- What is the process or sequence of a phenomenon?
- How can individuals serve as their own experts on the phenomenon?
- How can individuals be involved in the research team?
- How do data shape an evolving theory or thick description of a phenomenon?
- How does the researcher's participation influence how data are collected and analyzed?
- What can be done to maximize the validity of the study?
- To what degree does one include participants' narratives in the findings?

TABLE 8.7 Characteristics of Qualitative Research.

- Study of issues in depth and detail
- Contextual
- Discovery-oriented approach
- How social experience is created and given meaning
- Thick description
- Fieldwork
- Research design constantly evolving
- Inductive analysis
- Researcher as instrument
- Participants as experts/partners in research
- Participant observation
- Interviewing
- Document analysis
- Purposeful sampling
- Reflexivity
- Themes vs. numbers
- Trustworthiness

Source: Maxwell, 2005; Patton, 2002.

Additional characteristics of qualitative research are presented in Table 8.7. Many of the terms presented in the table are defined in the following subsections. In this section we discuss research traditions, sampling methods, data collection methods, data management and analysis strategies, and strategies for establishing trustworthiness.

8.7.1 Qualitative Research Traditions

Research traditions are an important part of qualitative research design as they guide sampling, data collection, and data analysis decisions. Seven major research traditions are covered in this section: case study, phenomenology, grounded theory, consensual qualitative research, ethnography, biography, and participatory action research.

- The *case study* approach represents one of the most universal methods of qualitative inquiry. A *case* is a distinct system of an event, process, setting, or individuals or a small group of individuals. For example, cases can include the implementation of No Child Left Behind legislation or exploration of a counseling process, a classroom, or individuals' progress in a grief group. Although cases may be used in SSRD (see section 8.4), the case study approach is more often cited as a qualitative tradition. The uniqueness of this approach is that those involved in a case are active participants in data collection.
- **Phenomenology** is an approach used to discover or describe the meaning or essence of participants' lived experiences with the goal of understanding individual and collective human experiences for various phenomena. Qualitative researchers strive to assess participants' intentionality (i.e., internal experience of being conscious of something). An example of phenomenology is studying

clients' perspectives on the grief process after recently surviving the loss of a loved one.

- **Grounded theory** is one of the most influential approaches in qualitative research. Its purpose is to generate theory that is grounded in data from participants' perspectives for a particular phenomenon. It is an inductive approach. The theories that are generated often explain a process or action surrounding an experience or a sequence of events pertaining to a particular topic. An example of grounded theory is evaluating data from the use of a counseling theory with adolescents; the approach might yield theory regarding the most effective components of the theory for this population.

- **Consensual qualitative research (CQR)** is an approach that combines elements of phenomenology and grounded theory. It involves researchers selecting participants who are very knowledgeable about a topic and remaining close to data without major interpretation with some hope of generalizing to a larger population. CQR varies slightly from other grounded theory and phenomenological approaches as researchers often reflect on their own experiences with a phenomenon when developing interview questions. Consensus is key to this approach, as qualitative researchers use rigorous methods to facilitate agreement in interpretations among themselves, participants, and the general audience. One unique aspect of CQR is its emphasis on power in all aspects of the research process. With the use of research teams, researchers share power among themselves and participants.

- **Ethnography** is a research tradition in which the researcher describes and provides interpretations about the culture of a group or system. Participant observation is used by the researcher in describing the process and

experience of culture, particularly socialization processes. An ethnography example in a counseling setting is studying a local community to understand its method for addressing mental health concerns.

- A **biography** seeks to identify personal meanings individuals give to their social experiences. The counselor gathers stories and explores meanings for an individual as well as how the stories fit into a broader social or historical context. Biographical methods also include life history and oral history methods. A use of biographies in counseling includes the work of Daniel Levinson (1978), who studied developmental stages of men (see section 3.8.5).

- **Participatory action research (PAR)** is a research tradition that focuses on change of the participants and researcher as a result of qualitative inquiry. Essentially, the goals of PAR are emancipation and transformation, and the researcher is required to critically reflect on the power of research as a change agent. PAR involves a collaborative approach to problem solving between the researcher and other key stakeholders. An example of a PAR approach is working with a community agency and its clients to move toward improving the agency.

8.7.2 Purposive Sampling

The intention of **purposive sampling**, also known as purposeful sampling, is to obtain information-rich cases that allow for maximum depth and detail regarding a particular phenomenon. Counselors seek sample sizes that reach the point of redundancy of information, or **saturation**—that is, counselors continue to sample individuals until no new data refute findings of previously collected data. Researchers have developed approximately 15 types of purposive sampling. Table 8.8 provides an

TABLE 8.8 Examples of Purposive Sampling Methods.

Sampling Method	Hypothetical Sample
Convenience	Teachers from a local high school with which you have a preexisting relationship
Maximum variation	Teachers of diverse backgrounds from diverse types of high schools, with training in various grade levels and forms of math
Homogenous	Teachers that instruct a geometry class
Stratified purposeful	Six samples of teachers for each type of math course offered in high school
Purposeful random	Selection of 15 teachers randomly from high schools within four school districts
Comprehensive	All teachers at a particular private school
Typical case	Teachers of regular math courses having "average" expectations of their students
Intense case	Teachers of advanced math courses
Critical case	Teachers who assisted students who make significant progression in math achievement
Extreme or deviant case	Teachers of remedial and advanced math courses
Snowball, chain, or network	National award-winning teachers selected by networking with various superintendents
Criterion	Teachers who have at least 5 years of teaching advanced math at the high school level
Opportunistic or emergent	A high-profile teacher who is suddenly able to participate in your study
Theoretical	Teachers who can specifically address a theoretical component (such as changing expectations) of the theory
Confirming/disconfirming	Teachers whose expectations of students have changed in either a positive or negative manner throughout the academic year

example of each of these types using the following research question (or some modification of it) as a guide: How do math teachers' expectations influence high school students' math achievement?

- *Convenience sampling.* Sampling based on availability or accessibility. This is the least desirable method, and it is viewed as least trustworthy.
- *Maximum variation sampling.* Sampling a diverse group and searching for core patterns and individual perspectives based on unique participant characteristics.
- *Homogenous sampling.* Selecting participants for a specific subgroup with theoretically similar experiences.
- *Stratified purposeful sampling.* Identifying important variables pertaining to a research question and sampling subgroups that best isolate each variable. This is also referred to as "samples within samples."
- *Purposeful random sampling.* Identifying a sample and randomly selecting participants from that sample.
- *Comprehensive sampling:* Sampling all individuals within a system. This method is useful when the case has few participants.
- *Typical case sampling.* Selecting the "average" participants, or those who represent the typical experience for a phenomenon.
- *Intensity sampling.* Identifying those with intense (but not extreme) experiences of a phenomenon.
- *Critical case sampling.* Sampling those with intense and irregular experiences. This method allows illustrating a point well and/or gaining the most knowledge.
- *Extreme or deviant sampling.* Looking for the bounds of difference, or those with the most positive and negative experiences. Each pole of the continuum may be compared, or the counselor may focus on exploring one pole.
- *Snowball, chain, or network sampling.* A pool of participants is derived through obtaining recommendations from earlier participants. This method is often used when a sample is difficult to obtain.

- *Criterion sampling.* Developing criteria and selecting all cases that meet the criteria.
- *Opportunistic or emergent sampling.* Taking advantage of an unexpected opportunity and changing one's research design to include a particular individual in one's pool.
- *Theoretical sampling.* As theory evolves, sampling those who best contribute information for one's theory.
- *Confirming/disconfirming case sampling.* Including cases that confirm and add depth to one's evolving theory and also provide exceptions or potentially disconfirm elements of one's theory. This method may be done as part of theoretical sampling.

8.7.3 Qualitative Data Collection Methods

Qualitative data collection methods may be classified in three ways: interviews, observations, and unobtrusive methods (e.g., document analysis, photography). It is advisable to use multiple data collection methods in qualitative research. Table 8.9 presents the potential strengths and limitations of each.

8.7.3.1 QUALITATIVE INTERVIEWING Interviews vary in their amount of structure. The three types of interviews are *unstructured interviews* (no predetermined questions), *semi-structured interviews* (preset interview protocol with flexibility to change, add or remove questions), and *structured interviews* (standardized interview protocol and ensures the same level of depth and breadth of information are collected from each participant; also see Chapter 7).

- Interviews may involve individuals or focus groups. **Focus groups** typically include 6 to 12 members who can provide information and insight into a particular issue. Individual interviews may be better suited for more sensitive research topics, whereas focus group interviews may be helpful in assessing how social interaction facilitates data generation. It is important to note that these two forms of interviewing may yield different types of data.

TABLE 8.9 Qualitative Data Collection Methods.

Method	Strengths	Limitations
Interviews	• Can be adapted to include one individual or several individuals at one time • Allows participants to describe their perspectives directly • Encourages interaction between counselor and participant • May be cost effective	• May differ in the degree of structure as well as format and thus not provide similar amounts of data across participants • Depending on the type of interview, possible limit to number of questions asked
Observations	• Allows researcher to capture the context in which a phenomenon is occurring • Adds depth to qualitative data analysis	• Poorly established observation rubrics possibly leading to invalid observations • Difficult to focus on several aspects of an observation at one time
Unobtrusive methods	• Can guide future data collection methods • Allow for permanence and density of data • Corroborate findings from other data sources	• Some contextual information possibly missing from the source

Observer	Observer as Participant	Participant as Observer	Full Participant
← / _____	/ _____	/ _____	/ →

FIGURE 8.9 **The continuum of participant observation.**

8.7.3.2 OBSERVATIONAL METHODS The purpose of qualitative observations is to gather a detailed description of the setting or context in which a phenomenon is occurring. Counselors reflect on the content and process of the setting by engaging in fieldwork and memoing about the experience. To focus on particular aspects of a setting, counselors often will use observation rubrics based on the research question.

- Observing participants occurs on a continuum (Patton, 2002), as shown in Figure 8.9. An observer has little or no interaction with those being observed, whereas a full participant may function as a member of the group being studied while investigating the group. The points between these poles represent whether a counselor's role is primarily that of an observer or participant. **Participant observation** is the most common role of counselors engaging in observations.

8.7.3.3 UNOBTRUSIVE METHODS Unobtrusive data collection methods typically do not involve direct interactions with participants. Examples of data collection methods include collecting photographs, videos, documents (e.g., diaries, letters, newspapers, scrapbooks), archival data, and artifacts. (*Note:* Participants can be asked to produce some of these data sources. For example, participants can be asked to take pictures or produce diaries.)

8.7.4 Qualitative Data Management and Analysis

Because qualitative research often encompasses large amounts of data, data management strategies such as developing contact summary sheets and document summary forms become essential. Data management should continue as data are collected and analyzed. A **contact summary sheet** is a single-page snapshot of a specific contact, such as an interview or observation. Contact summary sheets are personalized by the counselor to include information such as specifics of the contact (e.g., time and date of contact, setting, and participant information) and a list of salient themes and reflections. A **document summary form** serves a similar purpose and is attached primarily to unobtrusive data sources, such as newsletters or artifacts.

- As data analysis occurs, counselors often use data displays as data management tools. A **data display** presents organized data in a table format or a figure containing interconnected nodes. Displays may be created for each participant (within-case display) as well as across a sample (cross-case display).
- An important term related to qualitative data analysis is inductive analysis. **Inductive analysis** is a common process among several research traditions, and it involves searching for keywords and potential themes from the

data without significant preconceived notions of what theory or theories fit the data—that is, the data allow notions of a phenomenon to emerge.

- Although the qualitative data can be analyzed in a variety of ways, McLeod (2001) provides generic steps of qualitative data analysis:
  - Writing memos throughout the research process
  - Constructing an initial summary or narrative for the data
  - Organizing and segmenting the text
  - Coding the data
  - Searching for themes and patterns to address research questions
  - Deciding on the main theme or themes, describing them in detail, and discussing any known relationships among the themes

8.7.5 Trustworthiness

One of the key ways to establish that a qualitative study is robust enough is to provide evidence of trustworthiness. **Trustworthiness** refers to the validity or truthfulness of findings—that is, why others should trust your data collection and analysis methods and why they should believe your results.

- The four components of trustworthiness are credibility, transferability, dependability and confirmability. *Credibility*, the main component of trustworthiness, refers to the "believability" of your findings: Do conclusions accurately represent the study at hand? *Transferability* is the degree to which data transfers to other contexts and participants, and it is similar to the concept of generalizability in quantitative research: Are all aspects of the research design described well enough so that findings can be potentially applied to other contexts? *Dependability* refers to the degree of consistency of results over time and across researchers: Would other counselors given the same data find similar results? *Confirmability* reflects that interpretation of the data is a genuine reflection of participants' views. How well have counselors' biases and assumptions been controlled? Table 8.10 outlines strategies to maximize these four components of trustworthiness.

8.7.6 Practice Multiple-Choice Items: Qualitative Research Design

1. Which of the following qualitative research traditions most assists the counselor to attend to participants' lived experiences while developing a theory on the processes of a phenomenon?
   a. Phenomenology
   b. Grounded theory

TABLE 8.10	**Strategies for Trustworthiness.**
Prolonged engagement	Focus on scope of context for an extended time frame to learn about the overall culture and phenomenon.
Persistent observation	Focus on depth of context to ascertain important details and characteristics related to a research question.
Triangulation	Test for consistency and inconsistency of data by using multiple participants, data sources, researchers or theories.
Peer debriefing	Check counselor's biases and findings with those outside of the study.
Member checking	Consult participants to verify the "truth" of the findings.
Negative case analysis	Look for inconsistencies and data that might refute preliminary findings.
Referential adequacy	Check findings against archived data collected at various points of the study.
Thick description	Describe in significant detail data collection and analysis procedures.
Auditing	Select an individual with no interest in the specific results of the study to review documents and proceedings (audit trail) for accuracy of interpretations.
Reflexive journal	Memo about reflections surrounding a qualitative inquiry to assist in minimizing the influence of counselor bias in data collection, analysis, and reporting.

c. Consensual qualitative research

d. Ethnography

2. Which of the following qualitative research traditions most assists the counselor to collaborate with participants to enact change in a setting?

a. Ethnography

b. Biography

c. Case study

d. Participatory action research

3. A data management tool that can serve as a cover sheet or snapshot for an event during data collection is a(n)

a. contact summary sheet.

b. memo.

c. reflexive journal.

d. audit trail.

4. The question "Why should I believe your qualitative findings?" is best answered by focusing on

a. credibility.

b. transferability.

c. dependability.

d. confirmability.

5. All of the following are characteristics of qualitative research EXCEPT

a. identifying researcher bias.

b. engaging in hypothesis testing.

c. managing and analyzing data throughout a qualitative study.

d. collaborating with participants and treating them as experts.

Answer Key: 1. c; 2. d; 3. a; 4. a; 5. b.

8.8   PROGRAM EVALUATION

Program evaluation involves assessment of a program at all stages of development and implementation with a primary goal of providing quality services to individuals in need. It refers to diagnosing programs, not individuals, for the individuals' benefit. With the increased attention on empirically supported treatment, accountability of counselors as a result of legislation such as the No Child Left Behind Act of 2001, and reliance on external funding to provide services, program evaluation is an important component of the counseling profession.

- Posavac and Carey (2007) highlight several questions that program evaluation findings may address, including the following:
  - Is a program needed?
  - Who should receive services and for how long?
  - Is a program implemented as planned?
  - Are resources being used properly?
  - What are the program outcomes?
  - Which programs produce the most favorable outcomes?
  - Are program benefits maintained over time?
  - What are the program costs?
  - Do the benefits outweigh the costs?

- Although counselors use research strategies in program evaluation, program evaluation differs from research in important ways. First, research (particularly quantitative research) involves the systematic and controlled investigation of phenomena, whereas findings often lead to narrow applicability or generalizability and, as a result, are likely of less relevance to the counselor. Thus, research may involve a primary purpose of investigating for the sake of knowing. Second, program evaluation tends to be diffused among many individuals who hold different roles, whereas research may be done in isolation.

- The following are the four major components or types of program evaluation (Posavac & Carey, 2007):
  - *Needs assessment.*   Often an initial step to explore whether a program is needed for a particular group of individuals.
  - *Process evaluation.*   Assessment of an ongoing program to ensure that program activities match plans.
  - *Outcome evaluation.*   Determination of program success by investigating how participants are performing with respect to themselves as well as others who are not involved in the program.

CASE 8.1
Violence Intervention Program

After reading several articles about the incidence and prevalence of bullying of gay, lesbian, bisexual, and transgender (GLBT) youths, you are interested in establishing a violence intervention program in your local community. Your agency director is very supportive of the program. However, she notes that minimal funding is available for the program and that you will have to generate most of the funds to support all initial and ongoing program costs. In addition, to document your involvement in the program and its overall effectiveness, you must conduct a comprehensive program evaluation.

- *Efficiency analysis.* Comparison of the costs of the program in relation to need, processes, and outcomes. Is there value added (i.e., do gains outweigh costs)?

In the remainder of this section, we discuss key terms of program evaluation; general steps in program evaluation; program evaluation components including needs assessment, process evaluation, outcome evaluation, and efficiency analysis; and program evaluation models and methods. Case 8.1 provides an organizing example to which these principles are applied throughout this section.

8.8.1   Key Terms of Program Evaluation

- **Accountability** refers to the process of providing feedback about a program to its stakeholders. As funding for counseling programs becomes more competitive for what little funds are available, professional counselors are even more accountable to program effectiveness overall and to its effectiveness compared to other programming options.
- **Stakeholders** are any individuals involved in or affected by the program. These are individuals to whom the professional counselor is accountable and can include parents, family members, principals, teachers, administrators, clients, community leaders, funding agencies, and so forth.
- **Formative evaluations** comprise the ongoing evaluation of a program throughout its implementation to ensure that it is being conducted as planned and acted upon as needed (needed changes must be made) based on stakeholder feedback. Since it makes no sense to evaluate a program that never existed (i.e., was not implemented as planned), formative evaluations are a necessary component in examining the success of a program.
- A **summative evaluation** is closely tied to outcome evaluation and involves the assessment of the entire program to determine the degree to which program goals and objectives have been met. Summative evaluations are used to decide if a program should be continued or chosen from among two or more alternatives.

8.8.2   General Steps in Program Evaluation

1. *Identify the program to be evaluated.* When planning an evaluation, it is important to gain as much information about the program as possible by meeting with several stakeholders. Who wants the evaluation to be conducted and why? What are the available resources and the estimated timeline for completing the evaluation?
2. *Plan the evaluation.* Planning the evaluation involves considering what type of research design one will use (i.e., qualitative, quantitative) and how many data sources one will collect to strengthen the validity of findings. It is also important to examine evaluations from similar programs to ensure the best program evaluation plan.
3. *Conduct a needs assessment and provide recommendations* (see section 8.8.3).
4. *Determine what "success" is.*
   - Co-develop program goals and objectives.
   - Program evaluators are interested in measures of both short-term and long-term success.
   - Program success is very difficult to determine. Criteria for success should be based on stakeholders' mutually agreed on objective and operational goals. In addition, the criteria will vary depending on the type of program and resources available.
   - Use multiple dependent or outcome variables to examine success, and measure them differently.
   - Use repeated measures designs to minimize validity threats (see section 8.2).
5. *Select data sources.*
   - Use multiple data sources to measure outcome variables.
   - Examples of data sources include participants, program staff, community statistics, program records, artifacts (e.g., essays, newspapers), program staff, and outside observers (e.g., experts, family members).
   - Useful assessments might include surveys, interviews, checklists, tests, and observation protocols.
   - These data sources can be used throughout the program evaluation process.
6. *Monitor and evaluate the program progress* (see section 8.8.4).
7. *Determine the degree to which a program is successful* (see section 8.8.5).
8. *Analyze the program's efficiency* (see section 8.8.6).
9. *Continue, revise, or stop the program based on findings.*

8.8.3   Needs Assessments

Determining a program need is a subjective and contextual process. Program evaluators should familiarize themselves with similar programs or communities to determine if resources are below some satisfactory and expected state. Also, evaluators should be sure not to duplicate existing services.

- Conducting a needs assessment involves identifying objectives to plan and develop services for clients.
- A needs assessment is an important part of program evaluation because it allows evaluators to understand needs of a client population and develop or revise program goals and objectives. These goals and objectives can be assessed by evaluators during other program evaluation components to determine if the program has met them.
- Program evaluators should establish an **advisory committee** composed of representatives from various stakeholder groups. Evaluators are encouraged to take into account the perspectives of all stakeholders in identifying needs and formulating goals and objectives.
- In preparing the needs assessment, the purpose of the evaluation must be identified and program details outlined. Who is interested in the needs assessment? What is the political and social context of the program? What target population(s) are being served (or will be served) by the program?
- Erford (2011) recommended using the **ABCD model** for developing program objectives, where A = audience (individuals influenced by the program objective), B = behavior (expected action or attitude), C = conditions (context or mode in which behavior will occur), and D = description (concrete performance criterion). The following are examples of objectives using the ABCD model:
  - The faculty member will spend approximately 20 minutes per class session reviewing comprehensive exam information as monitored through class observations by a third-party observer.
  - The client will demonstrate decreased substance use by two beers per week as reported by family members.
- Once needs are identified, program evaluators should develop an **executive summary** for the advisory committee. The report should contain background information about the needs assessment, information about data sources and data analyses used, and recommendations based on the findings for program implementation and future evaluation.
- Related to the case vignette presented in Case 8.1, one would conduct a thorough literature review and local community analysis of what bullying prevention programs in general exist as well as those specific to GLBT youth. Then, an advisory committee made up of stakeholders and members of the target population (e.g., agency representatives, professional counselors, community advocates, GLBT youth, parents of GLBT youth) would be organized to identify needs of this community and concrete objectives for the program. In addition, the needs assessment would involve investigating existing and needed resources for program development, implementation, maintenance, and evaluation.

8.8.4 Process Evaluation

A process evaluation focuses on the process of implementing the program to evaluate its progress at various points. It is also known as program monitoring.

- The evaluation examines whether the program was employed as planned and if it met its outcome expectations. Alternatives to the methods used also are investigated to ensure those methods being implemented are the best available.
- Government social programs routinely conduct this type of evaluation and often apply cost-benefit analysis (see section 8.8.5) to evaluate program performance.

8.8.5 Outcome Evaluation

An outcome evaluation measures the effectiveness of a program at the end of the program. Outcome evaluations use methods such as a posttest measure, exit interview, cost-benefit analysis, records review, or checklist.

- Program evaluation, at this stage, is usually determining one of three aspects: (a) the program was more effective than no intervention at all, (b) the program was more effective than another program, and (c) the degree to which the program was more effective than another program.

8.8.6 Efficiency Analysis

An **efficiency analysis (cost-benefit analysis)** allows one to quantitatively decide on a particular course of action. Put simply, it weighs the benefits of a particular course of action against the costs.

- In treatment decisions, for example, does more expensive or elaborate therapy necessarily lead to a better treatment outcome? It may, but typically, at some point, the return on treatment will diminish (i.e., the costs will exceed the benefit). The same can be said for test preparations. One could stay up all night cramming for a final examination, but at some point the costs of staying up will exceed the benefits of further study because the following morning, come test time, the student is likely to be too tired to perform well.
- In social research, those programs that provide the greatest benefit at the least cost are the most favorable. The costs do not have to be monetary costs; they can involve a number of other factors, such as time spent on the program or number of providers necessary to run the program. These other factors can be difficult to capture, and in these cases cost-benefit analysis may not be the most sensible evaluation method.

8.8.7 Program Evaluation Models and Strategies

Several evaluation models have been discussed in counseling literature. Some of the primary ones are described here (Heppner, Wampold, & Kivlighan, 2008; Posavac & Carey, 2007). Examples based on Case 8.1 are used to illustrate each model.

- ***Treatment package strategy or social science research model.*** Control and treatment groups are compared to determine if a program is effective. *Example:* Your GLBT bullying prevention program is implemented in one community, and the number of bullying incidences is compared for two communities.

- *Comparative outcome strategy.* Two or more programs or interventions are compared to assess which is effective. *Example:* GLBT bullying prevention program outcomes are compared to those of a program in another community.

- *Dismantling strategy.* Various program components from different perspectives are evaluated to determine the effective (and ineffective) parts of a program. *Example:* GLBT individuals, parents of these individuals, community leaders, professional counselors, and school administrators are interviewed about several aspects of the program (e.g., public service announcements, workshops, support groups, diversity training).

- *Constructive strategy.* A new component is added to an already effective program and assessed for "added value." *Example:* During the second year of your program, you decide to include a required community service project for perpetrators to examine if victimization will decrease more.

- *Parametric strategy.* A program evaluated at different stages is reviewed to determine the most appropriate times to evaluate it. *Example:* Throughout a 5-year period, you have devised different methods for evaluating programs, including conducting evaluations once per 6 months, once per month, and once per week. You are curious as to which method is most suitable for future program evaluations.

- *Common factors control group strategy.* A program is evaluated to determine whether a specific component or common factors of a program resulted in its effectiveness. *Example:* GLBT youth are surveyed about services provided by the professional counselor and specific workshops to determine what was most beneficial for them.

- *Moderation design strategy.* Participants and other stakeholders are assessed to consider who might benefit most from a program. *Example:* You interview various individuals involved in the program and look for the degree to which they perceived a program to be effective.

- *Objectives-based evaluation model.* This is the most common model used, whereas professional counselors determine if goals and objectives were met. *Example:* You measure the number of times a GLBT individual is victimized and compare it to the specific reduction objective set at the beginning of an evaluation.

- *Expert-opinion model.* An outside and neutral expert examines the program process and outcome. *Example:* Experts in bullying interventions review your program and determine if it should receive additional funding.

- *Success case method.* Information is sought from those individuals who benefited most from a program. *Example:* You observe professional counselors who seem to be intervening in bulling reports most effectively.

- *Improvement-focused approach.* Ineffective program components are reviewed to figure out what went wrong. *Example:* You interview a perpetrator after a bullying incident to understand why a program may not be preventing her behavior.

8.8.8 Practice Multiple-Choice Items: Program Evaluation

1. _____ refers to providing feedback to stakeholders.
   a. Accountability
   b. Efficiency
   c. Summation
   d. Advising

2. During the needs assessment process, a(n) _____ is typically given to stakeholders.
   a. process evaluation
   b. executive summary
   c. outcome evaluation
   d. treatment package

3. _____ is not part of the ABCD model.
   a. Behavior
   b. Content
   c. Condition
   d. Audience

4. Monitoring if a program is running as planned is known as
   a. process evaluation.
   b. executive summary.
   c. outcome evaluation.
   d. treatment package.

5. Determining if a program should be continued again is known as
   a. process evaluation.
   b. executive summary.
   c. outcome evaluation.
   d. treatment package.

Answer Key: 1. a; 2. b; 3. b; 4. a; 5. c.

8.9 KEY POINTS FOR CHAPTER 8: RESEARCH AND PROGRAM EVALUATION

- Research and program evaluation has undergone a transformation in philosophy, ethics, and law within the past few centuries. Today, researchers are attending more to the human element of research and being more morally, ethically, and legally accountable to participants.

- With quantitative research designs, counseling researchers make considerations about the variables of interest (e.g., independent, dependent, extraneous), the type of research questions to pose and hypotheses to test, sampling characteristics, and internal and external validity threats.

- Quantitative research designs are characterized by non-experimental and experimental (pre-experimental, quasi-experimental and true experimental) designs. Each of these designs varies in the use of random assignment and random selection.

- No matter the type of quantitative design, descriptive and/or inferential statistics are typically used. Descriptive statistics often serve as a precursor for organizing and summarizing data that will subsequently be assessed to determine what information might be inferred about a population based on a particular sample.

- Descriptive data can be presented in several ways, including tables and graphs (e.g., frequency distributions, histograms, bar graphs), measures of central tendency (i.e., mean, median, mode), measures of variability (e.g., range, standard deviation), and data distributions to determine degree of normality, skewness, and kurtosis.
- One of the key concepts for understanding inferential statistics is correlation. A correlation represents the relationship between two variables and the strength and direction of that relationship. Many statistical tests assess various associations or correlations among variables.
- An extension of correlation is regression. Regression involves the predictive nature of various independent variables based on the relationships among them and their relationship to a dependent variable.
- Inferential statistics involve both parametric and nonparametric statistics. Often, these tests mirror each other, with the exception that nonparametric statistics fail to satisfy particular statistical assumptions.

- Factor analysis, a procedure for reducing variables to a parsimonious number of factors, and meta-analysis, a procedure for condensing study findings to ascertain an overall sense of the effectiveness of a particular intervention, are associated with inferential statistics.
- For qualitative research designs, professional counselors select a research tradition (e.g., case study, ethnography, grounded theory), purposive sampling method(s) (e.g., criterion, maximum variation, homogenous), data collection method(s) (e.g., interviews, observations, documents), and data management and analysis procedures. When constructing a research design, professional counselors must attend to strategies for trustworthiness (e.g., member checking, triangulation).
- Program evaluation is a key process for professional counselors to assess the overall need and effectiveness of various programs and interventions. The four components include a needs assessment, process evaluation, outcome evaluation, and efficiency analysis.

Practice Tests of the National Counselor Examination and the Counselor Preparation Comprehensive Examination

ANSWER FORM FOR NCE SAMPLE TEST—FORM A

Circle the correct response for each test question.

Sum the number correct for each row.

1. a b c d	41. a b c d	81. a b c d	121. a b c d	___
2. a b c d	42. a b c d	82. a b c d	122. a b c d	___
3. a b c d	43. a b c d	83. a b c d	123. a b c d	___
4. a b c d	44. a b c d	84. a b c d	124. a b c d	___
5. a b c d	45. a b c d	85. a b c d	125. a b c d	___
6. a b c d	46. a b c d	86. a b c d	126. a b c d	___
7. a b c d	47. a b c d	87. a b c d	127. a b c d	___
8. a b c d	48. a b c d	88. a b c d	128. a b c d	___
9. a b c d	49. a b c d	89. a b c d	129. a b c d	___
10. a b c d	50. a b c d	90. a b c d	130. a b c d	___
11. a b c d	51. a b c d	91. a b c d	131. a b c d	___
12. a b c d	52. a b c d	92. a b c d	132. a b c d	___
13. a b c d	53. a b c d	93. a b c d	133. a b c d	___
14. a b c d	54. a b c d	94. a b c d	134. a b c d	___
15. a b c d	55. a b c d	95. a b c d	135. a b c d	___
16. a b c d	56. a b c d	96. a b c d	136. a b c d	___
17. a b c d	57. a b c d	97. a b c d	137. a b c d	___
18. a b c d	58. a b c d	98. a b c d	138. a b c d	___
19. a b c d	59. a b c d	99. a b c d	139. a b c d	___
20. a b c d	60. a b c d	100. a b c d	140. a b c d	___
21. a b c d	61. a b c d	101. a b c d	141. a b c d	___
22. a b c d	62. a b c d	102. a b c d	142. a b c d	___
23. a b c d	63. a b c d	103. a b c d	143. a b c d	___
24. a b c d	64. a b c d	104. a b c d	144. a b c d	___
25. a b c d	65. a b c d	105. a b c d	145. a b c d	___
26. a b c d	66. a b c d	106. a b c d	146. a b c d	___
27. a b c d	67. a b c d	107. a b c d	147. a b c d	___
28. a b c d	68. a b c d	108. a b c d	148. a b c d	___
29. a b c d	69. a b c d	109. a b c d	149. a b c d	___
30. a b c d	70. a b c d	110. a b c d	150. a b c d	___
31. a b c d	71. a b c d	111. a b c d	151. a b c d	___
32. a b c d	72. a b c d	112. a b c d	152. a b c d	___
33. a b c d	73. a b c d	113. a b c d	153. a b c d	___
34. a b c d	74. a b c d	114. a b c d	154. a b c d	___
35. a b c d	75. a b c d	115. a b c d	155. a b c d	___
36. a b c d	76. a b c d	116. a b c d	156. a b c d	___
37. a b c d	77. a b c d	117. a b c d	157. a b c d	___
38. a b c d	78. a b c d	118. a b c d	158. a b c d	___
39. a b c d	79. a b c d	119. a b c d	159. a b c d	___
40. a b c d	80. a b c d	120. a b c d		
			160. a b c d	___

Total correct for each column ___ ___ ___ ___ ___ ___ ___ ___

Chapter   1   2   3   4   5   6   7   8

NCE SAMPLE TEST—FORM A

1. The first state to offer licensure to counselors was
   a. South Carolina.
   b. Virginia.
   c. Maryland.
   d. Delaware.

2. Viewing clients from one's own cultural background, which is believed to be superior to other cultures, and ignoring the client's personal cultural context is known as
   a. cultural identity.
   b. assimilation.
   c. introjection.
   d. cultural encapsulation.

3. A 53-year-old woman feels like she is 25 years old. Which category of aging does this statement represent?
   a. Biological aging
   b. Psychological aging
   c. Social aging
   d. All of the above

4. The _____ was founded in 1913 as the first career-guidance organization.
   a. National Vocational Guidance Association (NVGA)
   b. American Personnel and Guidance Association (APGA)
   c. National Career Development Association (NCDA)
   d. National Employment Counseling Association (NECA)

5. Stress management, self-worth, and leisure are dimensions of the _____ factor of the indivisible self model of wellness.
   a. social self
   b. essential self
   c. coping self
   d. creative self

6. When a member forms an unhealthy attachment in group work, this most likely means that the member
   a. has become involved in an abusive relationship with another member.
   b. feels dependent on the relationship formed in group.
   c. has developed a romantic attachment to another group member.
   d. All of the above.

7. James Bryant Conant believed he could create equal opportunities in access to college education through the development of
   a. the Scholastic Aptitude Test (SAT).
   b. the Iowa Test of Basic Skills (ITBS).
   c. the Educational Testing Service (ETS).
   d. TerraNova tests.

8. A researcher recruited two counseling groups with clients who self-reported to be test anxious. One group was instructed on the use of meditation prior to exams; the other was not (and served as controls). Students' anxiety level was assessed after the training just prior to final exams. What research design has just been described?
   a. Single group posttest
   b. Quasi-experimental
   c. Randomized experimental
   d. Pre-experimental

9. The civil rights law that mandates equal access for individuals with disabilities to opportunities and services is called
   a. FERPA.
   b. HIPAA.
   c. Section 504 of the *U.S. Rehabilitation Act.*
   d. CAPTA.

10. The _____ model refers to when persons reject both the customs and values of the new culture and their country of origin.
    a. separation
    b. marginalization
    c. biculturalism
    d. assimilation

11. The _____ controls higher order behavior and conscious thought.
    a. hindbrain
    b. midbrain
    c. forebrain
    d. limbic system

12. Williamson's Minnesota point of view is considered a
    a. nondirective counseling approach.
    b. cognitive-behavioral counseling approach.
    c. directive counseling approach.
    d. psychodynamic counseling approach.

13. An example of resistance is
    a. a client who refuses to talk.
    b. a client who frequently misses appointments.
    c. a client who tries to steer conversations toward irrelevant, "safe" topics.
    d. All of the above.

14. A counselor may choose to run a group because
    a. it is more cost efficient than individual counseling.
    b. it is time efficient.
    c. it presents members with a microcosm of society.
    d. All of the above.

15. Power tests
    a. use time to prevent perfect scores.
    b. are concerned with normal performance.
    c. assess how quickly the test-taker can understand the question and choose the right answer.
    d. prevent perfect scores by including difficult test items.

16. A counselor wants to explore the relationship between three types of counseling interventions and client satisfaction. Which of the following would represent a confounding variable?
    a. Client issue: each intervention addresses a different client problem
    b. Time of day: all interventions occur at 10:00 a.m.
    c. Medication use: Clients under study for each intervention are heterogeneous with respect to medications.
    d. Environmental factors: Clients vary in their experiences to trauma.

17. A child who has a documented learning disability but is doing well in all of his or her classes would most likely
    a. not qualify for special education services under IDEA or accommodations under Section 504.
    b. qualify for special education services under IDEA but not accommodations under Section 504.

c. not qualify for special education services under IDEA but would qualify for accommodations under Section 504.

d. qualify for special education services under IDEA and accommodations under Section 504.

18. In Ivan Pavlov's experiment with dogs, the unconditioned stimulus was the
   a. salivation.
   b. food.
   c. bell.
   d. None of the above.

19. An individual who enjoys acting would be demonstrating a manifest interest by
   a. stating out loud, "I enjoy acting."
   b. applying to a school that specialized in the performing arts.
   c. performing the lead role in a school play.
   d. talking to a career counselor about career options in theater.

20. A person who is friendly and empathetic would most likely score high on the _____ factor of the Five Factor model.
   a. openness
   b. affability
   c. conscientiousness
   d. agreeableness

21. Group member screening is
   a. a legal requirement.
   b. an ethical requirement.
   c. recommended but neither a legal nor an ethical requirement.
   d. both a legal and an ethical requirement.

22. The _____ is NOT an example of a subjective test.
   a. Rorschach inkblot test
   b. sentence completion test
   c. Mental Status Exam (MSE)
   d. Myers-Briggs Type Indicator

23. A sampling method in which participants from an entire population have an equal chance of being selected is known as _____ sampling.
   a. systematic
   b. simple random
   c. quota
   d. stratified

24. A counselor suspects that one of her minor clients is being physically abused, so she files a report with child protective services. CPS conducts an investigation and finds that no abuse has occurred or is occurring with that child. In this situation, the counselor
   a. would be held liable for making a false report.
   b. would not be held liable unless the report was made with malice.
   c. would receive a warning from CPS.
   d. would be investigated by an ethics committee.

25. Burnout can lead to
   a. physical exhaustion.
   b. emotional exhaustion.
   c. an increased sense of personal accomplishment.
   d. social withdrawal.

26. Assessment generally occurs during the _____ stage of counseling.
   a. action/intervention
   b. termination
   c. relationship-building
   d. intake

27. According to the Association for Specialists in Group Work, the four categories of group work are
   a. growth groups, counseling groups, T-groups, and psychotherapy groups.
   b. task groups, psychoeducational groups, counseling groups, and psychotherapy groups.
   c. self-help groups, psychotherapy groups, task groups, and psychoeducational groups.
   d. encounter groups, counseling groups, psychoeducational groups, and psychotherapy groups.

28. According to _____ test-users must have technical knowledge regarding the validity and reliability of test results.
   a. *Rights and Responsibilities of Test-Takers*
   b. *Responsibilities of Users of Standardized Tests* (RUST)
   c. *Tests Critiques*
   d. *Health Insurance Portability and Accountability Act* of 1996 (HIPAA)

29. Jenny wants to examine two scores for a group of adolescents in an after-school program based on pretest and posttest data. Which analysis is most appropriate?
   a. Independent t-test
   b. Dependent t-test
   c. Logistic regression design
   d. ANCOVA

30. In the _____ consultation model, there is no "expert"; all members are equally responsible for the outcome.
   a. collaborative-dependent
   b. collaborative-interdependent
   c. triadic-dependent
   d. triadic-interdependent

31. Which of the following is a closed-ended question?
   a. "What went through your mind when your girlfriend was breaking up with you?"
   b. "How many times have you fought with your daughter in the past week?"
   c. "What is your relationship with your brother like now?"
   d. "How do you feel about your decision to go back to school?"

32. In most states, for counselors to work in private practice, they must obtain
   a. licensure.
   b. certification.
   c. licensure and certification.
   d. neither licensure nor certification.

33. The counseling theory called _____ is deterministic.
   a. individual psychology
   b. psychoanalysis
   c. humanistic
   d. existential

34. Which of the following factors is NOT related to career salience?
   a. Participation: spending time and energy in a work role
   b. Commitment: an emotional attachment to the work role
   c. Interest: engaging in meaningful vocational activities
   d. Value expectation: the satisfaction gained from the vocational decisions and actions one makes throughout the course of one's lifespan

35. Licensure occurs at the
   a. national level.
   b. regional level.
   c. state level.
   d. county level.

36. The superego resides in a person's
   a. preconscious mind.
   b. conscious mind.
   c. unconscious mind.
   d. subconscious mind.

37. Which of the following is NOT true concerning construct validity?
   a. Construct validity is empirically established by examining the relationship between data collected from the instrument and a specific criterion.
   b. Construct validity is important to establish when an instrument measures an abstract construct.
   c. Construct validity is defined as the extent to which an instrument measures a theoretical construct.
   d. Construct validity can be determined through experimental design or factor analysis.

38. _____ have been trained to help clients work through their issues by uncovering and examining unconscious conflicts.
   a. Psychologists
   b. Psychoanalysts
   c. Psychiatrists
   d. Mental health counselors

39. _____ were considered by Freud to be the "royal road to the unconscious."
   a. Dreams
   b. Memories
   c. Early childhood recollections
   d. Fantasies

40. Ethnocentrism means
   a. believing that other cultures are more worthy than one's own.
   b. believing that one's own culture is superior to others.
   c. believing culturally appropriate research is only done through ethnography.
   d. believing that gender roles should be congruent with a culture.

41. A client tells his counselor that after thinking about all of the potential consequences, he has decided to engage in an extramarital affair. The counselor believes he will be making a huge mistake if he takes this course of action; however, after consideration, the counselor decides to accept and respect the client's decision and not try to convince the client to change his mind. In this situation, the counselor is upholding the ethical principle of
   a. independence.
   b. fidelity.
   c. autonomy.
   d. self-determination.

42. Spiritual bypass refers to
   a. a counselor not discussing spirituality with a client.
   b. a client not discussing spirituality with a counselor.
   c. an agency having an anti-discrimination policy that prohibits spirituality questions on the intake.
   d. avoiding problematic issues by using spirituality instead of facing problems.

43. When Thomas has a tantrum and throws toys around the house, his mother tells him that because of his behavior he will have to forfeit his outside play privileges for the day. What type of reinforcement is she using?
   a. Positive reinforcement
   b. Negative reinforcement
   c. Punishment, stimulus applied
   d. Punishment, stimulus removed

44. _____ is an example of an investigative occupation.
   a. Mechanic
   b. Accountant
   c. Biologist
   d. Real estate agent

45. Adler believed that a person's lifestyle is established by the age of
   a. 4 years.
   b. 5 years.
   c. 6 years.
   d. 7 years.

46. A _____ is established with the overarching purpose of accomplishing a specified goal.
   a. T-group
   b. task group
   c. psychoeducational group
   d. psychotherapy group

47. In the classical test theory equation, $X = T + e$, e represents the
   a. reliability of a test.
   b. reliability of a person's test score across several test administrations.
   c. amount of error present during test administration.
   d. observed test score.

48. Computing _____ allows a researcher to examine if statistically significant relationships are practically meaningful.
   a. effect size
   b. power
   c. p-value
   d. Cronbach's alpha

49. A counselor who decides to attend the graduation ceremony of one of his adult clients who, after many years of hard work, is finally graduating from college must ethically
   a. gain consent from the client to attend.
   b. document in writing his reason for attending.
   c. seek to repair any damages if they occur as a result of the nonprofessional interaction.
   d. All of the above.

50. Internalized oppression, or when minority members espouse the majority opinion, is also known as
   a. primary oppression.
   b. secondary oppression.
   c. tertiary oppression.
   d. double jeopardy.

51. A young child sees a dog and exclaims, "Look, Dad, a cat!" The child only noticed that the animal had four legs, like the family's pet cat. Which Piagetian concept does this scenario best exemplify?
   a. Assimilation
   b. Cognitive dissonance
   c. Accommodation
   d. Symbolic representation

52. According to the Myers-Briggs type theory, an individual who uses all five senses to take in information about the world uses the _____ dimension of perceiving.
   a. Sensing
   b. Intuition
   c. Thinking
   d. Feeling

53. Which of the following is NOT a true statement about the shadow archetype in Jungian analytic psychology?
    a. The shadow represents the parts of the self that people do not want to recognize or accept.
    b. The shadow contains only negative aspects of people's personalities.
    c. The shadow may be projected onto others if it is not brought into awareness.
    d. All of the above.

54. As a group enters the working stage, all of the following should occur EXCEPT
    a. the leader should transfer more power to group members.
    b. the leader should become less directive.
    c. the leader should become more active.
    d. group members should be given more responsibility.

55. If an individual's mean score after multiple test administrations is 84 and the SEM is 5, what can be said about the distribution of his observed scores?
    a. 95% of the time his observed scores will fall between 89 and 79.
    b. 68% of the time his observed scores will fall between 89 and 79.
    c. 68% of the time his observed scores will fall between 91 and 74.
    d. There is not enough information provided to make a determination.

56. If scores are piled up at the low end of the scale, the distribution is said to be
    a. negatively skewed.
    b. positively skewed.
    c. leptokurtic.
    d. platykurtic.

57. Bartering with a client may be reasonable under the following circumstances EXCEPT
    a. if it is suggested by the client.
    b. if it is an accepted convention in the community.
    c. if the counselor thinks it is in the client's best interest.
    d. if the exchange is fair.

58. A student has trouble answering questions on her midterm exam because of information she just learned for the final exam. This student is experiencing
    a. poor retrieval.
    b. retroactive inhibition.
    c. decay of memory traces.
    d. proactive inhibition.

59. Super's establishment stage involves
    a. the process of moving from a tentative career plan to a more specific occupational choice.
    b. moving into a position with added responsibilities and an increase in pay and status.
    c. contributing to the progress of the field through new developments.
    d. the clarification of different types of careers that are of interest to an individual.

60. _____ is NOT one of the four functions of Jung's personality typology.
    a. Thinking
    b. Feeling
    c. Behaving
    d. Intuition

61. The preferred group leadership style is
    a. authoritarian.
    b. democratic.
    c. laissez-faire.
    d. It depends on a variety of factors, such as the type of group and the stage of the group process.

62. The developer of a challenging test computes each item's difficulty. He finds that the majority of his test items have an item difficulty score ranging from .90 to .95. What can be said about the test?
    a. The test developer needs to make his test items more difficult.
    b. The test developer needs to make his test items easier.
    c. The test questions were not consistent.
    d. The item difficulty score is high, and the test developer does not need to make any corrections to the individual items.

63. Carlita would like to study domestic violence intervention in a community. She decides to interview survivors and their families, the mayor, local medical and mental health professionals, and a city council member. Which research tradition is most closely aligned with her design?
    a. Grounded theory
    b. Phenomenology
    c. Ethnography
    d. Biography

64. A records custodian is an individual appointed by a counselor to
    a. maintain and organize the counselor's records.
    b. inform the counselor about the legal requirements for record keeping.
    c. implement the counselor's plan regarding transfer of records and client care in the event of the counselor's death or impairment.
    d. All of the above.

65. A year ago, Jan's boss informed her that she would be promoted to senior analyst for her outstanding job performance; however, Jan was never promoted. According to Schlossberg, this is an example of a(n)
    a. nonevent.
    b. chronic hassle.
    c. unanticipated transition.
    d. anticipated transition.

66. According to _____, dreams have hidden symbolism.
    a. Perls
    b. Freud
    c. Jung
    d. All of the above.

67. _____ should be used to protect a group from a member's harmful behavior.
    a. Interpreting
    b. Blocking
    c. Confronting
    d. Providing feedback

68. An inventory that uses a Likert-type scale is likely to yield _____ data.
    a. interval
    b. ordinal
    c. nominal
    d. ratio

69. Which of the following research paradigms references reliability and validity considerations?
    a. Positivism
    b. Post-positivism
    c. Critical
    d. Constructivism

70. _____ involves removing a child so that he or she is no longer able to receive positive reinforcement
   a. Overcorrection
   b. Extinction
   c. Response cost
   d. Time out

71. "My wedding reception would have been wonderful if the DJ hadn't been late." This example best represents what type of distorted thinking?
   a. Overgeneralization
   b. Dichotomous thinking
   c. Magnification
   d. Selective abstraction

72. Which of the following scenarios is considered ethical according to the ACA *Code of Ethics*?
   a. Counselor educators who use their own textbooks in their classes
   b. Counselors who urge their clients to buy their products
   c. Counselors who solicit testimonials from current clients
   d. All of the above.

73. A counselor is working with a teenage client who finds herself ruminating obsessively about what would happen if her parents decided to get a divorce. These negative thought cycles are causing her considerable distress and are making it hard for her to focus in school. What cognitive technique might be most useful for this client to help her break out of these cycles when they occur?
   a. Cognitive rehearsal
   b. Thought stopping
   c. Cognitive disputation
   d. Shame attack exercises

74. Which career decision-making theory rests on the assumption that stress significantly contributes to the quality of the decision that is made—that is, high levels of stress can lead to a "defective" career decision?
   a. Janis and Mann's conflict model of decision making
   b. Gelatt's decision-making model
   c. Tiedeman and O'Hara's theory of career decision making
   d. Social learning theory

75. A counselor uses an assessment tool to evaluate a client whose cultural background is not represented in the test's norms. The counselor
   a. should not have used that assessment to evaluate the client.
   b. was justified in using the assessment if the client consented.
   c. should be careful when reporting the results to the client and be sure to frame the results in the proper perspective.
   d. should not report the results of the assessment to the client.

76. Which of the following words, when found in a client statement, would most likely indicate an irrational thought or belief?
   a. Want
   b. Would like
   c. Wish
   d. Must

77. What percentage of a normally distributed population's scores fall between ±3 standard deviations?
   a. 95%
   b. 99%
   c. 68%
   d. 2%

78. A fire alarm interrupts the administration of a standardized assessment. The counselor should do all of the following EXCEPT
   a. immediately reschedule the assessment.
   b. make a note of the disruption.
   c. consider the disruption when interpreting the results of the assessment.
   d. put the test results in the proper perspective when reporting them to the client.

79. The word *gestalt* can be defined as
   a. a whole that is greater than the sum of its parts.
   b. an adaptive pattern of behavior.
   c. the individual parts that make up each individual.
   d. All of the above.

80. One of the five stages of prejudice is _____, which indicates a person shares harmful views of a group with persons who have similar views but has not taken action.
   a. discrimination
   b. avoidance
   c. assimilation
   d. antilocution

81. Internet counselors should
   a. inform clients about how they can be reached should a session end due to a technological error.
   b. take steps to confirm the identity of their clients before sessions.
   c. provide clients with information about local counseling services.
   d. All of the above.

82. A cultural characteristic common within the African American community is
   a. harmony with nature.
   b. respect for the family.
   c. egalitarian gender roles.
   d. All of the above.

83. Language acquisition device, surface structures, and deep structures are all concepts associated with which theory of language development?
   a. Learning theory approach
   b. Nativist approach
   c. Interactionist approach
   d. Epigenetic approach

84. Which career theory proposes that occupational selection is heavily influenced by the psychological needs that develop from interactions between children and their parents?
   a. Personal construct psychology
   b. Roe's personality development and occupational classification
   c. Social learning theory
   d. Gottfredson's theory of circumscription, compromise, and self-creation

85. _____ is NOT one of the five basic human needs, as proposed by Glasser.
   a. Survival
   b. Spirituality
   c. Freedom
   d. Fun

86. Which quadrant of the Johari window increases as a result of self-disclosure?
   a. Public/open quadrant
   b. Private/hidden quadrant
   c. Blind quadrant
   d. Unknown/unconscious quadrant

87. If a student scored a 45 on an exam with a mean of 35 and a standard deviation of 5, what would be the student's z-score?
    a. +2
    b. −1
    c. 0
    d. +1.5

88. _____ research is most interested in baseline data.
    a. Quantitative
    b. Qualitative
    c. Single subject
    d. Longitudinal

89. The following is NOT a component that must be proved in a negligence or malpractice case.
    a. There was a legal duty owed to the plaintiff by the defendant.
    b. The plaintiff has or had a physical injury.
    c. The defendant breached the legal duty owed to the plaintiff.
    d. The defendant's breach of duty caused the plaintiff's injury.

90. Crises that arise due to unexpected situations, such as being fired, are considered to be
    a. developmental crises.
    b. existential crises.
    c. situational crises.
    d. environmental crises.

91. Most elementary school students are in the _____ stage of psychosocial development.
    a. identity vs. role confusion
    b. initiative vs. guilt
    c. industry vs. inferiority
    d. autonomy vs. shame and doubt

92. _____ contains three instruments that measure interest, abilities, and values and can be administered individually or together.
    a. The California Occupational Preference Survey (COPS)
    b. Kuder Career Search
    c. Keirsey Temperament Sorter II
    d. Career Thoughts Inventory

93. _____ is NOT one of the three core conditions of counseling.
    a. Encouragement
    b. Empathy
    c. Congruence
    d. Unconditional positive regard

94. When a group member uses sarcasm, it is usually an attempt to hide
    a. anger.
    b. neediness.
    c. a desire for control.
    d. a desire for attention.

95. What can we say about a fourth-grader who has completed 6 months of fourth grade and has a grade equivalent score of 6.1 in math?
    a. The student scored average in math when compared to her classmates.
    b. The student needs to be moved into sixth-grade math.
    c. The student is performing at the sixth-grade level in math.
    d. The student is performing higher in math than most students in the fourth grade.

96. A college counselor is interested in conducting a study on college administrators' attitudes toward Greek organizations. He conducts focus groups with several administrators and asks other administrators to complete rating scales regarding their satisfaction with these organizations. This is an example of _____ research.
    a. concurrent
    b. action

c. sequential exploratory
d. sequential explanatory

97. The legal case that established the counselor's duty to warn/protect in California was
    a. *Poddar v. Regents of the University of California.*
    b. *Tarasoff v. Poddar.*
    c. *Tarasoff v. Regents of the University of California.*
    d. *Regents of the University of California v. Tarasoff.*

98. After experiencing considerable pressure from his family, a high school graduate decides to attend his father's alma mater and pursue the same field of study as his father did so that he can eventually become a partner in the family business. This student is displaying the _____ status.
    a. identity diffusion
    b. identity moratorium
    c. identity foreclosure
    d. identity achievement

99. _____ inventories identify personal factors that may impede an individual's career development process.
    a. Interest
    b. Personality
    c. Values
    d. Career development

100. A man thinks something is wrong with him because he is more interested in spending time with his family and friends than excelling in his career. He says that he is embarrassed about his lack of ambition because he knows men are supposed to be the family breadwinners. Narrative therapists would describe his self-narrative as
    a. multilayered.
    b. thin.
    c. superficial.
    d. thick.

101. _____ is NOT a potential benefit of a heterogeneous group.
    a. Better generalization
    b. Better reality testing
    c. Decreased resistance
    d. More in-depth learning

102. What are the three types of aptitude testing?
    a. Readiness testing, vocational aptitude testing, and diagnostic testing
    b. Cognitive ability testing, vocational aptitude testing, and intelligence testing
    c. Survey batteries, cognitive ability testing, and intelligence testing
    d. Readiness testing, survey batteries, and diagnostic testing

103. A counseling researcher is interested in investigating the following research question: "What is the influence of socioeconomic status and school climate on academic achievement?" The independent variable is
    a. socioeconomic status.
    b. academic achievement.
    c. gender.
    d. geography.

104. Confidentiality and privileged communication belong to the
    a. counselor.
    b. client.
    c. court.
    d. client's attorney.

105. According to the Department of Labor's 2005 Occupational Projections, _____ occupations are expected to grow faster than any other occupational group.
    a. professional
    b. construction and extraction
    c. production
    d. service

106. It is extremely hard to work with clients until they have become
    a. customers.
    b. complainants.
    c. managers.
    d. visitors.

107. Which of the following may indicate that an individual is not appropriate for group work.
    a. Troublesome attention-seeking behavior
    b. Interpersonal problems
    c. Inadequate social skills
    d. All of the above.

108. Achievement tests are designed to
    a. assess what one has learned at the time of testing.
    b. identify academically at-risk students, but they cannot measure student academic growth.
    c. assess what a person is capable of learning.
    d. predict future performance in a school subject.

109. What is the key distinction between cluster and quota sampling methods?
    a. Use of individuals
    b. Statistical power
    c. Validity threats
    d. Randomization

110. Most family models of counseling are based on
    a. psychodynamic theories.
    b. strategic counseling theory.
    c. general systems theory.
    d. humanistic-existential theories.

111. Which of the following is NOT a fully accurate statement about family rules?
    a. Family rules help set expectations for family members.
    b. Family rules provide a basis for family interactions.
    c. Family rules provide families with predictability.
    d. Family rules are stated overtly.

112. A counselor who receives a legal document asking her to provide information about a client to the court has most likely been given a
    a. court order.
    b. search warrant.
    c. subpoena.
    d. summons.

113. It is best for family systems to
    a. be open.
    b. be closed.
    c. strike a balance between being fully open and fully closed.
    d. None of the above.

114. Which source of occupational information is published by JIST Works and has over 900 occupations that are classified into 14 interest categories and 83 work groups?
    a. Standard Occupational Classification System (SOC)
    b. *Occupational Outlook Handbook* (OOH)
    c. Occupational Information Network (O*NET)
    d. *Guide for Occupational Exploration* (GOE)

115. Heightened awareness of and interest in multicultural issues in counseling emerged in the
    a. 1950s.
    b. 1960s.
    c. 1970s.
    d. 1980s.

116. People who are "differentiated" are
    a. able to enter into emotional family situations without becoming overly affected or involved.
    b. cut off from their families.
    c. fused with their families.
    d. unable to balance logic and affect.

117. The _____ is NOT a diagnostic aptitude test?
    a. Key Math Diagnostic Test
    b. Test of Adult Basic Education
    c. Wide Range Achievement Test
    d. Metropolitan Achievement Test

118. Before changing its name to ACA in 1993 (as it is known today), this organization enacted its second name change in 1983 from APGA to
    a. American Mental Health Counselors Association (AMHCA).
    b. American Association of Counseling and Development (AACD).
    c. National Counseling Association (NCA).
    d. Counseling Association of America (CAA).

119. To help clients increase their level of differentiation, Bowen recommends
    a. back-home visits.
    b. creating a genogram.
    c. unbalancing.
    d. learning how to communicate congruently.

120. Whites who claim to be "color blind" would be best characterized by which of Helms' racial identity statuses?
    a. Disintegration
    b. Reintegration
    c. Autonomy
    d. Contact

121. The overarching spirit behind informed consent is to
    a. procure a physical document affirming the client's consent to be counseled.
    b. ensure that clients fully understand the counseling process and their right to decline treatment.
    c. protect counselors from lawsuits.
    d. inform clients about the potential harms of counseling.

122. In general, among American Indians honor and respect are gained through
    a. sharing.
    b. educational achievement.
    c. material wealth.
    d. None of the above.

123. The highest level of Kohlberg's stage theory of moral development is
    a. law and order.
    b. universal ethical principles.
    c. social/moral contract and system of laws.
    d. None of the above.

124. Which of the following is TRUE concerning information interviews?
    a. It is an employment interview.
    b. The goal of an informational interview is to obtain a job.

c. The informational interview is a tool used to assist clients in exploring occupations.

d. None of the above are true.

125. Experiential family counseling is most reminiscent of
    a. Gestalt therapy.
    b. narrative therapy.
    c. Adlerian psychology.
    d. humanistic counseling.

126. All of the following are examples of structural issues in group work EXCEPT
    a. the topic under discussion.
    b. type and function of group.
    c. size of group.
    d. open vs. closed group.

127. Which one of the following assessments describes the personality traits of nonpathological, well-adjusted individuals?
    a. California Psychological Inventory
    b. Million Clinical Multiaxial Inventory
    c. Minnesota Multiphasic Personality Inventory
    d. None of the above.

128. Children in Head Start programs show a significant improvement in academic skills. Regarding threats to internal validity, the success of Head Start might be most affected by
    a. diffusion of treatment.
    b. testing.
    c. instrumentation.
    d. statistical regression.

129. Eligibility for services under IDEA lasts from birth until age
    a. 16 years.
    b. 18 years.
    c. 21 years.
    d. 25 years.

130. Which of the following statements is true regarding the term *transgender*?
    a. It represents individuals who are attracted only to the opposite sex.
    b. It is solely synonymous with sex reassignment.
    c. It represents individuals who identify only with the opposite gender.
    d. It is an umbrella term for anyone permanently or periodically identifying with another gender.

131. The most harmful parenting style is
    a. authoritative.
    b. permissive.
    c. authoritarian.
    d. uninvolved.

132. The middle phase of career counseling is often referred to as the
    a. goal-setting stage.
    b. intervention stage.
    c. working stage.
    d. information-gathering stage.

133. After a long day at work, a wife comes home tired. Her husband notices her fatigue and cooks dinner for her. The next morning, the wife packs her husband a lunch, thankful for his kindness the previous night. Strategic family therapists refer to this reciprocal behavior as
    a. punctuation.
    b. the golden rule.
    c. quid pro quo.
    d. tit for tat.

134. Group cohesion is strengthened when
    a. group membership is stable.
    b. both group goals and personal goals are set.
    c. group members must work together to achieve established goals.
    d. All of the above.

135. Informal assessments are unlike formal assessments in that they
    a. provide a comparison to a broader group.
    b. are standardized tests.
    c. are used in high-stakes testing.
    d. are subjective assessment techniques used to identify the specific strengths and needs of a client.

136. A counselor is interested in measuring the success of a program on clients over time. As a select group of clients are studied, the way success is measured becomes more restrictive. What type of single subject research design does this best describe?
    a. A-B-C
    b. Changing criterion
    c. Between series
    d. Parametric

137. HIPAA is a federal law that applies to
    a. insurance companies.
    b. HMOs.
    c. mental health professionals.
    d. All of the above.

138. A homicide would be categorized as
    a. a situational crisis.
    b. an existential crisis.
    c. a developmental crisis.
    d. a psychiatric crisis.

139. Career placement services
    a. use career coaches, who devise strategies to help individuals overcome vocational barriers.
    b. integrate career-related information and activities into educational curricula.
    c. typically do not assist dislocated workers.
    d. focus on helping individuals obtain employment and are provided by public/private agencies and institutions of higher education.

140. Which of the following is NOT an accurate statement about paradoxical intention?
    a. Paradoxical intention should be used with caution.
    b. Paradoxical intention can reduce client resistance.
    c. Paradoxical intention helps clients understand that they have control over their behavior.
    d. Paradoxical intention is appropriate for almost all client problems.

141. A group leader notices an instance of resistance in a group member but finds that it does not hinder the group process. The leader should
    a. interpret it.
    b. ignore it.
    c. ask the group to discuss the behavior.
    d. meet individually with the group member to explore the resistant behavior.

142. A(n) _____ behavioral rating scale is administered to identify the problematic behavior, and a(n) _____ behavioral rating scale is subsequently administered to provide detailed information about the problematic behavior.
    a. broad-band; narrow-band
    b. unstructured; structured

    c. narrow-band; broad-band

    d. narrative; event

143. The minimum score for a data set is 5, whereas the maximum score is 25. The range would be

    a. 5.

    b. 25.

    c. 19.

    d. 21.

144. If a counselor suspects that a minor client is being abused, she should make a report to child protective services within ＿＿ hours of first having reason to suspect.

    a. 24

    b. 48

    c. 72

    d. 96

145. ＿＿＿＿＿ refers to the systematic process for identifying gaps between "what is" and "what should be."

    a. Program planning

    b. Program evaluation

    c. Needs assessment

    d. Program design

146. A counselor describes a child's temper tantrums as an attempt to bring her parents together. Milan systemic family counselors would call this

    a. a positive connotation.

    b. revealing.

    c. relabeling.

    d. None of the above.

147. In group work, process evaluations measure

    a. group effectiveness.

    b. group outcomes.

    c. group dynamics.

    d. level of group conflict and resistance.

148. During an intake meeting, your client discloses that he swallowed several sleeping pills just before coming to your office with the intent to end his life. What would be this client's suicide lethality?

    a. Low lethality

    b. Moderate lethality

    c. Moderate-high lethality

    d. High lethality

149. ＿＿＿＿＿ is not a component of trustworthiness.

    a. Credibility

    b. Dependability

    c. Reliability

    d. Transferability

150. Milan systemic family counselors believe that it is imperative to remain

    a. subjective.

    b. neutral.

    c. impassive.

    d. partisan.

151. Two teenage children believe that some of the family rules that they must abide by are so unfair that they have joined together to give their parents a hard time. Structural family counselors refer to this relationship as a(n)

    a. alignment.

    b. power struggle.

    c. alliance.

    d. coalition.

152. Being part of an HMO can result in all of the following EXCEPT

    a. limitations in client confidentiality.

    b. a steady flow of clients.

    c. limitations in the amount of time allowed to treat clients.

    d. the ability to treat clients without ever making a diagnosis.

153. Making hypotheses is a central component of which type of family counseling?

    a. Structural family counseling

    b. Strategic family therapy

    c. Milan systemic family counseling

    d. Bowen family systems therapy

154. Specific, measurable, action-oriented steps that must be attained to accomplish a program goal are referred to as

    a. formative evaluations.

    b. program objectives.

    c. summative evaluations.

    d. program mission statements.

155. Clinical mental health counselors work in

    a. community organizations.

    b. drug rehabilitation centers.

    c. hospitals.

    d. All of the above.

156. ＿＿＿＿＿ is NOT one of the seven domains in Lazarus' multimodal counseling?

    a. Sensations

    b. Interpersonal relationships

    c. Connections

    d. Imagery

157. Considering only applicant SAT scores for an academic scholarship perpetuates ＿＿＿＿＿ bias.

    a. ecological

    b. response

    c. examiner

    d. test

158. Counselors who work in ＿＿＿＿＿ are also considered to be educators

    a. college admissions counseling

    b. college counseling

    c. school counseling

    d. family counseling

159. An interaction between a boss who is operating from an adult ego state and an employee who is operating from a natural child ego state is an example of a(n) ＿＿＿＿＿ transaction.

    a. complementary

    b. covert

    c. ulterior

    d. crossed

160. A counselor who works at a community agency notices an unethical practice that commonly occurs at her place of work. She informs her supervisor, but her supervisor fails to rectify the problem, so the counselor files a complaint with an ethics committee. When the supervisor finds out, she fires the counselor. In this situation, the supervisor behaved in

    a. an ethical manner; the counselor should not have accepted employment there if she did not agree with the practices.

    b. an ethical manner; the counselor betrayed the supervisor's trust and went above her authority.

    c. an unethical manner; the counselor should not have been fired for trying to resolve an ethical concern in an appropriate manner.

    d. a legal manner but not an ethical one.

ANSWER KEY FOR NCE SAMPLE TEST—FORM A

1. b	21. b	41. c	61. d	81. d	101. c	121. b	141. b
2. d	22. d	42. d	62. a	82. d	102. b	122. a	142. a
3. b	23. b	43. d	63. c	83. b	103. a	123. b	143. d
4. a	24. b	44. c	64. c	84. b	104. b	124. c	144. c
5. c	25. b	45. b	65. a	85. b	105. a	125. d	145. c
6. b	26. a	46. b	66. b	86. a	106. a	126. a	146. a
7. a	27. b	47. c	67. b	87. a	107. a	127. a	147. c
8. b	28. b	48. a	68. b	88. c	108. a	128. d	148. d
9. c	29. b	49. d	69. b	89. b	109. d	129. c	149. c
10. b	30. b	50. c	70. d	90. c	110. c	130. d	150. b
11. c	31. b	51. a	71. d	91. c	111. d	131. d	151. d
12. c	32. a	52. a	72. a	92. a	112. c	132. c	152. d
13. d	33. b	53. b	73. b	93. a	113. c	133. c	153. c
14. d	34. c	54. c	74. c	94. a	114. d	134. d	154. b
15. d	35. c	55. b	75. c	95. d	115. c	135. d	155. d
16. a	36. c	56. b	76. d	96. a	116. a	136. b	156. c
17. a	37. a	57. c	77. b	97. c	117. d	137. d	157. a
18. b	38. b	58. b	78. a	98. c	118. b	138. a	158. c
19. c	39. a	59. b	79. a	99. d	119. a	139. d	159. d
20. d	40. b	60. c	80. d	100. b	120. d	140. d	160. c

ANSWER FORM FOR NCE SAMPLE TEST—FORM B

Circle the correct response for each test question.

Sum the number correct for each row.

1. a b c d	41. a b c d	81. a b c d	121. a b c d	___
2. a b c d	42. a b c d	82. a b c d	122. a b c d	___
3. a b c d	43. a b c d	83. a b c d	123. a b c d	___
4. a b c d	44. a b c d	84. a b c d	124. a b c d	___
5. a b c d	45. a b c d	85. a b c d	125. a b c d	___
6. a b c d	46. a b c d	86. a b c d	126. a b c d	___
7. a b c d	47. a b c d	87. a b c d	127. a b c d	___
8. a b c d	48. a b c d	88. a b c d	128. a b c d	___
9. a b c d	49. a b c d	89. a b c d	129. a b c d	___
10. a b c d	50. a b c d	90. a b c d	130. a b c d	___
11. a b c d	51. a b c d	91. a b c d	131. a b c d	___
12. a b c d	52. a b c d	92. a b c d	132. a b c d	___
13. a b c d	53. a b c d	93. a b c d	133. a b c d	___
14. a b c d	54. a b c d	94. a b c d	134. a b c d	___
15. a b c d	55. a b c d	95. a b c d	135. a b c d	___
16. a b c d	56. a b c d	96. a b c d	136. a b c d	___
17. a b c d	57. a b c d	97. a b c d	137. a b c d	___
18. a b c d	58. a b c d	98. a b c d	138. a b c d	___
19. a b c d	59. a b c d	99. a b c d	139. a b c d	___
20. a b c d	60. a b c d	100. a b c d	140. a b c d	___
21. a b c d	61. a b c d	101. a b c d	141. a b c d	___
22. a b c d	62. a b c d	102. a b c d	142. a b c d	___
23. a b c d	63. a b c d	103. a b c d	143. a b c d	___
24. a b c d	64. a b c d	104. a b c d	144. a b c d	___
25. a b c d	65. a b c d	105. a b c d	145. a b c d	___
26. a b c d	66. a b c d	106. a b c d	146. a b c d	___
27. a b c d	67. a b c d	107. a b c d	147. a b c d	___
28. a b c d	68. a b c d	108. a b c d	148. a b c d	___
29. a b c d	69. a b c d	109. a b c d	149. a b c d	___
30. a b c d	70. a b c d	110. a b c d	150. a b c d	___
31. a b c d	71. a b c d	111. a b c d	151. a b c d	___
32. a b c d	72. a b c d	112. a b c d	152. a b c d	___
33. a b c d	73. a b c d	113. a b c d	153. a b c d	___
34. a b c d	74. a b c d	114. a b c d	154. a b c d	___
35. a b c d	75. a b c d	115. a b c d	155. a b c d	___
36. a b c d	76. a b c d	116. a b c d	156. a b c d	___
37. a b c d	77. a b c d	117. a b c d	157. a b c d	___
38. a b c d	78. a b c d	118. a b c d	158. a b c d	___
39. a b c d	79. a b c d	119. a b c d	159. a b c d	___
40. a b c d	80. a b c d	120. a b c d		___
			160. a b c d	___

Total correct for each column ___ ___ ___ ___ ___ ___ ___ ___

Chapter 1   2   3   4   5   6   7   8

NCE SAMPLE TEST—FORM B

1. The concept of a free appropriate public education (FAPE) is associated with
   a. Section 504.
   b. FERPA.
   c. HIPAA.
   d. IDEA.

2. Acculturation level is LEAST influenced by
   a. disability status.
   b. number of years in the new country.
   c. country of origin.
   d. age at beginning of acculturation process.

3. Which part of the brain is least developed at birth?
   a. Hindbrain
   b. Midbrain
   c. Forebrain
   d. Thalamus

4. The _____ was passed in response to the U.S.S.R.'s launching of *Sputnik* and sought to increase the number of trained counselors in secondary schools to raise the number of students enrolled in higher education that were pursuing math and science careers.
   a. Wagner-Peyser Act of 1933
   b. National Defense Education Act (NDEA)
   c. Vocational Education Act of 1963
   d. Smith-Hughes National Vocational Education Act

5. Wellness is
   a. the absence of illness.
   b. a state of complete well-being—physical, cognitive, and psychological.
   c. easily achieved.
   d. All of the above.

6. _____ is the name of the ACA division dedicated to group work.
   a. American Group Psychotherapy Association
   b. Association for Specialists in Group Work
   c. National Group Work Association
   d. American Society of Group Psychotherapy and Psychodrama

7. This 19th-century pioneer is credited with recognizing that mental retardation was related to developmental deficiencies rather than mental illness.
   a. Edouard Seguin
   b. Charles Spearman
   c. Jean Esquirol
   d. Arthur Otis

8. The _____ design requires random assignment.
   a. single subject
   b. true experimental
   c. quasi-experimental
   d. ex post facto

9. Parents of a minor client demand to be informed by the counselor about what the client is talking about during counseling sessions. In this situation, the first thing the counselor should do is
   a. inform the parents about what is discussed in the sessions because the parents hold the legal right to know.
   b. tell the parents that the sessions are confidential and that their child holds the sole right to that confidentiality.
   c. explain the importance of confidentiality to the parents and, if they still insist, try to seek release from the child before disclosing any information to the parents.
   d. describe to the parents how the counseling relationship will suffer if confidentiality with the child is breached.

10. A person's genetics and biology make up a person's
    a. culture.
    b. acculturation level.
    c. race.
    d. gender role.

11. A teacher provides positive reinforcement every two times Katherine waits until she is called on to answer a question. What type of reinforcement schedule is the teacher using?
    a. Fixed ratio
    b. Variable ratio
    c. Fixed interval
    d. Variable interval

12. Which of the following is TRUE concerning the ethical use of career technology?
    a. Career counselors do not have to inform clients of the limitations related to maintaining confidentiality when using career technology.
    b. When using career technology, it is the client's responsibility to ensure reasonable access to computer applications.
    c. Career counselors do not have to verify their client's identity when using career technology as doing so would result in violating confidentiality.
    d. Career technology can be used to provide career information, vocational assessments, integrative career services, and databases of job openings.

13. Positive client outcomes can be best predicted by
    a. the counselor's theoretical orientation.
    b. the quality of the therapeutic alliance.
    c. the techniques used to help the client.
    d. the level of client resistance.

14. _____ may be an advantage of group work, rather than a challenge.
    a. Pressure to conform
    b. Breaking confidentiality
    c. Power of the peer group
    d. Reality distortion

15. According to the ACA and NBCC ethical guidelines related to testing and assessment, professional counselors
    a. are obligated to inform clients of the intended purpose of the assessment results only when the results will be released to a third party.
    b. do not need client consent to release test results when the results do not include any identifying client information.
    c. should use only assessment instruments in which they are expert.
    d. do not need to consider the multicultural limitations of the selected instrument when assessing a Caucasian male client.

16. A professional counselor tested a hunch that government counselors older than 60 years are far happier in their positions than their counterparts in private practice. The researcher interviewed 100 older workers from both occupations and found that indeed government counselors were happier than those in private practice in their later years. What additional information might indicate a history threat to internal validity?
    a. The government counselors had recently received a raise.
    b. The private practice counselors were from one geographic region.
    c. Several of the participants did not speak English as their first language.
    d. The survey was too long.

17. To become a National Certified Counselor (NCC), individuals must have
    a. passed the NCE.
    b. achieved an advanced degree in counseling.
    c. met the requirements for supervised experience.
    d. All of the above.

18. According to Albert Bandura, each of the following is a characteristic of an effective model EXCEPT
    a. perceived as competent.
    b. warm and friendly.
    c. have demographic characteristics that are unlike the observer's.
    d. perceived as having a high status.

19. The _____ prohibits employers from discriminating against a qualified individual who has a mental or physical disability.
    a. Americans with Disabilities Act of 1990
    b. Section 504 of the Rehabilitation Act of 1973
    c. Family and Medical Leave Act of 1993
    d. Individuals with Disabilities Education Improvement Act of 2004

20. _____ is NOT one of the five factors in the Five Factor model.
    a. Neuroticism
    b. Consideration
    c. Agreeableness
    d. Extraversion

21. ASGW Best Practice Guidelines recommend that leaders do all of the following EXCEPT
    a. conduct ecological assessments.
    b. create groups that meet community needs.
    c. put in writing the purpose and goals of any group they are running.
    d. choose a leadership style and use it consistently with all groups.

22. _____ assessments are often used to determine admission into graduate education programs.
    a. Achievement
    b. Intelligence
    c. Aptitude
    d. Personality

23. A sampling technique in which participants have an equal chance of being selected for a particular intervention group is referred to as
    a. random assignment.
    b. random selection.
    c. random probability.
    d. random purposeful.

24. Advocacy counseling may involve
    a. educating the public about the counseling profession.
    b. intervening with organizations that have unethical or unfair policies.
    c. working on behalf of clients to help them overcome barriers to their growth.
    d. All of the above.

25. Maria works as a crisis counselor for a local agency. Although she enjoys her job, she finds herself worrying about clients after work hours and is often tempted to check in on her clients over the weekend. Maria is experiencing
    a. role spillover.
    b. role congruence.
    c. role conflict.
    d. role overload.

26. An appropriate time to terminate the counseling relationship is when
    a. the client is resistant.
    b. the client does not improve after treatment.
    c. the client progresses too slowly.
    d. All of the above.

27. A _____ group is most commonly found in schools.
    a. task
    b. psychoeducational
    c. growth
    d. counseling

28. The Joint Committee on Testing Practices published
    a. *Rights and Responsibilities of Test-Takers.*
    b. *Test User Qualifications.*
    c. *Fair Code of Testing Practice in Education.*
    d. All of the above.

29. Dan has collected qualitative data on students' attitudes toward substance abuse. After he completes an analysis of each student, he presents some of the key themes with quotes for each participant on a single page. What data management tool has he most likely used?
    a. Case display
    b. Document summary form
    c. Contact summary sheet
    d. Codebook

30. The first thing a counselor should do when administering psychological first aid is
    a. connect individuals with family and friends.
    b. connect individuals with helpful community services.
    c. help individuals meet their primary needs.
    d. build rapport.

31. "It seems like you are having trouble in your current relationship because you haven't fully moved on from your past relationship." This is an example of
    a. an interpretation.
    b. a confrontation.
    c. a self-disclosure.
    d. giving feedback.

32. When presented with a gift from a client, the counselors should
    a. refuse to accept the gift under any circumstances.
    b. consider the possible impact on the counseling relationship before accepting or refusing the gift.
    c. only accept the gift if it is of small monetary value.
    d. accept the gift to avoid offending the client.

33. In psychoanalysis, transference is
    a. ignored.
    b. encouraged.
    c. discouraged.
    d. a sign of pathology.

34. _____ and _____ values are the primary values that affect an individual's occupational decision.
    a. Work; cultural
    b. Lifestyle; work
    c. Cultural; family
    d. Family; work

35. A client informs her counselor that she has been diagnosed with HIV and does not plan on telling her significant other, even though they are engaging in unprotected sex. The counselor
    a. is ethically obligated to keep the information confidential.
    b. is ethically obligated to warn the client's significant other because the client is posing a serious threat to that person.
    c. is ethically justified in telling, but not obligated to tell, the client's significant other.
    d. is legally required to warn the client's significant other.

36. _____ is NOT a common psychoanalytic technique.
    a. Interpretation
    b. Dream analysis
    c. Unbalancing
    d. Free association

37. Validity can be reported as a(n)
    a. regression equation.
    b. internal consistency coefficient.
    c. fraction.
    d. standard error of measurement.

38. A counselor decides to use a technique with some of her clients that is not based in theory and does not have any scientific support. In this situation, the counselor should _____ to uphold ethical standards.
    a. discuss any possible risks with her clients
    b. label the technique as unproven
    c. label the technique as developing
    d. All of the above.

39. The neo-Freudian approach known as _____contends that, under certain circumstances, the ego is able to function autonomously without being influenced by the id or superego.
    a. object relations theory
    b. self-psychology
    c. interpersonal psychoanalysis
    d. ego psychology

40. Having benefits, prestige, and a general belief that one's group is superior is termed
    a. racism.
    b. privilege.
    c. ethnocentrism.
    d. cultural encapsulation.

41. A counselor who has a Ph.D. in education refers to himself as Dr. Julian Lewis in advertisements for his counseling practice. The counselor in this situation is
    a. acting ethically; it is true that he has earned a Ph.D.
    b. acting unethically; the Ph.D. is not in counseling or a related field.
    c. acting ethically; counselors may represent themselves however they wish in advertisements.
    d. acting unethically; counselors should never advertise their services.

42. The _____ phase of culture shock includes feelings of belonging to multiple cultures.
    a. adaptation or resolution
    b. crisis or disintegration
    c. honeymoon
    d. reorientation and reintegration

43. A mother pours each of her two children a cup of chocolate milk. Although each cup holds the same amount of liquid, one is taller and skinnier. The child who does not receive the tall, skinny glass starts crying because she is convinced that her brother received more chocolate milk than she did. Which cognitive developmental concept does this child have trouble understanding?
    a. Reversibility
    b. Centration
    c. Conservation
    d. Classification

44. Unlike a lot of other career theories, the theory of work adjustment
    a. is concerned with actual performance on the job.
    b. considers the impact of gender and social class on career choice.
    c. exerts that early relationships play an important role in an individual's career development.
    d. focuses on the career decision-making process.

45. The Adlerian technique known as _____ helps clients understand that paying attention to positive thoughts, actions, memories, and feelings, rather than negative ones, is within their control.
    a. catching themselves
    b. spitting in the client's soup
    c. acting "as if"
    d. pushbutton

46. Members in a(n) _____ group normally have a *DSM* diagnosis.
    a. encounter
    b. counseling
    c. psychotherapy
    d. psychoanalysis

47. Valid tests are
    a. always reliable.
    b. never reliable.
    c. not credible.
    d. None of the above.

48. How would you describe a relationship between a sample of counselors' beginning and current salaries if the correlation coefficient was $r = .88, p < .01$
    a. There is a significant positive relationship between beginning and current salaries.
    b. There has been an increase in salaries for all of the participants.
    c. The distribution of each variable is platykurtic.
    d. There is a 1% chance of a relationship between beginning and current salaries.

49. A counselor decides to use an old version of a depression assessment with his clients. The assessment has had two substantial revisions since the version he wants to use was published, but the counselor does not want to spend money to purchase the newest version when he still has so many copies of the older one. In this situation, the counselor is acting
    a. ethically as long as he gains the clients' consent.
    b. ethically as long as he purchases the new version when he runs out of the old one.
    c. unethically because the test is outdated for the assessment of depression.
    d. None of the above.

50. Peer mediation is typically used
    a. in schools.
    b. at Alcoholics Anonymous meetings.
    c. when counseling divorcees.
    d. when counseling the incarcerated.

51. The _____ technique for improving memory involves guided visual imagery.
    a. eidetic images
    b. hunking
    c. method of loci
    d. All of the above.

52. According to Holland's theory of types, congruence refers to
    a. the degree of similarity between the six different Holland types.
    b. the relationship between an individual's personality and the work environment.
    c. the level of distinctiveness between each of the six Holland types.
    d. an individual's ability to match his or her interests with work environment characteristics.

53. According to Jung, complexes
    a. form around an archetype.
    b. represent problems that must be worked through.
    c. are repressed desires, thoughts, or impulses that combine in the unconscious.
    d. All of the above.

54. A task group is run by a leader who has expertise in the task to be accomplished. The group members have little or no experience with the task at hand. In addition, the group has very little time to complete the task. What leadership style would make the most sense in this situation?
    a. Authoritarian
    b. Democratic
    c. Laissez-faire
    d. Delegative

55. When using split-half reliability, a test developer must use the _____ to ensure that test length does not affect the accuracy of the reliability estimate.
    a. Kuder-Richardson formula 20 (KR-20)
    b. Spearman-Brown prophecy formula
    c. Cronbach's coefficient alpha
    d. standard error of measurement

56. A research design with at least one independent variable with three or more levels is referred to as a(n)
    a. ANOVA.
    b. MANCOVA.
    c. chi-square statistic.
    d. regression.

57. A counselor who does not believe in abortion gains a client who is considering having one and is seeking the counselor's support. The counselor feels exceedingly uncomfortable. She should
    a. seek consultation with a supervisor while working with this client.
    b. refer the client to another counselor.
    c. disclose her views to the client and give the client the option of seeking counseling elsewhere.
    d. contact an ethics committee for advice.

58. A person who takes turns in a conversation is using
    a. semantics.
    b. pragmatics.
    c. syntax.
    d. phonology.

59. Dan has spent the past 30 years working full time for a manufacturing company. He recently decided to focus on his leisure activities and took a part-time position within the company. Dan is in the _____ stage of Super's lifespan, life-space career theory.
    a. maintenance
    b. disengagement
    c. growth
    d. exploration

60. _____ represents a decision-making function in Jung's personality typology.
    a. Intuition
    b. Feeling
    c. Sensation
    d. Extraversion

61. Group leaders may use the _____ technique when they want to hear every group member's thoughts on a given topic or issue.
    a. pairing
    b. making the rounds
    c. linking
    d. drawing out

62. When calculating the item discrimination for a test item on an achievement test, the test developer will want
    a. more lower performing group members to answer the question correctly than higher performing group members.
    b. a positive item discrimination.
    c. a zero item discrimination
    d. a negative item discrimination

63. Which of the following research paradigms is least appropriate for qualitative research?
    a. Positivism
    b. Post-positivism
    c. Critical
    d. Constructivism

64. A counselor educator teaching a group counseling class makes student self-disclosure an integral part of the class. This decision is
    a. unethical under any circumstances.
    b. unethical unless the counselor educator engages in self-disclosure, too.
    c. ethical as long as the counselor educator does not grade the students on their self-disclosures.
    d. ethical, and the students may be graded on their self-disclosures; it was the students' choice to enter into a program that considers self-disclosure an important part of the learning process.

65. Transitions that create significant disruption and cause one to develop new methods of dealing with a career issue are referred to as a
    a. crisis.
    b. chronic hassle.
    c. occupational stress.
    d. career adaptation.

66. _____ is a technique that involves comparing a client's dream to myth, literature, and folklore to help unearth possible meanings of the dream.
    a. Active imagination
    b. Explication
    c. Amplification
    d. Free association

67. Which of the following behaviors may indicate resistance in a group member?
    a. Trying to solve other members' problems
    b. Dominating group discussions
    c. Missing group sessions
    d. All of the above.

68. Which of the following is a measurement occurring on a ratio scale?
    a. 32 degrees Fahrenheit
    b. 135 pounds
    c. The score from an inventory that measures career attitudes
    d. Marital status

69. A professional counselor has developed a survey and, before distributing it to an entire agency, wants to ensure the survey has no major problems. Administering the survey to 15 individuals first is an example of what type of research?
    a. Quantitative
    b. Qualitative
    c. Cross-sectional
    d. Pilot

70. A counselor recommends that a client who has trouble sleeping at night remove her TV, desk, and computer from her bedroom; thus, the client must engage in all nonsleeping activities in other areas of her house. This behavioral technique is called
    a. environmental planning.
    b. overcorrection.
    c. maintenance.
    d. shaping.

71. "My boss promoted me, but it's probably just because he likes me, not because I actually deserve it." This is an example of what type of distorted thinking?
    a. Labeling
    b. Discounting
    c. Selective abstraction
    d. Dichotomous thinking

72. Using deception as part of a research study is acceptable if
    a. the researcher gains informed consent from all participants.
    b. the study has educational value and the deception is unavoidable.
    c. the deception is never revealed to the clients.
    d. the researchers are conducting a study on an area that has never been studied before.

73. Rational-emotive behavior therapy was originally called
    a. rational behavior therapy.
    b. emotive behavior therapy.
    c. rational emotive therapy.
    d. None of the above; it has always been called rational-emotive behavior therapy.

74. Mitchell has to declare his major by the end of the semester. He discloses to his academic advisor that he feels very pressured and does not believe one semester is enough time to search and evaluate career alternatives. Which one of the coping patterns presented by Janis and Mann is Mitchell most likely to use given his situation?
    a. Unconflicted change
    b. Defensive avoidance
    c. Unconflicted adherence
    d. Hypervigilance

75. Laws overrule ethics
    a. in all circumstances.
    b. in most circumstances.

    c. is certain states.
    d. never.

76. Homework assignments play an important role in all of the following theories EXCEPT
    a. individual psychology.
    b. rational-emotive behavior therapy.
    c. cognitive therapy.
    d. strategic family therapy.

77. Which of the following is NOT a characteristic of a normal distribution?
    a. Most scores fall near the mean.
    b. The normal distribution forms a bell curve when graphed.
    c. The curve is symptotic, meaning that the tail touches the y-axis at ±3 standard deviations.
    d. The mean, median, and mode all fall at the center of the distribution

78. A reasonable defense for behaving in an unethical manner is
    a. not having anyone to consult with about a concern.
    b. not having read pertinent ethical codes.
    c. not fully understanding relevant ethical codes.
    d. None of the above.

79. REBT counselors use _____ to alter clients' irrational beliefs.
    a. circular questioning
    b. disputation
    c. restructuring
    d. scriptotherapy

80. The expectation of hopelessness is characterized in which worldview?
    a. Internal locus of control–Internal locus of responsibility
    b. Internal locus of control–External locus of responsibility
    c. External locus of control–Internal locus of responsibility
    d. External locus of control–External locus of responsibility

81. To ensure that no laws are violated, Internet counselors should
    a. be familiar with applicable laws in their state.
    b. be familiar with applicable laws in their clients' states.
    c. be familiar with applicable laws both in their state and their clients' state(s).
    d. only provide Internet counseling services to clients who live in their state.

82. Sara overhears a group making jokes about someone in her class who identifies as gay, yet she fails to do anything about it. Sara is demonstrating
    a. primary oppression.
    b. secondary oppression.
    c. tertiary oppression.
    d. double jeopardy.

83. At what stage of psychosocial development are family relationships and work performance of key importance?
    a. Intimacy vs. isolation
    b. Generativity vs. stagnation
    c. Industry vs. inferiority
    d. Integrity vs. despair

84. Goal setting, values clarification, and seeking occupational information are examples of
    a. associative learning experiences.
    b. task approach skills.
    c. environmental conditions.
    d. worldview generalizations.

85. Reality therapy is also called
    a. practical counseling.
    b. choice theory.
    c. planful therapy.
    d. decision theory.

86. Information that is known to others but unknown to self is found in which quadrant of the Johari window?
    a. Public/open quadrant
    b. Private/hidden quadrant
    c. Blind quadrant
    d. Unknown/unconscious quadrant

87. If a student scored an 82 on an exam with a mean of 80 and a standard deviation of 2, what would be the student's normal curve equivalent?
    a. 71.06
    b. 50
    c. +1.0
    d. 23.68

88. A sequential design is most closely associated with _____ research.
    a. quantitative
    b. qualitative
    c. mixed-methods
    d. single-subject

89. A counselor discovers that a colleague has published an opinion piece in the local newspaper making false accusations about her professional behavior and abilities. The counselor may be able to sue this person for
    a. slander.
    b. libel.
    c. malicious gossip.
    d. All of the above.

90. Which of the following terms does NOT coincide with the eugenics movement (1920s–1930s)?
    a. One drop rule
    b. Support of biracial individuals
    c. Laws against interracial marriages
    d. Connection between genes and intellectual and social traits

91. Although Madeline draws in her coloring book while Sophie builds a house with blocks, they sit near each other and carry on a conversation. This type of play is called
    a. associative play.
    b. nonsocial activity.
    c. cooperative play.
    d. parallel play.

92. The external conflict scale on the Career Thoughts Inventory indicates client difficulty in
    a. overcoming career decision-making barriers.
    b. balancing one's own views and vocational desires with others' input.
    c. initiating the career decision-making process.
    d. obtaining work-related skills.

93. Frankl believed that people could find meaning through
    a. suffering.
    b. achievement.
    c. creation.
    d. All of the above.

94. All of the following behaviors can be potentially problematic in group work EXCEPT
    a. advice giving.
    b. gatekeeping.

    c. informing.
    d. blocking.

95. Students must run a mile at least a minute faster in the spring than they did in the fall to pass their physical education fitness exam. This type of exam is an example a(n)
    a. norm-referenced test.
    b. raw score.
    c. criterion-referenced test.
    d. ipsative assessment.

96. A counseling researcher is interested in investigating the following research question: "What is the influence of socioeconomic status and school climate on academic achievement?" The dependent variable is
    a. socioeconomic status.
    b. academic achievement.
    c. gender.
    d. geography.

97. One of the first steps that counselors who receive subpoenas should take is
    a. to comply so as not to be held in contempt of court.
    b. to refuse to comply due to client confidentiality.
    c. to contact the client to see how he or she would like them to proceed.
    d. to comply but only provide the court with the most essential information.

98. Selfishness predominates the _____ stage of Gilligan's theory of moral development.
    a. goodness as self-sacrifice
    b. morality of nonviolence
    c. orientation to individual survival
    d. ethic of self-preservation

99. To assess a client's career interests, a counselor should administer (the)
    a. My Vocational Situation.
    b. Work Orientation and Values Survey (WOVS).
    c. Kuder Career Search.
    d. Career Beliefs Inventory.

100. Because she is upset about the amount of fighting she engages in with her teenage daughter (upwards of five fights each week), a client is seeing a counselor who uses a solution-focused brief counseling approach. After a few sessions, she reports to the counselor that she fought only once with her daughter since her last counseling session. The counselor responds by asking the client "How were you able to do that? What did you do to decrease the amount of fighting?" The counselor in this scenario is using the SFBT technique called
    a. compliments.
    b. positive blame.
    c. miracle question
    d. exception question.

101. Closed groups are often preferred when the leader is looking to encourage
    a. achievement of group goals.
    b. group process.
    c. group cohesion and trust.
    d. All of the above.

102. Readiness tests, which indicate the minimum level of skills needed to move from one grade level to another, have been
    a. removed from high-stakes testing.
    b. criticized for including cultural and language biases.

c. replaced by survey batteries.

d. applauded for cultural competence when assessing students from lower socioeconomic status (SES) groups.

103. The research question "How does ethnicity impact religiosity?" is an example of a _____ research question.
    a. causal
    b. relational
    c. descriptive
    d. structured

104. The 1970s court case that resulted in the deinstitutionalization of patients living in mental hospitals was
    a. *Jain v. State of Iowa.*
    b. *Tarasoff v. Regents of the University of California.*
    c. *Jaffee v. Redmond.*
    d. *Donaldson v. O'Connor.*

105. _____ needs occur when the demand for workers exceeds the number of existing workers and requires more workers to be added to the workforce.
    a. Occupational
    b. Growth
    c. Replacement
    d. Employment

106. Which of the following is an example of an externalizing question?
    a. "How long have you been depressed?"
    b. "How has impulsivity hindered you from forming intimate connections with others?"
    c. "In what situations are you the most anxious?"
    d. "When did you first start feeling sad?"

107. For optimal functioning, task groups should consist of at least _____ members.
    a. 3 to 4
    b. 4 to 5
    c. 5 to 6
    d. 6 to 7

108. Survey batteries
    a. are designed to identify student learning disabilities.
    b. are used to assess academic progress by measuring individuals' knowledge across broad content areas.
    c. provide an in-depth analysis of a student's skill competency in one academic subject.
    d. indicate the minimum level of skills needed to move from one grade level to another.

109. During a repeated measures design, counseling researchers note that participants' mental health symptoms are fluctuating significantly. Which type of validity threat would best account for this occurrence?
    a. History
    b. Instrumentation
    c. Attrition
    d. Selection

110. Family boundaries should be
    a. clear.
    b. communicated to all members.
    c. understood by all members.
    d. All of the above.

111. _____ is (are) NOT one of the eight core elements that Bowen believed affects a family's functioning.
    a. Triangles
    b. Circular causality

c. Differentiation of self

d. Sibling position

112. The _____ was passed following the launch of the *Sputnik* satellite that gave additional funding to schools, resulting in increased hiring of school counselors.
    a. National Defense Education Act (NDEA)
    b. Family Educational Rights and Privacy Act (FERPA)
    c. Individuals with Disabilities Education Act (IDEA)
    d. Section 504 of the Rehabilitation Act

113. When choosing a marriage partner, people are most likely to select someone with
    a. a higher level of differentiation.
    b. a lower level of differentiation.
    c. around the same level of differentiation.
    d. There is no relationship between level of differentiation and mate selection.

114. Which occupational classification system does the Occupational Information Network (O*NET) use?
    a. Occupational Network Classification System (ONCS)
    b. Standard Occupational Classification System (SOC)
    c. Occupational Classification System (OCS)
    d. Career Classification System (CCS)

115. Under HIPAA, patients/clients must
    a. be allowed to review their records.
    b. be given a privacy policy.
    c. sign a document declaring they have been given information about HIPAA.
    d. All of the above.

116. The multigenerational transmission process explains how
    a. people become triangulated.
    b. levels of differentiation are perpetuated.
    c. some individuals become emotionally cut off from their families.
    d. birth order affects the personalities of children.

117. Which of the following is true about the Armed Services Vocational Aptitude Battery (ASVAB)?
    a. It is a special aptitude test.
    b. It is administered to students in Grades 7 through 12.
    c. It was originally developed for the military but now measures the abilities required for a variety of both military and civilian jobs.
    d. It includes a career interest inventory that assesses student vocational strengths and determines possible careers that might interest the student.

118. CACREP-accredited counseling programs must apply for accreditation every
    a. 8 years.
    b. 2 years.
    c. 10 years.
    d. 5 years.

119. _____ is NOT the name of one of the four communication patterns that Satir describes as dysfunctional.
    a. Super-reasonable
    b. Blamer
    c. Comedian
    d. Placater

120. Acknowledgment of White privilege and a desire to relinquish privileges occurs in Helms'
    a. internalization status.
    b. autonomy status.

    c. immersion status.

    d. pseudo-independence status.

121. A student receiving services under IDEA is placed in a normal classroom because it has been determined that he can function well there with some accommodations. This scenario best exemplifies the concept of

    a. least restrictive environment.

    b. 504 plan.

    c. free appropriate public education.

    d. individualized education plan.

122. In terms of *time orientation,* American Indians and Native Alaskans are much more oriented toward the

    a. future.

    b. present.

    c. past.

    d. All of the above.

123. Which of the following is a FALSE statement about maternal employment?

    a. When accounting for job title and years of experience, women without children generally make the same amount of money as men.

    b. Mothers who work have increased life satisfaction compared to nonworking mothers.

    c. Marital satisfaction is the same for working mothers as it is for nonworking mothers.

    d. Working mothers are more stressed than nonworking mothers.

124. Clients' career issues

    a. often intersect with their personal lives.

    b. are unrelated to their personal lives.

    c. are not to be discussed in personal counseling.

    d. can only be resolved through career counseling.

125. According to Satir, the best communication style is

    a. empathic.

    b. congruent.

    c. caring.

    d. genuine.

126. Cohesion is likely to develop more quickly for

    a. small groups.

    b. medium-size groups.

    c. large groups.

    d. None of the above. Group cohesion develops at approximately the same rate, regardless of group size.

127. The Rorschach inkblot test uses _____ to score the client's responses.

    a. the location of the portion to which the client responds

    b. the determinants that the client used to describe what he or she saw

    c. the content of the client's response

    d. All of the above.

128. _____ is NOT an experimental design.

    a. Ex post facto

    b. Time series

    c. One group pretest-posttest

    d. Nonequivalent groups posttest only

129. Obtaining liability insurance is essential for

    a. new counselors.

    b. counselors who work in private practice.

    c. counselors who work with children.

    d. All of the above.

130. The stereotype of successful Asian Americans has the effect of

    a. upholding the belief that any minority can succeed if they merely work hard enough.

    b. pitting one minority against the other by holding up one as an example.

    c. shortchanging support for many Asian communities because of the view that all Asians are "successful."

    d. All of the above.

131. When someone does not fully resolve and work through a crisis situation, he or she may experience

    a. vicarious trauma.

    b. transcrisis.

    c. compassion fatigue.

    d. burnout.

132. According to the NCDA's Career Counseling Competencies, an effective career counselor should have knowledge of

    a. individual and group counseling skills.

    b. research and evaluation.

    c. career development theory.

    d. All of the above.

133. Which theory of family counseling would view a family's symptoms as the way that the family maintains its homeostasis?

    a. Human validation process model

    b. Strategic family therapy

    c. Symbolic-experiential family therapy

    d. Structural family therapy

134. Homogeneity of members, interdependence, and attractiveness of members refers to which factor of group cohesion?

    a. Group factors

    b. Interpersonal factors

    c. Group composition factors

    d. Group environment factors

135. Which type of observation records the number of times a client engages in the targeted behavior during a predetermined time interval?

    a. Indirect

    b. ABC

    c. Event

    d. Partial interval

136. A professional counselor wants to display nominal data. A _____ is the most suitable way to present that data.

    a. frequency polygon

    b. histogram

    c. bar graph

    d. None of the above.

137. Reciprocity refers to

    a. the ability for counselors licensed in one state to work in another state without having to apply for licensure again.

    b. bartering.

    c. the client–counselor relationship.

    d. None of the above.

138. A teenager who is embarrassed to go out to dinner with his family even though he does not know anyone else dining at the restaurant is experiencing

    a. a personal fable.

    b. magical thinking.

    c. an imaginary audience.

    d. All of the above.

139. Which career counseling intervention allows a client to gain insight into a particular work environment by observing a competent worker?
   a. Informational interviewing
   b. Job shadowing
   c. Job coaching
   d. Volunteer work

140. Families often get stuck because of their tendency to perpetuate dysfunctional patterns of behavior without attempting any change. Strategic family therapists refer to this as
   a. circular functioning.
   b. punctuation.
   c. the redundancy principle.
   d. ritualistic behavior.

141. _____ groups will place significant emphasis on examining member transference and resistance.
   a. Existential
   b. Adlerian
   c. Psychodynamic
   d. Gestalt

142. What is the biggest drawback to using a structured interview format to assess a client?
   a. The interviewer tends to rely on the client to determine the interview's focus.
   b. The structured interview does not provide the flexibility to ask follow-up questions or explore client issues more in depth.
   c. Structured interviews are considered to be less reliable than semi-structured interviews.
   d. The structured interview tends to cover a narrow range of topics.

143. In a normal distribution, approximately _____% of the scores will exceed two standard deviations above the mean.
   a. 1
   b. 2
   c. 8
   d. 14

144. If sufficiently trained, professional counselors are legally allowed to use psychological tests as part of their practice in
   a. a handful of states.
   b. most states.
   c. all states.
   d. None of the above. Only psychologists are permitted to use psychological tests.

145. _____ is NOT a method used to conduct needs assessments.
   a. Surveying the target group
   b. Conducting focus group interviews
   c. Hiring a consultant
   d. Reviewing peer-reviewed journal articles

146. In family counseling, circular questioning is used to
   a. help the counselor formulate a hypothesis.
   b. highlight the differences in perspectives among family members.
   c. create a more comprehensive understanding of the family system.
   d. All of the above.

147. Member satisfaction with the overall group experience is most commonly assessed
   a. toward the end of the group process.
   b. in the beginning of the group process.
   c. in the middle of the group process.
   d. throughout the group process.

148. What type of clinical interview format is most subject to interviewer error?
   a. Structured interviews
   b. Semi-structured interviews
   c. Unstructured interviews
   d. Closed interviews

149. "Going native" is a risk for which of the following data collection methods?
   a. Participant observation
   b. Document analysis
   c. Individual interviewing
   d. Random selection

150. Which of the following is NOT a true statement about structural family counseling?
   a. Marital roles should have complementarity.
   b. Parents should be at the top of the family hierarchy.
   c. Boundaries should be permeable.
   d. Older children should have more responsibilities and privileges than younger children.

151. Structural family counselors join families for all of the following reasons EXCEPT
   a. to help put them at ease.
   b. to establish rapport.
   c. to more easily form hypotheses.
   d. to reduce resistance.

152. The Community Mental Health Act of 1963 most significantly affected the counseling specialty area of
   a. school counseling.
   b. rehabilitation counseling.
   c. clinical mental health counseling.
   d. All of the above.

153. Structural maps do NOT include
   a. alignments.
   b. three generations of the family.
   c. coalitions.
   d. boundaries.

154. Which of the following steps is NOT included in the program evaluation phase?
   a. Determining program goals and objectives
   b. Determining the behaviors, skills, attitudes, and/or knowledge to be evaluated
   c. Determining the data sources and data collection tools that will be used during program evaluation
   d. Analyzing and interpreting the data gathered during the evaluation.

155. School counselors help all students with their
   a. academic needs.
   b. career needs.
   c. personal-social needs.
   d. All of the above.

156. A technique that uncovers the order of events that lead to the presentation of a problematic symptom to prevent the symptom from occurring in the future is called
   a. flagging the minefield.
   b. firing sequence.
   c. bridging.
   d. scripting.

157. To reduce bias in assessment, professional counselors can
    a. rely solely on cultural stereotypes.
    b. use assessments that were normed on White, middle-class individuals.
    c. use assessment instruments that use the most clear and understandable language for the client population.
    d. use a translated test.

158. When counselors encounter ethical dilemmas, they should
    a. consult with other professionals.
    b. use a decision-making model.
    c. examine codes of ethics and relevant laws.
    d. All of the above.

159. Feminist therapy does NOT involve
    a. social change.
    b. an equal relationship between the counselor and client.
    c. helping female clients become less passive and more aggressive.
    d. a teaching component.

160. When counselors have to break client confidentiality, they should ideally
    a. inform the client beforehand.
    b. inform the client after.
    c. not tell the client if at all possible because, even though it was ethically required, it might harm the counseling relationship.
    d. None of the above. Counselors should never break client confidentiality.

ANSWER KEY FOR NCE SAMPLE TEST—FORM B

1. d	21. d	41. b	61. b	81. c	101. d	121. a	141. c
2. a	22. c	42. a	62. b	82. b	102. b	122. b	142. b
3. c	23. a	43. c	63. a	83. b	103. a	123. d	143. b
4. b	24. d	44. a	64. c	84. b	104. d	124. a	144. b
5. b	25. a	45. d	65. a	85. b	105. b	125. b	145. d
6. b	26. b	46. c	66. c	86. c	106. b	126. a	146. d
7. c	27. b	47. a	67. d	87. a	107. b	127. d	147. a
8. b	28. d	48. a	68. b	88. c	108. b	128. a	148. c
9. c	29. c	49. c	69. d	89. b	109. b	129. d	149. a
10. c	30. c	50. a	70. a	90. b	110. d	130. d	150. c
11. a	31. a	51. c	71. b	91. a	111. b	131. b	151. c
12. d	32. b	52. b	72. b	92. b	112. a	132. d	152. c
13. b	33. b	53. d	73. c	93. d	113. c	133. a	153. b
14. c	34. a	54. a	74. d	94. b	114. b	134. b	154. a
15. b	35. c	55. b	75. a	95. d	115. d	135. d	155. d
16. a	36. c	56. a	76. a	96. b	116. b	136. c	156. b
17. d	37. a	57. b	77. c	97. c	117. c	137. a	157. c
18. c	38. d	58. b	78. d	98. c	118. a	138. c	158. d
19. a	39. d	59. b	79. b	99. c	119. c	139. b	159. c
20. b	40. b	60. b	80. d	100. b	120. b	140. c	160. a

ANSWER FORM FOR CPCE SAMPLE TEST—FORM A

Circle the correct response for each test question.

Sum the number correct for each row.

1. a b c d	41. a b c d	81. a b c d	121. a b c d	___
2. a b c d	42. a b c d	82. a b c d	122. a b c d	___
3. a b c d	43. a b c d	83. a b c d	123. a b c d	___
4. a b c d	44. a b c d	84. a b c d	124. a b c d	___
5. a b c d	45. a b c d	85. a b c d	125. a b c d	___
6. a b c d	46. a b c d	86. a b c d	126. a b c d	___
7. a b c d	47. a b c d	87. a b c d	127. a b c d	___
8. a b c d	48. a b c d	88. a b c d	128. a b c d	___

9. a b c d	49. a b c d	89. a b c d	129. a b c d	___
10. a b c d	50. a b c d	90. a b c d	130. a b c d	___
11. a b c d	51. a b c d	91. a b c d	131. a b c d	___
12. a b c d	52. a b c d	92. a b c d	132. a b c d	___
13. a b c d	53. a b c d	93. a b c d	133. a b c d	___
14. a b c d	54. a b c d	94. a b c d	134. a b c d	___
15. a b c d	55. a b c d	95. a b c d	135. a b c d	___
16. a b c d	56. a b c d	96. a b c d	136. a b c d	___

17. a b c d	57. a b c d	97. a b c d	___
18. a b c d	58. a b c d	98. a b c d	___
19. a b c d	59. a b c d	99. a b c d	___
20. a b c d	60. a b c d	100. a b c d	___
21. a b c d	61. a b c d	101. a b c d	___
22. a b c d	62. a b c d	102. a b c d	___
23. a b c d	63. a b c d	103. a b c d	___
24. a b c d	64. a b c d	104. a b c d	___

25. a b c d	65. a b c d	105. a b c d	___
26. a b c d	66. a b c d	106. a b c d	___
27. a b c d	67. a b c d	107. a b c d	___
28. a b c d	68. a b c d	108. a b c d	___
29. a b c d	69. a b c d	109. a b c d	___
30. a b c d	70. a b c d	110. a b c d	___
31. a b c d	71. a b c d	111. a b c d	___
32. a b c d	72. a b c d	112. a b c d	___

33. a b c d	73. a b c d	113. a b c d	___
34. a b c d	74. a b c d	114. a b c d	___
35. a b c d	75. a b c d	115. a b c d	___
36. a b c d	76. a b c d	116. a b c d	___
37. a b c d	77. a b c d	117. a b c d	___
38. a b c d	78. a b c d	118. a b c d	___
39. a b c d	79. a b c d	119. a b c d	___
40. a b c d	80. a b c d	120. a b c d	___

Total correct for each column ___ ___ ___ ___ ___ ___ ___ ___

Chapter   1   2   3   4   5   6   7   8

CPCE SAMPLE TEST—FORM A

1. In the early 1920s, the counseling profession consisted primarily of
   a. mental health counseling.
   b. vocational guidance counseling.
   c. school counseling.
   d. All of the above.

2. Culture is understood to be
   a. the same as race.
   b. the background of patterns, languages, psychological factors, and biological factors of a person.
   c. an irrelevant factor in diagnosis.
   d. factors that pertain to the here and now; historical contexts are not as salient.

3. Erikson's psychosocial developmental theory is an example of
   a. a continuous, active theory.
   b. a continuous, reactive theory.
   c. a discontinuous, active theory.
   d. a discontinuous, reactive theory.

4. _____ is considered the father of career guidance and the counseling profession.
   a. George Merrill
   b. Edmund Williamson
   c. Frank Parsons
   d. John Crities

5. Which of the following models of resistance is behavioral?
   a. Noncompliance
   b. Negative social influence
   c. Power struggle
   d. Anxiety control

6. Institutional barriers to group work may include all the following EXCEPT
   a. resistant group members.
   b. the need to obtain parental consent.
   c. belief by staff members that group work in not as effective as other activities.
   d. the lack of appropriate facilities.

7. William Wundt is known for
   a. developing the form broad, which is considered a predecessor to performance IQ testing.
   b. being the first to apply statistical concepts to psychological assessment.
   c. founding one of the first psychological laboratories to conduct experimental research.
   d. his work on the forgetting curve.

8. A construct, such as a treatment group, that can be manipulated in a study is most often referred to as a(n) _____ variable.
   a. outcome
   b. categorical
   c. criterion
   d. independent

9. Ethical principles that counselors are required to follow are called
   a. aspirational ethics.
   b. obligatory ethics.
   c. mandatory ethics.
   d. compulsory ethics.

10. The tripartite model of multicultural counseling competencies includes each of the following components EXCEPT
    a. an etic perspective.
    b. awareness.
    c. knowledge.
    d. skills.

11. For a researcher who has limited time and a low budget, the _____ research design might be most appropriate.
    a. cross-sectional
    b. longitudinal
    c. time-lag
    d. naturalistic

12. The Fair Labor Standards Act of 1938 was NOT responsible for
    a. establishing a national minimum wage.
    b. enforcing workplace safety and health standards.
    c. providing minimum standards for overtime entitlement.
    d. prohibiting the employment of minors.

13. A professional counselor consults with an experienced colleague about some problems she has encountered while working with a particular client. She is completely reliant on her colleague's expertise to help her move forward with her client. Which consultation model does this represent?
    a. Collaborative-dependent
    b. Collaborative-interdependent
    c. Triadic-dependent
    d. Triadic-interdependent

14. In group work, confidentiality is
    a. the ethical requirement of group leaders but not group members.
    b. the ethical requirement of group members but not group leaders.
    c. the ethical requirement of both group leaders and group members.
    d. not an ethical requirement for anyone involved in the process.

15. A(n) _____ does not compare an individual score to a norm group but relies on the judgment of the professional counselor to interpret the data.
    a. standardized test
    b. norm-referenced test
    c. ipsative assessment
    d. nonstandardized test

16. "Whereas 1 million white swans can indicate that all swans are white, one brown swan can falsify it." That is, we can only approximate truth. This description refers to the _____ paradigm.
    a. positivism
    b. post-positivism
    c. social constructivism
    d. critical theory

17. Accreditation is NOT
    a. voluntary.
    b. involuntary.
    c. a way for educational institutions to demonstrate their quality to the public.
    d. an accountability measure for schools.

18. Judging someone's worth by how closely he or she resembles European Americans is termed
    a. racism.
    b. colorism.
    c. eugenics.
    d. Jensenism.

19. What part of the brain regulates emotions and motivation?
    a. Temporal lobe
    b. Limbic system
    c. Reticular activating system
    d. Cerebellum

20. _____ is an example of an occupation.
    a. Addictions Counselor Level II
    b. Professional Counselor
    c. Assistant Director of Career Counseling
    d. Residential Treatment Counselor

21. Observing clients' verbal and nonverbal communication and verbally conveying empathy and understanding of clients' thoughts, feelings, and behaviors are all important elements of
    a. paraphrasing.
    b. reflecting.
    c. confronting.
    d. interpreting.

22. Group members' personal goals are generally
    a. overt.
    b. hidden from the group.
    c. agreed on by the entire group.
    d. None of the above.

23. Under the _____ a 3-year-old child who is suspected of having a disability is guaranteed to receive testing at the expense of the public school system.
    a. Family Educational Rights and Privacy Act of 1974 (FERPA)
    b. Americans with Disabilities Act of 1990 (ADA)
    c. No Child Left Behind Act of 2001
    d. Individuals with Disabilities Education Improvement Act of 2004 (IDEA)

24. Which of the following most represents a quasi-experimental design?
    a. Researchers compared the treatment group of low-fat meals with a randomized control group and found faster mental processing in the low-fat group.
    b. Researchers found that teachers at Henderson High favored the concept of year-round schooling.
    c. Researchers compared students' scores under Curriculum A with a matched comparison group and found better achievement for Curriculum A.
    d. Researchers found that clients' stories reflected strong motivation for change.

25. _____ is NOT one of the five principal ethics of the counseling profession.
    a. Nonmaleficence
    b. Constancy
    c. Justice
    d. Autonomy

26. _____ is (are) are based on biology, and _____ include(s) societal expectations of behavior.
    a. Gender roles; sex roles
    b. Gender identity; sexual identity
    c. Sex roles; gender roles
    d. Sexual identity; gender identity

27. Classical conditioning was developed by
    a. Ivan Pavlov.
    b. Albert Bandura.
    c. John B. Watson.
    d. Joseph Wolpe.

28. Individuals who demonstrate high career adaptability demonstrate
    a. concern for their future work life.
    b. confidence to pursue career goals.
    c. curiosity for exploring career possibilities.
    d. All of the above.

29. Freud contended that each individual possesses all of the following types of consciousness EXCEPT
    a. preconscious mind.
    b. conscious mind.
    c. unconscious mind.
    d. subconscious mind.

30. A _____ group is primarily remedial.
    a. psychotherapy
    b. counseling
    c. psychoeducational
    d. task

31. If a professional counselor would like to read critical test reviews of the Beck Depression Inventory, the counselor would be most interested in the publication known as
    a. *Tests.*
    b. *Mental Measurements Yearbook.*
    c. *Tests in Print.*
    d. *Standards for Educational and Psychological Testing.*

32. In a single-subject design, it is most important to
    a. have unequal time intervals between collections of baseline data.
    b. have the intervention be distinctive from what is naturally occurring for the subject.
    c. randomly assign subjects to interventions.
    d. All of the above.

33. A client tells her counselor that she is currently receiving counseling services from another mental health professional. According to ACA's ethical code, the counselor should
    a. terminate the counseling relationship with the client.
    b. ask the client to choose and continue seeing only one counselor.
    c. ask the client for permission to contact the other professional to establish a collaborative relationship.
    d. not do anything.

34. _____ is associated with meaningful experiences linked to a relationship with a divine entity, nature, or the universe, whereas _____ is more ritualistic and organized.
    a. Religion; spirituality
    b. Spirituality; religion
    c. Buddhism; Confucianism
    d. Christianity; Taoism

35. Operant conditioning is based on the belief that
    a. true learning does not require external reinforcement.
    b. learning depends on which behaviors are reinforced.
    c. learning occurs through observation.
    d. learning occurs when an unconditioned stimulus is repeatedly paired with a conditioned stimulus to produce a conditioned response.

36. According to the theory of work adjustment, tenure refers to
    a. an individual's ability to tolerate problematic and dissatisfying aspects of the job.

b. how long an individual will remain with a company.

c. how long an individual will endure unfavorable work conditions before changing jobs.

d. the degree to which the individual and work environment continue to meet each other's needs.

37. At the core of individual psychology is the concept of
    a. self-actualization.
    b. social interest.
    c. unconscious impulses.
    d. individuation.

38. According to Kurt Lewin, theory Z refers to a(n)
    a. democratic leadership style.
    b. authoritarian leadership style.
    c. autocratic leadership style.
    d. laissez-faire leadership style.

39. Which one of the following is true regarding reliability?
    a. Shorter tests are more reliable than longer tests.
    b. High reliability estimates are reported when test items vary greatly in content.
    c. The closer a reliability coefficient is to 0, the more reliable the instrument.
    d. Speed tests yield spuriously high reliability coefficients.

40. _____ is a sampling technique that involves identifying convenient, existing subgroups and then randomly selecting subgroups.
    a. Systematic sampling
    b. Stratified random sampling
    c. Cluster sampling
    d. Quota sampling

41. A counselor who is going through a divorce is ethically expected to
    a. stop providing counseling services if his or her emotions are likely to interfere with the ability to work with and help clients.
    b. stop providing counseling services until the situation has been resolved.
    c. seek supervision while working through this difficult time.
    d. continue providing counseling services so that clients do not feel abandoned.

42. Being able to revert to previous levels of functioning is termed
    a. motivation.
    b. resilience.
    c. harmony.
    d. participation.

43. Interpreting new information in a way that alters a person's existing cognitive framework is called
    a. adaptation.
    b. accommodation.
    c. organization.
    d. assimilation.

44. Katherine Briggs and Isabel Myers developed the Myers-Briggs type theory, which was derived from the work of
    a. Sigmund Freud.
    b. Alfred Adler.
    c. Albert Ellis.
    d. Carl Jung.

45. Jungian counselors help clients uncover elements of their unconscious minds through
    a. spirituality.
    b. dreams.

c. culture.

d. All of the above.

46. Showing group members the proper way to execute a specific skill or behavior to help them learn is called
    a. modeling.
    b. role-playing.
    c. initiating.
    d. instructing.

47. Validity
    a. refers to how accurately an instrument measures a given construct.
    b. refers to the consistency of test scores from one administration to the next.
    c. is concerned with the error found in instruments.
    d. is never reported in terms of the specific test purpose and target population.

48. The degree to which extraneous variables may be controlled (to accurately measure the relationship between independent variables and dependent variables) refers to
    a. internal validity.
    b. trustworthiness.
    c. external validity.
    d. statistical control.

49. Client records can be disposed of
    a. once the counseling relationship has been permanently terminated.
    b. only after the client has died.
    c. 5 years after the counseling relationship has ended.
    d. only if the counselor discontinues his or her practice.

50. _____ is similar to _____.
    a. Covert racism; extermination
    b. Physical attack; covert racism
    c. Avoidance; overt racism
    d. Overt racism; extermination

51. A family needs to buy a new car. It is having trouble deciding between two cars because both models are incredibly appealing to all family members. Which kind of conflict are they experiencing?
    a. Approach-avoidance conflict
    b. Approach-approach conflict
    c. Avoidance-avoidance conflict
    d. Avoidance-approach conflict

52. Gottfredson proposes that
    a. adolescents give up more accessible career alternatives for those that are more compatible with their interests.
    b. individuals will settle for a "good enough" career due to the limited accessibility of highly compatible career choices.
    c. when the compromise is severe, individuals will sacrifice interest and prestige before gender role.
    d. when the compromise is moderate, individuals will sacrifice prestige before interest.

53. At the core of cognitive therapy is the restructuring of clients'
    a. irrational beliefs.
    b. automatic thoughts.
    c. cognitive fictions.
    d. polarized thinking.

54. Which of the following types of co-leadership is often used for mentoring purposes?
    a. Experience with experience
    b. Experience with inexperience

c. Inexperience with inexperience

d. All of the above.

55. Sensitivity, a term used in decision accuracy, refers to

a. an instrument's ability to accurately identify the absence of a phenomenon.

b. the extent to which an instrument enhances the accuracy of prediction of a specific criterion.

c. the ratio of total correct decisions divided by the total number of decisions.

d. an instrument's ability to accurately identify the presence of a phenomenon.

56. A professor concluded that the time students spent reading a research text predicted final examination scores. These results might come from a _____ study.

a. comparative

b. regression

c. single-subject

d. time-series

57. A counselor hears one of her colleagues revealing confidential information about a client at a party. The first thing the counselor should do is

a. file a report with an ethics committee.

b. tell the colleague's client what happened.

c. try to resolve the issue with the colleague informally.

d. keep the knowledge private until the counselor can be certain that this is not an isolated incident.

58. Sabrina indicates that she is experiencing difficulty adjusting to leaving her own country and adapting to her host country's culture. She is very likely experiencing

a. *confianza* stress.

b. acculturative stress.

c. model minority myth.

d. dissociative disorder.

59. A teacher notices that one of his students is having trouble understanding a new mathematical concept. To help the child, he provides her with additional examples, gives her hints, and uses questions to assist her in working through problems. Once it is clear that she is able to complete these problems on her own, he stops providing her with the example, hints, and questions he offered before. This technique is called

a. shaping.

b. positive reinforcement.

c. zone of proximal development.

d. scaffolding.

60. Which of the following is TRUE regarding Super's lifespan, life-space career theory?

a. The theory describes five life roles: child, student, parent, worker, and retiree.

b. The theory outlines five developmental stages and 16 substages.

c. The life-career rainbow illustrates how the self-concept changes and develops over time as individuals acquire experiences.

d. The theory emphasizes the role gender and prestige play in making career decisions.

61. "If I don't have a significant other or someone who is interested in dating me it means that I'm completely unlovable and undesirable." This is an example of what type of distorted thinking?

a. Overgeneralization

b. Magnification

c. Dichotomous thinking

d. Selective abstraction

62. A group member is encouraged by the leader to refrain from giving advice to other members and instead focuses on self-disclosing about her own life. This member feels exceedingly uncomfortable talking about her life and prefers to try to help others solve their problems. This individual is experiencing

a. role ambiguity.

b. role dissonance.

c. role conflict.

d. role overload.

63. Which of the following is NOT an example of a measurement occurring on a nominal scale?

a. Socioeconomic status

b. Gender

c. Ethnicity

d. Eye color

64. In a frequency distribution, the sums of the frequencies for all intervals will _____ the total number of scores in the sample.

a. exceed

b. equal

c. be less than

d. be less than or equal to

65. A client meets with a counselor and, during one of their sessions, reveals that her husband sometimes physically abuses her. The client says she is not ready to contact any authorities or leave her husband. In this situation, the counselor is

a. legally obligated to file a report with the police.

b. ethically obligated to file a report with the police.

c. legally and ethically obligated to file a report with the police.

d. neither legally nor ethically obligated to file a report with the police.

66. A stressor that affects international students with greater frequency than other groups is

a. low self-worth.

b. terminal illness.

c. language.

d. substance abuse.

67. _____ memory only retains information for 1 or 2 seconds.

a. Short-term

b. Long-term

c. Executive

d. Sensory

68. Gelatt proposed that a career decision can be terminal or investigatory. An investigatory career decision

a. is final.

b. calls for additional information.

c. is prescriptive.

d. is not recommended by Gelatt.

69. Which of the following is NOT a primary goal of Gestalt therapy?

a. Helping clients identify and attend to their most pressing needs

b. Helping clients make appropriate contact and withdrawal from their environments

c. Helping clients identify exceptions to their problems

d. Helping clients resolve their unfinished business

70. Which of the following resources is commonly used by leaders to teach members about appropriate self-disclosure?

a. Sharing diagram

b. Hill interaction matrix

    c. Self-disclosure guidelines
    d. Johari window

71. The standard error of measurement
    a. can be used to report validity.
    b. is a measure of central tendency.
    c. is the standard deviation of an individual's repeated test scores when administered the same instrument multiple times.
    d. represents an individual's true test score.

72. The central goal of _____ is to describe holistically a culture or cultural group.
    a. ethnography
    b. grounded theory
    c. phenomenology
    d. critical study

73. Which of the following did NOT lead to the development of vocational guidance?
    a. World War I
    b. Industrial Revolution
    c. Social reform movements
    d. None of the above. All led to the development of vocational guidance.

74. The three phases of trauma counseling include all of the following EXCEPT
    a. Remembrance and mourning.
    b. Establishing a safe environment.
    c. Reconnection with ordinary life.
    d. Engaging in anger management.

75. A child who has a low vocabulary for her age and trouble forming sentences may have
    a. a phonological disorder.
    b. a problem with stuttering.
    c. an expressive language disorder.
    d. a mixed receptive-expressive language disorder.

76. In narrative career counseling, the narrator of the client's story is referred to as the
    a. storyteller.
    b. agent.
    c. instrument.
    d. raconteur.

77. Humanistic-existential counselors
    a. avoid interpreting or analyzing clients' motives or behavior.
    b. focus on the present rather than the past.
    c. believe that clients should direct counseling sessions.
    d. All of the above.

78. It may be appropriate to interpret _____ in a group member during group time.
    a. resistance
    b. sarcasm
    c. monopolization
    d. All of the above.

79. A _____ is calculated by dividing the number of correct test items by the total number of test items.
    a. percentile rank
    b. raw score
    c. standard score
    d. percentage score

80. The assessment of the ongoing progress of a program is referred to as a(n)
    a. needs assessment.
    b. process evaluation.
    c. outcome evaluation.
    d. efficiency analysis.

81. Under FERPA, which of the following is NOT true about directory information?
    a. It includes students' honors and awards.
    b. It includes students' grades and test scores.
    c. Schools are required to send an annual notice to parents, and/or students regarding directory information.
    d. Schools can release directory information without student and/or parent consent.

82. Characteristics such as facial expression, posture, characteristics of movement, gestures, and eye contact are
    a. kinesics.
    b. paralanguage.
    c. chronemics.
    d. proxemics.

83. A woman who is unhappy with her marriage accuses her husband of wanting a divorce, even though he has never shown any indication of wanting to take such a course of action. What defense mechanism is the wife displaying?
    a. Projection
    b. Reaction formation
    c. Displacement
    d. Rationalization

84. Which of the following career assessments does not use Holland's six personality types?
    a. Vocational Preference Inventory
    b. Self-Directed Search
    c. Campbell Interest and Skill Survey
    d. Strong Interest Inventory

85. _____ do not have any desire to change and are unwilling to admit that a problem exists.
    a. Customers
    b. Visitors
    c. Complainants
    d. Preservers

86. A _____ is NOT an example of a planned theme group.
    a. grief and loss group
    b. growth group for adolescent females
    c. social skills group
    d. divorce group

87. It a student scored a 48 on an exam for which the mean was 56 and the standard deviation was 4, what can be said about the student's score?
    a. The score fell two standard deviations below the mean.
    b. The score fell close to the 95th percentile.
    c. The score fell two standard deviations above the mean.
    d. The score fell at the 50th percentile.

88. An example of _____ research is examining the relationship between number of play therapy sessions and children's behavioral problems.
    a. quantitative
    b. qualitative
    c. single-subject research design
    d. None of the above.

89. In regard to IDEA, all of the following terms apply EXCEPT
    a. least restrictive environment.
    b. impairment of a major life activity.
    c. free appropriate public education.
    d. individualized education plan.

90. According to the Hardiman's white racial identity development model, the _____ stage is characterized by a conscious belief in the democratic ideal that everyone has an opportunity to succeed.
    a. naiveté
    b. acceptance
    c. resistance
    d. redefinition

91. Which of the following is a true statement about self-actualization?
    a. Self-actualization usually occurs during middle adulthood, if at all.
    b. Self-actualization can only be achieved when all of the lower needs on Maslow's hierarchy have been met.
    c. Some people never become self-actualized.
    d. All of the above.

92. Which career inventory assesses the psychological barriers that adults may face during a career transition, as well as the resources individuals possess to make a successful transition?
    a. Career Orientation Placement and Evaluation Survey (COPES)
    b. Transition-to-Work Inventory
    c. Career Development Inventory
    d. Career Transitions Inventory

93. A skeleton key in solution-focused brief counseling is
    a. a technique that can be used to help all clients, no matter what their presenting problem.
    b. a technique that encourages clients to look for times when their problem does not occur or is less severe.
    c. a technique that is specifically designed for clients based on their unique situation.
    d. None of the above.

94. If co-leaders are used, the group size
    a. should stay the same.
    b. should be reduced.
    c. can be increased by over 50%.
    d. None of the above.

95. Deviation IQ scores have
    a. a mean of 0 and a standard deviation of 1.
    b. a mean of 100 and a standard deviation of 50.
    c. a mean of 50 and a standard deviation of 10.
    d. a mean of 100 and a standard deviation of 15.

96. An agency counselor interviews adolescents, then administers a survey packet to them. This is an example of _____ research.
    a. concurrent exploratory
    b. concurrent explanatory
    c. sequential exploratory
    d. sequential explanatory

97. In some states, minors who have reached a specified age can agree to receive certain services (e.g., counseling) without parental consent. These laws are called
    a. youth consent laws.
    b. minor consent laws.
    c. informed minor laws.
    d. juvenile consent laws.

98. Internal locus of control (IC) refers to
    a. people's ability to shape their own fate.
    b. a fatalistic perspective.
    c. self-worth.
    d. people's ability to control their level of self-esteem.

99. Children who have disorganized attachments to their caregivers would display which of the following kind of behavior?
    a. They would feel securely attached to their caregivers and become upset on separation from their caregivers.
    b. They would not display much expression on separation from caregivers and would seem puzzled on their return.
    c. They would not pay attention to either the departures or the returns of their caregivers.
    d. They would act clingy when caregivers leave and become extremely upset after separation from them.

100. _____ factors influence occupational projections.
    a. Technological
    b. Economic
    c. Population
    d. All of the above.

101. A counselor asks a family member to physically arrange his or her family members in the room to help better understand family dynamics. This technique is called
    a. family sculpting.
    b. the pretend technique.
    c. an enactment.
    d. an ordeal.

102. It is most important that pregroup interviews involve
    a. icebreakers.
    b. the presentation of an informed consent agreement.
    c. high levels of member interaction.
    d. None of the above.

103. Which of the following is a characteristic of Raymond Cattell's term *crystallized intelligence*?
    a. Innate ability that is not influenced by experience or education
    b. Intelligence that is gained through learning and is greatly affected by life experiences and culture
    c. Decreases with age
    d. Consists of reasoning ability, memory capacity, and speed of information processing.

104. A(n) _____ hypothesis is designed to consider extraneous or additional independent variables.
    a. null
    b. research
    c. alternative
    d. organismic

105. _____ help clients with disabilities live more independently and find employment.
    a. Rehabilitation counselors
    b. School counselors
    c. Occupational therapists
    d. Clinical mental health counselors

106. "I never felt Chinese. I was always surrounded by my mother's family from Puerto Rico, often traveling there, and speaking Spanish with my friends at school. The only Chinese people we knew were the delivery men." This statement most closely reflects the _____ stage in Poston's (1990) model of biracial identity development.
    a. personal identity
    b. choice of group categorization
    c. enmeshment/denial
    d. integration

107. Morality is judged by a person's intentions in the _____ stage of Piaget's theory of moral development.
- **a.** moral realism
- **b.** premoral
- **c.** moral intentionality
- **d.** moral relativism

108. The _____ is published by the Bureau of Labor Statistics and provides occupational information on 270 broad occupations that are grouped into 11 different career clusters.
- **a.** Standard Occupational Classification System (SOC)
- **b.** *Occupational Outlook Handbook* (OOH)
- **c.** Occupational Information Network (O*NET)
- **d.** *Guide for Occupational Exploration* (GOE)

109. A well-functioning family develops, first and foremost, from a strong
- **a.** sibling subsystem.
- **b.** spousal subsystem.
- **c.** parental subsystem.
- **d.** All of the above.

110. Member resistance is an example of
- **a.** a contraindication to group work.
- **b.** process dynamics.
- **c.** a structural issue.
- **d.** a leader style issue.

111. The _____ is the most well-known intelligence test, whereas the _____ is the most widely used intelligence test.
- **a.** Stanford Achievement Test; Wide Range Achievement Test
- **b.** Wechsler Scale; Stanford-Binet
- **c.** Stanford Achievement Test; Wechsler Scale
- **d.** Stanford-Binet; Wechsler Scale

112. You find a significant relationship between socioeconomic status and a particular mental health disorder. You can conclude that
- **a.** socioeconomic status causes a mental health disorder.
- **b.** the relationship between socioeconomic status and the mental health disorder is proven.
- **c.** socioeconomic status and the mental health disorder may be associated.
- **d.** socioeconomic status shares variance with ethnicity.

113. Mental health practitioners from diverse specializations differ primarily in the
- **a.** types of problems they address.
- **b.** their ultimate goals for clients.
- **c.** the types of treatment they are trained to use.
- **d.** All of the above.

114. Which of the following is NOT typically experienced during the coming-out process?
- **a.** The individual's relationships with friends are not seriously affected.
- **b.** The individual feels an overwhelming sense of isolation.
- **c.** The individual has feelings of anger, rejection, and grief.
- **d.** The individual, who is emotionally and financially dependent on family, has less access to appropriate role models in the GLBT community.

115. Children generally begin talking
- **a.** at 6 months.
- **b.** between 7 and 12 months.
- **c.** at 12 months.
- **d.** between 13 and 18 months.

116. During the beginning phase of career counseling, the counselor
- **a.** establishes the therapeutic alliance.
- **b.** reviews the client's progress and prepares the client for future challenges.
- **c.** develops an action plan and provides interventions to address the client's concerns.
- **d.** proposes and implements several interventions that address the client's concerns.

117. In a family counseling session, the counselor notices that the father sits between his two children while the mother sits off to the side. A common theme that emerges during the session is that the father allows the children to override the mother in making many important family decisions. To begin to establish a more appropriate hierarchy, the counselor asks the father to sit by his wife. This technique is called
- **a.** unbalancing.
- **b.** restructuring.
- **c.** family sculpting.
- **d.** an ordeal.

118. High levels of group cohesion can result in
- **a.** increased attendance.
- **b.** increased self-disclosure.
- **c.** increased effectiveness of the group.
- **d.** All of the above.

119. The Myers-Briggs type indicator is
- **a.** based on Carl Jung's psychological types.
- **b.** used to assess for clinical symptomatology.
- **c.** written at a fourth-grade reading level.
- **d.** All of the above.

120. If participants' scores are approximately equally distributed across a set of test score values, the data distribution is likely
- **a.** platykurtic.
- **b.** mesokurtic.
- **c.** leptokurtic.
- **d.** bimodal.

121. Professional associations do NOT
- **a.** provide professional development opportunities.
- **b.** license counselors.
- **c.** publish journals.
- **d.** engage in advocacy.

122. European Americans likely possess what type of time orientation?
- **a.** Past
- **b.** Present
- **c.** Future
- **d.** None of the above.

123. Children who have _____ parents are often rebellious and low achievers.
- **a.** authoritative
- **b.** permissive
- **c.** authoritarian
- **d.** uninvolved

124. The majority of career interventions used in the United States are driven by
- **a.** collectivism.
- **b.** inequity.
- **c.** affluence.
- **d.** the notion that leisure is a salient aspect of people's lives.

125. Arnold Lazarus is responsible for the development of
    a. eye movement desensitization and reprocessing.
    b. multimodal therapy.
    c. eclectic counseling.
    d. transactional analysis.

126. _____ conflict can lead to growth within groups.
    a. Moderate
    b. Aggressive
    c. Hostile
    d. None of the above.

127. Based on the risk factors associated with committing suicide, which client is LEAST likely to commit suicide?
    a. A 75-year-old widowed African American female, who has a family history of suicides and is currently abusing prescription pain medications.
    b. An 18-year-old, single Caucasian male who was recently diagnosed with Antisocial Personality Disorder and has reported homicidal thoughts.
    c. A 31-year-old divorced Asian female who reports feelings of hopelessness and has a low tolerance for psychological pain.
    d. A 63-year-old married Latino male, who recently lost his job and has thoughts of suicide.

128. Which of the following is NOT a statistical assumption in inferential statistics?
    a. An independent variable is normally distributed.
    b. A dependent variable is normally distributed.
    c. A ratio scale of measurement is used.
    d. An interval scale of measurement is used.

129. The ACA ethical code encourages counselors to develop their counseling plans
    a. by themselves.
    b. with the help of a colleague or supervisor.
    c. with their clients.
    d. with the help of a treatment manual.

130. A(n) _____ is typically an objective third party in conflict resolution.
    a. mediator
    b. arbitrator
    c. facilitator
    d. None of the above.

131. Which of the following is NOT one of the five dimensions of wellness in the indivisible self-model?
    a. Creative
    b. Social
    c. Practical
    d. Essential

132. Which of the following is an example of a career development program objective?
    a. Clients will obtain gainful employment.
    b. Clients will improve their job search and interviewing skills by the end of this program.
    c. Clients will increase their number of employer contacts by 25% within a 3-week period.
    d. Clients will reach a career decision by reviewing occupational information.

133. According to transactional analysis, the _____ ego state is characterized by logical thought and an unemotional approach to making decisions.
    a. adult
    b. parent
    c. natural child
    d. adapted child

134. Which of the following is NOT a true statement about outcome evaluation?
    a. Outcome evaluation can demonstrate accountability.
    b. The results of outcome evaluation should be used to improve a program.
    c. Outcome evaluation is synonymous with formative evaluation.
    d. Outcome evaluation is conducted to help determine whether to retain a program.

135. Bias in assessment can result from
    a. the test.
    b. the examiner.
    c. global systems that affect the examinee.
    d. All of the above.

136. Which component of trustworthiness generally refers to the believability of qualitative research findings?
    a. Credibility
    b. Dependability
    c. Reliability
    d. Transferability

ANSWER KEY FOR CPCE SAMPLE TEST—FORM A

1. b	18. b	35. b	52. c	69. c	86. b	103. b	120. a
2. b	19. b	36. b	53. b	70. d	87. a	104. c	121. b
3. c	20. b	37. b	54. b	71. c	88. a	105. a	122. c
4. c	21. b	38. d	55. d	72. a	89. b	106. a	123. c
5. a	22. a	39. d	56. b	73. a	90. b	107. d	124. c
6. a	23. d	40. c	57. c	74. d	91. d	108. b	125. b
7. c	24. c	41. a	58. b	75. c	92. d	109. b	126. a
8. d	25. b	42. b	59. d	76. b	93. a	110. b	127. c
9. c	26. c	43. b	60. b	77. d	94. c	111. d	128. a
10. a	27. a	44. d	61. c	78. d	95. d	112. c	129. c
11. a	28. d	45. d	62. c	79. d	96. c	113. c	130. b
12. b	29. d	46. a	63. a	80. b	97. b	114. a	131. c
13. c	30. a	47. a	64. b	81. b	98. a	115. b	132. c
14. a	31. b	48. a	65. d	82. a	99. b	116. a	133. a
15. d	32. b	49. c	66. c	83. a	100. d	117. a	134. c
16. b	33. c	50. d	67. d	84. c	101. a	118. d	135. d
17. b	34. b	51. b	68. b	85. b	102. b	119. a	136. a

ANSWER FORM FOR CPCE SAMPLE TEST—FORM B

Circle the correct response for each test question.

Sum the number correct for each row.

1. a b c d	41. a b c d	81. a b c d	121. a b c d	___
2. a b c d	42. a b c d	82. a b c d	122. a b c d	___
3. a b c d	43. a b c d	83. a b c d	123. a b c d	___
4. a b c d	44. a b c d	84. a b c d	124. a b c d	___
5. a b c d	45. a b c d	85. a b c d	125. a b c d	___
6. a b c d	46. a b c d	86. a b c d	126. a b c d	___
7. a b c d	47. a b c d	87. a b c d	127. a b c d	___
8. a b c d	48. a b c d	88. a b c d	128. a b c d	___
9. a b c d	49. a b c d	89. a b c d	129. a b c d	___
10. a b c d	50. a b c d	90. a b c d	130. a b c d	___
11. a b c d	51. a b c d	91. a b c d	131. a b c d	___
12. a b c d	52. a b c d	92. a b c d	132. a b c d	___
13. a b c d	53. a b c d	93. a b c d	133. a b c d	___
14. a b c d	54. a b c d	94. a b c d	134. a b c d	___
15. a b c d	55. a b c d	95. a b c d	135. a b c d	___
16. a b c d	56. a b c d	96. a b c d	136. a b c d	___
17. a b c d	57. a b c d	97. a b c d		___
18. a b c d	58. a b c d	98. a b c d		___
19. a b c d	59. a b c d	99. a b c d		___
20. a b c d	60. a b c d	100. a b c d		___
21. a b c d	61. a b c d	101. a b c d		___
22. a b c d	62. a b c d	102. a b c d		___
23. a b c d	63. a b c d	103. a b c d		___
24. a b c d	64. a b c d	104. a b c d		___
25. a b c d	65. a b c d	105. a b c d		___
26. a b c d	66. a b c d	106. a b c d		___
27. a b c d	67. a b c d	107. a b c d		___
28. a b c d	68. a b c d	108. a b c d		___
29. a b c d	69. a b c d	109. a b c d		___
30. a b c d	70. a b c d	110. a b c d		___
31. a b c d	71. a b c d	111. a b c d		___
32. a b c d	72. a b c d	112. a b c d		___
33. a b c d	73. a b c d	113. a b c d		___
34. a b c d	74. a b c d	114. a b c d		___
35. a b c d	75. a b c d	115. a b c d		___
36. a b c d	76. a b c d	116. a b c d		___
37. a b c d	77. a b c d	117. a b c d		___
38. a b c d	78. a b c d	118. a b c d		___
39. a b c d	79. a b c d	119. a b c d		___
40. a b c d	80. a b c d	120. a b c d		___

Total correct for each column ___ ___ ___ ___ ___ ___ ___ ___

Chapter 1 2 3 4 5 6 7 8

CPCE SAMPLE TEST—FORM B

1. _____ is considered to be the "father of vocational guidance."
   a. Frank Parsons
   b. Donald Super
   c. E. G. Williamson
   d. Jesse B. Davis

2. Incorporating the culture of the client into the session would suggest that the counselor is
   a. using the assimilation model.
   b. operating from an etic perspective.
   c. operating from an emic perspective.
   d. color blind.

3. Learning theories of human development are generally considered to be
   a. inactive theories.
   b. reactive theories.
   c. proactive theories.
   d. active theories.

4. _____ transformed America's agriculturally based economy into a manufacturing economy and initiated the U.S. career-guidance movement.
   a. World War II
   b. Industrial Revolution
   c. Great Depression
   d. World War I

5. Resistance is displayed by
   a. very few clients.
   b. approximately 10% of clients.
   c. approximately 50% of clients.
   d. almost all clients at some point during the counseling process.

6. Psychodrama was invented by
   a. Fritz Perls.
   b. J. L. Moreno.
   c. Wilfred Bion.
   d. Kurt Lewin.

7. _____ developed the first modern intelligence test, the Binet-Simon scale. This scale was later revised by _____, who renamed the scale the Stanford-Binet intelligence test.
   a. Alfred Binet; Theophile Simon
   b. Alfred Binet; Lewis Terman
   c. Theophile Simon; Lewis Terman
   d. Theophile Simon; Alfred Binet

8. A professional counselor wondered how the general trait of happiness was related to intelligence. Young adults' intelligence was measured using a traditional IQ scale; their level of happiness was also measured on a self-report scale ranging from 1 to 20. The researcher found no link between the results of the two measures. What research design has just been described?
   a. Causal-comparative
   b. Descriptive
   c. Correlational
   d. Regression

9. HIPAA is to medical records as FERPA is to
   a. educational records.
   b. counseling records.
   c. legal records.
   d. None of the above.

10. _____ promotes a current status quo related to social class. An example of this would be being grandfathered into an organization.
    a. Internalized classism
    b. Modern classism
    c. Structural classism
    d. Socioeconomic status

11. A _____ research design allows for comprehensive analysis and observation but probably lacks generalizability.
    a. survey
    b. cross-sectional
    c. correlational
    d. case study

12. _____ developed the Career Maturity Inventory and endorsed comprehensive career counseling.
    a. Mark Savickas
    b. Donald Super
    c. John Krumboltz
    d. John Crites

13. The crisis intervention approach known as psychological first aid is useful for helping individuals who have experienced
    a. a terrorist attack.
    b. a natural disaster.
    c. a traumatic event.
    d. All of the above.

14. Confidentiality in group work is
    a. guaranteed.
    b. required.
    c. unnecessary.
    d. strived for.

15. Who developed the Minnesota Multiphasic Personality Inventory (MMPI), an objective measure of personality structure?
    a. Carl Jung and Henry Murray
    b. Starke Hathaway and Charnley McKinley
    c. Henry Murray and Starke Hathaway
    d. Frank Parsons and Carl Jung

16. A(n) _____ variable results when an extraneous variable is allowed to change with the independent variable.
    a. constant
    b. dependent
    c. confounding
    d. outcome

17. Personal notes kept on students by counselors in a school setting
    a. always become part of students' educational records.
    b. never become part of students' educational records because they are considered an expansion of the counselor's memory.
    c. do not become part of students' educational records if they are kept separate from the educational records in a locked, secure place.
    d. sometimes become part of students' educational records, depending on the school principal's policies.

18. All of the following are components of sexual identity EXCEPT
    a. biological makeup.
    b. sexual orientation.
    c. gender roles.
    d. cognitions.

265

19. _____ is characterized by the body's incapacity to metabolize fatty substances.
   a. Phenylketonuria
   b. Klinefelter's syndrome
   c. Tay-Sachs disease
   d. Sickle cell anemia

20. Which of the following personality factors is NOT associated with the experience of occupational stress and burnout?
   a. Internal locus of control
   b. Low self-esteem
   c. Type A personality
   d. Neuroticism

21. It may be appropriate for counselors to use self-disclosure when
   a. they have gone through an experience that is similar to the client's current situation.
   b. they feel a strong connection with the client.
   c. they think their experience might benefit the client by providing the client with a new outlook or perspective.
   d. All of the above.

22. _____ is NOT classified as a curative factor in groups.
   a. Universality
   b. Confidentiality
   c. Instillation of hope
   d. Imitative behavior

23. According to the *Rights and Responsibilities of Test Takers,* which of the following is NOT a test-taker responsibility?
   a. Being familiar with the use of test results
   b. Following the test instructions
   c. Asking questions related to test administration
   d. None of the above.

24. _____ sampling refers to selecting every *n*th element of a population.
   a. Systematic
   b. Quota
   c. Stratified
   d. Nonprobability

25. If a child discloses to a counselor that he or she is being physically abused, the counselor is
   a. legally but not ethically required to file a report with child protective services.
   b. ethically but not legally required to file a report with child protective services.
   c. legally and ethically required to file a report with child protective services.
   d. neither legally nor ethically required to file a report with child protective services.

26. The faith whose core precept is that of karma and who believes in Brahman as the creator of Earth is
   a. Hinduism.
   b. Judaism.
   c. Taoism.
   d. Buddhism.

27. Developed by Joseph Wolpe, _____ is very effective for treating phobias.
   a. flooding
   b. counterconditioning
   c. systematic desensitization
   d. firing sequence

28. Career is referred to as
   a. the primary activity that engages one's time.
   b. the activities that serve as one's regular source of livelihood.
   c. the lifetime pursuits of an individual.
   d. activities that a person does for fun.

29. The _____ operates according to the pleasure principle.
   a. anima
   b. id
   c. superego
   d. ego

30. _____ groups can be preventative, growth oriented, or remedial.
   a. Counseling and task
   b. Task and psychotherapy
   c. Counseling and psychoeducational
   d. Counseling and psychotherapy

31. As a school counselor you must provide students with testing information that is in their primary language. Which court case mandated this requirement?
   a. *Bakke v. California* (1978)
   b. *Larry P. v. Riles* (1984)
   c. *Griggs v. Duke Power Company* (1971)
   d. *Sharif v. New York State Educational Department* (1989)

32. An instructor creates an exam with too many easy questions. A graph of the distribution would indicate a curve that was
   a. positively skewed.
   b. negatively skewed.
   c. normal.
   d. a scattergram.

33. The organization responsible for the accreditation of counseling programs in the United States is the
   a. Council for the Accreditation of Counseling and Related Educational Programs.
   b. American Counseling Association.
   c. American Psychological Association.
   d. Association for Counseling Program Accreditation.

34. _____ refers to devaluing cultural artifacts such as art, media, or religion if they do not equate to White-held values.
   a. Cultural racism
   b. Discrimination
   c. Internalized racism
   d. Prejudice

35. The reinforcement schedule most resistant to extinction is
   a. fixed ratio.
   b. fixed interval.
   c. variable ratio.
   d. variable interval.

36. Which Holland code is most consistent?
   a. ERS
   b. CAS
   c. ARI
   d. IAS

37. According to Adler's theory of birth order, _____ generally receive the same amount of attention as firstborns.
   a. second children
   b. middle children
   c. youngest children
   d. None of the above.

38. _____ groups usually have formal member roles.
    a. Psychoeducational
    b. Counseling
    c. Psychotherapy
    d. Task

39. To establish content validity
    a. a test must look valid.
    b. test items must reflect all major content areas covered by the domain.
    c. a test must predict future performance.
    d. factor analysis must show that the instrument's subscales are statistically related to each other.

40. A(n) _____ is an analysis technique that compares two means for one group based on pretest and posttest data.
    a. independent t-test
    b. dependent t-test
    c. logistic regression design
    d. ANCOVA

41. A counselor who gains and preserves a client's trust is upholding the ethical principle of
    a. dependability.
    b. altruism.
    c. fidelity.
    d. loyalty.

42. Racism occurs at three levels, including all of the following EXCEPT
    a. institutional.
    b. contextual.
    c. individual.
    d. cultural.

43. _____ is NOT one of the four components of effective modeling
    a. Retention
    b. Attention
    c. Motivation
    d. Shaping

44. For an ESFP, which letter indicates an auxiliary function?
    a. E
    b. S
    c. F
    d. P

45. The _____ is an archetype in Jungian analytic psychology that represents the female traits that exist in the collective unconscious of males.
    a. shadow
    b. persona
    c. anima
    d. animus

46. Norms are established in groups as means to
    a. bring group members into the here and now.
    b. accomplish an executive function.
    c. build a group culture.
    d. All of the above.

47. Which of the following is NOT a characteristic of test-retest reliability?
    a. Test-retest reliability determines the relationship between the scores obtained from two different administrations of the same test.
    b. Test-retest reliability is subject to participant memory and practice effects.

c. Test-retest reliability is used to calculate the degree of consistency of ratings between two or more persons observing the same behavior or assessing an individual through observational or interview methods.
    d. Test-retest reliability is most effective when the instrument assesses stable characteristics.

48. In a smooth yet skewed distribution, the most representative measure of central tendency is the
    a. mean.
    b. median.
    c. mode.
    d. semi-interquartile range.

49. While working with a client, the counselor meets a relative of the client whom she becomes interested in romantically. The ACA *Code of Ethics* states that counselors in this situation
    a. are prohibited from proceeding with the relationship until 5 years after the counseling relationship with the client has ended.
    b. are free to pursue the relationship because it does not involve the client.
    c. are free to pursue the relationship once the counseling relationship with the client has been terminated.
    d. must never pursue the relationship, even after the counseling relationship with the client has ended.

50. Microaggression is
    a. against individuals of color and women.
    b. the belief that aggression is beneficial to some relationships.
    c. aggression through assertiveness.
    d. a phenomenon that occurred often during the 1950s but is not present anymore.

51. The ability to order and classify new information is called
    a. adaptation.
    b. accommodation.
    c. organization.
    d. assimilation.

52. A young adult in Ginzberg's realistic stage
    a. considers the availability, demand, and benefits of certain careers.
    b. is able to assess and consider his or her capabilities in relation to career aspirations.
    c. engages in career exploration to narrow down his or her career choices.
    d. bases career decisions on likes and dislikes.

53. Stress inoculation training, a cognitive-behavioral technique, was developed by
    a. Ellis.
    b. Beck.
    c. Meichenbaum.
    d. Glasser.

54. A group leader assists group members in setting group goals and facilitating group discussions. Members are encouraged to share responsibility for the outcomes of the group with the leader. Which leadership style is this leader using?
    a. Democratic
    b. Authoritarian
    c. Laissez-faire
    d. Autocratic

55. When the reliability coefficient is found to be 1.0, what can be said about an individual's observed score and true score?
    a. The observed score is higher than the true score.
    b. The true score is higher than the observed score.

c. The true sore and observed score are equal.

d. The error during test administration was high.

56. Amber wants to understand what factors promote school counselor retention and decides to develop close relationships with the school counselors in her study. Which strategy for trustworthiness is she using?

    a. Triangulation

    b. Prolonged engagement

    c. Thick description

    d. Referential adequacy

57. Before starting a counseling group, counselors must do all of the following EXCEPT

    a. screen potential members.

    b. inform potential members that confidentiality is guaranteed.

    c. only invite individuals to join who will likely benefit from the group.

    d. not invite any individual to join the group who may be harmed by the experience.

58. Traditional mental health practices

    a. value individual responsibility and autonomy.

    b. view the problem as residing primarily in the environment.

    c. overemphasize the exploration of therapist values and beliefs.

    d. mesh well with the more collectivistic orientation of ethnic minorities.

59. _____ is NOT a theory of forgetting.

    a. Storage failure theory

    b. Decay of memory theory

    c. Interference theory

    d. Retrieval theory

60. People who demonstrate career maturity

    a. have a highly differentiated Holland code.

    b. have a willingness and ability to deal with career transitions.

    c. have the ability to use the knowledge gained from career exploration activities to make career plans.

    d. All of the above.

61. "I should never have shared my sales idea at today's department meeting at work. I just know that my boss thought my suggestion was ridiculous." This is an example of what type of distorted thinking?

    a. Mind reading

    b. Fortune telling

    c. Minimization

    d. Labeling

62. _____ is commonly used by group leaders to encourage quiet members to participate.

    a. Linking

    b. Questioning

    c. Drawing out

    d. Initiating

63. A (n) _____ scale has equivalent units of measurement but does not have an absolute zero point

    a. nominal

    b. ratio

    c. ordinal

    d. interval

64. If a professional counselor was interested in trainees' multicultural competency, a sample consisting of members from the American Counseling Association might involve a _____ threat.

    a. selection

    b. statistical regression

c. maturation

d. history

65. A new counselor is offered a job as a counseling supervisor. The counselor does not have any experience or training in supervision, but she does have a solid educational background and practical experiences as a counselor. Ethically, the counselor should

    a. accept the job; her educational background will support her in this new role.

    b. accept the job; the company would not have hired her if it did not think she was qualified.

    c. not accept the job; she does not have the requisite qualifications or professional experience.

    d. consult with trusted family and friends about the situation.

66. Worldview can be defined broadly as

    a. how an individual understands his or her race.

    b. how a person perceives his or her relationship to nature, institutions, people, and the experiential world.

    c. one's degree of comfort in an unfamiliar cultural environment.

    d. one's values as shaped solely by religion.

67. A woman is upset after losing her job, but she is not surprised. She says that she has failed at every job that she has ever had because she is dumb and there is nothing she can do about it. Her attribution is

    a. stable, external, and uncontrollable.

    b. unstable, internal, and controllable.

    c. stable, internal, and uncontrollable.

    d. unstable, external, and controllable.

68. _____ is NOT one of Krumboltz's four career determinants.

    a. Genetic endowment

    b. Task approach skills

    c. Planned happenstance

    d. Environmental conditions

69. Which of the following is a TRUE statement about reality therapy?

    a. Reality therapists should penalize clients for not following through on their plans.

    b. Reality therapists use the WBET system.

    c. Determinism is emphasized.

    d. Clients are not allowed to make excuses for themselves.

70. A major challenge with self-disclosure in groups is that members often

    a. share too much.

    b. share too little.

    c. do not know how much to share.

    d. None of the above.

71. The _____ scale measures multiple dimensions of an attitude by employing a paired comparison method.

    a. Guttman

    b. semantic differential

    c. Likert

    d. Thurstone

72. Which of the following research paradigms most values multiple realities?

    a. Positivism

    b. Post-positivism

    c. Modernism

    d. Constructivism

73. A counselor meets with a client who divulges that he is planning to kill one of his friends, who he believes stole his girlfriend. During the session, the counselor learns the name of the client's friend. It is the counselor's legal responsibility in most states to

a. keep the information confidential.

b. warn the identified friend.

c. warn the identified friend and take additional steps to protect him, such as calling the police.

d. keep the information confidential but try to talk the client out of his decision.

74. U.S. society is characterized by which worldview?

a. Internal locus of control–Internal locus of responsibility

b. Internal locus of control–External locus of responsibility

c. External locus of control–Internal locus of responsibility

d. External locus of control–External locus of responsibility

75. _____ is NOT a category of language development theory.

a. Learning theory approach

b. Nativist approach

c. Interactionist approach

d. Epigenetic approach

76. Roe's occupational classification system comprises eight _____ that classify the primary focus of activity involved in each occupation and six _____ that classify the amount of responsibility and ability required by the occupation.

a. groups; levels

b. levels; groups

c. occupational categories; skill levels

d. skill levels; occupational categories

77. Most importantly, counselors with a phenomenological perspective try to

a. understand the important events in clients' lives.

b. pay attention to the patterns and themes in clients' stories.

c. ascertain how clients perceive important events in their lives.

d. place clients' problems in a social context.

78. Self-disclosure results in the shrinking of which quadrant of the Johari window?

a. Public/open quadrant

b. Private/hidden quadrantc

c. Blind quadrant

d. Unknown/unconscious quadrant

79. Standard scores

a. compare individual raw scores to a predetermined cutoff score.

b. do not allow comparison of an individual's scores on different types of tests.

c. include age-equivalent and grade-equivalent scores.

d. compare individual scores to a norm group by converting raw scores to a new score based on the normal curve.

80. An example of _____ research is interviewing counselor trainees on their experiences in a training program.

a. quantitative

b. qualitative

c. single-subject

d. None of the above.

81. Anyone can be sued for _____, but only certain professionals can be sued for _____.

a. negligence; malpractice

b. malpractice; negligence

c. slander; libel

d. libel; slander

82. A White individual who becomes defensive and demonstrates increased racial intolerance as a result of a racialized event is likely in which Helms status?

a. Disintegration

b. Reintegration

c. Encounter

d. Crisis

83. At what stage of psychosexual development does that superego emerge?

a. Anal stage

b. Phallic stage

c. Latency stage

d. Oral stage

84. The Transition-to-Work Inventory

a. matches respondents' top vocational interests with occupational clusters.

b. is particularly useful for those with limited work experience, those who are seeking a new career, or those who are engaging in retirement planning.

c. primarily measures career interests but also includes self-estimates of abilities and competencies.

d. measures self-reported vocational interests and skills.

85. Outside witnesses in narrative therapy are usually

a. counselors' previous clients.

b. family members.

c. friends of the client.

d. All of the above.

86. Leaders can address a group member who exhibits manipulative behavior by

a. blocking the behavior.

b. confronting the member about the behavior.

c. initiating concurrent individual group counseling with the member.

d. All of the above.

87. If the average test score on a 100-item English test is 65, what is the percentile rank of an individual who scored a 65?

a. 65

b. 50

c. 100

d. None of the above.

88. A counseling researcher is interested in investigating the following research question: "What is the influence of socioeconomic status and school climate on academic achievement?" What might be an example of an extraneous variable?

a. Socioeconomic status

b. School climate

c. Academic achievement

d. School budget cut

89. The legal concept that safeguards client–counselor communications under certain circumstances is called

a. privileged communication.

b. privacy.

c. confidentiality.

d. classified communication.

90. An autonomous counselor working with a disintegration client would likely

a. provide potential for client insight and knowledge around racial issues.

b. want to terminate prematurely with the client.

c. avoid discussing racial issues.

d. protect and nurture the client inappropriately.

91. Gender role development is influenced by
    a. parents.
    b. the media.
    c. teachers.
    d. All of the above.

92. Value inventories assist individuals in identifying and prioritizing their
    a. cultural values.
    b. lifestyle and cultural values.
    c. work values.
    d. None of the above.

93. Scaling questions are most commonly used in
    a. narrative therapy.
    b. reality therapy.
    c. Solution-focused brief counseling.
    d. cognitive therapy.

94. A group composed of members of the same age and gender who also have similar concerns is an example of a _____ group.
    a. homogeneous
    b. homologous
    c. heterogeneous
    d. multifarious

95. Unlike percentile ranks, NCEs
    a. divide the normal curve into 100 equal parts.
    b. range from 1 to 99.
    c. indicate how an individual ranked in relationship to his or her peers.
    d. can be converted from a z-score.

96. Accepting a null hypothesis when it is false refers to
    a. type II error.
    b. effect size.
    c. type I error.
    d. maturation.

97. The name of Frank Parsons' important publication on careers is
    a. *Vocational Choices.*
    b. *Choosing a Career.*
    c. *Choosing a Vocation.*
    d. *Career Match.*

98. In Native American culture, children who establish direct eye contact with an elder would probably be seen as displaying
    a. anger.
    b. disrespect.
    c. agreement.
    d. resentment.

99. _____ is NOT one of the five stages of grief.
    a. Denial
    b. Fear
    c. Hopelessness
    d. Bargaining

100. Employment rate refers to
    a. the number of individuals in the workforce.
    b. the number of individuals who are not actively seeking employment, including institutionalized individuals.
    c. the number of currently employed individuals divided by the total number of individuals who are of working age.
    d. the need to replace those who have left the workforce.

101. A client tells her counselor that every night before going to bed she eats a large quantity of junk food and cannot seem to stop. The counselor tells the client that she can have junk food before bed if she would like to but, before eating, she must clean one part of the house. If she does not, she is not allowed to eat anything. This technique is called
    a. the pretend technique.
    b. an ordeal.
    c. an enactment.
    d. a ritual.

102. It is recommended that group sessions not exceed
    a. 1 hour.
    b. 1½ hours.
    c. 2 hours.
    d. 2½ hours.

103. What are the key features of high stakes tests?
    a. No clear line is drawn between those who pass and those who fail.
    b. The test results have a direct consequence.
    c. Students receive only one opportunity to take the exam.
    d. None of the above.

104. You are studying the impact of cognitive therapy on those receiving mental health treatment in a community, and you would like to include a sample proportionate to the makeup of the community. What sampling method does this best describe?
    a. Systematic
    b. Stratified
    c. Cluster
    d. Quota

105. FERPA affects
    a. any school that does not receive federal funding.
    b. any school that receives federal funding.
    c. all schools regardless of federal funding.
    d. only Title 1 schools.

106. Which of the following is true for counselors working with GLBT clients?
    a. Counselors should be aware of the special issues faced by their clients.
    b. Counselors should include questions about sexual orientation, behavior, or attraction during the assessment.
    c. Counselors should address concerns such as mental health issues, substance use, and high-risk sexual behaviors with their clients.
    d. All of the above.

107. According to Kohlberg, individuals who base their actions on what is likely to please others are in the _____ stage of moral development.
    a. law and order
    b. "good boy, good girl"
    c. instrumental hedonism
    d. obedience and punishment

108. Using the Standard Occupational Classification System, the first and second digits indicate the
    a. broad occupation.
    b. detailed occupation.
    c. minor group.
    d. major group.

109. Enmeshed families often have boundaries that are
    a. permeable.
    b. semi-permeable.

c. impermeable.

d. None of the above.

110. Members who prematurely drop out of groups are more likely to
   a. be from a lower socioeconomic status.
   b. have low motivation.
   c. have poor social skills.
   d. All of the above.

111. The Kaufman Assessment Battery for Children
   a. uses basal and ceiling levels to determine starting and stopping points.
   b. is designed to evaluate adults with learning disabilities.
   c. allows the test administrator to use the Luria neuropsychological model and the Cattell/Horn/Carroll (CHC) approach to interpret the subtests.
   d. measures children's abstract thinking and reasoning abilities.

112. What is the key distinction between nonexperimental and experimental research designs?
   a. Presence of an intervention
   b. Description of a dependent variable
   c. Sampling
   d. Using a single-subject design

113. The following is a true statement about college counseling, a specialization within the profession:
   a. It aims to help high school students get accepted into college.
   b. It occurs at the postsecondary level.
   c. High school counselors spend a large percentage of their time engaged in college counseling.
   d. All of the above.

114. An obligation to family and parents is best termed
   a. confianza.
   b. marianismo.
   c. personalismo.
   d. filial piety.

115. Young adults must refute all of the following false assumptions EXCEPT
   a. "Safety can last forever."
   b. "My parents will always be there to help when things go wrong or not exactly as I want."
   c. "Adults will always live with their parents."
   d. "My parents can always offer a simplified version and solution to complicated inner realities."

116. _____ is a pictorial display of the client's family relationships that enables clients to understand familial influences on their career development process.
   a. Guided imagery
   b. Career hologram
   c. Career genogram
   d. Family graph

117. A counselor asks a family to re-create a common scenario at home that is causing problems. This technique is called a(n) _____ by structural family counselors.
   a. ritual
   b. enactment
   c. ordeal
   d. role play

118. _____ issues are the LEAST significant contributors to group dynamics.
   a. Process
   b. Content

c. Familial

d. Structural

119. The Big Five personality factors are
   a. neuroticism, introversion, openness to experience, achievement, and conscientiousness.
   b. narcissism, extraversion, openness to experience, socialization, and conscientiousness.
   c. neuroticism, extraversion, openness to experience, agreeableness, and conscientiousness.
   d. neuroticism, extraversion, openness to experience, achievement, and conscientiousness.

120. If a measure yields unreliable scores, it will likely underestimate the correlation between two variables. This is known as
   a. restriction of range.
   b. point-biserial concerns.
   c. diminished degrees of freedom.
   d. attenuation.

121. The mental health practitioners who most commonly operate from a systems theory perspective are
   a. psychiatric nurses.
   b. marriage and family therapists.
   c. psychoanalysts.
   d. school psychologists.

122. Physical challenges, cognitive issues, and grief and loss are common challenges in
   a. addictions counseling.
   b. gerontological counseling.
   c. school counseling.
   d. adolescent counseling.

123. Approximately what percentage of third marriages end in divorce?
   a. 50%
   b. 60%
   c. 70%
   d. 80%

124. Quality career development programming
   a. is cost ineffective in comparison to one-on-one counseling.
   b. requires the implementation of thoughtful and intentional designs.
   c. can be thrown together haphazardly.
   d. strives to positively affect participants but is not concerned with the larger community.

125. Multimodal therapy is an example of
   a. technical eclecticism.
   b. syncretism.
   c. theoretical integration.
   d. radical eclecticism.

126. As the size of a group increases, ordinarily
   a. group cohesion will increase.
   b. subgroupings will occur.
   c. rules will be enforced more stringently.
   d. resistance will increase.

127. Which of the following is NOT related to the nine key domains of the Mental Status Exam?
   a. The attitude domain refers to how the client interacts with the professional counselor during the interview.
   b. The thought content domain refers to experiencing hallucinations and derealizations.

   c. The perception domain refers to sensory experiences.
   d. The thought process domain refers to the connections between client thoughts.

128. Involving participants in data analysis is referred to as
   a. prolonged engagement.
   b. persistent observation.
   c. referential adequacy.
   d. member checking.

129. Counselors should terminate the counseling relationship if
   a. the client wants to do so.
   b. the client does not seem to be benefiting from counseling.
   c. the client no longer needs counseling.
   d. All of the above.

130. A needle exchange program is most representative of the_____ method.
   a. abstinence
   b. motivational interviewing
   c. harm reduction
   d. relapse prevention

131. A crisis
   a. has the potential to result in negative outcomes.
   b. is a temporary period of instability.
   c. can present an opportunity for growth.
   d. All of the above.

132. To determine whether or not the program is being implemented as planned, career counselors can attend to _____, which determines the extent to which participants were engaged in the program's content and activities.
   a. participant responsiveness
   b. program quality

   c. exposure
   d. adherence

133. Proponents of transactional analysis posit that problems arise when people operate from
   a. one ego state in almost all situations.
   b. two ego states.
   c. three ego states.
   d. all of their ego states.

134. A nonthreatening way to address resistance in groups is by
   a. reframing the resistant behavior.
   b. using paradoxical intention.
   c. asking members to interpret the behavior.
   d. interpreting the behavior for members.

135. Using the term *Dixie* to refer to the southern half of the United States on an exam is an example of _____ bias?
   a. ecological
   b. examiner
   c. test
   d. situational

136. Examining the costs and benefits of a program to determine its overall effectiveness is also referred to as
   a. process evaluation.
   b. efficiency analysis.
   c. needs assessment.
   d. outcome evaluation.

ANSWER KEY FOR CPCE SAMPLE TEST—FORM B

1. a	18. d	35. c	52. c	69. d	86. d	103. b	120. d
2. c	19. c	36. d	53. c	70. c	87. b	104. b	121. b
3. b	20. a	37. c	54. a	71. d	88. d	105. b	122. b
4. b	21. c	38. d	55. c	72. d	89. a	106. d	123. c
5. d	22. b	39. b	56. b	73. c	90. c	107. b	124. b
6. b	23. a	40. b	57. b	74. a	91. d	108. d	125. a
7. b	24. a	41. c	58. a	75. d	92. c	109. a	126. b
8. c	25. c	42. b	59. a	76. a	93. c	110. d	127. b
9. a	26. a	43. d	60. c	77. c	94. a	111. c	128. d
10. c	27. c	44. b	61. a	78. b	95. a	112. a	129. d
11. d	28. c	45. c	62. c	79. d	96. a	113. b	130. c
12. d	29. b	46. c	63. d	80. b	97. c	114. d	131. d
13. d	30. c	47. c	64. a	81. a	98. b	115. a	132. a
14. d	31. d	48. b	65. c	82. b	99. b	116. c	133. a
15. b	32. b	49. a	66. b	83. b	100. c	117. b	134. a
16. c	33. a	50. a	67. c	84. b	101. b	118. c	135. c
17. c	34. a	51. c	68. c	85. d	102. c	119. c	136. b

APPENDIX A

ACA Code of Ethics

As approved by the ACA Governing Council, 2005
American Counseling Association
www.counseling.org

Mission

The mission of the American Counseling Association is to enhance the quality of life in society by promoting the development of professional counselors, advancing the counseling profession, and using the profession and practice of counseling to promote respect for human dignity and diversity.

Contents

ACA Code of Ethics Preamble

The American Counseling Association is an educational, scientific, and professional organization whose members work in a variety of settings and serve in multiple capacities. ACA members are dedicated to the enhancement of human development throughout the life span. Association members recognize diversity and embrace a cross- cultural approach in support of the worth, dignity, potential, and uniqueness of people within their social and cultural contexts.

Professional values are an important way of living out an ethical commitment. Values inform principles. Inherently held values that guide our behaviors or exceed prescribed behaviors are deeply ingrained in the counselor and developed out of personal dedication, rather than the mandatory requirement of an external organization.

ACA Code of Ethics Purpose

The *ACA Code of Ethics* serves five main purposes:

1. The *Code* enables the association to clarify to current and future members, and to those served by members, the nature of the ethical responsibilities held in common by its members.
2. The *Code* helps support the mission of the association.
3. The *Code* establishes principles that define ethical behavior and best practices of association members.
4. The *Code* serves as an ethical guide designed to assist members in constructing a professional course of action that best serves those utilizing counseling services and best promotes the values of the counseling profession.
5. The *Code* serves as the basis for processing of ethical complaints and inquiries initiated against members of the association.

The *ACA Code of Ethics* contains eight main sections that address the following areas:

Section A: The Counseling Relationship
Section B: Confidentiality, Privileged Communication, and Privacy
Section C: Professional Responsibility
Section D: Relationships With Other Professionals
Section E: Evaluation, Assessment, and Interpretation
Section F: Supervision, Training, and Teaching
Section G: Research and Publication
Section H: Resolving Ethical Issues

Each section of the *ACA Code of Ethics* begins with an Introduction. The introductions to each section discuss what counselors should aspire to with regard to ethical behavior and responsibility. The Introduction helps set the tone for that particular section and provides a starting point that invites reflection on the ethical mandates contained in each part of the *ACA Code of Ethics*.

When counselors are faced with ethical dilemmas that are difficult to resolve, they are expected to engage in a carefully considered ethical decision-making process. Reasonable differences of opinion can and do exist among counselors with respect to the ways in which values, ethical principles, and ethical standards would be applied when they conflict. While there is no specific ethical decision-making model that is most effective, counselors are expected to be familiar with a credible model of decision making that can bear public scrutiny and its application.

Through a chosen ethical decision-making process and evaluation of the context of the situation, counselors are empowered to make decisions that help expand the capacity of people to grow and develop.

A brief glossary is given to provide readers with a concise description of some of the terms used in the *ACA Code of Ethics*.

Section A

The Counseling Relationship

Introduction

Counselors encourage client growth and development in ways that foster the interest and welfare of clients and promote formation of healthy relationships. Counselors actively attempt to understand the diverse cultural backgrounds of the clients they serve. Counselors also explore their own cultural identities and how these affect their values and beliefs about the counseling process.

Counselors are encouraged to contribute to society by devoting a portion of their professional activity to services for which there is little or no financial return (pro bono publico).

A.1. Welfare of Those Served by Counselors

A.1.a. Primary Responsibility

The primary responsibility of counselors is to respect the dignity and to promote the welfare of clients.

A.1.b. Records

Counselors maintain records necessary for rendering professional services to their clients and as required by laws, regulations, or agency or institution procedures. Counselors include sufficient and timely documentation in their client records to facilitate the delivery and continuity of needed services. Counselors take reasonable steps to ensure that documentation in records accurately reflects client progress and services provided. If errors are made in client records, counselors take steps to properly note the correction of such errors according to agency or institutional policies. *(See A.12.g.7., B.6., B.6.g., G.2.j.)*

A.1.c. Counseling Plans

Counselors and their clients work jointly in devising integrated counseling plans that offer reasonable promise of success and are consistent with abilities and circumstances of clients. Counselors and clients regularly review counseling plans to assess their continued viability and effectiveness, respecting the freedom of choice of clients. *(See A.2.a., A.2.d., A.12.g.)*

A.1.d. Support Network Involvement

Counselors recognize that support networks hold various meanings in the lives of clients and consider enlisting the support, understanding, and involvement of others (e.g., religious/spiritual/community leaders, family members, friends) as positive resources, when appropriate, with client consent.

A.1.e. Employment Needs

Counselors work with their clients considering employment in jobs that are consistent with the overall abilities, vocational limitations, physical restrictions, general temperament, interest and aptitude patterns, social skills, education, general qualifications, and other relevant characteristics and needs of clients. When appropriate, counselors appropriately trained in career development will assist in the placement of clients in positions that are consistent with the interest, culture, and the welfare of clients, employers, and/or the public.

A.2. Informed Consent in the Counseling Relationship

(See A.12.g., B.5., B.6.b., E.3., E.13.b., F.1.c., G.2.a.)

A.2.a. Informed Consent

Clients have the freedom to choose whether to enter into or remain in a counseling relationship and need adequate information about the counseling process and the counselor. Counselors have an obligation to review in writing and verbally with clients the rights and responsibilities of both the counselor and the client. Informed consent is an ongoing part of the counseling process, and counselors appropriately document discussions of informed consent throughout the counseling relationship.

A.2.b. Types of Information Needed

Counselors explicitly explain to clients the nature of all services provided. They inform clients about issues such as, but not limited to, the following: the purposes, goals, techniques, procedures, limitations, potential risks, and benefits of services; the counselor's qualifications, credentials, and relevant experience; continuation of services upon the incapacitation or death of a counselor; and other pertinent information. Counselors take steps to ensure that clients understand the implications of diagnosis, the intended use of tests and reports, fees, and billing arrangements.

Clients have the right to confidentiality and to be provided with an explanation of its limitations (including how supervisors and/or treatment team professionals are involved); to obtain clear information about their records; to participate in the ongoing counseling plans; and to refuse any services or modality change and to be advised of the consequences of such refusal.

A.2.c. Developmental and Cultural Sensitivity

Counselors communicate information in ways that are both developmentally and culturally appropriate. Counselors use clear and understandable language when discussing issues related to informed consent. When clients have difficulty understanding the language used by counselors, they provide necessary services (e.g., arranging for a qualified interpreter or translator) to ensure comprehension by clients. In collaboration with clients, counselors consider cultural implications of informed consent procedures and, where possible, counselors adjust their practices accordingly.

A.2.d. Inability to Give Consent

When counseling minors or persons unable to give voluntary consent, counselors seek the assent of clients to services, and include them in decision making as appropriate. Counselors recognize the need to balance the ethical rights of clients to make choices, their capacity to give consent or assent to receive services, and parental or familial legal rights and responsibilities to protect these clients and make decisions on their behalf.

A.3. Clients Served by Others

When counselors learn that their clients are in a professional relationship with another mental health professional, they request release from clients to inform the other professionals and strive to establish positive and collaborative professional relationships.

A.4. Avoiding Harm and Imposing Values

A.4.a. Avoiding Harm

Counselors act to avoid harming their clients, trainees, and research participants and to minimize or to remedy unavoidable or unanticipated harm.

A.4.b. Personal Values

Counselors are aware of their own values, attitudes, beliefs, and behaviors and avoid imposing values that are inconsistent with counseling goals. Counselors respect the diversity of clients, trainees, and research participants.

A.5. Roles and Relationships With Clients
(See F.3., F.10., G.3.)

A.5.a. Current Clients
Sexual or romantic counselor–client interactions or relationships with current clients, their romantic partners, or their family members are prohibited.

A.5.b. Former Clients
Sexual or romantic counselor–client interactions or relationships with former clients, their romantic partners, or their family members are prohibited for a period of 5 years following the last professional contact. Counselors, before engaging in sexual or romantic interactions or relationships with clients, their romantic partners, or client family members after 5 years following the last professional contact, demonstrate forethought and document (in written form) whether the interactions or relationship can be viewed as exploitive in some way and/or whether there is still potential to harm the former client; in cases of potential exploitation and/or harm, the counselor avoids entering such an interaction or relationship.

A.5.c. Nonprofessional Interactions or Relationships (Other Than Sexual or Romantic Interactions or Relationships)
Counselor–client nonprofessional relationships with clients, former clients, their romantic partners, or their family members should be avoided, except when the interaction is potentially beneficial to the client. *(See A.5.d.)*

A.5.d. Potentially Beneficial Interactions
When a counselor–client nonprofessional interaction with a client or former client may be potentially beneficial to the client or former client, the counselor must document in case records, prior to the interaction (when feasible), the rationale for such an interaction, the potential benefit, and anticipated consequences for the client or former client and other individuals significantly involved with the client or former client. Such interactions should be initiated with appropriate client consent. Where

unintentional harm occurs to the client or former client, or to an individual significantly involved with the client or former client, due to the nonprofessional interaction, the counselor must show evidence of an attempt to remedy such harm. Examples of potentially beneficial interactions include, but are not limited to, attending a formal ceremony (e.g., a wedding/commitment ceremony or graduation); purchasing a service or product provided by a client or former client (excepting unrestricted bartering); hospital visits to an ill family member; mutual membership in a professional association, organization, or community. *(See A.5.c.)*

A.5.e. Role Changes in the Professional Relationship
When a counselor changes a role from the original or most recent contracted relationship, he or she obtains informed consent from the client and explains the right of the client to refuse services related to the change. Examples of role changes include

1. changing from individual to relationship or family counseling, or vice versa;
2. changing from a nonforensic evaluative role to a therapeutic role, or vice versa;
3. changing from a counselor to a researcher role (i.e., enlisting clients as research participants), or vice versa; and
4. changing from a counselor to a mediator role, or vice versa.

Clients must be fully informed of any anticipated consequences (e.g., financial, legal, personal, or therapeutic) of counselor role changes.

A.6. Roles and Relationships at Individual, Group, Institutional, and Societal Levels

A.6.a. Advocacy
When appropriate, counselors advocate at individual, group, institutional, and societal levels to examine potential barriers and obstacles that inhibit access and/or the growth and development of clients.

A.6.b. Confidentiality and Advocacy
Counselors obtain client consent prior to engaging in advocacy efforts on behalf of an identifiable client to

improve the provision of services and to work toward removal of systemic barriers or obstacles that inhibit client access, growth, and development.

A.7. Multiple Clients
When a counselor agrees to provide counseling services to two or more persons who have a relationship, the counselor clarifies at the outset which person or persons are clients and the nature of the relationships the counselor will have with each involved person. If it becomes apparent that the counselor may be called upon to perform potentially conflicting roles, the counselor will clarify, adjust, or withdraw from roles appropriately. *(See A.8.a., B.4.)*

A.8. Group Work
(See B.4.a.)

A.8.a. Screening
Counselors screen prospective group counseling/therapy participants. To the extent possible, counselors select members whose needs and goals are compatible with goals of the group, who will not impede the group process, and whose well-being will not be jeopardized by the group experience.

A.8.b. Protecting Clients
In a group setting, counselors take reasonable precautions to protect clients from physical, emotional, or psychological trauma.

A.9. End-of-Life Care for Terminally Ill Clients

A.9.a. Quality of Care
Counselors strive to take measures that enable clients

1. to obtain high quality end-of-life care for their physical, emotional, social, and spiritual needs;
2. to exercise the highest degree of self-determination possible;
3. to be given every opportunity possible to engage in informed decision making regarding their end-of-life care; and
4. to receive complete and adequate assessment regarding their ability to make competent, rational decisions on their own behalf from a mental health professional who is experienced in end-of-life care practice.

A.9.b. Counselor Competence, Choice, and Referral
Recognizing the personal, moral, and competence issues related to

end-of-life decisions, counselors may choose to work or not work with terminally ill clients who wish to explore their end-of-life options. Counselors provide appropriate referral information to ensure that clients receive the necessary help.

A.9.c. Confidentiality

Counselors who provide services to terminally ill individuals who are considering hastening their own deaths have the option of breaking or not breaking confidentiality, depending on applicable laws and the specific circumstances of the situation and after seeking consultation or supervision from appropriate professional and legal parties. *(See B.5.c., B.7.c.)*

A.10. Fees and Bartering

A.10.a. Accepting Fees From Agency Clients

Counselors refuse a private fee or other remuneration for rendering services to persons who are entitled to such services through the counselor's employing agency or institution. The policies of a particular agency may make explicit provisions for agency clients to receive counseling services from members of its staff in private practice. In such instances, the clients must be informed of other options open to them should they seek private counseling services.

A.10.b. Establishing Fees

In establishing fees for professional counseling services, counselors consider the financial status of clients and locality. In the event that the established fee structure is inappropriate for a client, counselors assist clients in attempting to find comparable services of acceptable cost.

A.10.c. Nonpayment of Fees

If counselors intend to use collection agencies or take legal measures to collect fees from clients who do not pay for services as agreed upon, they first inform clients of intended actions and offer clients the opportunity to make payment.

A.10.d. Bartering

Counselors may barter only if the relationship is not exploitive or harmful and does not place the counselor in an unfair advantage, if the client requests it, and if such arrangements are an accepted practice among professionals in the community. Counselors consider the cultural implications of bartering and discuss relevant concerns with clients and document such agreements in a clear written contract.

A.10.e. Receiving Gifts

Counselors understand the challenges of accepting gifts from clients and recognize that in some cultures, small gifts are a token of respect and showing gratitude. When determining whether or not to accept a gift from clients, counselors take into account the therapeutic relationship, the monetary value of the gift, a client's motivation for giving the gift, and the counselor's motivation for wanting or declining the gift.

A.11. Termination and Referral

A.11.a. Abandonment Prohibited

Counselors do not abandon or neglect clients in counseling. Counselors assist in making appropriate arrangements for the continuation of treatment, when necessary, during interruptions such as vacations, illness, and following termination.

A.11.b. Inability to Assist Clients

If counselors determine an inability to be of professional assistance to clients, they avoid entering or continuing counseling relationships. Counselors are knowledgeable about culturally and clinically appropriate referral resources and suggest these alternatives. If clients decline the suggested referrals, counselors should discontinue the relationship.

A.11.c. Appropriate Termination

Counselors terminate a counseling relationship when it becomes reasonably apparent that the client no longer needs assistance, is not likely to benefit, or is being harmed by continued counseling. Counselors may terminate counseling when in jeopardy of harm by the client, or another person with whom the client has a relationship, or when clients do not pay fees as agreed upon. Counselors provide pretermination counseling and recommend other service providers when necessary.

A.11.d. Appropriate Transfer of Services

When counselors transfer or refer clients to other practitioners, they ensure that appropriate clinical and administrative processes are completed and open communication is maintained with both clients and practitioners.

A.12. Technology Applications

A.12.a. Benefits and Limitations

Counselors inform clients of the benefits and limitations of using information technology applications in the counseling process and in business/billing procedures. Such technologies include but are not limited to computer hardware and software, telephones, the World Wide Web, the Internet, online assessment instruments and other communication devices.

A.12.b. Technology-Assisted Services

When providing technology-assisted distance counseling services, counselors determine that clients are intellectually, emotionally, and physically capable of using the application and that the application is appropriate for the needs of clients.

A.12.c. Inappropriate Services

When technology-assisted distance counseling services are deemed inappropriate by the counselor or client, counselors consider delivering services face to face.

A.12.d. Access

Counselors provide reasonable access to computer applications when providing technology-assisted distance counseling services.

A.12.e. Laws and Statutes

Counselors ensure that the use of technology does not violate the laws of any local, state, national, or international entity and observe all relevant statutes.

A.12.f. Assistance

Counselors seek business, legal, and technical assistance when using technology applications, particularly when the use of such applications crosses state or national boundaries.

A.12.g. Technology and Informed Consent

As part of the process of establishing informed consent, counselors do the following:

1. Address issues related to the difficulty of maintaining the confidentiality of electronically transmitted communications.

2. Inform clients of all colleagues, supervisors, and employees, such as Informational Technology (IT) administrators, who might have authorized or unauthorized access to electronic transmissions.

3. Urge clients to be aware of all authorized or unauthorized users

including family members and fellow employees who have access to any technology clients may use in the counseling process.

4. Inform clients of pertinent legal rights and limitations governing the practice of a profession over state lines or international boundaries.

5. Use encrypted Web sites and e-mail communications to help ensure confidentiality when possible.

6. When the use of encryption is not possible, counselors notify clients of this fact and limit electronic transmissions to general communications that are not client specific.

7. Inform clients if and for how long archival storage of transaction records are maintained.

8. Discuss the possibility of technology failure and alternate methods of service delivery.

9. Inform clients of emergency procedures, such as calling 911 or a local crisis hotline, when the counselor is not available.

10. Discuss time zone differences, local customs, and cultural or language differences that might impact service delivery.

11. Inform clients when technology-assisted distance counseling services are not covered by insurance. *(See A.2.)*

A.12.h. Sites on the World Wide Web

Counselors maintaining sites on the World Wide Web (the Internet) do the following:

1. Regularly check that electronic links are working and professionally appropriate.

2. Establish ways clients can contact the counselor in case of technology failure.

3. Provide electronic links to relevant state licensure and professional certification boards to protect consumer rights and facilitate addressing ethical concerns.

4. Establish a method for verifying client identity.

5. Obtain the written consent of the legal guardian or other authorized legal representative prior to rendering services in the event the client is a minor child, an adult who is legally incompetent, or an adult incapable of giving informed consent.

6. Strive to provide a site that is accessible to persons with disabilities.

7. Strive to provide translation capabilities for clients who have a different primary language while also addressing the imperfect nature of such translations.

8. Assist clients in determining the validity and reliability of information found on the World Wide Web and other technology applications.

Section B
Confidentiality, Privileged Communication, and Privacy

Introduction

Counselors recognize that trust is a cornerstone of the counseling relationship. Counselors aspire to earn the trust of clients by creating an ongoing partnership, establishing and upholding appropriate boundaries, and maintaining confidentiality. Counselors communicate the parameters of confidentiality in a culturally competent manner.

B.1. Respecting Client Rights

B.1.a. Multicultural/Diversity Considerations

Counselors maintain awareness and sensitivity regarding cultural meanings of confidentiality and privacy. Counselors respect differing views toward disclosure of information. Counselors hold ongoing discussions with clients as to how, when, and with whom information is to be shared.

B.1.b. Respect for Privacy

Counselors respect client rights to privacy. Counselors solicit private information from clients only when it is beneficial to the counseling process.

B.1.c. Respect for Confidentiality

Counselors do not share confidential information without client consent or without sound legal or ethical justification.

B.1.d. Explanation of Limitations

At initiation and throughout the counseling process, counselors inform clients of the limitations of confidentiality and seek to identify foreseeable situations in which confidentiality must be breached. *(See A.2.b.)*

B.2. Exceptions

B.2.a. Danger and Legal Requirements

The general requirement that counselors keep information confidential does not apply when disclosure is required to protect clients or identified others from serious and foreseeable harm or when legal requirements demand that confidential information must be revealed. Counselors consult with other professionals when in doubt as to the validity of an exception. Additional considerations apply when addressing end-of-life issues. *(See A.9.c.)*

B.2.b. Contagious, Life-Threatening Diseases

When clients disclose that they have a disease commonly known to be both communicable and life threatening, counselors may be justified in disclosing information to identifiable third parties, if they are known to be at demonstrable and high risk of contracting the disease. Prior to making a disclosure, counselors confirm that there is such a diagnosis and assess the intent of clients to inform the third parties about their disease or to engage in any behaviors that may be harmful to an identifiable third party.

B.2.c. Court-Ordered Disclosure

When subpoenaed to release confidential or privileged information without a client's permission, counselors obtain written, informed consent from the client or take steps to prohibit the disclosure or have it limited as narrowly as possible due to potential harm to the client or counseling relationship.

B.2.d. Minimal Disclosure

To the extent possible, clients are informed before confidential information is disclosed and are involved in the disclosure decision-making process. When circumstances require the disclosure of confidential information, only essential information is revealed.

B.3. Information Shared With Others

B.3.a. Subordinates

Counselors make every effort to ensure that privacy and confidentiality of clients are maintained by subordinates, including employees, supervisees, students, clerical assistants, and volunteers. *(See F.1.c.)*

B.3.b. Treatment Teams

When client treatment involves a continued review or participation by a treatment team, the client will be informed of the team's existence and composition, information being shared, and the purposes of sharing such information.

B.3.c. Confidential Settings

Counselors discuss confidential information only in settings in which they can reasonably ensure client privacy.

B.3.d. Third-Party Payers

Counselors disclose information to third-party payers only when clients have authorized such disclosure.

B.3.e. Transmitting Confidential Information

Counselors take precautions to ensure the confidentiality of information transmitted through the use of computers, electronic mail, facsimile machines, telephones, voicemail, answering machines, and other electronic or computer technology. *(See A.12.g.)*

B.3.f. Deceased Clients

Counselors protect the confidentiality of deceased clients, consistent with legal requirements and agency or setting policies.

B.4. Groups and Families

B.4.a. Group Work

In group work, counselors clearly explain the importance and parameters of confidentiality for the specific group being entered.

B.4.b. Couples and Family Counseling

In couples and family counseling, counselors clearly define who is considered "the client" and discuss expectations and limitations of confidentiality. Counselors seek agreement and document in writing such agreement among all involved parties having capacity to give consent concerning each individual's right to confidentiality and any obligation to preserve the confidentiality of information known.

B.5. Clients Lacking Capacity to Give Informed Consent

B.5.a. Responsibility to Clients

When counseling minor clients or adult clients who lack the capacity to give voluntary, informed consent, counselors protect the confidentiality of information received in the counseling relationship as specified by federal and state laws, written policies, and applicable ethical standards.

B.5.b. Responsibility to Parents and Legal Guardians

Counselors inform parents and legal guardians about the role of counselors and the confidential nature of the counseling relationship. Counselors are sensitive to the cultural diversity of families and respect the inherent rights and responsibilities of parents/guardians over the welfare of their children/charges according to law. Counselors work to establish, as appropriate, collaborative relationships with parents/guardians to best serve clients.

B.5.c. Release of Confidential Information

When counseling minor clients or adult clients who lack the capacity to give voluntary consent to release confidential information, counselors seek permission from an appropriate third party to disclose information. In such instances, counselors inform clients consistent with their level of understanding and take culturally appropriate measures to safeguard client confidentiality.

B.6. Records

B.6.a. Confidentiality of Records

Counselors ensure that records are kept in a secure location and that only authorized persons have access to records.

B.6.b. Permission to Record

Counselors obtain permission from clients prior to recording sessions through electronic or other means.

B.6.c. Permission to Observe

Counselors obtain permission from clients prior to observing counseling sessions, reviewing session transcripts, or viewing recordings of sessions with supervisors, faculty, peers, or others within the training environment.

B.6.d. Client Access

Counselors provide reasonable access to records and copies of records when requested by competent clients. Counselors limit the access of clients to their records, or portions of their records, only when there is compelling evidence that such access would cause harm to the client. Counselors document the request of clients and the rationale for withholding some or all of the record in the files of clients. In situations involving multiple clients, counselors provide individual clients with only those parts of records that related

directly to them and do not include confidential information related to any other client.

B.6.e. Assistance With Records

When clients request access to their records, counselors provide assistance and consultation in interpreting counseling records.

B.6.f. Disclosure or Transfer

Unless exceptions to confidentiality exist, counselors obtain written permission from clients to disclose or transfer records to legitimate third parties. Steps are taken to ensure that receivers of counseling records are sensitive to their confidential nature. *(See A.3., E.4.)*

B.6.g. Storage and Disposal After Termination

Counselors store records following termination of services to ensure reasonable future access, maintain records in accordance with state and federal statutes governing records, and dispose of client records and other sensitive materials in a manner that protects client confidentiality. When records are of an artistic nature, counselors obtain client (or guardian) consent with regards to handling of such records or documents. *(See A.1.b.)*

B.6.h. Reasonable Precautions

Counselors take reasonable precautions to protect client confidentiality in the event of the counselor's termination of practice, incapacity, or death. *(See C.2.h.)*

B.7. Research and Training

B.7.a. Institutional Approval

When institutional approval is required, counselors provide accurate information about their research proposals and obtain approval prior to conducting their research. They conduct research in accordance with the approved research protocol.

B.7.b. Adherence to Guidelines

Counselors are responsible for understanding and adhering to state, federal, agency, or institutional policies or applicable guidelines regarding confidentiality in their research practices.

B.7.c. Confidentiality of Information Obtained in Research

Violations of participant privacy and confidentiality are risks of participation in research involving human participants. Investigators maintain all research records in a secure manner.

They explain to participants the risks of violations of privacy and confidentiality and disclose to participants any limits of confidentiality that reasonably can be expected. Regardless of the degree to which confidentiality will be maintained, investigators must disclose to participants any limits of confidentiality that reasonably can be expected. (See G.2.e.)

B.7.d. Disclosure of Research Information

Counselors do not disclose confidential information that reasonably could lead to the identification of a research participant unless they have obtained the prior consent of the person. Use of data derived from counseling relationships for purposes of training, research, or publication is confined to content that is disguised to ensure the anonymity of the individuals involved. (See G.2.a., G.2.d.)

B.7.e. Agreement for Identification

Identification of clients, students, or supervisees in a presentation or publication is permissible only when they have reviewed the material and agreed to its presentation or publication. (See G.4.d.)

B.8. Consultation

B.8.a. Agreements

When acting as consultants, counselors seek agreements among all parties involved concerning each individual's rights to confidentiality, the obligation of each individual to preserve confidential information, and the limits of confidentiality of information shared by others.

B.8.b. Respect for Privacy

Information obtained in a consulting relationship is discussed for professional purposes only with persons directly involved with the case. Written and oral reports present only data germane to the purposes of the consultation, and every effort is made to protect client identity and to avoid undue invasion of privacy.

B.8.c. Disclosure of Confidential Information

When consulting with colleagues, counselors do not disclose confidential information that reasonably could lead to the identification of a client or other person or organization with whom they have a confidential relationship unless they have obtained the prior consent of the person or organization or the disclosure cannot be avoided. They disclose information only to the extent necessary to achieve the purposes of the consultation. (See D.2.d.)

Section C
Professional Responsibility

Introduction

Counselors aspire to open, honest, and accurate communication in dealing with the public and other professionals. They practice in a nondiscriminatory manner within the boundaries of professional and personal competence and have a responsibility to abide by the ACA Code of Ethics. Counselors actively participate in local, state, and national associations that foster the development and improvement of counseling. Counselors advocate to promote change at the individual, group, institutional, and societal levels that improve the quality of life for individuals and groups and remove potential barriers to the provision or access of appropriate services being offered. Counselors have a responsibility to the public to engage in counseling practices that are based on rigorous research methodologies. In addition, counselors engage in self-care activities to maintain and promote their emotional, physical, mental, and spiritual well-being to best meet their professional responsibilities.

C.1. Knowledge of Standards

Counselors have a responsibility to read, understand, and follow the ACA Code of Ethics and adhere to applicable laws and regulations.

C.2. Professional Competence

C.2.a. Boundaries of Competence

Counselors practice only within the boundaries of their competence, based on their education, training, supervised experience, state and national professional credentials, and appropriate professional experience. Counselors gain knowledge, personal awareness, sensitivity, and skills pertinent to working with a diverse client population. (See A.9.b., C.4.e., E.2., F.2., F.11.b.)

C.2.b. New Specialty Areas of Practice

Counselors practice in specialty areas new to them only after appropriate education, training, and supervised experience. While developing skills in new specialty areas, counselors take steps to ensure the competence of their work and to protect others from possible harm. (See F.6.f.)

C.2.c. Qualified for Employment

Counselors accept employment only for positions for which they are qualified by education, training, supervised experience, state and national professional credentials, and appropriate professional experience. Counselors hire for professional counseling positions only individuals who are qualified and competent for those positions.

C.2.d. Monitor Effectiveness

Counselors continually monitor their effectiveness as professionals and take steps to improve when necessary. Counselors in private practice take reasonable steps to seek peer supervision as needed to evaluate their efficacy as counselors.

C.2.e. Consultation on Ethical Obligations

Counselors take reasonable steps to consult with other counselors or related professionals when they have questions regarding their ethical obligations or professional practice.

C.2.f. Continuing Education

Counselors recognize the need for continuing education to acquire and maintain a reasonable level of awareness of current scientific and professional information in their fields of activity. They take steps to maintain competence in the skills they use, are open to new procedures, and keep current with the diverse populations and specific populations with whom they work.

C.2.g. Impairment

Counselors are alert to the signs of impairment from their own physical, mental, or emotional problems and refrain from offering or providing professional services when such impairment is likely to harm a client or others. They seek assistance for problems that reach the level of professional impairment, and, if necessary, they limit, suspend, or terminate their professional responsibilities until such time it is determined that they may safely resume their work. Counselors assist colleagues or supervisors in recognizing their own professional impairment and provide consultation and assistance when warranted with colleagues or supervisors showing signs of impairment and intervene as appropriate to prevent imminent harm to clients. *(See A.11.b., F.8.b.)*

C.2.h. Counselor Incapacitation or Termination of Practice

When counselors leave a practice, they follow a prepared plan for transfer of clients and files. Counselors prepare and disseminate to an identified colleague or "records custodian" a plan for the transfer of clients and files in the case of their incapacitation, death, or termination of practice.

C.3. Advertising and Soliciting Clients

C.3.a. Accurate Advertising

When advertising or otherwise representing their services to the public, counselors identify their credentials in an accurate manner that is not false, misleading, deceptive, or fraudulent.

C.3.b. Testimonials

Counselors who use testimonials do not solicit them from current clients nor former clients nor any other persons who may be vulnerable to undue influence.

C.3.c. Statements by Others

Counselors make reasonable efforts to ensure that statements made by others about them or the profession of counseling are accurate.

C.3.d. Recruiting Through Employment

Counselors do not use their places of employment or institutional affiliation to recruit or gain clients, supervisees, or consultees for their private practices.

C.3.e. Products and Training Advertisements

Counselors who develop products related to their profession or conduct workshops or training events ensure that the advertisements concerning these products or events are accurate and disclose adequate information for consumers to make informed choices. *(See C.6.d.)*

C.3.f. Promoting to Those Served

Counselors do not use counseling, teaching, training, or supervisory relationships to promote their products or training events in a manner that is deceptive or would exert undue influence on individuals who may be vulnerable. However, coun-

selor educators may adopt textbooks they have authored for instructional purposes.

C.4. Professional Qualifications

C.4.a. Accurate Representation

Counselors claim or imply only professional qualifications actually completed and correct any known misrepresentations of their qualifications by others. Counselors truthfully represent the qualifications of their professional colleagues. Counselors clearly distinguish between paid and volunteer work experience and accurately describe their continuing education and specialized training. *(See C.2.a.)*

C.4.b. Credentials

Counselors claim only licenses or certifications that are current and in good standing.

C.4.c. Educational Degrees

Counselors clearly differentiate between earned and honorary degrees.

C.4.d. Implying Doctoral-Level Competence

Counselors clearly state their highest earned degree in counseling or closely related field. Counselors do not imply doctoral-level competence when only possessing a master's degree in counseling or a related field by referring to themselves as "Dr." in a counseling context when their doctorate is not in counseling or related field.

C.4.e. Program Accreditation Status

Counselors clearly state the accreditation status of their degree programs at the time the degree was earned.

C.4.f. Professional Membership

Counselors clearly differentiate between current, active memberships and former memberships in associations. Members of the American Counseling Association must clearly differentiate between professional membership, which implies the possession of at least a master's degree in counseling, and regular membership, which is open to individuals whose interests and activities are consistent with those of ACA but are not qualified for professional membership.

C.5. Nondiscrimination

Counselors do not condone or engage in discrimination based on age, culture, disability, ethnicity, race, religion/spirituality, gender, gender identity, sexual orientation, marital status/partnership, language preference,

socioeconomic status, or any basis proscribed by law. Counselors do not discriminate against clients, students, employees, supervisees, or research participants in a manner that has a negative impact on these persons.

C.6. Public Responsibility

C.6.a. Sexual Harassment

Counselors do not engage in or condone sexual harassment. Sexual harassment is defined as sexual solicitation, physical advances, or verbal or nonverbal conduct that is sexual in nature, that occurs in connection with professional activities or roles, and that either

1. is unwelcome, is offensive, or creates a hostile workplace or learning environment, and counselors know or are told this; or
2. is sufficiently severe or intense to be perceived as harassment to a reasonable person in the context in which the behavior occurred.

Sexual harassment can consist of a single intense or severe act or multiple persistent or pervasive acts.

C.6.b. Reports to Third Parties

Counselors are accurate, honest, and objective in reporting their professional activities and judgments to appropriate third parties, including courts, health insurance companies, those who are the recipients of evaluation reports, and others. *(See B.3., E.4.)*

C.6.c. Media Presentations

When counselors provide advice or comment by means of public lectures, demonstrations, radio or television programs, prerecorded tapes, technology-based applications, printed articles, mailed material, or other media, they take reasonable precautions to ensure that

1. the statements are based on appropriate professional counseling literature and practice,
2. the statements are otherwise consistent with the *ACA Code of Ethics,* and
3. the recipients of the information are not encouraged to infer that a professional counseling relationship has been established.

C.6.d. Exploitation of Others

Counselors do not exploit others in their professional relationships. *(See C.3.e.)*

C.6.e. Scientific Bases for Treatment Modalities

Counselors use techniques/procedures/modalities that are grounded in theory and/or have an empirical or scientific foundation. Counselors who do not must define the techniques/procedures as "unproven" or "developing" and explain the potential risks and ethical considerations of using such techniques/procedures and take steps to protect clients from possible harm. *(See A.4.a., E.5.c., E.5.d.)*

C.7. Responsibility to Other Professionals

C.7.a. Personal Public Statements
When making personal statements in a public context, counselors clarify that they are speaking from their personal perspectives and that they are not speaking on behalf of all counselors or the profession.

Section D
Relationships With Other Professionals

Introduction
Professional counselors recognize that the quality of their interactions with colleagues can influence the quality of services provided to clients. They work to become knowledgeable about colleagues within and outside the field of counseling. Counselors develop positive working relationships and systems of communication with colleagues to enhance services to clients.

D.1. Relationships With Colleagues, Employers, and Employees

D.1.a. Different Approaches
Counselors are respectful of approaches to counseling services that differ from their own. Counselors are respectful of traditions and practices of other professional groups with which they work.

D.1.b. Forming Relationships
Counselors work to develop and strengthen interdisciplinary relations with colleagues from other disciplines to best serve clients.

D.1.c. Interdisciplinary Teamwork
Counselors who are members of interdisciplinary teams delivering multifaceted services to clients, keep the focus on how to best serve the clients.

They participate in and contribute to decisions that affect the well-being of clients by drawing on the perspectives, values, and experiences of the counseling profession and those of colleagues from other disciplines. *(See A.1.a.)*

D.1.d. Confidentiality
When counselors are required by law, institutional policy, or extraordinary circumstances to serve in more than one role in judicial or administrative proceedings, they clarify role expectations and the parameters of confidentiality with their colleagues. *(See B.1.c., B.1.d., B.2.c., B.2.d., B.3.b.)*

D.1.e. Establishing Professional and Ethical Obligations
Counselors who are members of interdisciplinary teams clarify professional and ethical obligations of the team as a whole and of its individual members. When a team decision raises ethical concerns, counselors first attempt to resolve the concern within the team. If they cannot reach resolution among team members, counselors pursue other avenues to address their concerns consistent with client well-being.

D.1.f. Personnel Selection and Assignment
Counselors select competent staff and assign responsibilities compatible with their skills and experiences.

D.1.g. Employer Policies
The acceptance of employment in an agency or institution implies that counselors are in agreement with its general policies and principles. Counselors strive to reach agreement with employers as to acceptable standards of conduct that allow for changes in institutional policy conducive to the growth and development of clients.

D.1.h. Negative Conditions
Counselors alert their employers of inappropriate policies and practices. They attempt to effect changes in such policies or procedures through constructive action within the organization. When such policies are potentially disruptive or damaging to clients or may limit the effectiveness of services provided and change cannot be effected, counselors take appropriate further action. Such action may include referral to appropriate certification, accreditation, or state licensure organizations, or voluntary termination of employment.

D.1.i. Protection From Punitive Action
Counselors take care not to harass or dismiss an employee who has acted in a responsible and ethical manner

to expose inappropriate employer policies or practices.

D.2. Consultation

D.2.a. Consultant Competency
Counselors take reasonable steps to ensure that they have the appropriate resources and competencies when providing consultation services. Counselors provide appropriate referral resources when requested or needed. *(See C.2.a.)*

D.2.b. Understanding Consultees
When providing consultation, counselors attempt to develop with their consultees a clear understanding of problem definition, goals for change, and predicted consequences of interventions selected.

D.2.c. Consultant Goals
The consulting relationship is one in which consultee adaptability and growth toward self-direction are consistently encouraged and cultivated.

D.2.d. Informed Consent in Consultation
When providing consultation, counselors have an obligation to review, in writing and verbally, the rights and responsibilities of both counselors and consultees. Counselors use clear and understandable language to inform all parties involved about the purpose of the services to be provided, relevant costs, potential risks and benefits, and the limits of confidentiality. Working in conjunction with the consultee, counselors attempt to develop a clear definition of the problem, goals for change, and predicted consequences of interventions that are culturally responsive and appropriate to the needs of consultees. *(See A.2.a., A.2.b.)*

Section E
Evaluation, Assessment, and Interpretation

Introduction
Counselors use assessment instruments as one component of the counseling process, taking into account the client personal and cultural context. Counselors promote the well-being of individual clients or groups of clients by developing and using appropriate educational, psychological, and career assessment instruments.

E.1. General

E.1.a. Assessment

The primary purpose of educational, psychological, and career assessment is to provide measurements that are valid and reliable in either comparative or absolute terms. These include, but are not limited to, measurements of ability, personality, interest, intelligence, achievement, and performance. Counselors recognize the need to interpret the statements in this section as applying to both quantitative and qualitative assessments.

E.1.b. Client Welfare

Counselors do not misuse assessment results and interpretations, and they take reasonable steps to prevent others from misusing the information these techniques provide. They respect the client's right to know the results, the interpretations made, and the bases for counselors' conclusions and recommendations.

E.2. Competence to Use and Interpret Assessment Instruments

E.2.a. Limits of Competence

Counselors utilize only those testing and assessment services for which they have been trained and are competent. Counselors using technology assisted test interpretations are trained in the construct being measured and the specific instrument being used prior to using its technology based application. Counselors take reasonable measures to ensure the proper use of psychological and career assessment techniques by persons under their supervision. *(See A.12.)*

E.2.b. Appropriate Use

Counselors are responsible for the appropriate application, scoring, interpretation, and use of assessment instruments relevant to the needs of the client, whether they score and interpret such assessments themselves or use technology or other services.

E.2.c. Decisions Based on Results

Counselors responsible for decisions involving individuals or policies that are based on assessment results have a thorough understanding of educational, psychological, and career measurement, including validation criteria, assessment research, and guidelines for assessment development and use.

E.3. Informed Consent in Assessment

E.3.a. Explanation to Clients

Prior to assessment, counselors explain the nature and purposes of assessment and the specific use of results by potential recipients. The explanation will be given in the language of the client (or other legally authorized person on behalf of the client), unless an explicit exception has been agreed upon in advance. Counselors consider the client's personal or cultural context, the level of the client's understanding of the results, and the impact of the results on the client. *(See A.2., A.12.g., F.1.c.)*

E.3.b. Recipients of Results

Counselors consider the examinee's welfare, explicit understandings, and prior agreements in determining who receives the assessment results. Counselors include accurate and appropriate interpretations with any release of individual or group assessment results. *(See B.2.c., B.5.)*

E.4. Release of Data to Qualified Professionals

Counselors release assessment data in which the client is identified only with the consent of the client or the client's legal representative. Such data are released only to persons recognized by counselors as qualified to interpret the data. *(See B.1., B.3., B.6.b.)*

E.5. Diagnosis of Mental Disorders

E.5.a. Proper Diagnosis

Counselors take special care to provide proper diagnosis of mental disorders. Assessment techniques (including personal interview) used to determine client care (e.g., locus of treatment, type of treatment, or recommended follow-up) are carefully selected and appropriately used.

E.5.b. Cultural Sensitivity

Counselors recognize that culture affects the manner in which clients' problems are defined. Clients' socioeconomic and cultural experiences are considered when diagnosing mental disorders. *(See A.2.c.)*

E.5.c. Historical and Social Prejudices in the Diagnosis of Pathology

Counselors recognize historical and social prejudices in the misdiagnosis and pathologizing of certain individuals and groups and the role of mental health professionals in perpetuating these prejudices through diagnosis and treatment.

E.5.d. Refraining From Diagnosis

Counselors may refrain from making and/or reporting a diagnosis if they believe it would cause harm to the client or others.

E.6. Instrument Selection

E.6.a. Appropriateness of Instruments

Counselors carefully consider the validity, reliability, psychometric limitations, and appropriateness of instruments when selecting assessments.

E.6.b. Referral Information

If a client is referred to a third party for assessment, the counselor provides specific referral questions and sufficient objective data about the client to ensure that appropriate assessment instruments are utilized. *(See A.9.b., B.3.)*

E.6.c. Culturally Diverse Populations

Counselors are cautious when selecting assessments for culturally diverse populations to avoid the use of instruments that lack appropriate psychometric properties for the client population. *(See A.2.c., E.5.b.)*

E.7. Conditions of Assessment Administration

(See A.12.b., A.12.d.)

E.7.a. Administration Conditions

Counselors administer assessments under the same conditions that were established in their standardization. When assessments are not administered under standard conditions, as may be necessary to accommodate clients with disabilities, or when unusual behavior or irregularities occur during the administration, those conditions are noted in interpretation, and the results may be designated as invalid or of questionable validity.

E.7.b. Technological Administration

Counselors ensure that administration programs function properly and provide clients with accurate results when technological or other electronic methods are used for assessment administration.

E.7.c. Unsupervised Assessments

Unless the assessment instrument is designed, intended, and validated for self-administration and/or scoring, counselors do not permit inadequately supervised use.

E.7.d. Disclosure of Favorable Conditions

Prior to administration of assessments, conditions that produce most favorable assessment results are made known to the examinee.

E.8. Multicultural Issues/ Diversity in Assessment

Counselors use with caution assessment techniques that were normed on populations other than that of the client. Counselors recognize the effects of age, color, culture, disability, ethnic group, gender, race, language preference, religion, spirituality, sexual orientation, and socioeconomic status on test administration and interpretation, and place test results in proper perspective with other relevant factors. *(See A.2.c., E.5.b.)*

E.9. Scoring and Interpretation of Assessments

E.9.a. Reporting

In reporting assessment results, counselors indicate reservations that exist regarding validity or reliability due to circumstances of the assessment or the inappropriateness of the norms for the person tested.

E.9.b. Research Instruments

Counselors exercise caution when interpreting the results of research instruments not having sufficient technical data to support respondent results. The specific purposes for the use of such instruments are stated explicitly to the examinee.

E.9.c. Assessment Services

Counselors who provide assessment scoring and interpretation services to support the assessment process confirm the validity of such interpretations. They accurately describe the purpose, norms, validity, reliability, and applications of the procedures and any special qualifications applicable to their use. The public offering of an automated test interpretations service is considered a professional-to-professional consultation. The formal responsibility of the consultant is to the consultee, but the ultimate and overriding responsibility is to the client. *(See D.2.)*

E.10. Assessment Security

Counselors maintain the integrity and security of tests and other assessment techniques consistent with legal and contractual obligations. Counselors do not appropriate, reproduce, or modify published assessments or parts thereof without acknowledgment and permission from the publisher.

E.11. Obsolete Assessments and Outdated Results

Counselors do not use data or results from assessments that are obsolete or outdated for the current purpose. Counselors make every effort to prevent the misuse of obsolete measures and assessment data by others.

E.12. Assessment Construction

Counselors use established scientific procedures, relevant standards, and current professional knowledge for assessment design in the development, publication, and utilization of educational and psychological assessment techniques.

E.13. Forensic Evaluation: Evaluation for Legal Proceedings

E.13.a. Primary Obligations

When providing forensic evaluations, the primary obligation of counselors is to produce objective findings that can be substantiated based on information and techniques appropriate to the evaluation, which may include examination of the individual and/or review of records. Counselors are entitled to form professional opinions based on their professional knowledge and expertise that can be supported by the data gathered in evaluations. Counselors will define the limits of their reports or testimony, especially when an examination of the individual has not been conducted.

E.13.b. Consent for Evaluation

Individuals being evaluated are informed in writing that the relationship is for the purposes of an evaluation and is not counseling in nature, and entities or individuals who will receive the evaluation report are identified. Written consent to be evaluated is obtained from those being evaluated unless a court orders evaluations to be conducted without the written consent of individuals being evaluated. When children or vulnerable adults are being evaluated, informed written consent is obtained from a parent or guardian.

E.13.c. Client Evaluation Prohibited

Counselors do not evaluate individuals for forensic purposes they currently counsel or individuals they have counseled in the past. Counselors do not accept as counseling clients individuals they are evaluating or individuals they have evaluated in the past for forensic purposes.

E.13.d. Avoid Potentially Harmful Relationships

Counselors who provide forensic evaluations avoid potentially harmful professional or personal relationships with family members, romantic partners, and close friends of individuals they are evaluating or have evaluated in the past.

Section F
Supervision, Training, and Teaching

Introduction

Counselors aspire to foster meaningful and respectful professional relationships and to maintain appropriate boundaries with supervisees and students. Counselors have theoretical and pedagogical foundations for their work and aim to be fair, accurate, and honest in their assessments of counselors-in-training.

F.1. Counselor Supervision and Client Welfare

F.1.a. Client Welfare

A primary obligation of counseling supervisors is to monitor the services provided by other counselors or counselors-in-training. Counseling supervisors monitor client welfare and supervisee clinical performance and professional development. To fulfill these obligations, supervisors meet regularly with supervisees to review case notes, samples of clinical work, or live observations. Supervisees have a responsibility to understand and follow the *ACA Code of Ethics*.

F.1.b. Counselor Credentials

Counseling supervisors work to ensure that clients are aware of the qualifications of the supervisees who render services to the clients. *(See A.2.b.)*

F.1.c. Informed Consent and Client Rights

Supervisors make supervisees aware of client rights including the protection of client privacy and confidentiality in the counseling relationship. Supervisees provide clients with professional disclosure information and inform them of how the supervision process influences the limits of confidentiality. Supervisees make clients aware of who will have access to records of the counseling relationship and how these records will be used. *(See A.2.b., B.1.d.)*

F.2. Counselor Supervision Competence

F.2.a. Supervisor Preparation

Prior to offering clinical supervision services, counselors are trained in supervision methods and techniques. Counselors who offer clinical supervision services regularly pursue continuing education activities including both counseling and supervision topics and skills. *(See C.2.a., C.2.f.)*

F.2.b. Multicultural Issues/Diversity in Supervision

Counseling supervisors are aware of and address the role of multiculturalism/diversity in the supervisory relationship.

F.3. Supervisory Relationships

F.3.a. Relationship Boundaries With Supervisees

Counseling supervisors clearly define and maintain ethical professional, personal, and social relationships with their supervisees. Counseling supervisors avoid nonprofessional relationships with current supervisees. If supervisors must assume other professional roles (e.g., clinical and administrative supervisor, instructor) with supervisees, they work to minimize potential conflicts and explain to supervisees the expectations and responsibilities associated with each role. They do not engage in any form of nonprofessional interaction that may compromise the supervisory relationship.

F.3.b. Sexual Relationships

Sexual or romantic interactions or relationships with current supervisees are prohibited.

F.3.c. Sexual Harassment

Counseling supervisors do not condone or subject supervisees to sexual harassment. *(See C.6.a.)*

F.3.d. Close Relatives and Friends

Counseling supervisors avoid accepting close relatives, romantic partners, or friends as supervisees.

F.3.e. Potentially Beneficial Relationships

Counseling supervisors are aware of the power differential in their relationships with supervisees. If they believe nonprofessional relationships with a supervisee may be potentially beneficial to the supervisee, they take precautions similar to those taken by counselors when working with clients. Examples of potentially beneficial interactions or relationships include attending a formal ceremony; hospital visits; providing support during a stressful event; or mutual membership in a professional association, organization, or community. Counseling supervisors engage in open discussions with supervisees when they consider entering into relationships with them outside of their roles as clinical and/or administrative supervisors. Before engaging in nonprofessional relationships, supervisors discuss with supervisees and document the rationale for such interactions, potential benefits or drawbacks, and anticipated consequences for the supervisee. Supervisors clarify the specific nature and limitations of the additional role(s) they will have with the supervisee.

F.4. Supervisor Responsibilities

F.4.a. Informed Consent for Supervision

Supervisors are responsible for incorporating into their supervision the principles of informed consent and participation. Supervisors inform supervisees of the policies and procedures to which they are to adhere and the mechanisms for due process appeal of individual supervisory actions.

F.4.b. Emergencies and Absences

Supervisors establish and communicate to supervisees procedures for contacting them or, in their absence, alternative on-call supervisors to assist in handling crises.

F.4.c. Standards for Supervisees

Supervisors make their supervisees aware of professional and ethical standards and legal responsibilities. Supervisors of postdegree counselors encourage these counselors to adhere to professional standards of practice. *(See C.1.)*

F.4.d. Termination of the Supervisory Relationship

Supervisors or supervisees have the right to terminate the supervisory relationship with adequate notice. Reasons for withdrawal are provided to the other party. When cultural, clinical, or professional issues are crucial to the viability of the supervisory relationship, both parties make efforts to resolve differences. When termination is warranted, supervisors make appropriate referrals to possible alternative supervisors.

F.5. Counseling Supervision Evaluation, Remediation, and Endorsement

F.5.a. Evaluation

Supervisors document and provide supervisees with ongoing performance appraisal and evaluation feedback and schedule periodic formal evaluative sessions throughout the supervisory relationship.

F.5.b. Limitations

Through ongoing evaluation and appraisal, supervisors are aware of the limitations of supervisees that might impede performance. Supervisors assist supervisees in securing remedial assistance when needed. They recommend dismissal from training programs, applied counseling settings, or state or voluntary professional credentialing processes when those supervisees are unable to provide competent professional services. Supervisors seek consultation and document their decisions to dismiss or refer supervisees for assistance. They ensure that supervisees are aware of options available to them to address such decisions. *(See C.2.g.)*

F.5.c. Counseling for Supervisees

If supervisees request counseling, supervisors provide them with acceptable referrals. Counselors do not provide counseling services to supervisees. Supervisors address interpersonal competencies in terms of the impact of these issues on clients, the supervisory relationship, and professional functioning. *(See F.3.a.)*

F.5.d. Endorsement

Supervisors endorse supervisees for certification, licensure, employment, or completion of an academic or training program only when they believe supervisees are qualified for the endorsement. Regardless of qualifications, supervisors do not endorse supervisees whom they believe to be impaired in any way that would interfere with the performance of the duties associated with the endorsement.

F.6. Responsibilities of Counselor Educators

F.6.a. Counselor Educators

Counselor educators who are responsible for developing, implementing, and supervising educational programs are skilled as teachers and practitioners. They are knowledgeable regarding the ethical, legal, and regulatory aspects of the profession, are skilled in applying that knowledge, and make students and supervisees aware of their responsibilities. Counselor educators conduct counselor education and training programs in an ethical manner and serve as role models for professional behavior. *(See C.1., C.2.a., C.2.c.)*

F.6.b. Infusing Multicultural Issues/Diversity

Counselor educators infuse material related to multicultural/diversity into all courses and workshops for the development of professional counselors.

F.6.c. Integration of Study and Practice

Counselor educators establish education and training programs that integrate academic study and supervised practice.

F.6.d. Teaching Ethics

Counselor educators make students and supervisees aware of the ethical responsibilities and standards of the profession and the ethical responsibilities of students to the profession. Counselor educators infuse ethical considerations throughout the curriculum. *(See C.1.)*

F.6.e. Peer Relationships

Counselor educators make every effort to ensure that the rights of peers are not compromised when students or supervisees lead counseling groups or provide clinical supervision. Counselor educators take steps to ensure that students and supervisees understand they have the same ethical obligations as counselor educators, trainers, and supervisors.

F.6.f. Innovative Theories and Techniques

When counselor educators teach counseling techniques/procedures that are innovative, without an empirical foundation, or without a well-grounded theoretical foundation, they define the counseling techniques/procedures as "unproven" or "developing" and explain to students the potential risks and ethical considerations of using such techniques/procedures.

F.6.g. Field Placements

Counselor educators develop clear policies within their training programs regarding field placement and other clinical experiences. Counselor educators provide clearly stated roles and responsibilities for the student or supervisee, the site supervisor, and the program supervisor. They confirm that site supervisors are qualified to provide supervision and inform site supervisors of their professional and ethical responsibilities in this role.

F.6.h. Professional Disclosure

Before initiating counseling services, counselors-in-training disclose their status as students and explain how this status affects the limits of confidentiality. Counselor educators ensure that the clients at field placements are aware of the services rendered and the qualifications of the students and supervisees rendering those services. Students and supervisees obtain client permission before they use any information concerning the counseling relationship in the training process. *(See A.2.b.)*

F.7. Student Welfare

F.7.a. Orientation

Counselor educators recognize that orientation is a developmental process that continues throughout the educational and clinical training of students. Counseling faculty provide prospective students with information about the counselor education program's expectations:

1. the type and level of skill and knowledge acquisition required for successful completion of the training;
2. program training goals, objectives, and mission, and subject matter to be covered;
3. bases for evaluation;
4. training components that encourage self-growth or self-disclosure as part of the training process;
5. the type of supervision settings and requirements of the sites for required clinical field experiences;
6. student and supervisee evaluation and dismissal policies and procedures; and
7. up-to-date employment prospects for graduates.

F.7.b. Self-Growth Experiences

Counselor education programs delineate requirements for self-disclosure or self-growth experiences in their admission and program materials. Counselor educators use professional judgment when designing training experiences they conduct that require student and supervisee self-growth or self-disclosure. Students and supervisees are made aware of the ramifications their self-disclosure may have when counselors whose primary role as teacher, trainer, or supervisor requires acting on ethical obligations to the profession. Evaluative components of experiential training experiences explicitly delineate predetermined academic standards that are separate and do not depend on the student's level of self-disclosure. Counselor educators may require trainees to seek professional help to address any personal concerns that may be affecting their competency.

F.8. Student Responsibilities

F.8.a. Standards for Students

Counselors-in-training have a responsibility to understand and follow the *ACA Code of Ethics* and adhere to applicable laws, regulatory policies, and rules and policies governing professional staff behavior at the agency or placement setting. Students have the same obligation to clients as those required of professional counselors. *(See C.1., H.1.)*

F.8.b. Impairment

Counselors-in-training refrain from offering or providing counseling services when their physical, mental, or emotional problems are likely to harm a client or others. They are alert to the signs of impairment, seek assistance for problems, and notify their program supervisors when they are aware that they are unable to effectively provide services. In addition, they seek appropriate professional services for themselves to remediate the problems that are interfering with their ability to provide services to others. *(See A.1., C.2.d., C.2.g.)*

F.9. Evaluation and Remediation of Students

F.9.a. Evaluation

Counselors clearly state to students, prior to and throughout the training program, the levels of competency expected, appraisal methods, and timing of evaluations for both didactic and clinical competencies. Counselor educators provide students with ongoing performance appraisal and evaluation feedback throughout the training program.

F.9.b. Limitations

Counselor educators, throughout ongoing evaluation and appraisal, are aware of and address the inability of some students to achieve counseling competencies that might impede performance. Counselor educators

1. assist students in securing remedial assistance when needed,
2. seek professional consultation and document their decision to dismiss or refer students for assistance, and
3. ensure that students have recourse in a timely manner to address decisions to require them to seek assistance or to dismiss them and provide students with due process according to institutional policies and procedures. *(See C.2.g.)*

F.9.c. Counseling for Students

If students request counseling or if counseling services are required as part of a remediation process, counselor educators provide acceptable referrals.

F. 10. Roles and Relationships Between Counselor Educators and Students

F.10.a. Sexual or Romantic Relationships

Sexual or romantic interactions or relationships with current students are prohibited.

F.10.b. Sexual Harassment

Counselor educators do not condone or subject students to sexual harassment. *(See C.6.a.)*

F.10.c. Relationships With Former Students

Counselor educators are aware of the power differential in the relationship between faculty and students. Faculty members foster open discussions with former students when considering engaging in a social, sexual, or other intimate relationship. Faculty members discuss with the former student how their former relationship may affect the change in relationship.

F.10.d. Nonprofessional Relationships

Counselor educators avoid nonprofessional or ongoing professional relationships with students in which there is a risk of potential harm to the student or that may compromise the training experience or grades assigned. In addition, counselor educators do not accept any form of professional services, fees, commissions, reimbursement, or remuneration from a site for student or supervisee placement.

F.10.e. Counseling Services

Counselor educators do not serve as counselors to current students unless this is a brief role associated with a training experience.

F.10.f. Potentially Beneficial Relationships

Counselor educators are aware of the power differential in the relationship between faculty and students. If they believe a nonprofessional relationship with a student may be potentially beneficial to the student, they take precautions similar to those taken by counselors when working with clients. Examples of potentially beneficial interactions or relationships include, but are not limited to, attending a formal ceremony; hospital visits; providing support during a stressful event; or mutual membership in a professional association, organization, or community. Counselor educators engage in open discussions with students when they consider entering into relationships with students outside of their roles as teachers and supervisors. They discuss with students the rationale for such interactions, the potential benefits and drawbacks, and the anticipated consequences for the student. Educators clarify the specific nature and limitations of the additional role(s) they will have with the student prior to engaging in a nonprofessional relationship. Nonprofessional relationships with students should be time-limited and initiated with student consent.

F.11. Multicultural/Diversity Competence in Counselor Education and Training Programs

F.11.a. Faculty Diversity

Counselor educators are committed to recruiting and retaining a diverse faculty.

F.11.b. Student Diversity

Counselor educators actively attempt to recruit and retain a diverse student body. Counselor educators demonstrate commitment to multicultural/diversity competence by recognizing and valuing diverse cultures and types of abilities students bring to the training experience. Counselor educators provide appropriate accommodations that enhance and support diverse student well-being and academic performance.

F.11.c. Multicultural/Diversity Competence

Counselor educators actively infuse multicultural/diversity competency in their training and supervision practices. They actively train students to gain awareness, knowledge, and skills in the competencies of multicultural practice. Counselor educators include case examples, role-plays, discussion questions, and other classroom activities that promote and represent various cultural perspectives.

Section G
Research and Publication

Introduction

Counselors who conduct research are encouraged to contribute to the knowledge base of the profession and promote a clearer understanding of the conditions that lead to a healthy and more just society. Counselors support efforts of researchers by participating fully and willingly whenever possible. Counselors minimize bias and respect diversity in designing and implementing research programs.

G.1. Research Responsibilities

G.1.a. Use of Human Research Participants

Counselors plan, design, conduct, and report research in a manner that is consistent with pertinent ethical principles, federal and state laws, host institutional regulations, and scientific standards governing research with human research participants.

G.1.b. Deviation From Standard Practice

Counselors seek consultation and observe stringent safeguards to protect the rights of research participants when a research problem suggests a deviation from standard or acceptable practices.

G.1.c. Independent Researchers

When independent researchers do not have access to an Institutional Review Board (IRB), they should consult with researchers who are familiar with IRB procedures to provide appropriate safeguards.

G.1.d. Precautions to Avoid Injury

Counselors who conduct research with human participants are responsible for the welfare of participants throughout the research process and should take reasonable precautions to avoid causing injurious psychological, emotional, physical, or social effects to participants.

G.1.e. Principal Researcher Responsibility

The ultimate responsibility for ethical research practice lies with the principal researcher. All others involved in the research activities share ethical obligations and responsibility for their own actions.

G.1.f. Minimal Interference

Counselors take reasonable precautions to avoid causing disruptions in the lives of research participants that could be caused by their involvement in research.

G.1.g. Multicultural/Diversity Considerations in Research

When appropriate to research goals, counselors are sensitive to incorporating research procedures that take into account cultural considerations. They seek consultation when appropriate.

G.2. Rights of Research Participants

(See A.2, A.7.)

G.2.a. Informed Consent in Research

Individuals have the right to consent to become research participants. In seeking consent, counselors use language that

1. accurately explains the purpose and procedures to be followed,
2. identifies any procedures that are experimental or relatively untried,
3. describes any attendant discomforts and risks,
4. describes any benefits or changes in individuals or organizations that might be reasonably expected,
5. discloses appropriate alternative procedures that would be advantageous for participants,
6. offers to answer any inquiries concerning the procedures,
7. describes any limitations on confidentiality,
8. describes the format and potential target audiences for the dissemination of research findings, and
9. instructs participants that they are free to withdraw their consent and to discontinue participation in the project at any time without penalty.

G.2.b. Deception

Counselors do not conduct research involving deception unless alternative procedures are not feasible and the prospective value of the research justifies the deception. If such deception has the potential to cause physical or emotional harm to research participants, the research is not conducted, regardless of prospective value. When the methodological requirements of a study necessitate concealment or deception, the investigator explains the reasons for this action as soon as possible during the debriefing.

G.2.c. Student/Supervisee Participation

Researchers who involve students or supervisees in research make clear to them that the decision regarding whether or not to participate in research activities does not affect one's academic standing or supervisory relationship. Students or supervisees who choose not to participate in educational research are provided with an appropriate alternative to fulfill their academic or clinical requirements.

G.2.d. Client Participation

Counselors conducting research involving clients make clear in the informed consent process that clients are free to choose whether or not to participate in research activities. Counselors take necessary precautions to protect clients from adverse consequences of declining or withdrawing from participation.

G.2.e. Confidentiality of Information

Information obtained about research participants during the course of an investigation is confidential. When the possibility exists that others may obtain access to such information, ethical research practice requires that the possibility, together with the plans for protecting confidentiality, be explained to participants as a part of the procedure for obtaining informed consent.

G.2.f. Persons Not Capable of Giving Informed Consent

When a person is not capable of giving informed consent, counselors provide an appropriate explanation to, obtain agreement for participation from, and obtain the appropriate consent of a legally authorized person.

G.2.g. Commitments to Participants

Counselors take reasonable measures to honor all commitments to research participants. *(See A.2.c.)*

G.2.h. Explanations After Data Collection

After data are collected, counselors provide participants with full clarification of the nature of the study to remove any misconceptions participants might have regarding the research. Where scientific or human values justify delaying or withholding information, counselors take reasonable measures to avoid causing harm.

G.2.i. Informing Sponsors

Counselors inform sponsors, institutions, and publication channels regarding research procedures and outcomes. Counselors ensure that appropriate bodies and authorities are given pertinent information and acknowledgement.

G.2.j. Disposal of Research Documents and Records

Within a reasonable period of time following the completion of a research project or study, counselors take steps to destroy records or documents (audio, video, digital, and written) containing confidential data or information that identifies research participants. When records are of an artistic nature, researchers obtain participant consent with regard to handling of such records or documents. *(See B.4.a, B.4.g.)*

G.3. Relationships With Research Participants (When Research Involves Intensive or Extended Interactions)

G.3.a. Nonprofessional Relationships

Nonprofessional relationships with research participants should be avoided.

G.3.b. Relationships With Research Participants

Sexual or romantic counselor–research participant interactions or relationships with current research participants are prohibited.

G.3.c. Sexual Harassment and Research Participants

Researchers do not condone or subject research participants to sexual harassment.

G.3.d. Potentially Beneficial Interactions

When a nonprofessional interaction between the researcher and the research participant may be potentially beneficial, the researcher must document, prior to the interaction (when feasible), the rationale for such an interaction, the potential benefit, and anticipated consequences for the research participant. Such interactions should be initiated with appropriate consent of the research participant. Where unintentional harm occurs to the research participant due to the nonprofessional interaction, the researcher must show evidence of an attempt to remedy such harm.

G.4. Reporting Results

G.4.a. Accurate Results

Counselors plan, conduct, and report research accurately. They provide thorough discussions of the limitations of their data and alternative hypotheses. Counselors do not engage in misleading or fraudulent research, distort data, misrepresent data, or deliberately bias their results. They explicitly mention all variables and conditions known to the investigator that may have affected the outcome of a study or the interpretation of data. They describe the extent to which results are applicable for diverse populations.

G.4.b. Obligation to Report Unfavorable Results

Counselors report the results of any research of professional value. Results that reflect unfavorably on institutions, programs, services, prevailing opinions, or vested interests are not withheld.

G.4.c. Reporting Errors

If counselors discover significant errors in their published research, they take reasonable steps to correct such errors in a correction erratum, or through other appropriate publication means.

G.4.d. Identity of Participants

Counselors who supply data, aid in the research of another person, report research results, or make original data available take due care to disguise the identity of respective participants in the absence of specific authorization from the participants to do otherwise. In situations where participants self-identify their involvement in research studies, researchers take active steps to ensure that data is adapted/changed to protect the identity and welfare of all parties and that discussion of results does not cause harm to participants.

G.4.e. Replication Studies

Counselors are obligated to make available sufficient original research data to qualified professionals who may wish to replicate the study.

G.5. Publication

G.5.a. Recognizing Contributions

When conducting and reporting research, counselors are familiar with and give recognition to previous work on the topic, observe copyright laws, and give full credit to those to whom credit is due.

G.5.b. Plagiarism

Counselors do not plagiarize, that is, they do not present another person's work as their own work.

G.5.c. Review/Republication of Data or Ideas

Counselors fully acknowledge and make editorial reviewers aware of prior publication of ideas or data where such ideas or data are submitted for review or publication.

G.5.d. Contributors

Counselors give credit through joint authorship, acknowledgment, footnote statements, or other appropriate means to those who have contributed significantly to research or concept development in accordance with such contributions. The principal contributor is listed first and minor technical or professional contributions are acknowledged in notes or introductory statements.

G.5.e. Agreement of Contributors

Counselors who conduct joint research with colleagues or students/supervisees establish agreements in advance regarding allocation of tasks, publication credit, and types of acknowledgement that will be received.

G.5.f. Student Research

For articles that are substantially based on students course papers, projects, dissertations or theses, and on which students have been the primary contributors, they are listed as principal authors.

G.5.g. Duplicate Submission

Counselors submit manuscripts for consideration to only one journal at a time. Manuscripts that are published in whole or in substantial part in another journal or published work are not submitted for publication without acknowledgment and permission from the previous publication.

G.5.h. Professional Review

Counselors who review material submitted for publication, research, or other scholarly purposes respect the confidentiality and proprietary rights of those who submitted it. Counselors use care to make publication decisions based on valid and defensible standards. Counselors review article submissions in a timely manner and based on their scope and competency in research methodologies. Counselors who serve as reviewers at the request of editors or publishers make every effort to only review materials that are within their scope of competency and use care to avoid personal biases.

Section H
Resolving Ethical Issues

Introduction

Counselors behave in a legal, ethical, and moral manner in the conduct of their professional work. They are aware that client protection and trust in the profession depend on a high level of professional conduct. They hold other counselors to the same standards and are willing to take appropriate action to ensure that these standards are upheld.

Counselors strive to resolve ethical dilemmas with direct and open communication among all parties involved and seek consultation with colleagues and supervisors when necessary. Counselors incorporate ethical practice into their daily professional work. They engage in ongoing professional development regarding current topics in ethical and legal issues in counseling.

H.1. Standards and the Law
(See F.9.a.)

H.1.a. Knowledge

Counselors understand the *ACA Code of Ethics* and other applicable ethics codes from other professional organizations or from certification and licensure bodies of which they are members. Lack of knowledge or misunderstanding of an ethical responsibility is not a defense against a charge of unethical conduct.

H.1.b. Conflicts Between Ethics and Laws

If ethical responsibilities conflict with law, regulations, or other governing legal authority, counselors make known their commitment to the *ACA Code of Ethics* and take steps to resolve the conflict. If the conflict cannot be resolved by such means, counselors may adhere to the requirements of law, regulations, or other governing legal authority.

H.2. Suspected Violations

H.2.a. Ethical Behavior Expected

Counselors expect colleagues to adhere to the *ACA Code of Ethics*. When counselors possess knowledge that raises doubts as to whether another counselor is acting in an ethical manner, they take appropriate action. *(See H.2.b., H.2.c.)*

H.2.b. Informal Resolution

When counselors have reason to believe that another counselor is violating or has violated an ethical standard, they attempt first to resolve the issue informally with the other counselor if feasible, provided such action does not violate confidentiality rights that may be involved.

H.2.c. Reporting Ethical Violations

If an apparent violation has substantially harmed, or is likely to substantially harm a person or organization and is not appropriate for informal resolution or is not resolved properly, counselors take further action appropriate to the situation. Such action might include referral to state or national committees on professional ethics, voluntary national certification bodies, state licensing boards, or to the appropriate institutional authorities. This standard does not apply when an intervention would violate confidentiality rights or when counselors have been retained to review the work of another counselor whose professional conduct is in question.

H.2.d. Consultation

When uncertain as to whether a particular situation or course of action may be in violation of the *ACA Code of Ethics,* counselors consult with other counselors who are knowledgeable about ethics and the *ACA Code of Ethics,* with colleagues, or with appropriate authorities

H.2.e. Organizational Conflicts

If the demands of an organization with which counselors are affiliated pose a conflict with the *ACA Code of Ethics,* counselors specify the nature of such conflicts and express to their supervisors or other responsible officials their commitment to the *ACA Code of Ethics.* When possible, counselors work toward change within the organization to allow full adherence to the *ACA Code of Ethics.* In doing so, they address any confidentiality issues.

H.2.f. Unwarranted Complaints

Counselors do not initiate, participate in, or encourage the filing of ethics complaints that are made with reckless disregard or willful ignorance of facts that would disprove the allegation.

H.2.g. Unfair Discrimination Against Complainants and Respondents

Counselors do not deny persons employment, advancement, admission to academic or other programs, tenure, or promotion based solely upon their having made or their being the subject of an ethics complaint. This does not preclude taking action based upon the outcome of such proceedings or considering other appropriate information.

H.3. Cooperation With Ethics Committees

Counselors assist in the process of enforcing the *ACA Code of Ethics.* Counselors cooperate with investigations, proceedings, and requirements of the ACA Ethics Committee or ethics committees of other duly constituted associations or boards having jurisdiction over those charged with a violation. Counselors are familiar with the *ACA Policy and Procedures for Processing Complains of Ethical Violations* and use it as a reference for assisting in the enforcement of the *ACA Code of Ethics.*

Glossary of Terms

Advocacy – promotion of the well-being of individuals and groups, and the counseling profession within systems and organizations. Advocacy seeks to remove barriers and obstacles that inhibit access, growth, and development.

Assent – to demonstrate agreement, when a person is otherwise not capable or competent to give formal consent (e.g., informed consent) to a counseling service or plan.

Client – an individual seeking or referred to the professional services of a counselor for help with problem resolution or decision making.

Counselor – a professional (or a student who is a counselor-in-training) engaged in a counseling practice or other counseling-related services. Counselors fulfill many roles and responsibilities such as counselor educators, researchers, supervisors, practitioners, and consultants.

Counselor Educator – a professional counselor engaged primarily in developing, implementing, and supervising the educational preparation of counselors-in-training.

Counselor Supervisor – a professional counselor who engages in a formal relationship with a practicing counselor or counselor-in-training for the purpose of overseeing that individual's counseling work or clinical skill development.

Culture – membership in a socially constructed way of living, which incorporates collective values, beliefs, norms, boundaries, and lifestyles that are cocreated with others who share similar worldviews comprising biological, psychosocial, historical, psychological, and other factors.

Diversity – the similarities and differences that occur within and across cultures, and the intersection of cultural and social identities.

Documents – any written, digital, audio, visual, or artistic recording of the work within the counseling relationship between counselor and client.

Examinee – a recipient of any professional counseling service that includes educational, psychological, and career appraisal utilizing qualitative or quantitative techniques.

Forensic Evaluation – any formal assessment conducted for court or other legal proceedings.

Multicultural/Diversity Competence – a capacity whereby counselors possess cultural and diversity awareness and knowledge about self and others, and how this awareness and knowledge is applied effectively in practice with clients and client groups.

Multicultural/Diversity Counseling – counseling that recognizes diversity and embraces approaches that support the worth, dignity, potential, and uniqueness of individuals within their historical, cultural, economic, political, and psychosocial contexts.

Student – an individual engaged in formal educational preparation as a counselor-in-training.

Supervisee – a professional counselor or counselor-in-training whose counseling work or clinical skill development is being overseen in a formal supervisory relationship by a qualified trained professional.

Supervisor – counselors who are trained to oversee the professional clinical work of counselors and counselors-in-training.

Teaching – all activities engaged in as part of a formal educational program designed to lead to a graduate degree in counseling.

Training – the instruction and practice of skills related to the counseling profession. Training contributes to the ongoing proficiency of students and professional counselors.

APPENDIX B

CODE OF ETHICS

PREAMBLE

The National Board for Certified Counselors (NBCC) is a professional certification board which certifies counselors as having met standards for the general and specialty practice of professional counseling established by the Board. The counselors certified by NBCC may identify with different professional associations and are often licensed by jurisdictions which promulgate codes of ethics. The NBCC code of ethics provides a minimal ethical standard for the professional behavior of all NBCC certificants. This code provides an expectation of and assurance for the ethical practice for all who use the professional services of an NBCC certificant. In addition, it serves the purpose of having an enforceable standard for all NBCC certificants and assures those served of some resource in case of a perceived ethical violation. This code is applicable to National Certified Counselors and those who are seeking certification from NBCC.

The NBCC Ethical Code applies to all those certified by NBCC regardless of any other professional affiliation. Persons who receive professional services from certified counselors may elect to use other ethical codes which apply to their counselor. Although NBCC cooperates with professional associations and credentialing organizations, it can bring actions to discipline or sanction NBCC certificants only if the provisions of the NBCC Code are found to have been violated.

The National Board for Certified Counselors, Inc. (NBCC) promotes counseling through certification. In pursuit of this mission, the NBCC:

- Promotes quality assurance in counseling practice
- Promotes the value of counseling
- Promotes public awareness of quality counseling practice
- Promotes professionalism in counseling
- Promotes leadership in credentialing

Section A: General

1.   Certified counselors engage in continuous efforts to improve professional practices, services, and research. Certified counselors are guided in their work by evidence of the best professional practices.

2.   Certified counselors have a responsibility to the clients they serve and to the institutions within which the services are performed. Certified counselors also strive to assist the respective agency, organization, or institution in providing competent and ethical professional services. The acceptance of employment in an institution implies that the certified counselor is in agreement with the general policies and principles of the institution. Therefore, the professional activities of the certified counselor are in accord with the objectives of the institution. If the certified counselor and the employer do not agree and cannot reach agreement on policies that are consistent with appropriate counselor ethical practice that is conducive to client growth and development, the employment should be terminated. If the situation warrants further action, the certified counselor should work through professional organizations to have the unethical practice changed.

3.   Ethical behavior among professional associates (i.e., both certified and non-certified counselors) must be expected at all times. When a certified counselor has doubts as to the ethical behavior of professional colleagues, the certified counselor must take action to attempt to rectify this condition. Such action uses the respective institution's channels first and then uses procedures established by the NBCC or the perceived violator's profession.

4.   Certified counselors must refuse remuneration for consultation or counseling with persons who are entitled to these services through the certified counselor's employing institution or agency. Certified counselors must not divert to their private practices, without the mutual consent of the institution and the client, legitimate clients in their primary agencies or the institutions with which they are affiliated.

5.   In establishing fees for professional counseling services, certified counselors must consider the financial status of clients. In the event that the established fee status is inappropriate for a client, assistance must be provided in finding comparable services at acceptable cost.

6.   Certified counselors offer only professional services for which they are trained or have supervised experience. No diagnosis, assessment, or treatment should be performed without prior training or supervision. Certified counselors are responsible for correcting any misrepresentations of their qualifications by others.

7.   Certified counselors recognize their limitations and provide services or use techniques for which they are qualified by training and/or supervision. Certified counselors recognize the need for and seek continuing education to assure competent services.

8.   Certified counselors are aware of the intimacy in the counseling relationship and maintain respect for the client. Counselors must not engage in activities that seek to meet their personal or professional needs at the expense of the client.

9.   Certified counselors must insure that they do not engage in personal, social, organizational, financial, or political activities which might lead to a misuse of their influence.

10.   Sexual intimacy with clients is unethical. Certified counselors will not be sexually, physically, or romantically intimate with clients, and they will not engage in sexual, physical, or romantic intimacy with clients within a minimum of two years after terminating the counseling relationship.

11.   Certified counselors do not condone or engage in sexual harassment, which is defined as unwelcome comments, gestures, or physical contact of a sexual nature.

12.   Through an awareness of the impact of stereotyping and unwarranted discrimination (e.g., biases based on age, disability, ethnicity, gender, race, religion, or sexual orientation), certified counselors guard the individual rights and personal dignity of the client in the counseling relationship.

13.   Certified counselors are accountable at all times for their behavior. They must be aware that all actions and behaviors of the counselor reflect on professional integrity and, when inappropriate, can damage the public trust in the counseling profession. To protect public confidence in the counseling profession, certified counselors avoid behavior that is clearly in violation of accepted moral and legal standards.

14.   Products or services provided by certified counselors by means of classroom instruction, public lectures, demonstrations, written articles, radio or television programs or other types of media must meet the criteria cited in this code.

15.   Certified counselors have an obligation to withdraw from the practice of counseling if they violate the Code of Ethics, or if the mental or physical condition of the certified counselor renders it unlikely that a professional relationship will be maintained.

16.   Certified counselors must comply with all NBCC policies, procedures and agreements, including all information disclosure requirements.

Section B: Counseling Relationship

1.   The primary obligation of certified counselors is to respect the integrity and promote the welfare of clients, whether they are assisted individually, in family units, or in group counseling. In a group setting, the certified counselor is also responsible for taking reasonable precautions to protect individuals from physical and/or psychological trauma resulting from interaction within the group.

2.   Certified counselors know and take into account the traditions and practices of other professional disciplines with whom they work and cooperate fully with such. If a person is receiving similar services from another professional, certified counselors do not offer their own services directly to such a person. If a certified counselor is contacted by a person who is already receiving similar services from another professional, the certified counselor carefully considers that professional relationship as well as the client's welfare and proceeds with caution and sensitivity to the therapeutic issues. When certified counselors learn that their clients are in a professional relationship with another counselor or mental health professional, they request release from the clients to inform the other counselor or mental health professional of their relationship with the client and strive to establish positive and collaborative professional relationships that are in the best interest of the client. Certified counselors discuss these issues with clients and the counselor or professional so as to minimize the risk of confusion and conflict and encourage clients to inform other professionals of the new professional relationship.

3.   Certified counselors may choose to consult with any other professionally competent person about a client and must notify clients of this right. Certified counselors avoid placing a consultant in a conflict-of-interest situation that would preclude the consultant serving as a proper party to the efforts of the certified counselor to help the client.

4.   When a client's condition indicates that there is a clear and imminent danger to the client or others, the certified counselor must take reasonable action to inform potential victims and/or inform responsible authorities. Consultation with other professionals must be used when possible. The assumption of responsibility for the client's behavior must be taken only after careful deliberation, and the client must be involved in the resumption of responsibility as quickly as possible.

5.   Records of the counseling relationship, including interview notes, test data, correspondence, audio or visual tape recordings, electronic data storage, and other documents are to be considered professional information for use in counseling. Records should contain accurate factual data. The physical records are property of the certified counselors or their employers. The information contained in the records belongs to the client and therefore may not be released to others without the consent of the client or when the counselor has exhausted challenges to a court order. The certified counselors are responsible to insure that their employees handle confidential information appropriately. Confidentiality must be maintained during the storage and disposition of records. Records should be maintained for a period of at least five (5) years after the last counselor/client contact, including cases in which the client is deceased. All records must be released to the client upon request.

6.   Certified counselors must ensure that data maintained in electronic storage are secure. By using the best computer security methods available, the data must be limited to information that is appropriate and necessary for the services being provided and accessible only to appropriate staff members involved in the provision of services. Certified counselors must also ensure that the electronically stored data are destroyed when the information is no longer of value in providing services or required as part of clients' records.

7.   Any data derived from a client relationship and used in training or research shall be so disguised that the informed client's identity is fully protected. Any data which cannot be so disguised may be used only as expressly authorized by the client's informed and uncoerced consent.

8.   When counseling is initiated, and throughout the counseling process as necessary, counselors inform clients of the purposes, goals, techniques, procedures, limitations, potential risks and benefits of services to be performed, and clearly indicate limitations that may affect the relationship as well as any other pertinent information. Counselors take reasonable steps to ensure that clients understand the implications of any diagnosis, the intended use of tests and reports, methods of treatment and safety precautions that must be taken in their use, fees, and billing arrangements.

9.   Certified counselors who have an administrative, supervisory and/or evaluative relationship with individuals seeking counseling services must not serve as the counselor and should refer the individuals to other professionals. Exceptions are made only in instances where an individual's situation warrants counseling intervention and another alternative is unavailable. Dual relationships that might impair the certified counselor's objectivity and professional judgment must be avoided and/or the counseling relationship terminated through referral to a competent professional.

10.   When certified counselors determine an inability to be of professional assistance to a potential or existing client, they must, respectively, not initiate the counseling relationship or immediately terminate the relationship. In either event, the certified counselor must suggest appropriate alternatives. Certified counselors must be knowledgeable about referral resources so that a satisfactory referral can be initiated. In the event that the client declines a suggested referral, the certified counselor is not obligated to continue the relationship.

11.   When certified counselors are engaged in intensive, short-term counseling, they must ensure that professional assistance is available at normal costs to clients during and following the short-term counseling.

12.   Counselors using electronic means in which counselor and client are not in immediate proximity must present clients with local sources of care before establishing a continued short or long-term relationship. Counselors who communicate with clients via Internet are governed by NBCC standards for Web Counseling.

13.   Counselors must document permission to practice counseling by electronic means in all governmental jurisdictions where such counseling takes place.

14.   When electronic data and systems are used as a component of counseling services, certified counselors must ensure that the computer application, and any information it contains, is appropriate for the respective needs of clients and is non-discriminatory. Certified counselors must ensure that they themselves have acquired a facilitation level of knowledge with any system they use including hands-on application, and understanding of the uses of all aspects of the computer-based system. In selecting and/or maintaining computer-based systems that contain career information, counselors must ensure that the system provides current, accurate, and locally relevant information. Certified counselors must also ensure that clients are intellectually, emotionally, and physically compatible with computer applications and understand their purpose and operation. Client use of a computer application must be evaluated to correct possible problems and assess subsequent needs.

15.   Certified counselors who develop self-help/stand-alone computer software for use by the general public, must first ensure that it is designed to function in a stand-alone manner that is appropriate and safe for all clients for which it is intended. A manual is required. The manual must provide the user with intended outcomes, suggestions for using the software, descriptions of inappropriately used applications, and descriptions of when and how other forms of counseling services might be beneficial. Finally, the manual must include the qualifications of the developer, the development process, validation date, and operating procedures.

16.   The counseling relationship and information resulting from it remains confidential, consistent with the legal and ethical obligations of certified counselors. In group counseling, counselors clearly define confidentiality and the parameters for the specific group being entered, explain the importance of confidentiality, and discuss the difficulties related to confidentiality involved in group work. The fact that confidentiality cannot be guaranteed is clearly communicated to group members. However, counselors should give assurance about their professional responsibility to keep all group communications confidential.

17.   Certified counselors must screen prospective group counseling participants to ensure compatibility with group objectives. This is especially important when the emphasis is on self-understanding and growth through self-disclosure. Certified counselors must maintain an awareness of the welfare of each participant throughout the group process.

Section C: Counselor Supervision

NCCs who offer and/or provide supervision must:

a. Ensure that they have the proper training and supervised experience through contemporary continuing education and/or graduate training

b. Ensure that supervisees are informed of the supervisor's credentials and professional status as well as all conditions of supervision as defined/outlined by the supervisor's practice, agency, group, or organization

c. Ensure that supervisees are aware of the current ethical standards related to their professional practice

d. Ensure that supervisees are informed about the process of supervision, including supervision goals, paradigms of supervision and the supervisor's preferred research-based supervision paradigm(s)

e. Provide supervisees with agreed upon scheduled feedback as part of an established evaluation plan (e.g., one (1) hour per week)

f. Ensure that supervisees inform their clients of their professional status (i.e., trainee, intern, licensed, non-licensed, etc.)

g. Establish procedures with their supervisees for handling crisis situations

h. Render timely assistance to supervisees who are or may be unable to provide competent counseling services to clients and

i. Intervene in any situation where the supervisee is impaired and the client is at risk

In addition, because supervision may result in a dual relationship between the supervisor and the supervisee, the supervisor is responsible for ensuring that any dual relationship is properly managed.

Section D: Measurement and Evaluation

1.   Because many types of assessment techniques exist, certified counselors must recognize the limits of their competence and perform only those assessment functions for which they have received appropriate training or supervision.

2.   Certified counselors who utilize assessment instruments to assist them with diagnoses must have appropriate training and skills in educational and psychological measurement, validation criteria, test research, and guidelines for test development and use.

3.   Certified counselors must provide instrument specific orientation or information to an examinee prior to and following the administration of assessment instruments or techniques so that the results may be placed in proper perspective with other relevant factors. The purpose of testing and the explicit use of the results must be made known to an examinee prior to testing.

4.   In selecting assessment instruments or techniques for use in a given situation or with a particular client, certified counselors must carefully evaluate the specific theoretical bases and characteristics, validity, reliability and appropriateness of the instrument.

5.   When making statements to the public about assessment instruments or techniques, certified counselors must provide accurate information and avoid false claims or misconceptions concerning the meaning of the instrument's reliability and validity terms.

6   Counselors must follow all directions and researched procedures for selection, administration and interpretation of all evaluation instruments and use them only within proper contexts.

7.   Certified counselors must be cautious when interpreting the results of instruments that possess insufficient technical data, and must explicitly state to examinees the specific limitations and purposes for the use of such instruments.

8.   Certified counselors must proceed with caution when attempting to evaluate and interpret performances of any person who cannot be appropriately compared to the norms for the instrument.

9.   Because prior coaching or dissemination of test materials can invalidate test results, certified counselors are professionally obligated to maintain test security.

10.   Certified counselors must consider psychometric limitations when selecting and using an instrument, and must be cognizant of the limitations when interpreting the results. When tests are used to classify clients, certified counselors must ensure that periodic review and/or retesting are made to prevent client stereotyping.

11.   An examinee's welfare, explicit prior understanding, and consent are the factors used when determining who receives the test results. Certified counselors must see that appropriate interpretation accompanies any release of individual or group test data (e.g., limitations of instrument and norms).

12.   Certified counselors must ensure that computer-generated test administration and scoring programs function properly thereby providing clients with accurate test results.

13.   Certified counselors who develop computer-based test interpretations to support the assessment process must ensure that the validity of the interpretations is established prior to the commercial distribution of the computer application.

14.   Certified counselors recognize that test results may become obsolete, and avoid the misuse of obsolete data.

15.   Certified counselors must not appropriate, reproduce, or modify published tests or parts thereof without acknowledgment and permission from the publisher, except as permitted by the fair educational use provisions of the U.S. copyright law.

Section E: Research and Publication

1.   Certified counselors will adhere to applicable legal and professional guidelines on research with human subjects.

2.   In planning research activities involving human subjects, certified counselors must be aware of and responsive to all pertinent ethical principles and ensure that the research problem, design, and execution are in full compliance with any pertinent institutional or governmental regulations.

3.   The ultimate responsibility for ethical research lies with the principal researcher, although others involved in the research activities are ethically obligated and responsible for their own actions.

4.   Certified counselors who conduct research with human subjects are responsible for the welfare of the subjects throughout the experiment and must take all reasonable precautions to avoid causing injurious psychological, physical, or social effects on their subjects.

5.   Certified counselors who conduct research must abide by the basic elements of informed consent:

    a.   fair explanation of the procedures to be followed, including an identification of those which are experimental

    b.   description of the attendant discomforts and risks
    c.   description of the benefits to be expected
    d.   disclosure of appropriate alternative procedures that would be advantageous for subjects with an
              offer to answer any inquiries concerning the procedures
    e.   an instruction that subjects are free to withdraw their consent and to discontinue participation in
              the project or activity at any time

6..   When reporting research results, explicit mention must be made of all the variables and conditions known to the investigator that may have affected the outcome of the study or the interpretation of the data.

7.   Certified counselors who conduct and report research investigations must do so in a manner that minimizes the possibility that the results will be misleading.

8.   Certified counselors are obligated to make available sufficient original research data to qualified others who may wish to replicate the study.

9.   Certified counselors who supply data, aid in the research of another person, report research results, or make original data available, must take due care to disguise the identity of respective subjects in the absence of specific authorization from the subjects to do otherwise.

10.   When conducting and reporting research, certified counselors must be familiar with and give recognition to previous work on the topic, must observe all copyright laws, and must follow the principles of giving full credit to those to whom credit is due.

11.   Certified counselors must give due credit through joint authorship, acknowledgment, footnote statements, or other appropriate means to those who have contributed to the research and/or publication, in accordance with such contributions.

12.   Certified counselors should communicate to other counselors the results of any research judged to be of professional value. Results that reflect unfavorably on institutions, programs, services, or vested interests must not be withheld.

13.   Certified counselors who agree to cooperate with another individual in research and/or publication incur an obligation to cooperate as promised in terms of punctuality of performance and with full regard to the completeness and accuracy of the information required.

14.   Certified counselors must not submit the same manuscript, or one essentially similar in content, for simultaneous publication consideration by two or more journals. In addition, manuscripts that have been published in whole or substantial part should not be submitted for additional publication without acknowledgment and permission from any previous publisher.

Section F: Consulting

Consultation refers to a voluntary relationship between a professional helper and a help-needing individual, group, or social unit in which the consultant is providing help to the client(s) in defining and solving a work-related problem or potential work-related problem with a client or client system.

1.   Certified counselors, acting as consultants, must have a high degree of self awareness of their own values, knowledge, skills, limitations, and needs in entering a helping relationship that involves human and/or organizational change. The focus of the consulting relationship must be on the issues to be resolved and not on the person(s) presenting the problem.

2.   In the consulting relationship, the certified counselor and client must understand and agree upon the problem definition, subsequent goals, and predicted consequences of interventions selected.

3.   Certified counselors acting as consultants must be reasonably certain that they, or the organization represented, have the necessary competencies and resources for giving the kind of help that is needed or that may develop later, and that appropriate referral resources are available.

4.   Certified counselors in a consulting relationship must encourage and cultivate client adaptability and growth toward self-direction. Certified counselors must maintain this role consistently and not become a decision maker for clients or create a future dependency on the consultant.

Section G: Private Practice

1.   In advertising services as a private practitioner, certified counselors must advertise in a manner that accurately informs the public of the professional services, expertise, and techniques of counseling available.

2.   Certified counselors who assume an executive leadership role in a private practice organization do not permit their names to be used in professional notices during periods of time when they are not actively engaged in the private practice of counseling unless their executive roles are clearly stated.

3.   Certified counselors must make available their highest degree (described by discipline), type and level of certification and/or license, address, telephone number, office hours, type and/or description of services, and other relevant information. Listed information must not contain false, inaccurate, misleading, partial, out-of-context, or otherwise deceptive material or statements.

4.   Certified counselors who are involved in a partnership/corporation with other certified counselors and/or other professionals, must clearly specify all relevant specialties of each member of the partnership or corporation.

Appendix: Certification Examination

Applicants for the NBCC Certification Examinations must have fulfilled all current eligibility requirements, and are responsible for the accuracy and validity of all information and/or materials provided by themselves or by others for fulfillment of eligibility criteria.

Approved on July 1, 1982 Amended on February 21, 1987, January 6, 1989, October 31, 1997, June 21, 2002, February 4, 2005 and October 8, 2005

Acknowledgment
Reference documents, statements, and sources for development of the NBCC Code of Ethics were as follows:

The Ethical Standards of the American Counseling Association, Responsible Uses for Standardized Testing (AAC), codes of ethics of the American Psychological Association and the National Career Development Association, Handbook of Standards for Computer-Based Career Information Systems (ACSCI) and Guidelines for the Use of Computer Based Information and Guidance Systems (ACSCI).

APPENDIX C

Multicultural Counseling Competencies

I. COUNSELOR AWARENESS OF OWN CULTURAL VALUES AND BIASES

A. Attitudes and Beliefs

1. Culturally skilled counselors believe that cultural self-awareness and sensitivity to one's own cultural heritage is essential.

Explanatory Statements

a. Can identify the culture(s) to which they belong and the significance of that membership including the relationship of individuals in that group with individuals from other groups, institutionally, historically, educationally, etc. (include A, 13, and C Dimensions as do the other suggestions in this section).

b. Can identify the specific cultural group(s) from which counselor derives fundamental cultural heritage and the significant beliefs and attitudes held by those cultures that are assimilated into their own attitudes and beliefs.

c. Can recognize the impact of those beliefs on their ability to respect others different from themselves?

d. Can identify specific attitudes, beliefs and values from their own heritage and cultural learning which support behaviors that demonstrate respect and valuing of differences and those that impede or hinder respect and valuing of differences?

e. Actively engage in an ongoing process of challenging their own attitudes and beliefs that do not support respecting and valuing of differences.

f. Appreciate and articulate positive aspects of their own heritage that provide them with strengths in understanding differences.

g. In addition to their cultural groups, can recognize the influence of other personal dimensions of identity (PDI) and their role in cultural self-awareness.

2. Culturally skilled counselors are aware of how their own cultural background and experiences have influenced attitudes, values, and biases about psychological processes.

Explanatory Statements

a. Can identify the history of their culture in relation to educational opportunities and its impact on their current worldview (includes A and some B Dimensions).

b. Can identify at least five personal, relevant cultural traits and can explain how each has influenced cultural values of the counselor.

c. Can identify social and cultural influences on their cognitive development and current information processing styles and can contrast that with those of others (includes A, B, and C Dimensions).

d. Can identify specific social and cultural factors and events in their history that influence their view and use of social belonging, interpretations of behavior, motivation, problem solving and decision methods, thoughts and behaviors (including subconscious) in relation to authority and other institutions and can contrast these with the perspectives of others. (A and B Dimensions).

e. Can articulate the beliefs of their own cultural and religious groups around differences, such as sexual orientation, religion able-bodiedness, and so forth, and the impact of these beliefs in a counseling relationship.

3. Culturally skilled counselors are able to recognize the limits of their multi-cultural competency and expertise.

a. Can recognize in a counseling or teaching relationship, when and how their attitudes, beliefs and values are interfering with providing the best service to clients. (Primarily A and B Dimensions).

b. Can identify preservice and inservice experiences which contribute to expertise and can identify current specific needs for professional development.

c. Can recognize and use referral sources that demonstrate values, attitudes, and beliefs that will respect and support the client's developmental needs.

d. Can give real examples of cultural situations in which they recognize their limitations and referred the client to more appropriate resources.

B. Knowledge

1. Culturally skilled counselors have specific knowledge about their own racial and cultural heritage and how it personally and professionally affects their definitions and biases of normality/abnormality and the process of counseling.

a. Have knowledge regarding their heritage: for example, A Dimensions in terms of ethnicity, language, and so forth, and C Dimensions in terms of knowledge regarding the context of the time period in which their ancestors entered the established United States and/or North American continent.

b. Can recognize and discuss their family's and culture's perspectives of acceptable (normal) codes of conduct and what are unacceptable (abnormal) and how this may or may not vary from those of other cultures and families.

c. Can identify at least five specific features of culture-of-origin and explain how those features impact the relationship with culturally different clients.

Explanatory Statements

2. Culturally skilled counselors recognize their sources of discomfort with differences that exist between themselves and clients in terms of race, ethnicity and culture.
   a. Able to recognize their sources of comfort/discomfort with respect to differences in terms of race, ethnicity and culture.
   b. Able to identify differences (along A and B Dimensions) and is nonjudgmental about those differences.
   c. Communicate acceptance and respect of differences both verbally and nonverbally.
   d. Can identity at least five specific cultural differences, the needs of culturally different clients, and how these differences are handled in the counseling relationship.

Explanatory Statements

3. Culturally skilled counselors possess knowledge and understanding about how oppression, racism, discrimination, and stereotyping affect them personally and in their work. This allows individuals to acknowledge their own racist attitudes, beliefs, and feelings. Although this standard applies to all groups, for White counselors it may mean that they understand how they may have directly or indirectly benefited from individual, institutional, and cultural racism as outlined in White identity development models.
   a. Can specifically identify, name, and discuss privileges that they personally receive in society due to their race, socioeconomic background, gender, physical abilities, sexual orientation, and so forth.
   b. Specifically referring to White counselors, can discuss White identity development models and how they relate to one's personal experiences.
   c. Can provide a reasonably specific definition of racism, prejudice, discrimination and stereotype. Can describe a situation in which they have been judged on something other than merit. Can describe a situation in which they have judged someone on something other than merit.
   d. Can discuss recent research addressing issues of racism, White identity development, anti-racism, and so forth, and its relation to their personal development and professional development as counselors.

3. Culturally skilled counselors possess knowledge about their social impact upon others. They are knowledgeable about communication style differences, how their style may clash with or foster the counseling process with persons of color or others different from themselves based on the A, B and C, Dimensions , and how to anticipate the impact it may have on others.
   a. Can describe the A and B Dimensions of Personal Identity with which they most strongly identify.
   b. Can behaviorally define their communication style and describe both their verbal and nonverbal behaviors, interpretations of others behaviors, and expectations.
   c. Recognize the cultural bases (A Dimension) of their communication style and the differences between their style and the styles of those people different from themselves.
   d. Can describe the behavioral impact and reaction of their communication style on clients different from themselves. For example, the reaction of an older (60's) Vietnamese male recent immigrant to continuous eye contact from the young female counselor.
   e. Can give examples of an incident where communication broke down with a client of color and hypothesize about the causes.
   f. Can give 3–5 concrete examples of situations in which they modified their communication style to compliment that of a culturally different client, how they decided on the modification, and the result of that modification.

C. Skills

1. Culturally skilled counselors seek out educational, consultative, and training experiences to improve their understanding and effectiveness in working with culturally different populations. Being able to recognize the limits of their competencies, they (a) seek consultation, (b) seek further training or education, (c) refer out to more qualified individuals or resources, or (d) engage in a combination of these.

Explanatory Statements

a. Can recognize and can identify characteristics or situations in which the counselor's limitations in cultural, personal, or religious beliefs and/or issues of identity development require referral.
b. Can describe objectives of at least two multicultural-related professional development activities attended over the past 5 years and can identity at least two adaptations to their counseling practices as a result of these professional development activities.
c. Have developed professional relationships with counselors from backgrounds different from their own and maintain a dialogue regarding multicultural differences and preferences.
d. Maintain an active referral list and continuously seek new referrals relevant to different needs of clients along A and B Dimensions.
e. Understand and communicate to the client that the referral is being made because of the counselor's limitations rather than communicating that it is caused by the client.
f. On recognizing these limitations, the counselor actively pursues and engages in professional and personal growth activities to address these limitations.
g. Actively consult regularly with other professionals regarding issues of culture in order to receive feedback about issues and situations and whether or where referral may be necessary.

Explanatory Statements

2. Culturally skilled counselors are constantly seeking to understand themselves as racial and cultural beings and are actively seeking a nonracist identity.

   a. Actively seek out and participate in reading and activities designed to develop cultural self-awareness and work toward eliminating racism and prejudice.

   b. Maintain relationships (personal and professional) with individuals different from themselves and actively engage in discussions allowing for feedback regarding the counselor's behavior (personal and professional) concerning racial issues. (For example, a white counselor maintaining a personal/professional relationship with a Latina counselor that is intimate enough to request and receive honest feedback regarding behaviors and attitudes and their impact on others, I seem to have difficulty retaining Latina students in my class, given how I run my class, can you help me find ways that I may make it a more appropriate environment for Latina students?" or "When I said, _____, how do you think others perceived that comment?") This requires the commitment to develop and contribute to a relationship that allows for adequate trust and honesty in very difficult situations.

   c. When receiving feedback the counselor demonstrates a receptivity and willingness to learn.

Strategies to Achileve the Competencies and Objectives (I)

Read materials regarding identity development. For example: a European American counselor may read materials on White or Majority Identity Development, an African American may read materials on Black Identity Development, etc. to gain an understanding of own development. Additionally, reading about others' identity development processes is essential. The following are some resources specifically for European American or White counselors:

- Carter, R. T. (1990). The relationship between racism and racial identity among white Americans: An exploratory investigation. *Journal of Counseling and Development,* 69, 46–50.
- Corvin, S., & Wiggins, F. (1989). An anti racism training model for White professionals. *Journal of Multicultural Counseling and Development,* 17, 105–114.
- Helms, J. (1990). *White identity development.* New York: Greenwood Press.
- Pedersen, P. B. (1988). A *handbook for development multicultural awareness.* Alexandria, VA: American Association for Counseling and Development.
- Pope-Davis, D. B., & Ottavi, T. M. (1992). The influence of white racial identity attitudes on racism among faculty members: A preliminary examination. *Journal of College Student Development, 33,* 389–394.
- Sabnani, H. B., Ponterotto, J. G., & Borodovsky, L. G. (1991). White racial identity development and cross-cultural training. *The Counseling Psychologist, 19,* 76–102.
- Wrenn, C. G. (1962). The culturally encapsulated counselor. *Harvard Educational Review, 32,* 444–449.

Other Professional Activities

Attend annual conferences and workshops such as:

- Annual Conference on Race and Ethnicity in Higher Education sponsored by the *Center for Southwest Studies Oklahoma* (1995, *Santa Fe*)
- Third World Counselor's Association Annual Conference (Palm Springs, 1995)
- AMCD Annual Western Summit

  Engage a mentor from your own culture who you identify as someone who has been working toward becoming cross culturally competent and who has made significant strides in ways you have not.

  Engage a mentor or two from cultures different from own who are willing to provide honest feedback regarding your behavior, attitudes, and beliefs. And, be willing to listen and work toward change!

  Film: "The Color of Fear" by Lee Mun Wah

  Film: A Class Divided by PBS

  Film: True Colors — 20/20 Special

  Video: The Triad Model by Paul Pederson

Dimensions of Personal Identity

"A" Dimensions:	Age
	Culture
	Gender
	Language
	Physicality
	Race
	Sexual Orientation
	Social Class
	Education Background
	Geographic Location
	Relationship Status
"B"Dimensions:	Religion
	Work Experience
	Hobbies/Recreational Interests
"C"Dimensions:	Historical Moments/Eras

II. COUNSELOR AWARENESS OF CLIENT'S WORLDVIEW

A. Attitudes and Beliefs

1. Culturally skilled counselors are aware of their negative and positive emotional reactions toward other racial and ethnic groups that may prove detrimental to the counseling relationship. They are willing to contrast their own beliefs and attitudes with those of their culturally different clients in a nonjudgmental fashion.

Explanatory Statements

a. Identify their common emotional reactions about individuals and groups different from themselves and observe their own reactions in encounters. For example, do they feel fear when approaching a group of three young African American males? Do they assume that the Asian American clients for whom they provide career counseling will be interested in a technical career?

b. Can articulate how their personal reactions and assumptions are different from those who identify with that group (e.g., if the reaction upon approaching three young African American males is fear, what is the reaction of a young African American male or female in the same situation? What might the reaction be of an African American female approaching a group of White young men?).

c. Identify how general emotional reactions observed in oneself could influence effectiveness in a counseling relationship. (Reactions may be regarding cultural differences as well as along A and B Dimensions).

d. Can describe at least two distinct examples of cultural conflict between self and culturally different clients, including how these conflicts were used as "content" for counseling. For example, if a Chicana agrees to live at home rather than board at a four year college in order to support her mother. Can an counselor be nonjudgmental?

2. Culturally skilled counselors are aware of their stereotypes and preconceived notions that they may hold toward other racial and ethnic minority groups.

Explanatory Statements

a. Recognize their stereotyped reactions to people different than themselves. (e.g., silently articulating their awareness of a negative stereotypical reaction . . . I noticed that I locked my car doors when that African American teenager walked by.).

b. Consciously attend to examples that contradict stereotypes.

c. Can give specific examples of how their stereotypes (including "positive" ones), referring to the A and B Dimensions can impact the counselor-client relationship. d. Recognize assumptions of those in a similar cultural group but who may differ based on A or B Dimension.

B. Knowledge

1. Culturally skilled counselors possess specific knowledge and information about the particular group with which they are working. They are aware of the life experiences, cultural heritage, and historical background of their culturally different clients. This particular competency is strongly linked to the "minority identity development models" available in the literature.

Explanatory Statements

a. Can articulate (objectively) differences in nonverbal and verbal behavior of the five major different cultural groups most frequently seen in their experience of counseling.

b. Can describe at least two different models of "minority identity development" and their implications for counseling with persons of color or others who experience oppression or marginalization.

c. Understand and can explain the historical point of contact with dominant society for various ethnic groups and the impact of the type of contact (enslaved, refugee, seeking economic opportunities, conquest, etc.) on current issues in society.

d. Can identify within-group differences and assess various aspects of individual clients to determine individual differences as well as cultural differences. For example, the counselor is aware of differences with in Asian Americans: Japanese Americans, Vietnamese Americans, and so forth; differences between first generation refugees vs. second or third generation; differences between Vietnamese refugees coming in the "first wave" 1975, versus Vietnamese refugees coming to the United States in 1990. e. Can discuss viewpoints of other cultural groups regarding issues such as sexual orientation, physical ability/ disability, gender, and aging.

2. Culturally skilled counselors understand how race, culture, ethnicity, and so forth may affect personality formation, vocational choices, manifestation of psychological disorders, help seeking behavior, and the appropriateness or inappropriateness of counseling approaches.

Explanatory Statements

a. Can distinguish cultural differences and expectations regarding role and responsibility in family, participation of family in career decision making, appropriate family members to be involved when seeking help, culturally acceptable means of expressing emotion and anxiety, and so forth. (primarily along A Dimension and portions of B Dimension).

b. Based on literature about A Dimensions, can describe and give examples of how a counseling approach may or may not be appropriate for a specific group of people based primarily upon an A Dimension.

c. Understand and can explain the historical point of contact with dominant society for various ethnic groups and the impact of the type of contact (enslaved, refugee, seeking economic opportunities, conquest, etc.) on potential relationships and trust when seeking help from dominant culture institutions.

d. Can describe one system of personality development, the populations(s) on which the theory was developed, and how this system relates or does not relate to at least two culturally different populations.

e. Can identify the role of gender, socioeconomic status, and physical disability as they interact with personality formation across cultural groups.

3. Culturally skilled counselors understand and have knowledge about sociopolitical influences that impinge upon the life of racial and ethnic minorities. Immigration issues, poverty, racism, stereotyping, and powerlessness may impact self esteem and self concept in the counseling process.

Explanatory Statements

a. Can identify implications of concepts such as internalized oppression, institutional racism, privilege, and the historical and current political climate regarding immigration, poverty, welfare (public assistance).

b. Can explain the relationship between culture and power. Can explain dynamics of at least two cultures and how factors such as poverty and powerlessness have influenced the current conditions of individuals of those cultural groups.

c. Understand the economic benefits and contributions gained by the work of various groups, including migrant farm workers, to the daily life of the counselor and the country at large.

d. Can communicate an understanding of the unique position, constraints and needs of those clients who experience oppression based on an A or B dimension alone (and families of clients) who share this history.

e. Can identify current issues that impact groups of people (A and B Dimensions) in legislation, social climate, and so forth, and how that affects individuals and families to whom the counselor may be providing services.

f. Are aware of legal legislation issues that impact various communities and populations (for example, in California it is essential for a counselor to understand the ramifications of the recent passage of Proposition 187 and how that will affect not only undocumented individuals but also families, and anyone that has Chicano features, a Mexican American accent, and speaks Spanish. In addition, the counselor must be aware of how this will affect health issues, help-seeking behaviors, participation in education, and so forth)

g. Counselors are aware of how documents such as the book, The Bell Curve. and affirmative action legislation impact society's perception of different cultural groups.

C. Skills

1. Culturally skilled counselors should familiarize themselves with relevant research and the latest findings regarding mental health and mental disorders that affect various ethnic and racial groups. They should actively seek out educational experiences that enrich their knowledge, understanding, and cross-cultural skills for more effective counseling behavior.

Explanatory Statements

a. Can discuss recent research regarding mental health, career decision making, education and learning, and so forth. that focuses on issues related to different cultural populations and as represented in A and B dimensions.

b. Complete (at least 15 hours/ year) workshops, conferences, classes, inservice regarding multicultural counseling skills and knowledge. These should span a variety of topics, cultures, and include discussions of wellness rather than focusing only on negative issues (medical model) related to these cultures.

c. Can identify at least five multicultural experiences in which counselor has participated within past 3 years.

d. Can identify professional growth activities and information which is presented by professionals respected and seen as credible by members of the communities being studied. (e.g., the book The Bell Curve may not represent accurate and helpful information regarding individuals from non-White cultures).

e. Can describe in concrete terms how one has applied various information gained through current research in mental health, education, career choices, and so forth, based on differences noted in A Dimension.

2. Culturally skilled counselors become actively involved with minority individuals outside the counseling setting (e.g., community events, social and political functions, celebrations, friendships, neighborhood groups, and so forth) so that their perspective of minorities is more than an academic or helping exercise.

a. Can identify at least five multicultural experiences in which counselor has participated within the past three years. These include various celebrations, political events, community activities involving individuals and groups from racial and cultural backgrounds different from their own, such as political fund-raisers, Tet celebrations, and neighborhood marches against violence. b. Actively plan experiences and activities that will contradict negative stereotypes and preconceived notions they may hold.

Strategies to Achieve the Competencies and Obilecteves (1I)

The following reading list may be helpful for counselors to broaden their understanding of different world views (some of these materials would also be helpful in developing culturally appropriate intervention strategies):

- Atkinson, D., Morten, G., & Sue, D. W. (1989). *Counseling American minorities: A cross-cultural perspective.* Dubuque, IA: Brown.
- Collins, P. (1990). *Black feminist thought Knowledge, consciousness and the politics of empowerment* Boston: Unwin Hyman.

- Sue, D. W., & Sue, D. (1990). *Counseling the culturally different Theory and practice (2nd ed.).* New York: Wiley.

Attend conferences and workshops such as:

- Annual Conference on Race and Ethnicity in Higher Education sponsored by the Center for Southwest Studies Oklahoma (1995, Santa Fe)
- Third World Counselor's Association Annual Conference (Palm Springs, 1995)
- AMCD Annual Western Summit

Enroll in ethnic studies courses at local community colleges or universities that focus on cultures different from your own (if none are offered, communicate to that school your expectation that they will offer them in the future).

Spend time in communities different from your own, (e.g., shopping in grocery stores, attending churches, walking in marches).

Read newspapers and other periodicals targeting specifics population different from your own, (i.e., Spanish language newspapers, "Buffalo Soldier", "Lakota Times").

Engage in activities and celebrations within communities different from own (e.g., Juneteenth, Tet, Cinco de Mayo).

Engage a mentor or two from cultures different from own who are also working toward cross cultural competency (be sure to discuss with them your contribution to the relationship).

Accept that it is your responsibility to learn about other cultures and implications in counseling and do not expect or rely on individuals from those cultures to teach you.

Learn a second or third language relevant to clients to begin to understand the significance of that language in the transmission of culture.

Seek out and engage in consultation from professionals from cultures relevant to your client population.

Spend time in civil service offices observing service orientation toward individuals of color (Chicano/Latino; African American; Asian American; Native American) and contrast that with service orientation toward white individuals. Also observe any differences on service orientation that may be based on class issues (e.g., someone alone and well dressed versus a woman with children wearing older clothing, somewhat disheveled.

Film: "The Color of Fear"by Lee Mun Wah"
Film: "El Norte"
Film: *"Stand and Deliver"*
Film: "Roots"
Film: *"Lakota Woman"*
Film: "Daughters of the Dust"

III. CULTURALLY APPROPRIATE INTERVENTION STRATEGIES

A. Beliefs and Attitudes

1. Culturally skilled counselors respect clients' religious and/or spiritual beliefs and values, including attributions and taboos, because they affect worldview, psychosocial functioning, and expressions of distress.
2. Culturally skilled counselors respect indigenous helping practices and respect help-giving networks among communities of color.
3. Culturally skilled counselors value bilingualism and do not view another language as an impediment to counseling (monolingualism may be the culprit).

Explanatory Statements

1. Can identity the positive aspects of spirituality (in general) in terms of wellness and healing aspects.
2. Can identify in a variety of religious and spiritual communities the recognized form of leadership and guidance and their clients relationship (if existent) with that organization and entity.
   a. Can describe concrete examples of how they may integrate and cooperate with indigenous helpers when appropriate.
   b. Can describe concrete examples of how they may use intrinsic help giving networks from a variety of client communities.
   c. Communicate to clients and colleagues values and assets of bilingualism (if client is bilingual).

B. Knowledge

1. Culturally skilled counselors have a clear and explicit knowledge and understanding of the generic characteristics of counseling and therapy (culture bound, class bound, and monolingual) and how they may clash with the cultural values of various cultural groups.
   a. Can articulate the historical, cultural, and racial context in which traditional theories and interventions have been developed.
   b. Can identify, within various theories, the cultural values, beliefs and assumptions made about individuals and contrast these with values, beliefs, and assumptions of different racial and cultural groups.
   c. Recognize the predominant theories being used within counselor's organization and educate colleagues regarding the aspects of those theories and interventions that may clash with the cultural values of various cultural and racial minority groups.
   d. Can identify and describe primary indigenous helping practices in terms of positive and effective role in at least five A or B Dimensions, relevant to counselor's client population.
2. Culturally skilled counselors are aware of institutional barriers that prevent minorities from using mental health services.

Explanatory Statements

a. Can describe concrete examples of institutional barriers within their organization that prevent minorities from using mental health services and share those examples with colleagues and decision making bodies within the institution.

b. Recognize and draw attention to patterns of usage (or non usage) of mental health services in relation to specific populations.

c. Can identify and communicate possible alternatives that would reduce or eliminate existing barriers within their institution and within local, state, and national decision making bodies.

3. Culturally skilled counselors have knowledge of the potential bias in assessment instruments and use procedures and interpret findings keeping in mind the cultural and linguistic characteristics of the clients.

a. Demonstrate ability to interpret assessment results including implications of dominant cultural values affecting assessment/interpretation, interaction of cultures for those who are bicultural, and impact of historical institutional oppression.

b. Can discuss information regarding cultural, racial, gender profile of normative group used for validity and reliability on any assessment used by counselor.

c. Understand the limitations of translating assessment instruments as well as the importance of using language that includes culturally relevant connotations and idioms.

d. Use assessment instruments appropriately with clients having limited English skills.

e. Can give examples, for each assessment instrument used, of the limitations of the instrument regarding various groups represented in A and B Dimensions.

f. Recognize possible historical and current sociopolitical biases in *DSM (Diagnostic & Statistical Manual of Mental Disorder)* system of diagnosis based on racial, cultural sexual orientation, and gender issues.

Explanatory Statements

4. Culturally skilled counselors have knowledge of family structures, hierarchies, values, and beliefs from various cultural perspectives. They are knowledgeable about the community where a particular cultural group may reside and the resources in the community.

5. Culturally skilled counselors should be aware of relevant discriminatory practices at the social and community level that may be affecting the psychological welfare of the population being served.

a. Are familiar with and use organizations that provide support and services in different cultural communities.

b. Can discuss the traditional ways of helping in different cultures and continue to learn the resources in communities relevant to those cultures.

c. Adequately understand client's religious and spiritual beliefs to know when and what topics are or are not appropriate to discuss regarding those beliefs.

d. Understand and respect cultural and family influences and participation in decision making.

e. Are aware of legal issues that impact various communities and populations (for example, in Proposition 187 California described earlier).

C.   Skills

1. Culturally skilled counselors are able to engage in a variety of verbal and nonverbal helping responses. They are able to send and receive both verbal and nonverbal messages accurately and appropriately. They are not tied down to only one method or approach to helping, but recognize that helping styles and approaches may be culture bound. When they sense that their helping style is limited and potentially inappropriate, they can anticipate and modify it.

Explanatory Statements

a. Can articulate what, when, why and how they apply different verbal and nonverbal helping responses based on A and B Dimensions.

b. Can give examples of how they may modify a technique or intervention or what alternative intervention they may use to more effectively meet the needs of a client.

c. Can identify and describe techniques in which they have expertise for providing service that may require minimal English language skills (e.g., expressive therapy).

d. Can communicate verbally and nonverbally to the client the validity of a client's religious and/or spiritual beliefs.

e. Can discuss with the client aspects of their religious/ spiritual beliefs that have been helpful to the client in the past.

2. Culturally skilled counselors are able to exercise institutional intervention skills on behalf of their clients. They can help clients determine whether a "problem" stems from racism or bias in others (the concept of healthy paranoia) so that clients do not inappropriately personalize problems.

Explanatory Statements

a. Can recognize and discuss examples in which racism or bias may actually be imbedded in an institutional system or society.

b. Can discuss a variety of coping and survival behaviors used by a variety of individuals from their A and B Dimensions to cope effectively with bias or racism.

c. Communicate to clients an understanding of the necessary coping skills and behaviors viewed by dominant society as dysfunctional that they may need to keep intact.

d. Can describe concrete examples of situations in which it is appropriate and possibly necessary for a counselor to exercise institutional intervention skills on behalf of a client.

3. Culturally skilled counselors are not averse to seeking consultation with traditional healers or religious and spiritual leaders and practitioners in the treatment of culturally different clients when appropriate.

a. Participate or gather adequate information regarding indigenous or community helping resources to make appropriate referrals (e.g., be familiar with the American Indian community enough to recognize when, how and to whom it may be appropriate to refer a client to indigenous healers).

4. Culturally skilled counselors take responsibility for interacting in the language requested by the client and, if not feasible, make appropriate referrals. A serious problem arises when the linguistic skills of the counselor do not match the language of the client. This being the case, counselors should (a) seek a translator with cultural knowledge and appropriate professional background or (b) refer to a knowledgeable and competent bilingual counselor.

a. Are familiar with resources that provide services in languages appropriate to clients.

b. Will seek out, whenever necessary, services or translators to ensure that language needs are met.

c. If working within an organization, actively advocate for the hiring of bilingual counselors relevant to client population.

5. Culturally skilled counselors have training and expertise in the use of traditional assessment and testing instruments. They not only understand the technical aspects of the instruments but are also aware of the cultural limitations. This allows them to use test instruments for the welfare of culturally different clients.

Explanatory Statements

a. Demonstrate ability to interpret assessment results including implications of dominant cultural values affecting assessment/interpretation, interaction of cultures for those who are bicultural, and the impact of historical institutional oppression.

b. Can discuss information regarding cultural, racial, gender profile of norm group used for validity and reliability on any assessment used by counselor.

c. Understand that although an assessment instrument may be translated into another language, the translation may be literal without an accurate contextual translation including culturally relevant connotations and idioms.

6. Culturally skilled counselors should attend to as well as work to eliminate biases, prejudices, and discriminatory contexts in conducting evaluations and providing interventions, and should develop sensitivity to issues of oppression, sexism, heterosexism, elitism and racism.

a. Recognize incidents in which clients, students and others are being treated unfairly based on race, ethnicity, and physical disability, and take action by directly addressing the incident or perpetrator, filing informal complaint, filing formal complaint, and so forth.

b. Work at an organizational level to address, change, and eliminate policies that discriminate, create barriers, and so forth.

c. If an organization's policy created barriers for advocacy, the counselor works toward changing institutional policies to promote advocacy against racism, sexism, and so forth.

7. Culturally skilled counselors take responsibility for educating their clients to the processes of psychological intervention, such as goals, expectations, legal rights, and the counselor's orientation.

a. Assess the client's understanding and familiarity with counseling and mental health services and provides accurate information regarding the process, limitations, and function of the services into which the client is entering.

b. Ensure that the client understands client rights, issues and definitions of confidentiality, and expectations placed upon that client. In this educational process, counselors adapt information to ensure that all concepts are clearly understood by client. This may include defining and discussing these concepts.

Strategies to Achieve the Competencies and Objectives (III)

The following reading list may be helpful for building a foundation to develop and apply culturally appropriate interventions:

- Atkinson, D., Morten, G., & Sue, D. W. (1989). *Counseling American minorities: A cross-cultural perspective.* Dubuque, IA: Brown.
- Ibrahim, F. A., & Arredondo, P. M. (1990). Ethical issues in multicultural counseling. In B. Herlihy & L. Golden (Eds.), *Ethical standards casebook* (pp. 137–145). Alexandria, VA: American Association for Counseling and Development.
- Katz, J.(1978). *White awareness: Handbook for anti-racism training.* Norman, Oklahoma: Oklahoma.
- LaFromboise,T. D., & Foster, S. L. (1990). Cross-cultural training: Scientist-practitioner model and methods. *The Counseling Psychologist, 20,* 472–489.
- LaFromboise, T. D., & Foster, S. L. (1989). Ethics in multicultural counseling. In P. B. Pedersen, W. J. Lonner, & J. E. Trimble (Eds.), *Counseling across cultures* (3rd ed., pp. 115–136). Honolulu, H 1: University of Hawaii Press.
- Meet with leaders and heads of organizations that specifically focus on providing service to individuals of certain cultural groups (for example in San Jose, CA, AACI-Asian Americans for Community Involvement) to discuss how you may work cooperatively together and what support you may provide the organization.

- Conduct informal research of your clientele, your organizations' clientele, to determine if there are patterns of use or non use along cultural and/or racial lines.

Overall Strategies for Achieving Competencies and Objectives in all Three Areas

- Assess self in terms of Cross Cultural Counseling competencies either by reviewing the competencies and giving examples in each area and/or utilizing any of the following resources regarding assessment instruments:
- Ho, M. K. (1992) *Minority children and adolescents in therapy.* Newbury Park: Sage.
- LaFromboise, T. D., Coleman, H. L. K., & Hernandez, A. (1991). Development and factor structure of the Cross Cultural Counseling Inventory – Revised. *Professional Psychology. Research and Practice, 22,* 380–388.
- Ponterotto, J. G., Rieger, B. P., Barrett, A., & Sparks, R. (1994). Assessing multicultural counseling competence: A review of instrumentation. *Journal of Counseling and Development, 72,* 316–322.
- Learn a second or third language relevant to clients.
- Communicate to conference organizers and workshop providers that you will attend only if the activity addresses cross cultural aspects of the topic.
- Actively communicate in your organization the need for training in cross cultural training relevant to that organization.
- Speak up in your organization when you observe that clients, students etc. are being treated unfairly based on race, ethnicity, physical ableness, etc.
- Become a member of AMCD, Division 45/APA, or state and local organizations that provide cross cultural exchanges.

REFERENCES

Arredondo, P. And Glauner, T, (1992). *Personal Dimensions of Identity Model.* Boston: Empowerment Workshops.

Graham, L. (November 1994). Comments made in presentation to the Boston Human Resource Association.

Johnston, W.B. and Packer, A.H. (1987). *Workforce 2000: Work and Workers for the 21st Century,* Indiana: Hudson Institute.

Sue, D.W., Arredondo, P. and McDavis, R.J. (1992). Multicultural Counseling Competencies and Standards: A call to the profession. Journal of *Counseling and Development,* 70(4), 477–483.

BIBLIOGRAPHY

Texts and Chapters

Acosta, F. X., Yamamoto, J. and Evans, L. A. (1982). *Effective psychotherapy for low-income and minority patients.* New York, NY: Plenum Press.

Asante, M. (1987). *The Afrocentric idea.* Philadelphia: Temple University Press.

Atkinson, D., Morten, G. and Sue, D. (1989). *Counseling American minorities: A cross-cultural perspective.* (2nd Ed.) Dubuque, IA: W. C. Brown.

Cross, W. E. Jr. (1991). *Shades of Black.* Philadelphia: Temple University Press.

Cross, W. E. Jr. (1995) The psychology of Nigrescence: Revising the Cross model. In J. Ponterotto, M. Casas, L. Suzuki, and C. Alexander (Eds.) *Handbook of multicultural counseling.* Thousands Oaks, CA: Sage.

Cheatham, H. (1990) Empowering Black families. In H. Cheatham and J. Stewart (Eds.) *Black families: Interdisciplinary perspectives.* New Brunswick, N.J.: Transaction.

Ferris, F. (1987). *The central American refugees.* New York: Praeger Publishers.

Freire, P. (1970) *Pedagogy of the oppressed.* New York: Continuum.

Freire, P. (1994) *Educationfor critical consciousness.* New York: Continuum.

Hall, E. T. & Hall, M. R. (1990). ME.: Intercultural Press. Understanding cultural differences. Yarmouth

Helms, J. (1990) *Black and white racial identity: Theory, research, and practice.* Westport, CT: Greenwood.

Helms, J. (1992). *A race is a nice thing to have.* Topeka: Content Communications.

Hofstede, G. (1984). *Culture's consequences.* Cross-Cultural Research and Methodology Series 5. Newbury Park, CA: Sage.

Ivey, A. (1995). Psychotherapy as liberation. In J. Ponterotto, M. Casas, L. Suzuki, and C. Alexander. (Eds.). *Handbook of Multicultural Counseling.* Thousand Oaks, CA: Sage.

Jackson, M. L. (1995). Multicultural counseling: Historical perspective. In J. Ponterotto, M. Casas, L. Suzuki, and C. Alexander (Eds.) *Handbook of Multicultural Counseling.* Thousands Oaks, CA: Sage.

Klein, J. (1989). *Jewish identity and self-esteem: Healing wounds through ethnotherapy.* New York: Institute for American Pluralism of the American Jewish Committee.

Kohls, L. R. (1984). *The values Americans live by.* Washington, DC: Meridian House International.

Koslow, D. R. and Salett, E. P. (Eds.). (1989). *Crossing cultures in mental health.* Washington, DC: SIETAR International.

Lee, C. C., & Richardson, B. L. (Eds.). (1991). *Multicultural issues in counseling: New approaches to diversity.* Alexandria, VA: ACA Press.

Locke, D. C. (1992). *Increasing multicultural understanding.* Thousand Oaks, CA: Sage.

Marsella, A. J. and Pedersen, P. B. (Eds.). (1981). *Cross-cultural counseling and psychotherapy.* New York: Pergamon Press.

McGoldrick, M., Pearce, J., and Giordano, J. (1982). *Ethnicity and family therapy.* New York: Guilford.

Nobles, W. (1986). *African psychology: Inward its reclamation. Reassension and Revitaliation.* Oakland: Black Family Institute.

Padilla, A. M. (Ed.). (1995). *Hispanic psychology.* Thousand Oaks, CA: Sage.

Paniagua, F. (1994). *Assessing and treating culturally diverse clients.* Thousand Oaks, CA: Sage.

Pedersen, P., Draguns, J., Lonner, J., and Trimble, J. (1989). *Counseling across cultures. (3rd Ed.)* Honolulu: University of Hawaii Press.

Pedersen, P., & Ivey, A. (1993). *Culture-centered counseling.* New York: Greenwood.

Ponterotto, J., Casas, M., Suzuki, L. and Alexander, C. (Eds) (1995). *Handbook of multicultural counseling.* Thousand Oaks, CA: Sage.

Sue, D. W., Ivey, A., and Pedersen, P. (Eds.) (1996). *A theory of multicultural counseling and therapy.* Pacific Grove, CA: Brooks/Cole.

Sue, D. W. & Sue, D. (1990). *Counseling the culturally different.* New York: Wiley.

White, J. and Parham, T. (1990). *The psychology of Blacks.* Englewood Cliffs, N.J.: Princeton Hall.

Zambrana, R. E. (Eds.). (1995). *Understanding Latinofamilies.* Thousand Oaks, CA: Sage.

BIBLIOGRAPHY

Articles and Manuscripts

Arredondo, P., Psalti, A. & Cella K. (1993). The woman factor in multicultural counseling. *Counseling and Human Development, 25,* 1–8.

Arredondo-Dowd, P. M. and Gonsalves, J. (1980). Preparing culturally effective counselors. *Personnel and Guidance Journal, 58,* 657–662.

Arredondo-Dowd, P. M. (1981). Personal loss and grief as a result of immigration. *Personnel and Guidance Journal, 59,* 376–378.

Arredondo, P. M., Orjuela, E., & Moore, L. (1989). Family therapy with Central American war refugee families. *Journal of Strategic and Systemic Therapies, 8,* 28–35.

Bennett, M. J. (1986). A developmental approach to training for intercultural sensitivity. *International Journal of Intercultural Relations, 10,* 179–196.

Christiansen, C. P. (1989). Cross cultural awareness development: A conceptual model. *CounselorEducation and Supervision, 28*, 270–287.

D'Andrea, M. & Daniels, J. (1991). Exploring the different levels of multicultural counseling training. *Journal of Counseling & Development, 70*, 143–150.

D'Andrea, M. & Daniels, J. (1987). The different faces of racism in higher education. *The NEA Higher Education Journal.*

Fiske, S. T. (1993). Controlling other people. *American Psychologist, 48*, 621628.

Ford, Jr., D. L. (1978). Cultural influences on organizational behavior. *NTL Institute For Applied Behavioral Science.* 8, 2–8.

Fukuyama, M. A. (1990). Taking a universal approach to multicultural counseling. *Counselor Education and Supervision, 30*, 6–17.

Gaines, S. O., Jr. & Reed, E. S. (1995). Prejudice: From Allport to DuBois. *American Psychologist, 50*, 96–103.

Gibbs, J. T. (1987). Identity and marginality: Issues in the treatment of biracial adolescents. *American Journal of Orthopsychiatry, 57*, 265–278.

Hardiman, R. (1979). *White identity development theory.* Amherst, MA.: New Perspectives, Inc.

Herring, R. D. (1992). Counseling biracial youth within the interracial family. *The, New York State Journal of Counseling and Development, 7*, 43–5 1.

Ibrahim, F. (1985). Effective cross-cultural counseling and psychotherapy: A framework. *The Counseling Psychologist.* 13, 4, 625–638.

Ibrahim, F. A. (1991). Contribution of cultural worldview to generic counseling and development. *Journal o Counseling and Development, 70*, 13–19.

Langman, P. F. (1995). Including Jews in multiculturalism. *Journal of Multicultural Counseling and Development, 23*, 4, 222–236.

Lloyd, A. P. (1987). Multicultural counseling: Does it belong in a counselor education program? *Counselor Education and Supervision.* 26, 164–167.

Locke, D. (1990). A not so provincial view of multicultural counseling. *Counselor Education and Supervision, 30*, 18–25.

McRae, M. B. and Johnson, S. D., Jr. (1991). Toward training for competence in multicultural counselor education. *Journal of Counseling and Development, 70*, 131–35.

Myers, L. J., Speight, S. L., Highlen, P. S., Cox, C. I., Reynolds, A. L., Adams, E. M. and Hanley, C. P. (1991). Identity development and worldview: Toward an optimal conceptualization. *Journal of Counseling & Development, 70*, 54–63.

Nwachuku, U., and Ivey, A. (1991). Culture specific counseling: An alternative approach. *Journal of Counseling and Development, 70*, 106–51.

Ochs, N. G. (1994). The incidence of racial issues in white counseling dyads: An exploratory survey. *Counselor Education and Supervision, 33*, 305–313.

Paradis, F. (1981). Themes in the training of culturally effective psychotherapists. *Counselor Education and Supervision, 21*, 136–151.

Parham, T. (1989). Cycles of psychological Nigrescence. *The Counseling Psychologist, 17*, 187–26.

Pederson, P. B. (1991). Multiculturalism as a generic approach to counseling. *Journal of Counseling & Development, 70*, 6–12.

Ponterotto, J. G. (1991). The nature of prejudice revisited: Implications for counseling intervention. *Journal of Counseling & Development, 70*, 216–224.

Ruiz, A. S. (1990). Ethnic identity: Crisis and resolution. *Journal of Multicultural Counseling and Development, 18*, 29–40.

Seigel, R. (1986). Antisemitism and sexism in stereotypes of Jewish women. *Women and Therapy, 5*, 249–257.

Skillings, J. H. and Dobbins, J. E. (1991). Racism as disease: Etiology and treatment implications. *Journal of Counseling & Development, 70*, 206–212.

Smart, J. F. and Smart, D. W. (1995). Acculturative stress of Hispanics: Loss and challenge. *Journal of Counseling & Development, 73*, 390–396.

Spence, J. (1985). Achievement American style. *American Psychologist, 40*, 1285–1295.

Sue, D., Arredondo, P., & McDavis, R. (1992). Multicultural counseling competencies and standards: A call to the profession. *Journal of Multicultural Counseling and Development, 20*, 64–88.

Sue, S. and Zane, N. (1987). The role of culture and cultural techniques in psychology. *American Psychologist, 42*, 37–45.

Thomas, R. R., Jr. (1990). From affirmative action to affirming diversity. *Harvard Business Review,* March/April, 107–117.

Vontress, C.E. (1969). Cultural barriers in the counseling relationship. *Personnel and Guidance Journal, 48*, 153–180.

Weinrach, S. (1990). A psychosocial look at the Jewish dilemma. *Journal of Counseling & Development, 68*, 548–9.

Whitfield, D. (1994). Toward integrated approach to improving multicultural counselor education. *Journal of Multicultural Counseling and Development, 22*, 239–252.

Wrenn, C. (1962). The culturally encapsulated counselor. *Harvard Educational Review, 32*, 444–449.

DEFINITION OF TERMS
Patricia Arredondo, Ed.D.

Bias: a preference in the form of likes, dislikes, interests and/or priorities.

Culture: patterns of learned thinking and behavior of people communicated across generations through traditions, language and artifacts.

Cross cultural flexibility: involves the elements of Awareness, Respect and Adaptation (Arredondo & Glauner, 1992).

Diversity: describes individual differences. In the context of organizational life, diversity is about individual differences that can be drawn upon and developed to promote the goals of an organization.

Ethnocentrism: a) the development of standards based on cultural background; b) a belief that your personal culture is "right" or "best", and c) a lack of flexibility about other approaches/mindsets.

Feedback: communication that can be verbal or non-verbal, positive or negative.

Hot buttons: refers to sensitivities all people have. If a "hot button" is pushed, we tend to react emotionally.

Minority Groups: those who are identified as such by the federal government because they are members of a group that is numerically less than that of other groups in the total population. In the United States, individuals are categorized as minorities based on their ethnic/racial group identity.

Multicultural Counseling: refers to preparation and practices that integrate multicultural and culture-specific awareness, knowledge, and skills into counseling interactions (Arredondo, Toporek, et al, 1996).

Multicultural, in the context of counseling preparation and application, refers to five major cultural groups in the United States and its territories: African/Black, Asian, Caucasian/European, Hispanic/Latino and Native American or indigenous groups who have historically resided in the continental United States and its territories (Arredondo, Toporek, et al, 1996).

Organization: serves human need for comfort or camaraderie, inspiration or education, products or services — through people who perform some function or work" (Harris & Moran, 1979, p. 123).

People of Color: the term used by many individuals and groups to self-define based on cultural, ethnic, and racial heritage. This term is prefen-ed to "minorities" in some circles.

Personal culture: the organized totality of a person's identity comprised by historical mornents, unchangeable human factors and a range of developmental, sociocultural, political and economic dimensions including religion, work experience, parental status, and so forth. The interaction of these dimensions makes for a dynamic versus static personal culture and workplace.

Racism: the doctrine that race is the basic determinant of human abilities and that, therefore, the various racial groups constitute a hierarchy in which one group is properly regarded as superior to others. Mere is no scientific validity to the classification of the races.

Self-esteem: the value we give to ourselves based on feedback and experiences.

Self-fulfilling prophecy: the outcome of expectations and assumptions that are not necessarily true as stated, but which evoke behavior such that the original statement of expectation becomes true.

Stereotype: a preconceived, standardized, idea about the alleged essential nature of those making up a whole category of persons. Typically the idea is generalized to an entire group without regard to individual differences among those making up the category and is usually emotion charged. Stereotypes have a controlling function.

World View: A world view consists of presuppositions and assumptions an individual holds about the makeup of his or her world (Sire, 1976), "how a person perceives his or her relationship to the world (nature, institutions, other people, things, etc.), (Sire, 1978). It is culturally based and learned.

About The Self-Assessment

The self-assessment has been designed to assist individuals in gathering information about areas of strength and limitation in reference to the Multicultural Counseling Competencies. There are no right or wrong answers. Rather, through the assessment process, an individual can set objectives for professional development and enhancement.

The items on the Self-Assessment correspond to each of the Competencies and to the Explanatory Statements. Therefore, it is feasible to identify areas that may require attention. It is recommended that this assessment be used on a pre- and post-test basis for students in a multicultural counseling class experience.

GLOSSARY

A

ABCD Model: Used for developing program objectives and includes A = audience (individuals influenced by the program objective), B = behavior (expected action or attitude), C = conditions (context or mode in which behavior will occur), and D = description (concrete performance criterion).

ABCDEs of REBT: An acronym used to explain the core beliefs of rational emotive behavior therapy (REBT). The activating event (A) is any event or experience that elicits negativity or unease. People's belief systems (B) can be either rational or irrational in response to (A) and are what contribute to an emotional consequence (C) that is either beneficial or detrimental. By delineating this idea to clients, clients can see that (C) actually results from (B) and not (A), as often thought by clients. Next, irrational beliefs must be disputed (D) with the goal of developing (E), an effective new philosophy that allows people to replace their irrational beliefs with rational beliefs.

Ability Assessment: A broad category of assessment instruments that measure the cognitive domain (e.g., knowledge, comprehension, application, analysis, synthesis, and evaluation of information). Assessment of ability includes tests that measure achievement.

Ableism: The belief that individuals with disabilities are limited in what they can do and undervalues their abilities.

ACA *Code of Ethics*: A set of guidelines established by the American Counseling Association (ACA) to guide the professional practice of counselors in order to ensure the welfare and safety of clients.

Accommodation: An individual perceives and interprets new information in a way that causes the restructuring of existing cognitive structures.

Accountability: From a program evaluation perspective, a process of providing feedback about a program to its stakeholders.

Accreditation: A process that eligible educational institutions and organizations can elect to undergo (i.e., it is voluntary) to demonstrate that the institution meets set standards.

Acculturation: A process by which groups of individuals from differing cultures exchange cultural attributes as a result of continuously close contact. Typically, the minority group's adoption of the dominant culture's beliefs, values, and language; however, the dominant group can also adopt minority cultural patterns.

Acculturative Stress: The cognitive and affective consequences associated with leaving one's own country and entering a host country. Individuals with acculturative stress have to adapt to the values, norms, and behaviors of a new culture and lose some of their cultural identity in the process.

Achievement Tests: Assess the knowledge and skills an individual has acquired in a particular area due to instruction or training experiences.

Acting "As If": An Adlerian counseling technique that encourages clients to act "as if" they are the person they hope to be someday. This technique helps clients realize that they are capable of changing and being the person they want to be.

Action Research: Research carried out in an effort to improve practice or organizational efficiency. It is used as a means to test new approaches, theories, or ideas and reflect on one's own teachings in an effort to enhance effectiveness.

Active Imagination: A Jungian technique that requires clients to actively talk to the characters in their dreams.

Active Listening: A counseling technique used in both individual and group therapy in which the counselor attends to the nonverbal and verbal behaviors of clients to show that the counselor is paying attention.

Active Theories: Developmental theories that portray people as active in regulating or governing their behavior.

Adaptation: According to Piaget, individuals must adapt their existing cognitive structures when new information is encountered. The adaptation of cognitive structures occurs through two complimentary processes known as assimilation and accommodation. Assimilation and accommodation assist an individual in reducing the disequilibrium that results from encountering new information, which challenges previously existing ways of thinking.

Adaptive Information Processing (AIP): AIP theory holds that the brain is capable of adapting and learning from the events in our life. Pathology develops when this adaptive process has not occurred or has not been completed around a traumatic or stressful event.

Addiction: The psychological or physiological dependence on a substance or activity to maintain normal functioning. Addiction is generally associated with increased tolerance and the experience of withdrawal symptoms when the drug is removed.

Adler, Alfred: A Viennese psychologist (1870–1937) who developed the theory of individual psychology (also known as Adlerian psychology). Adler was the first major figure to break away from Freudian psychoanalysis because he disagreed with Freud over the importance of sexuality in motivating human behavior.

Advisory Committee: Used in program development and evaluation. Typically, the committee is composed of representatives from various stakeholder groups and varies widely in form and function.

Advocacy Counseling: Promotes the needs of clients, communities, and the counseling profession at the local, state, regional, and national levels.

Affectional Orientation: The suggested term used to describe sexual minorities, as it acknowledges that all relationships involve attraction, emotional stability, communication styles, and other interpersonal factors and feelings in addition to sexual attraction.

Ageism: The stereotyping and discrimination against individuals or groups as a result of their age. Ageism is based on the false notion that chronological age determines an individual's characteristics and value.

Aggression: Taking actions with the intent to cause pain or harm. Aggression can be verbal, physical, or relational.

Aggressiveness: Displayed in a group as frequent disagreement with, and forceful attempt to impose ideas upon, the leader and other members.

Aging: A set, predictable process involving growth and change in an organism over time. Aging is categorized as biological (how the body functions and changes over time), psychological (one's perception of personal age), and social (how one's chronological age is viewed within the societal, or cultural context). Two primary theories of aging have been proposed: disengagement theory (views withdrawal from social system as a natural process) and activity theory (suggests that people prefer to remain socially active as they age).

Agnosticism: The belief that any ultimate being is unknown or unknowable.

Ainsworth, Mary: Described four patterns of infant attachment: secure, avoidant, ambivalent, and disorganized.

Alcoholics Anonymous (AA): An organization that provides self-help groups and resources to persons who abuse alcohol. AA assists individuals with gaining and maintaining control over their lives through sobriety.

Alignments: Alliances between family members (i.e., the ways family members join with and oppose each other).

Alliances: The subgrouping of members in group therapy. Positive alliances can provide sources of support and strength and lead to high levels of group performance and cohesion, serving much the same intimacy function as friendships and families. However, alliances that are exclusionary can prevent members from forming productive relationships and achieving individual and group goals.

Alternative Hypothesis: A hypothesis developed in order to be eliminated; it addresses the question "What else could be causing the results?" Alternative hypotheses usually involve outlining potential extraneous variables. It is notated as (H_1).

American Association of State Counseling Boards (AASCB): Created to connect together states that have licensure boards in order to promote communication to the public and collaboration among states regarding counseling licensure laws and legal matters.

American College Counseling Association (ACCA): A division of ACA, the ACCA is a professional association for counselors working in higher education.

American Counseling Association (ACA): The largest professional association for counselors. Established in 1952, ACA was established to promote the growth and development of the profession.

American Group Psychotherapy Association (AGPA): An interdisciplinary organization promoting research and practice in group psychotherapy for individuals with mental disorders.

American Mental Health Counselors Association: The division of the American Counseling Association (ACA) that serves as the professional association for mental health counselors.

American Personnel and Guidance Association (APGA): Known today as the American Counseling Association (ACA).

American Rehabilitation Counseling Association (ARCA): A division of ACA, ARCA is the professional association for rehabilitation counselors, educators, and students.

American School Counselor Association (ASCA): The division of ACA that serves as the professional association for school counselors committed to increasing student achievement and success.

American Society of Group Psychotherapy and Psychodrama (ASGPP): Founded by J. L. Moreno, this professional association promotes standards in training, research, and practice in psychodrama, sociometry, and group psychotherapy.

Americans with Disabilities Act (ADA) of 1990: Prohibits discrimination against persons with disabilities in employment, public services, and telecommunications, and requires accommodations for access.

Amplification: A technique in which Jung compared the dreamer's image to stories or images in myths, fairy tales, literature, art, and folklore. Amplification helps the analyst identify central archetypes and possible meanings behind dreams.

Analysis of Covariance (ANCOVA): A statistical test that includes an independent variable as a *covariate*, or a variable that needs to be statistically adjusted and controlled in order to look at the relationship of other independent variables and the dependent variable.

Analysis of Variance (ANOVA): A statistical test that involves having at least one independent variable in a study with three or more groups or levels. An ANOVA provides an *F ratio*, which indicates if two or more of the group means are statistically different. With more than one independent variable, a *factorial ANOVA* is used. Factorial ANOVAs yield both main effects and *interaction effects* (i.e., significant differences among groups across two or more independent variables).

Androgyny: An individual's embodiment and expression of both male and female traditional characteristics (e.g., being strong and emotionally vulnerable).

Annulment: The voiding of a marriage.

Aptitude Tests: Assess what a person is capable of learning and attempt to predict how well that individual will perform in the future.

Arbitration: Use of a third party to make decisions that resolve a conflict for the involved individuals.

Archetypes: A Jungian concept used to refer to innate, universal templates for human thought and behaviors. Archetypes are patterns of human experience and interpretations that have existed since the origin of humankind. Some of the most prominent archetypes found within the collective unconscious are *The Self* (the regulating center of the psyche, which contains both conscious and unconscious aspects of a person); *The Shadow* (characterized as the repressed or unknown aspects of each person and which often

contains qualities that the individual possesses but does not identify with); *The Anima* (comprised of female traits that exist in the collective unconscious of men); *The Animus* (comprised of male traits that exist in the collective unconscious of women); and *The Persona* (the psychological masks that all humans wear and which allow people to change their behavior depending on the social situation).

Army Alpha: Developed by Yerkes, the Army Alpha is an intelligence test used during World War I to screen the cognitive ability of military recruits.

Army Beta: The language-free version of the intelligence test used during World War I to screen the cognitive ability of military recruits who could not read or speak English.

Asking the Question: The question that is often asked of clients in Adlerian psychology: "How would your life be different if you were well?" Many variations of this question are used, with the primary goals being to help clients think about the possibility of no longer having their problem and to show clients that they have the ability to change their lives. This question also helps counselors gain a clearer picture of what the client would like to change and whether the problem is physiological or psychological.

Aspirational Ethics: The optimal standard of behavior and the highest professional standards of conduct to which professional counselors can aspire.

Assertiveness Training: The use of behavioral techniques such as shaping, modeling, and behavioral rehearsal to assist clients in learning how to be assertive and speak up for themselves in an appropriate manner without being passive or aggressive.

Assessment: The systematic process of gathering and documenting information regarding a client's knowledge, skills, attitudes, and/or beliefs.

Assimilation: An individual perceives and interprets new information through previously existing cognitive structures.

Assimilation Model: A model of acculturation in which highly acculturated individuals identify solely with the new culture, so one group adopts values and customs of another, more dominant group.

Association for Adult Development and Aging (AADA): A division of ACA that was founded in 1986 to improve the counseling services available to adults at all stages of life through advancing counselor education and preparation related to human development and aging.

Association for Assessment in Counseling and Education (AACE): A division of ACA that was founded in 1965 to guide the proper development, training, and use of assessment in the realms of counseling and education.

Association for Counselor Education and Supervision (ACES): A division of ACA founded to enhance counseling services in all specializations through the promotion of quality education, supervision, and credentialing of counselors.

Association for Counselors and Educators in Government (ACEG): A division of ACA founded to connect counselors and educators working in government and military settings.

Association for Creativity in Counseling (ACC): This professional association, a division of ACA, was founded to promote imaginative and creative approaches to counseling and is comprised of counseling professionals from diverse specializations, including dance, art, music, and play therapy.

Association for Lesbian, Gay, Bisexual, and Transgendered Issues in Counseling (ALGBTIC): A division of ACA established to fight in the crusade for recognition of sexual minority issues within the counseling profession.

Association for Multicultural Counseling and Development (AMCD): A division of ACA created to raise awareness about multicultural issues in counseling.

Association for Specialists in Group Work (ASGW): A division of ACA founded in 1973 for the advancement of professionalism in group work.

Association for Spiritual, Ethical, and Religious Values in Counseling (ASERVIC): A division of ACA created to promote the incorporation of spiritual, religious, and ethical values into counselors' educational programs and professional practice.

Atheism: The disbelief in the existence of God.

Attending: A basic counseling skill that involves the counselor's use of verbal and nonverbal behaviors to convey to the client that the counselor is actively listening and is interested in client self-disclosures. Nonverbal attending behaviors include eye contact, an open stance, head nodding, gestures, and silence; verbal attending behaviors include "door openers" (e.g., "Tell me more about that.") and minimal encouragers (e.g., "Okay, I see.").

Attention-Seeking Behaviors: Call attention to the group member and away from other members.

Attenuation: A misleading correlation that occurs when unreliable measures indicate a lower relationship between two variables than actually exists.

Attribution Theory: Concerned with how people perceive their own as well as other's behaviors. It also examines the cause an individual attributes to events and how these cognitive perceptions shape one's behavior.

Authoritarian: A group leadership style in which the group leader takes control of and responsibility for the group; sets the agenda, goals, and rules; and serves as the conduit for member interaction (i.e., discussion occurs through the leader).

Automatic Thoughts: A term used in cognitive therapy to refer to immediate personal beliefs and ideas that are unexamined and dysfunctional.

Autonomy: The ability of clients to exercise free will and act independently.

Autosomal Diseases: Genetic disorders that involve a chromosome other than the sex chromosome. Examples of autosomal diseases are phenylketonuria, sickle cell anemia, and Tay-Sachs disease.

B

Back Home Visits: A technique used in Bowen family systems therapy that requires clients who have unresolved issues to visit their family of origin in order to increase the client's differentiation.

Bandura, Albert: Developed social learning theory, which is based on the principle that people learn through observation, imitation, and modeling.

Bar Graph: A graph that displays nominal data. Each bar represents a distinct (noncontinuous) response, and the height of the bar indicates the frequency of that response.

BASIC ID: An acronym used to describe the seven assessment domains in multimodal therapy: behavior, affect, sensations, imagery, cognitions, interpersonal relationships, and drugs/biological functions/nutrition/exercise.

Behavioral Rehearsal: A technique used by the client to practice or rehearse new behaviors until confident enough to try the new behaviors outside of the counseling environment.

Behaviorism: A scientific, research-based theory of counseling that aims to modify clients' maladaptive behaviors. Behaviorists focus only on overt, observable client behaviors and specify that all client behavior is learned and, therefore, can be unlearned. Often referred to as the "second force" in counseling.

Belmont Report: Prompted by the ethical issues arising from the Tuskegee syphilis study, this report was created by the former U.S. Department of Health, Education, and Welfare to outline ethical principles and guidelines for research involving human participants.

Beneficence: In contrast to nonmaleficence, means doing only good.

Berne, Eric: Developed transactional analysis (TA).

Between-Groups Design: A general category of experimental research designs that involves exploring the effects of a treatment or intervention between two groups or among more than two groups.

Bias: In assessment, a broad term that refers to an individual or group being deprived of the opportunity to demonstrate their true skills, knowledge, abilities, and personalities on a given assessment.

Biculturalism: A model of acculturation in which individuals identify with both their own culture and that of the host culture.

Biography: A qualitative research tradition that seeks to identify personal meanings individuals give to their social experiences. The researcher gathers stories and explores meanings for an individual as well as how the stories fit into a broader social or historical context.

Biological Aging: Categorization of aging as biological (how the body functions and changes over time).

Biracial Individuals: Individuals who are the biological children of parents from two different racial backgrounds.

Birth Order: Also referred to as sibling position, is a counseling term used to describe the position children occupy in their families of origin. Alfred Adler believed that where individuals fall chronologically in their family influences their personalities. He proposed five ordinal positions: firstborns, second children, middle children, youngest children, and only children.

Bisexual: Individual is attracted to members of the same and opposite sex.

Blind Study: The participants are not aware of the condition (treatment or control group) to which they have been assigned.

Blocking: A technique used in group counseling to stop a counterproductive member behavior in order to protect other members from potentially damaging interactions.

Boundaries: The physical and psychological factors that separate the family system from outsiders, as well as define roles and responsibilities within a family unit. Boundaries can be either rigid (closed family system) or flexible (open family system).

Bowen Family Systems Therapy: Developed by Murray Bowen, this theory proposes that healthy peoples' thoughts are differentiated from their feelings. Healthy individuals have also resolved their family of origin issues and do not experience undue anxiety when relationships with others become stressful.

Bowen, Murray: Developed Bowen family systems therapy, which maintains that people are affected by their family of origin and must resolve any issues from childhood to keep from repeating dysfunctional patterns of interaction in future relationships.

Bowlby, John: Described infants' innate ability to bond with their caregiver.

Bridging: A technique used in multimodal therapy by which counselors match their approach to a client's preferred domain in order to strengthen the therapeutic alliance and increase the client's comfort with the counseling process.

Burnout: A type of work-related strain stemming from repeated exposure to stressful circumstances that results in emotional exhaustion, depersonalization, and reduced personal accomplishment. Burnout has been empirically linked to several mental, behavioral, and physical symptoms.

C

Caplan, Gerard: Expanded Eric Lindemann's work by applying public health and preventative psychiatry principles.

Career: The lifetime pursuits of an individual. While the term can be broadly defined to include all the roles people play throughout their lifetime, many theorists maintain that the term *career* is largely concerned with an individual's work and leisure roles.

Career Adaptability: An individual's readiness and available resources for coping with changing work and employment conditions. It involves the ability to cope with predictable career development tasks (e.g., preparing and locating a job) as well as a future orientation that permits individuals to continually capitalize on their skills and abilities.

Career Adjustment: A worker's ability to adapt or adjust to the work environment.

Career Assessment: A broad process of systematically collecting career-related information using multiple methods. Career-assessment results can provide an individual with information concerning career options, career-planning courses, personality type, aptitudes, career-related beliefs, interests, work values, career-development stage, and career barriers. Three commonly used methods in career assessment include interviewing, formal testing, and self-assessment.

Career Choice: The decisions individuals make at any point in their career about which work and leisure activities to pursue.

Career Construction Theory: Mark Savikas' (2005) narrative career counseling approach maintains that individuals construct their careers by imposing meaning on vocational behaviors. This approach emphasizes individual personality types, life themes, and career adaptability.

Career Counseling: The process by which professional counselors facilitate an individual's development of a life career; specifically, counselors focus on assisting clients with defining their role as a worker and understanding how that role interacts with their other life roles.

Career Decision-Making Self-Efficacy: The degree to which individuals feel competent in their ability to make a career decision. Persons with high career decision-making self-efficacy will readily engage in career decision-making behaviors, whereas those with low career decision-making self-efficacy may give up easily if they run into barriers or avoid engaging in these behaviors altogether.

Career Decision-Making Theories: A group of career theories that focus on the decision-making process and are less concerned with the careers people actually choose. Theories falling within this category can be prescriptive (describe ideal approaches to decision making) or descriptive (explain how individuals actually make vocational choices).

Career Development: A process by which individuals grow and change to cope with and accommodate career issues that arise throughout their lifetime.

Career Development Inventories: A group of inventories that identify personal factors that may impede or facilitate an individual's career development process. Typically these inventories measure factors related to faulty career beliefs, anxiety, career maturity, and career barriers.

Career Development Theory: Developed by Ginzberg, Ginsburg, Axelrad, and Herma (1951), this lifespan theory focuses on the career decision-making process of children and adolescents. The theory proposes that career decision making involves three developmental stages: fantasy, tentative, and realistic.

Career Interests: Preferences for particular life activities and are thought to play a key role in career decision making and choice. Three types of career interests are typically distinguished: expressed, manifested, and tested.

Career Intervention: A counseling intervention that is specifically meant to facilitate clients' career development processes and the attainment of their counseling goals. Career counseling interventions can be implemented in an individual or group session.

Career Maturity: An individual's readiness to make good career choices.

Career Salience: The significance or importance an individual places on the role of career in relationship to other life roles. Career salience is often defined by an individual's participation, commitment, and value expectations.

Career Transition: A move from one developmental stage to the next. Transitions can be smooth and seamless (e.g., a job promotion) or chaotic and disruptive (e.g., being fired).

Carl D. Perkins Vocational and Technical Education Act of 1984: Provides access to vocational assessment, counseling, and placement services for the economically disadvantaged, those with disabilities, individuals entering non-traditional occupations, adults in need of vocational training, single parents, those with limited English proficiency, and incarcerated individuals.

Case Study: (a) Used in human development research to collect data on a developmental change from a single individual, or a single group of individuals experiencing a similar developmental phenomenon. (b) A qualitative research approach that describes a case, a distinct system of an event, process, setting, or individuals or small group of individuals.

Catching Oneself: An Adlerian counseling technique that encourages clients to catch themselves when they are engaging in the behaviors that are perpetuating their presenting problem.

Central Nervous System: A part of the nervous system that consists of the brain and spinal cord.

Central Tendency: Measures of the typical or middle value of the data set. Measures of central tendency include the mean, median, and mode.

Certified Rehabilitation Counselor (CRC): Professionals who seek to help individuals with disabilities work through personal and vocational issues they may encounter as a result of impairment.

Child Abuse: Involves harm to an individual under the age of 18 years, caused by either exploitation, neglect, or physical, sexual, or emotional abuse.

Child Abuse Prevention and Treatment Act (CAPTA): Federal legislation that addresses the prevention, assessment, investigation, and prosecution of child abuse and neglect. The act mandates counselors to report suspicions of child abuse and/or neglect to their local child protective services (CPS).

Child Protective Services (CPS): A state agency that investigates reports of child abuse and neglect. Any counselor who suspects child abuse or neglect is required by law to report their suspicion to their local CPS agency within 72 hours from the time they first became aware of the potentially abusive or neglectful event.

Chi Sigma Iota (CSI): The international honor society for professional counselors, counselor educators, and counseling students. CSI was created in 1985 to foster achievement and scholarship within the profession as well as to acknowledge exceptional leaders in the field.

Chi-Square Test: A nonparametric statistical test used to determine whether two or more categorical or nominal variables are statistically independent.

Chronemics: How individuals perceive, structure, and react to time. Monochromic time refers to an orientation toward time in a linear fashion (use of schedules, advanced planning of activities), and polychromic time refers to the value of time as secondary to relationships among people. These orientations affect individuals' punctuality, willingness to wait, and interactions.

Circular Causality: A term used in general systems theory to describe the notion that each family member's behavior is influenced by other family members. In other words, causality is not a linear process; each family member affects the others' behavior in a circular manner.

Circular Questioning: A Milan family therapy technique that uses questions to highlight family connections and differences among family members.

Clarifying: A counseling technique used in individual or group therapy to help the counselors check their understanding of what clients have said.

Classical Conditioning: A learning process, first described by Ivan Pavlov, that occurs when an environmental stimulus is consistently associated with a naturally occurring stimulus. Specifically, classical conditioning involves the pairing of an *unconditional stimulus* (US) that automatically elicits an *unconditioned response* (UR), with a neutral, *conditioned stimulus* (CS) that, after a number of pairings, results in the CS eliciting the UR, now called the *conditioned response* (CR).

Classification Systems: Used to assess the presence or absence of an attribute.

Classism: A form of oppression based on a person's social status. Classism can take two forms: structural and internalized.

Client-Centered Counseling: Also referred to as person-centered counseling, the client-centered counseling approach was developed by Carl Rogers and proposes that clients, not counselors, set the pace for counseling and determine the focus of each session. Client-centered counseling downplays the use of techniques, instead focusing on the development of a trusting, genuine, and accepting therapeutic relationship to facilitate change.

Clinical Assessment: The process of assessing clients through multiple methods such as personality testing, observation, interviewing, and performance in order to increase client self-awareness or assist the professional counselor in client conceptualization and treatment planning.

Clinical Interviewing: The process by which a professional counselor uses clinical skills to obtain information from a client that will facilitate the course of counseling, such as a client's demographic characteristics, presenting problems, current life situation, family, educational status, occupational background, physical health, and mental health history.

Closed Groups: Leaders allow a set number of members to participate from the group's beginning to termination and expect consistent attendance throughout the group experience.

Coalitions: Occur when some family members form an alignment against another family member.

Coefficient of Determination: The amount of shared variance between the two variables; computed by squaring the correlational coefficient.

Cognitive Ability Tests: Make predictions about an individual's ability to perform in future grade levels, colleges, and graduate schools.

Cognitive-Behavior Modification: A cognitive-behavioral approach created by Donald Meichenbaum that trains clients to alter their internal cognitions—that is, self-talk—in order to change the way they react and respond to situations.

Cognitive-Behavioral Theories: A counseling approach that seeks to alter both the thoughts and actions of clients through the use of cognitive and behavioral techniques.

Cognitive Dissonance: Conflict or discomfort experienced when a discrepancy is noticed between what an individual already knows and new information being received. The theory of cognitive dissonance exerts that individuals are motivated to reduce dissonance either by changing their existing beliefs and attitudes to accommodate the new information or by justifying their beliefs and attitudes by rejecting the new information.

Cognitive Rehearsal: A cognitive technique that assists clients in practicing their new thoughts before implementing them in an actual situation.

Cognitive Restructuring: A technique used in cognitive-behavior modification to help clients adjust their self-talk. The process involves targeting the client's self-statements that result in problematic behaviors or feelings and replace the self-statements with new statements that are more rational, logical, and positive.

Cognitive Therapy: A type of therapy developed by Aaron Beck which posits that peoples' emotions and behaviors are a direct result of their cognitions. Cognitive therapy seeks to assist clients in identifying, testing, and restructuring their distorted, dysfunctional thoughts.

Cohort Study: Involves assessing the same population over time.

Co-Leadership: Occurs when more than one leader shares or helps to facilitate the group process.

Collaborative-Interdependent Consultation Model: A model of consultation that provides clinicians with a way to work in concert with community organizations to solve complicated problems that affect many clients on a variety of levels. The model calls for diverse professionals to join together as equals to solve presenting issues of individuals and work interdependently to develop a way forward.

Collective Trauma: A community's reaction to a crisis.

Collective Unconscious: A Jungian term used to refer to the part of an individual's unconscious that is shared by the entire human race. The collective unconscious is a product of ancestral experience and contains archetypes.

Color Blindness: Involves the equal treatment of individuals by ignoring racial differences. Professional counselors who endorse this assumption are likely to adopt the attitude that race no longer matters, and in doing so perpetuate a continuing distrust of White counselors for clients of color, diminish the importance that the client's cultural background has on the client's worldview, and fail to create therapeutic goals that are met with culturally appropriate treatments.

Color Consciousness: A process by which Whites experience guilt for their role in perpetuating racial discrimination for racial minorities and, as a result, begin to focus solely on racial differences.

Colorism: A form of discrimination in which individuals receive differential treatment based on skin color. Traditionally, individuals whose skin color approximates that of Whites receive preferential treatment.

Coming Out Process: The process of recognizing oneself as a sexual minority and disclosing one's sexual identity to others. Aspects of the coming out process include becoming aware of attraction to the same sex; being sexually involved; becoming familiar with the sexual minority community; self-identifying as gay, lesbian, bisexual, or transgender; and coming out to others.

Commission on Rehabilitation Counselor Certification (CRCC): A nonprofit organization that was formed in 1974 to certify rehabilitation counselors who meet particular professional standards and have achieved adequate education and work experience related to rehabilitation. CRCC is the equivalent of the National Board for Certified Counselors (NBCC) for rehabilitation counselors seeking certification.

Common Rule: A part of Title 45: Public Health Part 46: Protection of Human Subjects of the *Code of Federal Regulations*, it outlines policies that guide researchers who use human subjects. It requires these studies to be approved by an institutional review board (IRB).

Communication Disorders: A group of disorders that involve problems in speech, language, and hearing. Four Communication Disorders are discussed in the *DSM-IV-TR*: Expressive Language Disorder, Mixed Receptive-Expressive Language Disorder, Phonological Disorder, and Stuttering.

Comparative Design: A type of nonexperimental design that allows the researcher to investigate group differences for a particular variable in order to determine if there is a difference between the groups.

Compassion Fatigue: Occurs when helping professionals experience overwhelming feelings after being exposed to client crisis states (e.g., pain, suffering). Professionals may experience hopelessness, a decrease in pleasure, constant stress and anxiety, and a pervasive negative attitude.

Complainants: A term used in SFBT to characterize clients who recognize the existence of a problem and can define it but have yet to commit to solving it.

Complementary Relationships: Relationships in a family between unequals, where one member is "one down" and the other is "one up." Although this description appears negative, complementary relationships are not necessarily objectionable.

Complex: A Jungian term used to describe amalgamating unconscious feelings, thoughts, and desires. Jung proposed the existence of many kinds of complexes and that each complex revolves around a universal experience, or archetype (e.g., "mother complex"). Complexes symbolize issues that a person needs to resolve.

Compromise: A method professional counselors can use to help group members detach their ideas from their egos in order to promote group goals and enhance the group process.

Computer Adaptive Testing: Have the ability to adapt the test structure and items to the examinee's ability level (e.g., GRE).

Computer-Assisted Career Guidance (CACG) Systems: Computer-based systems that provide vocational assessments, occupational and educational information, and career planning tools. Commonly used CACG systems include DISCOVER, SIGI PLUS, Choices, and Guidance Information Service.

Computer-Based Testing (CBT): A method for administering, analyzing, and interpreting tests through the use of computer technology, software programs, or Internet sites. Also known as *computer-based assessment* (CBA).

Confianza: A value in the Latino culture that refers to possessing trust and confidence in those with whom one is in a relationship.

Confidentiality: An ethical principle that requires professional counselors to maintain the privacy of information shared by the client during counseling sessions. Confidentiality promotes establishment of a trusting environment and facilitates the development of the therapeutic alliance. However, exceptions to client confidentiality are allowable in certain instances, including suicidal or homicidal ideation, child abuse, elder abuse, and dependent adult abuse.

Confirmatory Bias: A person's likelihood of screening for information that confirms previously held beliefs (i.e., hearing what one wants to hear).

Conflict: An intrapersonal struggle in which an individual must make a decision between at least two choices, or an interpersonal struggle between at least two persons who are striving to achieve opposing goals.

Conflict Resolution: The way individuals seek resolution to interpersonal differences. Usually involves negotiating, mediating, facilitating, and arbitrating.

Confronting: A counseling skill that involves informing clients about discrepancies in their words, behaviors, feelings, or nonverbal communication in order to increase client self-awareness so the client can become more congruent.

Congruence: A term used in Holland's theory of types to refer to the relationship between an individual's personality and the work environment. The more similar an individual's personality traits are to the work environment characteristics, the more congruent the relationship.

Conscious Mind: Awareness of everything occurring in the present.

Consciousness: A total awareness of one's self. Psychoanalytic theory proposes that individuals have a conscious mind (awareness of everything occurring in the present), a preconscious mind (contains forgotten memories and vast stores of knowledge and information that can be easily recalled with assistance or cues) and an unconscious mind (contains memories, instincts, and drives that are exceedingly difficult to bring to a person's conscious awareness).

Consensual Qualitative Research (CQR): A qualitative approach that combines elements of phenomenology and grounded theory and involves researchers selecting participants who are very knowledgeable about a topic and remaining close to data without major interpretation with some hope of generalizing to a larger population.

Consistency: The degree of similarity between the six different Holland types. Holland developed the hexagon model to illustrate the degree of similarity among the different types.

Constructivism: A philosophical paradigm that contends there are multiple realities or perspectives for any given phenomenon. Truth differs for individuals and is an internal manifestation, as opposed to positivism and post-positivism, which propose that truth is external to the individual.

Contact Summary Sheet: A data management tool used in qualitative research that provides a single-page snapshot of a specific contact, such as an interview or observation.

Continuous Development: Emphasizes the small shifts or gradual, sequential, changes that occur in behaviors and abilities over time and that are difficult to separate.

Control Group: Used in experimental designs, this group comprises those participants in a study who share very similar attributes with the experimental group but do not receive treatment. Three types of control groups are commonly used: (a) *wait list control group* (individuals who are awaiting treatment, but not receiving any treatment at all); (b) *placebo control group* (individuals who receive some "treatment" that will not affect the dependent variable [e.g., sugar pill]); and (c) *treatment as usual* (TAU) *control group* (individuals receive whatever treatment they would ordinarily receive if they sought treatment but do not receive the special treatment under study).

Conversion Therapy: Also known as reparative therapy.

Consultation: A formal process by which professional helpers and individuals/ groups form a relationship voluntarily in order to solve a problem. Typically the professional helper (consultant) assists the individual/group (consultee) with defining and resolving an issue. The three primary models of consultation are the triadic-dependent model, the collaborative-dependent model, and the collaborative-interdependent model.

Consultation Process: The process of consulting can be divided into four steps: (a) The consultant establishes rapport with the consultee, explains the consultation process, and defines the responsibilities of each member. (b) The consultant works with the consultee to assess and define the problem in clear, specific terms and to set a goal related to the identified problem. (c) The consultant and consultee brainstorm, evaluate, select, and implement solutions. (d) The consultant and consultee determine the solution's effectiveness and whether it makes sense to terminate the consultative relationship because the goal has been achieved or to return to the drawing board to devise and try another strategy.

Continuous Development: Some theorists maintain that human development is a smooth and continuous process without distinct stages. They emphasize the small shifts or gradual changes that occur over time.

Contingency Contracts: A behavioral technique that uses a chart or table to note whether desired behaviors were achieved. The contingency contact also describes the conditions that must be met for the individual to be rewarded.

Core Counseling Conditions: Rogers exerted that counselors must possess core helping conditions in order to promote client change, growth, and self-actualization. The core counseling conditions include (a) genuineness/congruence (being honest with clients and ensuring that a counselor's verbal and nonverbal communication is congruent), (b) respect/unconditional positive regard (the ability to communicate acceptance of the client as a person, regardless of their actions or beliefs), and (c) empathy (the ability to enter the client's worldview and convey an understanding of a client's thoughts, feelings, and actions).

Correlational Research Design: A type of nonexperimental research design that allows the researcher to describe the relationship between two

variables. The variables are not experimentally manipulated; therefore, the researcher cannot determine a causal relationship. Instead, this design computes a correlation coefficient that describes the strength and direction of a relationship.

Correlation Coefficient: A numerical index that represents the relationship between two variables. Index values range from -1.00 and $+1.00$, with $+1.00$ indicating a perfect positive relationship and a -1.00 indicating a perfect negative relationship. Four commonly used types of correlation coefficients include (a) Pearson product moment correlation coefficient (commonly referred to as Pearson r), (b) Spearman r (for comparing rank-order variables), (c) biserial correlation coefficients (comparing one continuous and one dichotomous or dummy coded variable), and (d) point biserial correlation coefficients (relating one continuous and one true dichotomous variable). A correlation provides information about the relationship between two variables, including whether there is a relationship at all, the direction of that relationship, and the strength of the relationship.

Correspondence: The degree to which the individual and work environment continue to meet each other's needs.

Council for Accreditation of Counseling and Related Educational Programs (CACREP): An independent accrediting agency that provides accreditation for master's-level counseling programs and doctoral-level counselor education programs.

Counseling Association for Humanistic Education and Development (C-AHEAD): This "heart and conscience of the counseling profession" looks after the mental health and wellness of both clients and counselors.

Counseling Groups: Groups that are designed to help members work on interpersonal problems (e.g., family issues, difficult relationships, stress-related problems) and promote behavioral changes related to these problems. Counseling groups are typically problem oriented, helping members explore their problems and seek resolution but also can be preventive, growth oriented, or remedial.

Counselors for Social Justice (CSJ): A division of ACA since 2002, CSJ was established with the mission of "confronting oppressive systems of power and privilege" relevant to counselors and their clients.

Counselor Supervisors: Experienced professional counselors who provide training to novice counselors. Counselor supervisors promote the improvement of supervisee clinical skills and facilitate the novice counselor's professional development. Counselor supervisors are legally and ethically responsible for the well-being of their supervisees and the clients served by their supervisees.

Counterparadox: Counselors employ a counterparadox when they ask family members not to change too quickly in order to assist the family in avoiding resistance.

Countertransference: A psychoanalytic term used to describe the emotions and fantasies a counselor unconsciously transfers to the client. Typically, these feelings stem from the counselor's own unresolved conflicts and past relationships.

Crisis: A stressful or traumatic event that compromises a person's previously effective coping mechanisms. An individual trauma refers to an individual's response to a crisis, while a collective trauma refers to a community's reaction to a crisis.

Crisis Counseling Program (CCP): A model of crisis intervention that focuses on restoring a sense of safety in the aftermath of a natural disaster. Under this model, professional counselors work as a team to identify the problem, inventory the available resources, help reduce the disorder and confusion, assist victims in adjusting to their new life situations, provide victims with support and empathy, and educate individuals about common and atypical reactions to crisis and what to do should they need extra help.

Crisis Team: A group of professionals from different backgrounds (e.g., mental health professionals, medical professionals, etc.) who have been trained to respond to those in crisis.

Criterion-Referenced Assessment: Provides information about an individual's score by comparing it to a predetermined standard or set criterion.

Crites, John: A leading vocational psychologist of the 20th century who researched the area of career maturity and developed the Career Maturity Inventory.

Critical/Ideological Paradigm: A philosophical paradigm that centers on researchers taking a proactive role and confronting the social structure and conditions facing oppressed or underprivileged groups.

Cross-Sectional Design Studies: A research method that allows the researcher to simultaneously compare several groups from differing levels of development (e.g., 20-year-olds, 30-year-olds, 40-year-olds) with respect to the independent variable(s).

Crystallized Intelligence: A type of intelligence proposed by Cattell (1971) that is gained through learning and is greatly affected by life experiences and culture.

Cultural Encapsulation: Occurs when the dominant cultural view is regarded in counseling as more important than minority values. Cultural encapsulation can lead counselors to evaluate and treat diverse clients from the dominant perspective, disregarding clients' individual cultures and values.

Cultural Identity: Derived from an individual's sense of belonging to specific subgroups of various cultural groups or categories.

Culture: The shared attitudes, values, expectations, habits, customs, and rituals of a group that are transmitted from one generation to the next and provide members with rules for living and adapting to the environment.

Culture Shock: The experience of disorientation and psychological symptoms such as anxiety and depression that occurs when one adjusts to a new culture where rules, customs, and language are unknown.

Customers: A term used in SFBT to characterize the most ideal clients; such clients recognize a problem that needs to be fixed and are committed to finding a solution. Until clients become customers, it is difficult to help them effectively improve their lives.

D

Data Display: A data management tool used in qualitative research to present organized data in a table format or a figure containing interconnected nodes. Displays may be created for each participant (within-case display) as well as across a sample (cross-case display).

Decay of Memory Theory: Suggests that traces of information held in memory simply decay over time and that the memory eventually disappears forever.

Decision Accuracy: The accuracy of an instrument in supporting counselor decisions. Decision accuracy often assesses sensitivity (the instrument's ability to accurately identify the presence of a phenomenon); specificity (the instrument's ability to accurately identify the absence of a phenomenon); false positive error (an instrument inaccurately identifies the presence of a phenomenon); false negative error (an instrument inaccurately identifies the absence of a phenomenon); efficiency (the ratio of total correct decisions divided by the total number of decisions); incremental validity (the extent to which an instrument enhances the accuracy of prediction of a specific criterion).

Defamation: A type of tort that refers to marring an individual's reputation through the intentional spreading of falsehoods. Libel refers to defamation through writing, while slander is defamation through spoken statement(s).

Definitional Ceremony: A technique used in narrative therapy, in which clients tell their new stories to an audience of outside witnesses.

Degrees of Freedom (*df*): An important concept used in inferential statistics, this term refers to the number of IVs "free to vary." Computing *df* depends on the statistical test used.

Demand Characteristics: Cues that participants pick up from the researcher or research setting that motivate them to behave or respond in certain ways.

Democratic: A group leadership style in which the group leader facilitates member interactions. With the leader's guidance, members make decisions, take responsibility, set agenda, as well as establish goals, and rules.

Derived Score: A converted raw score that gives meaning to test scores by comparing an individual's score with those of the norm group.

Descriptive Design: The most prevalent category of nonexperimental research design that includes thoroughly describing a variable at one time (*simple descriptive* design) or over time (*longitudinal design*).

Descriptive Research: A type of nonexperimental research that is used to describe a phenomenon and does not involve an intervention (treatment). This type of research can only present what is and how often something occurs; it cannot capture the reason a particular situation is occurring. Often descriptive research is conducted as either a precursor to or in conjunction with other research methods. Types of descriptive research designs include *simple descriptive designs* (i.e., "one-shot" surveys of a variable), *cross-sectional designs*, and *longitudinal designs*.

Descriptive Statistics: Organize and summarize a data set. Descriptive statistics are calculated as an initial method for interpreting a data set.

DeShazer, Steve: Developed solution-focused brief therapy (SFBT).

Determinism: A philosophical position that argues people's actions are predetermined by an external, uncontrollable force, such as genetics or biology. The deterministic perspective is endorsed by psychoanalytic theories.

Detriangulation: In Bowen family systems therapy, learning how to avoid involvement in triangles and how to avoid triangulating others.

Developmental Scores: Place an individual's raw score along a developmental continuum in order to derive meaning from the score. Developmental scores directly evaluate an individual's score against the scores of those of the same age or grade level. The two commonly used types of developmental scores are *age-equivalent scores* (compare an individual's score with the average raw score at a certain age) and *grade-equivalent scores* (compare an individual's score with the average raw score of those at a certain grade level).

Developmental Supervision Approaches: Emphasize counselor-trainees' progress through a series of stages as they become more experienced, competent, and independent.

Deviation IQ: A type of standardized score that has a mean of 100 and standard deviation of 15.

Diagnostic Tests: Identify learning disabilities or specific learning difficulties by providing an in-depth analysis of student skill competency in a given academic area.

Differentiation: An individual or work environment's level of distinctiveness between each of the six Holland types. Differentiation is calculated by subtracting the lowest score of any type from the highest score of any type on the Self Directed Search or Vocational Preference Inventory. Low scores are indicative of undifferentiation, which can lead to career indecision.

Differentiation of Self: A term used in Bowen family systems therapy to refer to individuals' ability to separate themselves from their family of origin without cutting themselves off from their families. Differentiated individuals maintain healthy family boundaries and are able to encounter emotionally charged family situations by balancing emotions with logic and rationality.

Directives: Homework assignments.

Direct Observation: Assesses an individual's behavior in real time and usually occurs in a naturalistic setting.

Directory Information: Information that schools can release about students without parental consent. Directory information includes the student's name, address, telephone number, date of birth, place of birth, honors or awards, and dates of attendance at the school.

Disability: A physical, mental, or behavioral challenge that limits an individual's ability to function in the activities associated with daily living.

Discontinuous Development: Portrays changes in behaviors and abilities as qualitatively different from previous or subsequent behaviors and abilities. Theorists who endorse this view of human development categorize developmental changes into distinct stages.

Discrimination Model: A supervision model that requires the supervisor to be aware of the supervisee's intervention, conceptualization, and personalization skills and address supervisee needs by adopting the role of either teacher, counselor, or consultant as needed.

Disputing Irrational Beliefs: A technique used in REBT in which the counselor challenges a client's irrational beliefs.

Distorted Thinking: Inaccurate thoughts or ideas that maintain dysfunctional thinking and negative emotions. Specific types of distorted thinking include: dichotomous thinking (thinking in absolute terms, such as "always" and "never"); selective abstraction (focusing on only the negative aspects of a situation in order to support distorted thinking); overgeneralization (using isolated cases to make broad generalizations); magnification/minimization (exaggerating or understating personal characteristics or situations); labeling (occurs when people define themselves based on perceived imperfections); mind reading (occurs when people believe that they know what others are thinking about them without any evidence); and negative predictions (occurs when people anticipate that something bad will happen without any evidence and alter their behaviors accordingly).

Divorce: The formal, legal termination of a marriage. Individuals may progress through four emotional stages (shock and disbelief, initial adjustment, active re-organization, life reformation) as they work through the divorce process.

Document Summary Form: A data management tool used in qualitative research that is similar to a contact summary sheet but is used to document salient themes and reflections from unobtrusive data sources, such as newsletters or artifacts.

Dollard, John, and Neal Miller: Proposed that anxiety and psychological disturbances were learned from experiences. They are best known for identifying and describing three types of conflicts: (a) approach-approach conflicts occur when two positive choices are presented, but only one can be chosen, even though they may be equally appealing; (b) approach-avoidance conflicts occur when a person wants something appealing but fears being punished or being negatively evaluated for obtaining it; and (c) avoidance-avoidance conflicts occur when the person loses no matter which choice is made.

Dominant Narratives: Narratives involving cultural customs that affect a client's life and worldview.

Double Blind Study: Neither the researcher nor the participant knows if the participant belongs to the experimental group or the control group, which helps to combat subjective bias by both the researcher and the participant in the study.

Double Jeopardy: Individuals who are marginalized as a result of dual minority statuses (e.g., being an African American female).

Drawing Out: The group leader directly interacting with a member to get the member to contribute to a discussion topic or activity.

Dream Analysis: A psychoanalytic technique in which dreams are explored and interpreted according to manifest (literal/obvious meaning) and latent content (hidden meaning).

Dream Interpretation: A Jungian technique that involves helping clients understand the personal meaning behind their dreams. Jung believed that dreams reflected both the personal and collective unconscious; therefore, archetypes such as The Animus, The Anima, and The Shadow manifested themselves in dreams as symbols or figures. To assist individuals in determining the reason why certain objects appeared in their dreams, Jung used a technique called explication. Amplification (i.e., comparing a dreamer's image to stories/images in myths, literature, and the arts) was used to help the analyst identify central archetypes and possible meanings behind dreams. Jung also used a technique called active imagination that requires clients to actively talk to the characters in their dreams in order to help them connect with their unconscious.

DSM-IV-TR: *The Diagnostic and Statistical Manual of Mental Disorders, Fourth Edition, Text Revision* (American Psychiatric Association, 2000), is the most commonly used nosological system by mental health practitioners in the United States. The *DSM-IV-TR* defines mental disorders and describes symptoms and diagnostic criteria for each condition.

E

Eclectic Counseling: A counseling approach that draws from an assortment of theories in order to assist clients. Rather than approaching clients from one primary theoretical perspective, eclectic counselors use numerous theories to attempt to improve their clients' functioning. Two main types of eclecticism are technical eclecticism, in which counselors use just the techniques from a wide range of theories, and theoretical integration, in which counselors strive to combine at least two theories into a unified whole.

Educational Accreditation: A process by which educational programs and services are evaluated by an external agency to determine whether certain standards are being maintained. CACREP, an independent agency, provides accreditation for master's and doctoral counseling programs.

Educational Record: Any document or information kept by the school relating to a student, such as attendance, achievement, behavior, activities, and assessment.

Effect Size: A measure of the strength of the relationship between two variables in a population.

Efficiency Analysis (Cost-Benefit Analysis): Used in program evaluation to weigh the benefits of a particular course of action (i.e., maintaining a program; terminating a program) against the costs.

Ego: A term used in psychoanalysis to refer to the conscious part of the personality. The ego operates on the reality principle, moderating the wishes and desires of the id and moral demands of the superego. The ego is the logical, rational part of the personality that allows the person to function effectively in society.

Ego Psychology: A neo-Freudian theory that was developed after Freud's id, ego, and superego personality model. The psychoanalyst most responsible for the development of ego psychology was Heinz Hartmann. Hartmann, unlike Freud, exerted that the ego could act independently from the id and superego under normal, favorable conditions. He also believed the ego included innate capacities such as perception, attention, memory, concentration, motor coordination, and language.

Ellis, Albert: An American psychologist who founded rational emotive behavior therapy (REBT). His original theory was known as rational-emotive therapy (RET). Ellis maintained that individuals must modify their irrational self-talk in order to achieve healthy functioning.

Emic: A multicultural perspective that maintains counseling approaches should be specific to a client's culture. A counselor working from an emic perspective would tailor counseling approaches that are consistent with a specific client's worldview.

Emotional Control Cards: A technique used in REBT to reinforce the disputation of irrational beliefs outside of counseling sessions. These cards list both appropriate and inappropriate feelings, which can serve as reminders to clients who are having a difficult time.

Emotional Cutoff: Occurs when children, who are highly fused with their families, may try to emotionally cut themselves off from their family of origin through moving, refusing to talk to family members, or only interacting with family members on a surface level in order to improve or maintain their well-being.

Empathy: One of the core counseling conditions; the counselor's ability to understand and effectively communicate back a client's thoughts, feelings, and worldview.

Employment Rate: The number of currently employed individuals divided by the total number of individuals who are of working age (i.e., 16 years of age and older).

Empty Chair: A technique used in Gestalt therapy in which a client is asked, through role play, to talk to conflicting parts of their personality or to an individual with whom they are in conflict.

Enactment: A deliberate process by which the counselor encourages the family to play out its problem in the session.

Encode: The process of compacting information in a meaningful way so that it can be stored and retrieved efficiently during transfer from short-term to long-term memory.

Encouragement: An Adlerian technique whereby the counselor conveys to clients his or her belief and conviction that the client can make important lifestyle changes.

Environmental Planning: A behavioral technique that involves having clients rearrange their environments to encourage or discourage certain behaviors.

Epston, David: With Michael White, developed narrative therapy, a postmodern and social constructionist approach.

Equilibration: A process, ordinarily accomplished through a combination of assimilation and accommodation, through which motivated people attempt to make sense of new information (adapting thoughts to reduce the conflict or disequilibrium).

Erickson, Milton: Developed strategic family therapy.

Erikson, Erik: Developmental psychologist and psychoanalyst known for his psychosocial theory of human development.

Esalen Institute: Uses a humanistic approach to enrich and explore human potential through multidisciplinary workshops, forums, and retreats.

Ethics: Moral principles that guide an individual's behavior. For professional counselors, the ACA (2005) *Code of Ethics* guides practice to ensure the welfare and safety of clients as well as counseling professionals.

Ethnic Identity: Self-perceived sense of membership in an ethnic group, including feelings and attitudes associated with that membership.

Ethnicity: An individual's identification with a group of people who have common social ties due to geographic origins, cultural heritage, language, values, or religious belief.

Ethnocentrism: The belief that one's cultural group is right or superior to all other cultures. Ethnocentrism represents a lack of flexibility and openness to other perspectives and worldviews.

Ethnography: A qualitative research tradition in which the researcher describes and provides interpretations about the culture of a group or system.

Ethological Theories: Developmental theories that emphasize the role of instinct and innate capacities in human development. Well-known ethological theorists include Konrad Lorenz (carried out a set of experiments concerning gosling imprinting and critical periods); John Bowlby (described infants' innate ability to bond with their caregiver); Mary Ainsworth (described four patterns of infant attachment: secure, avoidant, ambivalent, and disorganized); and Harry Harlow (studied attachment patterns of infant rhesus monkeys and found that, when frightened, the infants preferred contact with a terrycloth surrogate mother to a wire mother that provided food).

Etic: A multicultural perspective that endorses the idea of cultural neutrality and maintains that universal qualities of counseling can be generalized across cultures. Counselors who work from this perspective minimize individual cultural differences, and instead focus on basic counseling processes and strategies that can be broadly applied.

Eugenics Movement: A social movement that attempted to preserve the purity of the Caucasian race by monitoring a person's innate characteristics and dictating who could marry and reproduce.

Evaluating: The group leader's continuous monitoring and assessment of group progress, process, and outcomes.

Evaluation: (1) Includes the sharing of insights or judgments about whether a group is accomplishing agreed-on goals. (2) Making a determination of worth or significance based on the result of a measurement.

Executive Summary: A report that is developed by program evaluators for the advisory committee after the needs assessment is completed. The report should contain background information about the needs assessment, information about data sources and data analyses used, and recommendations based on the findings for program implementation and future evaluation.

Exercises: Techniques in Gestalt therapy that are planned prior to a therapy session. Exercises used by Gestalt therapists often include psychodrama, role-playing, and the empty chair technique.

Existential Counseling: An approach to counseling that assists clients in addressing universal questions about life, death, and freedom and helps them find meaning in their lives.

Existential Vacuum: A term associated with existential counseling describing the experience of life as empty, meaningless, purposeless, and so on.

Experiment: A technique in Gestalt therapy that occurs spontaneously in session.

Experimental Research Designs: Quantitative research designs that assess the cause-and-effect relationships among variables through manipulating research conditions and variables.

Experiential Family Counseling: A counseling model that is less concerned with techniques and more concerned with establishing a genuine relationship with clients and helping them bring their problems into the here-and-now.

Explication: A Jungian technique used to help clients determine the reason why certain objects appeared in their dreams.

Ex Post Facto Research Designs: Also referred to as *causal-comparative designs*. Nonexperimental research designs that involve looking at potential causes of a dependent variable after the fact (after data have been collected). Specifically, this design examines how an independent variable affects a dependent variable by assessing whether one or more pre-existing conditions possibly caused differences in groups. Unfortunately, independent variables or conditions cannot be manipulated as the data have already been collected.

External Validity: The ability to generalize the results of a study to a larger group. Two types of external validity include *population external validity* (involves the population to which one can generalize) and *ecological external validity* (involves the conditions or settings to which one can generalize). Threats to external validity include novelty effect, experimenter effect, history by treatment effect, measurement of the dependent variable, and time of measurement by treatment effect.

Extinction: The termination of a behavior by withholding reinforcement. In classical conditioning, extinction describes the eventual elimination of the conditioned response (CR) through repeated presentations of the conditioned stimulus (CS) without the unconditioned stimulus (US).

Eye Movement Desensitization and Reprocessing (EMDR): A technique that attempts to simulate REM (i.e., rapid eye movement) sleep, the sleep cycle thought to be most restorative and helpful in working through troubling matters in the unconscious.

F

Face Validity: A superficial measure that is concerned with whether an instrument looks valid or credible. Face validity is NOT a true type of validity.

Facilitation: The use of counseling-related skills, especially in groups, to analyze the conflict, find compromise and solutions, and elicit commitment among individuals.

Factor Analysis: A statistical test used to reduce a larger number of variables (often items on an assessment) to a smaller number of factors (groups or factors). The two forms of factor analysis are (a) *exploratory factor analysis* (EFA), which involves an initial examination of potential models (or factor structures) that best categorize the variables and (b) *confirmatory factor analysis* (CFA), which refers to confirming the EFA results.

Familismo: A value commonly endorsed by Latin Americans that refers to a strong connection to extended families. This value reflects the collectivist nature of this cultural group.

Family Educational Rights and Privacy Act (FERPA): Also known as the Buckley Amendment, FERPA is a federal law that protects the privacy of student educational records. Specifically, the act provides parents and students the right to access the student's educational records, petition to have incorrect information found in the record amended, and ensure that certain information is not released to outside agencies without permission.

Family of Origin (FOO): The family in which a person grows up.

Family Projection Process: Occurs when undifferentiated parents project their tension and anxiety onto their most susceptible or sensitive child.

Family Sculpting: A technique used to help the counselor and family fully understand one family member's impression of family relationships.

Family Theories: Counseling theories that provide practitioners with a systemic way of conceptualizing problems within a family.

Family Therapy: A group of counseling theories that provide practitioners with a systemic way of conceptualizing problems within a family. These systems theories aim to ameliorate the functioning of entire family units, rather than the one "symptomatic" individual within the family.

Feedback: A counseling skill that involves sharing thoughts, feelings, and impressions about the client directly with the client to help the client gain increased self-awareness, confront inconsistencies, and reinforce progress.

Femininity: Attributions that are commonly associated with a woman, such as relational, nurturing, and emotional. In the Latino culture, this term is referred to as "marianismo."

Feminist Theory: A psychological theory pioneered by Carol Gilligan (1982) that espouses equality for all individuals and is particularly dedicated to eliminating sexism. The theory aims to help clients become more aware of the effect of gender on their lives as well as to empower them to improve their lives and the lives of others.

Fidelity: Facilitating trust, keeping one's word, and fulfilling obligations to clients.

Filial Piety: A cultural value commonly endorsed by Asian Americans whereby the needs of an individual are often secondary to those of the family (especially to parents and elders).

Firing Sequence: A technique used in multimodal counseling in which a counselor works with the client to determine the chain of events leading to a stressor that affects the client's life in a maladaptive way.

Five Factor Model: An evidence-based model of personality that breaks down the construct of personality into five factors: openness, conscientiousness, extraversion, agreeableness, and neuroticism (OCEAN). This model is often referred to as the "Big Five." The NEO Personality Inventory–Revised (NEO-PI-R) is commonly used to measure these factors in clients, and clinicians can use the results to help formulate useful interventions to help clients improve the quality of their lives.

504 Plan: Dictates the accommodations or other special considerations the student is entitled to receive under the Rehabilitation Act of 1973.

Fluid Intelligence: A type of intelligence proposed by Cattell that refers to innate ability that is not influenced by experience and education. It consists of reasoning ability, memory capacity, and speed of information processing.

Focus Groups: An interview method used in research that typically includes 6 to 12 participant members who can provide information and insight into a particular issue.

Focusing on Others: A group member's attempt to avoid self-focus and self-disclosure.

Forebrain: Part of the brain that consists of the cerebrum, which is responsible for higher order behavior and conscious thought. The cerebrum consists of the left and right hemispheres, the corpus callosum, and the cerebral cortex.

Formative Evaluations: The ongoing evaluations of a program throughout its implementation to ensure that the program is being conducted as planned and that any changes needed based on stakeholder feedback may be made.

Forming and Orienting Stage: The beginning developmental stage of a group. This stage is characterized by group member anxiety, insecurity, and preoccupation with personal issues. Group rules and goals are also established.

FRAMES: An acronym for a model (Feedback, Responsibility, Advice, Menu, Empathy, Self-Menu) that was developed to guide timely and effective interventions.

Frankl, Victor: A Holocaust survivor and Austrian psychiatrist who trained under Alfred Alder. Frankl is one of the key figures in existential therapy and founded logotherapy, which focuses on individuals' search for meaning in their lives. His book *A Man's Search for Meaning* chronicles his experiences in a Nazi concentration camp as he searches for meaning in life.

Free Appropriate Public Education (FAPE). Education that addresses students' individual needs and helps ready them for higher levels of education or employment.

Free Association: A psychoanalytic technique that encourages clients to say anything that comes to mind, without thinking. This technique is used to uncover unconscious, repressed thoughts and feelings.

Free Will: Self-determination.

Frequency Distribution: Tabulation of the number of observations (or number of participants) per distinct response for a particular variable. It is presented in a table format with rows indicating each distinct response and columns presenting the frequency for which that response occurred.

Frequency Polygon: A line graph of the frequency distribution that is used to visually display data that are ordinal, interval, or ratio. The X-axis typically indicates the possible values and the Y-axis typically represents the frequency count for each of those values.

Freud, Sigmund: An Austrian psychiatrist who is considered to be the father of psychoanalysis. He stated that personality develops through the interaction of innate drives and also maintained that environment and past experiences play a key role in an individual's current behaviors. Freud theorized that psyche was comprised of the id (operates on the pleasure principle), ego (operates on the reality principle), and superego (operates on the morality principle).

Friedman's Rank Test: A nonparametric statistical test similar to Wilcoxon's signed-ranks test in that it is designed for repeated measures. It may be used with more than two comparison groups.

Fused: Enmeshed.

G

Games: In transactional analysis, ulteriorly motivated transactions that appear complementary on the surface but end up in bad feelings.

Gatekeeping: Occurs when members and leaders insist on adherence to the established group norms.

Gelatt's Decision-Making Model: Proposes that all decisions have similar qualities in that a choice, which has two or more possible courses of action, must be made and an individual must rationally analyze information to accurately predict the outcome of choice.

Gender: The psychological and social characteristics often associated with an individual's biological sex but usually derived from cultural rules and norms.

Gender Identity: A psychological awareness of one's maleness or femaleness. Gender identity is typically solidified around age three years, when a child self-refers as a boy or girl, and contains an environmental and cultural component.

Gender Roles: The expectations placed on individuals by society regarding how they should behave, think, and be treated because of their biological sex.

Gender Schema Theory: Sandra Bem (1974) proposed children learn from society what it means to be male or female. As children begin to internalize these assumptions, they adjust their behavior to conform to society's gender norms and expectations.

Gender Self-Confidence: The degree to which an individual defines oneself according to traditional views of masculinity and femininity and accepts those views.

General Systems Theory: Developed by Ludwig von Bertalanffy, this theory provides a basic framework for understanding the interactions and issues that occur within family systems. The theory examines family relationships and transactions between members rather than scrutinizing the personalities or actions of any one family member in isolation.

Generational Poverty: Occurs when poverty has been a factor in several generations.

Genogram: Developed by Bowen, genograms are visual representations of approximately three generations of a family. Genograms can help professional counselors and families become aware of patterns of interaction that have occurred throughout a family's history and then work to resolve any dysfunction that becomes apparent.

Gerontological Counseling: A specialty area in counseling that is tailored for working with individuals 65 years of age and older.

Gesell, Arnold: American psychologist and pediatrician who believed that human development reflects a genetic unfolding of, and maturational readiness for, physical, cognitive, language, and social-emotional characteristics or milestones with only slight environmental influence. He developed a well-known set of assessments, known as the Gesell Scales.

Gilligan, Carol: An American feminist, ethicist, and psychologist best known for her work with and against Lawrence Kohlberg on ethical community and ethical relationships, and certain subject-object problems in ethics.

Giving Information: A counseling skill through which counselors provide clients with information to help them achieve their goals.

Glasser, William: An American psychiatrist who is known for developing reality therapy and choice theory. His ideas focus on the role of personal choice, responsibility, and transformation in an individual's life.

Gottfredson's Theory of Circumscription, Compromise, and Self-Creation: A lifespan theory that outlines the career development processes of children and adolescents. Gottfredson proposes that career development occurs through circumscription (i.e., the process by which individuals eliminate career alternatives they believe are not compatible with their self-concept) and compromise (i.e., the process by which adolescents give up highly preferred career alternatives for those that are less compatible but more accessible). Gottfredson emphasizes the role that gender and prestige play in making career decisions.

Gould, Roger: An American writer and psychiatrist who studied more than 1,000 adults and discovered that they strove to eliminate false assumptions (protective devices), usually relating to parental dependency, that restricted young and middle adult development. He viewed adult development as a series of task resolutions that allowed adults to correct these false assumptions and ultimately take control of their lives.

Grounded Theory: A qualitative approach used for the purpose of generating theory that is grounded in data from participants' perspectives for a particular phenomenon.

Group Climate Measures: Help assess which stage of group process the members have entered and provide leaders with member perceptions of group climate.

Group Cohesion: Feelings of belonging and inclusion that members and leaders experience through group interactions.

Group Dynamics: The interaction among and movement between members in a group. Many factors contribute to group dynamics, including group structure, content, and process. Structure issues include group size, function (i.e., task, psychoeducational, counseling, psychotherapy), voluntary/involuntary, and open/closed groups. Content issues involve the "what" or actual subject under discussion by the group members. Group process issues involve the interplay of forces or dynamics between and among members and leaders—or "how" the interaction is occurring in the here and now.

Group Member Roles: The various positions or expected patterns of behavior group members may adopt during group work. Formal roles are specific roles assigned to a group member; for example, many task groups have a chair and someone who records minutes of the meeting. Informal roles are not specified but are developed through interactions with other group members, such as an advice giver or aggressor.

Group Member Screening: A process conducted by the leader(s) to ensure the appropriateness of member and group fit.

Group Size: The number of people included in a therapy group. Group size varies depending upon the model, purpose, member age, and intensity of planned interactions.

Group Tests: Tests that are administered to two or more test-takers at a time.

Growth Needs: Occur in the labor market when the demand for workers exceeds the number of existing workers and requires more workers to be added to the workforce.

Guide for Occupational Exploration (GOE): A print-only source of occupational information. The GOE is published by JIST Works and offers information on over 900 occupations.

Guttman Scale: Measures the intensity of a variable being measured. Items are presented in a progressive order so that a respondent, who agrees with an extreme test item, will also agree with all previous, less extreme items.

H

Haley, Jay: Helped found the Bateson Group, the Mental Research Institute (MRI), and the Family Research Institute and contributed to the development of MRI Interactional Family Therapy.

Halo Effect: A type of experimenter effect wherein the researcher's subjective, usually positive and initial, perceptions of the participant are generalized to other traits and characteristics.

Harlow, Harry: Described classic experiments with infant rhesus monkeys that were placed into cages with wire surrogate mothers, one with a bottle to provide food (oral gratification and sustenance) and another with a terrycloth covering (comfort and warmth). The infant monkeys would move to the wire monkey for food but preferred contact comfort with the terrycloth monkey, spending the vast majority of time with and running to the terrycloth monkey when frightened.

Harm Reduction: A set of public health policies and pragmatic interventions that are designed to reduce the harms associated with drug use and other high risk activities.

Harris-Bowlsbey, Joanne: Developed computerized vocational systems such as CVIS, DISCOVER, and VISIONS, and is known for her work in training career development facilitators internationally and for writing print-based career curriculum for high school and college-age students.

Havighurst, Robert: American professor, physicist, educator, and aging expert, who proposed a series of developmental tasks that humans achieve as they grow and develop from infancy through late adulthood.

Hawthorne Effect: A type of experimenter effect in which the presence of the investigator affects participant responses independent of any intervention. Sometimes called *reactivity*.

Health Insurance Portability and Accountability Act (HIPAA): A federal law that protects the privacy of individuals' medical and mental health records. Under this law, counselors must allow clients to view their records and petition for changes to the counselor's notes if they believe any information is false or inaccurate. Counselors must also provide clients with a copy of a HIPAA privacy policy, which outlines with whom their protected health information may be shared.

Health Maintenance Organization (HMO): An HMO is a type of managed care organization that provides members access to health services at a lower cost.

Here and Now Therapy: A Gestalt approach used to encourage clients to discuss only what is bothering them in the present moment.

Herman, Judith: Author of *Trauma and Recovery*, Herman believed that healing from a psychologically traumatic situation occurs in three phases (establishment of safety, remembrance and mourning, reconnection with ordinary life) that are ongoing and not necessarily ever completed.

Heterogeneous Group: Consists of members with diverse characteristics (e.g., age, gender, race, socioeconomic, and sexual orientation) and concerns.

Heterosexism: Discriminatory attitudes and beliefs toward persons who do not fall within the "mainstream" heterosexual category. Typically, heterosexism endorses the notion that homosexuality and bisexuality are inferior and less desirable than heterosexuality.

Heterosexual: Individual is attracted to members of the opposite sex.

Hierarchy of Needs: Proposes that higher order needs (e.g., achievement, self-actualization) cannot be attained until lower order needs (e.g., food, shelter, safety) are met. Developed by Abraham Maslow (1947).

High-Context Communication: Involves relying on factors other than explicit speech to convey a message. Individuals using high-context communication often infer, imply, or deliver nonverbal cues to convey unspoken messages.

High Stakes Testing: The use of standardized test outcomes to make a major educational decision concerning promotion, retention, educational placement, and entrance into college; as a result, high stakes testing can have serious consequences for the students being tested.

Hindbrain: The brain stem, which consists of the medulla oblongata, cerebellum, pons, and reticular activating system, which act collectively to coordinate maintenance and survival functions such as motor activity, posture, sleep patterns, and essential unconscious activities (e.g., breath, blood circulation).

Histogram: A graph of connecting bars that shows the frequency of scores for a variable. Taller bars indicate greater frequency or number of responses. Histograms are used with quantitative and continuous variables (ordinal, interval, or ratio).

Holland, John: Known for developing a theory of vocational types, which involves matching persons to work environments.

Holland's Theory of Types: Developed by John Holland (1966), this trait and type career theory exerts that individuals should "match" their personality type with the work environment. Holland proposed that there are six personality and work environment types: Realistic, Investigative, Artistic, Social, Enterprising, and Conventional (RIASEC). Career satisfaction is dependent on the degree of congruence between an individual's personality type and work environment.

Homeostasis: The tendency of a family system to sustain normal functioning and patterns of interaction by continually taking inventory of, prioritizing, and tending to their needs so as to maintain health and well-being. Families will resist change unless someone or something intervenes in order to maintain a state of equilibrium.

Homework (Directives): Assignments given to clients to be completed outside of counseling sessions to reinforce learning and skill acquisition.

Homogeneous Group: Consists of members with similar characteristics (e.g., sex, age, sexual orientation, race, physical ability) and concerns.

Homophobia: An excessive fear of associating with homosexuals and/or being homosexual. Homophobia is often accompanied by a hatred of sexual minorities and can result in hate crimes.

Homoprejudice: A term that has recently emerged in research as scholars suggest that prejudice is more of the cause of discrimination than an actual phobia (i.e., homophobia).

Homosexual: Individual is attracted to members of the same sex.

Humanistic Counseling: A group of counseling theories focusing on experiences that are unique to humans (e.g., self-actualization, wellness, hope, love, creativity). Humanistic counselors believe in human goodness and the ability of all individuals to strive toward self-actualization given the proper environment. Humanistic counseling is frequently referred to as the "third force" in counseling.

Human Validation Process Model: Developed by Virginia Satir, this approach views symptoms as ways to preserve the family's homeostasis and as obstructions to growth. Thus, these blockages must be unclogged to allow development to occur. Satir strove to create a welcoming environment in which families will feel comfortable exploring their issues and beginning the process of change.

Hypothesizing: In Milan family therapy, counselors formulate hypotheses to help family members change and gain more insight into their behavior; these hypotheses are not supposed to be accepted as absolute truths.

Hypothesis Testing: Involves the decision-making process of determining if the null hypothesis is to be retained or rejected based on significance level and the critical value.

I

Id: A term used in psychoanalysis to refer to the part of the personality that is present from birth and operates on the pleasure principle. The id involves innate drives (e.g., food, sex, aggression) and is concerned solely with achieving pleasure, no matter what the consequences.

Identity: An understanding of oneself as a separate, distinct individual. Erikson (1950) described identity development as occurring during adolescence when individuals must recognize and integrate a sense of personal uniqueness and future direction. Those who fail to do so experience confusion and question their purpose and direction. Marcia (1966, 1980) expanded Erikson's conceptualization of identity, proposing four types of identity: identity achievement, identity moratorium, identity foreclosure, and identity diffusion.

Imaginary Audience: A belief maintained by adolescents that everyone is watching and critically judging them.

Implosion or Implosive Therapy: A behavioral technique that teaches clients to vividly imagine hypothetical scenarios that would cause them severe anxiety (often referred to as flooding). Consequently, the client becomes desensitized to and less anxious about this fearful scenario.

Inclusion: A member's sense of connectedness to the group.

Indirect Observation: Assesses an individual's behavior through self-report or the use of informants such as family, friends, or teachers.

Individualized Education Plan (IEP): Delineates what services a student with specials needs will receive, when, and how often, as well as yearly goals for the student's learning, all of which are updated and reviewed.

Individuals with Disabilities Education Improvement Act (IDEA) of 2004: A civil rights law that guarantees students with disabilities access to a free appropriate public education (FAPE), an Individualized Educational Plan (IEP), and receipt of the benefits of education in the least restrictive environment (LRE).

Individual Tests: Tests that are administered to one examinee at a time.

Individual Trauma: An individual's response to a crisis.

Individuation: A Jungian concept that describes the process of discovering one's true, inner self. Jung believed that as individuals move through life they lose touch with important parts of themselves; therefore, he suggested, through listening to the messages of dreams and waking imagination, individuals can reestablish contact with these different parts. Individuation is seen as a life goal and is thought to have a holistic, healing effect on individuals.

Inductive Analysis: A common process among several research traditions that involves searching for keywords and potential themes from the data without significant preconceived notions of what theory or theories fit the data.

Industrial Revolution: Transformed America's agriculturally based economy into an industrial and manufacturing economy.

Inferential Statistics: Statistical procedures that are used to draw inferences about a population from a sample.

Inferiority Complex: A term associated with individual psychology that refers to an individual who is unable to move beyond feelings of inferiority. An inferiority complex interferes with an individual's ability to live a healthy, socially interested, and goal-directed life. An inferiority complex can lead to overcompensation, which results in a superiority complex.

Informal Assessments: Subjective assessment techniques that are developed to identify the strengths and needs of clients.

Informational Interviewing: An informal method of obtaining occupational information that provides one the opportunity to interview people who are currently employed in a career field of interest. Informational interviews, unlike job interviews, assist persons in exploring career options.

Information Seeking: Occurs when group members ask for clarification or help to promote self-disclosure in oneself or other members.

Informed Consent: Guarantees a client the right to choose whether to enter into or remain in a counseling relationship, and it ensures the active involvement of the client in decisions made during the counseling process. Informed consent is initially covered in the first counseling session but should be utilized throughout the counseling process. When working with minors, counselors must obtain informed consent from parents/legal guardians and assent from the minor.

Informing: Occurs when a member talks about other members outside of group. Leaders should remind all members that what happens in group stays in group and underscore the importance of confidentiality to group work success and goal accomplishment.

In-Group: The group to which an individual feels similar.

Initiation: Occurs when group members make suggestions or take action to move the group toward goals.

Initiating: A group leader technique that can provide direction for members by initiating group topics or activities, thereby allowing members to focus energy and achieve desired outcomes.

Institutional Review Board (IRB): Any institution receiving federal funding must sponsor an IRB in order to approve proposals to conduct research with human subjects. An IRB consists of five members and typically operates under the same general guidelines.

Integration Model: A model of acculturation in which individuals identify with both their own culture and that of the host culture.

Intelligence Tests: Broadly assess an individual's cognitive abilities and yield a single summary score, commonly called an intelligence test (IQ). Also see DEVIATION IQ.

Intentional Tort: A tort in which the counselor's action would result in harm to the client, even if the counselor did not intend to injure the client.

Interest Assessments: Assessments that facilitate students' personal exploration of career options in concert with their interests.

Interest-Based Negotiations: A form of conflict resolution that involves the process of finding a commonality between the individuals involved.

Interest Inventories: A group of inventories that are used to identify an individual's work-related interests, as well as what one finds enjoyable and motivating. Interest inventories solicit an individual's preferences and do not necessarily correlate with ability or job success.

Interference Theory: Proposes that learned information is inhibited by other learning experiences.

Internalized Classism: A form of classism in which individuals come to believe the negative attributes associated with their social class.

Internalized Homophobia: The process by which sexual minorities accept heterosexist messages; this can hinder their sexual identity development.

Internalized Racism: The taking in of majority beliefs about minority groups that will cause the minority group to believe stereotypes concerning itself, resulting in low self-esteem, feelings of worthlessness, and lowered motivation levels.

Internal Validity: The degree to which changes in the dependent variable are due to the effects of the independent variable. Threats to internal validity include history, selection, statistical regression, testing, instrumentation, attrition, maturation, diffusion of treatment, experimenter effects, and subject effects.

International Association of Addiction and Offender Counselors (IAAOC): A division of ACA that was chartered in 1974 to promote suitable services for and treatment of clients addressing these issues and also to forward this counseling specialization by endorsing ongoing research, training, advocacy, prevention, and intervention related to these groups.

International Association of Marriage and Family Counselors (IAMFC): A division of ACA that encourages leadership and distinction in marriage and family counseling.

International Students: Individuals who leave their home country to pursue higher education in a host country.

Interpersonal Psychoanalysis: A neo-Freudian approach that is based on the work of Henry Stack Sullivan. Sullivan contended that people's mental disorders stem from dysfunctional patterns of interpersonal interactions. Consequently, analysts assist clients by focusing on client relationships and personal interactions rather than past events.

Interpretation: Plays a critical role in psychoanalysis. Psychoanalysts interpret the meaning of clients' thoughts, emotions, behavior, and dreams to increase their self-awareness and understanding of their unconscious desires.

Interpreting: (1) A counseling skill that involves suggesting possible reasons for client behavior, thoughts, or feelings or helping clients recognize hidden meaning in their actions. Psychoanalysts often use interpretation in psychoanalysis to increase client self-awareness and understanding of their unconscious desires. (2) A part of the assessment process wherein the professional counselor assigns meaning to the data yielded by evaluative procedures.

Interquartile Range: The distance between the 75th percentile and the 25th percentile (i.e., the range of the middle 50% of the data). The interquartile range may be a more accurate estimate of variability when dealing with outliers or extreme values as it eliminates the top and bottom quartiles.

Interval Scale: Includes all ordinal scale qualities and has equivalent intervals—that is, interval scale measures have an equal distance between each point on the scale (e.g., temperature).

Intimate Partner Violence (IPV): A predominant form of adult domestic violence, defined as any behavior that is physically, emotionally, or sexually abusive in nature and used to gain authority over one's relationship with an intimate partner.

Ipsative Assessment: Compares individuals' test scores to their previous test scores.

IS PATH WARM: A mnemonic method to remember the warning signs of suicide: Ideation, Substance abuse, Purposelessness, Anxiety, Trapped, Hopelessness, Withdrawal, Anger, Recklessness, and Mood change.

I-Statement: Using the first person singular "I" to express thoughts and feelings.

Item Analysis: A procedure that involves statistically examining test-taker responses to individual test items with the intent to assess the quality of test items as well as the test as a whole. Item analysis is frequently used to eliminate confusing, easy, and difficult items from a test that will be used again.

Item Difficulty: The percentage of test-takers who answer a test item correctly, calculated by dividing the number of individuals who correctly answered the item by the total number of test-takers.

Item Discrimination: The degree to which a test item is able to correctly differentiate test-takers who vary according to the construct measured by the test. It is calculated by subtracting the performance of the top quarter of total scores from the bottom quarter of total scores on a given test item.

J

Janis and Mann's Conflict Model of Decision Making: A decision-making approach that describes how individuals handle stress when making career decisions. The model proposes that stress significantly contributes to the quality of the decision that is made; therefore, high levels of stress can lead to a "defective" career decision. People use five patterns to cope with this stress: unconflicted adherence, unconflicted change, defensive avoidance, hypervigilance, and vigilance.

Jewish Chronic Disease Hospital Study: An infamous, unethical research study in which both healthy and unhealthy patients were injected with live cancer cells so that researchers could better understand the impact of cancer based on health status. Participants never provided informed consent and were not told they were being injected with cancer cells.

Jim Crow Laws: Enacted after slavery ended in 1865, these laws sought to maintain separate and unequal social and economic situations for Blacks.

Job: Refers to positions that require a specific skill set and are within an organization or company.

Job Satisfaction: How content individuals are with their jobs. Job satisfaction is said to result from a match between individuals' self-concept and the characteristics of their work environments.

Job Shadowing: A temporary, unpaid experience in which one observes a competent worker and/or work environment to learn more about a career.

Job Training Partnership Act (JTPA) of 1982: Law passed by the U.S. government to address the needs of disadvantaged students, technical education programs, and unemployed workers.

Johari Window: A model used to describe levels of client awareness. These levels are represented by four quadrants: the public self, the blind self, the private self, and the unknown self. The model proposes that as individuals interact with group members, the public, blind, and private selves grow while the unknown self decreases.

Joining: Imitating the manner, style, affective range, or content of a family's communications for purposes of solidifying the therapeutic alliance.

Joint Committee on Testing Practices (JCTP): Disbanded in 2007 after publishing several documents concerning testing standards in educational, psychological, and counseling fields. The most notable of the JCTP's publications include *Rights and Responsibilities of Test Takers, Test User Qualifications*, and the *Code for Fair Testing Practices in Education*.

Jung, Carl Gustav: Swiss psychiatrist (1875–1961) who was a follower of Freud but eventually broke those ties after disagreements over some of the central tenets of Freud's psychoanalytic theory. Jung went on to develop Jungian Analytic Psychology.

Jungian Analytic Psychology: Originating from the ideas of Carl Jung, this psychoanalytic theory focuses on the role of the larger culture, spirituality, dreams, and symbolism in understanding the human psyche. Jung believed that through exploring the unconscious, people's psychological health could be improved. Thus, the goal of analytic psychology is to help people develop appropriate contact with their unconscious so that they are neither overwhelmed by it nor completely unaware of its forces.

Justice: Counselors adhering to the principle of justice will not discriminate against clients and will ensure that all clients receive equal treatment.

K

Keat, Donald: Adapted the BASIC ID for use with children by using the acronym HELPING (Health, Emotions, Learning, Personal, Imagery, Need to Know, Guidance of ABCs) to indicate the same seven modalities as the BASIC ID.

Kinesics: Involves postures; body movements and positions such as facial expressions, eye contact, and gazes; and touch. Many cultures have norms that dictate the expression of kinesics. For example, in many cultures it is considered disrespectful to look a person directly in the eye.

Kohlberg, Lawrence: Proposed a stage theory of moral development (1981), which suggests that developmental improvements in cognitive functioning lead to increases in moral development. Kohlberg's theory outlines three levels of development (i.e., preconventional, conventional, and postconventional), and each level has two stages. While Kohlberg's theory of moral development is the most influential, it has been criticized for being too male centered.

Kolmogorov-Smirnov Z Procedure: A nonparametric statistical test that is similar to the Mann-Whitney U test but more appropriate to use when samples are smaller than 25 participants.

Krumboltz, John: Developed the social learning theory of career counseling. Krumboltz espoused that individuals' learned experiences lead them to develop specific career beliefs, which influence their career decisions.

Krumboltz's Social Learning Career Theory: A career decision-making theory that focuses on the learning process and emphasizes the role of behavior and cognitions in career decision making. Social learning theory teaches clients how to implement career decision making techniques in their own life.

Kruskal-Wallis Test: A nonparametric statistical test analogous to an ANOVA and used when there are three or more groups per independent variable as well as an ordinal scaled dependent variable.

Kübler-Ross, Elisabeth: A Swiss-born psychiatrist who is known for her work on grief. She proposed that individuals facing loss (e.g., death, loss of a loved one, unexpected life transition) will experience grief. The Kübler-Ross model outlines the stages of grief: shock and denial, anger, bargaining and guilt, hopelessness, and acceptance.

Kurtosis: The degree of peakedness of a distribution. Distributions can be *mesokurtic* (normal curve), *leptokurtic* (tall and thin), and *platykurtic* (flat and wide).

L

Labor Market: Involves a geographic location (local, regional, state, national, international) where workers compete for paid work and employers compete for qualified workers.

Laissez-Faire: A group leadership style in which the group leader takes little or no leadership/responsibility for the group agenda, goals, or rules.

Language Development: Language development has been conceptualized through three differing theoretical approaches. *Learning theory* approaches exert that children acquire language skills by observing and imitating others who are using language. *Nativist* approaches maintain that children are born with an innate language acquisition device, predisposing them to language acquisition. *Interactionist* approaches propose that a combination of learning and nativist approaches are responsible for language development through social and cultural influences.

Latent Content: The symbolism in dreams that is harder to understand and interpret.

Law of Effect: Introduced by Edward L. Thorndike, proposes that if a response to stimuli results in a satisfying state/reward, the response is likely to be repeated in a similar situation. On the other hand, a response that results in an unpleasant consequence is unlikely to be repeated again.

Lazarus, Arnold: Created multimodal therapy.

Learning: A relatively permanent change in behavior or thinking resulting from an individual's experiences.

Least Restrictive Environment: A term that mandates students, as much as possible, remain in regular classrooms if their needs could be met there with only limited accommodation.

Leisure: Engaging in activities as a means of passing time; leisure activities are often referred to as hobbies.

Levinson, Daniel: American born, studied adult male development and presented a combination task/stage theory.

Lewin, Kurt: Credited with the invention of training groups (T-groups), which gave rise to the encounter and sensitivity groups of the 1960s and 1970s. His research resulted in the identification of predictable stages of group work and specific change markers for individual clients.

Liability: Professional counselors have the legal obligation to act with due care in professional practice. Professional counselors who fail to practice due care can be held legally and financially responsible for any damages to the client that were incurred during the counseling process.

Liability Insurance: A form of insurance that is designed to provide protection from third-party claims arising from unintentional injuries or damages to a client.

Libel: Defamation through writing.

Licensure: The process by which a government agency grants a counselor permission to practice and/or render specific counseling services. A license protects the public by ensuring that only qualified professionals can legally provide counseling services.

Life-Career Rainbow: A concept developed by Donald Super (1953) to illustrate how an individual's six major life roles (i.e., child, student, leisurite, citizen, worker, and homemaker) can vary over a person's lifetime.

Life Script: A term created by Eric Berne that refers to a script individuals develop at a young age based on their interactions with others, which forms a blueprint for future interactions with people.

Lifespan, Life-Space Career Theory: Developed by Donald Super (1953), this developmental theory exerts that individuals engage in a lifelong process of career development. As a result, the theory includes five developmental stages (i.e., growth, exploration, establishment, maintenance, disengagement) and 16 substages that extend from birth to death.

Lifestyle Analysis: An Adlerian technique that is used to interview clients about early life memories (prior to the age of 10 years), perceptions of their relationships with their parents and siblings, family dynamics, experiences in school and society, and beliefs about themselves.

Likert Scale: Commonly used to measure attitudes or opinions, this scale typically includes a statement regarding the concept in question followed by answer choices that range from strongly agree to strongly disagree. Sometimes called a Likert-type scale.

Lindemann, Eric: A pioneer in the development of crisis models, he observed that mental health professionals can help those people affected by traumatic events to grieve and mourn properly, thereby preventing further mental health complications.

Linking: A counseling technique used in group therapy to connect member themes, issues, and similarities to facilitate shared perspectives, commonalities, and goals.

Live Observation: Supervisors meet privately with supervisees to discuss particular cases, meet with supervisees in a group format, watch videotapes of supervisee counseling sessions, and/or actually sit in during a supervisee session with a client.

Locus of Control: The degree of control an individual believes he/she has over their environment.

Locus of Responsibility: Who or what is accountable for events that occur in an individual's life.

Loevinger, Jane: A developmental psychologist who proposed 10 stages of ego development, which stressed the internalization of social norms and the maturing conscience in personality development.

Logotherapy: An existential approach developed by Victor Frankl that focuses on individuals' search for meaning in their lives. Logotherapy assists clients in restoring meaning to their lives by viewing their problems from a larger spiritual context.

Longitudinal Design Studies: A research method that involves repeated observations of a population over long periods of time. Longitudinal designs can be categorized further as trend (i.e., involves assessing the *general population* over time), where new individuals are sampled each time data is collected, cohort (i.e., involves assessing the *same population* over time), or panel studies (i.e., involves studying the *same individuals* over time).

Long-Term Memory: Enables an individual to store a large amount of information for relatively permanent amounts of time, depending upon how efficiently the person learned the information.

Lorenz, Konrad: Carried out a famous set of experiments on imprinting, the process by which a duck or gosling attaches to the first moving object it encounters shortly after hatching.

Low-Context Communication: Style of communication that values the explicit, literal meaning of a word. In low-context communication, individuals "say what they mean, and mean what they say." There is little to be read into the verbal message.

M

Machismo: A traditional Latin American gender role, in which males are competitive, powerful, and decision makers and breadwinners for the family.

Maintenance: A behaviorist term that refers to clients' ability to perform desired behaviors without continual reinforcement or help from others.

Major Life Activity: Walking, seeing, hearing, speaking, breathing, working, performing manual tasks, learning, and caring for oneself.

Making the Rounds: A technique used in group counseling where group members take turns sharing their perspectives on a given focused topic.

Malpractice: Occurs when professional counselors fail to follow accepted professional standards and do not provide the expected standard of care, resulting in injury to the client.

Mandatory Ethics: The minimum standards that a counseling professional must adhere to in order to practice in an ethical manner.

Manifest Content: The symbolism in dreams with meaning that is easily perceived.

Manipulation: A challenging group member behavior that typically stems from the need for control and anger and promotes group tension and conflict.

Mann-Whitney U Test: A nonparametric statistical test that compares two groups on a variable that is ordinally scaled. This test is analogous to a parametric independent t-test.

Marathon Group: A type of group therapy used in the 1960s and 1970s that involved meeting together for extended periods of time, usually between 24 and 48 consecutive hours, throughout which members were expected to become more authentic and engage in true self-disclosure.

Marginalization Model: A model of acculturation in which individuals reject cultural values and customs of both cultures.

Marianismo: A traditional Latin American gender role, in which females are nurturing, emotional, and sexually pure.

Marriage and Family Therapist: Works with individuals, couples, and families from a systems theory perspective, helping clients develop more effective patterns of interaction with significant others and family members.

Masculinity: The features typically affiliated with a male, such as aggression, rationality, competitiveness, and independence. In the Latino culture, this term is referred to as *machismo*.

Maslow, Abraham: A humanistic theorist who is known for the development of the hierarchy of needs. The hierarchy of needs proposes that higher order needs (e.g., achievement, self-actualization) cannot be attained until lower order needs (e.g., food, shelter, safety) are met. Maslow also coined the term *self-actualization*, which refers to recognizing and moving toward one's full potential.

Maximal Performance Test: A type of assessment that yields information regarding the client's best attainable score/performance (e.g., on an achievement or aptitude test).

May, Rollo: An American psychologist who was a leader in the existential counseling approach. May studied the concept of anxiety in depth, noticing that it often interferes with people's ability to accomplish goals. However, May also believed that experiencing moderate amounts of anxiety was beneficial. His book *The Meaning of Anxiety* describes the role of anxiety as a motivator.

Mean: The arithmetic average of a set of scores. It is computed by summing the values of all scores and then dividing this sum by the total number of scores.

Measurement: The process of defining and estimating the magnitude of human attributes and behavioral expressions.

Med-Arb: Uses both mediation and arbitration to resolve conflict.

Median: The middlemost score when the scores are ordered from smallest to largest, or largest to smallest.

Mediation: The use of an objective, uninvolved person to help with conflict resolution with the goal of working toward determining specific desires and good solutions.

Mental Disorder: A "clinically significant behavioral or psychological syndrome or pattern that occurs in an individual and that is associated with present distress (e.g., a painful symptom) or disability (i.e., impairment in one or more important areas of functioning) or with a significantly increased risk of suffering death, pain, disability, or an important loss of freedom. In addition, this syndrome or pattern must not be merely an expectable and culturally sanctioned response to a particular event, for example, the death of a loved one" (APA, 2000, p. xxxi).

Mental Health Practitioner: A person trained to treat individuals with mental health issues and mental illnesses.

Mental Measurements Yearbook (MMY): An informational resource that provides assessment information on commercially available instruments. The *MMY* includes information regarding the test name, acronym, test author and publisher, copyright date, purpose, intended test population, administration time, forms, prices, test reliability and validity, norming data, scoring and reporting services, and available foreign language versions.

Mental Status Exam (MSE): Used by professional counselors to obtain a snapshot of a client's mental symptoms and psychological state. The MSE addresses the following areas: appearance, attitude, movement and behavior, mood and affect, thought content, perceptions, thought processes, judgment and insight, and intellectual functioning and memory.

Merrill, George A.: A pioneer and forerunner in career guidance. He developed a curriculum that combined academic instruction with technical and vocational training.

Mestizo: A person who is born of Native American and Caucasian parents.

Meta-Analysis: Involves statistically comparing the results across several similar studies for particular outcome or dependent variables.

Microaggression: Involves insults and aggressive acts against minorities. Microaggression is a subtle form of racism and is often automatic and unconscious. Examples include invalidating racial issues and maintaining stereotypic assumptions.

Midbrain: Portion of the brain that connects the hindbrain and forebrain, controls eye muscles, and relays auditory and visual information to the brain's centers for higher level thinking.

Milan Systemic Family Counseling: Developed by the Milan group in Italy, this model of family counseling focuses on exploring family members' perceptions of each other and their interactional patterns, as well as asking questions to increase their awareness of unhealthy family behaviors. The Milan approach is sometimes referred to as long brief therapy because counselors only meet with families once per month.

Milgram Obedience Study: An infamous, unethical research study in which Stanley Milgram sought to investigate blind obedience through a series of shocks (15-450 volts). "Learners" (who were a part of Milgram's team) pretended to be shocked by "teachers" (participants) when responding with incorrect answers. Although most participants showed signs of internal struggle, 65% "shocked" learners at the maximum level. There was no debriefing of the study.

Minnesota Model (MM): A forceful confrontation-based counseling model.

Minnesota Point of View: A career guidance theory considered a directive counseling approach, derived by Edmund Williamson from the work of Frank Parsons. It proposes that counselors should share their wisdom with clients to help them reach a career decision.

Minor Consent Laws: State laws that allow minors of a certain age to consent to various community health services, including mental health treatment, without parental consent.

Minuchin, Salvador: Developed structural family counseling.

Miracle Question: A technique used in SFBT to help clients begin to think about how to solve their problems. Usually, the question is some variation of "If a miracle happened and you woke up to find that your problem was solved, what would be different?"

Mixed-Method Research: Blends or mixes designs from quantitative and qualitative research. The most important characteristic of mixed-method research is that it can strengthen what either of the research designs provides individually. Generally two types of mixed-method research designs are considered: (a) *concurrent design* (quantitative and qualitative data are collected at the same time) and (b) *sequential design* (either quantitative or qualitative data are collected first). When researchers employ qualitative research strategies first, they are using an exploratory design. When researchers introduce a study with quantitative research strategies, they are using an explanatory design.

Mode: The most frequently occurring score. If a data set has two most frequently occurring scores, it is said to be *bimodal*. If a data set has more than two frequently occurring scores, it is *multimodal*.

Modeling: Demonstration of a particular skill or behavior so that it may be learned and passed on.

Model Minority Myth: The common perception that Asian Americans have excelled in U.S. society and experience few difficulties in relation to adjustment. The myth perpetuates the notion that Asian Americans no longer experience discrimination and thus no longer need social services.

Model of Adult Transitions: Developed by Hopson and Adams (1977), this model outlines seven developmental stages (i.e., immobilization, minimization, self-doubt, letting go, testing out, search for meaning, and internationalization) that conceptualize how individuals handle crises.

Modern Classism: A theory of classism that proposes those of lower status may exhibit classism as well as those of upper status.

Monochromic Time: An orientation toward time in a linear fashion (use of schedules, advanced planning of activities).

Monopolizing: Occurs when group members demonstrate behaviors such as neediness, demandingness, excessive talkativeness, and control through a focus on the self. These behaviors usually involve underlying anxieties.

Moral Development: The emergent process of distinguishing right from wrong, and acting in accordance with those distinctions. Prominent theories of moral development include Kohlberg's cognitive approach, Gilligan's feminist approach, Piaget's cognitive approach, and Freud's psychoanalytic approach.

Moreno, J. L.: Created the Theater of Spontaneity, the earliest form of psychodrama.

Motivational Interviewing (MI): A counseling approach used in addiction counseling that is rooted in person-centered principles yet is distinctly directive.

MRI Interactional Family Therapy: A strategic family therapy approach developed by Jay Haley. MRI encourages the exploration of family interactional patterns to understand and effectively resolve family issues.

Mulatto: A person with both White and African lineages.

Multicultural Counseling: The awareness and incorporation into the counseling process of diverse cultural identities. All counseling can be viewed as multicultural counseling in that all helping relationships involve two or more individuals with different worldviews as a result of ethnicity, race, social class, gender, sexual orientation, and religion. Often referred to as the "fourth force" in counseling. Often referred to as the "fourth force" in counseling.

Multigenerational Transmission Process: In Bowen family systems therapy, this term refers to a process by which family emotional patterns and levels of differentiation are transferred and maintained over generations.

Multimodal Therapy: A form of technical eclecticism developed by Arnold Lazarus. Using this model, clients are assessed in seven domains, which can be easily remembered by the acronym BASIC ID: behavior, affect, sensations, imagery, cognitions, interpersonal relationships, and drugs/biological functions/nutrition/exercise. By determining which domains clients think they need most assistance with, counselors develop a multimodal treatment plan that draws techniques and interventions from myriad theories to target the concerns in each domain.

Multiple Analysis of Covariance (MANCOVA): A statistical test similar to an ANCOVA but involving multiple dependent variables.

Multiple Analysis of Variance (MANOVA): A statistical test similar to an ANOVA but involving multiple dependent variables.

Multiracial: Individuals who are from multiple racial lineages.

Myelination: Insulation of neurons to enhance speed of neural transmissions.

Myers-Briggs Type Indicator (MBTI): A paper-and-pencil personality inventory that is based on Carl Jung's personality theory. The MBTI informs people about their preferences for thinking and acting. Specifically, the inventory yields scores on the dimensions of introversion (I) v. extraversion (E), sensing (S) v. intuition (N), thinking (T) v. feeling (F), and judging (J) v. perceiving (P).

Myers-Briggs Type Theory: A psychological theory derived from the work of Carl Jung by Katharine Briggs and her daughter, Isabel Myers. The theory proposes that four dimensions shape what individuals pay attention to in the world and how they make decisions about what they see. These dimensions include introversion (I) v. extroversion (E), sensing (S) v. intuition (N), thinking (T) v. feeling (F), and judging (J) v. perceiving (P). The four dichotomous dimensions yield a total of 16 different psychological types, which are denoted by an abbreviation of four letters (e.g., INFP). Briggs and Myers theorized that for each of the 16 psychological types, one guiding or dominant function usually develops as does a secondary, auxiliary function.

N

Narrative Career Counseling: Based on the principles of social constructivism, this theory views a client's career as a story that includes a client's past, present, and future career development. Therapy focuses on restoring the client's vocational story.

Narrative Therapy: A postmodern and social constructionist approach developed by Michael White and David Epston, narrative therapy is concerned with how individuals author their lives, proposing that people construct stories about themselves and their lives. This approach encourages people to reauthor their problem-saturated stories in order to promote greater wellness.

National Association for College Admission Counseling (NACAC): The professional association for individuals who work in the college admission specialization. NACAC is not affiliated with ACA.

National Board for Certified Counselors (NBCC): A credentialing organization for professional counselors seeking certification. The NBCC's leading credential is the National Certified Counselor (NCC). To obtain this credential, counselors must meet specific educational criteria as well as pass the National Counselor Examination (NCE).

National Career Development Association: A division of ACA that promotes career development throughout the lifespan. This professional organization offers professional development activities, publications, research, public information, professional standards, and advocacy to the public and professionals who deliver career services.

National Certified Counselor (NCC): A counselor who has been certified by the National Board for Certified Counselors (NBCC).

National Counselor Examination (NCE): An exam that a counselor must pass to receive the National Certified Counselor (NCC) credential.

National Defense Education Act (NDEA) of 1958: Passed in response to the Soviet Union's launching of *Sputnik;* sought to expand K–12 counselor education programs by offering reimbursement to programs that offered counselor training institutes and stipends to graduate students.

National Employment Counseling Association (NECA): A professional association chartered by ACA in 1966 to make strides in the field of employment counseling by providing members with helpful resources, promoting research and knowledge related to effective career counseling techniques and tools to best serve job seekers and society, staying abreast of legislation affecting employment counselors, and creating a community in which professionals can network and share ideas

National Rehabilitation Counseling Association (NRCA): A division of ACA founded in 1958 to help individuals with disabilities become as independent and self-reliant as possible through counseling interventions and advocacy.

National Training Laboratory (NTL): A professional organization that offers a certificate program for business professionals and a master's degree in organizational development.

National Vocational Guidance Association (NVGA): The first career-guidance organization, it worked to legitimize and increase the number of guidance counselors by offering credentialing.

Naturalistic Study: A type of study in which the researcher observes and documents a behavior or phenomenon in its natural setting.

Nature vs. Nurture: A controversial debate concerning the importance of nature (innate qualities) versus nurture (environmental characteristics) in determining individual differences in human development.

Nazi Medical War Crimes: Involved exploiting and deceiving prisoners during World War II in Nazi Germany to understand how the human body would react to various conditions.

Needs Assessment: The systematic process for identifying gaps between "what is" and "what should be" in a program. It allows the professional counselor to explore the target population's perception of the problem and determine whether or not needs are currently being met by an existing program.

Negative Reinforcement: Occurs when the removal of a stimulus (e.g., loud noise) increases the likelihood that a behavior will reoccur.

Neglect: The most prevalent type of abuse, involves not taking care of a child's needs, either physically, medically, educationally, or emotionally.

Negligence: Occurs when professional counselors fail to use reasonable care and/or protect a client from foreseeable harm, resulting in injury to the client.

Negotiation: A form of conflict resolution that involves compromise by involved individuals.

Neo Personality Inventory–Revised (NEO-PI-R): Commonly used to measure the "Big Five" (openness, conscientiousness, extraversion, agreeableness, and neuroticism) in clients. Clinicians can use the results to help formulate useful interventions to help clients improve the quality of their lives.

Neutrality: In Milan family counseling, the objective position that counselors adhere to when working with families.

Nigrescence: A racial identity model that provides a description of stages that Blacks experience as they come to understand and embrace their Black identity.

No Child Left Behind (NCLB) Act of 2001: NCLB aims to improve the quality of U.S. primary and secondary schools by increasing the accountability standards of states, school districts, and schools and requiring states to develop and administer assessments in basic skills to all students.

Nominal Scale: Classifies data without respect for order or equal interval units (e.g., gender).

Nonexperimental Research Designs: A type of quantitative research design that is intended to observe and outline the properties of a variable. No intervention is involved, and thus no variables or conditions are manipulated.

Nonlabor Force: The number of individuals who are not actively seeking employment. This includes institutionalized individuals (e.g., those in prisons or psychiatric hospitals), stay-at-home spouses, children, and those serving in the military.

Nonmaleficence: The foundational principle upon which counselors operate. It means to do no harm to clients.

Nonparametric Statistics: Statistical tests that are used when researchers are only able to make a few assumptions about the distribution of scores in the underlying population. Specifically, their use is suggested when nominal or ordinal data are involved or when interval or ratio data are not distributed normally (i.e., are skewed).

Nonprobability Sampling: A quantitative sampling method that typically involves accessible, convenient samples and does not use randomization. Nonprobability sampling methods include *convenience* (the selection of an easily accessible population that most likely does not fully represent the population of interest); *purposeful* (the selection of a sample from a population based on who will be most informative about a topic of interest; participants are selected because they represent needed characteristics); and *quota* (drawing the needed number of participants with the needed characteristic [e.g., gender, race] from the convenience sample).

Nonstandardized Tests: Unlike standardized tests, these tests allow for variability and adaptation in test administration, scoring, and interpretation. Nonstandardized tests do not permit an individual's score to be compared to a norm group.

Normal Curve (Bell Curve): When a normal distribution is graphed, it forms a normal (bell-shaped) curve. The normal curve is symmetrical, with the highest point occurring at the graph's center. The lowest points lie on either side of the graph. The curve is also asymptotic, meaning that the tail approaches the horizontal axis without ever touching it.

Normal Curve Equivalent: A type of standardized score that ranges from 1 to 99 and has a mean of 50 and a standard deviation of 21.06.

Normal Distribution: A distribution that forms a bell-shaped curve, with nearly all scores falling close to the average and very few scores falling toward either extreme of the distribution.

Norm-Referenced Assessment: A test in which an individual's score is compared to the average score (i.e., the mean) of the test-taking group.

Norms: (1) The rules for individual member and group behavior, communicating to members what is and is not socially acceptable within the group environment. (2) The typical score/performance against which all other test scores are evaluated.

Nuclear Family Emotional System: The basic emotional unit of a family system. It is formed based on the parental subsystem's degree of differentiation. Bowen asserted that individuals are normally attracted to partners who have the same level of differentiation as they do.

Null Hypothesis: A statement that "There is no relationship" between an independent variable (IV) and a dependent variable (DV). It is notated as H_0.

Nuremberg Code: A set of ethical principles for research using humans that resulted from the Nuremberg trials following World War II. The code guarantees research participants' choice to be involved in a research study (i.e., voluntary consent) as well as the right to terminate their participation in the study at any time.

O

OARES: An acronym for a counseling model (Open-Ended Questions, Affirm, Reflective Listening, Elicit Self-Motivational Statements, Summarize) that outlines motivation interviewing (MI) techniques.

Objective Personality Tests: Standardized, self-report instruments that often use multiple-choice or true/false formats to assess various aspects of personality to identify personality types, personality traits, personality states, and self-concept.

Objective Tests: Tests that include questions that have one correct answer (e.g., multiple choice, true/false, matching). An objective test provides consistency in administration and scoring to ensure freedom from the examiner's own beliefs or biases.

Object Relations: A neo-Freudian theory that maintains individual's personalities are developed through early parent-child interactions. Therefore, healthy personality development is dependent on satisfying interpersonal relationships. Objects are defined as people or things that meet a child's need; object relations theorists are concerned with how children represent and relate to the objects in their environment. Major contributors to this theory are W. R. D. Fairbairn, Otto Kernberg, Melanie Klein, Margaret Mahler, and D. W. Winnicott.

Observation: Includes member and leader feedback to the group.

Observational Learning: Learning that occurs as a function of observing, retaining, and, in some situations, replicating novel behavior executed by others.

Occupation: The primary activity that engages one's time. Often, occupations refer to a group of similar positions/jobs found across different organizations and industries (e.g., manager).

Occupational Information: Facts about a position, job task, career field, or industry used to assist clients in making decisions regarding future employment. Occupational information commonly includes, but is not limited to, duties and nature of work, work settings and conditions, education and training, methods of entry, salary and benefits, advancement opportunities, and employment outlook.

Occupational Information Network (O*NET): An electronic source of occupational information that houses current information and skill requirements for 1,170 occupations. The O*NET database is published by the U.S. Department of Labor and is updated semiannually.

Occupational Outlook Handbook (OOH): A U.S. government source for career information that provides occupational information on 270 broad occupations. The OOH is published by the U.S. Bureau of Labor Statistics and is revised every two years.

Occupational Stress: The chronic physiological and psychological strain that results from ongoing job-related stressors. The experience of ongoing occupational stress can lead to a phenomenon known as burnout.

One Drop Rule: A hierarchical social system that implied being Black was unfortunate, and as a result those possessing one drop of Black blood were labeled as Black and of a lower social status.

One-Stop Delivery System: U.S. Employment Service program that provides a variety of labor exchange services under one roof in easy-to-find locations.

Open Groups: Leaders allow members to enter and leave at various points while continuing a primary group focus.

Operant Conditioning: Developed by B. F. Skinner, this theory of learning maintains that all learning is contingent on the consequence of a particular behavior. As a result, operant conditioning uses consequences to modify the occurrence and type of behavior.

Opinion Seeking: Involves self- or other-disclosure of group member values in relation to a group task. Often, members want to know what others believe or value in order to gain insights into others' worldviews.

Oppression: The condition of being subject to a group of people who have access to social power and authority. Oppression can occur *by force* (i.e., imposing a role, experience or condition on someone) or *by deprivation* (i.e., not providing someone with a necessary experience or resource).

Ordeal: A paradoxical technique that asks clients to complete an undesirable, but health-promoting task before participating in the worrisome behavior.

Ordinal Scale: Classifies and assigns rank-order to data (e.g., Likert-type scales).

Organization: According to Piaget, one's ability to order and classify new information.

Outcome Evaluation: A type of program evaluation that measures the effectiveness of a program at the conclusion of the program.

Out-Group: The group to which an individual feels least similar.

Outlier: An extreme data point that distorts the mean by inflating or deflating the typical score.

Outside Witness: A technique used in solution-focused therapy that involves bringing in family members, friends, or even previous clients to help current clients gain outside perspectives on themselves.

Overcorrection: An aversive behavioral technique that requires the client to return the environment to its original condition prior to the undesirable behavior and then to make the environment better. Alternatively, the client who engages in an inappropriate behavior (e.g., does not hang up a coat in the closet) may be asked to repeatedly practice a positive behavior (e.g., hang up the coat 10 times).

P

Pacing: The pace or rate at which the group process moves. At times, leaders will speed up the pace, while at other times the leader will slow the pace to allow group members to focus on a particularly relevant topic.

Pairing: Used in group therapy to form smaller groups within the larger group to engage in activities or focused sharing.

Panel Study: Involves studying the same individuals over time.

Paradoxical Intention: A therapeutic technique in which counselors prescribe the symptom (e.g., client suffering from insomnia is asked to stay up all night). By asking clients to actively engage in the symptom behavior, they are able to recognize the control they possess over the symptom.

Paralanguage: The nonverbal cues used in communication to convey meaning and emotions. Examples of paralanguage include volume, tempo, intonation of speech, prolongation of sound, disfluencies (e.g., utterances such as *uh* and *um*), and pitch (highness or lowness of one's voice).

Paraphrasing: A basic counseling skill that involves repeating back the essence of what a client has said in the counselor's own words to convey understanding, check the accuracy of the counselor's comprehension, and summarize the significant elements that have been disclosed by the client.

Parenting Styles: Four parenting styles have been proposed: authoritarian (parents are restrictive and lack outward expressions of warmth; authoritative (parents display warmth and moderate control, explaining the reasoning behind their decisions to the child); permissive (parents display little control and, at most, moderate warmth); and uninvolved (parents show little if any interest in their children and are indifferent or rejecting toward them).

Parsons, Frank: Referred to as the "father" of vocational guidance, Parsons is known for his trait and factor approach, which proposes that individuals choosing a career must obtain self-understanding, an understanding of the world of work, and true reasoning (i.e., the ability to combine an understanding of self with knowledge about the world of work). Parsons also authored the well-known book *Choosing a Vocation*.

Participant Observation: A role that researchers may play in observational research by which they both actively participate in the experience they are studying and observe the experience.

Participatory Action Research (PAR): A qualitative research tradition that focuses on change of the participants and researcher as a result of qualitative inquiry. PAR involves a collaborative approach to problem solving between the researcher and other key stakeholders.

Pavlov, Ivan: A Russian physiologist best known for first describing the phenomenon of classical conditioning through his studies on the salivation of dogs.

Peer Mediation: Involves an objective, third-party individual who helps individuals in conflict to negotiate, compromise, and problem solve. Peer mediation is typically used in the school system to instill better conflict resolution skills in students.

Percentage Score: The raw score (i.e., the number of correct items) divided by the total number of test items.

Percentile Rank: Indicates the percentage of scores falling at or below a given score. Percentile ranks range from less than 1 to greater than 99 and have a median score of 50.

Performance Assessments: Nonverbal form of assessment that entails minimal verbal communication to measure broad attributes. The client is required to perform a task rather than answer questions using pencil-and-paper methods.

Peripheral Nervous System: The part of the nervous system consisting of a network of nerves that connect the central nervous system to the rest of the body.

Perls, Fritz: A German psychiatrist/psychotherapist known for developing Gestalt therapy. Perls created Gestalt therapy as a reaction to psychodynamic approaches. Perls stressed taking into account the whole person in therapy.

Personal Construct Psychology: Based on the work of George Kelly (1955), this theory proposes that individuals develop constructs (i.e., theories) to understand how the world works and to anticipate events. Constructs are comprised of two bipolar points (i.e., happy versus sad); individuals place events and people at either extreme or a point in between.

Personal Fable: An egocentric belief by which adolescents believe they are personally unique and exempt from the consequences of risky behaviors. Examples include the thought "Nobody understands me" or the belief that one cannot contract STDs from having unprotected sex.

Personalismo: A value in the Latino culture that refers to the importance of having compassion and caring for those in the community.

Personality Inventories: A group of inventories that identify a person's unique characteristics and styles of relating to others, tasks, and situations. Personality inventories are frequently administered in career counseling to facilitate the vocational decision-making process.

Personality Tests: See PERSONALITY INVENTORIES.

Personality Typology: Devised by Carl Jung, consists of two attitudes (introversion and extraversion) and four functions comprised of two pairs (sensation/intuition and thinking/feeling).

Personal Unconscious: A Jungian term that is synonymous with Freud's unconscious. The personal unconscious is unique to the individual and includes information (e.g., memories, desires, drives) that, at one time, has been conscious but has been forgotten or repressed.

Person-Centered Therapy: Another term for the client-centered counseling developed by Carl Rogers.

Phenomenological Perspective: In client-centered counseling, how counselors approach clients from the perspective of how they *perceive* an event rather than the event itself.

Phenomenological Philosophy: The notion that a person's perceptions of an event are more important than the event itself.

Phenomenology: A qualitative approach used to discover or describe the meaning or essence of participants' lived experiences with the goal of understanding individual and collective human experiences for various phenomena.

Physical Abuse: Involves causing injury and harm in the form of bruising, sprained muscles, bones being broken, burns, cuts, being shaken, hit, thrown, asphyxiation, and genital mutilation.

Piaget, Jean: The Swiss philosopher and scientist known for his theory of cognitive development. Piaget's theory, which describes cognitive development of children, proposed that cognitive growth is dependent on a child's ability to order and classify new information (i.e., organization). Piaget proposed that children moved through a series of four developmental stages: sensorimotor, preoperational, concrete operational, and formal operational.

Pilot Study: Smaller than a full-scale study, designed to assess the feasibility of expanding a small study to a much larger scale.

Placebo Effect: The positive effects of a treatment felt by participants even though no treatment is actually administered.

Planned Happenstance: The ability to capitalize on a chance event that is unpredictable. Krumboltz maintained that exercising planned happenstance would lead to an increase in career options as well as opportunities.

Planned Themed Group: A group that is planned around a content theme and focuses on helping members resolve problems in a specific area. Membership in such a group is restricted to individuals with a demonstrated need in this themed area.

Play Therapy: A therapeutic approach that uses play to help the client (usually a child) to give voice to and work through their concerns with the assistance of the counselor. Some play therapists select the toys and activities with which the client engages (i.e., directive play therapy), whereas other counselors allow the child to choose the toys and guide the play (i.e., nondirective play therapy). Many counselors include both directive and nondirective components in their sessions.

Polychromic Time: The value of time as secondary to relationships among people.

Positive Blame: A technique used in SFBT to reinforce clients' capabilities when successfully making a change or engaging in a behavior that brings them closer to their goal.

Positive Connotations: Similar to reframing, counselors attach positive motives to a family member's problematic behavior.

Positive Reinforcement: Occurs when the addition of a stimulus (e.g., reward) immediately following the response increases the likelihood that the behavior will reoccur.

Positivism: A philosophical paradigm that proposes an objective truth exists and can only be understood if directly observable (i.e., "truth" must be directly measurable). Positivism has been closely tied to quantitative research.

Post Hoc Analysis: Allows examination of every possible pairing of group means for a particular independent variable after one has concluded that there are *main effects* (i.e., significant difference among two or more groups comprising a single independent variable) in an ANOVA.

Post-Positivism: A philosophical paradigm that proposes truth can only be approximated because of inherent errors present when measuring reality. The concept of measurement error in terms of validity and reliability is emphasized.

Poverty: The struggle to meet and maintain basic needs such as food, clothing, and shelter. May also include a lack of access to educational and employment opportunities.

Power: (1) In the group context, power is viewed as having control over the resources the group values or desires (e.g., materials, role/position, information, ability, punishment/reward). (2) A term related to errors in hypothesis testing, referring to the likelihood of detecting a significant relationship between variables when one is really there.

Power Negotiations: A form of conflict resolution that occurs when individuals vie to have the strongest influence on the outcome and may involve deceitful tactics like relaying false information and cheating.

Power Tests: Assessments that are designed to prevent test-takers from attaining perfect scores by including difficult test items that few individuals can answer correctly.

Practice Effects (Memory Effects): Research participants know what to expect and learn something from a pretest that helps to improve their performance on future tests.

Preconscious Mind: Combines characteristics of both the conscious and unconscious minds.

Pre-Experimental Designs: A type of experimental design that does not use random assignment, thus failing to control for internal validity threats. Three common types of pre-experimental designs include (a) *one-group posttest only design* (a group receives an intervention and change is measured), (b) *one-group pretest-posttest design* (a group is evaluated before and after an intervention), and (c) *nonequivalent groups posttest-only design* (no attempt is made to begin the study with equivalent groups of participants, one group receives an intervention and change is measured, while another group serves as a control and receives no intervention yet is assessed at the same time as the other group).

Prejudice: Involves the formulation of preconceived opinions or judgments about an individual or group without sufficient knowledge.

Prescribing the Symptom: In strategic family counseling, the counselor tells clients to keep engaging in their troublesome behavior; by following the counselor's advice, clients recognize that they are *choosing* to perpetuate the problem.

Pretend Technique: Encourages clients to simulate their symptoms in order to realize that they are able to exert some control over what they say and do, as well as over the outcome of the situation.

Primary Reinforcer: Reinforcers that satisfy a primary need (such as food).

Privacy Policy: For HIPAA, outlines with whom protected health information may be shared.

Privilege: The ability of an individual to receive benefits, which are not as readily available to others, as a result of his or her membership in a dominant group.

Privileged Communication: A legal term that protects counselors from having to reveal information about a client during a legal proceeding.

Proactive Inhibition: A loss of memory that occurs when old information interferes with newly learned information.

Probability Sampling: A type of quantitative sampling that involves sampling a known population using randomization. Probability sampling methods include (a) *simple random sampling* (every member of the population has an equal chance of being selected); (b) *systematic sampling* (every *n*th element is chosen); (c) *stratified random sampling* (a population is divided into subgroups and the professional counselor draws randomly from the subgroups); and (d) *cluster sampling* (the professional counselor identifies existing subgroups and not individual participants. Cluster sampling can involve multiple stages; this might include a two-stage random sample (e.g., randomly select 60 schools and then 20 classes from those schools), three-stage random sample (e.g., randomly selecting 200 school districts, then 20 schools from each district, and then 10 classes per school), and so forth.

Problem Externalization: A technique used in narrative therapy in which the counselor seeks to help clients distance themselves from their problems. Problems, in relation to clients, are seen as a separate, outside entity. Counselors use externalizing questions (e.g., "How has depression been holding you back these past few months?") to separate the problem from the client.

Problem-Saturated Stories: A term used in narrative counseling to refer to self-narratives that are harmful and detrimental to client well-being.

Process Evaluation: A type of program evaluation that focuses on the process of implementing the program to evaluate its progress at various points. Also known as process monitoring.

Professional Associations: Counseling organizations that seek to further the counseling profession by uniting members through a shared identity, advocating on behalf of the profession, providing professional development opportunities, and offering access to counseling-related resources.

Professional Counselor: A professional who works with individuals and families to overcome developmental and unexpected life changes in order to facilitate client wellness and personal growth. Specifically, professional counselors work to prevent psychological problems and promote healthy human development.

Program Goals: Broad statements that indicate how the career intervention program will respond to population's needs.

Program Objectives: Specific, measurable, action-oriented steps that must be attained to accomplish a particular program goal.

Projective Personality Tests: Test that assess personality factors by interpreting a client's response to ambiguous stimuli. These personality tests are rooted in psychoanalytic psychology and ensure that the ambiguity of the presented stimuli will tap into the unconscious attitudes and motivations of the client.

Prosocial Behavior: Demonstrating a concern for the welfare of others and acting in a way that benefits others. Prosocial behaviors initially occur in early childhood but are not consistently demonstrated until later childhood.

Protected Health Information (PHI): Individually identifiable health information protected by HIPAA.

Proxemics: The physical distance between people as they interact. Cultural norms often dictate how close individuals will stand to each other when communicating.

Psychiatric Nursing: A specialization within the nursing profession that is concerned with the prevention and treatment of psychiatric disorders. Psychiatric nurses specialize in the identification of mental health issues and delivery of services to patients with severe psychological disorders.

Psychiatrist: Trained medical doctors licensed to treat clients with severe mental disorders. Unlike other mental health professionals, psychiatrists are able to prescribe medications, perform physical examinations, and order laboratory testing for clients.

Psychoanalyst: Professionals trained to assist clients in resolving issues through psychoanalysis (i.e., exploring client unconscious conflicts). Psychoanalysts are required to earn a terminal degree in the mental health field, train at a psychoanalysis institute, and engage in personal psychoanalysis by a trained psychoanalyst.

Psychodrama: (1) An exercise used in Gestalt therapy that asks clients to act out their internal conflicts and related emotions in order to gain clarity on their unfinished business.(2) An approach used in group therapy to bring about mental and emotional catharsis for the purpose of tension relief.

Psychodynamic Model: One of the earliest theories of family counseling, developed by Nathan Ackerman. This model was based on the key concepts of Freud's psychoanalytic theory and explores the role of anxiety, defense mechanisms, and unconscious conflicts and desires in the functioning of individuals and families.

Psychoeducational Groups: A group work model that emphasizes skill development through various nonthreatening skill-building exercises but at the same time encourages discussion, sharing, and feedback among members. The goal of psychoeducational group work is to prevent psychological disturbance by increasing self-awareness, knowledge, and skills about specific developmentally relevant issues.

Psychological Aging: Categorization of aging based on one's perception of personal age.

Psychological First Aid (PFA): A crisis response method that focuses first on meeting individuals' survival needs (e.g., food, water, shelter, safety), then on psychological needs, and finally on establishing support networks.

Psychologist: A mental health professional who specializes in diagnosing and treating emotional disturbances, behavioral problems, and learning disorders. Psychologists may have a master's degree or doctorate in psychology.

Psychosexual Theory: Freud's theory of personality development. Freud proposed that people need to resolve psychological conflicts resulting from the psychic energy focused within different parts of the body as one matures. Freud proposed a model of five stages of development—oral, anal, phallic, latent, and genital—and theorized that failure to resolve the psychological conflicts encountered in each stage can result in fixation.

Psychotherapy Groups: Groups that are designed to treat those who may be experiencing severe or chronic problems in their lives. Ordinarily, members in psychotherapy groups display more dysfunctional behavior and typically carry a psychiatric (i.e., *DSM*) diagnosis.

Punctuation: The conviction by individuals that their verbal communication, especially during a conflict, occurs in reaction to someone else.

Punishment: The addition or removal of a stimulus that decreases the frequency of a given behavior. It is also commonly referred to as an aversive behavioral technique.

Purposive Sampling: Also known as purposeful sampling, this sampling method is used primarily in qualitative research to obtain information-rich cases that allow for maximum depth and detail regarding a particular phenomenon. Among the approximately 15 types of purposive sampling are convenience, maximum variation, homogenous, stratified purposeful, purposeful random, comprehensive, typical case, intensity, critical case, extreme or deviant, snowball, criterion, opportunistic, theoretical, confirming/disconfirming case.

Pushbutton Technique: An Adlerian counseling technique used to teach clients that they play a role in maintaining their problems. Specifically, clients are encouraged to focus on their positive feelings and push the positive pushbutton rather than the negative pushbutton.

Q

Qualitative Research: A type of research that is concerned with how behavior occurs, uses data that is represented in words rather than numbers, and usually takes the form of interview transcripts, field notes, pictures, video, or artifacts. The sampling is usually not randomized like that of a quantitative study, and the research can be more exploratory, meaning a hypothesis is not being tested.

There is also greater subjectivity as the professional counselor plays a key role in the research.

Quantitative Research: Focuses on capturing the relationship between two variables that can be measured numerically. Typically quantitative research tests a hypothesis looking at a descriptive or causal relationship among variables. Results usually involve numbers that are typically displayed in a statistically significant manner.

Quasi-Experimental Designs: A type of experimental design that is used when it is impossible or inappropriate to randomly assign participants to groups. Quasi-experimental designs are often used with nested data (e.g., classrooms, counseling groups) or naturally occurring groups (e.g., males, African-Americans, adolescents). Two common types of quasi-experimental designs include (a) *nonequivalent groups pretest-posttest control* (sometimes called *comparison group designs*), in which the counselor keeps groups intact, administers a pretest, administers treatment to one group (control group design) or to at least two groups (comparison group designs), and then gives the groups a posttest and (b) *time series design*, characterized by repeatedly measuring before and after an intervention for one group (one group interrupted time series design) or including a control group for comparison (control group interrupted time series design).

Questioning: (1) A basic counseling skill in which counselors ask open-ended (invite client to elaborate on a topic) and closed-ended (gather factual/specific information and elicit a minimal response) questions to obtain further information from clients, often for clarification or to encourage deeper exploration of topics. (2) When an individual questions his or her sexual orientation.

Quid Pro Quo: The propensity of individuals to treat others like they are treated. This "reciprocal behavior" is present in all families, and often it is unspoken.

R

Race: A social and political classification that identifies individuals by distinguishing physical characteristics such as skin color, facial features, hair texture, or eye shape.

Racial Identity: A sense of belongingness and communality that is derived from one's identification with one or more racial groups.

Racial Interaction Theory: Developed by Helms (1995), this theory conceptualized how Whites and people of color, at various racial identity development statuses, might interact and if those interactions would be adaptive or maladaptive.

Racism: Involves the belief that a group of people are inferior to one's own group due to recognized or perceived differences in physical characteristics. Racism also involves the ability to act on such beliefs overtly or covertly, intentionally or unintentionally.

Random Assignment: Involves assigning participants to different groups, such as a treatment or control group, to ensure that groups (errors) are equal and that any systematic group differences are due to chance.

Random Selection: Involves selecting participants from a population so that every member of the population has an equal chance of being selected.

Range: The most basic indicator of variability that is computed by subtracting the largest value from the smallest value and adding 1 place value.

Rating Scales: Used to evaluate the quantity of an attribute. Rating scales can measure a broad range of behavioral domains (broad-band rating scales) or a specific dimension of targeted behaviors (narrow-band behavioral rating scales).

Rational Emotive Behavior Therapy (REBT): A counseling theory developed by Albert Ellis, which addresses the relationship between thinking and emotion. REBT, formerly known as rational-emotive therapy (RET), exerts that somewhere between the activating event and the emotional consequence, people engage in self-talk, either rational or irrational, that triggers certain emotions. These rational beliefs (rBs) or irrational beliefs (iBs) are what produce people's emotional responses to any given event. Therefore, REBT seeks to reduce clients' interpersonal difficulty by modifying their irrational thoughts.

Rational Emotive Imagery: A technique used in rational emotive behavior therapy (REBT) to assist clients in disputing their irrational beliefs. Clients are asked to imagine their worst fears and to stay with the difficult, painful emotions that surface. The counselor requests that the client begin to repeat the new

rational belief over and over until a shift from "dysfunctional" emotion to a "self-helping" emotion occurs.

Ratio Scale: A scale that possesses the qualities of nominal, ordinal, and interval scales and has an absolute zero point (e.g., height).

Raw Score: A score that has not been converted into a derived score.

Reactive Theories: Theories of human development, such as Skinner's operant conditioning, that propose that people are passive and react to environmental stimuli to accommodate to changes.

Readiness Tests: A group of criterion-referenced achievement assessments that indicate the minimum level of skills needed to move from one grade level to the next.

Reality Distortion: Occurs when a therapeutic group provides an example of social reality that is not achievable in the outside world.

Reality Therapy: Based upon choice theory, the basic premise of reality therapy is that people make choices in order to meet their five basic needs: survival, belonging, power, freedom, and fun. According to Glasser, the founder of reality therapy, people can make decisions that result in healthy, positive lives, or they can make decisions that result in self-destructive, unhappy lives.

Reciprocal Inhibition: A principle development by Wolpe that assumes a person cannot engage in two mutually exclusive events simultaneously. Reciprocal inhibition is used in systematic desensitization, a technique used to treat phobias.

Reciprocity: Allows a counselor who is licensed in one state to work in another state without having to reapply for licensure or fulfill additional requirements.

Recycling: A term used by Donald Super to refer to the idea that an individual can reenter a developmental stage they have been through before.

Redundancy Principle: A family's tendency to interact with each other in the same way. It is unusual for those patterns of behavior to change or expand.

Reflecting: A basic counseling skill that involves verbal responses to clients that indicate that the professional counselor understands their emotions, thoughts, or the meaning behind their disclosures.

Regression Studies: Used to predict outcomes (dependent variable) from a predictor variable(s) (independent variable). The three types of regression include (a) *bivariate regression* (how well scores from an independent variable [predictor variable] predict scores on the dependent variable [criterion variable]), (b) *multiple regression* (involves more than one predictor variable when each predictor variable is weighted [*beta weights*] in a regression equation to determine the contribution of each variable to the criterion variable), and (c) *logistic regression* (used when the dependent variable is dichotomous, this form of regression may be similar to a bivariate or multiple regression).

Rehabilitation Act of 1973 (PL 93-122): Prohibits the discrimination of persons with disabilities in federally sponsored programs. Sometimes referred to as Section 504.

Reinforcement Schedule: Dictates when and how often a behavior is reinforced. A continuous schedule of reinforcement administers a reinforcer immediately following each desired response. An intermittent reinforcement schedule does not administer a reinforcer every time a desired response occurs. The four types of intermittent schedules are (a) *fixed ratio* (reinforcer is administered each time a participant makes a certain number of responses), (b) *variable ratio* (reinforcements are presented periodically, occurring every *n*th time), (c) *fixed interval* (reinforce individuals after a fixed period of time), and (d) *variable interval* (vary the time interval of the reinforcement administration).

Reinforcer: A term used in operant conditioning referring to a stimulus that increases the likelihood that a behavior will reoccur. Reinforcers can be primary or secondary.

Relabeling/Reframing: A strategic family therapy technique that involves interpreting a family's situation in a new way to encourage family members to view their problem in a more favorable light.

Relational Approaches: Propose that relationships play an important role in the career development and decision-making processes of children and adolescents.

Reliability: The consistency of scores attained by the same person on different administrations of the same test. Reliability is concerned with measuring the difference between (error) an individual's observed test score and true test score: X = T + e. There are several different types of reliability: (a) *test-retest reliability* (sometimes called *temporal stability*) determines the correlation between the scores obtained from two different administrations of the same test, thus evaluating the consistency of scores across time; (b) *alternate form reliability* (sometimes called *equivalent form reliability* or *parallel form reliability*) compares the consistency of scores from two alternate, but equivalent, forms of the same test; (c) *internal consistency* measures the consistency of responses within a single administration of the instrument; two common types of internal consistency are *split-half reliability* and *interitem reliability* (e.g., KR-20 and coefficient alpha); and (d) *inter-scorer reliability*, sometimes called *inter-rater reliability,* is used to calculate the degree of consistency of ratings between two or more persons observing the same behavior or assessing an individual through observational or interview methods.

Reliability Coefficient: Used to report reliability of a set of scores on a test, a reliability coefficient ranges from 0 to 1.00. The closer the coefficient is to 1.00, the more reliable the scores.

Religion: The institutionalized expression of an organized set of beliefs and ritualized practices that guide a person or group's understanding of reality. Major religions include Buddhism, Christianity, Confucianism, Hinduism, Islam, Judaism, and Taoism.

Reparative Therapy: Sometimes referred to as conversion therapy, this type of therapy attempts to change one's sexual orientation. Reparative therapy is not empirically supported, and the American Psychiatric Association considers it to be ineffective and potentially harmful to the client.

Replacement Needs: Occur in the labor market when workers are needed to replace those who have left the workforce due to retirement, returning to school, assuming household and child-raising duties, or choosing not to work.

Research Hypothesis: A testable, concise statement involving the expected relationship between two or more variables. Research hypotheses can be *nondirectional* (e.g., "There is a significant relationship between amount of sleep and career satisfaction") or *directional* (i.e., "There is a significant *positive* relationship between amount of sleep and career satisfaction").

Research Question: A statement that identifies what a research study hopes to examine. There are three major types of research questions: (a) *relational research questions* examine the relationship between variables; (b) *descriptive research questions* examine and describe what already exists; and (c) *causal research questions* attempt to determine the cause-and-effect relationship among variables.

Resilience: An individual's ability to adapt to negative life conditions or spring back from adverse situations in order to return to a positive level of functioning.

Resiliency Factors: Assist an individual in overcoming risk factors and maintaining positive functioning in spite of adverse circumstances.

Resistance: Clients' unwillingness to work on their problems; characterized by behaviors that remove discomfort or conflict (e.g., missing a counseling session). Resistance prevents clients from initiating change in their own lives.

Response Cost: A behavioral technique that reduces undesirable behaviors by removing a positive reinforcement. Response cost is often used in conjunction with a token economy.

Responsibilities of Users of Standardized Tests (RUST): A policy statement published by the Association for Assessment in Counseling and Education (AACE) to ensure counselors use standardized tests with clients in an accurate, fair, and responsible manner.

Restructuring: An intervention that involves actively working to change the structure of a family system.

Retrieval Theory: Asserts that information is held permanently in long-term storage and that forgetting is the result of insufficient cues that fail to retrieve the information. The tip-of-the-tongue phenomenon is commonly associated with this theory of forgetting.

Retroactive Inhibition: A loss of memory that occurs when new information interferes with information previously learned.

Reverse Role-Playing: A technique used in rational emotive behavior therapy (REBT) to help clients dispute their irrational beliefs. Typically, the counselor pretends to be the client and holds dearly to the client's irrational beliefs while the client plays the counselor and attempts to persuade the "client" to think in a more rational manner.

Rights Negotiations: A form of conflict resolution that involves the legality of what is right and uses norms, policies, and rules.

Risk Factors: Include characteristics that place individuals at a high risk of developing mental disorders, academic problems, or personal-social difficulties.

Ritual Prescriptions: Paradoxical assignments that indicate certain actions to be taken on specific days and times by particular family members. The goal of rituals is to help families try new ways of behaving and interacting.

Roe and Lunneborg's Occupational Classification System: A relational approach to career development that sought to predict occupational choices from biological, sociological, and psychological differences. Ultimately, Roe and Lunneborg (1990) desired to show that individuals in certain occupations have commonalities in the way they were raised. They proposed three parental attitudes (concentration, avoidance, and acceptance), as well as an occupational classification system that is comprised of eight Groups (i.e., the groups classify the primary focus of activity involved in each occupation) and six Levels (i.e., the Levels classify the amount of responsibility and ability required by the occupation).

Rogers, Carl: An American psychologist who founded the client-centered approach to counseling. Rogers emphasized the importance of the client in counseling sessions and implemented a nondirective counseling approach, which placed the responsibility for personal growth on the client. Rogers maintained that a professional counselor should demonstrate empathy, unconditional positive regard, and genuineness.

Role: Broadly refers to a set of interconnected behaviors, rights, and obligations that are associated with a particular social situation. Super (1953) described six major roles (i.e., child, student, leisurite, citizen, worker, homemaker) that individuals play throughout their lifetime. Individuals are often required to play multiple roles in their day-to-day life and can experience (a) role overload (expectations associated with multiple roles exceed an individual's time and energy as well as ability to perform the role adequately); (b) role conflict (demands and expectations of an individual's multiple roles conflict with each other); or (c) role spillover (carryover of one role's demands and expectations into another role).

Role Ambiguity: Occurs when a group member is not sure of the role expectations or behavior requirements they should fulfill.

Role Conflict: Occurs when group members experience conflicting demands of various roles, such as when a member who prefers to avoid emotional expression is encouraged to self-disclose reactions to emotionally laden group content and process; that is, the roles a member plays come into conflict with each other.

Role Differentiation: A term used in group counseling to describe the process of group members adopting different roles (e.g., storyteller, advice giver, leader) within the group.

Role-Playing: A behavioral technique used in counseling in which the counselor demonstrates specific skills and applications. The counselor then has the client practice these skills and applications in a safe environment so that the client can gain experience and feedback, which allows for the application of skills and behaviors outside of a therapeutic environment.

Role Salience: The importance individuals assign to each life role throughout their lifetime.

Rules: A term used in general systems theory to refer to the unique family rules every family establishes and expects its members to abide by. Family rules establish a template of expected family behavior and provide members with predictability and a foundation for interacting with each other. Some rules preserve and enhance family functioning, while others do the opposite.

S

Sarcasm: An attempt to mask and not express anger.

Satisfaction: In the theory of work adjustment, an employee's contentment with the work environment.

Satisfactoriness: In the theory of work adjustment, the employer's satisfaction with an individual's job performance.

Satir, Virginia: An American psychotherapist who believed in the innate goodness of humans, their desire to grow and learn, and their ability to change. Satir identified four types of dysfunctional communication patterns that family members often adopt: (a) Placaters agree with and try to please everyone; they also mollify people, are unsure of themselves, and often lack self-confidence. (b) Blamers are critical of other people, charge others with wrongdoing, and fail to take any responsibility for their actions. (c) Intellectualizers or super-reasonables approach situations in a detached manner, rationalizing everything and never allowing their emotions to be shown. (d) Distracters want to avoid dealing with situations, so they distract others by introducing unrelated, irrelevant topics. Satir worked with family members to replace these toxic styles of communication with a more health-enhancing one, the congruent communicator.

Saturation: In qualitative research refers to data collection reaching a point of redundancy—that is, researchers have reached the point where no new data refute findings of previously collected data.

Saving Face: A cultural value commonly endorsed by Asian Americans whereby an individual's behaviors are seen as being reflective of the family and thus one should protect the honor of the family.

Scale: A collection of items or questions that combine to form a composite score on a single variable. Scales can measure discrete or continuous variables and can describe data quantitatively or qualitatively.

Scaling Questions: A technique used in narrative therapy and SFBT that asks clients to approximate their progress. The question is used to keep track of clients' progress and help them continue making small changes. An example of a scaling question is "On a scale of 1 to 10 (with 10 meaning that your problem is solved), how close are you to meeting your goal?"

Schema: A mental structure that processes or integrates experiences, information, or perceptions. Schemas are often adapted as new information is encountered.

Schlossberg's Transition Theory: Proposes four different types of transitions that can occur throughout an individual's life: anticipated, unanticipated, chronic hassles, and nonevents. Schlossberg (1984) maintained that an individual's willingness and ability to deal with transitions depends on the situation, self, support, and strategies.

School-to-Work Act of 1994: Provides all students with equal opportunities to participate in programs that combine academic and occupational education, combine school-based learning with work-based learning, and prepare students for postsecondary education.

Screening and Selection Measures: Help leaders assess potential member attitudes toward groups, assess pro-social attitudes and problematic group member interpersonal behaviors, and select group members.

Scriptotherapy: A cognitive technique, commonly referred to as therapeutic writing, through which clients are asked to write down their thoughts for clarity and self-reflection.

Secondary Reinforcers: Reinforcers associated with a primary need (e.g., a token that can be traded in for food).

Section 504 (of The U.S. Rehabilitation Act of 1973): A civil rights act that protects individuals with disabilities from being discriminated against or denied equal access to services and opportunities because of their disability.

Seek Unique Outcomes (Exception Questions): A technique used in solution-focused brief therapy that asks clients to identify times when their problems were not present or were less pronounced.

Self-Categorization: An important piece of social identity theory, in which the "self" is seen as an object to be classified into membership in a social group that gives worth to the person.

Self-Disclosure: A counseling skill that involves sharing personal information with clients to help connect with the client, give feedback, or provide the client with alternative perspectives or ideas.

Self-Efficacy: Term developed by Bandura that refers to an individual's confidence in his or her ability to perform a given behavior or accomplish a given task.

Self-Instructional Training: A technique used in cognitive-behavior modification to teach clients how to alter their maladaptive thoughts and behavior in order to replace negative self-talk with self-enhancing cognitions.

Self-Narratives: In narrative therapy, the stories clients construct about themselves and their lives. Self-narratives assist clients in developing a consistent identity. *Thin descriptions* refer to internalized self-narratives that are imposed on a person by others (e.g., society). *Thick descriptions* refer to more complex self-narratives that involve both the client's interpretations of themselves and the labels that are put on them by others.

Self-Psychology: A neo-Freudian approach developed by Heinz Kohut that asserts psychological disorders result from unsatisfied developmental needs (e.g., a lack of empathy in the caregiver-child relationship). Diverging from Freud, Kohut believed that clients benefit more from analyst empathy than interpretation.

Self-Talk: Also referred to as self-statements, this concept refers to the internal messages people give themselves.

Semantic Differential: A scaling technique that is rooted in the belief that people think dichotomously and commonly includes the statement of an affective question followed by a scale that asks test-takers to place a mark between two dichotomous adjectives. Also referred to as *self-anchored scales*.

Semi-Structured Interviews: Use pre-established questions and topic areas; however, the professional counselor can customize the interview by modifying questions, altering the interview sequence, or adding follow up questions.

Sensory Memory (Trace Memory): The ability to retain environmental stimuli that is detected by sensory receptors (e.g., background music, the color of shoes other people are wearing). While the sensory memory has a large capacity for unprocessed information, it is only able to retain this information for a few seconds.

Separation: A legal process that allows couples to remain legally married while living separate lives.

Separation Anxiety: Occurs developmentally in most infants, ages 12 to 24 months, and involves extreme distress when they are separated from a primary caregiver.

Separation Model: A model of acculturation in which individuals refuse to adapt to cultural values outside of their own cultural values.

Setting Tone: The group leader setting a style of interaction (i.e., structure) for group members to follow.

Sex: An individual is biologically a male or female as determined by hormones, genetics, and physical makeup.

Sex Chromosomal Diseases: Genetic disorders that involve some genetic anomaly occurring on the sex-determining pair of chromosomes and usually affecting male or female characteristic displays or sexual reproduction. Common examples include Turner syndrome (XO) and Klinefelter's syndrome (XXY).

Sex Roles: Derived from an individual's biological makeup and physiological functioning (e.g., a woman's sex role would include her ability to conceive and birth a child.)

Sexual Abuse: Occurs when any adult in a position of power engages in sexual activity (e.g., incest, sexual assault, fondling) with a minor. Sexual abuse is not restricted to physical contact and can include exposure, voyeurism, and child pornography.

Sexual Exploitation: Forcing a child into prostitution or pornography.

Sexual Identity: Encompasses physical identity (biological makeup of an individual), gender identity (belief about one's gender), social sex role identity (sex roles individuals adopt due to culture), and sexual orientation identity (sexual and emotional attraction to individuals of the same and/or opposite sex).

Sexual Minority Individuals: Include lesbian, gay, bisexual, queer, and those questioning their sexual orientation.

Sexual Orientation: An individual's consistent attachment and sexual attraction to members of the same or opposite gender or to both gender(s). Sexual orientation can be thought of as a continuum that has four orientations: homosexual (individual is attracted to members of the same sex), bisexual (individual is attracted to members of the same and opposite sex), heterosexual (individual is attracted to members of the opposite sex), and questioning (individual is questioning his or her sexual orientation).

Shame Attack Exercise: A technique used in REBT that involves asking clients to participate in an activity that normally creates anxiety in order to help them realize that the outcomes are not nearly as embarrassing or devastating as they imagine.

Shaping: Gradually changing an individual's existing behavior by reinforcing responses that are similar to the desired response. Shaping is often referred to as successive approximation.

Short-Term Memory: A temporary information storage system that allows information to be retained for seconds to minutes. The limit of short-term recall is disputable but is most likely 7 ± 2 bits of information. The transfer of information from short-term to long-term memory occurs more efficiently if an individual encodes and rehearses this information.

Significance Level: A threshold used for rejecting the null hypothesis in hypothesis testing, with values associated with a (typically .001, .01, or .05).

Single-Subject Research Designs (SSRD): Used to measure how either receiving treatment or not receiving treatment affects a single subject (client) or group of subjects (clients) who can be treated as a single unit. There are three commonly used types of SSRDs: (a) *within-series designs* examine the effectiveness of one intervention or program; (b) *between-series designs* compare the effectiveness of two or more interventions for a single variable; and (c) *multiple-baseline designs* assess data for a particular target behavior across various situations or individuals.

Situational Poverty: Occurs when lack of resources is due to an extenuating circumstance, such as a divorce, unexpected unemployment, or a death.

Skeleton Keys: Using techniques that have worked before and, as a result, may work in a variety of different contexts and situations.

Skewness: An asymmetrical distribution in which the data points do not cluster systematically around a mean. Distributions can be *positively skewed* with a greater number of data points clustering around the lower end or *negatively skewed* with a greater number of data points clustering around the higher end of the distribution.

Skinner, B. F.: Developed the theory of operant conditioning.

Slander: Defamation through a spoken statement(s).

SLAP: A helpful acronym to remind counselors of the major areas covered during a suicide risk assessment: Specific details, Lethality of plan, Availability of method, and Proximity to obtaining help.

Slavson, S. R.: Founder of the American Group Psychotherapy Association. He also provided group therapy to children and concluded that it was as equally effective as individual counseling.

Social Aging: Categorization of aging based on how one's chronological age is viewed within the societal, or cultural context.

Social Constructionism: A theory that refers to an individual making meaning of knowledge within a social context.

Social Identity Theory: Rooted in social psychology, this theory was created to understand discrimination within groups. Specifically, social identity theory proposes that people sort themselves into groups based on similar characteristics, such as ethnicity or gender.

Social Influence Model: Based on social psychology, this model was formulated by Stanley Strong in the 1960s and asserts that if counselors are viewed as having expertise and being attractive, they will have greater influence on the client.

Social Justice: The belief in an equitable world for all individuals and the corresponding goal of promoting fairness by addressing privilege and oppression.

Social Learning Theory: Developed by Albert Bandura, this theory is based on the notion that learning occurs through observation, imitation, and modeling. Specifically, if an individual observes a behavior that leads to a desired outcome, the individual will be more likely to observe, imitate, and model the behavior.

Social Worker: A professional who works to address and alleviate social injustice. Social workers help people overcome societal barriers, pursue social reform, and affect public policy.

Societal Regression: Occurs when a society that is experiencing too much stress regresses in its level of differentiation. Like families, Bowen thought that societies, too, could be either differentiated or undifferentiated.

Sociodramatic Play: Maintains that play is an imitation of adult tasks, facilitating mature social interactions between children. Parten (1933) described social play categories: nonsocial activity, parallel play, associative play, and cooperative play.

Socioeconomic Class or Status (SES): The hierarchical distinctions between cultural groups in society. Individuals in each SES can have a different worldview, conceptions of problems, perceptions of themselves, and needs to be met. The distinctions between classes are often determined by income, occupation, and education. Individuals in the same social class often share a variety of common assumptions, norms, and values.

Sociogram: A graphical representation of group member interaction patterns that are used to display member relationships and educate group members about the intricacies of group dynamics.

Sociometric Test: A study of actual behavior.

Sociometry: Gauges the extent of relationship among people or groups, or how people relate to one another, via a sociogram, which is a scientific, visual way to analyze and display these relationships.

Solution-Focused Brief Therapy (SFBT): A counseling theory developed by Steve deShazer that is based on the assumption that all individuals possess the ability and resources to solve their problems. SFBT maintains that people become immobilized by unsuccessful attempts to solve problems and that they need only find new solutions to achieve change and progress. Therefore, this theory is not concerned about the history of a problem or seeking insight into why a problem has arisen; the primary goal is client change and instilling hope in clients that change will happen. SFBT, as its name suggests, is short term, usually lasting no more than 10 sessions.

Soul: The quintessential nature of a person.

Speed Tests: Assessments that are designed to prevent test-takers from attaining perfect scores by including too many items to answer in the allotted time. Speed tests assess how quickly the test-taker can understand the question and choose the right answer.

Spiritual Bypass: The misuse of spiritual beliefs and practices to avoid addressing problematic psychological, physical, emotional, cognitive, relational, or behavioral issues.

Spiritual Identity: The degree of connection individuals have with their spiritual force.

Spirituality: A process that involves the continual search for meaning and deepens one's connection to the inner self, others, and the world. Spirituality also encompasses a sense of well-being and fulfillment.

Spitting in the Client's Soup: An Adlerian counseling technique used to point out certain client behaviors so that the behavior no longer seems as desirable to the client.

Split-Plot Design: A general category of experimental research designs that involve assessing a general intervention on the whole plot and assessing other treatments to subplots within the whole plot.

Splitting: A psychoanalytic term in which object representations are viewed dichotomously (e.g., all good or all bad, "black or white").

Spontaneous Content Group: Groups that do not have planned content themes and are designed to provide personal growth and support. Membership in a spontaneous group is generally dictated by the need for general development and member characteristics.

Spontaneous Recovery: In classical conditioning, this occurs when the previously weakened CS/CR connection is reestablished very quickly causing the CR reemerge.

Spurious Correlation: Occurs when a correlation overrepresents or underrepresents the actual relationship.

Stakeholders: Any individuals involved in or affected by the program. These are individuals to whom the program evaluator is accountable.

Standard Deviation: The most frequently reported indicator of variability for interval or ratio data.

Standard Error of Estimate: A statistic that indicates the expected margin of error in a predicted criterion score due to the imperfect validity of the test.

Standard Error of Measurement (SEM): A statistic that indicates how scores from repeated administrations of the same instrument to the same individual are distributed around the true score. The standard error of measurement is computed using the standard deviation and reliability coefficient of the test instrument.

Standardization: The process of converting raw scores to standard scores by finding the typical score attained by a group of test-takers and comparing future scores to the typical score.

Standardized Scores: Compare individual scores to a norm group through the use of formulas that convert the raw score to a new score. The standardized score specifies the number of standard deviations a score is above or below the mean.

Standardized Tests: A type of assessment that is designed to ensure the conditions for administration, test content, scoring procedures, and interpretations are consistent

Standard Occupational Classification (SOC) System: The classification system used by the O*NET to classify occupations. The SOC system uses a six-digit code to classify occupations into four levels: major group, minor group, broad occupation, and detailed occupation.

Standards for Educational and Psychological Testing: A set of standards designed to promote the appropriate and ethical use of tests, as well as to provide professionals with a set of guidelines for test development, evaluation, and use. These standards were developed through collaboration between the American Educational Research Association (AERA), American Psychological Association (APA), and the National Council of Measurement in Education (NCME).

Stanine: A type of standard score that divides the normal distribution into nine intervals with a mean of 5 and a standard deviation of 2.

Statistical Significance: The cutoff point (i.e., critical value); any value that exceeds the cutoff point will be noted as statistically significant.

Stimulus Discrimination: In classical conditioning, stimulus discrimination refers to the absence of the CR when a new stimulus, which resembles the original CS, is presented. In Little Albert's case, stimulus discrimination would have occurred if he had reacted to a white rat (the original CS) but not a white rabbit.

Stimulus Generalization: In classical conditioning, stimulus generalization refers to the tendency for the CS/CR connection to be generalized to other stimuli, which are similar to the original CS. For example, Little Albert was originally conditioned to fear a white rat but later generalized his response, leading him to also fear a white rabbit.

Stranger Anxiety: A phenomenon that occurs in infants around six months of age. Theorists purport that infants' fear of strangers is due to enhanced visual acuity, onset of object permanence, and increasing cognitive awareness.

Strategic Family Therapy: Developed by Milton Erickson, this approach emphasizes altering behavior and resolving presenting symptoms rather than helping clients gain insight and personal awareness. Using directive strategies tailored to each family, strategic family therapists aim to resolve the problem as quickly as possible. Consequently, this type of family counseling is generally short term in nature.

Strengths-Based Approach: A multicultural counseling approach that focuses on honing in and building on client strengths and successes to initiate change.

Stress Inoculation Training (SIT): A process that combines cognitive and behavioral techniques (e.g., cognitive restructuring, relaxation training, problem solving) in order to help clients learn how to cope with stress. Clients then begin using these new techniques while imagining stressful situations and are eventually asked to apply them to real life situations that trigger stress.

Structural Classism: A form of classism that maintains the current *status quo* or arrangement of classes.

Structural Family Counseling: Developed by Salvador Minuchin, this approach is concerned with examining and changing the structure and organization of families, including their hierarchies and subsystems. It is believed that dysfunction results from faulty organization; therefore, the counselor works to restructure the family's organization to bring about improved functioning.

Structural Maps: Visual representations of a family's coalitions, alignments, boundaries, and conflicts. Counselors use these maps to help assess the family's strengths, weaknesses, and needs.

Structure: How a family organizes itself. A family's structure involves elements such as how members interact with one another, family rules and rituals, who exerts authority, how permeable the boundaries are, and what subsystems exist. Ideally, Minuchin believed that a family's structure should have an internal hierarchy whereby the parents serve as the main sources of authority.

Structured Interviews: Use a series of pre-established questions that cover broad topic areas and are presented in an invariable, sequential order during each interview.

Subjective Tests: Tests that include open-ended questions that have more than one correct answer (e.g., essay questions). A subjective test is sensitive to rater and examinee beliefs.

Subpoena: A legal document that commands a person to appear in court to serve as a witness or provide the court with certain documents.

Subsystems: Distinct and somewhat independent parts of a larger system. In family therapy the most important subsystems are the spousal subsystem (i.e., husband and wife, partners), the parental subsystem (i.e., mother and father, partners), and the sibling subsystem.

Suicide: The taking, whether intentional or unintentional, of one's own life.

Suicide Assessment: Determining a client's potential for committing suicide.

Suicide Lethality: The likelihood that a client will die as a result of suicidal thoughts and behaviors.

Summarizing: A basic counseling skill that involves condensing the important aspects discussed over a substantial period of time into a succinct synopsis. Summarizing is often used at the end of a session to recap the important topics that were discussed, but it can also be used at the beginning and middle of a session to tie together important themes, patterns, feelings, facts, and plans.

Summative Evaluation: Involves the assessment of the entire program to determine the degree to which program goals and objectives have been met.

Sum of Squares (SS): The sum of the squared deviation scores, computed by subtracting the mean from each data point (deviation scores), squaring each deviation score, and adding them together.

Super, Donald: One of the first career theorists to develop a lifespan developmental approach to career counseling. He also proposed a career rainbow that represented the many roles an individual has throughout life. Super also developed several career inventories: Work Values Inventory, Career Development Inventory, and Adult Career Concerns Inventory.

Superego: A term used in psychoanalysis to refer to the conscience part of an individual's personality. The superego operates on the morality principle and, like the id, also exists in the unconscious.

Superiority Complex: In some individuals, when feelings of inferiority lead to overcompensation.

Survey Batteries: A collection of tests that measure individuals' knowledge across multiple subject areas and, as a result, do not assess any one subject in great depth.

Survey Research: A method of collecting quantitative data, in which a researcher selects a sample of participants and administers a series of questions to them. Survey research can be conducted via interviews or through administration of questionnaires and involves sampling a pool of participants to assess and understand their thoughts, feelings, and perceptions regarding the variable(s) under study.

Symbolic-Experiential Family Therapy: A family therapy approach developed by Carl Whitaker to help families strike a balance between independence and togetherness and to learn how to interact with each other in a meaningful and natural way, while moving away from the tendency to behave in the same monotonous patterns that led to the dysfunction.

Symmetrical Relationships: Relationships in a family between equals. These types of relationships may become competitive because there is not a dominant member.

Syncretism: A careless process by which counselors use theories and techniques they are unable to implement adeptly or by which they randomly use a diverse range of techniques without giving sufficient thought to why they are using them or how they will work together.

Systematic Desensitization: A technique developed by Joseph Wolpe to treat phobias. It is based on the principle of reciprocal inhibition (i.e., a person cannot engage in two mutually exclusive events simultaneously) and involves client exposure to increasingly fearful objects (i.e., fear hierarchy) while maintaining a simultaneous state of relaxation. Thus, the fear is systematically deconditioned using reciprocal inhibition—that is, the client cannot be fearful and relaxed at the same time.

T

Task Groups: Groups designed around and focused on accomplishing a specific task in an efficient and effective manner. Task groups use principles of group dynamics and incorporate such methods as collaboration, problem solving, and team building exercises to reach goals.

Tavistok Institute: An organization that promotes interdisciplinary training in group dynamics and leadership coaching for businesses.

Technology-Assisted Distance Counseling: Counseling occurring over the phone or online through e-mail, video, or chat programs.

Tenure: In the theory of work adjustment, how long an individual will remain with a company. Dawis and Lofquist (1984) proposed that the degree of an employee's contentment with the employer (satisfaction) and the degree of an employer's satisfaction with the worker (satisfactoriness) predict tenure. Tenure is said to be the principal indicator of work adjustment.

Termination Stage: The final stage in group development, which is characterized by closure of group process and the relationships members have established throughout the group experience.

Test: A subset of assessment used to yield data regarding an examinee's responses to test items.

Test Adaptation: The process of altering a test for a population that differs significantly from the original test population in terms of cultural background and language. The process includes translating language as well as empirically evaluating the cultural equivalence of the adapted test.

Test Bias: Occurs when the properties of a test cause an individual or particular group of individuals to score lower (negative bias) or higher (positive bias) on the test than the average score for the total population. This disparity in scores is due to factors that are not related to the true attribute being measured. The following are common types of test bias: (a) *examiner bias* occurs when the examiner's beliefs or behaviors influence test administration; (b) *interpretive bias* occurs when the examiner's interpretation of the test results provides unfair advantage or disadvantage to the client; (c) *response bias* occurs when clients use a response set (e.g., all yes or no) to answer test questions; (d) *situational bias* occurs when testing conditions or situations differentially affect the performance of individuals from a particular group; and (e) *ecological bias* occurs when global systems prevent members of a particular group of individuals from demonstrating their true skills, knowledge, abilities, and personalities on a given assessment.

Test Critiques: An informational resource that is designed to be a companion text to *Tests*. Each entry in *Test Critiques* contains an overview of the assessment, practical applications (e.g., intended population, administration, scoring, and interpretation procedures), and information regarding the instrument's reliability and validity.

Test Theory: Assumes that test constructs, in order to be considered empirical, must be measurable for quality and quantity (Erford, 2007); consequently, test theory strives to reduce test error and enhance construct reliability and validity. The two common types of test theory are (a) *classical test theory*, which postulates that an individual's observed score is the sum of the true score and the amount of error present during test administration, and (b) *item response theory*, also referred to as *modern test theory*, which applies mathematical models to the data collected from assessments in order to evaluate how well individual test items and the test as a whole work.

Test Translation: A process of reducing cultural bias in testing by translating test items into the language spoken by examinees.

Tests: An assessment resource that contains information on thousands of assessment instruments in the psychology, education, and business industries. *Tests* provides quick access to concise instrument descriptions that include the test title, author, publisher, intended test population, purpose, major features, administration time, scoring method, cost, and availability.

Tests in Print (TIP): A companion to the MMY, TIP offers a comprehensive listing of all published and commercially available tests in psychology and education. It provides information regarding the test title, intended population, publication date, acronym (if applicable), author, publisher, foreign adaptations, and references.

Theory-Based Models of Supervision: Extend the basic counseling theories to the supervisory relationship.

Theory of Career Decision Making: Developed by Tiedeman and O'Hara (1963), this theory is a descriptive approach that proposes two career decision-making stages: anticipating the choice and adjusting to the choice.

Theory of Psychosocial Development: Developed by Erik Erikson (1950), this personality theory is concerned with the impact of an individual's social experiences on ego development. Specifically, Erikson believed that the ego develops through a series of psychosocial crises, which are encountered throughout the lifespan. These crises are outlined in Erikson's eight stages of development.

Theory of Work Adjustment (TWA): A career development theory developed by Dawis and Lofquist (1984) that describes the relationship between individuals and their work environments. Specifically, TWA proposes that this relationship is reciprocal (i.e., complementary); therefore, both the individual and work environment must continue to meet each other's needs (i.e., correspondence).

Therapeutic Alliance: The relationship between the client and the professional counselor. The therapeutic alliance depends largely on the counselor's ability to express warmth and empathy, confront when necessary, make accurate interpretations and reflections, listen actively, work with clients to set goals, and recognize and reinforce client successes.

Therapeutic Factor: An element, generally created by the group leader or relationships with other members, which improves a group member's overall condition. Yalom (Yalom & Leszcz, 2005) classified therapeutic or curative factors as the instillation of hope, imparting of information, altruism, family reenactment, development of socialization techniques, imitative behavior, interpersonal learning, group cohesiveness, catharsis, and existential factors.

Therapeutic Letters: A technique used in narrative therapy in which the counselor writes letters to the client following counseling sessions. These letters review what was discussed in the session and highlight important moments. The ultimate goal of these letters is to keep the work that occurred during the session going long after the session has ended.

Thick Description: A self-narrative that involves clients' interpretations of themselves and the labels that are put on them by others.

Thin Description: A self-narrative that is imposed on a person by others (e.g., society) that the individual then internalizes.

Thorndike, Edward: Introduced the law of effect, which proposes that if a response to stimuli results in a satisfying state/reward, the response is likely to be repeated in a similar situation and that, on the other hand, a response that results in an unpleasant consequence is unlikely to be repeated again.

Thorne, Frederick: An early proponent of eclectic counseling.

Thought Stopping: A cognitive technique used to teach clients how to interrupt a pattern of negative self-statements or thinking; it usually involves the substitution of one thought for another.

Thurstone Scale: Measures multiple dimensions of an attitude by asking respondents to express their beliefs through agreeing or disagreeing with item statements. The Thurstone scale has equal-appearing, successive intervals and employs a paired comparison method.

Time-Lag Studies: Commonly used in developmental research, this type of study involves replications of previous studies on a modern-day cohort using the same parameters as the previous study.

Time-Out: A type of punishment procedure that removes the child from a rewarding context and places in an alternative context (e.g., a time-out chair) so that he or she is no longer able to receive any kind of positive reinforcement.

Token Economy: A behavioral technique that provides clients with rewards for demonstrating desired behavior. Specifically, a contract is arranged between the counselor and client, which establishes the number of tokens a client will receive in exchange for demonstrating certain behavioral goals. The client can then cash in tokens for a reward.

Tort: An act that results in injury to another person, property, or reputation, entitling the injured party to compensation. Torts are not considered criminal wrongdoings and cover both intentional and unintentional acts.

Tracking: A counseling technique that allows the counselor to keep up with and clarify client content through verbal clarifications.

Trait and Factor Theory: A career theory that is heavily influenced by the work of both Frank Parsons and Edmund G. Williamson. This theory maintains that an individual must gain self-understanding, knowledge about the world of work, and integrate this information (i.e., self-understanding and world of work) in order to choose an occupation that will result in satisfaction and success.

Trait and Type Career Theories: Also known as person-environment fit theories, this group of career theories assesses the traits or characteristics of individuals in order to "match" them with an occupation that has similar characteristics. Theories falling under the person-environment fit classification include the trait and factor theory, theory of work adjustment, Holland's theory of types, and Myers-Briggs type theory.

Transactional Analysis (TA): A cognitive theory developed by Eric Berne with roots in psychoanalysis. The focus of TA is on examining how clients interact with others. It is believed that if clients can change their styles of interaction, the result will be improved functioning. According to Berne, people operate from three common ego states in their interactions: parent, adult, or child.

Transactions: The interactions that occur between two or more people. Transactions between people can be complementary, crossed, or covert. *Complementary transactions* occur when two people interact with each other using the same, or complementary, ego state. *Crossed transactions* occur when someone functions from an ego state that is undesirable or unsuitable for the others' wants or needs. *Ulterior transactions* occur when people seemingly operate from one ego state but are actually just concealing their true ego state.

Trans-Affirmative Approach: Involves the counselor taking on the role of an advocate by being involved politically, teaching the client how to advocate, and rallying for equal community resources.

Transcrisis: Occurs when the traumatic event of an initial crisis is not fully dealt with and becomes submerged into a client's subconscious. Subsequent similar events then trigger these subconscious feelings.

Transference: A psychoanalytic term used to describe the displacement of emotions from one individual to another. Transference often occurs in counseling when a client brings feelings from a past relationship into the counseling relationship, often transferring those feelings onto the clinician. For example, a client might say to the counselor, "You treat me just like my father did when I was a child."

Transformation-Based Negotiations: A form of conflict resolution that deals with promoting "empowerment and recognition" of involved persons. Empowerment raises consciousness of what people can do and their personal value. Recognition deals with being able to connect to the situation and engage in true listening.

Transgender: A term used to describe a broad continuum of individuals whose gender identity and roles, to varying degrees, do not conform to cultural norms and expectations associated with their biological sex.

Transition Stage: The second group development stage that is characterized by the testing of boundaries and power structures that can range from subtle testing to full-blown rebellion and conflict. Group work authors have referred to this stage as storming, conflict, resistance, or power and control.

Transphobia: Discrimination against transsexual or transgendered individuals, based on their nonalignment with cultural expectations regarding gender and sexuality.

Trauma: A long-term crisis for which there is no resolution or balance of stressors and available resources. Persons experiencing a trauma often experience severe emotional and mental stress.

Trend Study: Involves assessing the general population over time, with new individuals sampled each time data are collected.

Triangle: A term used in Bowen family systems therapy to refer to a relationship system comprised of three people. Triangles are created when two family members are experiencing stress in their relationship and draw in a third member to help release the emotional tension. Bowen proposed that clients need to detriangulate, learn how to avoid becoming involved in triangles, and learn how to avoid triangulating others.

Tripartite Model of Multicultural Counseling Competence: Outlines three standards that inform multiculturally competent counselors, including self-awareness (e.g., the counselor is aware of his/her values and biases), knowledge (e.g., seeks to understand and appreciate the client's worldview), and skills (e.g., employs culturally appropriate assessments and interventions).

Triple Jeopardy: Individuals who are marginalized as a result of having triple minority status (e.g., being a racial minority, female, and having a disability).

True Experimental Designs: Also referred to as *randomized experimental designs*, these are the gold standard in that they involve at least two groups for comparison and random assignment. Common types of true experimental designs include (a) *randomized pretest-posttest control group design* (participants are assigned to two groups [one group serves as the control], and both groups are measured before and after an intervention), (b) *randomized pretest-posttest comparison group design* (participants are assigned to one of at least two groups, each group receives a distinct intervention, and the effectiveness of interventions is compared through the use of pre- and posttests), (c) randomized posttest-only control group design (involves the random assignment of participants to a treatment or control group, administering an intervention to one group and then measuring the outcome), (d) randomized posttest-only comparison group design (similar to a randomized posttest-only control group design but with at least two groups for comparison and no control group), and (f) Solomon four-group design (uses four randomly assigned groups so the presence of a pretest and the presence of an intervention can be assessed more rigorously).

Trustworthiness: The validity or truthfulness of qualitative findings. The four components of trustworthiness are (a) credibility (the "believability" of your findings), (b) transferability (the degree to which data transfer to other contexts and participants), (c) dependability (the degree of consistency of results over time and across researchers), and (d) confirmability (reflects that interpretation of the data is a genuine reflection of participants' views).

T Score: A type of standardized score that has an adjusted mean of 50 and a standard deviation of 10.

T-Test: Compares two means for one variable. *Independent t-tests* involve comparing two independent groups (usually assigned randomly) on one dependent variable. *Dependent t-tests* involve similar groups paired or matched in some meaningful way or the same group tested twice. T-tests provide a t-ratio.

Tuskegee Syphilis Study: An infamous, unethical research study in which physicians studying the long-term effects of syphilis (i.e., data from autopsies) told 400 African-American males with syphilis they were receiving treatment for "bad blood." Participants were never informed of their actual diagnosis and, even when penicillin was discovered as a treatment in the 1940s, the participants never received the drug.

Type I Error: A type of error (alpha, α) associated with hypothesis testing that occurs when a decision is made to reject a null hypothesis when that null hypothesis is in fact true.

Type II Error: A type of error (beta, β) associated with hypothesis testing that occurs when a decision is made to retain the null hypothesis that should have been rejected because the null hypothesis was indeed false.

Typical Performance Test: A type of assessment that measures one's normal performance.

U

Unbalancing: A restructuring technique used to better establish a proper family hierarchy.

Unconscious Mind: The most nebulous part of a person's mind. It contains memories, instincts, and drives that are exceedingly difficult to bring to a person's conscious awareness.

Unemployment Rate: The level of unemployment (i.e., workforce minus the number of currently employed individuals) divided by the workforce.

Unfinished Business: A term used in Gestalt therapy to refer to past, unresolved issues that interfere with an individual's present functioning. The purpose of Gestalt psychology is to help individuals with neuroses become integrated and self-supportive through resolving their unfinished business.

Unintentional Tort: A tort not planned or aimed to cause harm to the client.

Unstructured Interviews: Use no pre-established questions and tend to rely on the client's lead to determine a focus for the interview.

U.S. Rehabilitation Act of 1973 (Section 504): A civil rights act that protects individuals with disabilities from being discriminated against or denied equal access to services and opportunities because of their disability.

V

Validity: How accurately an instrument measures a given construct. Validity is concerned with what an instrument measures, how well it does so, and the extent to which meaningful inferences can be made from the instrument's results. The three main types of validity are (a) *content validity*, the extent to which an instrument's content seems appropriate to its intended purpose; (b) *criterion validity*, the effectiveness of an instrument in predicting an individual's performance on a specific criterion, either predictive or concurrent; (c) and *construct validity*, the extent to which an instrument measures a theoretical construct (i.e., idea or concept).

Validity Coefficient: Often used to report validity, this coefficient is a correlation between a test score and the criterion measure.

Values: Beliefs that guide an individual's behavior and emotional responses. Work values specifically reflect needs that a work environment must reinforce to ensure an individual's work satisfaction and success. They can be intrinsic (values satisfied from performing the work itself) or extrinsic (values satisfied as a result of completing the work).

Values Inventories: A group of inventories that assist individuals in identifying and prioritizing work-related values.

Variability: Measures the amount of spread in a distribution of scores or data points. The more dispersed the data points, the more variability a distribution has. The three main indicators of variability are range, standard deviation, and variance.

Variable: A construct that has at least two levels or categories and, therefore, can vary and be measured. The three primary types of variables are (a) independent variable (IV) (a construct that is manipulated or controlled in some way by the researcher); (b) dependent variable (DV) (the outcome variable that is influenced by an independent variable); and (c) extraneous variables (a variable that could affect the dependent variable and mask the affect of the independent variable on the dependent variable). Confounding variables, a type of extraneous variable, occur when two or more variables both affect the dependent variable simultaneously, but the effects cannot be distinguished.

Variance: A type of variability that is the standard deviation squared.

Vicarious Trauma: A stress reaction resulting from exposure to client disclosures of traumatic events. Counselors experiencing vicarious trauma experience long-term and pervasive attitudinal shifts.

Violence: Involves a premeditated or spur-of-the-moment intent to cause harm.

Visitors: A term used in SFBT to characterize clients who do not recognize that a problem exists and are not ready or willing to change.

Vocational Aptitude Testing: A set of predictive tests that are designed to measure one's potential for occupational success. Employers frequently use these tests to assist in the process of screening for competent, well-suited employees. Vocational aptitude testing can assess several distinct aspects of ability at one time (i.e., multiple aptitude tests) or assess one homogenous area of aptitude (i.e., special aptitude tests).

Vocational Construct System: A group of constructs proposed by George Kelly (1955) that assist individuals in finding purpose at work, evaluating career decisions and tasks, and developing a sense of identity.

Vocational Education Act of 1963: Expanded career education programs to include career services for elementary schools, technical institutions, and public community colleges.

Vygotsky, Lev: A Russian psychologist known for his constructionist, cognitive developmental theory, which purported that cognitive processes occur in a social context and are facilitated by language development. Vygotsky coined the term *zone of proximal development,* which refers to tasks children encounter that are too difficult for them to master alone. He maintained that children need the guidance and assistance of adults to learn these tasks (i.e., scaffolding).

W

Watson, John B.: Often referred to as the "father of American behaviorism," Watson avidly campaigned for his idea that psychology should only deal with what can be observed and accurately measured. Watson is also well known for his controversial "Little Albert" experiment, which attempted to condition a phobia into an 11-month-old infant.

WDEP System: The predominant technique used in reality therapy. W stands for wants: counselors ascertain what clients want and need and what actions they have been taking to fulfill their needs. D stands for doing: counselors examine clients' actions, thoughts, and feelings. E stands for evaluation: counselors encourage clients to evaluate their current behavior and whether it is healthy and responsible, often through the use of questioning. P stands for plan: clients come up with a plan for meeting their needs in new ways.

Wellness: A balance between the mind, body, and spirit, resulting in positive well-being. The field of counseling stems from a wellness perspective, viewing the client as searching for a balanced lifestyle rather than being mentally ill.

Whitaker, Carl: Developed symbolic-experiential family therapy.

White, Michael: With David Epston, developed narrative therapy, a postmodern and social constructionist approach.

Wilcoxon's Signed-Ranks Test: A nonparametric statistical test that is equivalent to a dependent t-test. This test involves ranking the amount and direction of change for each pair of scores.

Williamson, Edmund: Best known for his directive approach to counseling, the Minnesota point of view. Williamson's theory outlines five steps: assessing the problem and obtaining/reviewing client records and testing results; organizing and synthesizing the client information gathered to fully understand the problem; interpreting the problem; providing counseling to assist the client in reaching a solution; and following up with the client after a solution is reached.

Willowbrook Study: An unethical research study in which researchers used a school for children with mental disabilities, Willowbrook, to study the effects of hepatitis in a controlled setting. Parents who wanted to enroll their children in the school signed an informed consent to allow their children to be injected with the hepatitis virus. Parents were never informed of their right to decline the injections for their children, nor were they told the long-term effects of hepatitis.

Within-Subject Design: A general category of experimental designs that involve assessing changes that occur within the participants in a group as they experience some intervention.

Wolpe, Joseph: Applied classical conditioning procedures to psychotherapy.

Work: Activities that serve as one's regular source of livelihood; commonly associated with a job position.

Work Adjustment: The continuous process by which an individual achieves and maintains correspondence with the work environment.

Workforce: The workers who make up the labor market. It includes employed individuals as well as those seeking gainful employment.

Working Stage: A stage of group development characterized by committed members who work to accomplish personal and group goals and help other member to do so by giving feedback, working as a cooperative team, and facilitating a supportive environment of positive change.

Worldview: An individual's conceptualization of his or her relationship with the world. Two worldview models are typically incorporated into counseling programs: (a) Sue (1978) proposed that an individual's worldview was influenced by two intersecting dimensions: *locus of responsibility* (i.e., who or what is accountable for events that occur in an individual's life) and *locus of control* (i.e., the degree of control an individual believes he/she has over their environment); and (b) Kluckhohn and Strodtbeck (1961) maintained that individuals combine five components (i.e., human nature, relationship to nature, sense of time, activity, and social relationships) to create a unique worldview.

X

X-Linked Diseases: Genetic disorders that are passed through the maternal X-chromosome to males. Common examples include male pattern baldness and hemophilia.

Y

Yerkes-Dodson Law: States that memory and performance are optimized when an individual attains a moderate state of arousal. Low and high states of arousal are thought to suppress performance.

Z

Z-Score: A standardized score for which the distribution has a mean of 0 and a standard deviation of 1; it represents the number of standard deviation units above or below the mean at which a given score falls.

REFERENCES

Abudabbeh, N., & Aseel, H. A. (1999). Transcultural counseling and Arab Americans. In J. McFadden (Ed.), *Transcultural counseling* (pp. 283–296). Alexandria, VA: American Counseling Association.

Ainsworth, M. D. S. (1989). Attachment beyond infancy. *American Psychologist, 44,* 709–716.

Allport, G. W. (1979). *The nature of prejudice.* Cambridge, MA: Perseus Books.

American Association of State Counseling Boards. (2009). *Welcome to AASCB.* Retrieved August 27, 2009, from http://www.aascb.org

American Association of Suicidology. (2006). *Assessing and managing suicide risk.* Washington, DC: American Association of Suicidology.

American College Counseling Association (ACCA). (2006). *Supporting and enhancing the practice of college counseling.* Retrieved August 27, 2009, from http://www.collegecounseling.org

American Counseling Association. (2003). *Advocacy competencies.* Alexandria, VA: Author.

American Counseling Association (ACA). (2005). *Code of ethics.* Alexandria, VA: Author.

American Counseling Association (ACA). (2009). *About us.* Retrieved July 30, 2009, from http://www.counseling.org/AboutUs

American Educational Research Association, American Psychological Association, National Council on Measurement and Evaluation. (1999). *Standards for educational and psychological testing* (3rd ed.). Washington, DC: American Psychological Association.

American Mental Health Counselors Association (AMHCA). (2004). *Why use a mental health counselor?* Retrieved January 21, 2010, from http://www.amhca.org/public_resources/why_use_a_mental_health_counselor.aspx

American Psychiatric Association (APA). (2000). *Diagnostic and statistical manual of mental disorders, Fourth Edition–Text Revision* (*DSM-IV-TR*). Washington, DC: American Psychiatric Association.

American Rehabilitation Counseling Association. (2005). *Welcome to ARCA.* Retrieved August 27, 2009, from http://www.arcaweb.org

American School Counselor Association (ASCA). (2004). *The role of the professional school counselor.* Retrieved August 25, 2009, from http://www.schoolcounselor.org/content.asp?pl=325&sl=133&contentid=240

American School Counselor Association (ASCA). (2005). *The ASCA national model: A framework for school counseling programs* (2nd ed.). Alexandria, VA: Author.

American School Counselor Association. (2009). *About ASCA.* Retrieved August 28, 2009, from http://www.schoolcounselor.org/content.asp?pl=325&sl=127&contentid=127

Arredondo, P. (1999). Multicultural counseling competencies as tools to address oppression and racism. *Journal of Counseling and Development, 77,* 102–108.

Arredondo, P., Toporek, R., Brown, S. P., Jones, J., Locke, D., Sanchez, J., & Stadler, H. (1996). Operationalization of the multicultural counseling competencies. *Journal of Multicultural Counseling and Development, 24,* 42–78.

Association for Adult Development and Aging (AADA). (2005). *The Association for Adult Development and Aging.* Retrieved August 28, 2009, from http://www.aadaweb.org

Association for Assessment in Counseling and Education (AACE). (2003). *Responsibilities of users of standardized tests* (3rd ed.) (RUST-3). Alexandria, VA: Author.

Association for Assessment in Counseling and Education (AACE). (2008). *AACE statements of purpose.* Retrieved August 28, 2009, from http://www.theaaceonline.com/about.htm

Association for Counselor Education and Supervision (ACES). (2005). *About ACES.* Retrieved August 28, 2009, from http://www.acesonline.net/about.asp

Association for Counselors and Educators in Government (ACEG). (2009). *About the ACEG.* Retrieved August 28, 2009, from http://www.dantes.doded.mil/dantes_web/organizations/aceg/index.htm

Association for Creativity in Counseling (ACC). (2004). *The development and growth of ACC.* Retrieved August 28, 2009, from http://www.aca-acc.org/AboutACC.htm

Association for Lesbian, Gay, Bisexual and Transgender Issues in Counseling (ALGBTIC). (2009). *About ALGBTIC.* Retrieved August 29, 2009, from http://www.algbtic.org/index.htm

Association for Multicultural Counseling and Development (AMCD). (2009). *A historical sketch* (1972–2007). Retrieved July 1, 2009, from http://www.amcdaca.org/amcd/history.cfm

Association for Play Therapy. (2009). *About play therapy overview.* Retrieved February 10, 2009, from http://www.a4pt.org/ps.playtherapy.cfm?ID=1158

Association for Specialists in Group Work. (ASGW). (1998). *Principles for diversity competent group workers.* Retrieved February 8, 2010, from http://www.asgw.org/diversity.htm

Association for Specialists in Group Work. (ASGW). (2000). *Professional standards for the training of group workers.* Retrieved February 8, 2010, from http://www.asgw.org/training_standards.htm

Association for Specialists in Group Work (ASGW). (2007). *Best practice guidelines.* Retrieved February 8, 2010, from http://www.asgw.org/PDF/Best_Practices.pdf

Association for Specialists in Group Work (ASGW). (2009). *Purpose of ASGW.* Retrieved August 29, 2009, from http://www.asgw.org/purpose.asp

Association for Spiritual, Ethical, and Religious Values in Counseling (ASERVIC). (2010). *Historical development of the Association for Spiritual, Ethical, and Religious Values in Counseling (ASERVIC).* Retrieved January 22, 2010, from http://www.aservic.org/history.html

Atchley, R. C. (1975). Adjustment to loss of job at retirement. *International Journal on Aging and Human Development, 6,* 17–27.

Bales, R. F. (1950). *Interaction process analysis: A method for the study of small groups.* Cambridge, MA: Addison-Wesley.

Bales, R. F., Cohen, S. P., & Williams, S. A. (1979). *SYMLOG: A system for the multiple level observation of groups.* New York: Free Press.

Bandura, A. (1977). *Social learning theory.* Englewood Cliffs, NJ: Prentice Hall, Inc.

Bandura, A. (1986). *Social foundations of thought and action: A social cognitive theory.* Upper Saddle River, NJ: Prentice Hall.

Bem, S. (1974). The measurement of psychological androgyny. *Journal of Cognitive Psychotherapy, 1,* 2–27.

Billow, R. M. (2003). Rebellion in group. *International Journal of Group Psychotherapy, 53,* 331–351.

Bolman, L. (1971). Some effects of trainers on their T-groups. *Journal of Applied Behavioral Science, 7,* 309–325.

Bowlby, J. (1988). *A secure base: Parent-child attachment and healthy human development.* New York: Basic Books.

Broverman, I. K., Broverman, D. M., Clarkson, F. E., Rosenkrantz, P. S., & Vogel, S. R. (1970). Sex-role stereotypes and clinical judgments of mental health. *Journal of Consulting and Clinical Psychology, 34*(1), 1–7.

Brown, D. (2002). The role of work and cultural values in occupational choice, satisfaction, and success: A theoretical statement. *Journal of Counseling and Development, 80,* 48–56.

Budman, S. H., & Gurman, A. S. (1988). *The theory and practice of brief therapy.* New York: Guilford Press.

Carter, E., & McGoldrick, M. (1998). *The expanded family life cycle: Individual, family and social perspectives* (3rd ed.). Boston: Allyn & Bacon.

Cashwell, C. (2010). Spiritual diversity. In D. G. Hays & B. T. Erford (Eds.), *Developing multicultural counseling competence: A systems approach* (pp. 367–388). Columbus, OH: Pearson Merrill.

Cass, V. C. (1979). Homosexual identity formation: A theoretical model. *Journal of Homosexuality, 4,* 219–235.

Castellano, C., & Plionis, E. (2006). Comparative analysis of three crisis intervention models applied to law enforcement first responders during 9/11 and Hurricane Katrina. *Brief Treatment and Crisis Intervention, 6,* 326–336.

Cattell, R. B. (1963). Theory of fluid and crystallized intelligence: A critical experiment. *Journal of Educational Psychology, 54,* 1–22.

Cattell, R. B. (1971). *Abilities: Their structure, growth and action.* Boston: Houghton-Mifflin.

Center for Credentialing and Education. (2009). *Counselor preparation comprehensive examination (CPCE)*. Retrieved July 30, 2009, from http://www.cce-global.org/cpce

Centers for Disease Control. (2006). Homicides and suicides: National violence death reporting system, United States, 2003–2004. *MMWR Weekly, 55*(26), 721–724.

Chaney, M. P., & Maszsalek, J. (2010). Sexual orientation and heterosexism. In D. G. Hays & B. T. Erford (Eds.), *Developing multicultural counseling competence: A systems approach* (pp. 113–141). Columbus, OH: Pearson Merrill.

Cheek, J. R. (2009). Resilience. In American Counseling Association (Ed.), *The ACA encyclopedia of counseling* (p. 458). Alexandria, VA: American Counseling Association.

Chi Sigma Iota. (2008). *What is CSI?* Retrieved October 23, 2009, from http://csi-net.org/displaycommon.cfm?an=1

Child Welfare Information Gateway. (2007). *Definitions in federal law*. Retrieved August 6, 2009, from http://www.childwelfare.gov/can/defining/federal.cfm

Chomsky, N. (2006). *Language and mind* (3rd ed.). New York: Cambridge University Press.

Cochran, L. (1997). *Career counseling: A narrative approach*. Newbury Park, CA: Sage Publications.

Commission on Rehabilitation Counselor Certification. (2003). *Scope of practice for rehabilitation counseling*. Retrieved August 22, 2009, from http://www.crccertification.com/pages/31research.html

Commission on Rehabilitation Counselor Certification. (2010). *FAQ index*. Retrieved February 19, 2010, from http://www.crccertification.com/pages/faqs/3.php

Connors, J. V., & Caple, R. B. (2005). A review of group systems theory. *Journal for Specialists in Group Work, 30*, 93–110.

Cooney, N. L., Kadden, R. M., Litt, M. D., & Getter, H. (1991). Matching alcoholics to coping skills or interactional therapies: Two-year follow-up results. *Journal of Consulting & Clinical Psychology, 59*, 598-601.

Corey, G., Corey, M. S., Callahan, P., & Russell, J. M. (2004). *Group techniques* (3rd ed.). Belmont, CA: Thompson Brooks/Cole.

Corey, M. S., & Corey, G. (1987). *Group counseling: Process and practice* (3rd ed.) Monterey, CA: Brooks/Cole.

Corey, M. S., & Corey, G. (2006). *Groups: Process and practice* (7th ed.). Belmont, CA: Thomson Brooks/Cole.

Costa, P. T., & McCrae, R. R. (1992). *Manual for the NEO PI-R*. Odessa, FL: Psychological Assessment Resources.

Council for Accreditation of Counseling and Related Educational Programs (CACREP). (2008). *CACREP: Council for Accreditation of Counseling and Related Educational Programs*. Retrieved August 20, 2009, from http://www.cacrep.org/index.html

Council for Accreditation of Counseling and Related Educational Programs (CACREP). (2009). *2009 standards*. Retrieved January 20, 2010, from http://www.cacrep.org/doc/2009%20Standards.pdf

Counseling Association for Humanistic Education and Development (C-AHEAD). (2009). *What is the Counseling Association for Humanistic Education and Development (C-AHEAD)?* Retrieved September 2, 2009, from http://www.c-ahead.com

Counselors for Social Justice (CSJ). (2007). *Welcome to Counselors for Social Justice*. Retrieved September 2, 2009, from http://counselorsforsocialjustice.com

Creswell, J. W. (2003). *Research design: Qualitative, quantitative and mixed-method approaches*. Thousand Oaks, CA: Sage.

Crethar, H. C. (2009). Social justice in counseling. In American Counseling Association (Ed.), *The ACA encyclopedia of counseling* (pp. 504–505). Alexandria, VA: American Counseling Association.

Crites, J. O. (1981). *Career counseling: Models, methods, and materials*. New York: McGraw-Hill.

Cross, W. E., Jr. (1971). The Negro-to-Black conversion experience: Toward a psychology of Black liberation. *Black World, 20,* 13–27.

Cross, W. E., Jr. (1995). The psychology of nigrescence: Revising the Cross model. In J. M. Ponterotto, J. M. Casas, L. A. Suzuki, & C. M. Alexander (Eds.), *Handbook of multicultural counseling* (pp. 93–122). Thousand Oaks, CA: Sage.

Dane, A. V., & Schneider, B. H. (1998). Program integrity in primary and early secondary prevention: Are implementation effects out of control? *Clinical Psychology Review, 18,* 23–45.

Dawis, R. V., & Lofquist, L. H. (1984). *A psychological theory of work adjustment*. Minneapolis, MN: University of Minnesota Press.

DeLucia-Waack, J. L. (1997). What do we need to know about group work? A call for future research and theory. *Journal for Specialists and Group Work, 22,* 146–148.

DeLucia-Waack, J. L. (1999). *Group psychotherapy and outcome measures*. Paper presented at the annual convention of the American Psychological Association, Boston.

DeLucia-Waack, J. L., Gerrity, D. A., Kalodner, C. R., & Riva, M. T. (Eds.). (2004). *Handbook of group counseling and psychotherapy*. Thousand Oaks, CA: Sage.

Downing, N. E., & Roush, K. L. (1985). From passive-acceptance to active commitment: A model of feminist identity development for women. *The Counseling Psychologist, 13,* 695–709.

Elkind, D., & Bowen, R. (1979). Imaginary audience behavior in children and adolescents. *Developmental Psychology 15*(1), 38–44.

Ellis, A. (1996). *Better, deeper, and more enduring brief therapy: The rational emotive behavior therapy approach*. New York: Brunner/Mazel.

Ellis, A., & Blau, S. (Eds.). (1998). *The Albert Ellis reader: A guide to well-being using rational emotive behavior therapy*. Secaucus, NJ: Carol Publishing Group.

Ellis, A., & Harper, R. A. (1975). *A new guide to rational living*. North Hollywood, CA: Wilshire Book Company.

Erford, B. T. (Ed.). (2006). *The counselor's guide to clinical, personality, and behavioral assessment*. Boston: Houghton Mifflin/Lahaska Press.

Erford, B. T. (Ed.). (2007). *Assessment for counselors*. Boston: Houghton Mifflin/Lahaska Press.

Erford, B. T. (Ed.). (2008*). Research and evaluation in counseling*. Boston, MA: Houghton Mifflin/Lahaska Press.

Erford, B. T. (Ed.). (2010). *Group work in the schools*. Columbus, OH: Pearson Merrill.

Erford, B. T. (Ed.). (2011). *Transforming the school counseling profession* (3rd ed.). Columbus, OH: Pearson Merrill Prentice Hall.

Erford, B. T., Eaves, S. H., Bryant, E., & Young, K. (2010). *35 techniques every counselor should know*. Columbus, OH: Pearson Merrill Prentice Hall.

Erikson, E. (1950). *Childhood and society*. New York: Norton.

Everly, G. S., Phillips, S. B., Kane, D., & Feldman, D. (2006). Introduction to and overview of group psychological first aid. *Brief Treatment & Crisis Intervention, 6,* 130–136.

Eysenck, H. J. (1952). *The scientific study of personality*. London: Routledge and Kegan Paul.

Family Business Institute, Inc. (2004). *The 4 Ps of marketing: Product, place, promotion, price*. Retrieved May 13, 2009 from http://www.family-business-experts.com/4-Ps-of-marketing.html

Festinger, L. (1957). *A theory of cognitive dissonance*. Stanford, CA: Stanford University Press.

French, J. R. P., & Raven, B. (1968). The bases of social power. In D. Cartwright & A. Zander (Eds.), *Group dynamics: Research and theory* (3rd ed., pp. 607–623). New York: Harper & Row.

Freud, S. (1925). An autobiographical study. In J. Strachey (Ed. and Trans.), *The standard edition of the complete psychological works of Sigmund Freud* (Vol. 20, pp. 3–70). London: Hogarth Press.

Friedan, B. (1963). *The feminine mystique*. New York: Norton.

Fuhriman, A., & Burlingame, G. M. (Eds.) (1994). *Handbook of group psychotherapy*. New York: Wiley.

Garrett, M. (2010). Native Americans. In D. G. Hays & B. T. Erford (Eds.), *Developing multicultural counseling competence: A systems approach* (pp. 301–332). Columbus, OH: Pearson Merrill.

Gazda, G. M., Ginter, E. J., & Horne, A. M. (2008). *Group counseling and group psychotherapy: Theory and application* (2nd ed.). Boston: Allyn & Bacon.

Gelatt, H. B. (1962). Decision-making: A conceptual frame of reference for counseling. *Journal of Counseling Psychology, 9,* 240–245.

Gilligan, C. (1982). *In a different voice: Psychological theory and women's development*. Cambridge, MA: Harvard University Press.

Ginzberg, E., Ginsburg, S. W., Axelrad, S., & Herma, J. (1951). *Occupational choice: An approach to a general theory.* New York: Colombia University Press.

Gladding, S. T. (2005). *Counseling theories: Essential concepts and applications.* Upper Saddle River, NJ: Pearson.

Gladding, S. T. (2008). *Groups: A counseling specialty* (5th ed.). Upper Saddle River, NJ: Merrill Prentice Hall.

Goldenberg, H., & Goldenberg, I. (2008). *Family therapy: An overview* (7th ed.). Belmont, CA: Thomson Higher Education.

Gottfredson, L. S. (1981). Circumscription and compromise: A developmental theory of occupational aspirations. *Journal of Career Assessment, 5,* 419–441.

Granello, P. F., & Witmer, J. M. (1998). Standards of care: Potential implications for the counseling profession. *Journal of Counseling and Development, 76,* 371–380.

Griffith, B. A., & Griggs, J. (2001). Religious identity status as a model to understand, assess, and interact with client spirituality. *Counseling and Values, 46,* 14–25.

Grosch, W. N., & Olsen, D. C. (1994). *When helping starts to hurt: A new look at burnout among psychotherapists.* New York: Norton.

Gysbers, N. C., Heppner, M. J., & Johnson, J. A. (2003). *Career counseling: Process, issues, and techniques* (2nd ed.). Boston: Allyn & Bacon.

Hanna, F. J., Talley, W. B., & Guindon, M. H. (2000). The power of perception: Toward a model of cultural oppression and liberation. *Journal of Counseling and Development, 78,* 430–441.

Hardiman, R. (1994). White racial identity development in the United States. In E. P. Salett & D. R. Koslow (Eds.), *Race, ethnicity, and self: Identity in multicultural perspective* (pp. 117–140). Washington, DC: National Multicultural Institute.

Havighurst, R. J. (1972). *Developmental tasks and education.* Philadelphia: McKay.

Hays, D. G., Chang, C. Y., & Dean, J. K. (2004). White counselors' conceptualization of privilege and oppression: Implications for counselor training. *Counselor Education and Supervision, 43,* 242–257.

Hays, D. G., & Gray, G. M. (2010). Multicultural counseling. In B. T. Erford (Ed.), *Orientation to the counseling profession* (pp. 163–192). Columbus, OH: Pearson Merrill.

Hays, D. G., & McLeod, A. L. (2010). The culturally competent counselor. In D. G. Hays & B. T. Erford (Eds.), *Developing multicultural counseling competence: A systems approach* (pp. 1–31). Columbus, OH: Pearson Merrill.

Heider, F. (1967). *The psychology of interpersonal relations.* Hoboken, NJ: Wiley.

Helm, K., & James, L., Jr. (2010). Individuals and families of African descent. In D. G. Hays & B. T. Erford (Eds.), *Developing multicultural counseling competence: A systems approach* (pp. 193–215). Columbus, OH: Pearson Merrill.

Helms, J. E. (1995). An update of Helms' White and people of color racial identity. In J. G. Ponterotto, J. M. Casas, & C. M. Alexander (Eds.), *Handbook of multicultural counseling* (pp. 181–198). Thousand Oaks, CA: Sage.

Heppner, P. P., Wampold, B. E., Kivlighan, D. M. (2008). *Research design in counseling* (3rd ed.). Belmont, CA: Thomson/ Brooks Cole.

Herlihy, B., & Corey G. (2006). *ACA ethical standards casebook* (6th ed.). Alexandria, VA: American Counseling Association.

Herman, J. (1997). *Trauma and recovery.* New York: Basic Books.

Herr, E. L., & Erford, B. T. (2011). Historical roots and future issues. In B. T. Erford (Ed.), *Transforming the school counseling profession* (3rd ed.) (pp. 20–46). Columbus, OH: Pearson Merrill.

Hill, R. (1949). *Families under stress.* Westport, CT: Greenwood.

Hill, W. F. (1965). *Hill Interaction Matrix.* Los Angeles: University of Southern California.

Hill, W. F. (1966). *Hill Interaction Matrix (HIM) monograph.* Los Angeles: University of Southern California, Youth Studies Center.

Hill, W. F. (1973). *Hill Interaction Matrix* (HIM) conceptual framework for understanding groups. In J. W. Pfeiffer, & J. E. Jones (Eds.), *The 1973 annual handbook for group facilitators* (pp. 159–176). San Diego, CA: University Associates.

Hoffman, R. M. (2006). Gender self-definitions and gender self-acceptance in women: Intersections with feminist, womanist, and ethnic identities. *Journal of Counseling and Development, 84,* 358–372.

Holland, J. L. (1966). *The psychology of vocational choice.* Waltham, MA: Blaisdell.

Hopson, B., & Adams, J. D. (1977). Towards an understanding of transitions: Defining some boundaries of transition. In J. Adams, J. Hayes, & B. Hopson (Eds.), *Transition: Understanding and managing personal change* (pp. 1–19). Montclair, NJ: Allenheld & Osmun.

Inman, A., & Alvarez, A. (2010). Individuals and families of Asian descent. In D. G. Hays & B. T. Erford (Eds.), *Developing multicultural counseling competence: A systems approach* (pp. 246–276). Columbus, OH: Pearson Merrill.

Institute of International Education. (2007). *Open doors 2007: International students in the United States.* Retrieved April 25, 2009, from Open Doors online Web site: http://opendoors.iienetwork.org

International Association of Addiction and Offender Counselors (IAAOC). (2009). *IAAOC identity, mission, and vision.* Retrieved September 2, 2009, from http://www.iaaoc.org/mission.asp

International Association of Marriage and Family Counselors (IAMFC). (2002). *Strategic plan.* Retrieved September 3, 2009, from http://www.iamfc.com/strategic_plan.html

Ivey, A. E., & Ivey, M. B. (2007). *Intentional interviewing and counseling: Facilitating client development in a multicultural society* (6th ed.). Belmont, CA: Brooks/Cole.

James, R. K., & Gilliland, B. E. (2005). *Crisis intervention strategies* (5th ed.). Belmont, CA: Wadsworth/Thomson Learning.

Janis, I. L., & Mann, L. (1977). *Decision making: A psychological analysis of conflict, choice, and commitment.* New York: Norton.

Joint Committee on Testing Practices (JCTP). (1998). *Rights and responsibilities of test takers.* Washington, DC: American Psychological Association.

Joint Committee on Testing Practices (JCTP). (2000). *Test user qualifications.* Washington, DC: American Psychological Association.

Joint Committee on Testing Practices (JCTP). (2004). *Code of fair testing practices in education.* Washington, DC: American Psychological Association.

Jung, C. G. (1971). *Psychological types: The collected works of C. G. Jung* (Vol. 6, H. B. Baynes, Trans., revised by R. F. Hull). Princeton, NJ: Princeton University Press.

Kelly, G. A. (1955). *The psychology of personal constructs.* New York: Norton.

Kent, M. M. (2007). Immigration and America's Black population. *Population Reference Bureau, 62*(4), 2–15.

Kivlighan, D. M., Jr., & Goldfine, D. C. (1991). Endorsement of therapeutic factors as a function of stage of group development and participant interpersonal attitudes. *Journal of Counseling Psychology, 38,* 150–158.

Kluckhohn, F. R., & Strodtbeck, F. L. (1961). *Variations in value orientations.* Evanston, IL: Row, Petersen.

Kohlberg, L. (1969). Stage and sequence: The cognitive developmental approach to socialization. In D. A. Goslin (Ed.), *Handbook of socialization research* (pp. 347–480). Chicago: Rand McNally.

Kohlberg, L. (1981). *The philosophy of moral development: Moral stages and the idea of justice.* San Francisco: Harper and Row.

Krumboltz, J. D. (1976). A social learning theory of career choice. *Counseling Psychologist, 6,* 71–80.

Kübler-Ross, E. (1969). *On death and dying.* New York: Simon & Schuster.

Lese, K. L., & McNair-Semands, R. R. (2000). The Therapeutic Factors Inventory: Development of the scale. *Group, 24,* 303–317.

Levinson, D. (1978). *The seasons of a man's life.* New York: Random House.

Lewin, K. (1943). Defining the "Field at a given time." *Psychological Review, 50,* 292–310.

Lewis, T. F., & Osborn, C. J. (2004). Solution-focused counseling and motivational interviewing: A consideration of confluence. *Journal of Counseling and Development, 82*(1), 38–48.

Linde, L. (2007). Ethical, legal, and professional issues in school counseling. In B. T. Erford (Ed.), *Transforming the school counseling profession* (2nd ed., pp. 39–62). Columbus, OH: Merrill Prentice Hall.

Lindeman, E. (1944). Symptomatology and management of acute grief. *American Journal of Psychiatry, 101,* 141–148.

Liu, W. M., Soleck, G., Hopps, J., Dunston, K., Jr., & Pickett, T. (2004). A new framework to understand social class in counseling: The social class worldview model and modern classism. *Journal of Multicultural Counseling and Development, 32*(2), 95–122.

Loevinger, J. (1979). The idea of the ego. *The Counseling Psychologist, 8,* 3–5.

Luft, J. (1984). *Group processes: An introduction to group dynamics* (3rd ed.). Palo Alto, CA: Mayfield.

MacKenzie, K. R. (1983). The clinical application of a group climate measure. In R. R. Dies, & K. R. MacKenzie (Eds.), *Advances in group psychotherapy: Integrating research and practice* (pp. 159–170). New York: International Universities Press.

MacKenzie, K. R. (1990). *Introduction to time limited group psychotherapy.* Washington, DC: American Psychiatric Press.

Makuch, L. (1997). Measuring dimensions of counseling and therapeutic group leadership style: Development of a leadership characteristics inventory. Unpublished doctoral dissertation, Indiana University.

Marcia, J. E. (1966). Development and validation of ego identity status. *Journal of Psychology and Social Psychology, 3,* 551-558.

Marcia, J. E. (1980). Identity in adolescence. In J. Adelson (Ed.), *Handbook of adolescent psychology* (pp. 159-187). New York: Wiley.

Maslach, C. (1982). *Burnout: The cost of caring.* Englewood Cliffs, NJ: Prentice Hall.

Maslach, C., & Leiter, M. P. (1997). *The truth about burnout.* San Francisco: Jossey-Bass.

Maslow, A. (1947). A theory of human motivation. *Psychological Review, 50,* 375–377.

Maxwell, J. A. (2005). *Qualitative research design: An interactive approach* (2nd ed.). Thousand Oaks, CA: Sage.

McCarn, S. R., & Fassinger, R. E. (1996). Re-visioning sexual minority identity formation: A new model of lesbian identity and its implications for counseling and research. *The Counseling Psychologist, 24,* 508–534.

McIntosh, P. (1988). *White privilege and male privilege: A personal account of coming to see correspondences through work in women's studies.* Working papers #189, Wellesley College Center for Research on Women, Wellesley, MA.

McLeod, J. (2001). *Qualitative research in counselling and psychotherapy.* London: Sage.

McMahon, H. G., Paisley, P., & Molina, B. (2010). Individuals and families of European descent. In D. G. Hays & B. T. Erford (Eds.), *Developing multicultural counseling competence: A systems approach* (pp. 333–366). Columbus, OH: Pearson Merrill.

Meichenbaum, D. (1996). Stress inoculation training for coping with stressors. *The Clinical Psychologist, 49,* 4–7.

Mentor Research Institute. (2009). *Confidentiality: The risks of using mental health insurance.* Retrieved August 21, 2009, from http://www.oregoncounseling.org/Consumer/RisksConfidentiality.htm

Mio, J. S., Trimble, J. E., Arredondo, P., Cheatham, H. E., & Sue, D. (1999). *Key words in multicultural interventions: A dictionary.* Westport, CT: Greenwood Press.

Mitchell, A., Levin, A., & Krumboltz, J. D. (1999). Planned happenstance: Constructing unexpected career opportunities. *Journal of Counseling and Development, 77,* 115–124.

Moos, R. H. (1986). *Group Environment Scale manual.* Palo Alto, CA: Consulting Psychologists Press.

Myers, J. E., & Sweeney, T. J. (2005a). *Counseling for wellness: Theory, research, and practice.* Alexandria, VA: American Counseling Association.

Myers, J. E., & Sweeney, T. J. (2005b). The indivisible self: An evidence-based model of wellness. *Journal of Individual Psychology, 60,* 234–244.

Nassar-McMillan, S. (2009). Counseling Arab Americans. In American Counseling Association (Ed.), *ACA encyclopedia of counseling* (pp. 28–30). Alexandria, VA: American Counseling Association.

Nassar-McMillan, S., Gonzales, L., & Mohamed, R. (2010). Individuals and families of Arab descent. In D. G. Hays & B. T. Erford (Eds.), *Developing multicultural counseling competence: A systems approach* (pp. 216–245). Columbus, OH: Pearson Merrill.

National Association for College Admission Counseling. (2008). *Guiding the way to higher education.* Retrieved August 25, 2009, from http://www.nacacnet.org/memberportal/default.htm

National Board for Certified Counselors (NBCC). (2005). *National Board for Certified Counselors Code of Ethics.* Retrieved January 22, 2010, from http://www.nbcc.org/AssetManagerFiles/ethics/nbcc-codeofethics.pdf

National Board for Certified Counselors (NBCC). (2007a). *General information.* Retrieved August 22, 2009, from http://www.nbcc.org

National Board for Certified Counselors (NBCC). (2007b). *The practice of Internet counseling.* Retrieved January 22, 2010, from http://www.nbcc.org/AssetManagerFiles/ethics/internetCounseling.pdf

National Board for Certified Counselors. (2009a). *National counselor exam (NCE).* Retrieved January 20, 2010, from http://www.nbcc.org/certifications/ncc/NCE.aspx

National Board for Certified Counselors. (2009b). *National Certified Counselor 2009 application.* Retrieved January 20, 2010, from http://www.nbcc.org/certifications/ncc/Default.aspx

National Career Development Association (NCDA). (1997). *Career counseling competencies.* Retrieved April 2, 2009, from http://associationdatabase.com/aws/NCDA/asset_manager/get_file/3397

National Career Development Association (NCDA). (2007). *Code of ethics.* Retrieved March 1, 2009 from http://associationdatabase.com/aws/NCDA/asset_manager/get_file/3395

National Career Development Association (NCDA). (2010). *About NCDA.* Retrieved January 22, 2010, from http://associationdatabase.com/aws/NCDA/pt/sp/about

National Child Traumatic Stress Network and National Center for PTSD. (2006). *Psychological first aid: Field operations guide* (2nd ed.). Retrieved February 8, 2009, from http://www.ptsd.va.gov/professional/manuals/psych-first-aid.asp

National Employment Counseling Association (NECA). (2008). *Bylaws of the National Employment Counseling Association.* Retrieved September 5, 2009, from http://www.geocities.com/employmentcounseling/subpages/necabylaws

National Rehabilitation Counseling Association (NRCA). (2009). *Organization information.* Retrieved September 5, 2009, from http://nrca-net.org

Otani, A. (1989). Client resistance in counseling: Its theoretical rationale and taxonomic classification. *Journal of Counseling and Development, 67,* 458–461.

Page, B. J., & Hulse-Killacky, D. (1999). Development and validation of the Corrective Feedback Self-Efficacy Instrument. *Journal for Specialists in Group Work, 24,* 37–54.

Page, B. J., Pietrzak, D. R., & Lewis, T. F. (2001). Development of the group leader self-efficacy instrument. *Journal for Specialists in Group Work, 26,* 168–184.

Paniagua, F. A. (2005). *Assessing and treating culturally diverse clients: A practical guide* (3rd ed.). Thousand Oaks, CA: Sage.

Parsons, F. (1909). *Choosing a vocation.* Boston: Houghton Mifflin.

Parten, M. (1933). Social play among preschool children. *Journal of Abnormal and Social Psychology, 28,* 136–147.

Patton, M. Q. (2002). *Qualitative research and evaluation methods* (3rd ed.). Thousand Oaks, CA: Sage.

Pavlov, I. P. (1960). *Conditioned reflexes: An investigation of the physiological activity of the cerebral cortex.* New York: Dover Publications.

Pedersen, P. B. (1995). *The five stages of culture shock.* Westport, CT: Greenwood Press.

Perls, F. (1973). *The Gestalt approach and eye witness to therapy.* Palo Alto, CA: Science and Behavior Books.

Pew Hispanic Center. (2005). *Hispanics: A people in motion.* Washington, DC: Author.

Pew Hispanic Center. (2006). *Hispanics at mid-decade.* Washington, DC: Author.

Piaget, J. (1963). *The origins of intelligence in children.* New York: W. W. Norton & Company.

Poll, J. B., & Smith, T. B. (2003). The spiritual self: Toward a conceptualization of spiritual identity development. *Journal of Psychology and Theology, 31,* 129–142.

Ponterotto, J. G. (1997). Multicultural counseling training: A competency model and national survey. In D. B. Pope-Davis & H. L. K. Coleman (Eds.), *Multicultural counseling competencies: Assessment, education and training, and supervision* (pp. 111–130). Thousand Oaks, CA: Sage.

Posavac, E. J., & Carey, R. G. (2007). *Program evaluation: Methods and case studies* (7th ed.). Upper Saddle River, NJ: Pearson Prentice Hall.

Poston, W. S. C. (1990). The biracial identity development model: A needed addition. *Journal of Counseling and Development, 69,* 152–155.

Ramsey, M. (2009). Key ethical issues in social and cultural foundations. In American Counseling Association (Ed.), *The ACA encyclopedia of counseling* (pp. 496–499). Alexandria, VA: American Counseling Association.

Ratts, M., D'Andrea, M, & Arredondo, P. (2004, July). Social justice counseling: A "fifth force" in the field. *Counseling Today, 47*(1), 28–30.

Reeves, T. J., & Bennett, C. E. (2004). *We the people: Asians in the United States, Census 2000 special reports CENSR-17*. Washington, DC: U.S. Department of Commerce.

Rich, P. (2002). *Divorce counseling homework planner*. New York: Wiley.

Ridley, C. R. (Ed.). (2005). *Overcoming unintentional racism in counseling and therapy: A practitioner's guide to intentional intervention* (2nd ed.). Thousand Oaks, CA: Sage.

Roe, A. (1957). Early determinants of vocational choice. *Journal of Counseling Psychology, 4,* 212–217.

Roe, S., & Lunneborg, P. W. (1990). Personality development and career choice. In D. Brown, L. Brooks, & Associates (Eds.), *Career choice and development: Applying contemporary theories to practice* (2nd ed., pp. 68–101). San Francisco: Jossey-Bass.

Romano, J. L., & Sullivan, B. A. (2000). Simulated group counseling for group work training: A four-year research study of group development. *Journal for Specialists in Group Work, 25,* 366–375.

Savickas, M. L. (2005). The theory and practice of career construction. In S. D. Brown & R. W. Lent (Eds.), *Career development and counseling: Putting theory and research to work* (pp. 42–69). Hoboken, NJ: John Wiley.

Schein, E. H. (1969). *Process consultation: Its role in organization development*. Reading, MA: Addison-Wesley.

Schlossberg, N. K. (1984). *Counseling adults in transition*. New York: Springer.

Schutz, W. (1992). Beyond FIRO-B-three new theory derived measures— element b: Behavior, element f: Feelings, element s: Self. *Psychological Reports, 70,* 915–937.

Search Institute. (2005). *Technical manual for creating a great place to learn survey*. Minneapolis, MN: Author.

Shapiro, F. (2001). *Eye-movement desensitization and reprocessing: Basic principles, protocols, and procedures* (2nd ed.). New York: Guilford Press.

Sheehy, G. (1976). *Passages: Predictable crises of adult life*. New York: Dutton.

Simon, A., & Agazarian, Y. (1974). Sequential Analysis of Verbal Interaction (SAVI). In A. E. Simon & G. Boyer (Eds.), *Mirrors for behavior III: An anthology of observation instruments*. Philadelphia: Humanizing Learning Program, Research for Better Schools.

Skinner, B. F. (1953). *Science and human behavior*. New York: Macmillan.

Slocum, Y. S. (1987). A survey of expectations about group therapy among clinical and non-clinical populations. *International Journal of Group Psychotherapy, 37,* 39–54.

Smaby, M. H., Maddux, C. D., Torres-Rivera, E., & Zimmick, R. (1999). A study of the effects of a skills-based versus a conventional group counseling training program. *Journal for Specialists in Group Work, 24,* 152–163.

Smith, M. L., & Glass, G. V. (1977). Meta-analysis of psychotherapy outcome studies. *American Psychologist, 32,* 752–760.

Soldz, S., Budman, S., Davis, M., & Demby, A. (1993). Beyond the interpersonal circumplex in group psychotherapy: The structure and relationship to outcome of the individual group member interpersonal process scale. *Journal of Clinical Psychology, 49,* 551–563.

Spearman, C. (1927). *The abilities of man: Their nature and measurement*. New York: Macmillan.

Stone, M. H., Lewis, C. M., & Beck, A. P. (1994). The structure of Yalom's Curative Factors Scale. *International Journal of Group Psychotherapy, 44,* 239–245.

Strauss, W., & Howe, N. (1991). *Generations: The history of America's future, 1584 to 2069*. New York: William Morrow.

Strong, S. (1968). Counseling: An interpersonal influence process. *Journal of Counseling Psychology, 15,* 215–224.

Sue, D. W. (1978). Eliminating cultural oppression in counseling: Toward a general theory. *Journal of Counseling Psychology, 25,* 419–428.

Sue, D. W., Arredondo, P., & McDavis, R. J. (1992). Multicultural counseling competencies and standards: A call to the profession. *Journal of Counseling and Development, 70,* 477–486.

Sue, D. W., Bernier, J. E., Durran, A., Feinberg, L., Pedersen P., Smith, E. J., & Vasquez-Nuttal, E. (1982). Position paper: Cross-cultural counseling competencies. *The Counseling Psychologist, 10,* 45–52.

Super, D. E. (1953). A theory of vocational development. *American Psychologist, 8,* 185–190.

Tanigoshi, H., Kontos, A. P., & Remley Jr., T. P. (2008). The effectiveness of individual wellness counseling on the wellness of law enforcement officers. *Journal of Counseling & Development, 86,* 64–74.

Tavris, C. (1992). *The mismeasure of woman*. New York: Simon & Schuster.

Terndrup, A., Ritter, K., Barrett, B., Logan. C., & Mate, R. (1997). *Competencies in counseling gay, lesbian, bisexual, and transgendered clients*. Retrieved April 25, 2009, from http://www.algbtic.org/competencies.html

Tewari, N., Inman, A. G., & Sandhu, D. S. (2003). South Asian Americans: Culture, concerns and therapeutic strategies. In J. Mio & G. Iwamasa (Eds.), *Culturally diverse mental health: The challenges of research and resistance* (pp. 191–209). New York: Brunner-Routledge.

Thompson, R. A. (2004). *Crisis intervention and crisis management: Strategies that work in schools and communities*. New York: Brunner-Routledge.

Thorndike, E. L. (1911). *Animal intelligence*. New York: Macmillan.

Tiedeman, D. V., & O'Hara, R. P. (1963). *Career development: Choice and adjustment*. New York: Teachers College Press.

Troiden, R. R. (1989). The formation of homosexual identities. *Journal of Homosexuality, 17,* 159–178.

Trotzer, J. P. (1999). *The counselor and the group* (4th ed.). Philadelphia: Accelerated Development.

Tuckman, B., & Jensen, M. (1977). Stages of small group development revisited. *Group and Organizational Studies, 2,* 419–427.

U. S. Bureau of Indian Affairs. (1988). *American Indians today*. Washington, DC: Author.

U.S. Census Bureau. (2001). *Population profile of the United States*. Washington, DC: U.S. Government Printing Office.

U.S. Census Bureau. (2003). *The Arab population: 2000*. Retrieved April 17, 2009, from http://www.census.gov/prod/2003pubs/c2kbr-23.pdf

U.S. Census Bureau. (2004). *U.S. interim projections by age, sex, race, and Hispanic origin: 2000–2050*. Retrieved January 23, 2010, from http://www.census.gov/ipc/www/usinterimproj

U.S. Census Bureau. (2008). *U.S. Hispanic population surpasses 45 million: Now 15 percent total*. Retrieved April 25, 2009, from http://www.census.gov/Press-Release/www/releases/archives/population/011910.html

U.S. Department of Education. (2000). *A guide to the individualized education program*. Retrieved August 2, 2009, from http://www.ed.gov/parents/needs/speced/iepguide/index.html

U.S. Department of Education. (2007). *Family Educational Rights and Privacy Act (FERPA)*. Retrieved August 2, 2009, from http://www.ed.gov/policy/gen/guid/fpco/ferpa/index.html

U.S. Department of Health and Human Services. (2000). *Your rights under section 504 and the Americans with Disabilities Act*. Retrieved January 20, 2010, from http://www.hhs.gov/ocr/civilrights/resources/factsheets/504ada. pdf

U. S. Department of Health and Human Services (USDHHS). (2001). *Mental health: Culture, race and ethnicity—A supplement to mental health: A report of the Surgeon General*. Rockville, MD: Author.

U.S. Department of Health and Human Services. (2006). *What does the HIPAA privacy rule do?* Retrieved January 20, 2010, from http://www.hhs.gov/hipaafaq/about/187.html

U.S. Department of Health and Human Services, Administration on Children, Youth and Families. (2007). *Child maltreatment 2005*. Washington, DC: Author.

U. S. Department of Labor. (2005). *Industry specific materials*. Retrieved March 27, 2009, from http://www.dol.gov/asp/programs/drugs/working-partners/stats/is.asp

U.S. Department of Labor. (2010). *Occupational outlook handbook, 2008–09 edition: Counselors*. Retrieved January 10, 2010, from http://www.bls.gov/oco/ocos067.htm

Valente, S. I. (2009). Addiction counseling. In American Counseling Association (Ed.), The *ACA encyclopedia of counseling* (pp. 4–7). Alexandria, VA: American Counseling Association.

Van Dyck, B. J. (1980). An analysis of selection criteria for short-term group counseling clients. *The Personnel & Guidance Journal, 59,* 226–230.

Vygotsky, L. S. (1978). *Mind in society: The development of higher psychological processes.* Cambridge, MA: Harvard University Press.

Vygotsky, L. S. (1997). In R. W. Rieber (Ed.) and M. Hall (Trans.), *The collected works of L. S. Vygotsky: The history of the development of higher mental functions* (Vol. 4). New York: Plenum Press.

Watson, J. B., & Rayner, R. (1920). Conditioned emotional reactions. *Journal of Experimental Psychology, 3*(1), 1–14.

Weinberg, M. S., Williams, C. J., & Pryor, D. W. (1994). *Dual attraction: Understanding bisexuality.* New York: Oxford University Press.

Wheeler, A. M., & Bertram, B. (2008). *The counselor and the law: A guide to legal and ethical practice* (5th ed.). Alexandria, VA: American Counseling Association.

Williamson, E. G. (1939). *How to counsel students.* New York: McGraw-Hill.

Wolpe, J. (1958). *Psychotherapy by reciprocal inhibition.* Stanford, CA: Stanford University Press.

Worthington, R. L., Bielstein-Savoy, H., Dillion, F. R., & Vernaglia, E. R. (2002). Heterosexual identity development: A multidimensional model of individual and social identity. *The Counseling Psychologist, 30,* 496–531.

Wright, B. (2004). Compassion fatigue. How to avoid it. *Palliative Medicine, 16,* 3–4.

Wubbolding, R. (2004). Professional school counselors and reality therapy. In B. T. Erford (Ed.), *Professional school counseling: A handbook of theories, programs & practices* (pp. 211–220). Austin, TX: Pro-Ed.

Yalom, I. D., & Leszcz, M. (2005). *The theory and practice of group psychotherapy* (5th ed.). New York: Basic Books.

Yalom, I. D., Tinklenberg, J., & Gilula, M. (1968). Curative factors in group psychotherapy. Unpublished manuscript.

Young, M. E. (2005). *Learning the art of helping: Building blocks and techniques.* Upper Saddle River, NJ: Pearson.

INDEX